THE COMPLETE

Astrological Handbook

FOR THE TWENTY-FIRST CENTURY

THE COMPLETE

Astrological Handbook

FOR THE TWENTY-FIRST CENTURY

*Understanding and Combining
the Wisdom of Chinese, Tibetan,
Vedic, Arabian, Judaic, and
Western Astrology*

Anistatia R Miller, RMAFA,
and Jared M. Brown

Schocken Books
New York

Copyright © 1999 by Anistatia R Miller and Jared M. Brown

All rights reserved under International and Pan-American Copyright Conventions. Published in the United States by Schocken Books Inc., New York, and simultaneously in Canada by Random House of Canada Limited, Toronto. Distributed by Pantheon Books, a division of Random House, Inc., New York.

Schocken and colophon are registered trademarks of Random House, Inc.

Library of Congress Cataloging-in-Publication Data
Miller, Anistatia R, 1952–
The complete astrological handbook for the twenty-first century: understanding and combining the wisdom of Chinese, Tibetan, Vedic, Arabian, Judaic, and Western astrology / Anistatia R Miller, RMAFA, and Jared M. Brown.
    p.   cm.
  Includes bibliographical references and index.
  ISBN 0-8052-1086-5 (pbk.)
  1. Astrology.   I. Brown, Jared M., 1964– . II. Title.
BF 1708.1.M55 1999
133.5′9—dc21   99-17725
              CIP

Random House Web Address: www.randomhouse.com

Book design by Anistatia R Miller and Jared M. Brown/Between the Covers

Printed in the United States of America
First Edition
9 8 7 6 5 4 3 2 1

Contents

Table of Figures

Preface and Acknowledgments

Jared and I are born skeptics. To both of us, mysticism is simply pragmatism wrapped in the black velvet of charlatanism. No wonder the great illusionist Harry Houdini spent the last few years of his life exposing the plethora of fake mediums and soothsayers that preyed upon the affluent and the gullible in the early part of the twentieth century. However, the death of someone very close prompted me to turn to psychics, Ouija boards, and freemasonry, looking for guidance at a very vulnerable time. Skepticism won the battle in almost every instance. A change in the atmosphere of a room could easily be dispelled as a physical manifestation of my own anxiety. Veiled messages from the departed, devoid of any meaningful insight, were merely the accurate guesses of an observant person posing as a conduit to "the other world."

In 1972, however, the owner of the Occult Bookstore in Chicago directed me to a number of astrology books on his shelves, particularly a small volume titled *The Story of Astrology*, written by the American astrologer Manly Palmer Hall in 1933. He suggested I should learn more about this science and consult a professional astrologer for advice, which I did.

During the consultation, I realized that no obvious logic would explain how this practitioner could conjecture that my spouse had recently died. I hadn't mentioned that I was ever married, let alone widowed. (Before our meeting, he had only asked for the date, time, and location of my birth.) He justified his comment by stating that the Sun was positioned in the Eighth House of my natal chart and was adversely aspected. Therefore, the early death of my spouse or partner had been part of my destiny since birth.

Since that initial encounter, I have spent much time studying the various astrological traditions, and have researched both exoteric and esoteric concepts, applying and assessing each method through the most scientific of all processes: trial and more trial, both at home and with clients.

Together, Jared and I have also tested the methods used by astrologers around the world, looking for strengths and flaws in the resulting interpretations. This book is the culmination of what we have discovered so far. As with any pursuit, the fact that we have written this book does not mean we have completed our studies of these ancient traditions; we have simply documented what we have observed so far in the hope that others might be inspired to conduct their own course of study in what is a logical and precise science.

We would like to thank our editor, Cecelia Cancellaro, and editorial director, Arthur Samuelson, for having the faith and the patience to champion this massive project. We also appreciate the hard work and efforts of our copyeditor David Smith, production editor Jeanne Morton, proofreader Robert Legault, managing editor Altie Karper, design director Kristen Bearse, and production manager Kathy Grasso for nurturing this project from manuscript to finished pages.

The people who read the many stages and segments of this book deserve our deepest admiration. Their insights provoked much thought and re-examination. Many thanks to Linda Johnsen, Vedic editor for *The Mountain Astrologer*; William L. Cassidy; Stephanie Ager; Margaret Richardson; and Valerie Vaughn, who has been championing a greater comprehension of astrology's cultural and historical roots by the astrological community.

Anistatia R Miller
Boise, Idaho, 1998

Introduction

There is no question that the celestial bodies that make up our solar system affect life on Earth. Ocean tides are the result of the gravitational pull exerted by the Moon as it revolves around the Earth. The phenomena known as sunspots not only change the polarity of the Sun's magnetic field and affect the Earth's climate, but the resulting solar flares seem to have a profound effect on the Earth's magnetic field, causing periodic radio interference, computer crashes, and other technological mayhem.[1] The planets themselves also generate magnetic radiation in varying degrees. Not surprisingly, the solar photon radiation that continuously showers the Earth seems to be altered when two planets' orbital paths cross each other at particular angles, creating magnetic storms.[2]

Humans are electrochemical beings. In fact, every muscle and organ in the human body functions because minute electrical impulses generated by both internal and external forces flow through the complex internal network that is the central nervous system. The brain transmits information to the rest of the body through minute electrical charges that not only control motion and speech, but stimulate emotion and behavior as well. Thus, humans are subtly and profoundly affected by any changes in the solar system's electromagnetic field.

---

1. During a seventy-year period in the 1700s, no sunspots were visible on the Sun's surface. Modern science has theorized that there was a direct correlation between this event and the well-documented global cooling that occurred during the same period.

2. According to Carl G. Jung, Professor Max Knoll proved that if two planets' orbital paths create a conjunction (matching paths and locations along the ecliptic), an opposition (paths that are on exactly opposite locations on the ecliptic), or a quartile angle or aspect (paths that are positioned at a 90-degree angle from each other), a magnetic storm may result.

The effects of the ebb and flow of energy produced by celestial motion upon this intricate neural system have been observed, documented, argued, and refined by scientists, physicians, theologians, and astrologers over thousands of years. This— the cumulative body of their work—is astrology.

Legitimate astrology is founded on logical observation and deductive reasoning, not superstition or magic. It is a body of knowledge (which, in its strictest sense, is science) that charts the positions of the planets at the exact time and place of a person's birth, and determines the overall effect of celestial electromagnetic forces on a given individual's personality and behavior throughout the course of his or her life, drawing on hundreds, even thousands, of years of cumulative research.

The term *astrology* is derived from the Greek words *astron* and *logos,* which literally mean "stars" and "study." Originally, astrologers documented and named the celestial bodies that they perceived as moving through the sky, and charted the diurnal (daytime) and nocturnal (nighttime) movements of large "stars" like the planets Venus and Mercury. But it wasn't long before scientists and mathematicians in locations as diverse as Beijing, Bombay, Babylon, and Bogotá noticed striking correlations between celestial activity and human behavior.

For example, ancient Greek and Roman physicians referred to intermittent bouts of insanity as "lunacy," accepting as fact the parity between erratic human behavior and the occurrence of the Full Moon or a lunar eclipse. Ancient Hindu believers associated an intoxicating herbal drink called *soma* with the Moon god Candra. Consumed by both gods and worshipers, *soma* reputedly produced a mild form of dementia. Those who drank *soma* felt invincible and supernatural, according to many passages in the Vedas. And Chinese tradition contains numerous legends about the Moon's effect on human beings. The most famous of these concerns the eighth-century A.D. poet Li Po, who invited the Moon and its inhabitant, the goddess Ch'ang-O, to have a drink with him. He was so intoxicated by the Moon's beauty—and by the liquor he was imbibing—that he drowned in a lake while attempting to capture the Moon itself. Even in modern times, major metropolitan police departments such as those of New York and Los Angeles add on extra staff to handle the perceived monthly increase in criminal, violent, and otherwise chaotic behavior that many people believe coincides with each Full Moon.

It is not a young science. In fact, astrology gave birth to the more modern science of astronomy as astrologers were the first scientists to document the planets' motions with mathematical accuracy. The oldest continuous written records of astral observations and practice were discovered in India and China. Numerous astrological manuscripts found in royal Indian libraries date back to the Indo-Aryans, who settled in the Indus River valley around 1500 B.C. Similarly, documentation of celestial observations and methods of astrological delineation which were found in Chinese archives are over four thousand years old.

Monarchs and military leaders, including the Macedonian emperor Alexander the Great and the Mongol emperor Genghis Khan, consulted astrologers prior to making strategic decisions. During the Middle Ages and into the Renaissance, Western European and Mediterranean physicians, clergy, and scholars applied astrological methods to their various professions, expanding their collective knowledge over the centuries by translating works imported from distant lands, including Arabia, India, and China. Even the great Mayan and Aztec civilizations in the New World developed their own unique forms of astrological calculation and interpretation. Today, interest in a variety of astrological practices is on a decided upswing.

So why do modern-day, realistic world leaders, corporate CEOs, physicists, and physicians consult personal astrologers about critical situations before acting or reacting? Why do highly educated individuals around the world turn to such an ancient science, looking for guidance or for glimpses into destiny? Is it hope, fear, or an intuitive belief that astrology is logical and realistic that spurs even skeptical twentieth-century intellectuals to consult a horoscope at critical crossroads in life?

As Kenneth Miller pointed out in a *Life* magazine article (July 1997): "It turns out astrology is experiencing its biggest boom in four hundred years. According to a recent poll, just 20 percent of Americans are flat-out nonbelievers; 48 percent say astrology is probably or definitely valid." The number of practicing professional astrologers in the United States alone has more than quintupled within the past two decades. Sun-sign horoscopes (timely predictions based strictly upon an individual's day of birth) cast by astrologers such as Sydney Omarr, Rob Brezsny, and the late Patrick Walker are published in numerous respectable magazines and newspapers. These general-advice columns are faithfully read by millions who often telephone the accompanying 900-number services for "more detailed forecasts."

The remarkable resurgence of interest in astrology at the end of the second millennium and the beginning of the third is predicted in the stars. According to Western astrological tradition, in late 1995, Pluto left an eleven-year cycle positioned in the sign of Scorpio, a cycle that highlighted military conflicts, possible biological warfare, and improved methods for increasing longevity. It then entered Sagittarius, commencing a thirteen-year period that turns the spotlight on a revived interest in spiritual, esoteric, and religious subjects, coupled with a worldwide drive toward familiarization with diverse ethnic cultures and a diffusion of national and racial distinctions. Within the sphere of Chinese and Tibetan astrological traditions, the Year of the Rat (1996) gave rise to a twelve-year cycle dominated by an intellectual interest in philosophical subjects.

But to comprehend and appreciate this new wealth of information, one needs to understand the basics: the history, methodology, intended purpose, and efficacy of the major astrological traditions, as well as their similarities and differences. Until now, this would have required the acquisition of numerous volumes, because the fundamentals of these six major Western and Eastern traditions have never before been compiled in one place, even though much can be gained from comparing those rich traditions while studying or practicing astrology. In this book you will find the cumulative results of our research into this science. Essential questions will be answered, such as these: When and where did astrology originate? Who were its champions and detractors? What do the various traditions have in common, and how are they dissimilar? How is a horoscope cast in the various traditions, and how is it interpreted? What can be gained by applying more than one tradition to an individual's astrological profile?

Part One introduces six of the world's major astrological traditions. Chapter 1, "The Celestial River," briefly details the origins of the Chinese, Tibetan, Vedic (Hindu), Arabian, Judaic, and Western astrological traditions, which include Chaldean, Babylonian, Greek, Egyptian, and Roman. This chapter explains how each tradition played a significant role in the history of the world's religions and governments, and contributed to the development of other sciences such as medicine, mathematics, and astronomy.

Chapter 2, "The Children of the Moon and the Children of the Sun," describes the various branches of astrology from natal (birth) charts and predictive astrology to medical and political astrology. It discusses the difference between exoteric astrology and esoteric astrology as well as the physical distinction between the tropical zodiac and the sidereal zodiac. This chapter also introduces a new method for categorizing these astrological traditions. Based on the level of importance placed on the Sun's versus the Moon's effect on human behavior and personality, we present our own unique divisions—the Sun school and the Moon school—along with the reasons why this new classification is useful to both astrological researchers and practitioners.

Part Two explains the basic steps involved in calculating and constructing a horoscope in each of the six traditions. We present commonly used chart construction procedures and generic interpretations of the resulting planetary positions: data that each practitioner customizes for presentation after years of observation and synthesis.

Beginning with one of the earliest forms of astrology, chapter 3 describes one of the many branches of Chinese astrology called *Tzu P'ing*, which concentrates on the relationship between an individual's life forces and surroundings as well as his or her destiny. The construction of a chronology based on decade-long "fate cycles" is also included, along with the two forms of daily prediction used in China: the *sieu* (lunar mansion) and the *chien-ch'ü* (daily indicator).

Chapter 4 presents Tibetan astrology, which was adapted from the Chinese tradition. But, unlike its predecessor, this method concentrates solely on the quality and type of life forces that an individual possesses from birth and their relationship to a specific point in time.

Chapter 5 describes the two types of natal horoscopes constructed and interpreted by Vedic astrologers, and also presents six additional charts that are often cast to enhance the astrological profile produced for an individual. One in particular, the *vimsottari dasa,* is a chronology that can foretell the general tone of events surrounding a person's life over periods as broad as years or as specific as hours.

Chapter 6 presents the calculation and interpretation of thirty-seven Arabian Parts, which were used to fine-tune or verify the prognostications of Arabian natal profiles and bear a close resemblance to modern-day Western and Judaic horoscopes. Chapter 7 explains the Judaic horoscope, which differs subtly from the Western horoscope, and the interpretation of the Ascendant (rising sign) according to the Judaic tradition. Chapter 8 takes you through the process of casting and interpreting a Western natal horoscope.

Part Three shows how the information in Part Two can be applied to the development of an individual personality profile. Chapter 9 demonstrates how the chronologies and personality profiles derived from the various astrological traditions are presented, using the late Diana, Princess of Wales, as the test subject. And chapter 10 suggests ways in which you can apply this vast body of knowledge to answer key questions about work, home, love, marriage, health, and many other essential facets of life.

Because so many unique terms are used in astrology, we have included a glossary for quick reference. A selected bibliography is provided to direct you on your way if you wish to further your own independent study of this subject.

One word of caution: Just as one physician seeks out another for a diagnosis of his or her own illness, and a good psychologist seeks professional counseling on someone else's couch, even the most experienced astrologer benefits from consulting another practitioner about his or her own horoscope. Therefore, if you are interested in uncovering your astrological profile or need astrological guidance concerning a specific question, you should consult a professional practitioner and use this book as a reference to help you understand what to expect from such a consultation. Anyone who tries to be his or her only astrologer cannot gain all that the science of astrology has to offer.

The Universal Search
Astrology Throughout the Ages

The Celestial River

A Brief History of Astrology

The influence of the celestial bodies on human beings has been astrology's broad focus for thousands of years, spanning many cultures and continents. The rise and fall of vast empires, as well as the births of conquerors and prophets, were often foretold by astral observations and recorded by astrologers. The development of modern science and medicine resulted in part from astrological observations and prognostications. It is a science that is embraced by two major religions (Hinduism and Buddhism), cautiously sanctioned by another (Judaism), and uniformly rejected by two more (Christianity and Islam).

The six major traditions discussed in this volume are by no means the world's only forms of astrology. But they do share common bonds: each was influenced by the other traditions during its development; and because of this interwoven relationship, each can trace its lineage as far back as 2700 B.C. Around that time, a form of astrology based on the apparent path of the Moon past certain groups of stars was first documented by Huang Ti (the Yellow Emperor) in China.[1] The people of China's agriculturally based culture relied on an adherence to the natural order of the universe: the orbits of the Moon and other celestial bodies were considered to influence profoundly many forces that controlled the existence and destiny of plants, animals, and human beings. Astrology provided human beings with the

---

1. The emperor Huang Ti (born c. 2704 B.C.) is the third of China's so-called Legendary Emperors, who were predynastic leaders between the twenty-seventh and twenty-second centuries B.C. Besides Huang Ti (a patron saint of Taoism, credited with having created the Chinese calendar), Fu Hsi (alleged inventor of pictograms and regulated marriages), and Shen Nung (said to have developed the agricultural system) are also members of this exclusive group.

information necessary to maintain cosmic and thus spiritual balance within the en-tire universe. But this was not the only astrological tradition to emerge at that time.

Although little documentation remains of the tradition practiced by the Chaldeans in the Near East, historians agree that they were responsible for an as-trological tradition that first emerged around 2500 B.C., based on the mean move-ments of the Sun. In the Old Testament, astrologers were called chaldeans, and were consulted to foretell the outcome of future events. Though astrology was practiced in both Babylonia and Chaldea, the latter's astrological methods became renowned throughout the known world. The early forms of Western astrology later practiced by the Egyptians, Greeks, and Romans fundamentally followed the Chaldeans' solar-based formulas. Even the early astrological traditions practiced in Arabia and Achaemenia (Persia) emerged from this same source.

A descendant of the Chaldean tradition, Greek astrology had a profound affect on the traditions that developed in Arabia and Achaemenia around 500 B.C. The determination of the midpoint between the exact location of an individual or event at a particular moment in time and a given planet—called a Lot by ancient Greek astrologers—became the basis for a prodigious collection of equations that were used by Arabian and Achaemenian astrologers to disclose everything of material importance from the potential outcome of a battle or a marriage proposal to the es-timated yield of a barley harvest. But despite its mathematical prowess, the sway of Greek astrology diminished as it spread farther East.

The oral traditions of the Indo-Aryans who settled in northern India were first narrated prior to 2000 B.C., but it wasn't until these myths about the origins of the Sun, the Moon, and the planets were written down five centuries later that the basis for Hindu astrology (now called Vedic astrology) was officially documented. The Hindu connection between the spiritual and the celestial was, in many ways, similar to Chinese ideology, which held that the spiritual destiny of human beings was closely linked to the forces of nature and the universe. But this lunar-based form of astrology was the first tradition to adapt methods imported from a Western culture. Taught by scholars living in Alexander the Great's Greco-Macedonian set-tlements in northern India, Vedic astrologers integrated the mathematical proce-dures used in Greek astrological tradition around 325 B.C. But because Hindu dogma and Vedic astrology both attach a great deal of spiritual and physical signifi-cance to lunar activity, the level of importance placed on the Sun's movements by the Greek school was discounted by the Vedics as insignificant.

The spread of trade from the Macedonian and Achaemenian empires to China shortly after Alexander left India enabled Vedic practitioners to share their newly synthesized knowledge with other scholars, influencing both the Chinese tradition and the unique form of astrology that had emerged around 642 A.D. in Tibet.

Combining the zodiac and the theoretical aspects of Chinese astrology with the mathematical concepts of the Vedic tradition, Tibetan astrology developed in a simplified, albeit rarefied atmosphere. According to Tibetan belief, human destiny and the forces of nature closely interact: the positive and negative flow of various elements must be kept in balance because the outcome of any event is determined by the level of harmony that is achieved.

Although abbreviated, this history of astrology provides a reasonable foundation from which to analyze each tradition, and studying these traditions together can serve as a steppingstone to expanding upon the world's current astrological knowledge.

THAT WHICH IS UNDER HEAVEN: THE ORIGINS OF CHINESE ASTROLOGY

The earliest surviving record of Chinese astrological activity dates back to the year 2677 B.C., when the Chinese emperor Huang Ti introduced a method for structuring time into orderly segments of sixty-year cycles, or *yüan*. The system relied on the position of asterisms (star clusters) and lunar movements that had been observed and recorded more than 1,500 years earlier. Beginning with the New Moon that occurs at the midpoint between the winter solstice and the vernal equinox, the Emperor's luni-solar[2] calendar consisted of twelve lunar cycles (or months) consisting of twenty-seven to thirty days each, with an "intercalary month" inserted every thirty months to ensure that the vernal equinox always took place within the second lunar month of any given year. But Huang Ti's fascination with T'ien Hsia ("that which is under Heaven" or the universe) did not end with the development of one of the world's earliest known calendars (which is still in use today) and the documentation of the Moon's orbit.

The emperor and his prime minister, Tajao, studied the stars from an observatory they erected in 2608 B.C. Using the Pleiades star cluster as the focal point from which the positions and relative distances of other stars could be determined, they identified four arcs of asterisms that were formed by bright, fixed stars. They associated the four groupings with the seasons of the year and the four compass directions: the Green Dragon[3] or Azure Dragon (spring/east), the Red Bird[4] or Vermilion Bird (summer/south), the White Tiger[5] (autumn/west), and the Dark

---

2. This term refers to the calendar's dual-natured basis, rectifying the movements of the Sun over the course of 365.25 days with the variable movements of the Moon over the course of twenty-seven to thirty days.
3. The Green Dragon arc consists of the asterisms Ch'io, K'ang, Ti, Fang, Hsin, Wei, and Chi, which correlate to fixed stars in the modern-day constellations Virgo, Scorpio, and a portion of Sagittarius.
4. The Red Bird arc includes the asterisms Ching, Kuei, Liu, Hsing, Chang, I, and Chen, which correlate to fixed stars in the modern-day constellations Gemini, Cancer, Hydra, Crater, and Corvus.
5. The White Tiger arc includes the asterisms K'uei, Lou, Wei, Mao, Pi, Tui, and Shen, which correlate to fixed stars found in the modern-day constellations of Andromeda, Aries, Taurus, and Orion.

Warrior[6] or Black Warrior (winter/north). The fixed stars themselves formed the basis for timing lunar activity as each became known as one of the Moon's "mansions" or *sieu*.

Emperor Huang Ti's contribution to the technical development of Chinese astrology (and astronomy) also had a dark side. According to legend, when Huang Ti became emperor, he deliberately ordered the burning of all existing books and documents. He believed that by removing any trace of written thought prior to his enthronement, he could stem the tide of misdirected analysis or comparison that might endanger the integrity of his school of thought. The only documents that were spared in this literary holocaust were quasi-astrological books (which included rudimentary astronomical texts) based on peasant folklore. Huang Ti believed that astrology came from the same celestial origins as the emperor himself, and the subject was seen as a vehicle by which humans could attain the natural order and harmony that he dreamt could exist for the people in his empire.

China is a primarily agrarian culture where the peasants have relied for thousands of years on a rich oral tradition that clearly outlines the natural and celestial omens dictating the most auspicious times to prepare the soil, plant, and harvest. (This same tradition also prescribed certain activities during specific lunar or seasonal periods and clearly imposed corporeal or spiritual punishment on anyone who did not follow the natural order of the universe.) It was an obvious progression, then, for the governing nobility to develop a rich scholarly culture reflecting this strong association with nature, order, and harmony.

The interrelationship between human beings and nature was the central focus of the Mandate of Heaven, which dictated the duties of the emperor.[7] As the "Son of Heaven," the emperor served as the intermediary between Heaven and Earth. He religiously followed the Sun's movements, moving from one of his thirteen residences to the next in the five palaces located on the imperial grounds. His path followed the same sequential direction as the Sun itself, moving from the east to the south, to the center, to the west, to the north, and back to the east.

During the spring, he lived in the three residences of the Eastern Palace, where he wore green and ate foods that were said to enhance the power of the Wood Planet (Jupiter), which bestows abundance. In the early summer, he lived in the three southern residences, where he wore red and ate chicken and peas to honor

---

6. The mythical turtle-snake, called the Dark Warrior, is an arc that includes the asterisms Tou, Niu, Nü, Hsü, Wei, Shih, and Pi, which correlate to fixed stars in the modern-day constellations Capricorn, Aquarius, Pegasus, and the remaining portion of Sagittarius.

7. According to the Confucian philosopher Mencius (371–289 B.C.), an emperor who lacked virtue forfeited his right to the throne. The mandate to rule was then awarded by Heaven to the conqueror who established the next dynasty, solving the philosophical problem of transferring loyalty from one dynasty to the next and passing with it specific responsibilities attached to the spiritual health of the empire.

the Fire Planet (Mars), which endows the Earth with light and energy. During the "dog days" of summer, he moved to the singular central residence known as the Temple of the Ancestors, ate beef and millet, and dressed in imperial yellow in reverence to the Earth Planet (Saturn), which is the immovable and unchanging land. When autumn arrived, the Emperor resided in the three Western Palace residences, wore white, and ate sesame and dog: symbols of the Metal Planet (Venus), which represents both the time of harvest and the time for war.[8] And when winter fell upon the earth, the Emperor moved to the three residences of the Northern Palace, eating sorghum and pork, and donning black garments to symbolize the Water Planet (Mercury), which governed the period of hibernation prior to the beginning of another year.

The imperial altar used by the emperor and his court to celebrate the new year also paid homage to the heavens. Positioned in the Temple of the Ancestors, the altar was decorated with symbols of the five planets that the Chinese had worshiped as gods (the White, Green, Black, Red, and Yellow Rulers) since 4000 B.C.; the twenty-eight *sieu*, which were considered to be the homes of gods who defeated the rebel patriarch T'ung-t'ien Chiao-chu during the Battle of the Ten Thousand Immortals; the fixed stars of Ursa Major, which are considered the home of the Fates; and the luminaries Jih-kung Ch'ih-chiang of the Sun Palace and Yüeh-fu Ch'ang-O of the Moon Palace. Like his peasant subjects, the emperor was required to maintain harmony between the forces of Heaven and Earth. It was believed that if the emperor did not follow the precepts of the Mandate of Heaven, there would be a disruption in the relationship, causing famine, earthquakes, floods, or plague.

The spiritual and scientific connections between the emperor and the stars continued long after Huang Ti's death. Over a century after Huang Ti documented the existence of the four arcs of asterisms, the emperor Chuan Hsü published an ephemeris (a daily listing of the motions and locations of each planet as it travels along the Sun's apparent path in the heavens), based on both his predecessors' and his own observations of the orbits made by the planets Mercury, Venus, Mars, Jupiter, and Saturn in the year 2513 B.C. As mentioned earlier, these planets were associated with the terrestrial elements of water, metal, fire, wood, and earth, which the Chinese call the *wu hsing*, or Five Agents. The system originated from oral traditions based on predynastic concepts of natural order and served as the foundation for the organization of the days of the week. Because all things in nature must achieve a harmonious existence, each *hsing* is not only endowed with its

---

8. This coupling was a way of life for two reasons: Peasants were generally drafted into the infantry after the harvest was finished. Wars, therefore, were fought during the nonfarming months of late autumn. Another reason wars were waged during that season was that armies were assured that food supplies could be commandeered easily after the harvest.

natural *yin* or *yang* properties, but also contains *yin* and *yang* aspects. The wood *hsing,* for example, has an essential *yin* life force, but there are also *yin* wood and *yang* wood. Treated as separate entities, these ten subdivisions of the five elements are called the *t'ien kan* (Celestial Stems). Besides ruling individual days, the *t'ien kan* dictate the relationships of the *wu hsing* with each other. By documenting the movements of the *wu hsing,* the emperor Chueni contributed the second major evolutionary step in the technical development of Chinese astrology.

When the five original canonical works that form the heart of classic Chinese literature were compiled and published around 1100 B.C., astrology was already recognized as a scholarly science. References to the asterisms and to astrology itself appear in the *I Ching* (Book of Changes, the only surviving book from a divination trilogy that included the *Lien Shan* [Manifestation of the Mountain] and the *Kuei Tsang* [Flow and Return to Womb and Tomb]); in the *Shih Ching* (Book of Poetry, which was later rewritten and republished by Confucius); in the *Shu Ching* (Book of Documents, or Great Plan, which was reputedly written by the first Legendary Emperor Fu Hsi (2852–2738 B.C.); in the *Li Chi* (Book of Rites); and in the *Ch'un Ch'iu* (Spring and Autumn Annals).[9]

Because China remained relatively isolated from actual physical contact with Western civilization until the thirteenth century A.D., the first European visitors discovered a body of astrological knowledge that was truly unique. By the second century A.D., Chinese astrologers had already observed and documented the position of 11,520 individual stars, and by the time Marco Polo arrived in China in A.D. 1275, astrology had already matured into an exacting science that incorporated numerous systems of calculation and delineation. As the Italian adventurer remarked in his journal: "These astrologers are very skillful in their business, and often their words come to pass, so the people have great faith in them."

It wasn't until the Silk Road was opened to trade by the Mongol Khanate, which was founded by Genghis Khan in A.D. 1206 and thrived until his grandson Kublai Khan died in A.D. 1294, that the calculation methods employed by Indian and Arabian practitioners who had independently developed forms of astrology and stellar observation were added to the already vast body of Chinese celestial knowledge, which had grown to include a reorganization of the division of daily hours. Prior to the Han dynasty (206 B.C.–A.D. 220), a twenty-four-hour day was segmented into ten *k'o* (time periods). This was changed to twelve *k'o* around A.D. 100. The periods were known as *ti chih* (Terrestrial Branches). Three centuries later, refined descriptions of the functions and characteristics of the *ti chih*

---

9.   The balance of this body of literature was completed nearly nine centuries later with the addition of the four *Shu,* which include the *Lun Yü* (Sayings of Confucius), *Ta Hsüeh* (Great Learnings), *Chung Yung* (Doctrine of the Mean), and *Meng Tzu* (Works of Mencius).

appeared in written texts throughout the empire. These were later distilled to form the popular astrological system called the *Ming Shu* (Circle of Animals), which is similar to modern-day Western Sun-sign astrology. Based on the peasant lunar calendar, this astrological method didn't require a knowledge of scholarly subjects, so it was quickly adopted by the less-educated rural population and lower-class city dwellers.

During the early years of the Ch'ing (Manchu) dynasty (c. A.D. 1670), Western science was introduced to Emperor Hsüan Yeh. Persuaded by his Western astronomical adviser, Father Ferdinand Verbiest, a Dutch Jesuit missionary,[10] Hsüan Yeh divided the day into ninety-six *k'o* or time periods of fifteen minutes of clock time each, thus precisely matching the Chinese clock to the Western clock. But the spirit of the twelve *ti chih* was so firmly interwoven into the cultural fabric that it was not abandoned. Within the nation, the people continued to mark time according to the traditional *ti chih* and, subsequently, the popular *ming shu*.

NO TURNING BACK:
THE BEGINNINGS OF TIBETAN ASTROLOGY

Tibetan astrology was born around A.D. 642, when the *Ming Shu* was introduced in Tibet by the Chinese princess Hun-shin Kun-ju (or Kong Jo), who married Tibet's king Srang-Tsan Gampo. This simple form of astrological delineation was quickly embraced in this remote mountainous Himalayan region, inhabited mostly by farmers and herders whose lives revolved around a comparatively short and tenuous growing season in the sparse pockets of vegetation around the foothills. Tibetans were no strangers to the concept of an interrelationship between the extreme elements of nature and human life. Their oral tradition reflected the association, creating a very animated spiritual realm populated by animal-faced gods and goddesses. Each deity ruled a particular portion of the physical world, and possessed either positive or negative behavioral traits. Thus, Tibetans readily embraced a concept such as the *Ming Shu* that so closely correlated with their reverence for natural phenomena (wind, rain, snow, etc.), their understanding of the lunar cycles, and their unswerving devotion to spirits whose animal and human natures needed constant appeasement.

Having little need for intellectual complexity in a culture so driven by natural extremes and the desire for harmonic survival, Tibetan scholars quickly adopted the orderly flow of natural forces and human behavioral patterns defined in the *Ming Shu* as well as the relationships of the *t'ien kan*. These two subjects created the

---

10.   Father Ferdinand Verbiest (whose Chinese name was Nan Huai-jen) replaced Adam Schall von Bell, another Jesuit missionary, as the emperor's adviser and director of the Imperial Board of Astronomy. In addition to his scientific services, Verbiest was also the official Chinese translator during treaty negotiations with Russia in 1678.

basis for *jung-tsi* (the spiritual side of Tibetan astrology). At around the same time, Tibetans adopted the non-astrologically-based set of eight trigrams employed by Chinese fortune tellers specializing in *I Ching* divination, and Tibetan scholars also developed a form of predictive astrology based on the nine prime numbers used in *lo shu,* a form of Chinese numerological divination. Additionally, the Tibetan calendar was changed to match the Chinese sixty-year, 354-day-per-year luni-solar calendar system.

While Chinese astrology was rapidly embraced because of its spiritual rapport with the Tibetan understanding of cosmology, Vedic (Hindu) astrology was also received with great reverence in Tibet, because of its mathematical precision and accuracy. This perceived accuracy may have been the result of Tibet's proximity to the Indian celestial observatories. The location of the fixed stars from a longitude and latitude in northern India would have appeared more precise to Tibetan eyes than those defined by observers in distant Beijing.

It was shortly after Lamaism (Tibetan Buddhism) developed in the eighth century that Vedic astrology was introduced into Tibet. When the Tantric Buddhist scholar Padmasambhava and the Mahayana Buddhist scholar Santiraksita arrived from India (c. A.D. 749), they brought with them a body of Hindu knowledge that expanded the already large retinue of Tibetan deities. But they also provided astrological scholars with technical data such as tables of lunar phases and ephemerides that documented both solar and lunar eclipses, forming the foundation for *kar-tsi* (the technical side of Tibetan astrology). With the exception of three Indian gods, the *naksatras* (lunar mansions), and the Vedic studies of the planets, however, little of the rich religious foundation of Vedic astrology was adopted in Tibet.

THE TIMES OF ISSUING-FORTH, CONTINUANCE, AND DESTRUCTION: VEDIC ASTROLOGY'S BEGINNINGS

Documents found in the libraries of the Punjabi maharajas date astrological practice in India as far back as the four Vedas: the liturgical texts that form the basis of Hinduism, which evolved from the spiritual practices of an Indo-Aryan cult that drank *soma* (a sacred intoxicating drink distilled from an unknown plant) and made animal sacrifices to a number of natural deities such as wind, sun, fire, rain, war, and creation. Based on four Brahmin-caste[11] oral traditions that originated prior to 3100 B.C. and were finally written and published around 1500 B.C., the *Rig Veda* (the Veda of Hymns, which is composed of one thousand hymns dedicated to the various deities), *Yajur Veda* (the Veda of Sacrificial Formulas, which is a manual of rites and rituals), *Sama Veda* (the Veda of Chants, which is an abridg-

---

11.   Generally, this is the caste of priests and scholars.

ment of the *Rig Veda*), and *Atharva Veda* (the Veda of Spells, which is an anthology of excerpts from the three previous volumes) are the primary sources of Indian spiritual knowledge. Each book portrays humankind's wonder at the greatness of the natural world, using rich visual imagery to describe the relationship of Heaven and Earth. Within the verses of these sacred texts are numerous references to the *ayanamsa* (the steady axial movement of the Earth's north-south poles) as well as the movements of the stars and the planets, particularly the Moon and its *naksatras* (lunar mansions)—in direct connection with the deities that rule every level of the Indian spiritual and physical worlds. Consequently, *jyotisa* or Vedic astrology is integral to the scholarly knowledge of Indian culture, and is as essential to Hindu religious dogma as is the study of the *brahmanas* (the protocol for the execution of rituals by the priests), which were written between 800 B.C. and 600 B.C.

But, despite voluminous references in these ancient texts, the Vedic techniques for astrological calculation that are still used today did not develop until an early form of Western astrology—Greek astrology—was introduced in India through the publication of the *Yavanajataka* (literally, "Ionian natal astrology" or "Greek natal astrology") in A.D. 269, during India's Maurya dynasty. This work was translated by Sphujidhvaja[12] from a Greek astrological text written by Yavanesvara ("Lord of the Greeks") that dated back to Alexander the Great's establishment of Greco-Macedonian settlements in northern India in 327 B.C. According to Sphujidhvaja, Yavanesvara had received his knowledge of the stars from Surya, the Sun, who had, in turn, received it from his twin sons, the Asvins, who had learned it from Prajapati, the Lord of Offspring.

Ancient Indian legends tell how some royal chiefs descended from the union of Surya and his two wives, while others descended from the marriage of Candra, the Moon, to his twenty-seven wives. Most Indian royal families can cite these tales, claiming to be descended from either the Suryavamsa (the Sun's dynasty) or the Candravamsa (the Moon's dynasty). (Noted exceptions, however, were the Pandava princes[13] [Arjuna and his half-brothers Yudhisthira, Bhma, Nakula, and Sahadeva] mentioned in the part-historic, part-legendary epic *Mahabharata*, who were born from the intermarriage of the solar dynasty's Maha and the lunar dynasty's Bharata.)

When the mathematical formulas found in the *Yavanajataka* were incorporated into the Vedic practice of astrology, the results revolutionized India's worldview. Scholars needed to justify the radical variations in placement among the visible

12. Sphujidhvaja was the ruler of a remnant Greek settlement situated in the Punjab that had been established when Alexander the Great conquered northern India.
13. More appropriately, these were clan chiefs of the Aryan tribe the Bharatas, who had settled in India's southern Punjab region.

constellations that appeared over Greece and Egypt to those situated over northern India and to the ones that passed over southern India. These observers hy-
pothesized that the world was round, not flat. Realizing that planetary positions
plotted from the Greek "ground zero" (Alexandria, Egypt) were of little value in
India, these scholars identified a new prime meridian from which to calculate the
planets' locations. Therefore, the Indian prime meridian was placed at Ujjayini
(now called Ujjain [23°11′N / 75°46′E]), which had been the capital of the Aryan
kingdom during the sixth century B.C. and was the site of numerous previously established celestial observatories.[14]

Since Vedic astrologers welcomed the mathematical precision of Greek astrology, for a time they reordered the *naksatras* so that the first of the twenty-seven
lunar mansions that make up the Vedic sidereal zodiac, the *naksatra* Asvini, began at
the same point as the first of the twelve tropical zodiac signs, 00°00′ Aries
(00°♈00′), used by Greek astrologers.[15] But eventually Indian scholars dropped the
practice of casting a tropical zodiac altogether. The Greeks' tropical zodiac (meaning
"circle of animals"), based on the Sun's synodic or mean movements, was of little interest to these devout Hindu scholars, who attached great religious significance to
the sidereal zodiac system's lunar movements, so vividly described in each of the
Vedas. This was partly due to a centuries-old prejudice against Greek culture, which
began when Alexander the Great invaded the Punjab during the Nanda dynasty
(fourth century B.C.) and grew during the subsequent Indo-Greek rule of portions of
northwestern India (c. 250–130 B.C.). It was also due to religious devotion to the
Hindu deities who were represented in the *naksatras* themselves. The final outcome
of this interchange and eventual schism between the two technical methodologies is
found in the written works of the sixth-century A.D. royal Indian astrologer, Varahamihira, whose techniques are still applied by modern-day Vedic practitioners.

The brief union of Vedic and Greek astrologies did not live out its entire existence
in India. Nor was Greek astrology the only "outside" tradition to be studied and partially adopted by Vedic scholars. During the Punjab's rule under the Muslim hege-
mony (c. A.D. 1200–1757), Tajika (Arabian) astrology was also introduced thanks to
the interchange of commerce and knowledge that developed when Turkish Ghurid
Muslims expanded their territorial interests to encompass northwest Indian territo-
ries occupied by the Achaemenians (Persians). Concurrently the Mongol expansion
from northern China to the Muslim-ruled Punjab (c. 1206–1227) exposed Chinese

---

14.   This city, which the Egyptian astrologer Ptolemy called Ozene, was the capital of the Western Satraps and a
major trade center by the first century A.D.

15.   In the *Atharva Veda* (published around 1500 B.C.), the *naksatra* Krttika (26°40′ Aries through 10°00′ Taurus
(26°♈40′–10°♉00′) was mentioned as the first lunar mansion, standing at the Vernal Point, 00°00′ Aries
(00°♈00′).

and Tibetan astrological scholars to both Arabian and Vedic practices. A form of sidereal astrology that appears to have been partially influenced by the Vedic *naksatras* and the Chinese *sieu* also developed during this period in Arabia.

THE GREAT CONJUNCTION: ARABIAN ASTROLOGY

There are few existing written records of the development of Tajika (Arabian) astrology. It is assumed that Arabian astrologers were initially influenced by the earliest forms of Western astrology, which were developed by the Chaldeans and Babylonians, whose astrological systems closely followed the Sun's mean movements and allegedly date as far back as 2500 B.C. Two thousand years later the science had developed to such a point that Arabian and Achaemenian (Persian) astrologers were considered to be the best practitioners of predictive astrology in the known world. One of the most notable was the royal astrologer to the Achaemenian king Darius I (550–486 B.C.). This scholar, whose name was Al'hakim[16] (Wise One; c. 540–480 B.C.), wrote many scientific and astrological works. But he is best remembered for the predictions he made in his book *Judicia Gjmaspia,* in which he foretold the end of the polytheistic Magian religion; the rise of monotheistic Zoroastrism during Darius's reign; the birth of Jesus Christ[17] five hundred years later; and the birth of Mohammed over a thousand years later.

By the time the prophet Mohammed was born, in A.D. 571, Arabian and Achaemenian scholars had already accumulated a thousand years of astrological knowledge. This scholarship was augmented by early forms of Western astrology found in books written by the Greek astrologer Hipparchus (110 B.C.) and the Egyptian scholar Claudius Ptolemy (A.D. 150), which had become readily available thanks to the expansive Arabian and Achaemenian mercantile trade that had developed over the centuries.

A growing merchant class and a wealthy nobility consulted their personal astrologers on a regular basis, seeking the future outcome of marriage contracts, business negotiations, battles, and the annual harvest. Arabian astrologers boasted that they could accurately predict the future by using the same methodology applied by ancient Greek astrologers in the calculation of the Seven Lots[18] many centuries

---

16.   This historical character is not to be confused with the caliph Al'hakim Bi'Amr Allah, the tyrannical ruler of Egypt between A.D. 985 and 1021.

17.   It has often been alleged by biblical scholars that the three Magi who traveled from Persia to Palestine seeking Jesus Christ had seen the celestial configuration foretold by Al'hakim.

18.   The Seven Lots were mathematically derived midpoints used by Greek astrologers to determine the relationship between the sign that represents the exact place and time of an individual's birth (the Ascendant) and another planet or an angle such as the Midheaven, the Descendant, or the Nadir. The Seven Lots were named the Lot of Daimon, the Lot of Audacity, the Lot of Eros, the Lot of Necessity, the Lot of Nemesis, the Lot of Victory, and the Lot of Fortune.

earlier (see "Guided by the Light of Ishtar," page 19) and by their Greek and Egyptian contemporaries, who employed more than forty equations derived from the same mathematical theory. Over the next few centuries, Arabian practitioners added to this body of knowledge by developing more than 143 equations to refine natal delineations, answer horary questions about the future of earthly activities, and verify planetary indicators in an individual's horoscope. Collectively called the "fate of the houses" or Arabian Parts, each of these mathematically derived corollary points (midpoints) focuses on the relationship of the Ascendant (an individual ruling zodiac sign based on the time and place of birth rather than the date) to other planetary positions or other constructed midpoints.

The Arabian thirst for knowledge continued. In A.D. 529 the closing of the Academy[19] in Athens by the Byzantine Roman emperor Justinian I (c. 483–565) was meant to curb paganism in polytheistic Greece and Macedonia. But it also forced many astrological, medical, and scientific scholars to seek more hospitable environs in Achaemenia and Arabia—which they readily found. Many classic Greek texts were translated into Arabic and distributed throughout the expanding Islamic empire in the centuries that followed.

During the eighth and ninth centuries A.D., two major series of works were translated into Arabic: the Abbasid caliph Al'mansur ordered the translation of the five fifth-century-A.D. Vedic astronomical treatises entitled the *Siddhantas;* and the Abbasid caliph Al'ma'mun ordered the translation of Ptolemy's astrological trilogy—*Tetrabiblos, Almagest,* and *Centiloquium.* The wealth of Western (i.e., Greek and Egyptian) as well as Vedic scientific and Hindu philosophic knowledge was digested and synthesized into an Arabian academic tradition encompassing logic; natural sciences such as rudimentary psychology and biology; metaphysics; and mathematical sciences such as music and astrology. This refined body of scholarship flourished among Muslims who embraced the concept of rational theology expounded by the Mu'tazilah ("those who stand apart"), a movement that segregated itself from the fanaticism of the Shi'ite, Gnostic, and Manichaean factions of the early Islamic faith. As defenders of "Allah's unity and justice," Mu'tazilah followers steadfastly defended the concept of free will, according to which human acts were physical proofs of spiritual faith, not results of divine predestination. Under this liberal viewpoint, astrology was considered an aid to the fulfillment of an individual's chosen path, not merely a prediction of his or her destiny.

It was within this ideological atmosphere that the ninth-century philosopher and mathematical scientist Al'kindi wrote lucid commentaries on the teachings of

---

19. This was the name for the pedagogic philosophy school that was considered to be the seat of Greek knowledge.

the Greek philosophers Plato and Aristotle. He also suggested that there was an acausal connection between the indeterminate yet constant spiritual world and the infinite yet ever-changing physical world.

One of his students also took full advantage of the intellectual freedom afforded by the times. The ninth-century Arabian astrologer Albumazar[20] wrote extensively on the calculation and interpretation of the Arabian Parts, claiming that at least ninety-seven of these corollary points were derived from Western sources such as ancient Egyptian and Babylonian texts. Albumazar's written works *Kitab al'Qiranat* (On the Great Conjunctions), *Kitab al'Madkhal al'Kabir'ala'ilm Ahkam Nujum* (The Great Introduction to the Science of Astrology), and *Kitab Tahawil Sini al'dlam* (The Revolutions of the World Years), were considered to be the greatest discourses ever produced about the Arabian Parts.[21]

The popularity of Albumazar's work among Arabian scholars was overwhelming. Inspired by his insights, additional Arabian Parts were developed and added to the already bloated repertoire. By the next century, the astrologer and historian Abu'l'rayhan Muhammad ibn Ahmad Al'biruni publicly scorned his peers' seemingly endless desire to create a part for nearly every human activity. He claimed that the increased dependence upon the Arabian Parts to predict daily life reduced the science of astrology to the superficial level attributed to divinatory oracles.

Born near Kath, in the northern portion of the Achaemenid empire that bordered northwestern India,[22] Al'biruni had been influenced at an early age by Magian and Vedic erudition as well as by the scholarship of the Khazarite Jews who inhabited the western shores of the Caspian Sea near his birthplace. This cross-cultural comprehension provided the young Al'biruni with a unique view of the known world.

In his monumental work, *Tafhim*,[23] Al'biruni applied his unique insight to the pure science of astrological chart construction: a pre-logarithmic approach to its calculation; a geometrically based justification of planetary positions; a logical approach to the organization and delineation of those positions; and an adaptation of the Vedic *naksatras*, which he called the *manazils*.

---

20.   Also known as Abu Ma'shar, this pivotal astrology scholar was born on August 10, A.D. 787, and died on March 9, 886.

21.   Albumazar was also famous for his theory of the Earth's creation and end. He believed that when the Earth was created, all seven traditional planets (the Sun, Moon, Mercury, Venus, Mars, Jupiter, and Saturn) simultaneously occupied 00°00′ Aries (00°♈00′) on the ecliptic. Further, life on Earth will come to an end when the same planets are concurrently positioned in 30°00′ Pisces (30°♓00′).

22.   This area south of the Ural Sea is now known as Khiva, Uzbekistan.

23.   This is the foreshortened Arabic title given to Al'biruni's book, *The Book of Instruction in the Elements of the Art of Astrology,* which was translated into English by R. Ramsay Wright (London: Luzac & Co., 1934).

By the time the Arabian astrologer and poet Anwari (as well as a number of Western astrologers from Spain, Greece, Rome, and Sicily) warned of a great storm that would occur when a conjunction of five planets took place in the sign of Libra (♎), Arabian astrology was already renowned for its mathematical accuracy. Anwari was ridiculed when the night in question (September 16, 1162)[24] passed without a breath of wind. However, he was later lauded for his remarkable prophecy when it was understood that on the night of this union of the Sun (00°♎25′), Jupiter (01°♎02′), Saturn (05°♎20′), Mars (10°♎40′), and the Moon (29°♎14′) a child named Temüjin was born.

The boy grew to become the Emperor Genghis Khan, who ruled China's Yüan (Mongol) dynasty from 1206 to 1227. As noted by Temüjin's family's astrologer, Sujujin, the so-called great conjunction was positioned in Temüjin's fourth house—the house of land and property—foretelling that he would be a great conqueror.[25] (The young Temüjin's personal knowledge of astrology was also extensive. His guardian and tutor was Sujujin's son, the astrologer Karasher.)

The entire doctrine of the Arabian Parts and the *manazils* were tragically lost in Europe and North Africa when Christian Crusaders destroyed many of the Arabian civilization's scholarly documents. In fact, what we now know of Arabian astrology can be credited to the work of the thirteenth-century Italian astrologer Guido Bonatti, who wrote an astrological treatise titled *Liber Astronomiae*, which included the extraction and delineation of the major Arabian Parts as well as a chronicle of the works of Albumazar, Al'biruni, and other Arabian astrologers that had been translated by Hebrew scholars who were seeking answers to their own questions concerning the interrelationship between human behavior and the mandates of a monotheistic God.

TO RULE BY DAY . . . TO RULE BY NIGHT: JUDAIC ASTROLOGY

The twelfth-century Jewish astrologer and biblical commentator Abraham ben Meir ibn Ezra was one of many writers whose works on the fundamentals of astrology, titled *Sefer Ha-te Amim* (Book of Reasons) and *Sefer Reshit Hokhmah* (Book of Nativities), had been translated during the thirteenth century by Henri Bate of Maline for the papal court of Orvieto, Italy. The views of Arabian astrologers who spent their lives predicting the outcome of future earthly events for their affluent clients were strongly contested by ibn Ezra, who called astrology a "sublime sci-

---

24. Genghis Khan's actual birth year is debatable, since there were no written records of the event. However, Mongolian historians generally accept the year as 1162, though some foreign scholars argue that his birth took place in 1155, 1162, 1167, or 1186.

25. The placement of this conjunction was also assumed by two twentieth-century astrologers: Sepharial and Manly Palmer Hall; the latter cast Genghis Khan's chart in his book *The Story of Astrology* (1933).

ence," pointing out that it had survived centuries of the rigorous Talmudic debates that began before the sixth century B.C. Unlike Western and Arabian astrologies, the Judaic tradition established the same strong connections between the celestial science and religious dogma as did Vedic astrology. In the eyes of ibn Ezra and other Jewish scholars, the numerous references to astrology found in the Torah (the Hebrew Bible) were irrefutable.

Throughout the first and last books of the Torah (Genesis and Deuteronomy), there are descriptions of the twelve sons of Jacob that more than superficially resemble the characteristics and symbols associated with the signs of the tropical zodiac used by the early Western astrological practitioners. As they appeared in the order of their birth, the general description of Jacob's son Reuben is associated with characteristics of the zodiac sign Shor (♉, Taurus), Simon with Teomin (♊, Gemini), Levi with Sarton (♋, Cancer), Judah with Ari (♌, Leo), Zebulon with Betulah (♍, Virgo), Issachar with Moznayim (♎, Libra), Dan with Akrab (♏, Scorpio), Gad with Kasshat (♐, Sagittarius), Asher with Gedi (♑, Capricorn), Naphthali with Deli (♒, Aquarius), Joseph with Dagim (♓, Pisces), and Benjamin with Taleh (♈, Aries).

The same texts explain that each of Jacob's sons headed a tribe of Israel that consequently became associated with the same zodiac sign. According to the book of Exodus, when the tribes of Israel traveled across the desert they divided themselves into four camps of three tribes each, corresponding to the four elements—fire, earth, air, and water—in the same manner that the Chaldean, Babylonian, and Egyptian zodiacs were subdivided.

Other biblical references were also noted by rabbinical scholars. For example, at one point in early Jewish history, the word *chaldean* meant astrologer. This correspondence led to a heated rabbinical discourse over a biblical passage that loosely narrated that "Abraham, the Chaldean, bore upon his breast a large astrological tablet on which the fate of every man might be read; for which reason . . . all the kings of the East and of the West congregated every morning before his door in order to seek advice."

Some ancient scholarly texts noted that the Hebrew term for constellations, *mazalot*, was derived from the word *nozeil*, which means "to drip steadily." From this connection it was believed that a flow of energy from divine sources moved from the heavens into the constellations, which reflected that energy onto earthly points below and consequently influenced time, events, and human nature.

The Jewish calendar is a luni-solar system, applying the nineteen-year Metonic Cycle developed by the Greeks to its calculation of lunar months and intercalary months in a format almost identical to the Chinese calendar. (The system begins with the traditional year of Creation, 3761 B.C.) Unlike the Chinese year, which begins with the second New Moon after the winter solstice, the Jewish ecclesiastical year begins with the first New Moon after the vernal equinox; while the civil year begins with the first New Moon following the autumnal equinox.

Each month in the Jewish calendar not only corresponds to important holy days, but also directly relates to a zodiac sign: Nisan to Taleh (♈, Aries), Iyyar to Shor (♉, Taurus), Sivan to Teomin (♊, Gemini), Tammuz to Sarton (♋, Cancer), Av to Ari (♌, Leo), Elul to Betulah (♍, Virgo), Tishrei to Moznayim (♎, Libra), Heshvan to Akrab (♏, Scorpio), Kislev to Kasshat (♐, Sagittarius), Tevet to Gedi (♑, Capricorn), Shevat to Deli (♒, Aquarius), and Adar to Dagim (♓, Pisces). An intercalary month, Ve-Adar, is added after Adar on the third, sixth, eighth, eleventh, fourteenth, seventeenth, and nineteenth years of the Metonic Cycle in the same manner that the Chinese and Vedic luni-solar calendars are periodically rectified.

The attainment of balance between individuals, between humans and animals, between humans and nature, and between humans and God lies at the heart of the Judaic faith, just as it does in Hindu and Buddhist dogma. Consequently an astrological comprehension of one's behavior in relation to other individuals, to the family, and to the community was deemed essential if it could be used to guide that person in Jewish law. Astrology was so commonly practiced among the people and the rabbinate that it was actually considered for inclusion as one of 613 precepts of Judaism. Numerous discussions of its application appear in the Talmud. The rabbis were cautious to differentiate astrology from fortune-telling. Divination practices such as snake-charming, necromancy, and animal auguries are listed in Deuteronomy as the magical arts of heathen nations, and are forbidden to the children of Israel. But the rabbinate agreed that a person's time and place of birth influenced both character and potential destiny, asserting in the Tractate Shabbath 156a that "the planet under which a person is born determines whether he is wise and rich, and the planets do affect the lives of the Israelites."

During the twelfth century A.D., while Abraham ibn Ezra's works were being translated, Kabbala (a form of Jewish mysticism claiming to reveal the "secret knowledge" of cosmology and the hidden meanings of biblical passages) was gaining popularity among European Jewish communities. Begun in Palestine during the first century A.D., the practice was originally based on contemplation of the *merkava*: a chariot envisioned by the prophet Ezekiel. Two centuries later the Kabbalic text *Sefer Yetzira* (Book of Formation) explained the original names of all the zodiac constellations as well as the secret codes of the divine numbers and alphabet, which were called the "thirty-two paths of secret wisdom." The *Sefer Ha-zohar* (Book of Splendor) offered explanations of the meanings of creation, salvation, and the functions of the divine numbers. Another text, the *Sefer Ha-bahir* (Book of

Brightness), introduced the concept of *gilgul* (transmigration of the soul) into Jewish scholarship. Unfortunately, the Kabbalistic practices of meditation and astrology, as well as the belief in reincarnation, were wrongly associated with magic and witchcraft by fanatical Catholic clergy and nobility determined to expunge non-Christian practices from European culture, especially in Spain. This resulted partially from Kabbalistic references found in the writings of curious non-Semitic alchemists and mystics that were seized during the thirteenth-century Papal Inquisition and the fifteenth-century Spanish Inquisition.

The balance between religious faith and heresy tipped against astrology as Christian scholars and scientists discovered and debated such forms of alleged mysticism. Tragically, the entire body of ancient Judaic, Arabian, and Western (particularly Greek and Egyptian) astrological knowledge was discounted as divination and witchcraft by a fearful and protective Roman Catholic Church. Despite this persecution, Jewish culture quietly prevailed throughout the centuries into modern days—including the study of the Kabbala and the casting of Western-style horoscopes by Judaic astrologers.

GUIDED BY THE LIGHT OF ISHTAR:
THE BIRTH OF WESTERN ASTROLOGY

The seeds of knowledge that eventually developed into the practice of Western astrology originated among the ancient Mesopotamian civilizations, where celestial omens are said to have been observed and categorized by the Chaldeans as far back as 3000 B.C. It was believed in those earliest of times that the gods conveyed messages to human beings through solar and lunar eclipses, comets, and other natural phenomena such as the rising and setting of the morning star (Venus). Consequently, rulers and military leaders consulted professional oracles who could read these prognostications about the potential outcome of a battle or political decision.

This popular practice made its way into the royal courts of the neighboring Babylonian empire several hundred years later, and was finally documented two thousand years later in a cuneiform text titled *Enuma Anu Enlil* (When the Gods Anu and Enlil) (c. 1000 B.C.). Many versions of this valuable work were handed down over the centuries, spreading from the Near East to the seats of early Western civilization: Greece, Macedonia, and Egypt. In each edition the omens were organized into four categories, representing four gods and their physical celestial representatives: Sin (the Moon), Shamash (the Sun), Adad (the weather), and Ishtar (Venus).

By 500 B.C., the *Enuma Anu Enlil* had been translated into Egyptian, Greek, and Sanskrit and disseminated throughout the growing Achaemenian empire that by then ruled much of northern Africa and the Near East between 559 and 330 B.C., and the subsequent Greco-Macedonian empire created by Alexander the Great, which included Egypt. But some scholars believed Western astrology was born in the Nile River valley. The British scientist Sir Isaac Newton wrote in his *Chronology* that "Nechepos, or Nicepsos, King of Sais by the assistance of Petosiris, a priest of Egypt, invented astrology, grounding it upon the aspects of the planets, and the qualities of the men and women they were dedicated; and in the beginning of the reign of Nabonassar, King of Babylon, about which time the Ethiopians, under Sason, invaded Egypt. . . . So Diodorus: 'they say that the Chaldean in Babylon, being colonies of Egyptians, became famous for astrology, having learned it from the priests of Egypt." According to Newton, this series of historic events places the Egyptian origins of astrology (as opposed to the reading of celestial omens) in the year 772 B.C., and its introduction in Babylon in 747 B.C.

A Chaldean priest named Berosus allegedly introduced astrology to the Greeks when he settled on the Greek island of Cos during the fourth century B.C. The time was ripe for the presentation of a subject that coincided with the Grecian desire to find new gods in the realm of science. What developed was a form of astrology that synthesized the interpretative accuracy of the Chaldeans with the famed geometric and mathematical prowess of the Greeks. The terminology was adopted for the twelve houses of the horoscope, the twelve zodiac signs, and the horoscope's four quadrants or angles (Ascendant, Descendant, Midheaven, and Nadir). A series of seven corollary points (midpoints) emanating from the Ascendant's relationship to other areas of the chart (the Seven Lots) were developed. Each was viewed as a secondary influence that substantiated a planetary position or a house prognostication. For example, the Lot of Fortune correlated a point between the Ascendant and the Moon. Similarly, the Lots of Necessity, Eros, Daimon, Audacity, Nemesis, and Victory followed a geometric formula. (As mentioned earlier in this chapter, the Seven Lots were the inspirational source for the eventual development of the Arabian Parts.)

Alexandria was the seat of all Egyptian knowledge. Under Macedonian rule by 330 B.C., the city became the intellectual capital of the known world. By the first century B.C., a wealth of Egyptian astrological knowledge was compiled and published in the second book of the Egyptian astrologer and geographer Claudius Ptolemy's seminal astrological work, *Tetrabiblos*, which, along with his previous work, the *Centiloquium*, served as the foundations of modern Western astrology.[26] Within these texts, Ptolemy documented the accumulated knowledge of the Baby-

---

26.   Ptolemy's study of geocentrically based astronomy and the technique for predicting celestial phenomena, the *Almagest*, and a companion work on the fixed stars, the *Geographic*, were widely referenced by European astronomers centuries after their publication.

Ionian celestial omens, including excerpts from the *Enuma Anu Enlil*, which he combined with scientific observations made by Egyptian and Chaldean astrologers, rather than truly originating theories and methods of his own. He presented this body of work within a framework of Stoic philosophy derived from the Greeks, which rationalized the relationship between the universe and human beings as a form of cosmic sympathy, thereby providing occidental astrology with a much-needed point of difference to separate it from divination or magic.

Ptolemy's work also derived much technical knowledge from Greek philosophers and scientists, applying Pythagoras's theoretical association of astrology, music, and medicine to the pure science of mathematics; Plato's geocentric view of the universe; Aristotle's view of the connection between the celestial bodies and the terrestrial world; and Hipparchus's documentation of 1,081 fixed stars (c. 140 B.C.).

In *Tetrabiblos*, Ptolemy also applied a variation of the Greek Lot of Fortune, which he called the Pars Fortuna (Part of Fortune). This suggests that the evolution of an astrology that combined the best of Arabian and European thought took place in a mere three hundred years.

The cumulative astrological knowledge disseminated by Ptolemy flourished for nearly four centuries in the Greek-speaking capital of the Byzantine Empire, Constantinople. The twelve-volume *Catalogue Codicum Astrologorum Graecorum* is a prime example of the rich literary treasury that had been produced in this Near Eastern stronghold. In 500 A.D. the Byzantine astrologer Rhetorius introduced a variation on Hippocrates' four humors (sanguine, choleric, phlegmatic, and melancholic) and Ptolemy's four influential elements (water, air, earth, and fire). His system categorized the zodiac signs into the triplicities that were air signs (Gemini, Libra, and Aquarius), fire signs (Leo, Aries, and Sagittarius), earth signs (Taurus, Virgo, and Capricorn), and water signs (Cancer, Scorpio, and Pisces).

As mentioned earlier in this chapter, however, the intellectual tide that nurtured this form of thinking was thwarted by A.D. 529, when the Byzantine emperor Justinian closed the Academy at Athens and banned the practice or study of astrology within the Byzantine Empire because of its early associations with pagan ideology. Justinian was not the first to attack astrology. The Ecumenical Council of Nicea, held in 325, banned the practice of astrology by devout Catholic Christians. And in 357, the Emperor Constantine grouped astrologers along with dream-diviners, magi, and other fortune-tellers, branding them as heretics and outcasts in his empire.

The Christian philosopher Saint Augustine condemned astrology in his writings during the fourth century, even though he admitted in his book *Confessions* (published in 397) that he studied the astrological science himself before turning to God and believed that the "lower bodies are moved by the higher [heavenly bodies]."

Augustine strongly criticized the words used by fortune-tellers who claimed they could predict a person's fate because it was written in the stars: such claims, he asserted, denied the Christian tenet of free will; and, further, they accused God of creating celestial entities that produced malefic characteristics in human beings (which was also antithetical to Christian belief). The philosopher attacked the scientific nature of astrological scholarship by questioning the effects of time, place, and date on the alleged fate of a human being, using the example of opposing fates in the biblical story of the twins Jacob and Esau. And he proposed that the Star of Bethlehem did not influence the birth of Christ, but rather that it was Christ's birth that directed the star to guide the three Magi to Bethlehem.

The tide of Christian fervor turned against the study of astrology in Byzantium. In 409, the emperor Theodosius ordered astrologers to burn their books before a gathering of bishops or face exile. And in 425, the emperor Valentinian banished a few notable astrologers as heretics. Justinian's mandate in the following century, and the increased use of Latin over Greek among the literate, dissipated the further expansion or study of astrology west of Constantinople until the eleventh and twelfth centuries. Portions of the astrological science did, however, survive in Europe during the Dark Ages as the liberal-arts study of astronomy.[27]

The translation of Ptolemy's *Tetrabiblos* during the twelfth century heralded the resurrection of interest in astrology within the growing community of European intellectuals. In fact, astrology—in the guise of astronomy—was included in the early curriculum at Oxford University when it opened its doors in 1249, even though the types of astrology used to foretell a person's reaction to the flow of daily events (predictive astrology) and the behavior of a culture or other secular body (judicial or mundane astrology) were opposed by the school's chancellor, Robert Grosseteste, because the precepts involved in each tradition denied God's will. Nevertheless, he regarded highly astrology's contributions and usefulness to the fields of medicine, alchemy, and meteorology.

The intellectual communities of both Islamic and Christian Europe seemed to welcome astrology's technical and scientific aspects. During the thirteenth century, the German theologian Albertus Magnus recommended that his students read Ptolemy's *Tetrabiblos* and *Almagest*. He admitted the influence of the planets on terrestrial events, but, like his predecessor, Saint Augustine, he denied the existence of planetary influence on human will. Albertus's most famous student, Saint Thomas Aquinas, took a completely different stance, however. In his seminal work, *Summa Theologica,* Aquinas stated in Question IX, Fifth Article, that the planets

---

27.   The seven liberal arts taught during the sixth century were grammar, rhetoric, dialectic, arithmetic, geometry, music, and astronomy.

and constellations indirectly influenced human character: "Now the majority of men are led by the passions, which the wise alone resist. Consequently, in the majority of cases predictions about human acts, gathered from the observation of the heavenly bodies, are fulfilled. Nevertheless, as Ptolemy says, the wise man governs the stars, as though to say that by resisting his passions, he opposes his will, which is free and in no way subject to the movement of the heavens, to such effects of the heavenly bodies."

During the same century, the British scholar Roger Bacon encouraged the use of medical astrology (a practice introduced by Hippocrates in ancient Greece that employed a patient's horoscope in the diagnosis and treatment of disease), and highly commended the mathematical prowess of his contemporary, the astrologer Campanus. The University of Bologna made a four-year curriculum in astrology a requisite for all medical students. (Its most famous professor was the astrologer Guido Bonatti, who translated the works of many Arabian practitioners.)

European nobility employed the services of astrologers just as their Egyptian, Greek, Roman, Achaemenian, Vedic, and Chinese predecessors and peers had done. For example, Frederick II of Sicily mentored the astrologer Michael Scot. A more interesting relationship occurred during the Third Crusade between England's King Richard I and the Sicilian theologian and astrologer Joachim de Fiore (Giocchino da Fiore).

A former abbot of a Cistercian monastery in Corazzo, Sicily, Joachim founded the monastic order of San Giovanni in the town of Fiore, Italy, after he left his administrative position for the contemplative life in 1191. It was around that time that de Fiore met King Richard the Lionhearted when the monarch was traveling to the Holy Land. This astrologer predicted the fall of the Saracen leader Saladin at King Richard's hand, and the monarch's subsequent abduction in Germany.

Joachim was also famous for his prediction of the advent of two monastic orders, the Dominicans and the Franciscans. After his death, he was condemned for his writings and prophecies, but nearly seven decades later he posthumously regained his elevated status when the two mendicant orders he predicted became a reality.

The Catholic Church still perceived the science to be a "black art," however, and predictive astrologers such as Cecco d'Ascoli were persecuted and burned at the stake by the Inquisition during the early 1300s. Yet Ptolemy's astrological works were studied in universities from Germany to Italy and from Austria-Hungary to Great Britain by physicians, philosophers, astronomers, and classicists. During the 1400s, under the mentorship of the powerful Medici family, Marsilio Ficino translated the works of Plato and wrote extensively on the affect of planetary motion on human health. His student Pico della Mirandola defended his teacher's faith in medical astrology and denounced predictive and judicial astrology as a fallible bastardization of the science in his book, *Disputationes Adversus Astrologiam Divinatricem*. Another astrologer who enjoyed the financial support of the Medici family was Nostradamus, who advised Catherine de Medici and her husband, King Henry II of France. He became best known for his prophetic poem, *Centuries*, as well as for his books on medical astrology.

On the other side of the coin, the German oculist, physician, and astrologer Henricus Cornelius Agrippa von Nettesheim contributed to the defense of judicial and predictive astrology. He served as a diplomat on behalf of Maximilian I between 1506 and 1510, and during this time he wrote his most influential work, titled *De Occulta Philosophia*, which was not officially published until 1533. A controversial figure, Agrippa was awarded doctorates in both law and medicine in 1515 while lecturing in Pavia, Italy, and aroused the ire of the Cologne Inquisition when, in 1520, he defended an accused witch.

In 1524, Agrippa was appointed physician and astrologer to Louise of Savoy, the queen mother of France. Two years later he wrote an esoteric work, titled *De Incertitudine et Vanitate Scientarum atque Artium Declamatio*, in which he denounced human knowledge and advocated blind faith in divine revelation. Agrippa made a lasting contribution to astrology, however, by establishing the relationship between archangels and angels to the zodiac signs in *De Occulta Philosophia*. This cosmological association has even been employed by modern-day esoteric astrologers. By connecting judicial and predictive astrology to occult arts such as palmistry, magic, and alchemy, however, he unknowingly aided in the ensuing separation of astrology and astronomy.

During the late 1500s, the Dominican theologian Tommaso Campanella wrote a six-volume treatise on the pure science of astrology, making no reference to the superstitious or divinatory aspects of Arabian or Judaic astrology. Titled *The Six Books of Astrology of Campanella of the Order of Preachers*, the work contained a statement defending the science despite the rising interest in heliocentric astronomy (a sun-centered versus a geocentric or earth-centered view of the solar system): "Whether the sun moves or stands still, it is to be supposed a moving Planet by us, considering the matter from our senses and our description; for the same happens whether it moves or the earth."

When Nicholas Copernicus introduced his heliocentric theory of planetary alignment during the late 1400s, it quietly shook the foundations of science and theology to their terrestrial roots. Its acceptance by the academic world, however, didn't occur until the 1600s, when Galileo Galilei and Johannes Kepler advocated this concept in their own theories and writings. (Kepler even attempted to develop a heliocentric form of astrology, which was rejected by the academic community.)

But the Church disapproved of Copernicus's theory and Galileo's defense of a heliocentric universe as much as it did judicial and predictive astrology, condemning all their adherents as heretics. To save the "science" of astrology, the British scholar Francis Bacon proposed a system stripped of superstition. He believed that astrology could be applied to predict large-scale changes and movements of planets and civilizations, but could not be employed to foretell individual behavior.

The Renaissance paved the way for the Reformation and the Enlightenment, during the seventeenth and eighteenth centuries. It was a time when European scholars sought "rational" explanations for everything in the known universe. Consequently, within the academic community there was little interest in a science that relied on synchronicity and ancient beliefs. The heads of Europe, however, including Charles I and Louis XI of France, Elizabeth I of England, and later Napoleon, continued to consult their personal astrologers before embarking on any major conquests. The common people followed suit.

Astrology survived in Europe and in the emerging American colonies thanks to the writings of the astrologer and physician Nicholas Culpeper, who applied medical astrology and herbology in his diagnosis and treatment of patients during the mid-1600s. In fact, the first American astrologers were found among the ranks of herbalists and physicians who relied on astrology as a routine portion of their diagnostic workup.

In the late 1600s a society known as the Rosicrucians was founded by astrologer and esotericist Johannes Kelpius in Germantown, Pennsylvania. Besides upgrading an existing American almanac (originally published by Daniel Leeds), a society member named Johann Seeling became well known in 1698 for casting a horoscope to determine the best date to begin construction of the Swedish Lutheran Church in Wiasco, Pennsylvania. The society's astrological works included the production of an American ephemeris, titled the *Simplified Scientific Rosicrucian Ephemeris*, which is published annually to this day.

During the eighteenth century, astrology gained broad acceptance among the colonists. American patriots and founding fathers George Washington, Thomas Jefferson, and Benjamin Franklin all had personal astrologers. (Franklin's *Poor Richard's Almanack* regularly contained astrological aspects and astrologically based weather predictions.)

The British astrologer James Wilson's seminal work, *A Complete Dictionary of Astrology* (1816), provided students with the basic information necessary for chart construction and delineation during these so-called "dark days of astrology." The astrologer Raphael (Robert C. Smith) wrote and distributed his first book, titled *Manual of Astrology*, around 1826. He published the first *Raphael's Ephemeris* shortly thereafter. It has been in continuous publication ever since.

Toward the end of the nineteenth century, the Theosophical Society (founded in 1875 by Madame Blavatsky in New York City) helped promote astrology as a requisite for all Western students of Hindu and Buddhist thought. And the astrologers Sepharial (Walter Gorn Old) and Alan Leo (William Frederick Allen) continued to expand the public's knowledge of astrology under the banner of theosophy well into the twentieth century.

When the Swiss psychologist Carl G. Jung presented his theory of synchronicity in the mid-twentieth century, he cited the study of astrology as a strong and convincing example of this existential concept. In his essay "On Synchronicity," he presented detailed evidence that there can be a parallelism of time and meaning between apparent and invisible events, which "scientific knowledge so far has been unable to reduce to a common principle." He believed there was a postulate connecting the macrocosmic world of the stars and planets and the microcosmic world of the individual human being.

This principle of "meaningful coincidence" wasn't his invention, however; it is the overriding ideological difference that separates the Western notion that every event has its cause and effect from the Eastern conviction that natural concurrences exist between seemingly unrelated events. This can be found throughout many facets of Asian culture—from medicine and architecture to the study of philosophy, religion, mathematics, and astrology.

Astrologers such as Max Heindel, Llewellyn George, Swami Ramacaraka, Manly Palmer Hall, Marc Edmund Jones, and Grant Lewi contributed greatly to the technical body of modern astrological knowledge during the first half of the twentieth century. At present, many more astrologers are integrating ancient Vedic, Chinese, Arabian, and Judaic methods into their Western practices. Astrology's figurative Tower of Babel continues to grow. No longer the focus of theological or scientific persecution and debate, astrology has regained its popularity among a broad spectrum of westerners, from corporate executives and politicians to housewives and high school students. Besides transcending language barriers and cultural differences along its five-thousand-year-old trail, the study of astrology has intersected the developmental course of civilizations, religions, trade systems, and science itself. Despite a global sentiment of "been there, done that," human beings still seek to fulfill a constant desire to understand the essence of human behavior, and to glimpse what tomorrow will bring.

The
Children of the Moon
and the
Children of the Sun

CHAPTER

2

R udyard Kipling once wrote, "East is East and West is West and never the twain shall meet." Perhaps this is a truism about cultural differences. In a discussion of astrology, however, it couldn't be further from the truth. There are substantial similarities between Eastern and Western forms of astrology, transcending linguistic, geographic, and political boundaries. But before delving too far into their commonalities and divergences, a short overview of the major branches of astrology is necessary.

THE PHYSICAL AND SPIRITUAL WORLDS: EXOTERIC AND ESOTERIC ASTROLOGY

To introduce the various branches, it's appropriate to employ the widely used and generally accepted categories that separate science from divination. Although this categorization is understood by Chinese, Tibetan, Vedic, and Arabian practitioners, only Western astrologers have developed terms to define these separate secular and spiritual factions, which they respectively call *exoteric* astrology and *esoteric* astrology.

Exoteric Astrology

Employing only known planets and stars, exoteric astrology concentrates on the potential physical and emotional experiences in an individual's life: centering on the circumstances surrounding a person's birth (natal), general progress (predictive), specific future (horary), health (medical), and the more generalized behavior of a culture or other secular body to which an individual belongs (mundane).

The natal horoscope establishes a foundational map of an individual based on the positions of the planets and constellations at his or her exact place, time, and date of birth. Natal (genethliacal) astrology deals with the individual's overall life including personality and appearance, potential for professional and personal achievement, ability to interact with other people, and ability to produce children. The basic chart constructed for this type of consultation is called a *natal horoscope, birth chart, geniture, radix,* or *nativity.* Unlike the other traditions, which employ only one chart for this purpose, Vedic astrologers use six to sixteen charts in their assessment of an individual's life. This compilation is known as *jataka.*

Predictive astrology analyzes the potential impact of planetary movements that occur after the moment of birth on an individual's life, forecasting shifts in the person's attitude or in his or her reaction to the flow of events occurring on a specific day, month, or year. This type of astrology takes many forms including but not limited to secondary progressions[1] and solar returns.[2] In a similar vein, horary astrology seeks to answer specific questions raised by an individual about the outcome of an existing or future event by casting a chart for an exact year, month, day, time, and location (if known). Delineations for this type of astrology differ from natal or predictive interpretations, forming a highly specialized branch of study. Another form of horary astrology, called *electional astrology,* concentrates on the actual selection of the optimal time to take action on a particular issue or event.

In addition to secondary progressions and solar returns (common methods used in Western, Judaic, and Arabian astrology) there are other forms of predictive astrology that practitioners frequently execute concurrently with the natal chart. For example, the Fate Cycles in Chinese astrology are frequently calculated to supplement the individual's natal information. This method progressively shifts the placement of the elements associated with a person's lunar month at ten-year intervals, creating a chronology that marks major changes of interest or action in the person's life. This progression is used in conjunction with other factors to create a form of electional astrology, using the Chinese solar calendar to determine smaller periods of time that might be auspicious or inauspicious for action. It is also used with daily almanac readings of the Moon's relative position to a fixed star.

Vedic astrologers apply similar methods of year-long prediction in the form of the solar return: an astrological branch called *varshaphala.* They also create a

---

1.   A secondary progression chart progresses the planetary positions that occurred on a person's birth date by one day for each year of that person's life. For example, to construct the secondary progression for a ten-year-old child born on January 1, 1961, the astrologer applies the actual planetary positions as they occurred ten days later, on January 11, 1961.

2.   A solar return chart presents the actual location of the planets on an individual's birthday for a specific year. For example, to construct the solar return for a ten-year-old child born on January 1, 1961, the astrologer would use the actual planetary positions as they occurred on January 1, 1971.

unique form of prediction based on a hypothetical life span of 120 years (need-less to say, death of the body is likely to occur long before the completion of this fixed life span), assigning specific planetary rulerships to fixed periods within that cycle. Known as *vimsottari dasa*, it is the most detailed of the prediction systems. Vedic practitioners devote more time than astrologers from other traditions to the chronological plotting of singular events and their outcomes. Estimated to within days and hours, a personal chronology is frequently combined with equally intricate methods of prediction such as *prasna* (horary astrology) and *muhurta* (electional astrology).

Tibetan astrologers combine a number of methods in their specific form of pre-diction. They review an individual's good and bad days of each month based on his or her birth year. They determine the governing *parkha* (a trigram derived from the Chinese *I Ching* form of divination) for the year, then advise the individual which deity to worship and which mantra to apply to counteract negative predictions and ensure a successful outcome of events during that period. They also locate the year's *mewa* (a nine-unit magic square that indicates good and bad compass direc-tions) to refine the above prognostications.

Medical astrology, or iatromathematics, was more common in the western hemisphere prior to the standardization of practices by the medical profession at the turn of the twentieth century. Many holistic physicians, however, regularly em-ploy this ancient method of natal delineation in combination with more conven-tional diagnostic procedures. This branch is still an integral part of medicine in eastern and central Asia. Since the information derived from a horoscope indicates which natural forces affect the patient and in what specific areas and ways, both urban and rural caregivers (mostly acupuncturists and traditional doctors) apply this data to the development of diet, medication, and other treatment programs.

Mundane astrology—commonly known as political, state, or judicial astrology—deals with secular or world affairs and the acts of a society or culture as a whole. Employed by court astrologers and political advisers for centuries, it now plays only a minor and relatively covert role in society. Though a surprising number of politi-cians and other public figures regularly consult astrologers, it has been centuries since astrologers were recognized as official members of governments.

Esoteric Astrology

Unlike exoteric astrology, esoteric or spiritual astrology exists only within the sphere of Western astrology. It applies astrological principles to quasi-religious or mystical endeavors such as the revelation of the zodiac's hidden symbology; the disclosure of an individual's prior lifetimes; or a forecast of a person's future beyond death. It also employs a number of asteroids, hypothetical planets, and psychically

perceived entities. Its practitioners believe that an individual can achieve enlightenment by following the practices that were revealed to select adepts through visions, dreams, and trances. Gaining prominence in Europe during the late 1800s,
this astrological division is often associated with Masonic traditions practiced by
Neoplatonic (Gnostic), Hermetic, and Kabbalistic orders as well as by the theosophical and spiritualist movements that sought to integrate Eastern ideologies into
Western spiritual thought. This particular form of astrology was broadly evange-
lized by eighteenth- and nineteenth-century practitioners such as Anton Mesmer,
Emanuel Swedenborg, and Madame Blavatsky. In North America, nineteenth-
century esoteric astrology was practiced by quasi-religious sects such as the Rosicrucians, the Brotherhood of Light, and the Order of the Magi.

One form of American esoteric astrology in particular gained a wide audience
of admirers during the first half of the twentieth century. In 1898, a Welsh psychic
named John Thomas (who wrote under the pseudonym Charubel) published a volume of esoteric delineations titled *The Degrees of the Zodiac Symbolized* (London:
Fowler, 1898). These so-called symbols were simply phrases such as "an adobe mis-
sion" or "an unexpected thunderstorm," to which deeper meanings were attributed.
The symbols were favorably received and considered highly reliable interpretive
elements, despite the sometimes strong underlying moral tone given to their delineation. The entries were originally intended to be used as Ascendant interpretations, but few attempts were made to expand their scope for use in daily prediction
and progression work.

It wasn't until 1925, when a new set of symbolic interpretations, called the
Sabian Symbols, was introduced by the American astrologer Marc Edmund Jones,
that interest in symbolic astrology grew (in fact, Sabian Symbols became synony-
mous with symbolic astrology). A small group of practitioners living in Los Angeles
distributed copies of this work, successfully testing the symbols' use in a variety
of applications. In 1931, Jones mimeographed copies of the interpretations—
collectively entitled *Symbolical Astrology*—and sent a copy to his colleague Dane
Rudhyar, who in turn published an abridged version of the lessons in his book *Astrology of Personality* (New York: Lucis, 1936). A final version was compiled and
published by Marc Edmund Jones in 1951, titled *Sabian Symbols*, and is employed
by some Western practitioners who believe that the symbols impart insight into the
individual's soul.

Another example of esoteric astrology is the application of hypothetical planets,
asteroids, and other psychically perceived entities in the construction and delineation of a horoscope. Known as Uranian astrology, this particular branch delineates the specific degree a planet occupies, rather than the elements and qualities
that planet is said to exert in more conventional forms. It also assesses midpoints,

which are similar to the Arabian Parts in their calculation and use. The practitioners of this system also interpret eight "undiscovered" planets that are alleged to exist beyond the planet Neptune. These include Admetos, Apollon, Cupido, Hades, Kronos, Poseidon, Vulkanus, and Zeus.

Esoteric astrology in all of its forms has garnered the most public attention because it is said to be steeped in mystery and secret orders from ancient times. Mainly, however, it was developed by nineteenth- and twentieth-century psychics and esotericists who had little to do with the science of astrology and much in common with the early Greek oracles and Babylonian soothsayers.

POLE TO POLE: THE TROPICAL AND SIDEREAL ZODIACS

The vernal equinox marks one of two moments in the year in which the plane created by the apparent path of the Sun (the ecliptic) intersects the plane created by the Earth's equator. This phenomenon also occurs approximately six months later, when it is called the autumnal equinox. The vernal equinox marks the beginning or zero-point of the Sun's apparent 360°00′ circular path across the Earth's sky, taking 365 days, 5 hours, 48 minutes, and 4.5 seconds until the next vernal equinox. This, however, is where the general comprehension of solar activity ends and another segregation of astrological technique begins.

There is one branch of astrology that concentrates on this form of solar activity. Called tropical astrology, its practitioners deem the vernal equinox, which occurs on or about March 20, as the starting point of the tropical zodiac and divide the ecliptic into twelve segments of 30°00′ each. The starting point of the tropical zodiac was arbitrarily determined to be located at a position called 00°00′ Aries (00°♈00′). In this format, the mean solar path is static because its points of convergence—the ecliptic and the equator—do not fluctuate. Also, the path always ends at 30°00′ Pisces (30°♓00′) and begins a new cycle every year at 00°00′ Aries (00°♈00′) on the vernal equinox. The tropical zodiac is most commonly applied in Western, Judaic, and Arabian astrology, where the influence of Greek and Egyptian methodology is strongest.

Sidereal astrology, on the other hand, does not trace the Sun's apparent path according to its two annual intersections with the Earth's equator; instead, it marks the Sun's movements against the backdrop of the constellations, demarcating its transit from one constellation to another. Unlike the tropical zodiac, the sidereal zodiac segments the path into twelve constellations of unequal distance along the 360°00′ ecliptic. (Some theorists have even divided the path into thirteen constellational segments, adding the constellation Ophiuchus, which is near the constellations of Scorpio and Sagittarius.) The Sun takes 365 days, 6 hours, 8 minutes, and 24 seconds to complete an apparent round trip from any one fixed star (e.g., the Sun passes the fixed star Spica [α Virgo] around the same time every year), creating another variation on the concept of the solar year. In this pattern there has been visible evidence of a shift in celestial longitude: the actual point of the vernal equinox appears to retrograde (move backwards along its regular path) approximately 00°50′ per year. From a terrestrial vantage point, the Earth's north-south axis appears to have moved from its original position in relation to the placement of the constellations. Because the Earth is not a perfect sphere, the poles do move along an elliptical path, completing a 360-degree cycle every 25,920 years. Vedic and Judaic astrologers call this phenomenon the "Great Year."[3] Evidence of this incident can be found in the identification of the Pole Star in historical records: the present-day northern Pole Star is Polaris (α Ursa Minor), but in 3000 B.C. the Pole Star was Thuban (α Draconis). This means that the point at which the Sun returns to 00°00′ Aries (00°♈00′) has changed each year since the beginning of time.

As Fred Gettings stated in his work *The Arkana Dictionary of Astrology:* "Around this cosmic truth a wealth of astrological symbolism has been woven into a proliferation of ideologies which tends to obscure the fact that no one has adequately dated the time when the two zodiacs coincided at the same fiducial [or fixed star], and that there is little or no agreement as to the extent of the arcs involved in the constellational zodiac." Vedic astrologers called the difference between the two vernal points *ayanamsa* (portion of movement), which represented almost one complete zodiac sign (about 23°43′) at the time of this writing. In the casting of a tropical and a sidereal horoscope, this difference can reflect a change of not only the Ascendant's ruling sign, but the placement of the planets within the shifted houses as well. This means that an individual's personality profile can change radically depending on whether a tropical or sidereal chart is erected for interpretation.

No one knows the exact date when the point of vernal equinox in the tropical zodiac coincided with the same point in the sidereal zodiac. That would mean being privy to the day the universe was born. Of course, many ancient and modern theorists have postulated the answer, debating not only the date of inception, but the exact rate of speed, which varies from 00°50′ to 00°50.2388′ to 00°50.27′ per year.

The shifting of the vernal equinox and the sidereal zodiac likewise affect the calculation of the Moon's path along the same series of fixed stars: a critical consideration in Vedic astrological interpretation. It does not, however, influence the Chinese or Tibetan calculation of solar or lunar activity. They are charted by their relation to the Pole Star as it was observed over four thousand years ago against ter-

---

3.   The Great Year is divided into precessional ages of 2,160 years each, which are sometimes called Astrological Ages. In Judaic astrology, these periods are called the Prophetic Ages.

restrial rather than celestial longitude. (The concept of the ecliptic was not introduced into Chinese astrology until the 1100s, over three thousand years after the celestial entities had been painstakingly observed and documented.)

Since Chinese, Tibetan, and Vedic astrologers chose to place the greatest emphasis upon lunar motion in their astrological practices, it's no wonder that these same traditions use a form of the sidereal zodiac in their calculations. Judaic, Arabian, and all forms of Western astrology (Chaldean, Greek, Egyptian, and Roman), on the other hand, most commonly employ the tropical zodiac in chart construction. There are, however, a few modern-day exceptions among the many variations of Western astrology that are being practiced today.

THE DYNASTIES OF THE SUN AND THE MOON: SOLAR-BASED AND LUNAR-BASED ASTROLOGIES

Having defined the established boundaries between exoteric and esoteric astrology as well as sidereal and tropical zodiacs, it seems appropriate to propose a new categorization for the world's major exoteric astrologies, using a metaphor that invites both cultural and technical comparison. As previously mentioned, most Indian royal families claim to be descended from either the Suryavamsa (the Sun's dynasty) or the Candravamsa (the Moon's dynasty). The world's major astrologies can similarly be divided between those that concentrate on the Sun's apparent movements and those that concentrate on the transits of the Moon.

Based on this physical focus, Western and Arabian astrologies constitute the "Sun school," while Chinese, Tibetan, and Vedic are all members of the "Moon school." The same division similarly serves to identify two diverse ideologies: those who espouse the concept of free will and those who embrace a belief in patterns of destiny. The point of fusion between these two schools of thought is Judaic astrology, which appears to have synthesized the disparate influences of the other cultures. In somewhat romantic terms, Judaic astrology's lineage can be compared to that of the princes in the Hindu epic *Mahabharata*, who were born from the intermarriage of the solar and lunar dynasties.

The Moon School: Chinese, Tibetan, and Vedic Astrologies

In Hindu mythology, the god Siva is closely associated with the Moon, embodying the powers of destruction and transformation and standing equal to Brahma the Creator and Vishnu the Protector. Siva married Sati, who was one of the sixty daughters fathered by Brahma's son Daksa. Sati was sister to all twenty-seven goddesses of the Lunar Mansions who married Candra the Moon, making Siva the brother-in-law of the Moon. Cursed by his father-in-law, Daksa, to suffer from periodic consumption as punishment for favoring one of his wives over the others,

Candra is seen waxing and waning in the nighttime sky. In later myths, Candra is called the Lord of Medicinal Plants and governs the making and imbibing of *soma*, the sacred drink of the Hindu gods. Some eighteenth-century Hindu works of art even depict the Moon as an emanation of Siva in his role as lord of the subconscious and mysterious side of the human mind.

The Moon has served as a nocturnal timing device for thousands of years not just in Hindu but in Chinese, Tibetan, Arabian, and Jewish cultures, where it is believed to govern the planting of crops as well as the highs and lows of human emotions. Because this concept is integral to the cultural ideologies of these regions, the astrologies practiced in China, India, and Tibet could be called the "Moon school." (Strongly influenced by Vedic astrology, both Arabian and Judaic practices applied similar lunar-oriented forms of calculation in their early incarnations. These methods were abandoned, however, as both forms adopted the solar-based methods practiced by the Egyptians and Greeks.)

The primary connecting principle among these practices is their perception of lunar activity. The Moon's orbital path was easily tracked by ancient celestial observers, who established a series of fixed stars (referred to as the lunar stations or lunar mansions) as checkpoints on their map of the nighttime skies. Chinese, Vedic, Arabian, and even medieval European astrologers charted this activity in similar ways, varying only slightly in their spatial perception of the Moon's transit from one star to the next. For example, Chinese, Arabian, Tibetan, and medieval European astrologers divided the path into twenty-eight mansions of 12°51′ each. Vedic practitioners segmented the path into twenty-seven mansions of 13°20′ each, plus an intercalary mansion that was only used to rectify the system with the Chinese and Arabian versions in studies written by early Vedic scholars, but was not applied by astrological practitioners.

The actual fixed stars used and their sequential order commence at two distinct points. The cycle of Chinese mansions begins with the fixed star Spica in the constellation Virgo (designated by modern astronomers and astrologers as α Virgo). The Vedic, Arabian, and medieval European mansions, however, begin with the fixed star Sharatan in the constellation Aries (designated by modern astronomers and astrologers as β Aries) (fig. 2.1). The difference between these two starting points can in some ways be attributed to the fact that Indian, Arabian, and Western observers used the Pole Star as their navigational starting point, while Chinese observers focused their attention on the Pleiades cluster. Some modern astronomical scholars have suggested that the topography surrounding Beijing made it impossible to navigate the heavens by the Pole Star, the apparent horizon being obscured by massive mountain ranges. Although the majority of the lunar mansions pinpoint exactly the same fixed star along the Moon's path, variations appear to accommodate differences in location. For example, the Chinese mansion Shen is positioned at Alnitak (ζ Orion) while the Vedic mansion Ardra is situated at the nearby star of Betelgeuse (α Orion). The Indian observatory at Ujjayini was located at 23°11′N / 75°46′E and the Chinese observatory at Beijing was situated at 39°55′N / 116°25′E. Because of the distance between the two locations, the Moon appeared to intersect the visual path of two different fixed stars in the same constellation, a variance caused primarily by the Earth's curvature.

As shown in fig. 2.1, the Chinese, Vedic, Arabian, and medieval European systems of lunar mansions are identified by many of the same fixed stars. For example, the fixed star Spica (α Virgo) represents the first lunar mansion in the Chinese system and the fourteenth lunar mansion in the Vedic, Arabian, and medieval European systems. The mansions that do not share the same fixed point are, however, generally situated within the same constellation.

The lunar mansions became the basis for each civilization's calendar. And even in present-day astrological practice, the lunar mansions are considered to have a primary influence on an individual's personality and emotional makeup as well as the outcome of actions and events on a given day. Not surprisingly, this concept closely coincides with the philosophical and religious dogma of these same cultures.

Buddhist and Hindu ideologies place a great deal of emphasis on the interrelationship of an individual with family, other people, the community, nature, and the universe, both in past lives and in present time. So it should come as no surprise that the astrologies of China, Tibet, and India concentrate on an individual's emotional health, spiritual satisfaction, karmic debt, ability to contribute to the good of humanity on numerous levels, and ability to lead a righteous and moral existence. These factors are analyzed within the context of fate or personal destiny.

A difficult concept for many westerners to accept, fate in Eastern cultures is not considered to be a doomsday machine or a loss of free will. It is believed that fate is simply part of a continuous natural process. Everything in nature exists according to a perceivable behavioral pattern that is structured by many contributing factors including physical characteristics, early training, and habitat. Because we are natural entities, humans follow similarly predictable but unique paths.

Astrology's role in this mindset is obvious. It offers empowerment through self-knowledge. One may have been born to follow a particular pattern of behavior within a prescribed series of circumstances, but being forewarned and prepared to comprehend and learn from those events—thus ensuring the perpetuation and regeneration of the cycle—requires primarily a knowledge of the personal, physical, and emotional equipment one can employ and, secondarily, a general understanding of event chronology.

FIGURE 2.1. FIXED STARS OF THE LUNAR MANSIONS.

FIXED STAR (CONSTELLATIONAL POINT)	CHINESE SIEU (BY SEQUENCE NUMBER AND NAME)	VEDIC NAKSATRA (BY SEQUENCE NUMBER AND NAME)	ARABIAN MANAZIL (BY SEQUENCE NUMBER AND NAME)	MEDIEVAL EUROPEAN LUNAR MANSION (BY SEQUENCE NUMBER AND NAME)
Spica (α Virgo)	1. Ch'io	14. Citra	14. Al'simak	14. Spica
Porrima (γ Virgo)	2. K'ang		13. Al'awwa	
Syrma (ι Virgo)			15. Al'ghafr	
Vindemiatrix (ε Virgo)				13. Canis
Arcturus (α Boötes)		15. Svati		
Zuben'elgenubi (α Libra)	3. Ti	16. Visakha	16. Al'jubana	16. Cornua scorpionis
Zuben'elchamali (β Libra)		16. Visakha		16. Cornua scorpionis
(π Scorpio)	4. Fang	17. Anuradha		
(δ Virgo)	5. Hsin		17. Iklil'al'jabha	15. Cooperta
Acrab (β Scorpio)		17. Anuradha		17. Corona super caput
Deschubba (δ Scorpio)				20. Trabs
Antares (α Scorpio)		18. Jyestha	18. Al'kalb	18. Cor scorpionis
(μ Scorpio)	6. Wei	19. Mula	19. Al'shaulah	19. Cauda scorpionis
Shaula (λ Scorpio)		19. Mula	19. Al'shaulah	19. Cauda scorpionis
Lesath (υ Scorpio)		19. Mula		
Kaus Borealis (Alnasi; λ Sagittarius)	7. Chi			
(φ Sagittarius)	8. Tou		21. Al'balda	
(π Sagittarius)			20. Al'na'am	
Nunki (Pelagus; σ Sagittarius)		20. Purvasadha		
Ascella (ζ Sagittarius)		21. Uttarasadha		
Dabith (β Capricorn)	9. Niu			21. Desertum
(σ Andromeda)	10. Nü			

Vega (α Lyra)	21a. Abhijit (intercalary)			
Altair (α Aquila)	22. Sravana			
Sualochin (α Delphinus)	23. Sravistha			
Rotanev (β Delphinus)	23. Sravistha			
Giedi (Algedi; α Capricorn)			22. Al'sa'd'aldhabih	22. Pastor et Aries
(μ Aquarius)			23. Al'sa'd'albula	25. Papilio
Sadachbia (γ Aquarius)	24. Satabhisaj			23. Glutiens
Sadalsuud (β Aquarius)		11. Hsü	24. Alsa'd'alsuud	24. Sidus fortunae
Sadalmelik (α Aquarius)		12. Wei	25. Alsa'd'aldahbiyah	
Markab (α Pegasus)	25. Purvabhadrapada	13. Shih		26. Hauriens primus
Algenib (γ Pegasus)	26. Uttarabhadrapada	14. Pi	26. Al'fargh'althani	
(γ Perseus)	26. Uttarabhadrapada			
Alpheratz (α Andromeda)			27. Al'fargh'al'mukdim	27. Hauriens secundus
Mirach (β Andromeda)			28. Albatn'alhut	28. Piscis
(η Andromeda)				
(ζ Pisces)	27. Revati	15. K'uei		
Sharatan (β Aries)	1. Asvini	16. Lou	1. Al'sharatain	1. Cornua arietis
Mesarthim (γ Aries)	1. Asvini			
(41 Aries)	2. Bharani	17. Wei		
Botein (δ Aries)			2. Al'butain	2. Veneter arietis
Alcyone (η Taurus)	3. Krttika	18. Mao	3. Al'thurayya	3. Caput tauri
Aldebaran (α Taurus)	4. Rohini		4. Al'dabaran	4. Cor tauri
(ε Taurus)		19. Pî		
(λ Orion)		20. Tsui		
Alhena (γ Gemini)	5. Mrgasiras		5. Al'hak'ah	5. Caput canis validi
Alnitak (ζ Orion)		21. Shen	6. Al'dhana	6. Sidus parvum lucis magnae

FIXED STAR (CONSTELLATIONAL POINT)	CHINESE SIEU (BY SEQUENCE NUMBER AND NAME)	VEDIC NAKSATRA (BY SEQUENCE NUMBER AND NAME)	ARABIAN MANAZIL (BY SEQUENCE NUMBER AND NAME)	MEDIEVAL EUROPEAN LUNAR MANSION (BY SEQUENCE NUMBER AND NAME)
Betelgeuse (α Orion)				
(μ Gemini)	22. Ching	6. Ardra		
Castor (α Gemini)		7. Punarvasu	7. Al'dhira	7. Brachium
Pollux (β Gemini)		7. Punarvasu		7. Brachium
Praesepe (M44 Cancer)			8. Al'nathrah	
(θ Cancer)	23. Kuei	8. Pusya		8. Nebulosa
Aselli Borealis (γ Cancer)		8. Pusya	9. Al'tarf	9. Oculus Leonis
Aselli Australis (δ Cancer)		8. Pusya		
(δ Hydra)	24. Liu	9. Aslesa		
Alphard (α Hydra)	25. Hsing			
(μ Hydra)	26. Chang			
Alkes (α Crater)	27. I			
Regulus (α Leo)		10. Magha	10. Al'jabhah	10. Frons Leonis
Zosma (δ Leo)		11. Purvaphalguni	11. Al'zubrah	11. Capillus Leonis
Denebola (β Leo)		12. Uttaraphalguni	12. Al'sarfa	12. Cauda Leonis
Gienah (γ Corvus)	28. Chen	13. Hasta		

A prime example of how "Moon school" astrology interacts with culture and society can be found in China, where it is believed that an individual's destiny must be carefully studied on three important occasions: on one's birth; before one marries; and when one dies. An individual's birth or adoption (either real or fictitious) into a family does not simply affect the person in question; it changes the destiny of the entire family. Marriage forms the union of two individual destinies sometimes called the "exchange of the eight signs" (a direct reference to the *ssu chu* (Four Pillars of Destiny) that are the backbone of Chinese astrology). In death, an individual continues to affect both family and friends by passing into another life. To make that final physical event an auspicious one for all its participants, the timing of the ceremony is only one critical consideration. The analysis of who may attend the ceremony itself, what direction the grave must face, and other details are also scrutinized.

Vedic astrologers are consulted when a child is born, to determine his or her general path in the present life, karmic debts and credits built up in past lives, and potential for fulfillment in the next life. A few years after the child is born, astrological charts are analyzed to determine the ideal marriage partner and the outcome of the match, in a practice known as *vivaha*. Since it is believed that each person exists for 120 years during any given lifetime, the time and effect of the individual's inevitable death upon loved ones and the community is also reviewed.

According to Hindu belief, this form of self-knowledge allows an individual to function more efficiently in the world because he or she fully comprehends his or her place in the universe. The lucid and logical nature of this process, which does not, however, segregate the physical and spiritual worlds into black and white, holds little weight in Western ideology.

The Sun School: Western and Arabian Astrologies

The Sun has served as a diurnal timing device since the ancient Egyptians selected its pattern of risings and settings to mark the passage of days. This same solar-based calendar was also the foundation for the present-day Gregorian calendar. The Sun's apparent motion is clearly visible. And this acceptance of physical reality is integral to the cultures of the Western hemisphere. Consequently, Arabian and Western astrologies could be called the "Sun school."

The ancient Egyptian calendar divided the Sun's apparent movements into twelve consecutive thirty-day segments, with five intercalary days added at the end of the annual cycle. The system was based on the annual sunrise reappearance of the fixed star Sirius (α Canis Major) on the eastern horizon, which marked the Nile River's annual flooding. A lunar calendar was also developed. Using thirty-six fixed stars as its foundation, the nighttime calendar marked the rise of each stellar body ten days after its predecessor on the horizon. It was, however, considered to be inferior by the Greeks and Romans, who readily adopted the Egyptians' solar template.

Not surprisingly, the Western and Arabian forms of astrology that evolved from these Egyptian origins also focused on the Sun. According to the Egyptian astrologer Ptolemy, "The power of the Sun however predominates, because it is more generally distributed; the others either cooperate with his power or diminish its effect: the Moon more frequently and more plainly performs this at her conjunction, at her first and last quarter, and at her opposition: the stars act also to a similar purpose, but at longer intervals and more obscurely than the Moon; and their operation principally depends upon the mode of their visibility, their occultation, and their declination." This radical opposition to the principles of Chinese, Tibetan, and Vedic astrologies[4] was rapidly adopted as scholarly gospel by European and Arabian intellectuals who sought a scientific meaning and purpose for the workings of the universe as well as the natures of God and humanity.

The Sun has represented both God and personal power in many European and Near Eastern cultures including Egyptian, Greek, Roman, Arabian, and Judaic. And astrologically, the Sun is believed to affect how an individual manifests his or her personal form of self-expression. Once again, this concept closely coincides with the philosophical and religious tenets of these Western cultures.

One similarity among the Christian, Islamic, and Judaic faiths is the concept of free will. According to this belief, every human being has a right to determine his or her own fate, because it is God's will that each individual should choose a personal form of self-expression. Based on this perception, every human being is capable of good and evil. Therefore, every human act involves a personal choice to do good or evil with a promise of reward or punishment. Within this context, the astrologies of the "Sun school" focus on expressions of the self and their consequences: how the individual physically appears to other people; how the individual learns from other people; how the individual reacts to both immediate surroundings and foreign environments; how the individual fulfills personal desires; and how the individual gains or loses personal freedom.

In Western and Arabian astrology it is presumed that individuals are predisposed by planetary influences to certain patterns of behavior, thought, and emotion. Christian, Muslim, and Jewish theologians have attempted to refute this concept of predictable conduct for centuries, as it challenges the concept that indi-

---

4. In the *Shu Ching* (Book of Documents or Great Plan), the hierarchy of Chinese astrological data was summed up in the description of the Five Disposers: "The first is called the year; the second is called the Moon; the third is the Sun; the fourth is the planetary hour; and the fifth is known as the astronomical dispositions."

viduals can choose their destinies and completely control their actions. Yet the desire for self-knowledge that astrology offers continues to entice people from a great variety of cultures.

Because Western cultures rely on written laws established for the good of groups and communities, and Western religions do not normally accept the concept of the "meaningful coincidence" between planetary motion and human behavior, the "Sun school" astrologies are not integrated into the cultural framework. Rather, astrology is part of the process of individuation: the search for personal identity and fulfillment. Consequently, "Sun school" astrologers play the roles of psychoanalyst, vocational counselor, financial consultant, sex therapist, and marriage counselor, advising individuals on a variety of ego-related matters.

Out of the Strong Came Forth Sweetness: Judaic Astrology

There is always one exception to every rule. In the case of the Sun and Moon schools, the exception exists in the structure and application of Judaic astrology.

The Jewish calendar uses a luni-solar structure which it shares with its Moon school (Chinese, Tibetan, and Vedic) counterparts, segregating itself from the solar structure of the Gregorian (Western) calendar. Judaic astrology, however, shares the use of the tropical zodiac with both Western and Arabian astrology, applying the Ascendant's decanate[5] in a manner of delineation similar to Vedic and some forms of Western astrology. It embraces the concept of free will, but allows for the integration of astrology into the cultural framework as a form of spiritual guidance, advising the individual on his or her path to a righteous life as God intended. Judaic astrologers also perceive the individual's role to be that of an interactive member of a family, a community, a culture, and a religious body rather than as an ego-based and ego-motivated entity.

The combination of free will and selfless spiritual responsibility in a single ideology may seem confused, but so was the last line of the riddle Samson presented to his Philistine wedding guests: "Out of the strong came forth sweetness."

— ✴ —

This comparison of the world's major astrologies is not meant to denigrate or elevate any single tradition or group of traditions. Neither is it intended to pinpoint strengths or weaknesses inherent in any practice. It is simply presented to demonstrate the unique qualities found in each tradition: to highlight both

---

5. An Ascendant sign is divided into three subsections of 10°00′ each, which are called decanates. A planetary subruler is assigned to each decanate. For example, Aquarius (♒) is ruled by the planet Uranus, but the sign's second decanate (11°♒00′–20°♒00′) is subruled by the planet Mercury. So a person born with an Ascendant in the second decanate of Aquarius receives planetary influences from both Uranus and Mercury.

conspicuous and subtle differences in ideology and approaches to delineation. The value of any acquired knowledge is in its application. The employment of two or more forms of astrology to the assessment of an individual personality is an ideal testing ground. To accomplish this task, however, it is necessary to have at least a rudimentary understanding of how each tradition identifies and interprets the knowledge gained from the year, month, day, and time an individual was born.

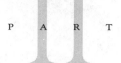

Delineating the Tower of Babel
Chart Construction and Interpretation

A person's time, date, and place of birth are the three essential elements used by all of the world's major astrological traditions. The actual methods used to derive the necessary interpretative data differ, however. This section concentrates on these diverse methods and variations as well as on the surprising number of interpretative similarities that have been passed along over the centuries and across cultures.

Two people's charts are constructed and analyzed throughout this section, not only to facilitate comprehension of the calculation methods described, but also to illustrate the comparisons and contrasts of interpretation found between traditions. The birth data on these two individuals are as follows:

Alice T., born in Chicago, Illinois, on June 15, 1952, at 10:45 P.M. Central Daylight Savings Time (CDT).

Peter C., born in Syracuse, New York, on August 27, 1964, at 7:45 P.M. Eastern Daylight Savings Time (EDT).

The
Wind
and the
Mountain

CHAPTER

<small>CHINESE FATE CALCULATION</small>

Chinese astrology is considered by many scholars to be one of the world's oldest forms. Unlike the other Moon-school traditions (Tibetan, Vedic, and Judaic), which couch astrology in religious dogma, Chinese astrology is purely secular: a direction shared by the Sun-school astrologies (Western and Arabian). Unlike Tibetan or Vedic astrologies, it does not focus its attention on karmic debt, nor does it attempt to integrate religious and cultural concepts, as does Judaic astrology. Instead, the Chinese tradition concerns itself with the individual's ability to achieve balanced relationships with family, friends, and the community within the context of present time.

Many forms of astrology are practiced in Chinese culture: some interpret the placement of various groups of stars along with the planets within the houses of an individual's chart; others simply interpret a person's year of birth; while others employ the Moon's placement at the time of an individual's birth. The rising popularity of *feng shui* (the Chinese art of environmental design, which applies portions of Chinese astrology in its calculation) in the western hemisphere is only one reason that some of these methods have attracted increased attention in the past decade. Another is that each type is reasonably simple to calculate and comprehend. The only data needed to begin are the year, month, day, and time an individual was born, as well as the general location of birth. Although there are scores of regional variants, in this volume we have decided to focus on three popular forms of Chinese astrology.

The method called the *Ming Shu* (Circle of Animals) is the practice most commonly recognized by westerners. This system is to Chinese astrology what Sun signs are to Western astrology: the practitioner needs only to know the year of a person's birth to create a personality profile. It employs twelve zodiac signs, representing a dozen general personality types, but knowing whether a person is a *lung* (Dragon) or a *niu* (Ox) is about as minimally revealing as knowing whether a person is a Virgo or a Taurus in Western astrology.

The second astrological method discussed in this chapter provides a more enhanced profile of an individual's personality, revealing the portion of luck the person receives at birth, the type of projects or events that will prove successful, the person's professional calling, emotional or physical strengths and weaknesses, and even his or her physical appearance, to name just a few facets. Known as the *Tzu P'ing,* it is a more precise form of fate calculation, and is commonly used in both rural and urban China. The system is based on *Ssu Chu* (Four Pillars of Destiny), which involves casting of the *ba tze* (eight characters), which are derived from the year, month, day, and hour of a person's birth. It is an age-old custom that when a child is born, the family consults a master astrologer to calculate the baby's *Ssu Chu.* Far simpler than its Western counterparts, the *Ssu Chu* is interpreted along with the Ten-Year Fate Cycles to develop a personality profile and subsequent life chronology.[1]

The third form of Chinese astrology to be discussed in this chapter involves locating the position of the Moon in relation to the constellations. For thousands of years, Chinese astrologers tracked the Moon's orbital path by documenting the date when it passed one of twenty-eight fixed stars or *sieu* (lunar mansions). Used throughout rural and urban China as a way to plan daily activities, the *sieu* are an extremely popular form of daily prediction.

A Chinese layperson is able to cast his or her own personal daily predictions, using either the *Tzu P'ing* or the daily *sieu* method, the latter of which employs a printed almanac for the current year. It would take years of study and practice for a Western layperson to accomplish the same level of personal prognostication on a daily basis using a natal chart, a progressed chart, at least two or three delineation reference books, and a printed ephemeris of the planets' daily motions throughout the current year.

---

1.   There are other, more complex astrological systems, closely resembling Vedic and Western chart constructions, that visually display not only an individual's *Ssu Chu,* but the placement of numerous fixed stars and planets within the twelve horoscope houses which are called the Houses of Fate. Critical aspects formed by these celestial bodies are also marked on these elaborate charts, which have taken more than a few dozen forms over the centuries.

The Basis of the *Tzu P'ing*: the *Ssu Chu*

At the hub of the *Ssu Chu* are two elements: the ten *t'ien kan* (Celestial Stems), as seen in fig. 3.1, and the twelve *ti chih* (Terrestrial Branches), as shown in fig. 3.2.[2] (The *ti chih* and their characteristics also serve as the basis for the popular *Ming Shu* form of astrology.)

FIGURE 3.1. THE TEN *T'IEN KAN*.

T'ien Kan Number	T'ien Kan Name	Hsing	Compass Direction	Ch'i
1	chia	wood	E	yang
2	yi	wood	E	yin
3	ping	fire	S	yang
4	ting	fire	S	yin
5	mou	earth	center	yang
6	chi	earth	center	yin
7	ken	metal	W	yang
8	hsin	metal	W	yin
9	jen	water	N	yang
10	kuei	water	N	yin

FIGURE 3.2. THE TWELVE *TI CHIH* AND THE *MING SHU*.

Ti Chih Number	Ti Chih Name	Ming Shu Sign	Hsing	Compass Direction	Ch'i
I	tzu	shu (rat)	water	N	yang
II	chou	niu (ox)	earth	NNE	yin
III	yin	hu (tiger)	wood	ENE	yang
IV	mao	t'u (hare)	wood	E	yin
V	ch'en	lung (dragon)	earth	ESE	yang
VI	ssu	she (snake)	fire	SSE	yin
VII	wu	ma (horse)	fire	S	yang
VIII	wei	yáng (ram)	earth	SSW	yin
IX	shen	hou (monkey)	metal	WSW	yang
X	yu	chi' (rooster)	metal	W	yin
XI	hsü	kou (dog)	earth	WNW	yang
XII	hai	chi (pig)	water	NNW	yin

2. To facilitate comprehension, the *t'ien kan* and *ti chih* will be referred to by Arabic and Roman numerals respectively, as seen in figures 3.1 and 3.2.

FIGURE 3.3. THE SIXTY *BA TZE* PAIRS.

Ba Tze Pair Number	T'ien Kan / Ti Chih (from figs. 3.1 and 3.2)	Ba Tze Pair Number	T'ien Kan / Ti Chih (from figs. 3.1 and 3.2)	Ba Tze Pair Number	T'ien Kan / Ti Chih (from figs. 3.1 and 3.2)
1	1/I	21	1/IX	41	1/V
2	2/II	22	2/X	42	2/VI
3	3/III	23	3/XI	43	3/VII
4	4/IV	24	4/XII	44	4/VIII
5	5/V	25	5/I	45	5/IX
6	6/VI	26	6/II	46	6/X
7	7/VII	27	7/III	47	7/XI
8	8/VIII	28	8/IV	48	8/XII
9	9/IX	29	9/V	49	9/I
10	10/X	30	10/VI	50	10/II
11	1/XI	31	1/VII	51	1/III
12	2/XII	32	2/VIII	52	2/IV
13	3/I	33	3/IX	53	3/V
14	4/II	34	4/X	54	4/VI
15	5/III	35	5/XI	55	5/VII
16	6/IV	36	6/XII	56	6/VIII
17	7/V	37	7/I	57	7/IX
18	8/VI	38	8/II	58	8/X
19	9/VII	39	9/III	59	9/XI
20	10/VIII	40	10/IV	60	10/XII

The *Ssu Chu* comprises *ba tze* (eight characters) that are divided into four pairs of one *t'ien kan* and one *ti chih* each. There are sixty potential *ba tze* pair combinations, as shown in fig. 3.3. When each *ba tze* pair is written down, the *t'ien kan* appears at the top and the *ti chih* appears at the bottom.

Only four pieces of personal data are required to calculate an individual's *Ssu Chu*: birth year, birth month, birthday, and birth hour. In fact, the *Ssu Chu*'s four pillars directly correspond to these time periods and are named *gen* (year pillar), *miao* (month pillar), *hua* (day pillar), and *guo* (hour pillar).

Unlike Western, Arabian, Judaic, or Vedic astrologies, relatively few calculations are needed to identify an individual's *Ssu Chu*, but there are dozens of ways to interpret those four pillars. This chapter concentrates only on the compilation of the *Ssu Chu* itself, and includes a general overview of the widely practiced *Tzu P'ing* form of interpretation.

STEP ONE: IDENTIFYING THE *SSU CHU* (FOUR PILLARS OF DESTINY) Locating and Interpreting the Birth *Gen* (Year Pillar)

The *gen* (year pillar) defines an individual's behavioral pattern, general appearance, and emotional state. Based on the year of an individual's birth, this pillar is interpreted by studying the natural elements, called *wu hsing* (Five Agents), that individually rule the *gen*'s *t'ien kan* (Celestial Stem) and the *ti chih* (Terrestrial Branch). A separate *hsing* (element) also governs the *ba tze* (eight characters) pair itself. Each of the five *hsing* (elements) represents an essential natural energy that animates the universe. These elemental forces are wood, fire, metal, earth, and water. Each *hsing* is ruled by a planet: Jupiter (♃) rules wood, Mars (♂) rules fire, Venus (♀) rules metal, Saturn (♄) rules earth, and Mercury (☿) rules water. An individual *hsing* also corresponds to one of five seasons of the year (spring, summer, dog days, autumn, and winter), one of five compass directions (east, west, north, south, and center), a color, a prime number, a particular taste sensation, *yin* and/or *yang* energy, and one or more body parts.[3]

Using fig. 3.4, identify the corresponding *t'ien kan* (fourth column) and *ti chih* (fifth column) for the individual's Western-calendar birth year. The resulting *ba tze* pair makes up the person's *gen* (year pillar). The birth year's *Ming Shu* sign (second column) and the given year's *hsing* (third column) are written down for future reference.

FIGURE 3.4. TABLE OF *MING SHU* SIGNS, *HSING*, *T'IEN KAN*, AND *TI CHIH* FOR THE YEARS 1924 THROUGH 2050.

Year	Ming Shu Sign	Hsing	T'ien Kan (from fig. 3.1)	Ti Chih (from fig. 3.2)	Starting Date
1924	*shu* (rat)	wood	I	I	Feb. 5
1925	*niu* (ox)	wood	2	II	Jan. 24
1926	*hu* (tiger)	fire	3	III	Feb. 13
1927	*t'u* (hare)	fire	4	IV	Feb. 2
1928	*lung* (dragon)	earth	5	V	Jan. 23
1929	*she* (snake)	earth	6	VI	Feb. 10
1930	*ma* (horse)	metal	7	VII	Jan. 30
1931	*yáng* (ram)	metal	8	VIII	Feb. 17
1932	*hou* (monkey)	water	9	IX	Feb. 6
1933	*chi'* (rooster)	water	10	X	Jan. 26

---

3. This doctrine was either compiled or created by Chou Yen (c. 350–270 B.C.) in a work titled the *Chou Tzu* (Master Chou's Writings).

Year	Ming Shu Sign	Hsing	T'ien Kan (from Fig. 3.1)	Ti Chih (from Fig. 3.2)	Starting Date
1934	kou (dog)	wood	1	XI	Feb. 14
1935	chi (pig)	wood	2	XII	Feb. 4
1936	shu (rat)	fire	3	I	Jan. 24
1937	niu (ox)	fire	4	II	Feb. 11
1938	hu (tiger)	earth	5	III	Jan. 31
1939	t'u (hare)	earth	6	IV	Feb. 19
1940	lung (dragon)	metal	7	V	Feb. 8
1941	she (snake)	metal	8	VI	Jan. 27
1942	ma (horse)	water	9	VII	Feb. 15
1943	yáng (ram)	water	10	VIII	Feb. 5
1944	hou (monkey)	wood	1	IX	Jan. 25
1945	chi' (rooster)	wood	2	X	Feb. 13
1946	kou (dog)	fire	3	XI	Feb. 2
1947	chi (pig)	fire	4	XII	Jan. 22
1948	shu (rat)	earth	5	I	Feb. 10
1949	niu (ox)	earth	6	II	Jan. 29
1950	hu (tiger)	metal	7	III	Feb. 17
1951	t'u (hare)	metal	8	IV	Feb. 6
1952	lung (dragon)	water	9	V	Jan. 27
1953	she (snake)	water	10	VI	Feb. 14
1954	ma (horse)	wood	1	VII	Feb. 3
1955	yáng (ram)	wood	2	VIII	Jan. 24
1956	hou (monkey)	fire	3	IX	Feb. 12
1957	chi' (rooster)	fire	4	X	Jan. 31
1958	kou (dog)	earth	5	XI	Feb. 18
1959	chi (pig)	earth	6	XII	Feb. 8
1960	shu (rat)	metal	7	I	Jan. 28
1961	niu (ox)	metal	8	II	Feb. 15
1962	hu (tiger)	water	9	III	Feb. 5
1963	t'u (hare)	water	10	IV	Jan. 25
1964	lung (dragon)	wood	1	V	Feb. 13
1965	she (snake)	wood	2	VI	Feb. 2
1966	ma (horse)	fire	3	VII	Jan. 21
1967	yáng (ram)	fire	4	VIII	Feb. 9
1968	hou (monkey)	earth	5	IX	Jan. 30
1969	chi' (rooster)	earth	6	X	Feb. 17
1970	kou (dog)	metal	7	XI	Feb. 6
1971	chi (pig)	metal	8	XII	Jan. 27
1972	shu (rat)	water	9	I	Feb. 15
1973	niu (ox)	water	10	II	Feb. 3
1974	hu (tiger)	wood	1	III	Jan. 23
1975	t'u (hare)	wood	2	IV	Feb. 11

Year	Ming Shu Sign	Hsing	T'ien Kan (from fig. 3.1)	Ti Chih (from fig. 3.2)	Starting Date
1976	*lung* (dragon)	fire	3	V	Jan. 31
1977	*she* (snake)	fire	4	VI	Feb. 18
1978	*ma* (horse)	earth	5	VII	Feb. 7
1979	*yáng* (ram)	earth	6	VIII	Jan. 28
1980	*hou* (monkey)	metal	7	IX	Feb. 16
1981	*chi'* (rooster)	metal	8	X	Feb. 5
1982	*kou* (dog)	water	9	XI	Jan. 25
1983	*chi* (pig)	water	10	XII	Feb. 13
1984	*shu* (rat)	wood	1	I	Feb. 2
1985	*niu* (ox)	wood	2	II	Feb. 20
1986	*hu* (tiger)	fire	3	III	Feb. 9
1987	*t'u* (hare)	fire	4	IV	Jan. 29
1988	*lung* (dragon)	earth	5	V	Feb. 17
1989	*she* (snake)	earth	6	VI	Feb. 6
1990	*ma* (horse)	metal	7	VII	Jan. 27
1991	*yáng* (ram)	metal	8	VIII	Feb. 15
1992	*hou* (monkey)	water	9	IX	Feb. 4
1993	*chi'* (rooster)	water	10	X	Jan. 23
1994	*kou* (dog)	wood	1	XI	Feb. 10
1995	*chi* (pig)	wood	2	XII	Jan. 31
1996	*shu* (rat)	fire	3	I	Feb. 19
1997	*niu* (ox)	fire	4	II	Feb. 7
1998	*hu* (tiger)	earth	5	III	Jan. 28
1999	*t'u* (hare)	earth	6	IV	Feb. 16
2000	*lung* (dragon)	metal	7	V	Feb. 5
2001	*she* (snake)	metal	8	VI	Jan. 24
2002	*ma* (horse)	water	9	VII	Feb. 12
2003	*yáng* (ram)	water	10	VIII	Feb. 1
2004	*hou* (monkey)	wood	1	IX	Jan. 22
2005	*chi'* (rooster)	wood	2	X	Feb. 9
2006	*kou* (dog)	fire	3	XI	Jan. 29
2007	*chi* (pig)	fire	4	XII	Feb. 18
2008	*shu* (rat)	earth	5	I	Feb. 7
2009	*niu* (ox)	earth	6	II	Jan. 26
2010	*hu* (tiger)	metal	7	III	Feb. 14
2011	*t'u* (hare)	metal	8	IV	Feb. 3
2012	*lung* (dragon)	water	9	V	Jan. 23
2013	*she* (snake)	water	10	VI	Feb. 10
2014	*ma* (horse)	wood	1	VII	Jan. 31
2015	*yáng* (ram)	wood	2	VIII	Feb. 19
2016	*hou* (monkey)	fire	3	IX	Feb. 8
2017	*chi'* (rooster)	fire	4	X	Jan. 28

Year	Ming Shu Sign	Hsing	T'ien Kan (from fig. 3.1)	Ti Chih (from fig. 3.2)	Starting Date
2018	*kou* (dog)	earth	5	XI	Feb. 16
2019	*chi* (pig)	earth	6	XII	Feb. 5
2020	*shu* (rat)	metal	7	I	Jan. 25
2021	*niu* (ox)	metal	8	II	Feb. 12
2022	*hu* (tiger)	water	9	III	Feb. 1
2023	*t'u* (hare)	water	10	IV	Jan. 22
2024	*lung* (dragon)	wood	1	V	Feb. 10
2025	*she* (snake)	wood	2	VI	Jan. 29
2026	*ma* (horse)	fire	3	VII	Feb. 17
2027	*yáng* (ram)	fire	4	VIII	Feb. 6
2028	*hou* (monkey)	earth	5	IX	Jan. 26
2029	*chi'* (rooster)	earth	6	X	Feb. 13
2030	*kou* (dog)	metal	7	XI	Feb. 3
2031	*chi* (pig)	metal	8	XII	Jan. 23
2032	*shu* (rat)	water	9	I	Feb. 11
2033	*niu* (ox)	water	10	II	Jan. 31
2034	*hu* (tiger)	wood	1	III	Feb. 19
2035	*t'u* (hare)	wood	2	IV	Feb. 8
2036	*lung* (dragon)	fire	3	V	Jan. 28
2037	*she* (snake)	fire	4	VI	Feb. 15
2038	*ma* (horse)	earth	5	VII	Feb. 4
2039	*yáng* (ram)	earth	6	VIII	Jan. 24
2040	*hou* (monkey)	metal	7	IX	Feb. 12
2041	*chi'* (rooster)	metal	8	X	Feb. 1
2042	*kou* (dog)	water	9	XI	Jan. 22
2043	*chi* (pig)	water	10	XII	Feb. 10
2044	*shu* (rat)	wood	1	I	Jan. 30
2045	*niu* (ox)	wood	2	II	Feb. 17
2046	*hu* (tiger)	fire	3	III	Feb. 6
2047	*t'u* (hare)	fire	4	IV	Jan. 26
2048	*lung* (dragon)	earth	5	V	Feb. 14
2049	*she* (snake)	earth	6	VI	Feb. 2
2050	*ma* (horse)	metal	7	VII	Jan. 23

Next, determine the *hsing* that results from the pairing of the *gen*'s *t'ien kan* and *ti chih* in fig. 3.4 (fourth and fifth columns). This is done by locating the *gen*'s *t'ien kan* and *ti chih* pair in fig. 3.5 (second column). As mentioned at the beginning of this section, the *gen* is interpreted by studying not only the *hsing* that individually rule the *gen*'s *t'ien kan* and the *ti chih*; it incorporates the *hsing* for the specific year as well.

Figure 3.5. Relationship of the *t'ien kan* and *ti chih*.

Ba Tze Pair Number	T'ien Kan/ Ti Chih (fig. 3.3)	Ch'i	Hsing	Poetic Name
1	1/I	yang	metal	gold at the bottom of the sea
2	2/II	yin	metal	gold at the bottom of the sea
3	3/III	yang	fire	fire of the furnace
4	4/IV	yin	fire	fire of the furnace
5	5/V	yang	wood	tree of the great forest
6	6/VI	yin	wood	tree of the great forest
7	7/VII	yang	earth	earth on the road side
8	8/VIII	yin	earth	earth on the road side
9	9/IX	yang	metal	steel of the sharp blade
10	10/X	yin	metal	steel of the sharp blade
11	1/XI	yang	fire	fire at the hilltop
12	2/XII	yin	fire	fire at the hilltop
13	3/I	yang	water	water which enters and fertilizes
14	4/II	yin	water	water which enters and fertilizes
15	5/III	yang	earth	earth on the city walls
16	6/IV	yin	earth	earth on the city walls
17	7/V	yang	metal	molded bronze
18	8/VI	yin	metal	molded bronze
19	9/VII	yang	wood	wood of poplar and willow
20	10/VIII	yin	wood	wood of poplar and willow
21	1/IX	yang	water	water of rain and springs
22	2/X	yin	water	water of rain and springs
23	3/XI	yang	earth	earth of the roof
24	4/XII	yin	earth	earth of the roof
25	5/I	yang	fire	fire of lightning
26	6/II	yin	fire	fire of lightning
27	7/III	yang	wood	wood of cedar and pine
28	8/IV	yin	wood	wood of cedar and pine
29	9/V	yang	water	running water
30	10/VI	yin	water	running water
31	1/VII	yang	metal	gold in the mine
32	2/VIII	yin	metal	gold in the mine
33	3/IX	yang	fire	fire at the foot of the hill
34	4/X	yin	fire	fire at the foot of the hill
35	5/XI	yang	wood	wood of the plain
36	6/XII	yin	wood	wood of the plain
37	7/I	yang	earth	earth of the wall
38	8/II	yin	earth	earth of the wall
39	9/III	yang	metal	metal of the mirror
40	10/IV	yin	metal	metal of the mirror
41	1/V	yang	fire	fire of the lamp

Ba Tze Pair Number	T'ien Kan/ Ti Chih (fig. 3.3)	Ch'i	Hsing	Poetic Name
42	2/VI	yin	fire	fire of the lamp
43	3/VII	yang	water	water of the celestial river
44	4/VIII	yin	water	water of the celestial river
45	5/IX	yang	earth	earth of the great roads
46	6/X	yin	earth	earth of the great roads
47	7/XI	yang	metal	metal of bracelets and hairpins
48	8/XII	yin	metal	metal of bracelets and hairpins
49	9/I	yang	wood	wood of mulberry
50	10/II	yin	wood	wood of mulberry
51	1/III	yang	water	water of streams
52	2/IV	yin	water	water of streams
53	3/V	yang	earth	earth buried in sand
54	4/VI	yin	earth	earth buried in sand
55	5/VII	yang	fire	fire in heaven
56	6/VIII	yin	fire	fire in heaven
57	7/IX	yang	wood	wood of pomegranate
58	8/X	yin	wood	wood of pomegranate
59	9/XI	yang	water	water of the ocean
60	10/XII	yin	water	water of the ocean

The *hsing* that individually rule the *gen's t'ien kan* and *ti chih,* as well as the *hsing* that rules the *gen's ba tze* pair are then interpreted as follows:

earth

The earth *hsing* is the source of all the other elements. The person is prudent and possesses the essential virtue of faith. The emotional state is desire. Earth corresponds to the afternoon and the "dog days" of summer, the center of the compass, both *yin* and *yang,* the color yellow, the number 5, the planet Saturn (♄), sweet and sugary tastes, the spleen, mouth, and flesh. The individual is professionally suited to be a businessperson or financier. An earth-influenced person is practical, conservative, and reliable. This individual moves cautiously and shrewdly, measuring each action for its potential result. He or she loves to delve deeply into any matter, seeking critical details as well as bits of trivia along the way. Physically, this *hsing* produces a person with a sallow complexion, thick features, round back, and flat belly, if no other *hsing* influences the *gen.*

fire

The fire *hsing* is a boiling, hot force that rises upwards. The person is enlightened and possesses wisdom. The emotional state is volatile. Fire corresponds to midday and summer, the south, *yang,* the color red, the number 7, the planet Mars (σ), bitter tastes, the heart, tongue, and blood. This person is suited to be a soldier or an adventurer. A fire-influenced person has natural leadership qualities such as decisiveness, motivation, aggressiveness, and optimism. This person is dynamic and egotistical. Physically, this *hsing* produces a person with a ruddy complexion, a face that is larger at the bottom, an aquiline nose, and detached earlobes, if no other *hsing* influences the *gen.*

metal

The metal *hsing* is inert, but adopts the shape imposed upon it. The person is energetic and possesses the essential virtue of rectitude. The emotional state is sadness. Metal corresponds to evening and autumn, the west, *yang,* the color white, the number 9, the planet Venus ($\female$), pungent or acrid tastes, the lungs, nose, skin, and hair. This person is best suited to become an attorney, a judge, or a juror. This *hsing* is most commonly associated with gold, bronze, or steel. A metal-influenced individual is guided by his or her feelings with passionate intensity. A determined and somewhat rigid, opinionated outlook guides this person through hard times and false starts. Ultimately, however, this individual finds success. Vigor, independence, and self-reliance are key issues. Physically, this *hsing* produces a person with a clear complexion, square face, straight ears, and small, square fingertips, if no other *hsing* influences the *gen.*

water

The water *hsing* is an infiltrating and dissolving force that sinks downward. The person is calm and possesses the essential virtue of respectability; the main emotional state is fear. Water corresponds to night and winter, the north, *yin,* the color black or blue, the number 6, the planet Mercury ($\mercury$), salty tastes, the kidneys, ears, and bones. This person is well suited to be an artisan or tradesperson. A water-influenced individual is a communicator who inspires others to act on his or her ideas. Contemplative and attentive, this person has a nose for future outcomes and knows how to move other people in the right direction. Opposition is met by quiet and steady work, infiltrating and wearing away problems and resistance. Physically, this *hsing* produces a round person with soft skin, glossy hair, thick lips, and large ears, if no other *hsing* influences the *gen*.

wood | The wood *hsing* is a live force that is easily shaped by outside influences, representing creative power. The person is relaxed and benevolent. The emotional state is anger. Wood corresponds to morning and spring, east, *yin*, the color green, the number 8, the planet Jupiter (♃), acid tastes, the liver, eyes, and muscles. This person is best suited to become an artist or a farmer. A wood-influenced person possesses high ethical and moral standards as well as self-confidence and compassion. A lover of nature and children, this is a rustic and creative person. Progressive in outlook, he or she knows how to delegate, diversify, and organize in an executive manner, making him or her an ideal manager of large-scale projects. Physically, this *hsing* produces a tall, thin, straight-standing person with a soft olive complexion, fine eyes, red lips, and small hands and feet, if no other *hsing* affects the *gen*.

Alice T. was born in 1952. According to fig. 3.4, her *gen*'s *ba tze* pair is 9/V (fourth and fifth columns), representing the ninth *t'ien kan*, which is ruled by the water *hsing* (fig. 3.1) and the fifth *ti chih*, which is ruled by the earth *hsing* (fig. 3.2). The data in fig. 3.4 also indicate that her *Ming Shu* sign (second column) is *lung* (Dragon), which is governed by the earth *hsing* (fig. 3.2), and her year *hsing* (third column) is water. These items are written down for future reference.

According to her *gen*'s *ba tze* pair (9/V) looked at separately, she is a prudent, faithful person because of the earth *hsing* that rules her *gen*'s *ti chih* (V in fig. 3.2). She is practical, conservative, and reliable, moving cautiously and shrewdly, measuring each action for its potential result. She loves delving deeply into any matter, finding critical details as well as bits of trivia along the way. The water *hsing* that rules her *gen*'s *t'ien kan* (9 in fig. 3.1) makes her behave calmly even though her primary emotion is fear. She is communicative, inspiring others to act. She has a nose for future outcomes and knows how to move other people in the right direction. Opposition is met by quiet and steady work, infiltrating and wearing away problems and resistance.

Her *gen*'s *ba tze* pair is governed by the water *hsing* and has the poetic name of "running water" (9/V in fig. 3.5, second column). Consequently, the water-influenced aspects of Alice's behavior and emotions mentioned earlier are stronger than the earth-related traits that are also present in her *gen*. Her physical appearance combines the two *hsing* (earth and water), but stresses the water-related influences. Therefore she possibly has soft skin, glossy hair, thick lips or features, a round back, and a flat stomach.

Peter C. was born in 1964. According to fig. 3.4, his *gen's ba tze* pair is 1/V (fourth and fifth columns), representing the first *t'ien kan*, which is ruled by the wood *hsing* (fig. 3.1) and the fifth *ti chih*, which is ruled by the earth *hsing* (fig. 3.2). The table in fig. 3.4 also indicates that his *Ming Shu* sign (second column) is *lung* (Dragon), which is governed by the earth *hsing* (fig. 3.2) and that his year *hsing* (third column) is wood. These facts are written down for future reference.

His *gen's ba tze* pair (1/V), looked at separately, indicates he is a prudent, faithful person because of the earth *hsing* that rules his *gen's ti chih* (V in fig. 3.2). He is practical, conservative, and reliable, moving cautiously and shrewdly, measuring each action for its potential result. He loves delving deeply into any matter, finding critical details as well as bits of trivia along the way. The wood *hsing* that rules his *gen's t'ien kan* (1 in fig. 3.1) strengthens his high ethical and moral standards as well as his self-confidence and compassion. It also makes him behave in a relaxed fashion, even though his primary emotion is anger. A lover of nature and children, Peter is a rustic and creative person. He knows how to delegate and organize.

His *gen's ba tze* pair is governed by the fire *hsing* and has the poetic name of "fire of the lamp" (1/V in fig. 3.5, second column). This affects Peter's behavior and emotions by introducing wisdom and volatility as well as strengthening the natural leadership qualities he possesses from the wood *hsing* influence exerted by his *gen's t'ien kan* (1 in fig. 3.1). The fire *hsing* also intensifies his self-confidence, making him somewhat egotistical. Physically, the combination of the two *hsing* (earth and wood) as well as this third *hsing* (fire) potentially creates a tall, thin, straight-standing person with soft skin, thick features, red lips, an aquiline nose, and a flat stomach.

Interpreting the *Ming Shu* (Circle of Animals)

There is another method for delineating the *gen*, which centers on the behavioral pattern of the person's *Ming Shu* sign and year *hsing*, written down earlier. Unlike the method described above, which strictly employs the interpretation of the *gen's* three *hsing* influences, this version assigns general characteristics to the *Ming Shu* sign in a manner identical to popular western Sun-sign astrology. The delineation is then augmented by elements controlled by the year *hsing*. Although both the *Ming Shu* system and the *Tzu P'ing* method of *Ssu Chu* interpretation are separately employed in China, there is no reason the two systems of interpretation cannot be compared in an interpretation.

Using the table in fig. 3.4 and the person's year of birth, the *Ming Shu* sign (second column) and year *hsing* (third column) are identified. The delineation material on the following pages for both the general characteristics of the sign and the combined influences of the sign's association with the year *hsing* are then used to synthesize a personality profile.

Ti Chih I: Shu (Rat)[4]

Shu serves as a symbol of wealth. A person born under the *Ming Shu* sign *shu* is a charming, nervous, nocturnal, intelligent, curious, secretive individual who is always on the lookout for money-making opportunities. But this person is generous and has a strong desire to experience the good things in life.

An earth-*hsing shu* (a *shu* born in a year ruled by the earth *hsing*) needs order and security to be happy. With both feet firmly planted on the ground, this person prefers to concentrate on one job at a time and work at it very thoroughly. The earth-*hsing shu* rarely takes risks and can be overly practical or overly concerned about maintaining a carefully nurtured reputation.

A fire-*hsing shu* is an active, dynamic person who loves to travel and is extremely independent. Besides possessing a strong ego, this person is also extremely competitive and refuses to take a mainstream or compromising stance on any issue.

A metal-*hsing shu* is intellectual, idealistic, very emotional, and is a masterful speaker—able to cover his or her true feelings with a cheerful smile. This person is also jealous, quick to anger, selfish, and possessive. He or she loves to impress others and has expensive tastes, but knows how to invest his or her finances.

A water-*hsing shu* possesses literary talent and a strong desire to learn. This person follows the mainstream, expressing a traditional and conservative outlook. However, the person is also shrewd, accommodating those who wield influence in the right places.

A wood-*hsing shu* can see far into the future, is egotistical and success-oriented. This person knows how to use every situation or raw material at hand and knows how to campaign for help when it's needed.

Ti Chih II: Niu (Ox or Buffalo)

Niu is a symbol of longevity. A *niu* person is hardworking, stubborn, and even-tempered. Despite a plodding, deliberate persona, this individual is very intelligent, using quiet analysis, caution, tenacity, and steady motion before moving forward. These people are very attached to home, family, and children.

An earth-*hsing niu* (a *niu* born in a year ruled by the earth *hsing*) needs security and stability to be happy, and is prepared to pay the price for success. Fidelity and

---

4. This sign is generally known as the Mouse in Vietnam and other neighboring regions.

constancy are strong traits in this person's character as are determination and sincerity.

A fire-*hsing niu* is driven to power, position, and material gain. Despite the fact that this individual is very protective of family and friends, he or she can be condescending toward others who do not help this person toward his or her personal goal.

A metal-*hsing niu* is a lover of the arts, but maintains a mental "stone wall," and would rather fight than change his or her personal viewpoint. A forceful personality is combined with a less-than-affectionate nature, making the person almost militant about life, unable to accept failure or defeat.

A water-*hsing niu* is shrewd, but possesses strong personal values. A little more flexible than those born in fire years, this person is open to practical suggestions that forward his or her personal goals. This person does not readily accept unconventional ideas, however.

A wood-*hsing niu* reacts quickly and possesses some compassion for other people's feelings. This ambitious, driven person also concedes to the consensus opinion.

Ti Chih *III*: Hu *(Tiger)*

Hu is the protector of children against evil spirits. A *hu* individual is a born leader. This person hates interference and is very protective of his or her personal reputation. But he or she is also courageous, generous, and self-sacrificing, even in love. Courage is an essential trait.

An earth-*hsing hu* (a *hu* born in a year ruled by the earth *hsing*) is a responsible realist unlike other *hu* personalities. Passionate and persistent, this person establishes relationships based on their usefulness rather than on adventurous or sentimental instincts. This individual also looks for status and recognition through systematic hard work rather than opportunism.

A fire-*hsing hu* has more enthusiasm and energy than most people. A traveler by nature, this person is very independent and eccentric. He or she is also extremely personable and generous.

A metal-*hsing hu* is a passionate, energetic person who presents an extremely glamorous persona. This individual is very direct and can occasionally be overly optimistic.

A water-*hsing hu* is an objective thinker with an open-minded attitude. An excellent judge of character who is perceptive of other people's feelings, this person excels at public communications.

A wood-*hsing hu* is practical and democratic, with a remarkable understanding of group dynamics. This person is an excellent corporate executive and negotiator.

Ti Chih *IV*: T'u *(Hare)*

A *t'u* person detests change. This individual is a discreet creature of comfort and a very intelligent observer of others' strengths and weaknesses. He or she can be highly touchy and secretly egotistical. This person is not a faithful spouse and has little understanding of domestic or familial pleasures. Virtue and prudence, however, are essential traits in his or her nature.

An earth-*hsing t'u* (a *t'u* born in a year ruled by the earth *hsing*) moves in a calculated fashion. This individual is more steadfast than other *t'u* personalities, but still aims toward the fulfillment of personal material desires.

A fire-*hsing t'u* is more outgoing than other *t'u* personalities. He or she may be temperamental and outspoken as well as easily moved by situations or perceptions.

A metal-*hsing t'u* is highly observant and uncompromising. He or she is totally preoccupied with fulfilling his or her own desires. But this person's ambition is well concealed.

A water-*hsing t'u* is emotionally quite fragile. Born with an empathic nature, this person's intuition and memory are very keen. He or she may dwell too much on the frailties of the past or on potential dangers of the future.

A wood-*hsing t'u* is both generous and compassionate. He or she may be somewhat intimidated by others who might take advantage of his or her overly generous nature.

Ti Chih *V*: Lung *(Dragon)*

The *lung* is the King of the Universe and the traditional symbol of the Chinese emperor.[5] A *lung* person can succeed at anything. This individual is highly intelligent and follows only his or her own personal judgment. Unless, however, his or her blunt personality edges are curbed and patience and tolerance are learned, success will elude this otherwise lucky person. A *lung* person is often loved, but seldom falls in love.

An earth-*hsing lung* (a *lung* born in a year ruled by the earth *hsing*) needs to control his or her environment. This person is quiet and understands the value of cooperation, but he or she still needs to lead in an executive and dignified manner.

A fire-*hsing lung* is highly dramatic and competitive. This person has elevated expectations, demanding to be heard and obeyed. The criticisms this person imparts are completely constructive, however, and all advice is objective.

A metal-*hsing lung* is strong-willed, critical, and very difficult to sway, but this person also inspires others. Everything must be done with integrity and honor; laziness and stupidity are never tolerated.

---

5.   In traditional Chinese symbology, the dragon's counterpart is the phoenix, which represents the empress.

A water-*hsing lung* believes in growth and expansion. To that end, this person puts aside personal opinion, but maintains a strong will and wields remarkable patience.

A wood-*hsing lung* has a creative mind and the ability to develop revolutionary ideas. This person is compulsively inquisitive at times and can be condescending toward others. He or she generally hides a domineering spirit, but can still be very outspoken.

Ti Chih VI: She *(Snake)*

The *she* is a symbol of wealth. A *she* person is stable and a good organizer, possessing substantial wisdom. This individual is highly intelligent and can occasionally be accused of having an overly moral outlook. The person listens carefully to the advice of other people, but he or she is a poor sport, incapable of losing gracefully. The *she* individual may know how to establish a relationship, but finds it difficult to maintain one.

An earth-*hsing she* (a *she* born in a year ruled by the earth *hsing*) is persistent and reliable. This person can handle any emergency, and bridges the gaps in a dire situation. He or she has well-calculated limits and the sort of charisma needed for success.

A fire-*hsing she* is extremely energetic and ambitious. Charismatic, exuding self-confidence, this person believes only in himself or herself and is jealous, power- and money-hungry, and extremely sensual.

A metal-*hsing she* has incredible willpower and a keen eye for opportunity. This person craves luxury and pursues wealth. He or she is also jealous and competitive, with a domineering streak. This person is also generous and cooperative, however.

A water-*hsing she* has remarkable charisma. Shrewd and materialistic, this person is very talented at handling finances. He or she can also maintain a grudge for a long period of time.

A wood-*hsing she* has a nose for history and a need for total intellectual freedom. As a spouse or lover, however, this person is completely loyal and affectionate.

Ti Chih VII: Ma *(Horse)*

The *ma* is a symbol of masculinity. A *ma* person is lively, passionate, quick-tempered, and very impatient. This individual needs to be the center of attention. Wit, brilliance, and elegance make the person attractive to others, but he or she may lack intellectual depth. The *ma* is naturally talented, however, at making the best of any opportunity presented.

An earth-*hsing ma* (a *ma* born in a year ruled by the earth *hsing*) is steadfast and slower-moving than other *ma* types. He or she moves cautiously and looks for options, but still vacillates at making a final decision. Abundant energy makes this person a great rebuilder.

A fire-*hsing ma* is flamboyant and adventurous. He or she is charismatic and smart, but also reckless. In fact, this person can be a competitive extremist who has a hard time concentrating on any task or controlling his or her mental volatility. This individual perceives trends and fashions easily.

A metal-*hsing ma* is socially popular, but very unruly and impetuous. There is a level of self-centeredness and stubbornness attached to this person, and he or she is in a constant state of activity, but deplores routine. Therefore, this person needs supervision in serious ongoing situations.

A water-*hsing ma* has a deep wanderlust. Besides being a nomad, this person constantly changes his or her mind without explanation. This same individual also has a remarkable ability to recognize and adopt fashions and trends.

A wood-*hsing ma* is systematic and self-disciplined, but resists domination. This person is always willing to try unconventional methods. He or she likes to start new projects, but has difficulty concentrating on the projects at hand or completing responsibilities.

Ti Chih VIII: Yáng *(Ram or Sheep)*

The *yáng* is a symbol of social and professional success. A *yáng* individual is naturally dependent on others. This person loves beauty and possesses artistic ability. He or she easily forgives and forgets. Eccentric and unstable, this person has problems establishing a close love relationship or maintaining a solid marriage. Art and refinement are essential in this person's nature.

An earth-*hsing yáng* (a *yáng* born in a year ruled by the earth *hsing*) is devoted to family and home, but also desires a level of personal independence. Cautious and conservative, this person does not scrimp, but is also not extravagant.

A fire-*hsing yáng* is confident enough to follow his or her intuition and instincts. He or she can accentuate strengths and conceal weaknesses very dramatically.

A metal-*hsing yáng* is aware of his or her talents, and exhibits immense self-confidence despite heightened sensitivity and a fragile ego. This person is always in search of aesthetic harmony and balance in daily life, as well as financial and domestic security. He or she can be overprotective and possessive of loved ones.

A water-*hsing yáng* is the sort of person other people want to mother and protect. However, this person is opportunistic, using this talent to develop a support network. He or she may suffer from a rejection complex if not allowed to have his or her own way.

A wood-*hsing yáng* wants to please others. This person is essentially generous and possesses high principles, but might make unwise personal sacrifices for others.

Ti Chih *IX:* Hou (*Monkey*)

The *hou* is a symbol of resourcefulness. A *hou* person has a superiority complex. This individual has a self-gratifying need for constant activity and friction. He or she is not afraid to lie or to create personas. This same individual also finds it difficult to maintain a love relationship because of his or her instability.

An earth-*hsing hou* (a *hou* born in a year ruled by the earth *hsing*) has a calm, collected persona. This individual secretly wants to be appreciated, and sulks if attention is not forthcoming. He or she values integrity and is less egotistical than other *hou* types.

A fire-*hsing hou* possesses such leadership traits as self-assured determination. He or she is also very inventive, but sometimes lets new concepts get out of hand. Despite a confident presence, this person lives with a morbid fear that others are deceptive.

A metal-*hsing hou* is independent and sophisticated. This person craves financial security and possesses a strong entrepreneurial spirit. A very convincing salesperson, this warm, lively individual works hard and always looks out for his or her interests.

A water-*hsing hou* believes that "one hand should wash the other." He or she invests in relationships that potentially yield a return, and conceals the true, self-gratifying motive.

A wood-*hsing hou* is resourceful and honorable. He or she strives for prestige and does not take setbacks lightly.

Ti Chih *X:* Chi' (*Rooster*)

The *chi'* is naturally honest and very intelligent, possessing an excellent memory. He or she is a showman with incredible vanity, and possesses remarkable candor. However, this person sometimes concentrates too much on the trees instead of the forest.

An earth-*hsing chi'* (a *chi'* born in a year ruled by the earth *hsing*) is capable of bearing heavy responsibilities. He or she digs for the root of every situation and carefully carries out every project to completion. This person can be hypercritical and overly strict, however.

A fire-*hsing chi'* is a highly motivated, single-minded person. This type of *chi'* person can be almost fanatical when it comes to details and investigation, causing problems with co-workers who do not share the same work ethic.

A metal-*hsing chi'* is an industrious person with incredible powers of deduction, but this person has a tendency to overdo everything from work to talking. He or she craves fame. Headstrong and critical, this person has a narrow view of the world.

A water-*hsing chi'* is a prolific writer and speaker who can sway other people into action, but this person sometimes spends too much time dwelling on details instead of viewing the big picture.

A wood-*hsing chi'* is considerate of others and is able to look beyond personal concerns. This individual tries to improve the general social conditions, but sometimes gets caught up in a maze of self-imposed details.

Ti Chih XI: Kou (Dog)

The *kou* is faithful. Rituals are very important to this person. Changes are not taken very well; neither are dishonesty and disloyalty. Extravagances are always appreciated, and ambition drives this person to succeed. Despite a warm, loving nature, this person is always anxious and is fundamentally a pessimist. In fact, if this person is born at night, he or she suffers from chronic anxiety.

An earth-*hsing kou* (a *kou* born in a year ruled by the earth *hsing*) bows to consensus opinion while remaining faithful to personal beliefs. This individual demands a high level of loyalty from others and is very secretive.

A fire-*hsing kou* is highly attractive and dramatic. This person is very popular with the opposite sex, but has the type of charisma that reaches out to everyone. When provoked, this individual can be a fierce opponent.

A metal-*hsing kou* is rigid in his or her beliefs, and unswerving in matters of law or principle. He or she takes everything very seriously. This person is selfless and charitable to others. He or she is somewhat overprotective of home and family, however.

A water-*hsing kou* is very sympathetic, even to his or her enemies. But it is also very difficult to form a close relationship with this person because an easygoing nature makes it hard for the individual to commit to strong personal bonds. Nevertheless, the physical beauty and mental versatility of this person attracts a large circle of acquaintances.

A wood-*hsing kou* may be reticent to commit to a close personal relationship at first, but once he or she has shed a natural wariness, this warm-hearted person maintains long-lasting bonds.

Ti Chih XII: Chi (Pig)

The *chi* serves as a symbol of family prosperity and good fortune. A *chi* person is very direct and extremely honest. Scrupulous and stable, this person is obstinate and likes to take the initiative. He or she can easily be deceived and is often mistaken, giving in to arguments and refusing to struggle. He or she is not a social person, however, and cares little about personal reputation.

An earth-*hsing chi* (a *chi* born in a year ruled by the earth *hsing*) believes that charity begins at home. This person works hard to maintain a level of material comfort for family and self. His or her perseverance inspires others.

A fire-*hsing chi* is essentially intrepid and steadfast. Motivated by love and a desire to acquire wealth, this individual succeeds against all odds.

A metal-*hsing chi* is a passionate, proud person who values personal reputation. This individual lacks tact, diplomacy, and/or refinements, but is very demonstrative with affections. He or she is ambitious and does not give in easily.

A water-*hsing chi* is a diplomat who is very adept at discovering others' personal desires. This individual believes in miracles and enjoys the company of friends.

A wood-*hsing chi* is concerned about personal ambitions, but spends a great deal of time concentrating on friends' needs. Unfortunately, some of those less-deserving friends drag the *chi* person down socially or professionally. This individual, however, has a remarkable talent for bringing the right people together at the right time.

As mentioned earlier, Alice T. was born in 1952 and Peter C. was born in 1964. According to the second column in fig. 3.4, these are both *lung* (dragon) years. Using the interpretative material above, this means that both people have the ability to succeed at nearly anything, are highly intelligent, and follow only their own personal judgment. They both have a tendency to speak bluntly or act impatiently, but these are not insurmountable traits. Both people are often loved by others, but seldom fall in love.

The third column in fig. 3.4 indicates that Alice's year *hsing* is water. This indicates that she puts aside personal opinion for the sake of growth, but maintains a strong will and wields remarkable patience. The same table shows that Peter's year *hsing* is wood. This suggests that he has a creative mind and the ability to develop revolutionary ideas. He is compulsively inquisitive at times and can be condescending toward others. He generally manages to conceal his domineering spirit despite being very outspoken.

Locating and Interpreting the Birth *Miao* (Month Pillar)

Generally speaking, the *miao* (month pillar) represents an individual's fate or destiny. Unlike the *gen*, the *miao* is simply used as the starting point. It is the main component used to create a personal chronology that is divided into ten-year cycles and is based on data derived from the lunar month of an individual's birth. In the *Tzu P'ing* method of astrology, the *miao* is not independently interpreted, but is used in conjunction with other elements.

FIGURE 3.6. TABLE OF *T'IEN KAN* AND *TI CHIH* FOR

Year	First Lunar Month	Second Lunar Month	Third Lunar Month	Fourth Lunar Month	Fifth Lunar Month	Sixth Lunar Month
1924*	Feb 5 3/III	Mar. 5 4/IV	Apr. 4 5/V	May 4 6/VI	Jun. 2 7/VII	Jul. 7 8/VIII
1925	Jan. 24 5/III	Feb. 23 6/IV	Mar. 24 7/V	Apr. 23—L** 8/VI	Jun. 21 9/VII	Jul 21 10/VIII
1926	Feb. 13 7/III	Mar. 14 8/IV	Apr. 12 9/V	May 12 10/VI	Jun. 10 1/VII	Jul. 10 2/VIII
1927	Feb. 2 9/III	Mar. 4 10/IV	Apr. 2 1/V	May 1 2/VI	May 31 3/VII	Jun. 29 4/VIII
1928	Jan. 23 1/III	Feb. 21—L 2/IV	Apr. 20 3/V	May 19 4/VI	Jun. 18 5/VII	Jul. 17 6/VIII
1929	Feb. 10 3/III	Mar. 11 4/IV	Apr. 10 5/V	May 9 6/VI	Jun. 7 7/VII	Jul. 7 8/VIII
1930	Jan. 30 5/III	Feb. 28 6/IV	Mar. 30 7/V	Apr. 29 8/VI	May 28 9/VII	Jun. 26—L 10/VIII
1931	Feb. 17 7/III	Mar. 19 8/IV	Apr. 18 9/V	May 17 10/VI	Jun. 16 1/VII	Jul. 15 2/VIII
1932	Feb. 6 9/III	Mar. 7 10/IV	Apr. 6 1/V	May 6 2/VI	Jun. 4 3/VII	Jul. 4 4/VIII
1933	Jan. 26 1/III	Feb. 24 2/IV	Mar. 26 3/V	Apr. 25 4/VI	May 24—L 5/VII	Jul. 22 6/VIII
1934	Feb. 14 3/III	Mar. 15 4/IV	Apr. 14 5/V	May 13 6/VI	Jun. 12 7/VII	Jul. 12 8/VIII
1935	Feb. 4 5/III	Mar. 5 6/IV	Apr. 3 7/V	May 3 8/VI	Jun. 1 9/VII	Jul. 1 10/VIII
1936	Jan. 24 7/III	Feb. 23 8/IV	Mar. 23—L 9/V	May 21 10/VI	Jun. 19 1/VII	Jul. 18 2/VIII
1937	Feb. 11 9/III	Mar. 13 10/IV	Apr. 11 1/V	May 10 2/VI	Jun. 9 3/VII	Jul. 8 4/VIII
1938	Jan. 31 1/III	Mar. 2 2/IV	Apr. 1 3/V	Apr. 30 4/VI	May 29 5/VII	Jun. 28 6/VIII
1939	Feb. 19 3/III	Mar. 21 4/IV	Apr. 20 5/V	May 19 6/VI	Jun. 17 7/VII	Jul. 17 8/VIII
1940	Feb. 8 5/III	Mar. 9 6/IV	Apr. 8 7/V	May 7 8/VI	Jun. 6 9/VII	Jul. 5 10/VIII
1941	Jan. 27 7/III	Feb. 26 8/IV	Mar. 28 9/V	Apr. 26 10/VI	May 26 1/VII	Jun. 25—L 2/VIII
1942	Feb. 15 9/III	Mar. 17 10/IV	Apr. 15 1/V	May 15 2/VI	Jun. 14 3/VII	Jul. 13 4/VIII
1943	Feb. 5 1/III	Mar. 6 2/IV	Apr. 5 3/V	May 4 4/VI	Jun. 3 5/VII	Jul. 2 6/VIII
1944	Jan. 25 3/III	Feb. 24 4/IV	Mar. 24 5/V	Apr. 23—L 6/VI	Jun. 21 7/VII	Jul. 20 8/VIII
1945	Feb. 13 5/III	Mar. 14 6/IV	Apr. 12 7/V	May 12 8/VI	Jun. 10 9/VII	Jul. 9 10/VIII

* Note: Leap years are designated with a double underscore in the first column.

** Note: Leap moons are designated by "—L" in the lunar month that contains the intercalation.

THE LUNAR MONTHS FROM 1924 THROUGH 2050.

Seventh Lunar Month	Eighth Lunar Month	Ninth Lunar Month	Tenth Lunar Month	Eleventh Lunar Month	Twelfth Lunar Month
Aug. 1 9/IX	Aug. 30 10/X	Sep. 29 1/XI	Oct. 28 2/XII	Nov. 27 3/I	Dec. 26 4/II
Aug. 19 1/IX	Sep. 18 2/X	Oct. 18 3/XI	Nov. 16 4/XII	Dec. 12 5/I	Jan. 14, 1926 6/II
Aug. 8 3/IX	Sep. 7 4/X	Oct. 10 5/XI	Nov. 11 6/XII	Dec. 12 7/I	Jan. 4, 1927 8/II
Jul. 29 5/IX	Aug. 27 6/X	Sep. 26 7/XI	Oct. 25 8/XII	Nov. 24 9/I	Dec. 24 10/II
Aug. 15 7/IX	Sep. 14 8/X	Oct. 13 9/XI	Nov. 12 10/XII	Dec. 12 1/I	Jan. 11, 1929 2/II
Aug. 5 9/IX	Sep. 3 10/X	Oct. 3 1/XI	Nov. 1 2/XII	Dec. 1 3/I	Dec. 31 4/II
Aug. 24 1/IX	Sep. 22 2/X	Oct. 22 3/XI	Nov. 20 4/XII	Dec. 20 5/I	Jan. 19, 1931 6/II
Aug. 14 3/IX	Sep. 12 4/X	Oct. 11 5/XI	Nov. 10 6/XII	Dec. 9 7/I	Jan. 8, 1932 8/II
Aug. 2 5/IX	Sep. 1 6/X	Sep. 30 7/XI	Oct. 29 8/XII	Nov. 28 9/I	Dec. 27 10/II
Aug. 21 7/IX	Sep. 20 8/X	Oct. 19 9/XI	Nov. 18 10/XII	Dec. 17 1/I	Jan. 15, 1934 2/II
Aug. 10 9/IX	Sep. 9 10/X	Oct. 8 1/XI	Nov. 7 2/XII	Dec. 7 3/I	Jan. 5, 1935 4/II
Jul. 30 1/IX	Aug. 29 2/X	Sep. 28 3/XI	Oct. 27 4/XII	Nov. 26 5/I	Dec. 26 6/II
Aug. 17 3/IX	Sep. 16 4/X	Oct. 15 5/XI	Nov. 14 6/XII	Dec. 14 7/I	Jan. 13, 1937 8/II
Aug. 6 5/IX	Sep. 5 6/X	Oct. 4 7/XI	Nov. 3 8/XII	Dec. 3 9/I	Jan. 2, 1938 10/II
Jul. 27—L 7/IX	Sep. 24 8/X	Oct. 23 9/XI	Nov. 22 10/XII	Dec. 22 1/I	Jan. 20, 1939 2/II
Aug. 15 9/IX	Sep. 13 10/X	Oct. 13 1/XI	Nov. 11 2/XII	Dec. 11 3/I	Jan. 9, 1940 4/II
Aug. 4 1/IX	Sep. 2 2/X	Oct. 1 3/XI	Oct. 31 4/XII	Nov. 29 5/I	Dec. 29 6/II
Aug. 23 3/IX	Sep. 21 4/X	Oct. 29 5/XI	Nov. 19 6/XII	Dec. 18 7/I	Jan. 17, 1942 8/II
Aug. 12 5/IX	Sep. 10 6/X	Oct. 10 7/XI	Nov. 8 8/XII	Dec. 8 9/I	Jan. 6, 1943 10/II
Aug. 1 7/IX	Aug. 31 8/X	Sep. 29 9/XI	Oct. 29 10/XII	Nov. 27 1/I	Dec. 27 2/II
Aug. 19 9/IX	Sep. 17 10/X	Oct. 17 1/XI	Nov. 16 2/XII	Dec. 15 3/I	Jan. 14, 1944 4/II
Aug. 8 1/IX	Sep. 6 2/X	Oct. 6 3/XI	Nov. 5 4/XII	Dec. 5 5/I	Jan. 3, 1946 6/II

Year	First Lunar Month	Second Lunar Month	Third Lunar Month	Fourth Lunar Month	Fifth Lunar Month	Sixth Lunar Month
1946	Feb. 2 7/III	Mar. 4 8/IV	Apr. 2 9/V	May 1 10/VI	May 31 1/VII	Jun. 29 2/VIII
1947	Jan. 22 9/III	Feb. 21—L 10/IV	Apr. 21 1/V	May 20 2/VI	Jun. 19 3/VII	Jul. 18 4/VIII
1948	Feb. 10 1/III	Mar. 11 2/IV	Apr. 9 3/V	May 9 4/VI	Jun. 7 5/VII	Jul. 7 6/VIII
1949	Jan. 29 3/III	Feb. 28 4/IV	Mar. 29 5/V	Apr. 28 6/VI	May 28 7/VII	Jun. 26 8/VIII
1950	Feb. 17 5/III	Mar. 18 6/IV	Apr. 17 7/V	May 17 8/VI	Jun. 15 9/VII	Jul. 15 10/VIII
1951	Feb. 6 7/III	Mar. 8 8/IV	Apr. 6 9/V	May 6 10/VI	Jun. 5 1/VII	Jul. 4 2/VIII
1952	Jan. 27 9/III	Feb. 25 10/IV	Mar. 26 1/V	Apr. 24 2/VI	May 24—L 3/VII	Jul. 22 4/VIII
1953	Feb. 14 1/III	Mar. 15 2/IV	Apr. 14 3/V	May 13 4/VI	Jun. 11 5/VII	Jul. 11 6/VIII
1954	Feb. 3 3/III	Mar. 5 4/IV	Apr. 3 5/V	May 3 6/VI	Jun. 1 7/VII	Jun. 30 8/VIII
1955	Jan. 24 5/III	Feb. 22 6/IV	Mar. 24—L 7/V	May 22 8/VI	Jun. 20 9/VII	Jul. 19 10/VIII
1956	Feb. 12 7/III	Mar. 12 8/IV	Apr. 11 9/V	May 10 10/VI	Jun. 6 1/VII	Jul. 8 2/VIII
1957	Jan. 31 9/III	Mar. 2 10/IV	Mar. 31 1/V	Apr. 30 2/VI	May 29 3/VII	Jun. 28 4/VIII
1958	Feb. 18 1/III	Mar. 20 2/IV	Apr. 19 3/V	May 19 4/VI	Jun. 17 5/VII	Jul. 17 6/VIII
1959	Feb. 8 3/III	Mar. 9 4/IV	Apr. 8 5/V	May 8 6/VI	Jun. 6 7/VII	Jul. 6 8/VIII
1960	Jan. 28 5/III	Feb. 27 6/IV	Mar. 27 7/V	Apr. 26 8/VI	May 25 9/VII	Jun. 24—L 10/VIII
1961	Feb. 15 7/III	Mar. 17 8/IV	Apr. 15 9/V	May 15 10/VI	Jun. 13 1/VII	Jul. 13 2/VIII
1962	Feb. 5 9/III	Mar. 6 10/IV	Apr. 5 1/V	May 4 2/VI	Jun. 2 3/VII	Jul. 2 4/VIII
1963	Jan. 25 1/III	Feb. 24 2/IV	Mar. 25 3/V	Apr. 24—L 4/VI	Jun. 21 5/VII	Jul. 21 6/VIII
1964	Feb. 13 3/III	Mar. 14 4/IV	Apr. 12 5/V	May 12 6/VI	Jun. 10 7/VII	Jul. 9 8/VIII
1965	Feb. 2 5/III	Mar. 3 6/IV	Apr. 2 7/V	May 1 8/VI	May 31 9/VII	Jun. 29 10/VIII
1966	Jan. 21 7/III	Feb. 20 8/IV	Mar. 22—L 9/V	May 20 10/VI	Jun. 19 1/VII	Jul. 18 2/VIII
1967	Feb. 9 9/III	Mar. 11 10/IV	Apr. 10 1/V	May 9 2/VI	Jun. 8 3/VII	Jul. 8 4/VIII
1968	Jan. 30 1/III	Feb. 28 2/IV	Mar. 29 3/V	Apr. 27 4/VI	May 27 5/VII	Jun. 26 6/VIII

SEVENTH LUNAR MONTH	EIGHTH LUNAR MONTH	NINTH LUNAR MONTH	TENTH LUNAR MONTH	ELEVENTH LUNAR MONTH	TWELFTH LUNAR MONTH
Jul. 28 3/IX	Aug. 27 4/X	Sep. 25 5/XI	Oct. 25 6/XII	Nov. 24 7/I	Dec. 23 8/II
Aug. 16 5/IX	Sep. 15 6/X	Oct. 14 7/XI	Nov. 13 8/XII	Dec. 12 9/I	Jan. 11, 1948 10/II
Aug. 5 7/IX	Sep. 3 8/X	Oct. 3 9/XI	Nov. 1 10/XII	Dec. 1 1/I	Dec. 30 2/II
Jul 26—L 9/IX	Sep. 22 10/X	Oct. 22 1/XI	Nov. 20 2/XII	Dec. 20 3/I	Jan. 18, 1950 4/II
Aug. 14 1/IX	Sep. 12 2/X	Oct. 11 3/XI	Nov. 10 4/XII	Dec. 9 5/I	Jan. 8, 1951 6/II
Aug. 3 3/IX	Sep. 1 4/X	Oct. 1 5/XI	Oct. 30 6/XII	Nov. 29 7/I	Dec. 28 8/II
Aug. 20 5/IX	Sep. 19 6/X	Oct. 19 7/XI	Nov. 17 8/XII	Dec. 17 9/I	Jan. 15, 1953 10/II
Aug. 9 7/IX	Sep. 8 8/X	Oct. 8 9/XI	Nov. 7 10/XII	Dec. 6 1/I	Jan. 5, 1954 2/II
Jul. 30 9/IX	Aug. 28 10/X	Sep. 27 1/XI	Oct. 27 2/XII	Nov. 25 3/I	Dec. 25 4/II
Aug. 18 1/IX	Scp. 16 2/X	Oct. 16 3/XI	Nov. 14 4/XII	Dec. 14 5/I	Jan. 13, 1955 6/II
Aug. 6 3/IX	Sep. 5 4/X	Oct. 4 5/XI	Nov. 3 6/XII	Dec. 2 7/I	Jan. 1, 1957 8/II
Jul. 27 5/IX	Aug. 25—L 6/X	Oct. 23 7/XI	Nov. 22 8/XII	Dec. 21 9/I	Jan. 20, 1958 10/II
Aug. 15 7/IX	Sep. 13 8/X	Oct. 13 9/XI	Nov. 11 10/XII	Dec. 11 1/I	Jan. 9, 1959 2/II
Aug. 4 9/IX	Sep. 3 10/X	Oct. 2 1/XI	Nov. 1 2/XII	Nov. 30 3/I	Dec. 30 4/II
Aug. 22 1/IX	Sep. 21 2/X	Oct. 20 3/XI	Nov. 19 4/XII	Dec. 18 5/I	Jan. 17, 1960 6/II
Aug. 11 3/IX	Sep. 10 4/X	Oct. 10 5/XI	Nov. 2 6/XII	Dec. 8 7/I	Jan. 6, 1962 8/II
Jul. 31 5/IX	Aug. 30 6/X	Sep. 29 7/XI	Oct. 28 8/XII	Nov. 27 9/I	Dec. 27 10/II
Aug. 19 7/IX	Sep. 18 8/X	Oct. 17 9/XI	Nov. 16 10/XII	Dec. 16 1/I	Jan. 15, 1964 2/II
Aug. 8 9/IX	Sep. 6 10/X	Oct. 6 1/XI	Nov. 4 2/XII	Dec. 4 3/I	Jan. 3, 1965 4/II
Jul. 28 1/IX	Aug. 28 2/X	Sep. 25 3/XI	Oct. 24 4/XII	Nov. 23 5/I	Dec. 23 6/II
Aug. 16 3/IX	Sep. 15 4/X	Oct. 14 5/XI	Nov. 12 6/XII	Dec. 12 7/I	Jan. 11, 1967 8/II
Aug. 6 5/IX	Sep. 4 6/X	Oct. 4 7/XI	Nov. 2 8/XII	Dec. 2 9/I	Dec. 31 10/II
Jul. 25—L 7/IX	Sep. 22 8/X	Oct. 22 9/XI	Nov. 20 10/XII	Dec. 20 1/I	Jan. 18, 1969 2/II

YEAR	FIRST LUNAR MONTH	SECOND LUNAR MONTH	THIRD LUNAR MONTH	FOURTH LUNAR MONTH	FIFTH LUNAR MONTH	SIXTH LUNAR MONTH
1969	Feb. 17 3/III	Mar. 18 4/IV	Apr. 17 5/V	May 16 6/VI	Jun. 15 7/VII	Jul. 14 8/VIII
1970	Feb. 6 5/III	Mar. 8 6/IV	Apr. 6 7/V	May 5 8/VI	Jun. 4 9/VII	Jul. 3 10/VIII
1971	Jan. 27 7/III	Feb. 25 8/IV	Mar. 27 9/V	Apr. 25 10/VI	May 24—l 1/VII	Jul. 22 2/VIII
1972	Feb. 15 9/III	Mar. 15 10/IV	Apr. 14 1/V	May 13 2/VI	Jun. 11 3/VII	Jul. 11 4/VIII
1973	Feb. 3 1/III	Mar. 5 2/IV	Apr. 3 3/V	May 3 4/VI	Jun. 1 5/VII	Jun. 30 6/VIII
1974	Jan. 23 3/III	Feb. 22 4/IV	Mar. 24 5/V	Apr. 22—L 6/VI	Jun. 20 7/VII	Jul. 19 8/VIII
1975	Feb. 11 5/III	Mar. 13 6/IV	Apr. 12 7/V	May 11 8/VI	Jun. 10 9/VII	Jul. 9 10/VIII
1976	Jan. 31 7/III	Mar. 1 8/IV	Mar. 31 9/V	Apr. 29 10/VI	May 29 1/VII	Jun. 27 2/VIII
1977	Feb. 18 9/III	Mar. 20 10/IV	Apr. 18 1/V	May 18 2/VI	Jun. 17 3/VII	Jul. 16 4/VIII
1978	Feb. 7 1/III	Mar. 9 2/IV	Apr. 7 3/V	May 7 4/VI	Jun. 6 5/VII	Jul. 5 6/VIII
1979	Jan. 28 3/III	Feb. 27 4/IV	Mar. 28 5/V	Apr. 26 6/VI	May 26 7/VII	Jun. 24—L 8/VIII
1980	Feb. 16 5/III	Mar. 17 6/IV	Apr. 15 7/V	May 14 8/VI	Jun. 13 9/VII	Jul. 12 10/VIII
1981	Feb. 5 7/III	Mar. 6 8/IV	Apr. 5 9/V	May 4 10/VI	Jun. 2 1/VII	Jul. 2 2/VIII
1982	Jan. 25 9/III	Feb. 24 10/IV	Mar. 25 1/V	Apr. 24—L 2/VI	Jun. 21 3/VII	Jul. 21 4/VIII
1983	Feb. 13 1/III	Mar. 15 2/IV	Apr. 13 3/V	May 13 4/VI	Jun. 11 5/VII	Jul. 10 6/VIII
1984	Feb. 2 3/III	Mar. 3 4/IV	Apr. 1 5/V	May 1 6/VI	May 31 7/VII	Jun. 29 8/VIII
1985	Feb. 20 5/III	Mar. 21 6/IV	Apr. 20 7/V	May 20 8/VI	Jun. 18 9/VII	Jul. 18 10/VIII
1986	Feb. 9 7/III	Mar. 10 8/IV	Apr. 9 9/V	May 9 10/VI	Jun. 7 1/VII	Jul. 7 2/VIII
1987	Jan. 29 9/III	Feb. 28 10/IV	Mar. 29 1/V	Apr. 28 2/VI	May 27 3/VII	Jun. 26—L 4/VIII
1988	Feb. 17 1/III	Mar. 18 2/IV	Apr. 16 3/V	May 16 4/VI	Jun. 14 5/VII	Jul. 14 6/VIII
1989	Feb. 6 3/III	Mar. 8 4/IV	Apr. 6 5/V	May 5 6/VI	Jun. 4 7/VII	Jul. 3 8/VIII
1990	Jan. 27 5/III	Feb. 25 6/IV	Mar. 27 7/V	Apr. 25 8/VI	May 24—L 9/VII	Jul. 22 10/VIII
1991	Feb. 15 7/III	Mar. 16 8/IV	Apr. 15 9/V	May 14 10/VI	Jun. 12 1/VII	Jul. 12 2/VIII

Seventh Lunar Month	Eighth Lunar Month	Ninth Lunar Month	Tenth Lunar Month	Eleventh Lunar Month	Twelfth Lunar Month
Aug. 13 9/IX	Sep. 12 10/X	Oct. 11 1/XI	Nov. 10 2/XII	Dec. 9 3/I	Jan. 8, 1970 4/II
Aug. 2 1/IX	Sep. 1 2/X	Sep. 30 3/XI	Oct. 30 4/XII	Nov. 29 5/I	Dec. 28 6/II
Aug. 21 3/IX	Sep. 19 4/X	Oct. 19 5/XI	Nov. 18 6/XII	Dec. 18 7/I	Jan. 16, 1972 8/II
Aug. 9 5/IX	Sep. 8 6/X	Oct. 7 7/XI	Nov. 6 8/XII	Dec. 6 9/I	Jan. 4, 1973 10/II
Jul. 30 7/IX	Aug. 28 8/X	Sep. 26 9/XI	Oct. 26 10/XII	Nov. 25 1/I	Dec. 24 2/II
Aug. 18 9/IX	Sep. 16 10/X	Oct. 15 1/XI	Nov. 14 2/XII	Dec. 14 3/I	Jan. 12, 1975 4/II
Aug. 7 1/IX	Sep. 6 2/X	Oct. 5 3/XI	Nov. 3 4/XII	Dec. 3 5/I	Jan. 1, 1976 6/II
Jul. 27 3/IX	Aug. 25—L 4/X	Oct. 23 5/XI	Nov. 21 6/XII	Dec. 21 7/I	Jan. 19, 1977 8/II
Aug. 15 5/IX	Sep. 13 6/X	Oct. 13 7/XI	Nov. 11 8/XII	Dec. 11 9/I	Jan. 9, 1978 10/II
Aug. 4 7/IX	Sep. 2 8/X	Oct. 2 9/XI	Nov. 1 10/XII	Nov. 30 1/I	Dec. 30 2/II
Aug. 23 9/IX	Sep. 21 10/X	Oct. 21 1/XI	Nov. 20 2/XII	Dec. 19 3/I	Jan. 18, 1980 4/II
Aug. 11 1/IX	Sep. 9 2/X	Oct. 9 3/XI	Nov. 8 4/XII	Dec. 7 5/I	Jan. 6, 1981 6/II
Jul. 31 3/IX	Aug. 29 4/X	Sep. 28 5/XI	Oct. 28 6/XII	Nov. 26 7/I	Dec. 26 8/II
Aug. 19 5/IX	Sep. 17 6/X	Oct. 17 7/XI	Nov. 15 8/XII	Dec. 15 9/I	Jan. 14, 1983 10/II
Aug. 9 7/IX	Sep. 7 8/X	Oct. 6 9/XI	Nov. 5 10/XII	Dec. 4 1/I	Jan. 3, 1984 2/II
Jul. 28 9/IX	Aug. 27 10/X	Sep. 25 1/XI	Oct. 24—L 2/XII	Dec. 22 3/I	Jan. 21, 1985 4/II
Aug. 16 1/IX	Sep. 15 2/X	Oct. 14 3/XI	Nov. 12 4/XII	Dec. 12 5/I	Jan. 10, 1986 6/II
Aug. 6 3/IX	Sep. 4 4/X	Oct. 4 5/XI	Nov. 2 6/XII	Dec. 2 7/I	Dec. 31 8/II
Aug. 24 5/IX	Sep. 23 6/X	Oct. 23 7/XI	Nov. 21 8/XII	Dec. 21 9/I	Jan. 19, 1988 10/II
Aug. 12 7/IX	Sep. 11 8/X	Oct. 11 9/XI	Nov. 9 10/XII	Dec. 9 1/I	Jan. 8, 1989 2/II
Aug. 1 9/IX	Aug. 31 10/X	Sep. 30 1/XI	Oct. 29 2/XII	Nov. 28 3/I	Dec. 28 4/II
Aug. 20 1/IX	Sep. 19 2/X	Oct. 18 3/XI	Nov. 17 4/XII	Dec. 17 5/I	Jan. 16, 1991 6/II
Aug. 10 3/IX	Sep. 8 4/X	Oct. 8 5/XI	Nov. 6 6/XII	Dec. 6 7/I	Jan. 5, 1992 8/II

Year	First Lunar Month	Second Lunar Month	Third Lunar Month	Fourth Lunar Month	Fifth Lunar Month	Sixth Lunar Month
1992	Feb. 4 9/III	Mar. 4 10/IV	Apr. 3 1/V	May 3 2/VI	Jun. 1 3/VII	Jun. 30 4/VIII
1993	Jan. 23 1/III	Feb. 21 2/IV	Mar. 23—L 3/V	May 21 4/VI	Jun. 20 5/VII	Jul. 19 6/VIII
1994	Feb. 10 3/III	Mar. 12 4/IV	Apr. 11 5/V	May 11 6/VI	Jun. 9 7/VII	Jul. 9 8/VIII
1995	Jan. 31 5/III	Mar. 1 6/IV	Mar. 31 7/V	Apr. 30 8/VI	May 29 9/VII	Jun. 28 10/VIII
1996	Feb. 19 7/III	Mar. 19 8/IV	Apr. 18 9/V	May 17 10/VI	Jun. 16 1/VII	Jul. 16 2/VIII
1997	Feb. 7 9/III	Mar. 9 10/IV	Apr. 7 1/V	May 7 2/VI	Jun. 5 3/VII	Jul. 5 4/VIII
1998	Jan. 28 1/III	Feb. 27 2/IV	Mar. 28 3/V	Apr. 26 4/VI	May 26—L 5/VII	Jul. 23 6/VIII
1999	Feb. 16 3/III	Mar. 18 4/IV	Apr. 16 5/V	May 15 6/VI	Jun. 14 7/VII	Jul. 13 8/VIII
2000	Feb. 5 5/III	Mar. 6 6/IV	Apr. 5 7/V	May 4 8/VI	Jun. 2 9/VII	Jul. 2 10/VIII
2001	Jan. 24 7/III	Feb. 23 8/IV	Mar. 25 9/V	Apr. 23—L 10/VI	Jun. 21 1/VII	Jul. 21 2/VIII
2002	Feb.12 9/III	Mar. 14 10/IV	Apr. 13 1/V	May 12 2/VI	Jun. 11 3/VII	Jul. 10 4/VIII
2003	Feb. 1 1/III	Mar. 3 2/IV	Apr. 2 3/V	May 1 4/VI	May 31 5/VII	Jun. 30 6/VIII
2004	Jan. 22 3/III	Feb. 20—L 4/IV	Apr. 19 5/V	May 19 6/VI	Jun. 18 7/VII	Jul. 17 8/VIII
2005	Feb. 9 5/III	Mar. 10 6/IV	Apr. 9 7/V	May 8 8/VI	Jun. 7 9/VII	Jul. 6 10/VIII
2006	Jan. 29 7/III	Feb. 28 8/IV	Mar. 29 9/V	Apr. 28 10/VI	May 27 1/VII	Jun. 26 2/VIII
2007	Feb. 18 9/III	Mar. 19 10/IV	Apr. 17 1/V	May 17 2/VI	Jun. 15 3/VII	Jul. 14 4/VIII
2008	Feb. 7 1/III	Mar. 8 2/IV	Apr. 6 3/V	May 5 4/VI	Jun. 4 5/VII	Jul. 3 6/VIII
2009	Jan. 26 3/III	Feb. 25 4/IV	Mar. 27 5/V	Apr. 25 6/VI	May 24—L 7/VII	Jul. 22 8/VIII
2010	Feb. 14 5/III	Mar. 16 6/IV	Apr. 14 7/V	May 14 8/VI	Jun. 12 9/VII	Jul. 12 10/VIII
2011	Feb. 3 7/III	Mar. 5 8/IV	Apr. 3 9/V	May 3 10/VI	Jun. 2 1/VII	Jul. 1 2/VIII
2012	Jan. 23 9/III	Feb. 22 10/IV	Mar. 22 1/V	Apr. 21—L 2/VI	Jun. 19 3/VII	Jul. 19 4/VIII
2013	Feb. 10 1/III	Mar. 12 2/IV	Apr. 10 3/V	May 10 4/VI	Jun. 9 5/VII	Jul. 8 6/VIII
2014	Jan. 31 3/III	Mar. 1 4/IV	Mar. 31 5/V	Apr. 29 6/VI	May 29 7/VII	Jun. 27 8/VIII

Seventh Lunar Month	Eighth Lunar Month	Ninth Lunar Month	Tenth Lunar Month	Eleventh Lunar Month	Twelfth Lunar Month
Jul. 30 5/IX	Aug. 28 6/X	Sep. 26 7/XI	Oct. 26 8/XII	Nov. 24 9/I	Dec. 24 10/II
Aug. 18 7/IX	Sep. 16 8/X	Oct. 15 9/XI	Nov. 14 10/XII	Dec. 13 1/I	Jan. 12, 1994 2/II
Aug. 7 9/IX	Sep. 6 10/X	Oct. 5 1/XI	Nov. 3 2/XII	Dec. 3 3/I	Jan. 1, 1995 4/II
Jul. 27 1/IX	Aug. 26—L 2/X	Oct. 24 3/XI	Nov. 22 4/XII	Dec. 22 5/I	Jan. 20, 1996 6/II
Aug. 14 3/IX	Sep. 13 4/X	Oct. 12 5/XI	Nov. 11 6/XII	Dec. 11 7/I	Jan. 9, 1997 8/II
Aug. 3 5/IX	Sep. 2 6/X	Oct. 2 7/XI	Oct. 31 8/XII	Nov. 30 9/I	Dec. 30 10/II
Aug. 22 7/IX	Sep. 21 8/X	Oct. 20 9/XI	Nov. 19 10/XII	Dec. 19 1/I	Jan. 17, 1999 2/II
Aug. 11 9/IX	Sep. 10 10/X	Oct. 9 1/XI	Nov. 8 2/XII	Dec. 8 3/I	Jan. 7, 2000 4/II
Jul. 31 1/IX	Aug. 29 2/X	Sep. 28 3/XI	Oct. 27 4/XII	Nov. 26 5/I	Dec. 26 6/II
Aug. 19 3/IX	Sep. 17 4/X	Oct. 17 5/XI	Nov. 15 6/XII	Dec. 15 7/I	Jan. 13, 2002 8/II
Aug. 9 5/IX	Sep. 7 6/X	Oct. 6 7/XI	Nov. 5 8/XII	Dec. 4 9/I	Jan. 3, 2003 10/II
Jul. 29 7/IX	Aug. 28 8/X	Sep. 26 9/XI	Oct. 25 10/XII	Nov. 24 1/I	Dec. 23 2/II
Aug. 16 9/IX	Sep. 14 10/X	Oct. 14 1/XI	Nov. 12 2/XII	Dec. 12 3/I	Jan. 10, 2005 4/II
Aug. 5 1/IX	Sep. 4 2/X	Oct. 3 3/XI	Nov. 2 4/XII	Dec. 1 5/I	Dec. 31 6/II
Jul.25—L 3/IX	Sep. 22 4/X	Oct. 22 5/XI	Nov. 21 6/XII	Dec. 20 7/I	Jan. 19, 2007 8/II
Aug. 13 5/IX	Sep. 11 6/X	Oct. 10 7/XI	Nov. 10 8/XII	Dec. 10 9/I	Jan. 8, 2008 10/II
Aug. 1 7/IX	Aug. 31 8/X	Sep. 29 9/XI	Oct. 29 10/XII	Nov. 28 1/I	Dec. 27 2/II
Aug. 20 9/IX	Sep. 19 10/X	Oct. 18 1/XI	Nov. 17 2/XII	Dec. 16 3/I	Jan. 15, 2010 4/II
Aug. 10 1/IX	Sep. 8 2/X	Oct. 8 3/XI	Nov. 6 4/XII	Dec. 6 5/I	Jan. 4, 2011 6/II
Jul. 31 3/IX	Aug. 29 4/X	Sep. 27 5/XI	Oct. 27 6/XII	Nov. 25 7/I	Dec. 25 8/II
Aug. 17 5/IX	Sep. 16 6/X	Oct. 15 7/XI	Nov. 14 8/XII	Dec. 13 9/I	Jan. 12, 2013 10/II
Aug. 7 7/IX	Sep. 5 8/X	Oct. 5 9/XI	Nov. 3 10/XII	Dec. 3 1/I	Jan. 1, 2014 2/II
Jul. 27 9/IX	Aug. 25 10/X	Sep. 24—L 1/XI	Nov. 22 2/XII	Dec. 22 3/I	Jan. 20, 2015 4/II

Year	First Lunar Month	Second Lunar Month	Third Lunar Month	Fourth Lunar Month	Fifth Lunar Month	Sixth Lunar Month
2015	Feb. 19 5/III	Mar. 20 6/IV	Apr. 19 7/V	May 18 8/VI	Jun. 16 9/VII	Jul. 16 10/VIII
2016	Feb. 8 7/III	Mar. 9 8/IV	Apr. 7 9/V	May 7 10/VI	Jun. 5 1/VII	Jul. 4 2/VIII
2017	Jan. 28 9/III	Feb. 26 10/IV	Mar. 28 1/V	Apr. 26 2/VI	May 26 3/VII	Jun. 24—L 4/VIII
2018	Feb. 16 1/III	Mar. 17 2/IV	Apr. 16 3/V	May 15 4/VI	Jun. 14 5/VII	Jul. 13 6/VIII
2019	Feb. 5 3/III	Mar. 6 4/IV	Apr. 5 5/V	May 5 6/VI	Jun. 3 7/VII	Jul. 3 8/VIII
2020	Jan. 25 5/III	Feb. 23 6/IV	Mar. 24 7/V	Apr. 23—L 8/VI	Jun. 21 9/VII	Jul. 21 10/VIII
2021	Feb. 12 7/III	Mar. 13 8/IV	Apr. 12 9/V	May 12 10/VI	Jun. 10 1/VII	Jul. 10 2/VIII
2022	Feb. 1 9/III	Mar. 3 10/IV	Apr. 1 1/V	May 1 2/VI	May 28 3/VII	Jun. 29 4/VIII
2023	Jan. 22 1/III	Feb. 20—L 2/IV	Apr. 20 3/V	May 19 4/VI	Jun. 18 5/VII	Jul. 18 6/VIII
2024	Feb. 10 3/III	Mar. 10 4/IV	Apr. 9 5/V	May 8 6/VI	Jun. 6 7/VII	Jul. 6 8/VIII
2025	Jan. 29 5/III	Feb. 28 6/IV	Mar. 29 7/V	Apr. 28 8/VI	May 25 9/VII	Jun. 25—L 10/VIII
2026	Feb. 17 7/III	Mar. 19 8/IV	Apr. 16 9/V	May 17 10/VI	Jun. 15 1/VII	Jul. 14 2/VIII
2027	Feb. 6 9/III	Mar. 8 10/IV	Apr. 7 1/V	May 6 2/VI	Jun. 5 3/VII	Jul. 4 4/VIII
2028	Jan. 26 1/III	Feb. 24 2/IV	Mar. 26 3/V	Apr. 25 4/VI	May 24—L 5/VII	Jul. 22 6/VIII
2029	Feb. 13 3/III	Mar. 15 4/IV	Apr. 14 5/V	May 13 6/VI	Jun. 12 7/VII	Jul. 11 8/VIII
2030	Feb. 3 5/III	Mar. 4 6/IV	Apr. 3 7/V	May 2 8/VI	Jun. 1 9/VII	Jul. 1 10/VIII
2031	Jan. 23 7/III	Feb. 21 8/IV	Mar. 23—L 9/V	May 21 10/VI	Jun. 20 1/VII	Jul. 19 2/VIII
2032	Feb. 11 9/III	Mar. 12 10/IV	Apr. 10 1/V	May 9 2/VI	Jun. 8 3/VII	Jul. 7 4/VIII
2033	Jan. 31 1/III	Mar. 1 2/IV	Mar. 31 3/V	Apr. 29 4/VI	May 28 5/VII	Jun. 27 6/VIII
2034	Feb. 19 3/III	Mar. 20 4/IV	Apr. 19 5/V	May 18 6/VI	Jun. 16 7/VII	Jul. 16 8/VIII
2035	Feb. 8 5/III	Mar. 10 6/IV	Apr. 8 7/V	May 8 8/VI	Jun. 6 9/VII	Jul. 5 10/VIII
2036	Jan. 28 7/III	Feb. 26 8/IV	Mar. 28 9/V	Apr. 26 10/VI	May 26 1/VII	Jun. 24—L 2/VIII
2037	Feb. 15 9/III	Mar. 17 10/IV	Apr. 16 1/V	May 15 2/VI	Jun. 14 3/VII	Jul. 13 4/VIII
2038	Feb. 4 1/III	Mar. 6 2/IV	Apr. 5 3/V	May 4 4/VI	Jun. 3 5/VII	Jul. 2 6/VIII

Seventh Lunar Month	Eighth Lunar Month	Ninth Lunar Month	Tenth Lunar Month	Eleventh Lunar Month	Twelfth Lunar Month
Aug. 14 1/IX	Sep. 13 2/X	Oct. 13 3/XI	Nov. 12 4/XII	Dec. 11 5/I	Jan. 10, 2016 6/II
Aug. 3 3/IX	Sep. 1 4/X	Oct. 1 5/XI	Oct. 31 6/XII	Nov. 29 7/I	Dec. 29 8/II
Aug. 22 5/IX	Sep. 20 6/X	Oct. 20 7/XI	Nov. 18 8/XII	Dec. 18 9/I	Jan. 17, 2018 10/II
Aug. 11 7/IX	Sep. 10 8/X	Oct. 9 9/XI	Nov. 8 10/XII	Dec. 7 1/I	Jan. 6, 2019 2/II
Aug. 1 9/IX	Aug. 30 10/X	Sep. 29 1/XI	Oct. 28 2/XII	Nov. 26 3/I	Dec. 26 4/II
Aug. 19 1/IX	Sep. 17 2/X	Oct. 17 3/XI	Nov. 15 4/XII	Dec. 15 5/I	Jan. 13, 2021 6/II
Aug. 8 3/IX	Sep. 7 4/X	Oct. 6 5/XI	Nov. 5 6/XII	Dec. 4 7/I	Jan. 3, 2022 8/II
Jul. 29 5/IX	Aug. 27 6/X	Sep. 26 7/XI	Oct. 25 8/XII	Nov. 24 9/I	Dec. 23 10/II
Aug. 15 7/IX	Sep. 15 8/X	Oct. 14 9/XI	Nov. 13 10/XII	Dec. 13 1/I	Jan. 11, 2024 2/II
Aug. 4 9/IX	Sep. 3 10/X	Oct. 3 1/XI	Nov. 1 2/XII	Dec. 1 3/I	Dec. 31 4/II
Aug. 23 1/IX	Sep. 22 2/X	Oct. 21 3/XI	Nov. 20 4/XII	Dec. 20 5/I	Jan. 19, 2026 6/II
Aug. 13 3/IX	Sep. 11 4/X	Oct. 10 5/XI	Nov. 10 6/XII	Dec. 9 7/I	Jan. 8, 2027 8/II
Aug. 2 5/IX	Sep. 1 6/X	Sep. 30 7/XI	Oct. 29 8/XII	Nov. 28 9/I	Dec. 28 10/II
Aug. 20 7/IX	Sep. 19 8/X	Oct. 18 9/XI	Nov. 16 10/XII	Dec. 16 1/I	Jan. 15, 2029 2/II
Aug. 10 9/IX	Sep. 8 10/X	Oct. 8 1/XI	Nov. 6 2/XII	Dec. 5 3/I	Jan. 4, 2030 4/II
Jul. 30 1/IX	Aug. 29 2/X	Sep. 27 3/XI	Oct. 27 4/XII	Nov. 25 5/I	Dec. 25 6/II
Aug. 18 3/IX	Sep. 17 4/X	Oct. 16 5/XI	Nov. 15 6/XII	Dec. 14 7/I	Jan. 13, 2032 8/II
Aug. 6 5/IX	Sep. 5 6/X	Oct. 4 7/XI	Nov. 3 8/XII	Dec. 3 9/I	Jan. 1, 2033 10/II
Jul. 26—L 7/IX	Sep. 23 8/X	Oct. 23 9/XI	Nov. 22 10/XII	Dec. 22 1/I	Jan. 20, 2034 2/II
Aug. 14 9/IX	Sep. 13 10/X	Oct. 12 1/XI	Nov. 11 2/XII	Dec. 11 3/I	Jan. 9, 2035 4/II
Aug. 4 1/IX	Sep. 2 2/X	Oct. 1 3/XI	Oct. 31 4/XII	Nov. 30 5/I	Dec. 29 6/II
Aug. 22 3/IX	Sep. 20 4/X	Oct. 19 5/XI	Nov. 18 6/XII	Dec. 17 7/I	Jan. 16, 2037 8/II
Aug. 11 5/IX	Sep. 10 6/X	Oct. 9 7/XI	Nov. 7 8/XII	Dec. 7 9/I	Jan. 5, 2038 10/II
Aug. 1 7/IX	Aug. 30 8/X	Sep. 29 9/XI	Oct. 28 10/XII	Nov. 26 1/I	Dec. 26 2/II

Year	First Lunar Month	Second Lunar Month	Third Lunar Month	Fourth Lunar Month	Fifth Lunar Month	Sixth Lunar Month
2039	Jan. 24 3/III	Feb. 23 4/IV	Mar. 25 5/V	Apr. 23 6/VI	May 23—L 7/VII	Jul. 21 8/VIII
2040	Feb. 12 5/III	Mar. 13 6/IV	Apr. 11 7/V	May 11 8/VI	Jun. 10 9/VII	Jul. 9 10/VIII
2041	Feb. 1 7/III	Mar. 2 8/IV	Apr. 1 9/V	Apr. 30 10/VI	May 31 1/VII	Jun. 28 2/VIII
2042	Jan. 22 9/III	Feb. 20—L 10/IV	Apr. 20 1/V	May 19 2/VI	Jun 18 3/VII	Jul. 17 4/VIII
2043	Feb. 10 1/III	Mar. 11 2/IV	Apr. 10 3/V	May 9 4/VI	Jun. 7 5/VII	Jul. 7 6/VIII
2044	Jan. 30 3/III	Feb. 28 4/IV	Mar. 29 5/V	Apr. 28 6/VI	May 27 7/VII	Jun. 25 8/VIII
2045	Feb. 17 5/III	Mar. 19 6/IV	Apr. 17 7/V	May 17 8/VI	Jun. 15 9/VII	Jul. 14 10/VIII
2046	Feb. 6 7/III	Mar. 8 8/IV	Apr. 6 9/V	May 6 10/VI	Jun. 4 1/VII	Jul. 4 2/VIII
2047	Jan. 26 9/III	Feb. 25 10/IV	Mar. 26 1/V	Apr. 25 2/VI	May 25—L 3/VII	Jul. 23 4/VIII
2048	Feb. 14 1/III	Mar. 14 2/IV	Apr. 13 3/V	May 13 4/VI	Jun. 11 5/VII	Jul. 11 6/VIII
2049	Feb. 2 3/III	Mar. 4 4/IV	Apr. 2 5/V	May 2 6/VI	May 31 7/VII	Jun. 30 8/VIII
2050	Jan. 23 5/III	Feb. 21 6/IV	Mar. 23—L 7/V	May 21 8/VI	Jun. 19 9/VII	Jul. 19 10/VIII

With its ancient agrarian origins, the Chinese luni-solar calendar is based on lunar cycles, unlike the Western calendar, which is founded upon mean solar motion. According to the traditional Chinese luni-solar calendar, the Moon generally takes twenty-nine days, twelve hours, and forty-four minutes to transit all of its phases from New Moon to New Moon. This particular time period varies from lunar month to lunar month as well as from year to year as indicated by the starting dates of the individual months in fig. 3.6. The Moon completes an entire cycle of these varying patterns once every nineteen years. Because the number of days in a given lunar month varies from twenty-seven to thirty days, an adjustment for any variation in time is added in "leap moons" or embolismic moons on the third, sixth, ninth, eleventh, fourteenth, seventeenth, and nineteenth years. The creators of the Chinese luni-solar calendar did this so that the vernal equinox always occurs during the second lunar month; the summer solstice occurs during the fifth lunar month; the autumn equinox occurs during the eighth lunar month; and the winter solstice occurs during the eleventh lunar month.[6]

---

6.   This system of calculation is identical to the Cycle of Meton developed by the ancient Greeks and Hebrews.

Seventh Lunar Month	Eighth Lunar Month	Ninth Lunar Month	Tenth Lunar Month	Eleventh Lunar Month	Twelfth Lunar Month
Aug. 20 9/IX	Sep. 18 10/X	Oct. 18 1/XI	Nov. 16 2/XII	Dec. 16 3/I	Jan. 14, 2040 4/II
Aug. 8 1/IX	Sep. 6 2/X	Oct. 6 3/XI	Nov. 5 4/XII	Dec. 4 5/I	Jan. 3, 2041 6/II
Jul. 28 3/IX	Aug. 27 4/X	Sep. 25 5/XI	Oct. 25 6/XII	Nov. 24 7/I	Dec. 23 8/II
Aug. 16 5/IX	Sep. 14 6/X	Oct. 14 7/XI	Nov. 13 8/XII	Dec. 12 9/I	Jan. 11, 2043 10/II
Aug. 5 7/IX	Sep. 3 8/X	Oct. 3 9/XI	Nov. 2 10/XII	Dec. 1 1/I	Dec. 31 2/II
Jul. 25—L 9/IX	Sep. 21 10/X	Oct. 21 1/XI	Nov. 19 2/XII	Dec. 19 3/I	Jan. 18, 2045 4/II
Aug. 13 1/IX	Sep. 11 2/X	Oct. 10 3/XI	Nov. 9 4/XII	Dec. 8 5/I	Jan. 7, 2046 6/II
Aug. 2 3/IX	Sep. 1 4/X	Sep. 30 5/XI	Oct. 29 6/XII	Nov. 28 7/I	Dec. 27 8/II
Aug. 21 5/IX	Sep. 20 6/X	Oct. 19 7/XI	Nov. 17 8/XII	Dec. 17 9/I	Jan. 15, 2048 10/II
Aug. 10 7/IX	Sep. 8 8/X	Oct. 8 9/XI	Nov. 6 10/XII	Dec. 5 1/I	Jan. 4, 2049 2/II
Jul 30 9/IX	Aug. 28 10/X	Sep. 27 1/XI	Oct. 27 2/XII	Nov. 25 3/I	Dec. 25 4/II
Aug. 17 1/IX	Sep. 16 2/X	Oct. 16 3/XI	Nov. 14 4/XII	Dec. 14 5/I	Jan. 13, 2051 6/II

Any lunar month that appears to be two months long is a "leap moon" month. For example, this occurred between the fifth and sixth lunar months in the year 1952 (fig. 3.6). In this instance, the fifth lunar month began on May 24, 1952, and ended on July 21, 1952. The sixth lunar month began on July 22, 1952, and ended on August 19, 1952.

The lunar months of the Chinese luni-solar calendar serve as the foundation for the second *Ssu Chu*, the *miao* (month pillar). Employing the individual's birth month and day, the *t'ien kan* and *ti chih* for the lunar month in which the birth took place are identified. This is done by consulting the table in fig. 3.6, in which the Western starting date of each lunar month is presented along with the relevant *ba tze* pair for ease of reference. The *miao*'s *ba tze* pair are then written down in the astrologer's notes.

According to the table in fig. 3.6, Alice T.'s *miao* for June 15, 1952, is the *ba tze* pair 3/VII, since she was born between the fifth lunar month, which began on May 24, 1952, and the sixth lunar month, which started on July 22, 1952.[7] This *ba*

---

7. Note that the fifth lunar month in 1952 was a "leap moon" month, meaning that one month was skipped between the two months shown in the table in fig. 3.6 to accommodate for the regular adjustment of the luni-solar calendar as discussed earlier in this chapter.

tze pair represents the third *t'ien kan* and the seventh *ti chih*. Peter C.'s *miao* for August 27, 1964, is the *ba tze* 9/IX, since he was born between the seventh lunar month, which began on August 8, 1964, and the eighth lunar month, which started on September 6, 1964. This *ba tze* pair represents the ninth *t'ien kan* and the ninth *ti chih*.

In most forms of Chinese astrology, an individual's life is divided into a series of ten-year fate cycles, progressing from the *miao* and placed within the twelve houses of fate. Each progressed cycle signifies the individual's potential areas of interest during a fixed period of his or her life. Although a fate cycle is ten years in duration, the first fate cycle does not always begin on a person's day of birth and end on his or her tenth birthday. The second fate cycle may in fact begin on the individual's third birthday and end on his or her thirteenth birthday. The third fate cycle may begin on the person's thirteenth birthday and end on his or her twenty-third birthday. Once the beginning of the second fate cycle is determined, all subsequent fate cycles follow in ten-year periods from that date. The *miao*'s *t'ien kan* and *ti chih* are progressed by one step at the turn of each fate cycle. Therefore, if an individual's birth or first fate-cycle *miao* is 3/VI, his or her second fate-cycle *miao* will be 4/VII. The third fate-cycle *miao* will be 5/VIII, and so forth.

To find the beginning of the second fate cycle, refer to the person's *gen t'ien kan* (see "Locating and Interpreting the Birth *Gen*," page 49). Using a separate sheet of paper, write down the number 1 if the *gen t'ien kan* is an odd digit. Write down the number 2 if the *gen t'ien kan* is an even digit. If the individual is male, add 1. If the person is female, add 2.

The Chinese solar calendar is divided into twenty-four *ch'i* (breaths), each of which is approximately fourteen days in duration. These periods are paired together into twelve *chieh* (monthly festivals) as shown in fig. 3.7. Each *chieh* generally begins at the midpoint of one of the twelve Western zodiac signs.

If the sum of the odd/even and male/female calculation above is odd, refer to the date of the *chieh* that occurs immediately before the person's birthday. If the sum is even, refer to the date of the *chieh* that occurs immediately after the person's birthday. The number of days between the person's day of birth and the selected *chieh* date are then counted and the sum divided by 3. The result is the age at which the person's second fate cycle begins.

For example, Alice T.'s *gen t'ien kan* is 9 (see "Locating and Interpreting the Birth *Gen*," page 49, and fig. 3.4). This is an odd number and she is female. Therefore, the odd sum (1 + 2 = 3) indicates the *chieh* that occurs before her day of birth, June 6 (fig. 3.7), should be used for calculation. There are nine days between June 6 and June 15 (Alice's day of birth). Divided by 3, the remainder indicates that Alice's second fate cycle begins when she is three years old.

FIGURE 3.7. THE TWELVE *CHIEH*.

CHIEH NUMBER	CHIEH STARTING DATE	CHIEH NAME (TRANSLATION)	SUN'S MEAN LOCATION IN THE TROPICAL ZODIAC
1	Feb. 4	Li Ch'un (beginning of spring)	16° ♒ 00'
2	Feb. 19	Yü Shui (rainwater)	01° ♓ 00'
3	Mar. 5	Ching Chih (movement of insects)	16° ♓ 00'
4	Mar. 20	Ch'un Fen (vernal equinox)	01° ♈ 00'
5	Apr. 5	Ch'ing Mong (serene clarity)	16° ♈ 00'
6	Apr. 20	Ku Yu (corn rain)	01° ♉ 00'
7	May 5	Li Hsia (beginning of summer)	16° ♉ 00'
8	May 21	Hsiao Man (corn sprouting)	01° ♊ 00'
9	Jun. 6	Mang Chung (grain in ear)	16° ♊ 00'
10	Jun. 21	Hsia Chih (summer solstice)	01° ♋ 00'
11	Jul. 7	Hsiao Shu (little heat)	16° ♋ 00'
12	Jul. 23	Ta Shu (great heat)	01° ♌ 00'
13	Aug. 7	Li Ch'iu (beginning of autumn)	16° ♌ 00'
14	Aug. 23	Ch'u Shu (heat finishes)	01° ♍ 00'
15	Sep. 7	Pai Lu (white dew)	16° ♍ 00'
16	Sep. 23	Ch'iu Fen (autumn equinox)	01° ♎ 00'
17	Oct. 8	Han Lu (cold dew)	16° ♎ 00'
18	Oct. 23	Shuang Chiang (frost descends)	01° ♏ 00'
19	Nov. 7	Li Tung (beginning of winter)	16° ♏ 00'
20	Nov. 22	Hsiao Hsüeh (little snow)	01° ♐ 00'
21	Dec. 7	Ta Hsüch (great snow)	16° ♐ 00'
22	Dec. 22	Thung Chih (winter solstice)	01° ♑ 00'
23	Jan. 5	Hsiao Han (little cold)	16° ♑ 00'
24	Jan 20	Ta Han (great cold)	01° ♒ 00'

Alice's birth *miao* (3/VII), which is found in fig. 3.6, and the age when the second fate cycle begins (explained above) are used to progress her fate cycles, one for every ten years of life. From the day of her birth to her third birthday, Alice's fate is influenced by her *miao*'s *ba tze* pair, 3/VII. Her second fate cycle begins on her third birthday. Therefore, from her third to her thirteenth birthday, Alice's fate is progressed to the next *ba tze* pair, 4/VIII. From her thirteenth to twenty-third birthdays, her fate is influenced by the next *ba tze* pair, 5/IX. This information is written down as shown in fig. 3.8. The *miao*'s *ba tze* pairs continue to be progressed in the same manner until all the boxes are filled.

Peter C.'s *gen t'ien kan* is 1 (see "Locating and Interpreting the Birth *Gen*," page 49, and fig. 3.4). This is an odd number and he is male. Therefore, the even sum (1 + 1 = 2) indicates that the *chieh* that occurs after his day of birth, September 7 (fig. 3.7), should be used for calculation. There are eleven days between August 27 and

FIGURE 3.8. ALICE T.'S FATE CYCLES.

FATE CYCLE	ONE	TWO	THREE	FOUR	FIVE	SIX	SEVEN	EIGHT	NINE	TEN
AGE	Birth	3 yrs.	13 yrs.	23 yrs.	33 yrs.	43 yrs.	53 yrs.	63 yrs.	73 yrs.	83 yrs.
MIAO T'IEN KAN	3 (from fig. 3.6)	4 (next in numeric sequence)	5 (next in numeric sequence)	6 (next in numeric sequence)	7 (next in numeric sequence)	8 (next in numeric sequence)	9 (next in numeric sequence)	10 (next in numeric sequence)	1 (next in numeric sequence)	2 (next in numeric sequence)
MIAO TI CHIH	VII (from fig. 3.6)	VIII (next in numeric sequence)	IX (next in numeric sequence)	X (next in numeric sequence)	XI (next in numeric sequence)	XII (next in numeric sequence)	I (next in numeric sequence)	II (next in numeric sequence)	III (next in numeric sequence)	IV (next in numeric sequence)

FIGURE 3.9. PETER C.'S FATE CYCLES.

FATE CYCLE	ONE	TWO	THREE	FOUR	FIVE	SIX	SEVEN	EIGHT	NINE	TEN
AGE	Birth	4 yrs.	14 yrs.	24 yrs.	34 yrs.	44 yrs.	54 yrs.	64 yrs.	74 yrs.	84 yrs.
MIAO T'IEN KAN	9 (from fig. 3.6)	10 (next in numeric sequence)	1 (next in numeric sequence)	2 (next in numeric sequence)	3 (next in numeric sequence)	4 (next in numeric sequence)	5 (next in numeric sequence)	6 (next in numeric sequence)	7 (next in numeric sequence)	8 (next in numeric sequence)
MIAO TI CHIH	IX (from fig. 3.6)	X (next in numeric sequence)	XI (next in numeric sequence)	XII (next in numeric sequence)	I (next in numeric sequence)	II (next in numeric sequence)	III (next in numeric sequence)	IV (next in numeric sequence)	V (next in numeric sequence)	VI (next in numeric sequence)

September 7. Divided by 3, the remainder rounds out to the nearest whole number and indicates that Peter's second fate cycle begins when he is four years old.

Peter's birth *miao* (9/IX), found in fig. 3.6, and the age when the second fate cycle begins are used to progress his fate cycles. Peter's first fate cycle lasts from his birth to his fourth birthday, when his fate is influenced by the *ba tze* pair 9/IX. His second fate cycle begins on his fourth birthday and ends on his fourteenth birthday. During that period, Peter's fate is influenced by the *ba tze* pair 10/X. During his third fate cycle, his fate is influenced by the *ba tze* pair 1/XI. This occurs between his fourteenth and twenty-fourth birthdays. This information is written down as shown in fig. 3.9. The *miao*'s *ba tze* pair continues to be progressed in the same manner until all the boxes are filled.

Similar to the twelve houses of the Western horoscope, the twelve houses of fate used in Chinese astrology influence various areas of an individual's life, as shown in fig. 3.10.

By using the number of the progressed *miao ti chih* as the number of the fate house that will be most influential during a given ten-year cycle in an individual's life, an astrologer derives a personal chronology that is similar to the Vedic *dasas* (time periods) (see "Constructing the *Vimsottari Dasa*" in chapter 5).

For example, Alice's *miao ti chih* at birth was VII, and progressed to VIII when she was three years old. This means that her seventh fate house (wives and concubines, in fig. 3.11) was most influential during the first three years of her life. The next ten years are affected by her eighth fate house (sickness and distress, in fig. 3.11). This same sequence is carried on through at least seven ten-year fate cycles as shown in fig. 3.11.

FIGURE 3.10. THE HOUSES OF FATE.

FATE HOUSE	INFLUENCE
I	fate (an individual's ultimate destiny)
II	riches and wealth
III	brothers and relatives (also emotions and affections)
IV	land and dwelling (also possessions and legacies)
V	sons and daughters (also charitable works)
VI	servants and slaves (also personal social status)
VII	wives and concubines
VIII	sickness and distress
IX	removal and change (also travel abroad)
X	official and reward (also profession)
XI	good fortune and virtue (also opportunities)
XII	manner and bearing

Peter's *miao ti chih* at birth was IX and progressed to X when he was four years old. This means that his ninth fate house (removal and change, in fig. 3.12) was most influential during the first four years of his life. The next ten years were affected by his tenth fate house (official and reward, in fig. 3.12). This same sequence is carried on through at least seven ten-year fate cycles as shown in fig. 3.12.

As mentioned at the beginning of this section, the *miao* is not interpreted as an independent entity; rather, it is progressed and employed in the construction of a personal chronology, which is interpreted in conjunction with the third of the *Ssu Chu* pillars, the *hua*.

FIGURE 3.11. ALICE T.'S PROGRESSION THROUGH THE HOUSES OF FATE.

FATE HOUSE (FROM FIG. 3.10)	INFLUENCE (FROM FIG. 3.10)	AGE (FROM FIG. 3.8)	MIAO TI CHIH AND ITS HSING (FROM FIGS. 3.8 AND 3.2)	HUA T'IEN KAN AND ITS HSING (FROM FIGS. 3.13 AND 3.1)	RELATIOSNHIP OF THE MIAO HSING (FIG. 3.11, FOURTH COLUMN) AND THE HUA HSING (FIG. 3.11, FIFTH COLUMN) (FROM FIG. 3.14)
VII	wives and concubines	birth	VII fire	7 metal	fire to metal negative
VII	sickness and distress	3 yrs.	VIII earth	7 metal	earth to metal positive
IX	removal and change (also travel abroad)	13 yrs.	IX metal	7 metal	metal to metal positive
X	official and reward (also profession)	23 yrs.	X metal	7 metal	metal to metal positive
XI	good fortune and virtue (also opportunities)	33 yrs.	XI earth	7 metal	earth to metal positive
XII	manner and bearing	43 yrs.	XII water	7 metal	water to metal positive
I	fate (an individual's ultimate destiny)	53 yrs.	I water	7 metal	water to metal positive
II	riches and wealth	63 yrs.	II earth	7 metal	earth to metal positive
III	brothers and relatives (also emotions and affections)	73 yrs.	III wood	7 metal	wood to metal negative
IV	land and dwelling (also possessions and legacies)	83 yrs.	IV wood	7 metal	wood to metal negative
V	sons and daughters (also charitable work)	NOT USED	NOT USED	N/A	NOT APPLICABLE
VI	servants and slaves (also personal social status)	NOT USED	NOT USED	N/A	NOT APPLICABLE

FIGURE 3.12. PETER C.'S PROGRESSION THROUGH THE HOUSES OF FATE.

FATE HOUSE (FROM FIG. 3.10)	INFLUENCE (FROM FIG. 3.10)	AGE (FROM FIG. 3.9)	MIAO TI CHIH AND ITS HSING (FROM FIGS. 3.9 AND 3.2)	HUA T'IEN KAN AND ITS HSING (FROM FIGS. 3.13 AND 3.1)	RELATIONSHIP OF THE MIAO HSING (FIG. 3.12, FOURTH COLUMN) AND HUA HSING (FIG. 3.12, FIFTH COLUMN) (FROM FIG. 3.14)
IX	removal and change (also travel abroad)	birth	IX metal	10 water	earth to metal positive
X	official and reward (also profession)	4 yrs.	X metal	10 water	earth to metal positive
XI	good fortune and virtue (also opportunities)	14 yrs.	XI earth	10 water	earth to water negative
XII	manner and bearing	24 yrs.	XII water	10 water	water to water positive
I	fate (an individual's ultimate destiny)	34 yrs.	I water	10 water	water to water positive
II	riches and wealth	44 yrs.	II earth	10 water	earth to water negative
III	brothers and relatives (also emotions and affections)	54 yrs.	III wood	10 water	wood to water positive
IV	land and dwelling (also possessions and legacies)	64 yrs.	IV wood	10 water	wood to water positive
V	sons and daughters (also charitable works)	74 yrs.	V earth	10 water	earth to water negative
VI	servants and slaves (also personal social status)	84 yrs.	VI fire	10 water	fire to water negative
VII	wives and concubines	NOT USED	VII fire	10 water	fire to water negative
VIII	sickness and distress	NOT USED	VIII earth	10 water	earth to water negative

Identifying and Locating the Birth *Hua* (Day Pillar)

The *hua* (day pillar) represents an individual's ego. Used in conjunction with the *miao*, a person's destiny can be determined in a pattern of ten-year-long cycles. It can also be disclosed on a daily basis. In fact, Chinese astrologers refer to the *hua*'s *t'ien kan* as *zu chu* (day master) because of its strong influence.

Using the individual's day of birth, the *hua*'s *ba tze* pair is identified by consulting the table in fig. 3.13. The resulting *t'ien kan* (second, fifth, or eighth columns in fig. 3.13) and *ti chih* (third, sixth, and ninth columns in fig. 3.13) that make up the *hua*'s *ba tze* pair are then written down in the astrologer's notes.

FIGURE 3.13. TABLE OF *T'IEN KAN* AND *TI CHIH* FOR EACH DAY OF THE YEAR.

Day	T'ien Kan	Ti Chih	Day	T'ien Kan	Ti Chih	Day	T'ien Kan	Ti Chih
Jan. 1	1	I	Feb. 1	2	VII	Mar. 1	10	XII
2	2	II	2	3	IX	2	1	I
3	3	III	3	4	X	3	2	II
4	4	IV	4	5	XI	4	3	III
5	5	V	5	6	XII	5	4	IV
6	6	VI	6	7	I	6	5	V
7	7	VII	7	8	II	7	6	VI
8	8	VIII	8	9	III	8	7	VII
9	9	IX	9	10	IV	9	8	VIII
10	10	X	10	1	V	10	9	IX
11	1	XI	11	2	VI	11	10	X
12	2	XII	12	3	VII	12	1	XI
13	3	I	13	4	VIII	13	2	XII
14	4	II	14	5	IX	14	3	I
15	5	III	15	6	X	15	4	II
16	6	IV	16	7	XI	16	5	III
17	7	V	17	8	XII	17	6	IV
18	8	VI	18	9	I	18	7	V
19	9	VII	19	10	II	19	8	VI
20	10	VIII	20	1	III	20	9	VII
21	1	IX	21	2	IV	21	10	VIII
22	2	X	22	3	V	22	1	IX
23	3	XI	23	4	VI	23	2	X
24	4	XII	24	5	VII	24	3	XI
25	5	I	25	6	VIII	25	4	XII
26	6	II	26	7	IX	26	5	I
27	7	III	27	8	X	27	6	II
28	8	IV	28	9	XI	28	7	III
29	9	V	(29)			29	8	IV
30	10	VI				30	9	V
31	1	VII				31	10	VI

For a leap year, add 1 day to the date of birth and apply the information for that day instead. To determine a leap year, refer to fig. 3.6.

If the year in question was a "leap year" (see the leap years in the first column of fig. 3.6, which are designated with a double underscore), add one day to the day of birth, and read the information on the corresponding line. For example, a person born on February 29 should refer to the *t'ien kan* and *ti chih* listed for March 1.

Since Alice was born on June 15, 1952, which was a leap year (first column in fig. 3.6), one day is added to her day of birth. The information listed on June 16 in

Day	T'ien Kan	Ti Chih	Day	T'ien Kan	Ti Chih	Day	T'ien Kan	Ti Chih
Apr. 1	1	VII	May 1	1	I	Jun. 1	2	VIII
2	2	VIII	2	2	II	2	3	IX
3	3	IX	3	3	III	3	4	X
4	4	X	4	4	IV	4	5	XI
5	5	XI	5	5	V	5	6	XII
6	6	XII	6	6	VI	6	7	I
7	7	I	7	7	VII	7	8	II
8	8	II	8	8	VIII	8	9	III
9	9	III	9	9	IX	9	10	IV
10	10	IV	10	10	X	10	1	V
11	1	V	11	1	XI	11	2	VI
12	2	VI	12	2	XII	12	3	VII
13	3	VII	13	3	I	13	4	VIII
14	4	VIII	14	4	II	14	5	IX
15	5	IX	15	5	III	15	6	X
16	6	X	16	6	IV	16	7	XI
17	7	XI	17	7	V	17	8	XII
18	8	XII	18	8	VI	18	9	I
19	9	I	19	9	VII	19	10	II
20	10	II	20	10	VIII	20	1	III
21	1	III	21	1	IX	21	2	IV
22	2	IV	22	2	X	22	3	V
23	3	V	23	3	XI	23	4	VI
24	4	VI	24	4	XII	24	5	VII
25	5	VII	25	5	I	25	6	VIII
26	6	VIII	26	6	II	26	7	IX
27	7	IX	27	7	III	27	8	X
28	8	X	28	8	IV	28	9	XI
29	9	XI	29	9	V	29	10	XII
30	10	XII	30	10	VI	30	1	I
			31	1	VII			

fig. 3.13 indicates that her *hua*'s *ba tze* pair is 7/XI. This represents the seventh *t'ien kan* (eighth column in fig. 3.13) and the eleventh *ti chih* (ninth column in fig. 3.13).

Similarly, Peter was born on August 27, 1964, which was also a leap year (first column in fig. 3.6). Therefore, one day is also added to his day of birth. The information listed on August 28 in fig. 3.13 indicates that his *hua*'s *ba tze* pair is 10/XII. This represents the tenth *t'ien kan* (second column in fig. 3.13) and the twelfth *ti chih* (third column in fig. 3.13).

Day	T'ien Kan	Ti Chih	Day	T'ien Kan	Ti Chih	Day	T'ien Kan	Ti Chih
Jul. 1	2	II	Aug. 1	3	IX	Sep. 1	4	IV
2	3	III	2	4	X	2	5	V
3	4	IV	3	5	XI	3	6	VI
4	5	V	4	6	XII	4	7	VII
5	6	VI	5	7	I	5	8	VIII
6	7	VII	6	8	II	6	9	IX
7	8	VIII	7	9	III	7	10	X
8	9	IX	8	10	IV	8	1	XI
9	10	X	9	1	V	9	2	XII
10	1	XI	10	2	VI	10	3	I
11	2	XII	11	3	VII	11	4	II
12	3	I	12	4	VIII	12	5	III
13	4	II	13	5	IX	13	6	IV
14	5	III	14	6	X	14	7	V
15	6	IV	15	7	XI	15	8	VI
16	7	V	16	8	XII	16	9	VII
17	8	VI	17	9	I	17	10	VIII
18	9	VII	18	10	II	18	1	IX
19	10	VIII	19	1	III	19	2	X
20	1	IX	20	2	IV	20	3	XI
21	2	X	21	3	V	21	4	XII
22	3	XI	22	4	VI	22	5	I
23	4	XII	23	5	VII	23	6	II
24	5	I	24	6	VIII	24	7	III
25	6	II	25	7	IX	25	8	IV
26	7	III	26	8	X	26	9	V
27	8	IV	27	9	XI	27	10	VI
28	9	V	28	10	XII	28	1	VII
29	10	VI	29	1	I	29	2	VIII
30	1	VII	30	2	II	30	3	IX
31	2	VIII	31	3	III			

Interpreting the Personal Chronology with the Birth Hua

As mentioned in the previous section, an individual's *miao* is progressed one step for every ten years of life, creating a personal chronology. The outcome of the events that might occur during that period, however, can only be interpreted in conjunction with the birth *hua*. This is determined by examining the relationship between the *hsing* that influence the *hua*'s *t'ien kan* and the *miao*'s *ti chih* (see "Locating and Interpreting the Birth *Miao*," page 65) during the course of each ten-year period. As the *miao* progresses through the fate houses every ten years, the relationship between these two elements changes, producing positive or negative

Day	T'ien Kan	Ti Chih	Day	T'ien Kan	Ti Chih	Day	T'ien Kan	Ti Chih
Oct. 1	4	X	Nov. 1	5	V	Dec. 1	5	XI
2	5	XI	2	6	VI	2	6	XII
3	6	XII	3	7	VII	3	7	I
4	7	I	4	8	VIII	4	8	II
5	8	II	5	9	IX	5	9	III
6	9	III	6	10	X	6	10	IV
7	10	IV	7	1	XI	7	1	V
8	1	V	8	2	XII	8	2	VI
9	2	VI	9	3	I	9	3	VII
10	3	VII	10	4	II	10	4	VIII
11	4	VIII	11	5	III	11	5	IX
12	5	IX	12	6	IV	12	6	X
13	6	X	13	7	V	13	7	XI
14	7	XI	14	8	VI	14	8	XII
15	8	XII	15	9	VII	15	9	I
16	9	I	16	10	VIII	16	10	II
17	10	II	17	1	IX	17	1	III
18	1	III	18	2	X	18	2	IV
19	2	IV	19	3	XI	19	3	V
20	3	V	20	4	XII	20	4	VI
21	4	VI	21	5	I	21	5	VII
22	5	VII	22	6	II	22	6	VIII
23	6	VIII	23	7	III	23	7	IX
24	7	IX	24	8	IV	24	8	X
25	8	X	25	9	V	25	9	XI
26	9	XI	26	10	VI	26	10	XII
27	10	XII	27	1	VII	27	1	I
28	1	I	28	2	VIII	28	2	II
29	2	II	29	3	IX	29	3	III
30	3	III	30	4	X	30	4	IV
31	4	IV				31	5	V

outcomes to the events occurring in a particular area of the person's life. For the sake of space, in this section only Alice and Peter's second and third fate cycles will be used as examples of how these relationships are interpreted. You will find a more complete interpretation in the personality profiles that appear later in the chapter. Practitioners actually analyze every ten-year period in the same manner, from the first through the ninth or tenth fate cycles.

Only the traits that are relevant to the fate house in question are presented from the characteristics for the various *hsing* found in the section titled "Locating and Interpreting the Birth *Gen*." In each case, the *hsing* associated with the *miao*'s *ti*

FIGURE 3.14. THE RELATIONSHIP OF THE *WU HSING*.

TYPE OF RELATIONSHIP	DESCRIPTION OF HSING RELATIONSHIP	FORM OF RELATIONSHIP
mutual production between two *hsing*	wood produces fire	positive
	fire creates earth	positive
	earth begets metal	positive
	metal runs like water	positive
	water nurtures wood	positive
mutual conquest between two *hsing*	wood burns earth	negative
	fire melts metal	negative
	earth absorbs water	negative
	metal cuts wood	negative
	water douses fire	negative
control among three *hsing*	wood burns earth, but metal cuts wood	neutral
	fire melts metal, but water douses fire	neutral
	earth absorbs water, but wood burns earth	neutral
	metal cuts wood, but fire melts metal	neutral
	water douses fire, but earth absorbs water	neutral
correction among three *hsing*	wood burns earth, but fire creates earth	neutral
	fire melts metal, but earth begets metal	neutral
	earth absorbs water, but metal runs like water	neutral
	metal cuts wood, but water nurtures wood	neutral
	water douses fire, but wood produces fire	neutral

chih takes precedence over the *hsing* that governs the *hua*'s *t'ien kan*, since the *miao*'s *ti chih* is the influential force that actually changes every ten years.

No one *hsing* is better or stronger than another. But astrologers believe that varying degrees of positive and negative energy flow as a result of the relationship between various *hsing*, as depicted in fig. 3.14.

In Alice's case, her *hua*'s *t'ien kan* is 7 (fig. 3.13), which is ruled by the metal *hsing* and *yang* (fig. 3.1). During her second fate cycle (from three to thirteen years of age), her progressed *miao ti chih* is VIII (fig. 3.11), which is ruled by the earth *hsing* and *yin* (fig. 3.2). Based on the data in fig. 3.14, the relationship between her earth *hsing* and metal *hsing* is positive and mutually productive. So although Alice's second fate cycle is placed in the eighth fate house (sickness and distress, in fig. 3.11), she gains strength despite the illness or stress she experiences during her third through thirteenth years because the *hsings*' relationship stimulates positive outcomes to difficult situations.

During her third fate cycle, Alice experiences many changes of residence and travels to foreign lands, since her *miao ti chih* (IX, in fig. 3.11) is governed by the metal *hsing* (fig. 3.2), which occupies the ninth fate house (removal, change, and travel in fig. 3.10) between the ages of thirteen and twenty-three. Since the metal *hsing* also rules her *hua*'s *t'ien kan* (figs. 3.13 and 3.1),[8] the events that occur during this ten-year period are filled with both energy and sadness. She is guided solely by her feelings with passionate intensity (see the interpretation of the *hsing* in "Locating and Interpreting the Birth *Gen*," page 49), because the relationship of the two *hsing* is static (metal *hsing* to metal *hsing*) and so has no complementary or contrasting energy to temper this prognostication.

The relationship between her *hua*'s *t'ien kan* and the progressed *miao ti chih* for Alice's fourth through ninth fate cycles (fig. 3.8) would be scrutinized for their influence on the various fate houses (fig. 3.11) in the same manner as shown above.

In Peter's case, his *hua*'s *t'ien kan* is 10 (figs. 3.13 and 3.1),[9] and is ruled by the water *hsing* and *yin* (fig. 3.1). During his second fate cycle, his progressed *miao ti chih* is X (fig. 3.12), which is ruled by the metal *hsing* and *yin* (fig. 3.2). This indicates that between his fourth through fourteenth birthdays, life concentrates on matters governed by his tenth fate house (official and reward, in fig. 3.13). The metal-*hsing* influence makes him act with passionate intensity. His determined and somewhat rigid, opinionated outlook guides him through hard times and false starts. Ultimately he receives honor, reward, and status during this period (see the interpretation of the *hsing* in "Locating and Interpreting the Birth *Gen*," page 49). The relationship of the two *hsing* is positive (fig. 3.14): the metal *hsing* to his water *hsing* indicates that he appears calm while exerting a great deal of energy during this period.

During his third fate cycle, his progressed *miao ti chih* is XI (see "Locating and Interpreting the Birth *Miao*," page 65, and fig. 3.12), which is also ruled by the earth *hsing* and *yang* (fig. 3.2). This indicates that between his fourteenth and twenty-fourth birthdays, life concentrates on matters governed by his eleventh fate house (good fortune and virtue, in fig. 3.12). The earth-*hsing* influence makes him move cautiously and shrewdly (see the interpretation of the *hsing* in "Locating and Interpreting the Birth *Gen*," page 49). The relationship of the earth *hsing* and the water *hsing* that rules his *hua*'s *t'ien kan* (10, in fig. 3.13) suggests that during this period his desires might override his ability to communicate and inspire others, because fig. 3.14 tells us that earth absorbs water. The relationship between his *hua*'s *t'ien kan*, which is ruled by the water *hsing* and the progressed *miao ti chih* for Peter's

---

8.   Alice was born in a leap year (1952 is a double-underscored year in fig. 3.6). Therefore, one day was added to her date of birth to determine her *hua*'s *tien kan* used in fig. 3.13.

9.   Peter was born in a leap year (1964 is a double-underscored year in fig. 3.6). Therefore, one day was added to his date of birth to determine his *hua*'s *tien kan*, used in fig. 3.13.

fourth through ninth fate cycles (fig. 3.9) would be scrutinized for their influence on the various fate houses (fig. 3.12) in the same manner as shown above.

Using the Birth Hua for Daily Prediction

An individual's birth *hua* is used not only to determine the outcome of events foretold by the ten-year fate cycles, but to plan daily activities. The method employs two cross-referenced elements: the person's birth *hua* and *chieh* (festivals) which divide the year into twenty-four segments. Using a chart similar to the one shown in fig. 3.15, a person locates the nearest *chieh* that precedes the day in question and cross-references it to his or her *hua*'s *ti chih*. The result is a letter that represents a *chien-ch'ü* (indicator), which outlines the potential outcome of the day's events.

There are twelve *chien-ch'ü* (indicators) that are commonly consulted on a daily basis in order to plan personal activities. Each *chien-ch'ü* is generally interpreted as follows:

A   An auspicious day for planning, but not for activating new projects. Established projects will prosper. Do not make or take loans; and do not make withdrawals from savings accounts. Settle old bills. Indoor activities will meet with success, but outdoor work will fail. Do not travel by plane or boat; errands by land will go well, however.

B   An auspicious day for cleaning house or clearing the decks in preparation for things to come. Not a good time for doing business or socializing. Attend to personal health, fitness, and appearance.

C   This is a most fortunate three-day period for large-scale social events such as weddings, receptions, or banquets. It's also a good time for long-distance travel and changes of residence. It's not, however, a time to work in the garden or in the fields. Don't bother with routine tasks if more urgent business needs attention.

D   This is a most fortunate period for large-scale social events and for decorating a new home, but not a time to work in the garden or in the fields. Don't bother with routine tasks if more urgent business needs attention.

E   Large-scale social events, long-distance travel, and changes of residence can reach successful conclusions. Routine tasks can be resumed. Keep personal opinions concealed, and do not meddle in other people's affairs.

FIGURE 3.15. THE TWELVE CHIEN-CH'Ü[10]

Chieh Number	Chieh Date	Hua Ti Chih I (from fig. 3.13)	Hua Ti Chih II (from fig. 3.13)	Hua Ti Chih III (from fig. 3.13)	Hua Ti Chih IV (from fig. 3.13)	Hua Ti Chih V (from fig. 3.13)	Hua Ti Chih VI (from fig. 3.13)	Hua Ti Chih VII (from fig. 3.13)	Hua Ti Chih VIII (from fig. 3.13)	Hua Ti Chih IX (from fig. 3.13)	Hua Ti Chih X (from fig. 3.13)	Hua Ti Chih XI (from fig. 3.13)	Hua Ti Chih XII (from fig. 3.13)
1	Feb. 4	K	L	A	B	C	D	E	F	G	H	I	J
2	Feb. 19	K	L	A	B	C	D	E	F	G	H	I	J
3	Mar. 5	J	K	L	A	B	C	D	E	F	G	H	I
4	Mar. 20	J	K	L	A	B	C	D	E	F	G	H	I
5	Apr. 5	I	J	K	L	A	B	C	D	E	F	G	H
6	Apr. 20	I	J	K	L	A	B	C	D	E	F	G	H
7	May 5	H	I	J	K	L	A	B	C	D	E	F	G
8	May 21	H	I	J	K	L	A	B	C	D	E	F	G
9	Jun. 6	G	H	I	J	K	L	A	B	C	D	E	F
10	Jun. 21	G	H	I	J	K	L	A	B	C	D	E	F
11	Jul. 7	F	G	H	I	J	K	L	A	B	C	D	E
12	Jul. 23	F	G	H	I	J	K	L	A	B	C	D	E
13	Aug. 7	E	F	G	H	I	J	K	L	A	B	C	D
14	Aug. 23	E	F	G	H	I	J	K	L	A	B	C	D
15	Sep. 7	D	E	F	G	H	I	J	K	L	A	B	C
16	Sep. 23	D	E	F	G	H	I	J	K	L	A	B	C
17	Oct. 8	C	D	E	F	G	H	I	J	K	L	A	B
18	Oct. 23	C	D	E	F	G	H	I	J	K	L	A	B
19	Nov. 7	B	C	D	E	F	G	H	I	J	K	L	A
20	Nov. 22	B	C	D	E	F	G	H	I	J	K	L	A
21	Dec. 7	A	B	C	D	E	F	G	H	I	J	K	L
22	Dec. 22	A	B	C	D	E	F	G	H	I	J	K	L
23	Jan. 5	L	A	B	C	D	E	F	G	H	I	J	K
24	Jan. 20	L	A	B	C	D	E	F	G	H	I	J	K

10. The actual dates of the twenty-four *chieh* vary by plus or minus one day each day. To find an exact date, practitioners commonly consult a Chinese almanac that lists the exact *chieh* for each day. Unfortunately, there are no versions printed in English or any other language than Chinese. However, this level of accuracy is not generally necessary for planning daily activities. The information found in fig. 3.15 is sufficient for application by a layperson.

F   Do not travel or change a situation at this time. Do not spend
           personal resources of any kind. It is an auspicious day for per-
           forming routine tasks, as well as work that can be done at a
           single location.

G   This is a time for rest and quiet; there are many conflicts and
           confrontations surrounding activities.

H   Rest and relax rather than partaking in current problems. Acci-
           dents and difficulties surround the workplace.

I   This is a very auspicious day to plan or prepare for large-scale
           activities. Avoid gossip. Start a long-distance trip. Lay new
           foundations.

J   This is an auspicious time to take loans, withdraw savings, or
           tap personal reserves to begin a new project. It's a fortunate
           time for business. Do not go to a doctor or health specialist dur-
           ing this time. Travel should also be avoided.

K   This is a very auspicious time for transacting business, traveling,
           practicing handicrafts, or playing musical instruments. Avoid
           depressing, offensive, or unhealthy activities.

L   This is an auspicious time for saving money, accumulating
           goods, starting a diet or new health program, and conducting
           funerals or memorial services.

For example, Alice wants to know how to proceed on June 10. Using her *hua*'s *ti
chih* (XI, from fig. 3.13)[11] and cross-referencing it to the closest *chieh* in fig. 3.15
(June 6), she finds the *chien-ch'ü* for the day in question is E (fig. 3.15). Employing
the above interpretative material, Alice is advised that successful conclusions to
large-scale social events, long-distance travel, and changes of residence can be
achieved and routine tasks can be resumed. However, she must keep her opinions
concealed and must not meddle in other people's affairs.

If Peter consults the chart in fig. 3.15 for the same day, he uses his *hua*'s *ti chih*
(XII, from fig. 3.13)[12] and cross-references to the closest *chieh* in fig. 3.15 (June 6).
The *chien-ch'ü* for the day in question, F, is identified. Consequently he is advised to
stick to performing routine tasks. Travel, changes, or the spending of personal resources are to be avoided.

---

11.   See footnote 8.
12.   See footnote 9.

Identifying and Applying the Birth *Guo* (Hour Pillar)

According to Chinese belief, each person is allotted a share of good fortune or luck in life. The birth *guo* (hour pillar) determines what direction that destiny might take, and to what extent the individual has been blessed by fate. Once the *guo* has been identified, it is then used in conjunction with a series of four images called the "Song of the Four Seasons" to define the quality and quantity of personal destiny.

Locating the Birth Guo *(Hour Pillar)*

Time is designated in pairs of hours in Chinese culture, starting with the period from 11:00 P.M. to 1:00 A.M. Each time period is also assigned a corresponding *ba tze* pair of one *t'ien kan* and one *ti chih*. To find the appropriate time period for a birth that did not occur in China, however, a few mathematical conversions must take place.

If the person was born during daylight savings time,[13] the time must be converted to standard time by subtracting one hour (01:00:00) from the birth time. The standard time of birth is then converted to naval time (i.e., 12:00 A.M. to 24:00:00, 1:15 P.M. to 13:15:00, etc.) to make the job of adding and subtracting hours easier.

The birth time is then converted to Greenwich Mean Time (GMT) (also called Universal Time or UT) by adding or subtracting hours as needed. For example, if the birth took place in North America's Atlantic Maritime Standard Time zone (Nova Scotia, New Brunswick, Prince Edward Island, or Newfoundland), 04:30:00 must be added to convert to GMT. If the person was born in North America's Eastern Standard Time zone (EST), 05:00:00 must be added to the birth time to convert to GMT. If the birth took place in North America's Central Standard Time zone (CST), then 06:00:00 must be added. If it took place in North America's Rocky Mountain Standard Time zone (MST), then 07:00:00 must be added. If it occurred in North America's Pacific Standard Time zone (PST), then 08:00:00 must be added. And if it occurred in the Alaska-Hawaii Standard Time zone (AST/HST), 10:00:00 must be added.[14]

Greenwich Mean Time is applied throughout the British Isles and Portugal. Therefore, a birth that occurs in either region needs no adjustment. However, if the

---

13.   Calculated by subtracting 01:00:00 from a given standard zone time during the summer growing and harvesting months (with exception of a few places in British Columbia, Canada, and portions of South America), daylight savings time occurs between late March and early October worldwide. During the First and Second World Wars, a similar daylight savings time adjustment, called war time, was enforced year-round. This took place during the period from March 31 to October 27, 1918; March 30 to October 26, 1919; and February 9, 1942, to September 30, 1945.
14.   Yukon Standard Time (YST) occupies a small segment of southeastern Alaska and the Canadian Yukon, extending from 127°30′W. If the birth took place in this time period, add 09:00:00. Bering Standard Time stretches along Alaska's far northwestern coast as well as the Aleutian Islands, from 157°30′W to 172°30′W. If the birth took place in this time zone, add 11:00:00.

birth occurred in the Central European Standard Time zone (CET), which extends from Spain to Poland and from Sweden and Norway to France and Italy, then 01:00:00 must be subtracted from the birth time to convert to GMT. If the person was born in the Eastern European Standard Time zone (EET), which includes Finland, Greece, Romania, Bulgaria, Egypt, the Sudan, South Africa, and the Middle East with the exception of Turkey, then 02:00:00 must be subtracted. If the birth occurred in the Russian Standard Time zone (or Baghdad Time), which applies in Turkey, the Balkan States, Russia, the Ukraine, Saudi Arabia, Iran, and Iraq, then 03:00:00 must be subtracted from the birth time to convert to GMT.

Finally, eight hours (08:00:00) are added to the GMT version of the birth time to convert it to Chinese Coastal Time (CCT). The result is the time used to determine the Chinese time period in which the individual was born.

For example, Alice was born at 10:45 P.M. in North America's Central Daylight Savings Time zone (CDT). Since she was born during daylight savings time, this birth time must be converted to Standard Time by subtracting one hour. This means that she was born at 9:45 P.M. Central Standard Time (CST). The 9:45 P.M. birth time is then converted into naval time, which is 21:45:00.

Because the birth took place in North America's Central Standard Time zone (CST), then 06:00:00 is added to 21:45:00 to convert the time to Greenwich Mean Time (GMT). Therefore, Alice was born at 27:45:00 GMT (03:45:00 GMT). Finally, 08:00:00 is added to this birth time to convert it to Chinese Coastal Time (CCT). In this case, Alice's birth time is converted to 11:45:00 CCT.

The converted birth time is then located in fig. 3.16. The *ti chih* for the corresponding time period is then written down. In this case, Alice's birth time occurs in

FIGURE 3.16. TABLE OF *TI CHIH* FOR EACH TIME PERIOD OF THE DAY.

Guo Ti Chih	China Time (CCT) in 24-Hour Marine Time	China Time (CCT) in Clock Time
I	23:00–01:00	11:00 P.M.–01:00 A.M.
II	01:00–03:00	01:00 A.M.–03:00 A.M.
III	03:00–05:00	03:00 A.M.–05:00 A.M.
IV	05:00–07:00	05:00 A.M.–07:00 A.M.
V	07:00–09:00	07:00 A.M.–09:00 A.M.
VI	09:00–11:00	09:00 A.M.–11:00 A.M.
VII	11:00–13:00	11:00 A.M.–01:00 A.M.
VIII	13:00–15:00	01:00 P.M.–03:00 P.M.
IX	15:00–17:00	03:00 P.M.–05:00 P.M.
X	17:00–19:00	05:00 P.M.–07:00 P.M.
XI	19:00–21:00	07:00 P.M.–09:00 P.M.
XII	21:00–23:00	09:00 P.M.–11:00 P.M.

the time period that begins at 11:00:00 and ends at 13:00:00 (found in column two). Therefore, Alice's *guo ti chih* is VII (column one in fig. 3.16).

To find the corresponding *guo t'ien kan* for Alice's birth hour, refer to the *hua t'ien kan*, which is 7 (see "Identifying and Locating the Birth *Hua*," page 83, and fig. 3.13), as well as the *guo ti chih*, which is VII (see fig. 3.16). Using fig. 3.17, find the *hua t'ien kan* in the first column and match it with the correct *guo ti chih* in the second column. Reading across, the third column provides the *guo t'ien kan*. In this case, Alice's *hua t'ien kan* (7, in the first column) is matched up with her *guo ti chih* (VII, in the second column), resulting in her *guo t'ien kan* (9, in the third column). Therefore, Alice's *guo* (hour pillar) is 9/VII.

The same method is also applied to Peter's birth time. He was born at 7:45 P.M. in North America's Eastern Daylight Savings Time zone (EDT). Since he was born during daylight savings time (DST), this birth time must be converted to standard time by subtracting one hour. This means that he was born at 6:45 P.M. Eastern Standard Time (EST). The 6:45 P.M. birth time is then converted into naval time, which is 18:45:00.

Because the birth took place in North America's Eastern Standard Time zone (EST), 05:00:00 is added to 18:45:00 to convert the time to Greenwich Mean Time. Therefore, Peter was born at 23:45:00 GMT. Finally, 08:00:00 is added to this birth time to convert it to Chinese Coastal Time (CCT). In this case, Peter's birth time is converted to 31:45:00 CCT (08:45:00 CCT).

The converted birth time is then located in fig. 3.16. The *ti chih* for the corresponding time period is then written down, which, in Peter's case, occurs in the time period that begins at 7:00:00 and ends at 9:00:00 (found in the second column). Therefore, Peter's *guo ti chih* is V (found in the first column).

To find the corresponding *guo t'ien kan* for Peter's birth hour, refer to his *hua t'ien kan*, which is 10 (see "Identifying and Locating the Birth *Hua*," page 83, and fig. 3.13) as well as the *guo ti chih*, which is V (see above). Using fig. 3.17, Peter's *hua t'ien kan* (10, in the first column) is matched up with his *guo ti chih* (V, in the second column), resulting in his *guo t'ien kan* (3, in the third column). Therefore, Peter's *guo ba tze* pair is 3/V.

Applying the Birth Guo (Hour Pillar) with the "Song of the Four Seasons"

Unlike Western astrological delineation, luck plays a significant role in the interpretation of an individual's horoscope in Chinese astrology. One of the oldest methods for determining a person's good fortune involves locating the individual's *guo ti chih* on one of four images depicting the Emperor Huang Ti. Chinese almanacs generally contain this series of images or "songs," which are called the "Song of the Four Seasons." Each image represents a particular season: Spring,

FIGURE 3.17. TABLE OF *T'IEN KAN* FOR EACH TIME PERIOD OF THE DAY.

HUA T'IEN KAN (FROM FIG. 3.13)	GUO TI CHIH (FROM FIG. 3.16)	GUO T'IEN KAN	HUA T'IEN KAN (FROM FIG. 3.13)	GUO TI CHIH (FROM FIG. 3.16)	GUO T'IEN KAN
1	I	1	1	IV	4
2	I	3	2	IV	6
3	I	5	3	IV	8
4	I	7	4	IV	10
5	I	9	5	IV	2
6	I	1	6	IV	4
7	I	3	7	IV	6
8	I	5	8	IV	8
9	I	7	9	IV	10
10	I	9	10	IV	2
1	II	2	1	V	5
2	II	4	2	V	7
3	II	6	3	V	9
4	II	8	4	V	1
5	II	10	5	V	3
6	II	2	6	V	5
7	II	4	7	V	7
8	II	6	8	V	9
9	II	8	9	V	1
10	II	10	10	V	3
1	III	3	1	VI	6
2	III	5	2	VI	8
3	III	7	3	VI	10
4	III	9	4	VI	2
5	III	1	5	VI	4
6	III	3	6	VI	6
7	III	5	7	VI	8
8	III	7	8	VI	10
9	III	9	9	VI	2
10	III	1	10	VI	4
1	VII	7	1	X	10
2	VII	9	2	X	2
3	VII	1	3	X	4
4	VII	3	4	X	6
5	VII	5	5	X	8
6	VII	7	6	X	10
7	VII	9	7	X	2
8	VII	1	8	X	4
9	VII	3	9	X	6
10	VII	5	10	X	8

Hua T'ien Kan (from fig. 3.13)	Guo Ti Chih (from fig. 3.16)	Guo T'ien Kan	Hua T'ien Kan (from fig. 3.13)	Guo Ti Chih (from fig. 3.16)	Guo T'ien Kan
1	VIII	8	1	XI	1
2	VIII	10	2	XI	3
3	VIII	2	3	XI	5
4	VIII	4	4	XI	7
5	VIII	6	5	XI	9
6	VIII	8	6	XI	1
7	VIII	10	7	XI	3
8	VIII	2	7	XI	5
9	VIII	4	9	XI	7
10	VIII	6	10	XI	9
1	IX	9	1	XII	2
2	IX	1	2	XII	4
3	IX	3	3	XII	6
4	IX	5	4	XII	8
5	IX	7	5	XII	10
6	IX	9	6	XII	2
7	IX	1	7	XII	4
8	IX	3	8	XII	6
9	IX	5	9	XII	8
10	IX	7	10	XII	10

Summer, Autumn, or Winter. The twelve *ti chih* are distributed in varying orders on the emperor's head, shoulders, belly, hands, groin, knees, and feet. These positions are listed in fig. 3.18 for easy reference, since the "Song of the Four Seasons," found in Chinese almanacs, is published only in Chinese, making it difficult for most westerners to use.

To find the share of good fortune allotted to an individual at birth, find the season in which the birth took place in the first column of fig. 3.18. Then locate the person's *guo ti chih* (see "Locating the Birth *Guo*," page 93) in the third column of fig. 3.18. Read across to the second column to find the appropriate body part and use the interpretative material listed below.

head   The person's life will pass without worry. There is good luck and a good future. Promotion and advancement to top positions is possible. Women born with this placement are very stable and will marry well.

FIGURE 3.18. SONG OF THE FOUR SEASONS.

SEASON OF THE YEAR	GUO TI CHIH (FROM FIG. 3.16)	LOCATION OF THE GUO TI CHIH ON THE EMPEROR'S BODY
Spring: Feb. 4–May 4	I	head
	IV or X	shoulders
	II or XII	belly
	VI or VIII	hands
	VII	groin
	V or XI	knees
	IX or III	feet
Summer: May 5–Aug. 7	VII	head
	IV or X	shoulders
	VIII or XII	belly
	VI or II	hands
	I	groin
	V or XI	knees
	III or IX	feet
Autumn: Aug. 8–Nov. 7	XII	head
	I or VII	shoulders
	IV or VIII	belly
	VI or II	hands
	IX	groin
	III or X	knees
	XI or V	feet
Winter: Nov. 8–Feb. 4	VI	head
	X or IV	shoulders
	III or IX	belly
	XII or VII	hands
	I	groin
	II or VIII	knees
	V or XI	feet

shoulders   Destiny improves with age, so the person may feel as if he or she is waiting for "Lady Luck" for a long time. The person can improve his or her fate by following two general rules: do not rely on other people for any reason, and avoid discouragement when encountering any obstacles. This person's children will have a better fate.

belly   Fame and fortune can be attained in the arts or music later in life. From simple yet satisfying beginnings, happiness increases as time passes.

hands	The person's quality of life improves if he or she leaves the place of birth. Business and trade are the primary sources for his or her fortune. The beginnings will be modest, but there is continued growth through the years. This person's family will enjoy abundance.
groin	This placement is an assurance of wealth. No destiny is unreachable or too farfetched. In older age, a very high position is awarded and the person's fortune will be passed on to his or her descendants.
knees	This placement portends an unsatisfied existence. All labors and efforts will be executed in vain. Seemingly in perpetual motion, there will be a lifelong search with only a little peace at the end.
feet	Happiness can be found only in the renunciation of all material or physical aspirations. Greater fortune is found in the intellectual and spiritual worlds. This person must move away from his or her birthplace and live in the wilderness or in seclusion, without ever turning back. He or she will have two spouses.

For example, Alice was born on June 15. Therefore, her birth occurred during the Summer season, which takes place between May 5 and August 7 (first column in fig. 3.18). Her *guo ti chih* (VII, from fig. 3.16) is placed on the emperor's head (second column in fig. 3.18). Based on the interpretative material above, this placement assures that Alice's life will pass without worry. She has good luck and good fortune. She is very stable and marries well.

Peter was born on August 27. Therefore his birth occurred during the Autumn season, which takes place between August 8 and November 7 (first column in fig. 3.18). His *guo ti chih* (V, from fig. 3.16) is located on the emperor's feet (second column in fig. 3.18). Based on the interpretative material above, this placement ensures that Peter's happiness can be found only in the renunciation of all material or physical aspirations. His fortune is in the intellectual and spiritual worlds. He must live in the wilderness or in seclusion.

STEP TWO: RECORDING THE *SSU CHU*

The individual's *Ssu Chu* pillars (*gen, miao, hua,* and *guo*), which have now been identified in the previous sections, are documented for future reference in an easy-to-read eight-unit grid, placing the four *ba tze* pairs of one *t'ien kan* and one *ti chih* for each pillar in the order shown in fig. 3.19.

FIGURE 3.19. *SSU CHU* GRID.

(Hour) GUO T'IEN KAN (FROM FIG. 3.17)	(Day) HUA T'IEN KAN (DAY MASTER) (FROM FIG. 3.13)	(Month) MIAO T'IEN KAN (FROM FIG. 3.6)	(Year) GEN T'IEN KAN (FROM FIG. 3.4)
(Hour) GUO TI CHIH (FROM FIG. 3.16)	(Day) HUA TI CHIH (FROM FIG. 3.13)	(Month) MIAO TI CHIH (FROM FIG. 3.6)	(Year) GEN TI CHIH (FROM FIG. 3.4)

For example, the first column of Alice's *Ssu Chu* grid (fig. 3.20) contains her birth *guo* (hour pillar), which is the *ba tze* pair 3/I (see "Locating the Birth *Guo*," page 93). The second column consists of her birth *hua* (day pillar), which is the *ba tze* pair 7/XI (see "Identifying and Locating the Birth *Hua*," page 83). The third column is made up of her birth *miao* (month pillar), which is the *ba tze* pair 3/VII (see "Locating and Interpreting the Birth *Miao*," page 65). And the fourth column is occupied by her birth *gen* (year pillar), which is the *ba tze* pair 9/V (see "Locating and Interpreting the Birth *Gen*," page 49).

In the same manner, the first column of Peter's *Ssu Chu* grid (fig. 3.21) contains his birth *guo* (hour pillar) which is the *ba tze* pair 10/XII (see "Locating the Birth *Guo*," page 93). The second column consists of his birth *hua* (day pillar), which is also the *ba tze* pair 10/XII (see "Identifying and Locating the Birth *Hua*," page 83). The third column is made up of his birth *miao* (month pillar), which is the *ba tze* pair 9/IX (see "Locating and Interpreting the Birth *Miao*," page 65). And the fourth column is occupied by his birth *gen* (year pillar), which is the *ba tze* pair 1/V (see "Locating and Interpreting the Birth *Gen*," page 49).

FIGURE 3.20. *SSU CHU* GRID FOR ALICE T.

3 (GUO T'IEN KAN FROM FIG. 3.17)	7 HUA T'IEN KAN FROM FIG. 3.13)	3 (MIAO T'IEN KAN FROM FIG. 3.6)	9 (GEN T'IEN KAN FROM FIG. 3.4)
I (GUO TI CHIH FROM FIG. 3.16)	XI (HUA TI CHIH FROM FIG. 3.13)	VII (MIAO TI CHIH FROM FIG. 3.6)	V (GEN TI CHIH FROM FIG. 3.4)

FIGURE 3.21. *SSU CHU* GRID FOR PETER C.

10 (GUO T'IEN KAN FROM FIG. 3.17)	10 (HUA T'IEN KAN FROM FIG. 3.13)	9 (MIAO T'IEN KAN FROM FIG. 3.6)	1 (GEN T'IEN KAN FROM FIG. 3.4)
XII (GUO TI CHIH FROM FIG. 3.16)	XII (HUA TI CHIH FROM FIG. 3.13)	IX (MIAO TI CHIH FROM FIG. 3.6)	V (GEN TI CHIH FROM FIG. 3.4)

STEP THREE: CREATING A PERSONALITY PROFILE FROM THE SSU CHU

When the *Ssu Chu* (Four Pillars of Destiny) have been identified (see "Step One: Identifying the *Ssu Chu*," page 49) and the fate cycles (see "Locating and Interpreting the Birth *Miao*," page 65) have been constructed as shown in the previous sections, the Chinese practitioner begins to unfold the individual's personality profile. This takes place most frequently on one of three important occasions: after the individual's birth, before the person is betrothed, and before the person is buried. During a consultation, the individual's profile is assessed by delineating the person's *Ming Shu* sign, personal *Ssu Chu*, and fate cycles as shown in the examples that follow.

Alice's Personality Profile

The *Ming Shu* system of astrology (see "Interpreting the *Ming Shu*," page 57) indicates that Alice was born in a *lung* (Dragon) year (1952, in fig. 3.4). This means that Alice can succeed at anything. She is highly intelligent and only follows her own personal judgment. However, unless her blunt personality edges are curbed and she learns patience and tolerance, success will elude this otherwise lucky person. Alice is often loved, but seldom falls in love.

Alice's year *hsing* is water (third column in fig. 3.4), which indicates that she believes in growth and expansion. To that end, Alice puts aside personal opinion, but maintains a strong will and wields remarkable patience.

Using a general version of the *Tzu P'ing* form of interpretation, Alice's *Ssu Chu* (fig. 3.20) reveals additional facets of her personal profile. According to the *gen's ba tze* pair (9/V in "Locating and Interpreting the Birth *Gen*," page 49) in Alice's *Ssu Chu* (fig. 3.20), she is a prudent, faithful person because of the earth *hsing* that rules her *gen's ti chih* (V in fig. 3.20). She is practical, conservative, and reliable, moving cautiously and shrewdly, measuring each action for its potential result. She loves delving deeply into any matter, finding critical details as well as bits of trivia along the way. The water *hsing* that rules her *gen's t'ien kan* (9 in fig. 3.20) makes her behave calmly, even though her primary emotion is fear. She is communicative, inspiring others to act. She has a nose for future outcomes and knows how to move other people in the right direction. Opposition is met by quiet and steady work, infiltrating and wearing away problems and resistance.

Her *gen's ba tze* pair is governed by the water *hsing* and has the poetic name of "running water" (9/V in fig. 3.5). Consequently, the water-influenced aspects of Alice's behavior and emotions mentioned earlier are stronger than the earth-related traits that are also present in her *gen*. Her physical appearance combines the two *hsing* (earth and water), but the water-related influences dominate. Therefore she possibly has soft skin, glossy hair, thick lips or features, a round back, and a flat stomach.

Alice's *Ssu Chu* (fig. 3.20) reveals that her *guo*'s *ti chih* is VII (first column in fig. 3.20) placed on the emperor's head (second column in fig. 3.18) in the "Song of the Four Seasons" (see "Applying the Birth *Guo* with the 'Song of Four Seasons,' " page 95). This placement ensures that Alice's life will pass without worry. She has good luck and good fortune. She is very stable and marries well.

At this point a Chinese practitioner consults Alice's Ten-Year Fate Cycles (fig. 3.11) to determine the quality and outcome of events from birth through her eighties or nineties. For the sake of space, only seventy years of this personal chronology will be discussed below.

Alice's *miao* for June 15, 1952, is the *ba tze* pair 3/VII (third column in fig. 3.20). Her *hua*'s *ba tze* pair is 7/XI (second column in fig. 3.20). According to the position of her *miao*'s *ti chih* (VII in fig. 3.20) at birth, women play an important role during Alice's first three years of life (VII in fig. 3.11). Since the relationship between the *hsing* that govern the birth *miao*'s *ti chih* (the fire *hsing* rules *ti chih* VII in fig. 3.2) and the birth *hua*'s *t'ien kan* (the metal *hsing* rules *t'ien kan* 7 in fig. 3.1) is negative (fig. 3.14), her encounters with women at this very early age have an adverse impact on her life.

Between the ages of three and thirteen, her progressed *miao*'s *ti chih* is VIII (see "Locating and Interpreting the Birth *Miao*," page 65). So although Alice's second fate cycle is placed in the eighth fate house (sickness and distress, in fig. 3.11), she gains strength despite the illness or stress she experiences during her third through thirteenth years because the *hsings*' relationship stimulates positive outcomes to difficult situations.

From the age of thirteen to her twenty-third birthday, her progressed *miao*'s *ti chih* is IX (see "Locating and Interpreting the Birth *Miao*," page 65). Therefore, during her third fate cycle, Alice experiences many changes of residence and travels to foreign lands since her *miao ti chih* (IX in fig. 3.11) is governed by the metal *hsing* (fig. 3.2) and occupies the ninth fate house (removal, change, and travel in fig. 3.10). Since the metal *hsing* also rules her *hua*'s *t'ien kan* (figs. 3.13 and 3.1),[15] the events that occur during this ten-year period are filled with both energy and sadness. She is guided solely by her feelings with passionate intensity (see the interpretation of the *hsing* in "Locating and Interpreting the Birth *Gen*," page 49), because the relationship of the two *hsing* is static (metal *hsing* to metal *hsing*) and so has no complementary or contrasting energy to temper this prognostication.

The fourth fate cycle, which governs Alice's life from age twenty-three until age

---

15. Alice was born in a leap year (1952 is a double-underscored year in fig. 3.6). Therefore, one day was added to her date of birth to determine her *hua*'s *tien kan* used in fig. 3.13.

thirty-three, is directed by her progressed *miao*'s *ti chih*, which is X (see "Locating and Interpreting the Birth *Miao*," page 65). Alice's fourth fate cycle (X in fig. 3.11) suggests that she develops her professional life during this period and receives rewards or a high position for her efforts. The relationship between the *hsing* that govern the progressed *miao*'s *ti chih* (the metal *hsing* rules *ti chih* X in fig. 3.2) and the birth *hua*'s *t'ien kan* (the metal *hsing* rules *t'ien kan* 7 in fig. 3.1) indicates that she is guided solely by her feelings with passionate intensity (see the interpretation of the *hsing* in "Locating and Interpreting the Birth *Gen*," page 49). This is because the relationship of the two *hsing* is also static, having no complementary or contrasting energy to temper the energy that governs her decisions.

Between the ages of thirty-three and forty-three, her progressed *miao*'s *ti chih* is XI (see "Locating and Interpreting the Birth *Miao*," page 65). Therefore, Alice's fifth fate cycle (XI in fig. 3.11) indicates that she experiences good fortune and encounters many opportunities during that period. Since the relationship between the *hsing* that govern the progressed *miao*'s *ti chih* (the earth *hsing* rules *ti chih* XI in fig. 3.2) and the birth *hua*'s *t'ien kan* (the metal *hsing* rules *t'ien kan* 7 in fig. 3.1) is mutually productive and positive (fig. 3.14), she gains strength and wisdom from her experiences.

From the age of forty-three to her fifty-third birthday, her progressed *miao*'s *ti chih* is XII (see "Locating and Interpreting the Birth *Miao*," page 65) and ruled by the water *hsing* (fig. 3.2). Therefore, Alice's sixth fate cycle (XII in fig. 3.11), which focuses on her manner and bearing, indicates that she is guided solely by her feelings with passionate intensity. She is a communicator who inspires others with her calm and respectability. Since the relationship between the *hsing* that govern the progressed *miao*'s *ti chih* (the water *hsing* rules *ti chih* XII in fig. 3.2) and the birth *hua*'s *t'ien kan* (the metal *hsing* rules *t'ien kan* 7 in fig. 3.1) is mutually productive and positive (fig. 3.14), she gains emotional strength from her experiences.

The seventh fate cycle, which governs Alice's life from ages fifty-three to sixty-three, is directed by her progressed *miao*'s *ti chih*, which is I (see "Locating and Interpreting the Birth *Miao*," page 65). Alice's seventh fate cycle (I in fig. 3.11) suggests that she encounters her ultimate destiny during this period. The relationship between the *hsing* that govern the progressed *miao*'s *ti chih* (the water *hsing* rules *ti chih* I in fig. 3.2) and the birth *hua*'s *t'ien kan* (the metal *hsing* rules *t'ien kan* 7 in fig. 3.1) is positive (fig. 3.14). She inspires others to act on her concepts, and her opinionated outlook guides her through hard times and false starts.

Peter's Personality Profile

According to the *Ming Shu* (see "Interpreting the *Ming Shu*," page 57), Peter was born in a *lung* (Dragon) year (1964 in fig. 3.4), which means that Peter can succeed at anything. He is highly intelligent and only follows his own personal judgment. However, unless his blunt personality edges are curbed and he learns both patience and tolerance, success will elude this otherwise lucky person. Peter is often loved, but seldom falls in love.

Peter's year *hsing* is wood (third column in fig. 3.4), which indicates that he has a creative mind and the ability to develop revolutionary ideas. Peter is compulsively inquisitive at times, and can be condescending toward others. He generally hides a domineering spirit, but can still be very outspoken.

Using a general version of the *Tzu P'ing* form of interpretation, Peter's *Ssu Chu* (fig. 3.21) reveals additional facets of his personal profile. His *gen's ba tze* pair (1/V in "Locating and Interpreting the Birth *Gen*," page 49) in his *Ssu Chu* (fig. 3.21), in-dicates he is a prudent, faithful person because of the earth *hsing* that rules his *gen's ti chih* (V in fig. 3.21). He is practical, conservative, and reliable, moving cautiously and shrewdly, measuring each action for its potential result. He loves delving deeply into any matter, finding critical details as well as bits of trivia along the way. The wood *hsing* that rules his *gen's t'ien kan* (1 in fig. 3.21) strengthens his high ethical and moral standards as well as his self-confidence and compassion. It also makes him behave in a relaxed fashion, even though his primary emotion is anger. A lover of nature and children, Peter is a rustic and creative person. He knows how to delegate and organize.

His *gen's ba tze* pair is governed by the fire *hsing* and has the poetic name of "fire of the lamp" (1/V in fig. 3.5). This affects Peter's behavior and emotions by intro-ducing wisdom and volatility as well as strengthening the natural leadership quali-ties he possesses from the wood-*hsing* influence exerted by his *gen's t'ien kan* (1 in fig. 3.21). The fire *hsing* also intensifies his self-confidence, making him somewhat egotistical. Physically, the combination of the two *hsing* (earth and wood) as well as this third *hsing* (fire) potentially create a tall, thin, straight-standing person with soft skin, thick features, red lips, aquiline nose, and a flat stomach.

Peter's *Ssu Chu* (fig. 3.21) reveals that his *guo's ti chih* is V (first column in fig. 3.21), placed on the emperor's feet (second column in fig. 3.18) in the "Song of the Four Seasons" (see "Applying the Birth *Guo* with the 'Song of the Four Seasons,'" page 95). This placement assures that Peter's fortune is in the intellectual and spiri-tual worlds. He must live in the wilderness or in seclusion.

At this point a Chinese practitioner consults Peter's Ten-Year Fate Cycles (fig. 3.12) to determine the quality and outcome of events from birth to his eighties or nineties. For the sake of space, only seventy years of this personal chronology will be discussed below.

Peter C.'s *miao* for August 27, 1964, is the *ba tze* pair 9/IX (third column in fig. 3.21). His *hua's ba tze* pair is 10/XII (second column in fig. 3.21). According to the position of his birth *miao*'s *ti chih* (IX), removal and change as well as travel abroad are his birthright (IX in fig. 3.12) from his birth until he's four years old. Since the relationship between the *hsing* that govern the birth *miao*'s *ti chih* (the metal *hsing* rules *ti chih* IX in fig. 3.2) and the birth *hua*'s *t'ien kan* (the water *hsing* rules *t'ien kan* 10 in fig. 3.1) is positive (fig. 3.14), the changes and opportunities for travel afforded him by his legacy yield positive results. The combined metal- and water-*hsing* influences make him appear calm and respectable while exerting energy with passionate intensity (see the interpretation of the *hsing* in "Identifying and Locating the Birth *Gen*," page 49).

During his second fate cycle, his progressed *miao ti chih* is X (fig. 3.12), which is ruled by the metal *hsing* and *yin* (fig. 3.2). This indicates that between his fourth and fourteenth birthdays, life concentrates on matters governed by his tenth fate house (official and reward, in fig. 3.13). The metal-*hsing* influence makes him act with passionate intensity. His determined and somewhat rigid, opinionated outlook guides him through hard times and false starts. Ultimately he receives honor, reward, and status during this period (see the interpretation of the *hsing* in "Locating and Interpreting the Birth *Gen*," page 49). The relationship of the two *hsing* is positive (fig. 3.14): the metal *hsing* to his water *hsing* (his *hua*'s *t'ien kan* is 10, fig. 3.13, and is ruled by the water *hsing* and *yin*, fig. 3.1) indicates that he appears calm while exerting a great deal of energy during this period.

During his third fate cycle, his progressed *miao ti chih* is XI (see "Locating and Interpreting the Birth *Miao*," page 65, and fig. 3.12), which is also ruled by the earth *hsing* and *yang* (fig. 3.2). This indicates that between his fourteenth and twenty-fourth birthdays, life concentrates on matters governed by his eleventh fate house (good fortune and virtue, in fig. 3.12). The earth-*hsing* influence makes him move cautiously and shrewdly (see the interpretation of the *hsing* in "Locating and Interpreting the Birth *Gen*," page 49). The relationship of the earth *hsing* and the water *hsing* that rules his *hua*'s *t'ien kan* (10 in fig. 3.13) suggests that during this period his desires might override his ability to communicate and inspire others, because fig. 3.14 tells us that earth absorbs water.

During his fourth fate cycle, his progressed *miao ti chih* is XII (fig. 3.12), which is ruled by the water *hsing* and *yin* (fig. 3.2). This indicates that between his twenty-fourth and thirty-fourth birthdays, life concentrates on matters governed by his twelfth fate house (manner and bearing, in fig. 3.14). He is a communicator who inspires others with his calm and respectability (see the interpretation of the *hsing* in "Locating and Interpreting the Birth *Gen*," page 49). Since the relationship between the *hsing* that govern the progressed *miao*'s *ti chih* (the water *hsing* rules *ti chih* I in fig. 3.2) and the birth *hua*'s *t'ien kan* (the water *hsing* rules *t'ien kan* 10 in fig. 3.1) is static, water *hsing* to water *hsing*, it has no complementary or contrasting energy.

Chinese practitioners believe that when the progressed *miao* enters the first fate house (destiny or fate), an individual develops his or her life potential during that ten-year period. From his thirty-fourth through forty-fourth birthdays, his progressed *miao*'s *ti chih* is I, which is ruled by the water *hsing* and *yin* (fig. 3.2). (See "Locating and Interpreting the Birth *Miao*," page 65 and fig. 3.12.) Peter's communication skills and his natural talents as an artisan or tradesperson are accentuated during this period (see the interpretation of the *hsing* in "Locating and Interpreting the Birth *Gen*," page 49). His ultimate destiny in life concentrates on these skills, and takes shape during this ten-year period. Since the relationship between the *hsing* that govern the progressed *miao*'s *ti chih* (the water *hsing* rules *ti chih* I in fig. 3.2) and the birth *hua*'s *t'ien kan* (the water *hsing* rules *t'ien kan* 10 in fig. 3.1) is static (water *hsing* to water *hsing*), there is no complementary or contrasting energy.

The sixth fate cycle, which governs Peter's life from the ages of forty-four to fifty-four, is directed by his progressed *miao*'s *ti chih*, which is II (see "Locating and Interpreting the Birth *Miao*," page 65). Peter's sixth fate cycle (II in fig. 3.12) suggests that he attains riches and wealth because of the efforts he exerts during this period. The relationship between the *hsing* that govern the progressed *miao*'s *ti chih* (the earth *hsing* rules *ti chih* II in fig. 3.2) and the birth *hua*'s *t'ien kan* (the water *hsing* rules *t'ien kan* 10 in fig. 3.1) is negative (fig. 3.14). His earth-*hsing* influence makes him driven by the desire to be a businessperson. This overrides his water-*hsing* ability to communicate and inspire other people (see "Locating and Interpreting the Birth *Gen*," page 49).

Between the ages of fifty-four and sixty-four, his progressed *miao*'s *ti chih* is III (see "Locating and Interpreting the Birth *Miao*," page 65). Therefore, Peter's seventh fate cycle (III in fig. 3.12) indicates that emotions and affections have great importance in his life during this period. Brothers and sisters also play a key role at that time. Since the relationship between the *hsing* that govern the progressed *miao*'s *ti chih* (the wood *hsing* rules *ti chih* III in fig. 3.2) and the birth *hua*'s *t'ien kan* (the water *hsing* rules *t'ien kan* 10 in fig. 3.1) is mutually productive and positive (fig. 3.14), he gains emotional strength and wisdom from his experiences.

After a personality profile like the two examples above has been created by the astrologer, answers to everyday matters are produced by consulting one of two forms of daily prediction, such as the day indicator, which employs the birth *hua* (see "Using the Birth *Hua* for Daily Prediction," page 90), or by applying a system called the daily *sieu*.

LOCATING AND INTERPRETING THE *SIEU* (LUNAR MANSION)

As mentioned at the beginning of this chapter, there are many forms of Chinese astrology that concentrate on determining an individual's behavioral patterns, emotional makeup, physical appearance, material wealth, and portion of good fortune. And, as shown in a previous section, the day that a person was born is also used to determine the potential outcome of daily activities. Another popular form of daily prediction used in China directs its attention to the Moon's orbital path to ascertain if the time is right to begin or end a large-scale project, to conduct a marriage or funeral, to ask for favors, or to travel.

The Moon's daily movements were documented and detailed nearly 4,400 years ago as it passed by each of twenty-eight *sieu* (lunar mansions) during its cyclical orbit.[16] Each *sieu* is ruled by a fixed star (see chapter 2, fig. 2.1), and each fixed star is located in one of the four arcs of constellations identified by ancient Chinese observers: the Green Dragon, the White Tiger, the Dark Warrior, and the Red Bird.[17] The *sieu* move in a parallel direction to the traditional sixty-year cycle of the Chinese luni-solar calendar (see "Locating and Interpreting the Birth *Miao*," page 65). All Chinese almanacs display the daily *sieu*, which are frequently used by both astrological practitioners and laypeople to ascertain the direction of a day's events. Since Chinese almanacs are only published in Chinese, making them difficult for most westerners to use, the charts found in figs. 3.22 and 3.23 can be used to determine the *sieu* for any given day between 1924 and 2050.

To identify the *sieu* for a specific day, find the day in fig. 3.22 (first, third, or fifth columns), below, noting the *sieu* in the right-hand column (second, fourth, or sixth columns). Then locate the year in question in fig. 3.23 (first, third, fifth, or seventh columns) and note the index number in the right-hand column (second, fourth, sixth, and eighth columns). Add the *sieu* and the index number together. If

---

16. The Moon travels through all 360 degrees of the constellational zodiac during its annual cycle. Since medieval times, Western astrologers have subdivided the Moon's annual path into twenty-eight transit points, which are positioned 13°00′ apart and were originally called "lunar mansions." In modern times they have evolved into the "critical degrees." Loosely, the medieval lunar mansions followed the same pattern as the Arabian *manazils*, the Vedic *naksatras*, and the Chinese *sieu*. Some early Western astrologers claimed that the critical degrees occurred only at the cusps of the first (Cornua Arietis [γ Aries]), eighth (Nebulosa [θ Cancer]), fifteenth (Cornua Scorpionis [α Libra]), and twenty-second (Pastor et Aries [α Capricorn]) medieval European lunar mansions. But most practitioners adopted the Arabian pattern.

Unlike the Chinese, Arabian, and Vedic methods, which apply the event's influence to the entire arc, a critical degree lasts only for the extent of its initial one-day transit, affecting a person's reaction to external forces, sudden and unexpected occurrences, and changes in plans. These events reach an intense peak at this juncture, so careful attention is paid if a critical degree appears in a natal chart. Rounded out to whole degrees, the modern-day critical degrees are located at 00°♈00′, 13°♈00′, 26°♈00′, 09°♉00′, 21°♉00′, 04°♊00′, 17°♊00′, 00°♋00′, 13°♋00′, 26°♋00′, 09°♌00′, 21°♌00′, 04°♍00′, 17°♍00′, 00°♎00′, 13°♎00′, 26°♎00′, 09°♏00′, 21°♏00′, 04°♐00′, 17°♐00′, 00°♑00′, 13°♑00′, 26°♑00′, 09°♒00′, 21°♒00′, 04°♓00′, and 17°♓00′.

17. Japanese astrologers adopted this system by the seventh century A.D., calling them *sei shuku* (moon stations), which are used for the same purposes.

FIGURE 3.22. TABLE OF *SIEU* FOR EACH DAY OF THE YEAR.

Day	Sieu	Day	Sieu	Day	Sieu	Day	Sieu	Day	Sieu	Day	Sieu
Jan. 1	1	Feb. 1	4	Mar. 1	4	Apr. 1	7	May 1	9	Jun. 1	12
2	2	2	5	2	5	2	8	2	10	2	13
3	3	3	6	3	6	3	9	3	11	3	14
4	4	4	7	4	7	4	10	4	12	4	15
5	5	5	8	5	8	5	11	5	13	5	16
6	6	6	9	6	9	6	12	6	14	6	17
7	7	7	10	7	10	7	13	7	15	7	18
8	8	8	11	8	11	8	14	8	16	8	19
9	9	9	12	9	12	9	15	9	17	9	20
10	10	10	13	10	13	10	16	10	18	10	21
11	11	11	14	11	14	11	17	11	19	11	22
12	12	12	15	12	15	12	18	12	20	12	23
13	13	13	16	13	16	13	19	13	21	13	24
14	14	14	17	14	17	14	20	14	22	14	25
15	15	15	18	15	18	15	21	15	23	15	26
16	16	16	19	16	19	16	22	16	24	16	27
17	17	17	20	17	20	17	23	17	25	17	28
18	18	18	21	18	21	18	24	18	26	18	1
19	19	19	22	19	22	19	25	19	27	19	2
20	20	20	23	20	23	20	26	20	28	20	3
21	21	21	24	21	24	21	27	21	1	21	4
22	22	22	25	22	25	22	28	22	2	22	5
23	23	23	26	23	26	23	1	23	3	23	6
24	24	24	27	24	27	24	2	24	4	24	7
25	25	25	28	25	28	25	3	25	5	25	8
26	26	26	1	26	1	26	4	26	6	26	9
27	27	27	2	27	2	27	5	27	7	27	10
28	28	28	3	28	3	28	6	28	8	28	11
29	1	(29)		29	4	29	7	29	9	29	12
30	2			30	5	30	8	30	10	30	13
31	3			31	6			31	11		

the year in question was or will be a leap year (double-underscored years in the first column of fig. 3.6), then add 1 to the sum. If the final total is greater than 28, subtract 28 from the sum. The remainder is the actual *sieu* for that date.

The day *sieu* is delineated according to both the literal and figurative interpretations of the traditional concepts presented in the following pages. As mentioned earlier, each *sieu* is associated with an arc of constellations and a fixed star. But it is also allied with a symbolic animal (not to be confused with the *Ming Shu* signs), a planet, and a variety of other activities.

Day	Sieu	Day	Sieu	Day	Sieu	Day	Sieu	Day	Sieu	Day	Sieu
Jul. 1	14	Aug. 1	17	Sep. 1	20	Oct. 1	22	Nov. 1	25	Dec. 1	27
2	15	2	18	2	21	2	23	2	26	2	28
3	16	3	19	3	22	3	24	3	27	3	1
4	17	4	20	4	23	4	25	4	28	4	2
5	18	5	21	5	24	5	26	5	1	5	3
6	19	6	22	6	25	6	27	6	2	6	4
7	20	7	23	7	26	7	28	7	3	7	5
8	21	8	24	8	27	8	1	8	4	8	6
9	22	9	25	9	28	9	2	9	5	9	7
10	23	10	26	10	1	10	3	10	6	10	8
11	24	11	27	11	2	11	4	11	7	11	9
12	25	12	28	12	3	12	5	12	8	12	10
13	26	13	1	13	4	13	6	13	9	13	11
14	27	14	2	14	5	14	7	14	10	14	12
15	28	15	3	15	6	15	8	15	11	15	13
16	1	16	4	16	7	16	9	16	12	16	14
17	2	17	5	17	8	17	10	17	13	17	15
18	3	18	6	18	9	18	11	18	14	18	16
19	4	19	7	19	10	19	12	19	15	19	17
20	5	20	8	20	11	20	13	20	16	20	18
21	6	21	9	21	12	21	14	21	17	21	19
22	7	22	10	22	13	22	15	22	18	22	20
23	8	23	11	23	14	23	16	23	19	23	21
24	9	24	12	24	15	24	17	24	20	24	22
25	10	25	13	25	16	25	18	25	21	25	23
26	11	26	14	26	17	26	19	26	22	26	24
27	12	27	15	27	18	27	20	27	23	27	25
28	13	28	16	28	19	28	21	28	24	28	26
29	14	29	17	29	20	29	22	29	25	29	27
30	15	30	18	30	21	30	23	30	26	30	28
31	16	31	19			31	24			31	1

1. *Ch'io*
(Horn)

Located in the eastern arc of the Green Dragon, its symbolic animal is the crocodile. This is a lucky day associated with the Wood Planet (Jupiter, ♃) and with favorable winds and rains, as well as agriculture and horticulture. It presides over marriage, birth, and growth. Partnerships and marriages taking place on this day result in numerous children or family endeavors. It's an ideal day to work on construction or to buy land. It brings glory and prosperity to projects started on this day. People who think

FIGURE 3.23. TABLE OF YEAR NUMBERS.

YEAR	INDEX NUMBER	YEAR	INDEX NUMBER	YEAR	INDEX NUMBER	YEAR	INDEX NUMBER
1924	5	1956	17	1988	1	2020	13
1925	7	1957	19	1989	3	2021	15
1926	8	1958	20	1990	4	2022	16
1927	9	1959	21	1991	5	2023	17
1928	10	1960	22	1992	6	2024	18
1929	12	1961	24	1993	8	2025	20
1930	13	1962	25	1994	9	2026	21
1931	14	1963	26	1995	10	2027	22
1932	15	1964	27	1996	11	2028	23
1933	17	1965	1	1997	13	2029	25
1934	18	1966	2	1998	14	2030	26
1935	19	1967	3	1999	15	2031	27
1936	20	1968	4	2000	16	2032	0
1937	22	1969	6	2001	18	2033	2
1938	23	1970	7	2002	19	2034	3
1939	24	1971	8	2003	20	2035	4
1940	25	1972	9	2004	21	2036	5
1941	27	1973	11	2005	23	2037	7
1942	0	1974	12	2006	24	2038	8
1943	1	1975	13	2007	25	2039	9
1944	2	1976	14	2008	26	2040	10
1945	4	1977	16	2009	0	2041	12
1946	5	1978	17	2010	1	2042	13
1947	6	1979	18	2011	2	2043	14
1948	7	1980	19	2012	3	2044	15
1949	9	1981	21	2013	5	2045	17
1950	10	1982	22	2014	6	2046	18
1951	11	1983	23	2015	7	2047	19
1952	12	1984	24	2016	8	2048	20
1953	14	1985	26	2017	10	2049	22
1954	15	1986	27	2018	11	2050	23
1955	16	1987	0	2019	12		

for a living may ask for favors from superiors. However, this *sieu* adversely influences endings and funerals, causing problems and even disasters within the next three years.

2. *K'ang* (Neck)

Located in the eastern arc of the Green Dragon, its symbolic animal is the dragon. It's an unlucky day associated with the Water Planet (Mercury, ☿), weather extremes, and the chemical industry. It presides over judgments and punishments. This *sieu* adversely influences construction, marriages, and funerals. Do not start anything on this day, and do not undertake anything for the next ten days because a disaster may occur. Marriages or partnerships and funerals or conclusions to projects cause untimely death.

3. *Ti*
(Base)

Located in the eastern arc of the Green Dragon, its symbolic animal is the badger. It is an unlucky day associated with the Earth Planet (Saturn, ♄) and strong rains and winds, as well as the aviation and patent-medicine industries. This *sieu* presides over proper actions and adversely influences marriages and travel on ships or boats. Do not start anything on this day. Marriages or partnerships bring calamities. Journeys on the water may result in a shipwreck. Funerals or conclusions to projects cause the impoverishment of the deceased's descendants.

4. *Fang*
(Room)

Located in the eastern arc of the Green Dragon, its symbolic animal is the hare or rabbit. It's a lucky day associated with the Sun, heat, and interior decorators. This *sieu* presides over building interiors. The planetary reference linked to this *sieu* varies. Projects started on this day bring wealth and abundant prosperity. Happiness, longevity, honor, riches and glory are forthcoming. If endings or funerals occur today, the people responsible are promoted.

5. *Hsin*
(Heart)

Located in the eastern arc of the Green Dragon, its symbolic animal is the fox. It's an unlucky day associated with the Moon and heads of state. This *sieu* presides over imperial power, and adversely influences ambitious plans. The planetary reference linked to this *sieu* varies. Projects started on this day lead to ruin sooner or later. Marriages or partnerships and funerals or endings are viewed as disastrous by others and assure three years of repeated calamities.

6. *Wei*
(Tail)

Located in the eastern arc of the Green Dragon, its symbolic animal is the tiger. It's a lucky day associated with the Fire Planet (Mars, ♂) and the heir apparent of a family. This *sieu* presides over boats, dams, legacies, mothers, and children. Projects started on this day are assured blessings and numerous progeny. Undertaking any business matter or planting assures prosperity to descendants. Funerals or endings and marriages or partnerships lead to the ennoblement of the entire family.

7. *Chi*
(Basket)

Located in the eastern arc of the Green Dragon, its symbolic animal is the leopard. It's a lucky day associated with the Water Planet (Mercury, ☿) and prosperity in general. This *sieu* presides over new projects and burials; it also adversely influences slander and gossip. Projects started on this day are assured power and good fortune. Marriages or partnerships and the repair of past projects are beneficial.

8. *Tou*
(Ladle)

Located in the northern arc of the Dark Warrior, its symbolic animal is the unicorn. It's a lucky day associated with the Wood Planet (Jupiter, ♃), rains and floods, rewards, and businesses that involve oil or wine. This *sieu* presides over building and digging. Starting projects on this day assures an abundance of wealth. To organize an ending or celebrate a conclusion ensures the prosperity of descendants. To open an establishment or factory ensures expansion in the future of some other enterprise. A marriage or partnership is guaranteed many overlapping happinesses.

9. *Niu*
(Buffalo)

Located in the northern arc of the Dark Warrior, its symbolic animal is the buffalo. It's an unlucky day associated with the Metal Planet (Venus, ♀) and the real-estate business. This *sieu* presides over roads, paths, and land; it adversely influences marriages. Projects started on this day produce nothing but danger. Cultivated projects or plantings do not reap a profit. A marriage, a partnership, or the opening of a business becomes a sea of troubles.

10. *Nü*
(Maiden)

Located in the northern arc of the Dark Warrior, its symbolic animal is the bat. It is an unlucky day associated with the Earth Planet (Saturn, ♄) and the weaving industry. This *sieu* presides over property and dowry; it adversely influences funerals. Starting a project on this day is damaging to women and will make men quarrel. Marriage or partnerships and funerals or endings cause luck to disappear, or create sudden removals.

11. *Hsü*
(Void)

Located in the northern arc of the Dark Warrior, its symbolic animal is the rat. It's an unlucky day associated with the Sun, rains and cold, undertakers, and frozen foods. This *sieu* presides over cemeteries and adversely influences marriages. The planetary reference linked to this *sieu* varies. Starting projects on this day is calamitous. A lack of organization or sense of order brings trouble.

12. *Wei*
(Roof)

Located in the northern arc of the Dark Warrior, its symbolic animal is the swallow. It's an unlucky day associated with the Moon and the building industry. This *sieu* presides over fortification, and adversely influences travel. The planetary reference linked to this *sieu* varies. Large projects should not be started on this day, and neither should large-scale endings. Either causes great losses. To open a business or to plant something new in the fields causes continual unhappiness and lawsuits.

13. *Shih*
(House)

Located in the northern arc of the Dark Warrior, its symbolic animal is the pig. It's a lucky day associated with the Fire Planet (Mars, ♂) and religious orders. This *sieu* presides over physical work in general. Projects started today bring long-lasting increases and general prosperity. Marriages or partnerships and funerals or endings take cares away forever.

14. *Pi*
(Wall)

Located in the northern arc of the Dark Warrior, its symbolic animal is the porcupine. It's a lucky day associated with the Water Planet (Mercury, ☿), literature, and the arts. This *sieu* presides over marriages and expansions. Projects or enterprises started on this day bring great prosperity. Marriages or partnerships cause peace and joy. Funerals or endings assure wealth and long-lasting prosperity.

15. *K'uei*
(Astride)

Located in the western arc of the White Tiger, its symbolic animal is the wolf. It's an unlucky day associated with the Wood Planet (Jupiter, ♃), cold weather, textiles, and shoes. This *sieu* presides over clothing, canals, and armaments; it adversely influences digging. Building on this day is very lucky, bringing harmony and prosperity to the home. Ending a project or celebrating a funeral produces a mysterious and unfortunate end. To conduct continuing business only attracts calamities.

16. *Lou*
(Mound)

Located in the western arc of the White Tiger, its symbolic animal is the dog. It's a lucky day associated with the Metal Planet

(Venus, ♀), wet and mildly cool weather, and the pharmacy business. This *sieu* presides over symphonic music and festivities. Building supports on an existing project increases its value and everything prospers if constructed on this day. Marriages and partnerships are fruitful. Children of the person born on this day gain honors and social promotion.

17. *Wei*
(Stomach)

Located in the western arc of the White Tiger, its symbolic animal is the pheasant. It's a lucky day associated with the Earth Planet (Saturn, ♄), floods, and the banking industry. This *sieu* presides over marriages, burials, investments, and earthworks. It adversely influences imprisonment. Projects started on this day generate a windfall of riches and glory. Endings or funerals assure social promotion. Marriages or partnerships usher in growth and flourishing harmony.

18. *Mao*
(Lights)

Located in the western arc of the White Tiger, its symbolic animal is the rooster. It's an unlucky day associated with the Sun and the legal profession. This *sieu* presides over judgments; it adversely influences marriages, funerals, family reunions, construction, and digging. The planetary reference linked to this *sieu* varies. Starting projects on this day allows slower, rigid-minded people to step all over the foundations, leading to calamities. Funerals and endings bring incessant worries. Marriages or partnerships bring misery.

19. *Pi*
(Net)

Located in the western arc of the White Tiger, its symbolic animal is the crow. It is a lucky day associated with the Moon, rains, and the military. This *sieu* presides over marriages and hunting; it adversely influences exiles, deserters, and frontiers. The planetary reference linked to this *sieu* varies. Projects started on this day bring light to their creator. Cultivating projects that already exist yields long-lasting abundance. Luck and blessings knock at the door. Marriages or partnerships and funerals or endings bring double longevity.

20. *Tsui*
(Beak)

Located in the western arc of the White Tiger, its symbolic animal is the monkey. It's an unlucky day associated with the Fire Planet (Mars, ♂) and animal breeding. This *sieu* presides over flocks and herds as well as the afflicted. It adversely influences executions. Starting a project today invites a lawsuit. Celebrating a funeral or ending invites collapse of the enterprise and the depletion of reserves.

21. *Shen* (Three Associates)

Located in the western arc of the White Tiger, its symbolic animal is the gibbon. It's a lucky day associated with the Water Planet (Mercury, ☿) and authorship. This *sieu* presides over labor, and adversely influences the completion of projects. Starting projects brings ample prosperity. Nurturing business that is already in existence occurs under happy auspices. But funerals or endings and marriages or partnerships shatter the family or business order. According to the ancient text, "The star of the lettered person will bring light."

22. *Ching* (Well)

Located in the southern arc of the Red Bird, its symbolic animal is the tapir. It's a lucky day associated with the Water Planet (Mercury, ☿), rains, the civil service, and veterinary surgery. This *sieu* presides over widows and examinations; it also adversely influences delays, postponements, and burials. Starting projects that will be steadily cultivated brings prosperity. Every enterprise brings money and numerous inheritors. Take extra care around funerals for those who have died violently, or endings that take place under volatile sentiments. According to the ancient text, "The family name is the first on the golden list."

23. *Kuei* (Ghosts)

Located in the southern arc of the Red Bird, its symbolic animal is the goat. It's an unlucky day associated with the Metal Planet (Venus, ♀). This *sieu* presides over respect for the dead. Starting a project on this day may cause disappearances as well as the loss of its creator. The celebration of funerals or endings creates advancement, but a marriage or partnership sees "a woman lonely in the nuptial chamber."

24. *Liu* (Willow)

Located in the southern arc of the Red Bird, its symbolic animal is the buck. It's an unlucky day associated with the Earth Planet (Saturn, ♄). Projects started on this day lead to trouble in the courts. Disasters and thieves put the "house" in danger. Marriages or partnerships and funerals or endings are a prelude to many miseries.

25. *Hsing* (Star)

Located in the southern arc of the Red Bird, its symbolic animal is the horse. It is an unlucky day associated with the Sun, heat, and the garment business. This *sieu* presides over bridges and dyestuffs; it adversely influences marriages and funerals. The planetary reference linked to this *sieu* varies. This is a good day for starting projects. Prosperity and advancement are noticed by those in authority. But, according to one translation, "a funeral or to proceed with [the] irrigation [of a rice or wheat field] causes the wife to abandon her hearth and look for another man."

26. *Chang* (Bow)   Located in the southern arc of the Red Bird, its symbolic animal is a stag. It is a lucky day associated with the Moon, and the business of the theater. This *sieu* also presides over festivities and entertainment. The planetary reference linked to this *sieu* varies. If building toward something specific on this day, everyone involved with the project is in favor with those in authority. Celebrating funerals or endings or nursing pet projects attracts money and riches. Marriages or partnerships are the cause of ceaseless happiness and harmony.

27. *I* (Wings)   Located in the southern arc of the Red Bird, its symbolic animal is the snake. It's an unlucky day associated with the Fire Planet (Mars, ♂) and politics. This *sieu* presides over ceremonial rites and adversely influences marriages, funerals, and leaving home. Don't start any lofty projects on this day. A new venture may bring about the demise of its creators. Marriages or partnerships and funerals or endings do not bring prosperity. And, according to the text, "Young girls run after boys away from home."

28. *Chen* (Carriage)   Located in the southern arc of the Red Bird, its symbolic animal is the earthworm. It's a lucky day associated with the Water Planet (Mercury, ☿) and wind and storms. It presides over travel, speed, marriage, digging, and construction. This *sieu* is also connected with the business of transport and landscape gardening. Starting projects on this day attracts promotion. A marriage or partnership receives the blessing of those in authority. To celebrate funerals or endings makes "bright the star of the lettered person." Prosperity is immense.

For example, to find the *sieu* associated with January 1, 2000, locate the day in fig. 3.22 (first column) and note the *sieu* (second column), which is 1. Find the year

2000 in fig. 3.23 (fifth column) and note the index number (sixth column), which is 16. Add 1 and 16 to get the sum 17. According to the first column in fig. 3.6, 2000 is a leap year. So add 1 to the sum (17) to get the *sieu*, 18.

Based on the material above, this *sieu* indicates that it is an unlucky day that adversely influences marriages, partnerships, funerals, conclusions to major projects, family reunions, construction, and digging. (Some modern astrologers would add that it's also a bad day to deal with courts, judgments of any kind, or research.) Starting projects on this day is also ill-advised because slower, rigid-minded people will step all over the main concept or foundations of the project, leading to calamities.

The same method of calculation is sometimes applied to ascertain the *sieu* that is associated with an individual's birth, loosely indicating the person's general luck with regard to large-scale projects, marriage, business, and funerals. For example, Alice was born on June 15, which is *sieu* 26 according to fig. 3.22 (fifth and sixth columns). The index number for her year of birth (1952) is 12 in fig. 3.23 (first and second columns). The sum of the two numbers is 38. Since her birth year was a leap year (a double-underscored year in the first column of fig. 3.6), 1 is added to the sum of 38. The final total is 39. Since there are only twenty-eight *sieu*, 28 is subtracted from the sum. The remainder, 11, is Alice's birth *sieu*.

Based on the interpretative material above, Alice is unlucky when it comes to marriage. The troubles that beset her in life stem primarily from a lack of organization or sense of order.

Peter was born on August 27, which is *sieu* 15 according to fig. 3.22 (third and fourth columns). And the index number for his year of birth (1964) is 25 in fig. 3.23 (second and third columns). The sum of the two numbers is 40. Since his birth year was a leap year (double-underscored years in the first column of fig. 3.6), 1 is added to the sum. The final total, 41, is greater than 28, so 28 is subtracted from the sum. The remainder, 13, is Peter's birth *sieu*. According to the interpretative material above, this indicates that he will experience long-lasting increases and general prosperity. It also suggests that marriages or partnerships take his cares away forever.

———— ✳ ————

The forms of Chinese astrology presented in this chapter are unique because of their relative simplicity, presenting a sharp contrast to western, Judaic, Arabian, and Vedic traditions, which require a person to know the exact hour and minute as well as the precise location of birth to assure an accurate calculation of a natal horoscope. Ancient Chinese peasants only needed to know the year of birth to consult the *Ming Shu*. The year, month, day, an idea of the hour, and the time zone in which the birth took place were the only elements required to practice *Tzu P'ing*.

There are more complex forms, such as the Great Bear method, that incorporate the placement of specific groups of stars or imaginary planets into charts that
closely resemble Western horoscopes. But many of those systems were developed
after the eighth century A.D. None of them were adopted outside of China, unlike
the *sieu*, which was exported to Japan, and the *Ming Shu*, which was introduced
into Tibet around 642 A.D. by the Chinese princess Hun-shin Kun-ju (Kong Jo),
who married Tibet's king Srang-Tsan Gampo.

The
Forces Within

TIBETAN CHART CONSTRUCTION

Adapted from the simplest form of Chinese astrology (the *Ming Shu*), the *jung-tsi* form of Tibetan astrology requires no calculations. Unlike Western, Judaic, Arabian, and Vedic astrologies, all the necessary data are derived from reference tables and the individual's birth year. This lucidity even carries over to the interpretation of the results; but it does not accommodate for as many modern-life questions and concerns over the timing of events as do the Chinese, Vedic, Arabian, Judaic, or Western traditions.

Tibetan astrology's "mother"—Chinese astrology—elevates the influence of the natural elements (fire, water, wood, metal, and earth) and their interrelationships into an intricate web that directs the flow of business, marriage, death, and numerous other specific daily activities. Tibetan astrology, on the other hand, provides valuable insights into the individual natural forces (life, power, luck, spirit, and health) that operate within a given personality, reviewing the "big picture" by identifying the hidden sources of personal power and, ultimately, individual destiny.

This form of astrology was also influenced by the Vedic tradition in its formative years. Evidence of this can be seen in the *Sidpaho*, which is a common Tibetan household accessory used to attract a positive flow of energy. The *Sidpaho* is a stylized image of the perceived universe, depicting the Chinese *Ming Shu* (see "Interpreting the *Ming Shu*" in chapter 3);[1] the eight trigrams that form the basis for *I Ching* divination; the nine prime numbers that form the basis of *lo shu* numerological

---

1. The *Ming Shu* was allegedly introduced in Tibet when the Chinese princess Hun-shin Kung-ju (Kong Jo) married the king of Tibet, Srang-Tsan Gampo, in 642 A.D.

divination;[2] and the *wu hsing* or Five Agents (see "Locating and Interpreting the Birth *Gen*" in chapter 3). Within the same image, Tibetan astrology's "father"—Vedic astrology—can also be found. The eight Vedic *navagrahas*[3] (planets); Manjushri,[4] the God of Divine Wisdom; Vajrapani, the God of Rain; and Chenrazigs, the protector of those who are in distress,[5] are given equal importance in this traditional Tibetan image of the universe.

Like other Moon-school astrologies (Chinese, Vedic, and Judaic), this practice concentrates on striking a harmonic balance between the individual and the universe. This goal is achieved by the careful analysis of the various forms of emotional, spiritual, and physical energy that flow in and out of a person as well as the portion of fate that an individual was allocated at birth by his or her deeds in a previous life.

As many forms of astrology are practiced in Tibet as in China, including *kar-tsi*, which is identical to Vedic astrology. This chapter, however, concentrates solely upon the most popular variation, which employs the Tibetan version of the *Ming Shu* and an individual's year of birth to determine the subject's personality and destiny. There are no formal charts constructed for a visual display of the astrologer's findings. Instead, the practitioner simply writes down the results in his or her interpretation notes.

STEP ONE: DETERMINING AN INDIVIDUAL'S ANIMAL SIGN

Tibetan astrologers use the same luni-solar calendar structure as their Chinese counterparts. An animal sign is designated for each year, as seen in fig. 4.1 (third column). Besides assigning a ruling element (fourth column) and gender (fifth column) for each animal sign, the relationships among the animal signs themselves are grouped into three categories: *thun-sun*, or friends (sixth column); *dun-zur*, or opposites (seventh column); and *shi-shey*, or enemies (eighth column). The Tibetan astrologer finds an individual's animal sign based on the person's year of birth. For example, Alice was born on June 15, 1952. According to fig. 4.1, 1952 (first column) was a *hBrul* (dragon) year (third column). Peter was born on August 27, 1964. According to fig. 4.1, 1964 (first column) was also a *hBrul* (dragon) year (third column).

---

2. According to legend, the nine prime numbers of *Lo Shu* (Writing of the Lo River) appeared to the Emperor Yü on the back of a tortoise in the form of a magic square:

4	9	2
3	5	7
8	1	6

The addition of three digits vertically, horizontally, or diagonally always totals 15.
3. The term used to describe the nine observed planets: Surya (Sun, ☉), Candra (Moon, ☽), Kuja (Mars, ♂), Buddha (Mercury, ☿), Guru (Jupiter, ♃), Sukra (Venus, ♀), Sani (Saturn, ♄), Rahu (Moon's North Node, ☊), and Ketu (Moon's South Node, ☋).
4. The name of this god is sometimes given as Manjushree.
5. This same god is also known as Avalokiteswara in portions of Nepal and India, and as the bodhisattva Kuan-yin in China (called Kannon in Japan).

Each animal sign in the Tibetan version of the *Ming Shu* is attributed with certain personality traits that are similar but not identical to the interpretations employed by Chinese astrologers (see "Interpreting the *Ming Shu*" in chapter 3):

by-bai (rat)	A nervous, intelligent, curious, secretive person who is constantly on the lookout for opportunities, but always misses the big ones. This person is kind but not generous; outspoken and forever searching.
gLan (ox)	He or she likes to sleep, and is stubborn and disobedient. Although difficult to change, this person is surprisingly agreeable when confronted. Slow and procrastinating, he or she has an even temper.
sTag (tiger)	He or she is courageous, brash, and thinks a great deal. This person is business-minded, enjoys gambling, and is very protective of loved ones.
yos (hare)	This person is egotistical, stingy, and extremely independent. The individual is not faithful, honest, nor direct. He or she appears to be quite generous on the surface, however.
hBrul (dragon)	This person listens well, but also talks a lot. He or she dutifully carries out what needs to be done when it needs doing, but does not spring into action. He or she is quick-tempered but well-meaning and good-natured.
sBrul (snake)	He or she is goodhearted but very bad-tempered, and won't reverse an opinion. This person has a self-destructive streak.
rTa (horse)	This person listens well, walks quickly, and loves to play. He or she is self-sacrificing and possesses remarkable endurance. This person's life is like a rollercoaster. Fortunately, the later portion of life is best.
lug (ram)	This person is good-natured, good-hearted, very laid back, and always late. He or she is very quiet and a good provider.
sPre (monkey)	This person is very intelligent and talkative, but also narrow-minded and, at times, untrustworthy, bad-tempered, and too playful. He or she always has big plans, needs self-gratification, and gossips a great deal.

FIGURE 4.1. TABLE OF TIBETAN YEAR NAMES,

YEAR	STARTING DATE	ANIMAL	RULING ELEMENT	GENDER
1924	Feb. 5	*by-bai* (rat)	wood	male
1925	Jan. 24	*gLan* (ox)	wood	female
1926	Feb. 13	*sTag* (tiger)	fire	male
1927	Feb. 2	*yos* (hare)	fire	female
1928	Jan. 28	*hBrul* (dragon)	earth	male
1929	Feb. 10	*sBrul* (snake)	earth	female
1930	Jan. 30	*rTa* (horse)	metal	male
1931	Feb. 17	*lug* (ram)	metal	female
1932	Feb. 6	*sPre* (monkey)	water	male
1933	Jan. 26	*bya* (rooster)	water	female
1934	Feb. 14	*khy* (dog)	wood	male
1935	Feb. 4	*phag* (pig)	wood	female
1936	Jan. 24	*by-bai* (rat)	fire	male
1937	Feb. 11	*gLan* (ox)	fire	female
1938	Jan. 31	*sTag* (tiger)	earth	male
1939	Feb. 19	*yos* (hare)	earth	female
1940	Feb. 8	*hBrul* (dragon)	metal	male
1941	Jan. 27	*sBrul* (snake)	metal	female
1942	Feb. 15	*rTa* (horse)	water	male
1943	Feb. 5	*lug* (ram)	water	female
1944	Jan. 25	*sPre* (monkey)	wood	male
1945	Feb. 13	*bya* (rooster)	wood	female
1946	Feb. 2	*khy* (dog)	fire	male
1947	Jan. 22	*phag* (pig)	fire	female
1948	Feb. 10	*by-bai* (rat)	earth	male
1949	Jan. 29	*gLan* (ox)	earth	female
1950	Feb. 17	*sTag* (tiger)	metal	male
1951	Feb. 6	*yos* (hare)	metal	female
1952	Jan. 27	*hBrul* (dragon)	water	male
1953	Feb. 14	*sBrul* (snake)	water	female
1954	Feb. 3	*rTa* (horse)	wood	male
1955	Jan. 24	*lug* (ram)	wood	female
1956	Feb. 12	*sPre* (monkey)	fire	male
1957	Jan. 31	*bya* (rooster)	fire	female
1958	Feb. 18	*khy* (dog)	earth	male
1959	Feb. 8	*phag* (pig)	earth	female
1960	Jan. 28	*by-bai* (rat)	metal	male
1961	Feb. 15	*gLan* (ox)	metal	female
1962	Feb. 5	*sTag* (tiger)	water	male
1963	Jan. 25	*yos* (hare)	water	female
1964	Feb. 13	*hBrul* (dragon)	wood	male
1965	Feb. 2	*sBrul* (snake)	wood	female

FRIENDS, OPPOSITES, AND ENEMIES.

Friends (Thun-Sun)	Opposite (Dun-Zur)	Enemies (Shi-Shey)
hBrul (dragon), sPre (monkey)	rTa (horse)	yos (hare), bya (rooster)
bya (rooster), sBrul (snake)	lug (ram)	hBrul (dragon), khy (dog)
rTa (horse), khy (dog)	sPre (monkey)	sBrul (snake), phag (pig)
lug (ram), phag (pig)	bya (rooster)	rTa (horse), by-bai (rat)
by-bai (rat), sPre (monkey)	khy (dog)	lug (ram), gLan (ox)
bya (rooster), gLan (ox)	phag (pig)	sPre (monkey), sTag (tiger)
sTag (tiger), khy (dog)	by-bai (rat)	bya (rooster), yos (hare)
yos (hare), phag (pig)	gLan (ox)	khy (dog), hBrul (dragon)
hBrul (dragon), by-bai (rat)	sTag (tiger)	phag (pig), sBrul (snake)
gLan (ox), sBrul (snake)	yos (hare)	by-bai (rat), rTa (horse)
rTa (horse), sTag (tiger)	hBrul (dragon)	gLan (ox), lug (ram)
lug (ram), yos (hare)	sBrul (snake)	sTag (tiger), sPre (monkey)
hBrul (dragon), sPre (monkey)	rTa (horse)	yos (hare), bya (rooster)
bya (rooster), sBrul (snake)	lug (ram)	hBrul (dragon), khy (dog)
rTa (horse), khy (dog)	sPre (monkey)	sBrul (snake), phag (pig)
lug (ram), phag (pig)	bya (rooster)	rTa (horse), by-bai (rat)
by-bai (rat), sPre (monkey)	khy (dog)	lug (ram), gLan (ox)
bya (rooster), gLan (ox)	phag (pig)	sPre (monkey), sTag (tiger)
sTag (tiger), khy (dog)	by-bai (rat)	bya (rooster), yos (hare)
yos (hare), phag (pig)	gLan (ox)	khy (dog), hBrul (dragon)
hBrul (dragon), by-bai (rat)	sTag (tiger)	phag (pig), sBrul (snake)
gLan (ox), sBrul (snake)	yos (hare)	by-bai (rat), rTa (horse)
rTa (horse), sTag (tiger)	hBrul (dragon)	gLan (ox), lug (ram)
lug (ram), yos (hare)	sBrul (snake)	sTag (tiger), sPre (monkey)
hBrul (dragon), sPre (monkey)	rTa (horse)	yos (hare), bya (rooster)
bya (rooster), sBrul (snake)	lug (ram)	hBrul (dragon), khy (dog)
rTa (horse), khy (dog)	sPre (monkey)	sBrul (snake), phag (pig)
lug (ram), phag (pig)	bya (rooster)	rTa (horse), by-bai (rat)
by-bai (rat), sPre (monkey)	khy (dog)	lug (ram), gLan (ox)
bya (rooster), gLan (ox)	phag (pig)	sPre (monkey), sTag (tiger)
sTag (tiger), khy (dog)	by-bai (rat)	bya (rooster), yos (hare)
yos (hare), phag (pig)	gLan (ox)	khy (dog), hBrul (dragon)
hBrul (dragon), by-bai (rat)	sTag (tiger)	phag (pig), sBrul (snake)
gLan (ox), sBrul (snake)	yos (hare)	by-bai (rat), rTa (horse)
rTa (horse), sTag (tiger)	hBrul (dragon)	gLan (ox), lug (ram)
lug (ram), yos (hare)	sBrul (snake)	sTag (tiger), sPre (monkey)
hBrul (dragon), sPre (monkey)	rTa (horse)	yos (hare), bya (rooster)
bya (rooster), sBrul (snake)	lug (ram)	hBrul (dragon), khy (dog)
rTa (horse), khy (dog)	sPre (monkey)	sBrul (snake), phag (pig)
lug (ram), phag (pig)	bya (rooster)	rTa (horse), by-bai (rat)
by-bai (rat), sPre (monkey)	khy (dog)	lug (ram), gLan (ox)
bya (rooster), gLan (ox)	phag (pig)	sPre (monkey), sTag (tiger)

Year	Starting Date	Animal	Ruling Element	Gender
1966	Jan. 21	*rTa* (horse)	fire	male
1967	Feb. 9	*lug* (ram)	fire	female
1968	Jan. 30	*sPre* (monkey)	earth	male
1969	Feb. 17	*bya* (rooster)	earth	female
1970	Feb. 6	*khy* (dog)	metal	male
1971	Jan. 27	*phag* (pig)	metal	female
1972	Feb. 15	*by-bai* (rat)	water	male
1973	Feb. 3	*gLan* (ox)	water	female
1974	Jan. 23	*sTag* (tiger)	wood	male
1975	Feb. 11	*yos* (hare)	wood	female
1976	Jan. 31	*hBrul* (dragon)	fire	male
1977	Feb. 18	*sBrul* (snake)	fire	female
1978	Feb. 7	*rTa* (horse)	earth	male
1979	Jan. 28	*lug* (ram)	earth	female
1980	Feb. 16	*sPre* (monkey)	metal	male
1981	Feb. 5	*bya* (rooster)	metal	female
1982	Jan. 25	*khy* (dog)	water	male
1983	Feb. 13	*phag* (pig)	water	female
1984	Feb. 2	*by-bai* (rat)	wood	male
1985	Feb. 20	*gLan* (ox)	wood	female
1986	Feb. 9	*sTag* (tiger)	fire	male
1987	Jan. 29	*yos* (hare)	fire	female
1988	Feb. 17	*hBrul* (dragon)	earth	male
1989	Feb. 6	*sBrul* (snake)	earth	female
1990	Jan. 27	*rTa* (horse)	metal	male
1991	Feb. 15	*lug* (ram)	metal	female
1992	Feb. 4	*sPre* (monkey)	water	male
1993	Jan. 23	*bya* (rooster)	water	female
1994	Feb. 10	*khy* (dog)	wood	male
1995	Jan. 31	*phag* (pig)	wood	female
1996	Feb. 19	*by-bai* (rat)	fire	male
1997	Feb. 7	*gLan* (ox)	fire	female
1998	Jan. 28	*sTag* (tiger)	earth	male
1999	Feb. 16	*yos* (hare)	earth	female
2000	Feb. 5	*hBrul* (dragon)	metal	male
2001	Jan. 24	*sBrul* (snake)	metal	female
2002	Feb. 12	*rTa* (horse)	water	male
2003	Feb. 1	*lug* (ram)	water	female
2004	Jan. 22	*sPre* (monkey)	wood	male
2005	Feb. 9	*bya* (rooster)	wood	female
2006	Jan. 29	*khy* (dog)	fire	male
2007	Feb. 18	*phag* (pig)	fire	female

Friends (Thun-Sun)	Opposite (Dun-Zur)	Enemies (Shi-Shey)
sTag (tiger), khy (dog)	by-bai (rat)	bya (rooster), yos (hare)
yos (hare), phag (pig)	gLan (ox)	khy (dog), hBrul (dragon)
hBrul (dragon), by-bai (rat)	sTag (tiger)	phag (pig), sBrul (snake)
gLan (ox), sBrul (snake)	yos (hare)	by-bai (rat), rTa (horse)
rTa (horse), sTag (tiger)	hBrul (dragon)	gLan (ox), lug (ram)
lug (ram), yos (hare)	sBrul (snake)	sTag (tiger), sPre (monkey)
hBrul (dragon), sPre (monkey)	rTa (horse)	yos (hare), bya (rooster)
bya (rooster), sBrul (snake)	lug (ram)	hBrul (dragon), khy (dog)
rTa (horse), khy (dog)	sPre (monkey)	sBrul (snake), phag (pig)
lug (ram), phag (pig)	bya (rooster)	rTa (horse), by-bai (rat)
by-bai (rat), sPre (monkey)	khy (dog)	lug (ram), gLan (ox)
bya (rooster), gLan (ox)	phag (pig)	sPre (monkey), sTag (tiger)
sTag (tiger), khy (dog)	by-bai (rat)	bya (rooster), yos (hare)
yos (hare), phag (pig)	gLan (ox)	khy (dog), hBrul (dragon)
hBrul (dragon), by-bai (rat)	sTag (tiger)	phag (pig), sBrul (snake)
gLan (ox), sBrul (snake)	yos (hare)	by-bai (rat), rTa (horse)
rTa (horse), sTag (tiger)	hBrul (dragon)	gLan (ox), lug (ram)
lug (ram), yos (hare)	sBrul (snake)	sTag (tiger), sPre (monkey)
hBrul (dragon), sPre (monkey)	rTa (horse)	yos (hare), bya (rooster)
bya (rooster), sBrul (snake)	lug (ram)	hBrul (dragon), khy (dog)
rTa (horse), khy (dog)	sPre (monkey)	sBrul (snake), phag (pig)
lug (ram), phag (pig)	bya (rooster)	rTa (horse), by-bai (rat)
by-bai (rat), sPre (monkey)	khy (dog)	lug (ram), gLan (ox)
bya (rooster), gLan (ox)	phag (pig)	sPre (monkey), sTag (tiger)
sTag (tiger), khy (dog)	by-bai (rat)	bya (rooster), yos (hare)
yos (hare), phag (pig)	gLan (ox)	khy (dog), hBrul (dragon)
hBrul (dragon), by-bai (rat)	sTag (tiger)	phag (pig), sBrul (snake)
gLan (ox), sBrul (snake)	yos (hare)	by-bai (rat), rTa (horse)
rTa (horse), sTag (tiger)	hBrul (dragon)	gLan (ox), lug (ram)
lug (ram), yos (hare)	sBrul (snake)	sTag (tiger), sPre (monkey)
hBrul (dragon), sPre (monkey)	rTa (horse)	yos (hare), bya (rooster)
bya (rooster), sBrul (snake)	lug (ram)	hBrul (dragon), khy (dog)
rTa (horse), khy (dog)	sPre (monkey)	sBrul (snake), phag (pig)
lug (ram), phag (pig)	bya (rooster)	rTa (horse), by-bai (rat)
by-bai (rat), sPre (monkey)	khy (dog)	lug (ram), gLan (ox)
bya (rooster), gLan (ox)	phag (pig)	sPre (monkey), sTag (tiger)
sTag (tiger), khy (dog)	by-bai (rat)	bya (rooster), yos (hare)
yos (hare), phag (pig)	gLan (ox)	khy (dog), hBrul (dragon)
hBrul (dragon), by-bai (rat)	sTag (tiger)	phag (pig), sBrul (snake)
gLan (ox), sBrul (snake)	yos (hare)	by-bai (rat), rTa (horse)
rTa (horse), sTag (tiger)	hBrul (dragon)	gLan (ox), lug (ram)
lug (ram), yos (hare)	sBrul (snake)	sTag (tiger), sPre (monkey)

Year	Starting Date	Animal	Ruling Element	Gender
2008	Feb. 7	*by-bai* (rat)	earth	male
2009	Jan. 26	*gLan* (ox)	earth	female
2010	Feb. 14	*sTag* (tiger)	metal	male
2011	Feb. 3	*yos* (hare)	metal	female
2012	Jan. 23	*hBrul* (dragon)	water	male
2013	Feb. 10	*sBrul* (snake)	water	female
2014	Jan. 31	*rTa* (horse)	wood	male
2015	Feb. 19	*lug* (ram)	wood	female
2016	Feb. 8	*sPre* (monkey)	fire	male
2017	Jan. 28	*bya* (rooster)	fire	female
2018	Feb. 16	*khy* (dog)	earth	male
2019	Feb. 5	*phag* (pig)	earth	female
2020	Jan. 25	*by-bai* (rat)	metal	male
2021	Feb. 12	*gLan* (ox)	metal	female
2022	Feb. 1	*sTag* (tiger)	water	male
2023	Jan. 22	*yos* (hare)	water	female
2024	Feb. 10	*hBrul* (dragon)	wood	male
2025	Jan. 29	*sBrul* (snake)	wood	female
2026	Feb. 17	*rTa* (horse)	fire	male
2027	Feb. 6	*lug* (ram)	fire	female
2028	Jan. 26	*sPre* (monkey)	earth	male
2029	Feb. 13	*bya* (rooster)	earth	female
2030	Feb. 3	*khy* (dog)	metal	male
2031	Jan. 23	*phag* (pig)	metal	female
2032	Feb. 11	*by-bai* (rat)	water	male
2033	Jan. 31	*gLan* (ox)	water	female
2034	Feb. 19	*sTag* (tiger)	wood	male
2035	Feb. 8	*yos* (hare)	wood	female
2036	Jan. 28	*hBrul* (dragon)	fire	male
2037	Feb. 15	*sBrul* (snake)	fire	female
2038	Feb. 4	*rTa* (horse)	earth	male
2039	Jan. 24	*lug* (ram)	earth	female
2040	Feb. 12	*sPre* (monkey)	metal	male
2041	Feb. 1	*bya* (rooster)	metal	female
2042	Jan. 22	*khy* (dog)	water	male
2043	Feb. 10	*phag* (pig)	water	female
2044	Jan. 30	*by-bai* (rat)	wood	male
2045	Feb. 17	*gLan* (ox)	wood	female
2046	Feb. 6	*sTag* (tiger)	fire	male
2047	Jan. 26	*yos* (hare)	fire	female
2048	Feb. 14	*hBrul* (dragon)	earth	male
2049	Feb. 2	*sBrul* (snake)	earth	female
2050	Jan. 23	*rTa* (horse)	metal	male

FRIENDS (THUN-SUN)	OPPOSITE (DUN-ZUR)	ENEMIES (SHI-SHEY)
hBrul (dragon), sPre (monkey)	rTa (horse)	yos (hare), bya (rooster)
bya (rooster), sBrul (snake)	lug (ram)	hBrul (dragon), khy (dog)
rTa (horse), khy (dog)	sPre (monkey)	sBrul (snake), phag (pig)
lug (ram), phag (pig)	bya (rooster)	rTa (horse), by-bai (rat)
by-bai (rat), sPre (monkey)	khy (dog)	lug (ram), gLan (ox)
bya (rooster), gLan (ox)	phag (pig)	sPre (monkey), sTag (tiger)
sTag (tiger), khy (dog)	by-bai (rat)	bya (rooster), yos (hare)
yos (hare), phag (pig)	gLan (ox)	khy (dog), hBrul (dragon)
hBrul (dragon), by-bai (rat)	sTag (tiger)	phag (pig), sBrul (snake)
gLan (ox), sBrul (snake)	yos (hare)	by-bai (rat), rTa (horse)
rTa (horse), sTag (tiger)	hBrul (dragon)	gLan (ox), lug (ram)
lug (ram), yos (hare)	sBrul (snake)	sTag (tiger), sPre (monkey)
hBrul (dragon), sPre (monkey)	rTa (horse)	yos (hare), bya (rooster)
bya (rooster), sBrul (snake)	lug (ram)	hBrul (dragon), khy (dog)
rTa (horse), khy (dog)	sPre (monkey)	sBrul (snake), phag (pig)
lug (ram), phag (pig)	bya (rooster)	rTa (horse), by-bai (rat)
by-bai (rat), sPre (monkey)	khy (dog)	lug (ram), gLan (ox)
bya (rooster), gLan (ox)	phag (pig)	sPre (monkey), sTag (tiger)
sTag (tiger), khy (dog)	by-bai (rat)	bya (rooster), yos (hare)
yos (hare), phag (pig)	gLan (ox)	khy (dog), hBrul (dragon)
hBrul (dragon), by-bai (rat)	sTag (tiger)	phag (pig), sBrul (snake)
gLan (ox), sBrul (snake)	yos (hare)	by-bai (rat), rTa (horse)
rTa (horse), sTag (tiger)	hBrul (dragon)	gLan (ox), lug (ram)
lug (ram), yos (hare)	sBrul (snake)	sTag (tiger), sPre (monkey)
hBrul (dragon), sPre (monkey)	rTa (horse)	yos (hare), bya (rooster)
bya (rooster), sBrul (snake)	lug (ram)	hBrul (dragon), khy (dog)
rTa (horse), khy (dog)	sPre (monkey)	sBrul (snake), phag (pig)
lug (ram), phag (pig)	bya (rooster)	rTa (horse), by-bai (rat)
by-bai (rat), sPre (monkey)	khy (dog)	lug (ram), gLan (ox)
bya (rooster), gLan (ox)	phag (pig)	sPre (monkey), sTag (tiger)
sTag (tiger), khy (dog)	by-bai (rat)	bya (rooster), yos (hare)
yos (hare), phag (pig)	gLan (ox)	khy (dog), hBrul (dragon)
hBrul (dragon), by-bai (rat)	sTag (tiger)	phag (pig), sBrul (snake)
gLan (ox), sBrul (snake)	yos (hare)	by-bai (rat), rTa (horse)
rTa (horse), sTag (tiger)	hBrul (dragon)	gLan (ox), lug (ram)
lug (ram), yos (hare)	sBrul (snake)	sTag (tiger), sPre (monkey)
hBrul (dragon), sPre (monkey)	rTa (horse)	yos (hare), bya (rooster)
bya (rooster), sBrul (snake)	lug (ram)	hBrul (dragon), khy (dog)
rTa (horse), khy (dog)	sPre (monkey)	sBrul (snake), phag (pig)
lug (ram), phag (pig)	bya (rooster)	rTa (horse), by-bai (rat)
by-bai (rat), sPre (monkey)	khy (dog)	lug (ram), gLan (ox)
bya (rooster), gLan (ox)	phag (pig)	sPre (monkey), sTag (tiger)
sTag (tiger), khy (dog)	by-bai (rat)	bya (rooster), yos (hare)

bya (rooster)	This person is enchanted by fashion, loves cleanliness, and has a strong sex drive. He or she tells others what to do, but rarely heeds his or her own counsel.
khy (dog)	This person tries to do things right, but the actions and outcomes never seem to turn out as intended. He or she walks fast and travels a great deal, is self-interested, and is always thinking too much. This person never seems to receive kindness despite being good-natured, and consequently can become mean and vengeful.
phag (pig)	This person is often greedy and takes advantage of others. Yet he or she can be good or bad; self-disciplined or gluttonous. This person lies.

Based on this interpretative material, Alice T. and Peter C. both listen well and talk a lot because each is born in a *hBrul* (dragon) year. This position also suggests that they execute their duties, but do not spring immediately into uncalculated action. Both are quick-tempered, but are generally well-meaning and good-natured.

STEP TWO: REVIEWING THE SIGN'S FORCES

Tibetan astrologers focus on five basic forces in an individual's life: *sok* (life force), *wang* (power), *lung ta* (luck), *la* (spirit), and *lü* (health). These forces are analyzed after the person's animal sign and the element attributed to that sign are identified.

Adapted from the *wu hsing* (Five Agents) used in Chinese astrology (see "Locating and Interpreting the Birth *Gen*" in chapter 3), the Tibetan practice's five elements characterize the essential energies that animate the entire universe: wood (*shing*), fire (*me*), metal (*chak*), earth (*sa*), and water (*chu*). Each element represents a repetitive and harmonious pattern of change, and indicates an animal sign's behavioral pattern, general appearance, and emotional state. Every one of an individual's five forces is ruled by a specific element that corresponds to the person's animal sign. Consequently, a person born in a *by-bai* (rat) year has a water-influenced *sok*, a wood-influenced *lung ta*, and so forth. The method used to determine each force and its governing element is outlined in the following pages.

Determining the *Sok* (Life Force)

The *sok* (life force) determines an individual's motive for taking action or following a particular direction in life, and is directly associated with the animal that rules the individual's year of birth. As mentioned earlier in this chapter, both Alice T. and Peter C. were born in *hBrul* (dragon) years (see "Step One: Determining an Individual's Animal Sign," page 120). According to fig. 4.2, the *sok* of people born in a *hBrul* (dragon) year (first column) is earth (second column).

Each element corresponds to a number of qualities, a color, and a portion of the physical anatomy:

earth *(sa)*   The earth element stabilizes and strengthens. It corresponds to the color yellow, the spleen, mouth, and flesh.

fire *(me)*   The fire element is strong, fast-moving, and hot. It corresponds to the color red, the heart and tongue.

metal *(chak)*   The metal element is strong, cutting, changeable, and direct. It corresponds to the color white, the bones and hair.

water *(chu)*   The water element is soft, keen-sighted, fluid, and placid. It corresponds to the color black or blue, and the blood.

wood *(shing)*   The wood element is changeable, long-lasting, and beautiful, and possesses a great deal of mental energy. It corresponds to the color green and the veins.

FIGURE 4.2. TABLE OF TIBETAN SOK (LIFE FORCE) ELEMENTS.

ANIMAL	ELEMENT
by-bai (rat)	water
gLan (ox)	earth
sTag (tiger)	wood
yos (hare)	wood
hBrul (dragon)	earth
sBrul (snake)	fire
rTa (horse)	fire
lug (ram)	earth
sPre (monkey)	metal
bya (rooster)	metal
khy (dog)	earth
phag (pig)	water

FIGURE 4.3. THE RELATIONSHIP OF THE FIVE ELEMENTS.

Element	Excellent Relationship	Very Beneficial Relationship	Good Relationship	Neutral Relationship	Bad Relationship	Very Bad Relationship
water (*chu*)	wood	earth	water	metal		fire
metal (*chak*)	water	fire		earth	metal	wood
earth (*sa*)	metal	wood	earth	fire		water
fire (*me*)	earth	water		wood	fire	metal
wood (*shing*)	fire	metal		water	wood	earth

Since Alice's and Peter's animal sign (*hBrul*) (first column in fig. 4.2) is governed by the earth element (second column in fig. 4.2), both people possess a stable, strong, grounded *sok*. A Tibetan practitioner might also review the quality of the relationship between the individual's *sok* and that of another person. Directly adapted from the Chinese astrological system, the table shown in fig. 4.3 would be used as a reference point.

Based on this material, the astrologer would advise both Alice and Peter, who both possess an earth-influenced *sok* (first column in fig. 4.3), that relationships with individuals who possess a metal-influenced *sok* (second column in fig. 4.3) are excellent; relationships with those who possess a wood-influenced *sok* (third column in fig. 4.3) are very beneficial; and relationships with those who possess an earth-influenced *sok* (fourth column in fig. 4.3) are good. However, people who have a water-influenced *sok* (seventh column in fig. 4.3) should be avoided. And those who have a fire-influenced *sok* (fifth column in fig. 4.3) are to be treated as neutral entities in relationships.

Determining the *Wang* (Power Force)

In the same manner that the *sok* (life force) influences an individual's motive for taking action or following a particular direction in life, the person's *wang* (power force) determines how that person overcomes obstacles and achieves success. The *wang* is determined by the element that is directly associated with the individual's year of birth (fourth column in fig. 4.1).[6]

For example, since Alice was born in 1952 (first column in fig. 4.1), her birth-year element is water (fourth column in fig. 4.1). The same interpretative material employed in the delineation of the *sok* (see "Determining the *Sok*," page 129) is also

6.   The element that is directly associated with the individual's year of birth is identical to the year *hsing* in Chinese astrology (see chapter 3, fig. 3.4).

used to assess her *wang*. In this instance, she overcomes obstacles and succeeds through keen-sightedness and soft, fluid actions that appear smooth on the surface, but move with the force of a river.

Peter was born in 1964 (first column in fig. 4.1). Therefore his birth-year element is wood (fourth column in fig. 4.1). Consequently, when the same interpretative material is applied to his profile, it indicates that he overcomes difficulties through his changeable but very long-lasting and self-perpetuating nature. He achieves everything by the energy of his thoughts.

Determining the *Lung Ta* (Luck Force)

Ideologically, the *lung ta* (luck force) is based on the Asian belief that every person is provided with a portion of positive or negative fortune at birth. The type and quality of *lung ta* is determined by the luck element that governs the individual's animal sign (fig. 4.4), which is different from the animal sign's element (fig. 4.2) or the birth year's element (fig. 4.1).

For example, Alice and Peter were born in a *hBrul* (dragon) year (1952 and 1964 in the first column in fig. 4.1), and their *sok* is ruled by earth (fig. 4.2). According to fig. 4.4, *hBrul* people have a *lung ta* that is ruled by wood. However, it's the relationship between the *sok* and *lung ta* elements that actually determines an individual's type of luck. Employing the data in fig. 4.3, a Tibetan astrologer would determine that the relationship between earth (first column) and wood (third column) is very beneficial. Therefore, both Alice and Peter are deemed to be people who enjoy good fortune throughout life.

FIGURE 4.4. TABLE OF TIBETAN LUNG TA (LUCK FORCE) ELEMENTS.

ANIMAL	ELEMENT
by-bai (rat)	wood
gLan (ox)	metal
sTag (tiger)	metal
yos (hare)	fire
hBrul (dragon)	wood
sBrul (snake)	metal
rTa (horse)	metal
lug (ram)	fire
sPre (monkey)	wood
bya (rooster)	metal
khy (dog)	metal
phag (pig)	fire

Determining the *La* (Spirit Force)

In Tibetan astrology, *la* (spirit force) governs an individual's emotional state. Practitioners determine this influence by locating the "mother" of the *sok* force (see "Determining the Sok," page 129). Based on the mutually productive relationships among the various elements in Chinese astrology (see chapter 3, fig. 3.14), the Tibetans believe that each element was actually born from another element. The relationship follows a circular path:

wood	water is wood's mother
water	metal is water's mother
metal	earth is metal's mother
earth	fire is earth's mother
fire	wood is fire's mother

Alice and Peter both have *soks* that are governed by earth (see "Determining the *Sok*," page 129). Therefore, both people have a *la* (spirit force) influenced by fire, since this element is earth's mother. Employing the interpretative material used in delineating the *sok* (see "Determining the *Sok*," page 129), a Tibetan astrologer would note that both people are quick-tempered, possessing intense and fiery emotions.

Determining the *Lü* (Health Force)

The source of physical health concerns is determined by the *lü* (health force). To identify this force, Tibetan astrologers employ the individual's animal sign (see "Step One: Determining an Individual's Animal Sign," page 120) and the *wang* (see "Determining the *Wang*," page 130). Applying the data in fig. 4.5, the astrologer refers to the individual's animal sign (first and fifth columns) and locates the person's *wang* (third and seventh columns). The relationship of the animal sign's "key element" (second and sixth columns) to the *wang* determines the individual's *lü* (fourth and eighth columns).

For instance, Alice's "key element" is metal (second column in fig. 4.5) because she was born in a *hBrul* (dragon) year (first column in fig. 4.5). Her *wang* (see "Determining the *Wang*," page 130) is water (third column in fig. 4.5) and her *lü* is also water (fourth column in fig. 4.5). Using the same interpretative material applied to the element that governs the *sok* force (see "Determining the *Sok*," page 129), the astrologer determines that Alice's bloodstream should be of primary concern in her overall health regimen.

Peter's "key element" is also metal (second column in fig. 4.5) because he is born in a *hBrul* (dragon) year (first column in fig. 4.5). But his *wang* is wood (see "Determining the *Wang*," page 130). Therefore, his *lü* is fire (fourth column in fig. 4.5). Using the same interpretative material applied to the element that governs the *sok* (see "Determining the *Sok*," page 129), the astrologer determines that Peter's heart and tongue should be his primary health concerns.

Creating a Tibetan Personality Profile

When the individual's animal sign has been identified (see "Step One: Determining an Individual's Animal Sign," page 120) and the five basic forces (see "Step Two: Reviewing the Sign's Forces," page 128) have been ascertained, the Tibetan practitioner unfolds the individual's personality profile as shown in the examples that follow.

FIGURE 4.5. TABLE OF TIBETAN LÜ (HEALTH FORCE) ELEMENTS.

ANIMAL SIGN	KEY ELEMENT	WANG (POWER ELEMENT)	LÜ (HEALTH ELEMENT)	ANIMAL SIGN	KEY ELEMENT	WANG (POWER ELEMENT)	LÜ (HEALTH ELEMENT)
by-bai (rat)	wood	fire	water	*rTa* (horse)	wood	fire	water
		water	wood			water	wood
		metal	earth			metal	earth
		earth	fire			earth	fire
		wood	metal			wood	metal
gLan (ox)	wood	fire	water	*lug* (ram)	wood	fire	water
		water	wood			water	wood
		metal	earth			metal	earth
		earth	fire			earth	fire
		wood	metal			wood	metal
sTag (tiger)	water	wood	water	*sPre* (monkey)	water	wood	water
		metal	wood			metal	wood
		earth	earth			earth	earth
		fire	fire			fire	fire
		water	metal			water	metal
yos (hare)	water	wood	water	*bya* (rooster)	water	wood	water
		metal	wood			metal	wood
		earth	earth			earth	earth
		fire	fire			fire	fire
		water	metal			water	metal
hBrul (dragon)	metal	water	water	*khy* (dog)	metal	water	water
		earth	wood			earth	wood
		fire	earth			fire	earth
		wood	fire			wood	fire
		metal	metal			metal	metal
sBrul (snake)	metal	water	water	*phag* (pig)	metal	water	water
		earth	wood			earth	wood
		fire	earth			fire	earth
		wood	fire			wood	fire
		metal	metal			metal	metal

Alice's Personality Profile

Alice was born in a *hBrul* (dragon) year (1952 in fig. 4.1). This means that she both listens well and talks a lot. It also suggests that she executes her duties, but does not spring immediately into uncalculated action. She is quick-tempered, but is generally well-meaning and good-natured.

The Tibetan astrologer would then assess the five basic forces that govern Alice's life: *sok* (life force), *wang* (power), *lung ta* (luck), *la* (spirit force), and *lü* (health force). Alice's animal sign, *hBrul* (first column in fig. 4.2), is governed by the earth element (second column in fig. 4.2), which means she has a stable, strong, grounded *sok* (see "Determining the *Sok*," page 129) This means that relationships with individuals who possess a metal-influenced *sok* (second column in fig. 4.3) are excellent; relationships with those who possess a wood-influenced *sok* (third column in fig. 4.3) are very beneficial; and relationships with those who possess an earth-influenced *sok* (fourth column in fig. 4.3) are good. However, people who have a water-influenced *sok* (seventh column in fig. 4.3) should be avoided. And those who have a fire-influenced *sok* (fifth column in fig. 4.3) are to be treated as neutral entities in relationships.

Since Alice was born in 1952 (first column in fig. 4.1), her birth-year element is water (fourth column in fig. 4.1). The same interpretative material employed in the delineation of the *sok* is used to ascertain her *wang* (see "Determining the *Wang*," page 130). These data indicate that she overcomes obstacles and succeeds through keen-sightedness and soft, fluid actions, which appear smooth on the surface but move with the force of a river.

Alice has a *lung ta* (luck) ruled by wood because she was born in a *hBrul* year (see "Determining the *Lung Ta*," page 131). Alice is deemed to be a person who enjoys good fortune throughout life because the relationship between the earth element that governs her *sok* (second column in fig. 4.2) and the wood element that rules her *lung ta* (second column in fig. 4.4) is very beneficial, according to the data in fig. 4.3.

Because the fire element is mother to Alice's earth-influenced *sok* according to Tibetan astrology (see "Determining the *La*," page 132), Alice has a fire-influenced *la* (spirit force). This means that she is quick-tempered, possessing intense and fiery emotions.

Alice's *lü* (health force) (see "Determining the *Lü*," page 132) is water. Using the same interpretative material applied to the element that governs the *sok* force (see "Determining the *Sok*," page 129), the astrologer determines that Alice's bloodstream should be of primary concern in her overall health regimen.

Peter's Personality Profile

Peter was born in a *hBrul* (dragon) year (1964 in fig. 4.1). This means that he both listens well and talks a lot. It also suggests that he executes his duties, but does not spring immediately into uncalculated action. He is quick-tempered, but is generally well-meaning and good-natured.

The Tibetan astrologer would then assess the five basic forces that govern Peter's life, including the *sok* (life force), *wang* (power), *lung ta* (luck), *la* (spirit force), and *lü* (health force). Peter's animal sign, *hBrul* (first column in fig. 4.2), is governed by the earth element (second column in fig. 4.2), which means he has a stable, strong, grounded *sok* (see "Determining the *Sok*," page 129). This means that relationships with individuals who possess a metal-influenced *sok* (second column in fig. 4.3) are excellent; relationships with those who possess a wood-influenced *sok* (third column in fig. 4.3) are very beneficial; and relationships with those who possess an earth-influenced *sok* (fourth column in fig. 4.3) are good. However, people who have a water-influenced *sok* (seventh column in fig. 4.3), should be avoided. And those who have a fire-influenced *sok* (fifth column in fig. 4.3) are to be treated as neutral entities in relationships.

Since Peter was born in 1964 (first column in fig. 4.1), his birth-year element is wood (fourth column in fig. 4.1). The same interpretative material employed in the delineation of the *sok* is used to ascertain his *wang* (see "Determining the *Wang*," page 130). These data indicate that he overcomes difficulties through his changeable, but very long-lasting and self-perpetuating nature. He achieves everything by the energy of his thoughts.

Peter has a *lung ta* (luck) ruled by wood because he was born in a *hBrul* year (see "Determining the *Lung Ta*," page 131, and fig. 4.4). Peter is deemed to be a person who enjoys good fortune throughout life because the relationship between the earth element that governs his *sok* (second column in fig. 4.2) and the wood element that rules his *lung ta* (second column in fig. 4.4) is very beneficial, according to the data in fig. 4.3.

Because the fire element is mother to Peter's earth-influenced *sok* according to Tibetan astrology (see "Determining the *La*," page 132), Peter has a fire-influenced *la* (spirit force). This means that he is quick-tempered, possessing intense and fiery emotions.

Peter's *lü* (health force) (see "Determining the *Lü*," page 132) is fire. Using the same interpretative material applied to the element that governs the *sok* force (see "Determining the *Sok*," page 129), the astrologer determines that Peter's heart and tongue should be his primary health concerns.

After a personality profile like the two examples above has been created by the astrologer, answers to everyday matters are generated by consulting one of two forms of daily prediction. One identifies the person's auspicious and inauspicious days during the course of any lunar month. This method is outlined below in "Step Three: Determining Good and Bad Days." The other locates the specific years in which a person may encounter lowered energy or many obstacles. This method is outlined below in "Step Four: Determining the *Parkhas*."

STEP THREE: DETERMINING GOOD AND BAD DAYS

Based on a person's animal sign (see "Determining an Individual's Animal Sign," page 120), practitioners can determine an individual's auspicious and inauspicious days during the course of any given lunar month. Using the luni-solar calendar (see chapter 3, fig. 3.6), find the first day of the lunar month and year in question. Then locate the person's animal sign in fig. 4.6 (first column). Reading across, the number listed in each column corresponds to a day in the lunar month, not to the actual date. The corresponding days in fig. 4.6 are categorized by quality: foundation, success, power, obstacle, enemy, and disturbance.

To find out what specific days within a given lunar month are auspicious or inauspicious, simply add the number in each column to the starting date of the specific lunar month (see chapter 3, fig. 3.6). For example, if Alice wants to determine the outcome of events during February 1998, a Tibetan practitioner would refer to the first lunar month of 1998, which begins on January 28 and ends on February 27 (chapter 3, fig. 3.6). She is born in a *hBrul* (dragon) year (1952 in fig. 4.1), so the practitioner would refer to that sign in the first column of fig. 4.6. Reading across from *hBrul*, it is determined that her Foundation Day (best day for starting new projects) occurs three days after January 28 (second column), or on January 31, 1998. Her Success Day (best day to finish a project) occurs seventeen days after January 28 (third column), or on February 14, 1998. Her Power Day (when she will be at her strongest) occurs twenty-four days after January 28 (fourth column), or on February 21, 1998. At the opposite end of her fortunes, her Obstacle Day (when she may encounter delays or obstacles) occurs eight days after January 28 (fifth column), or on February 5, 1998. Her Enemy Day (when she may encounter opposition to her projects) takes place eleven days after January 28 (sixth column), or on February 8, 1998. And her Disturbance Day (when chaos may occur) happens nine days after January 28 (seventh column), or on February 6, 1998. Because Peter was also born in a *hBrul* (dragon) year (1964 in fig. 4.1), the practitioner would derive exactly the same information for the same lunar month.

FIGURE 4.6. TABLE OF TIBETAN AUSPICIOUS DAYS.

Animal Sign	Foundation Day: Start a project on this day of any lunar month.	Success Day: Finish a project on this day of any lunar month.	Power Day: This is the day of any lunar month when an individual is mentally or physically at his or her peak.	Obstacle Day: This is the day of any lunar month when an individual encounters delays.	Enemy Day: This is the day of any lunar month when an individual encounters opponents to a project.	Disturbance Day: This is the day of any lunar month when an individual may encounter chaotic activities.
by-bai (rat)	20	3	6	26	23	10
gLan (ox)	17	12	14	12	5	18
sTag (tiger)	5	9	27	14	3	12
yos (hare)	11	12	27	26	18	25
hBrul (dragon)	3	17	24	8	11	9
sBrul (snake)	13	6	12	8	6	9
rTa (horse)	17	6	12	20	27	5
lug (ram)	8	2	1	20	27	5
sPre (monkey)	8	2	1	9	17	10
bya (rooster)	14	25	7	3	24	11
khy (dog)	9	5	27	11	12	3
phag (pig)	2	11	8	26	12	3

The figures shown in each column represent the number of days from the start of any given lunar month (fig. 3.6), not the actual day of a given lunar month. To determine the calendar date, add the figure shown in each column to the lunar month's starting date (fig. 3.6).

As mentioned earlier, this system can be applied to any lunar month of any given year, providing timely data that is similar to the reading of the birth *hua* (see "Using the Birth *Hua* for Daily Prediction" in chapter 3) or the daily *sieu* (see "Locating and Interpreting the *Sieu*" in chapter 3) in Chinese astrology.

STEP FOUR: DETERMINING THE PARKHAS (TRIGRAMS)

Another form of Tibetan predictive astrology determines bad or low-energy years that may occur during an individual's life. This method utilizes the eight trigrams developed by the Chinese that form the foundations of *I Ching* divination. In Tibet, these trigrams are called the *parkhas* (fig. 4.7). Each *parkha* comprises a combination of three broken lines (— —), which represent female energy, and/or unbroken lines (———), which represent male energy. Tibetan astrologers believe that the *parkha* governs a direction and a variety of positive or negative qualities and outcomes.

FIGURE 4.7. TABLE OF PARKHAS.

Trigram	Tibetan Parkha Name	Chinese Trigram Name	Compass Direction	Characteristics
——— / — — / ———	*lie*	*li*	S	fame; change of residence; artistic success; good publicity, writings, and communications; bad for concealing secrets
— — / — — / — —	*hon*	*k'un*	SW	creative; a time to harvest the benefits of completed projects; not always productive
— — / ——— / ———	*doha*	*tui*	W	relaxation; contemplation; accomplishment; satisfaction derived from accomplishments; joy
——— / ——— / ———	*khen*	*chen*	NW	ambition; promotion; firm purpose; dignity; pushing forward; potential of conflict via aggression
— — / ——— / — —	*kham*	*k'an*	N	obstacles; opposition; loss; difficulties; stasis or stagnation
——— / — — / — —	*gin*	*ken*	NE	a time for conclusions; finishing and beginning anew; internal change; coolness; drawing together
— — / — — / ———	*zin*	*ch'ien*	E	growth; initiative; movement; advancement; time to start new projects
——— / ——— / — —	*zon*	*sun*	SE	travel; mental action; concentration; good for emotions and business; steady progress

Parkhas are employed by Tibetan practitioners in many different ways. One method identifies the individual's birth *parkha* and pairs it with the *parkha* for a specific day, which is published in a Tibetan almanac. The resulting hexagram is used to disclose the outcome of the day in question by locating its corresponding verses and interpretation in the Chinese divination book *I Ching*.

Because Tibetan almanacs are not readily available in the western hemisphere and are nearly impossible to locate in languages outside of Tibetan, the following section will concentrate on another, more accessible method, which uses a progressed form of *parkha* called a *bap-par* (descending *parkhas*) to determine the outcome of events for a specific year during an individual's life.

Locating the *Bap-Par*

The method employed to identify the *bap-par* for the current or any given year depends on the gender of the individual in question. Using fig. 4.8 as a map, a man's *bap-par* for the current year is located by counting out his current age in a clockwise direction on the map starting from, but not including, the *lie parkha*. To find a woman's *bap-par* for the current year, use fig. 4.8 as a map and count out her current age in a counterclockwise direction beginning from, but not including, the *kham parkha*.

FIGURE 4.8. MAP OF BAP-PAR.

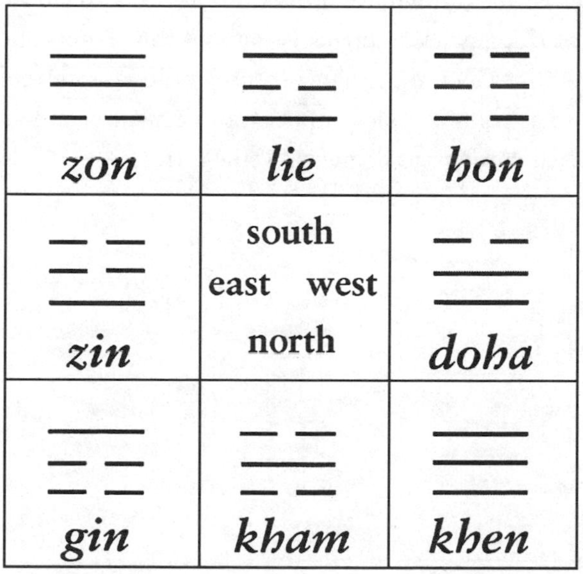

Using the year 2000 as a test case and following the method just described, Peter's *bap-par* for that year can be determined by counting out his age on the map in fig. 4.8. Born in 1964, Peter will be thirty-six years old in 2000. Therefore, the astrologer would count thirty-six squares in a clockwise fashion from the *lie parkha* (but not including it), arriving at the *kham parkha*. Thus, his *bap-par* for that year is the *kham parkha*.

Similarly, Alice's *bap-par* for the year 2000 can be determined by counting out her age on the map in fig. 4.8. Born in 1952, Alice will be forty-eight years old in the year 2000. Therefore, the astrologer would count forty-eight squares in a counterclockwise fashion from the *kham parkha* (but not including the *kham parkha*), arriving at the *kham parkha*. Thus, her *bap-par* for that year is the *kham parkha*.

Applying the interpretative material in fig. 4.7, the *kham parkha*, which applies to both Alice and Peter, indicates that the year 2000 is a time when obstacles and opposition are encountered that may lead to loss, difficulties, or stagnation of a project's progress.

The Tibetan tradition provides a view of the waxing and waning of an individual's spiritual and physical powers from birth to death without placing predetermined restraints on the person's professional, marital, or social destiny.

As mentioned at the beginning of this chapter, this tradition has dual origins. Although it is well founded in the animal-oriented Chinese zodiac as well as in the *I Ching* and *lo shu* forms of divination, this Moon-school tradition also embraces many facets of Vedic dogma including beliefs about the planets and their associated deities. Consequently, Tibetan astrology focuses on concrete reality, but is not as secular as Chinese astrology. It also concentrates on spiritual harmony, but is not as firmly entrenched in religious dogma as Vedic astrology.

Goddesses
of the
Lunar Mansions
VEDIC CHART CONSTRUCTION

Just as religious custom is interwoven into everyday routine in Judaic culture, Vedic (Hindu) dogma is integrated into both spiritual and physical life in India. Like Judaic and Tibetan astrologies, the primary purpose of Vedic astrology is to guide an individual toward spiritual enlightenment as well as appropriate secular interaction with family, friends, neighbors, and the community. Vedic astrology is a Moon-school tradition that employs a version of the lunar mansions, called the *naksatras,* that are similar to the Chinese *sieu* (see "The Moon School" in chapter 2). The *naksatras* are used for natal delineation and personal chronology development in this form of astrology.

The Vedic tradition includes three unique facets. Unlike other Moon-school astrologies (Chinese, Tibetan, or Judaic), Vedic practitioners employ a specialized lunar chart in the development of a woman's personality profile. Vedic astrology is more mathematically oriented than Chinese or Tibetan astrology, a trait that it shares with Judaic, Arabian, and Western methods. Vedic astrologers also create a personal chronology that reputedly tracks activities to the month and day without using any form of predictive astrology such as the Chinese daily *sieu* (see "Locating and Interpreting the *Sieu*" in chapter 3) or the Tibetan chart of auspicious and adverse days (see "Determining Good and Bad Days" in chapter 4).

Unlike Chinese astrology—a *secular* Moon-school tradition—or either of the Sun-school astrologies (Western and Arabian), the Vedic tradition focuses its attention on karmic debt: the accumulation of good fortune based upon the individual's actions during a previous life. The whole of Indian culture and ideology revolves around the interconnected cause-and-effect nature of all events in a manner similar to Tibetan ideology: karma is considered to be the main proponent of dharma.[1] This is the essential principle in the sacred scriptures known as the Vedas, which are a series of hymns originally passed down by oral tradition until they were documented around 1500 B.C., according to the nineteenth-century scholar Max Mueller. (However, orthodox Hindu dogma dictates that the compilation took place in 3100 B.C. and that the hymns are believed to be two thousand years older than that.) In Western terms, this relationship is viewed as a black-and-white concept: every action has a reaction. Within the realm of Vedic and Oriental thought, however, in general, karma and dharma embody the natural flow of life itself. Nothing can exist or discontinue without exerting an effect on something else within the whole of the universe.

Understanding this concept's importance, it is no wonder that *jyotisa*[2] (Vedic astrology) concentrates on the interrelationship between the heavens and an individual's dharma. It is tightly woven into the cultural, spiritual, and even scientific fabric of India's age-old civilization. The study of *jyotisastra* (the heavenly bodies) is a major branch of Indian learning, revered on par with *dharmasastra* (moral and ritual law), *athasastra* (government and politics), and *kamasastra* (the art of love and pleasure). The sciences of astrology, astronomy, and mathematics all fall within the general category of *jyotisastra*.

Within Vedic astrology are five basic subdivisions: *jataka* (natal),[3] *prasna* (horary), *varshaphala* (predictive), *muhurta* (electional), and *yatra* (mundane). Each subdivision has numerous methods and variations for the calculation and interpretation of data. For example, there are sixteen *sodasavargas*[4] (divisional charts) used in a *jataka* (natal) personality profile. Each *sodasavarga* (fig. 5.1) represents a specific area of life such as destiny, marriage, and education, and subdivides the 30 degrees attributed to each zodiac sign into smaller increments of degrees and minutes.

Only a handful of these *sodasavargas* are consulted on a regular basis by practitioners, however: the *rasicakra* (sign chart) or *bhavacakra* (house chart), *horacakra* (half-sign chart), *drekkanacakra* (third-sign chart), *saptamsacakra* (seventh-sign chart), *navamsacakra* (ninth-sign chart), *dasamsacakra* (tenth-sign chart), and *dvadasamsacakra* (twelfth-sign chart). The complexities of construction and inter-

---

1. In this instance, *karma* refers to past actions that affect an individual's fortunes or destiny in the present or future. *Dharma* refers to the way in which a person conducts his or her present life.
2. Pronounced "jyo-tee-sha."
3. This subdivision includes a special branch called *vivaha* (marriage) which concentrates on determining the compatibility of the intended couple and the appropriate time for the nuptial ceremony.
4. Pronounced "sho-dah-sha-var-gah," this term is often shortened to simply *varga* by practitioners.

FIGURE 5.1. THE SODASAVARGAS.

SODASAVARGA	APPLICATION
rasicakra or *bhavacakra*	general personality traits
horacakra	ability to acquire material wealth
drekkanacakra	relations with siblings and fulfillment of personal efforts
caturthamsacakra	portion of good luck and fortune
saptamsacakra	potential for offspring
navamsacakra	ultimate direction of life and marriage possibilities
dasamsacakra	profession and social status
dvadasamsacakra	hereditary traits, potential legacies, and parents
sodasamsacakra	ability to acquire property
vimsamsacakra	spirituality of the individual
caturvimsamsacakra	educational prospects
bhamsacakra	overall strength
trimsamsacakra	portion of good or bad luck
khavedamsacakra	auspicious effects
aksavedamsacakra	general indications
sastyamsacakra	general indications

pretation for all of the *sodasavargas* (divisional charts) that can be used in a *jataka* (natal) personality profile fills volumes of books not including the multitude of additional charts used in the other astrological subdivisions. Additionally, there is a great deal of knowledge concerning the interpretation of each chart type that has only been passed on by oral tradition from one astrologer to another and is carefully guarded by master practitioners.

This chapter provides a concise and usable primer on the development of a *jataka* (natal) personality profile by focusing on the construction of the first two types of *sodasavarga* (*rasicakra* and *bhavacakra*). The delineation of both the *rasicakra* and *bhavacakra* will include methods for interpreting the Ascendant's *naksatra* (lunar mansion); planetary positions by zodiac sign, by zodiac house, and by the position of each house's ruling planet; as well as the positions of the Moon's North and South Nodes by zodiac house. This chapter also includes the construction of a specialized chart that is primarily but not exclusively employed in women's personality profiles, called a *candralagna* (Moon chart). The construction of four additional *sodasavargas* (*navamsacakra, horacakra, drekkanacakra,* and *saptamsacakra*) will be outlined briefly. The processes by which Vedic astrologers analyze the strengths and weaknesses of the various planetary positions, which are collectively called the *shadbala* (*sthanabala, drigbala, naisargikabala, chestabala, dikbala,* and *kalabala*) will be reviewed. A brief explanation of how patterns of planetary positions or *yogas* are analyzed and applied. The construction and general interpretation of a personal chronology *(vimsottari dasa)* will conclude the presentation.

Throughout this chapter, you'll notice that the extra-Saturnian planets Uranus (♅), Neptune (♆), and Pluto (♇) are not commonly used in Vedic astrology. This is a characteristic that it shares with the Chinese and Tibetan traditions, which limit the planetary range outside of the Sun and Moon to five celestial bodies: Mercury (☿), Mars (♂), Venus (♀), Jupiter (♃), and Saturn (♄). Some modern Vedic practitioners have adopted Uranus, Neptune, and Pluto, incorporating them into their delineation work. However, the planetary rulerships for each of the twelve zodiac signs in this chapter follow the traditional pattern. (Interestingly, this arrangement was used by Western practitioners until the twentieth century because these planets were not discovered until 1781, 1846, and 1930, respectively.)

Unlike Chinese and Tibetan astrology, Vedic astrology treats the Moon's North Node (☊) and South Node (☋) as planets, even though they are not discrete celestial bodies. These are called Rahu and Ketu, respectively. Although the Moon's nodes are not considered to be as important as the planets, they are frequently interpreted not only in Vedic but in Western, Arabian, and Judaic natal delineations as well.

STEP ONE: ESTABLISHING THE POSITIONS OF THE PLANETS
Applying the *Ayanamsa*

Based on the Vedic (sidereal) zodiac, the data required to construct a *jataka* (natal) personality profile (which consists of either a *rasicakra* or a *bhavacakra* as well as four or more *sodasavargas*) can be directly derived from a Western natal horoscope erected according to the tropical zodiac. Therefore, for those of you who want to develop a *jataka*, you must first construct a Western natal chart (see instructions in chapter 8).

The simplest way to convert this Western information into usable Vedic data is to subtract the degrees and minutes of *ayanamsa*[5] from the Ascendant (cusp of House I), from each planetary position (Sun (☉), Moon (☽), Mercury (☿), Venus

---

5. Pronounced "ah-yah-nahm-sha," this term refers to the fluctuating position of the Vernal Point (Aries 00°00' [00°♈00']), placing the Sun's apparent path against the backdrop of the constellations, demarcating the Sun's transit from one constellation to another. The *ayanamsa* is the basis of Vedic astrological computation, and there are numerous methods used to calculate it. Some of the most common methods were developed by astrologers such as Fagan and Bradley, Lahiri, Raman, Usha-Shahi, Skri Yukteswra, Sundra Ragan, Krishnamurti, Shill Pond, Takra, and Djurhul Khul. The reason there are so many types is simple: no one agrees on the actual progressed position of the Vernal Point (Aries 00°00' [00°♈00']) along the Sun's apparent path. The *ayanamsa* formula used by modern Vedic astrologers such as Ronnie Gale Dreyer, however, is K. S. Krishnamurti's, which places the rate of precession at 00°00'50.2388" per year. But the most commonly applied *ayanamsa* method in India is the one developed by Lahiri, who was secretary of the Calendar Reform Committee and the person who compiled India's official ephemeris.

(♀), Mars (♂), Jupiter (♃), and Saturn (♄)) and from the Moon's North Node (☊) and South Node (☋), which are all expressed in degrees and minutes in the individual's Western natal chart, such as those constructed in chapter 8 (figs. 8.2 and 8.3).

FIGURE 5.2. TABLE OF AYANAMSAS FOR THE YEARS 1924 THROUGH 2050.

Year	Ayanamsa	Year	Ayanamsa	Year	Ayanamsa	Year	Ayanamsa
1924	22°42'	1955	23°08'	1987	23°35'	2019	24°02'
1925	22°43'	1956	23°09'	1988	23°35'	2020	24°03'
1926	22°44'	1957	23°10'	1989	23°36'	2021	24°04'
1927	22°44'	1958	23°10'	1990	23°37'	2022	24°05'
1928	22°45'	1959	23°11'	1991	23°38'	2023	24°05'
1929	22°46'	1960	23°12'	1992	23°39'	2024	24°06'
1930	22°47'	1961	23°13'	1993	23°40'	2025	24°07'
1931	22°48'	1962	23°14'	1994	23°41'	2026	24°08'
1932	22°49'	1963	23°15'	1995	23°41'	2027	24°09'
1933	22°49'	1964	23°15'	1996	23°42'	2028	24°10'
1934	22°50'	1965	23°16'	1997	23°43'	2029	24°10'
1935	22°51'	1966	23°17'	1998	23°44'	2030	24°11'
1936	22°52'	1967	23°18'	1999	23°45'	2031	24°12'
1937	22°53'	1968	23°19'	2000	23°46'	2032	24°13'
1938	22°54'	1969	23°20'	2001	23°47'	2033	24°14'
1939	22°54'	1970	23°20'	2002	23°47'	2034	24°15'
1940	22°55'	1971	23°21'	2003	23°48'	2035	24°16'
1941	22°56'	1972	23°22'	2004	23°49'	2036	24°16'
1942	22°57'	1973	23°23'	2005	23°50'	2037	24°17'
1943	22°58'	1974	23°24'	2006	23°51'	2038	24°18'
1944	22°59'	1975	23°25'	2007	23°52'	2039	24°19'
1945	22°59'	1976	23°25'	2008	23°53'	2040	24°20'
1946	23°00'	1977	23°26'	2009	23°53'	2041	24°21'
1947	23°01'	1978	23°27'	2010	23°54'	2042	24°22'
1948	23°02'	1979	23°28'	2011	23°55'	2043	24°22'
1949	23°03'	1980	23°29'	2012	23°56'	2044	24°23'
1950	23°04'	1981	23°30'	2013	23°57'	2045	24°24'
1951	23°04'	1982	23°30'	2014	23°58'	2046	24°25'
1952	23°05'	1983	23°31'	2015	23°59'	2047	24°26'
1953	23°06'	1984	23°32'	2016	23°59'	2048	24°27'
1954	23°07'	1985	23°33'	2017	24°00'	2049	24°28'
		1986	23°34'	2018	24°01'	2050	24°28'

The positions for Neptune (♆), Uranus (♅), and Pluto (♇), however, do not need to be converted, since they will not be used in the construction of any of the Vedic charts. The same is true for the cusps of House II through House XII, because only the Ascendant (House I) is used. For the sake of convenience, K. S. Krishnamurti's *ayanamsas* for the years 1924 through 2050 appear in fig. 5.2.

To facilitate the subtraction of the *ayanamsa* from each planetary position, node, and the Ascendant, the zodiac sign associated with each position is converted to a number as shown in fig. 5.3 (third column). Unlike Western or Judaic astrologers, Vedic practitioners do not use symbols for the zodiac signs throughout the process; instead, each of the twelve zodiac signs is simply represented by the sign's numeric position in the zodiac's sequential order (fig. 5.3, third column).

Each zodiac sign equals 30°00′[6] of the zodiac's 360°00′ circle. This is an important fact to remember when calculating these conversions. The result of the *ayanamsa*'s subtraction from the Western horoscope position must be in positive integers. In order to achieve this, sometimes it becomes necessary to transfer one sign's worth of degrees (30°00′) from the planetary position's zodiac sign to the planetary position's degrees. For example, Mercury's position (☿ 03°♋28′)[7] in fig. 8.1 is initially converted and written down as 04 03° 28′, because the zodiac sign number for Cancer (♋), which is 4 (fig. 5.3), is added to the degrees and minutes of the planetary position.

FIGURE 5.3 TABLE OF VEDIC SIGN NAMES AND NUMBERS.

ZODIAC SIGN IN ENGISH/VEDIC (SYMBOL)	TRANSLATION	ZODIAC SIGN NUMBER	ZODIAC SIGN'S PLANETARY RULER (SYMBOL)
Aries/*Mesa* (♈)	ram	1	Mars (♂)
Taurus/*Rsabha* (♉)	bull	2	Venus (♀)
Gemini/*Mithuna* (♊)	male-female couple	3	Mercury (☿)
Cancer/*Karkata* (♋)	crab	4	Moon (☽)
Leo/*Simha* (♌)	lion	5	Sun (☉)
Virgo/*Kanya* (♍)	maiden	6	Mercury (☿)
Libra/*Tula* (♎)	scales	7	Venus (♀)
Scorpio/*Vrscika* (♏)	scorpion	8	Mars (♂)
Sagittarius/*Dhanus* (♐)	archery bow	9	Jupiter (♃)
Capricorn/*Makara* (♑)	mythical beast that resembles a crocodile with an elephant's trunk	10	Saturn (♄)
Aquarius/*Kumbha* (♒)	water pot	11	Saturn (♄)
Pisces/*Mina* (♓)	fish	12	Jupiter (♃)

---

6. This figure is read as "thirty degrees, zero minutes." The zodiac sign's maximum degrees 30°00′ can also be represented as 29°60′ in a calculation, since 01°00′ is also equal to 00°60′.

7. This is read as "Mercury (☿) is in three degrees, twenty-eight minutes of the zodiac sign Cancer (♋)."

The remainder from each calculation must be a positive number. Since the 03° of the planet's position is less than the *ayanamsa*'s 23° to be subtracted below, this planetary position must be converted by transferring one sign's worth of degrees (30°00′) into degrees. Therefore, "04 03° 28′" is changed to "03 33° 28′" to facilitate calculation. The *ayanamsa* (fig. 5.2) can then be subtracted from Mercury's western position (fig. 8.1) to derive Mercury's Vedic position as a positive number, as shown below:

Mercury (☿ 03°♋28′)	03	33°	28′	*(converted from above)*
− *ayanamsa* (1952)	00	23°	05′	*(from fig. 5.2)*
	03	10°	23′	*(sidereal position* ☿ 10°♊23′)[8]

When 30°00′ is transferred from the sign and the *ayanamsa* is subtracted, the position's sign automatically reverts to the previous sign in this circular cycle, which is Gemini (♊) or "03." Therefore the remainder indicates that Mercury's Vedic position (☿ 10°♊23′) has moved one zodiac sign from its Western position (☿ 03°♋28′). This shift occurs frequently between a Vedic (sidereal) and a Western (tropical) planetary position.

The practitioner then proceeds to convert the Ascendant (cusp of House I), planets, and nodes as shown in the examples using Alice's and Peter's Western natal horoscopes (figs. 8.2 and 8.3).

Converting Planetary Positions from the Western to the Vedic Zodiac

Alice T. was born in 1952. Therefore, the *ayanamsa* for that year (23°05′ in fig. 5.2) is subtracted from the Western (tropical) planetary positions that appear in her natal chart (fig. 8.1) except for Uranus (♅), Neptune (♆), and Pluto (♇), which will not be used:

Ascendant (AS 01°♒57′)	11	01°	57′	*(from fig. 8.1, House I)*
	10	31°	57′	*(converted)*
− *ayanamsa*	00	23°	05′	*(from fig. 5.2)*
	10	08°	52′	*(sidereal position* AS 08°♑52′)[9]
Sun (☉ 24°♊55′)	03	24°	55′	*(from fig. 8.1)*
− *ayanamsa*	00	23°	05′	*(from fig. 5.2)*
	03	01°	50′	*(sidereal position* ☉ 01°♊50′)

---

8.   This is read as "Mercury (☿) is in ten degrees, twenty-three minutes of the zodiac sign Gemini (♊)."
9.   The zodiac sign Aquarius (♒) is converted to the number 11. When 30°00′ is transferred from the sign and the *ayanamsa* is subtracted, the position's sign automatically reverts to the previous sign in this circular cycle, which is Capricorn (♑) or 10.

Moon (☽ 11°♈28′)	01	11°	28′	(from fig. 8.1)
	12	41°	28′	(converted)[10]
− ayanamsa	00	23°	05′	(from fig. 5.2)
	12	18°	23′[11]	(sidereal position ☽ 18°♓23′)

Mercury (☿ 03°♋28′)	04	03°	28′	(from fig. 8.1)
	03	33°	28′	(converted)
− ayanamsa	00	23°	05′	(from fig. 5.2)
	03	10°	23′	(sidereal position ☿ 10°♊23′)[12]

Venus (♀ 22°♊31′)	03	22°	31′	(from fig. 8.1)
	02	52°	31′	(converted)
− ayanamsa	00	23°	05′	(from fig. 5.2)
	02	29°	26′	(sidereal position ♀ 29°♉26′)[13]

Mars (♂ 01°♏24′)	08	01°	24′	(from fig. 8.1)
	07	31°	24′	(converted)
− ayanamsa	00	23°	05′	(from fig. 5.2)
	07	08°	19′	(sidereal position ♂ 08°♎19′)[14]

Jupiter (♃ 10°♉52′)	02	10°	52′	(from fig. 8.1)
	01	40°	52′	(converted)
− ayanamsa	00	23°	05′	(from fig. 5.2).
	01	17°	47′	(sidereal position ♃ 17°♈47′)[15]

---

10. Because the zodiac sign that precedes Aries (♈ or 1) in the circular sequential order of the zodiac is Pisces (♓), which is designated by the sign number 12, Aries (♈) is converted to 12, and 30°00′ are added to the degrees to facilitate the *ayanamsa*'s subtraction.

11. The zodiac sign Aries (♈) is converted to the number 01. When 30°00′ is transferred from the sign and the *ayanamsa* is subtracted, the position's sign automatically reverts to the previous sign in this circular cycle, which is Pisces (♓) or 12.

12. The zodiac sign Cancer (♋) is converted to the number 04. When 30°00′ is transferred from the sign and the *ayanamsa* is subtracted, the position's sign automatically reverts to the previous sign in this circular cycle, which is Gemini (♊) or 03.

13. The zodiac sign Gemini (♊) is converted to the number 03. When 30°00′ is transferred from the sign and the *ayanamsa* is subtracted, the position's sign automatically reverts to the previous sign in this circular cycle, which is Taurus (♉) or 02.

14. The zodiac sign Scorpio (♏) is converted to the number 08. When 30°00′ is transferred from the sign and the *ayanamsa* is subtracted, the position's sign automatically reverts to the previous sign in this circular cycle, which is Libra (♎) or 07.

15. The zodiac sign Taurus (♉) is converted to the number 02. When 30°00′ is transferred from the sign and the *ayanamsa* is subtracted, the position's sign automatically reverts to the previous sign in this circular cycle, which is Aries (♈) or 01.

FIGURE 5.4. ALICE T.'S TROPICAL AND SIDEREAL PLANETARY POSITIONS.

ASCENDANT AND PLANETS IN CHART	POSITION IN WESTERN (TROPICAL) NATAL HOROSCOPE (FROM FIG. 8.2)	MINUS AYANAMSA FOR THE BIRTH YEAR 1952 (FIG. 5.2)	POSITION IN VEDIC (SIDEREAL) NATAL HOROSCOPE*
Ascendant (AS)	01°≈57'	23°05'	08°♑52'
Sun (☉)	24°♊55'	23°05'	01°♊50'
Moon (☽)	11°♈28'	23°05'	18°♓23'
Mercury (☿)	03°♋28'	23°05'	10°♊23'
Venus (♀)	22°♊31'	23°05'	29°♉26'
Mars (♂)	01°♏24'	23°05'	08°♎19'
Jupiter (♃)	10°♉52'	23°05'	17°♈47'
Saturn (♄)	08°♎12'	23°05'	15°♍07'
Moon's North Node (☊)	23°≈23'ʀ	23°05'	00°≈18'ʀ
Moon's South Node (☋)	23°♌23'ʀ	23°05'	00°♌18'ʀ

* See fig. 5.3 for the English and Vedic names for the symbols used to represent the zodiac signs in this chart.

Saturn (♄ 08°♎12')	07	08°	12'	(from fig. 8.1)
	06	38°	12'	(converted)
− ayanamsa	00	23°	05'	(from fig. 5.2)
	06	15°	07'	(sidereal position ♄ 15°♍07')[16]
Moon's North Node (☊ 23°≈23')	11	23°	23'	(from fig. 8.1)
− ayanamsa	00	23°	05'	(from fig. 5.2)
	11	00°	18'	(sidereal position ☊ 00°≈18')
Moon's South Node (☋ 23°♌23')	05	23°	23'	(from fig. 8.1)
− ayanamsa	00	23°	05'	(from fig. 5.2)
	05	00°	18'	(sidereal position ☋ 00°♌18')

The differences between Alice's Western (tropical) and Vedic (sidereal) positions can be quickly referenced by looking at the table in fig. 5.4.

Peter C. was born in 1964. Therefore the *ayanamsa* for that year (23°15' in fig. 5.2) is subtracted from the tropical planetary positions in his Western natal chart (fig. 8.2) except for Uranus (♅), Neptune (♆), and Pluto (♇), which will not be used:

16. The zodiac sign Libra (♎) is converted to the number 07. When 30°00' is transferred from the sign and the *ayanamsa* is subtracted, the position's sign automatically reverts to the previous sign in this circular cycle, which is Virgo (♍) or 06.

Ascendant(AS 02°♓49′)	12	02°	49′	(from fig. 8.2, House I)
	11	32°	49′	(converted)
— ayanamsa	00	23°	15′	(from fig. 5.2)
	11	09°	34′	(sidereal position AS 09°♒34′)[17]
Sun (☉ 04°♍41′)	06	04°	41′	(from fig. 8.2)
	05	34°	41′	(converted)
— ayanamsa	00	23°	15′	(from fig. 5.2)
	05	11°	26′	(sidereal position ☉ 11°♌26′)[18]
Moon (☽ 03°♉38′)	02	03°	38′	(from fig. 8.2)
	01	33°	38′	(converted)
— ayanamsa	00	23°	15′	(from fig. 5.2)
	01	10°	23′	(sidereal position ☽ 10°♈23′)[19]
Mercury (☿ 14°♍36′)	06	14°	36′	(from fig. 8.2)
	05	44°	36′	(converted)
— ayanamsa	00	23°	15′	(from fig. 5.2)
	05	21°	21′	(sidereal position ☿ 21°♌21′)[20]
Venus (♀ 18°♋53′)	04	18°	53′	(from fig. 8.2)
	03	48°	53′	(converted)
— ayanamsa	00	23°	15′	(from fig. 5.2)
	03	25°	38′	(sidereal position ♀ 25°♊38′)[21]
Mars (♂ 18°♋31′)	04	18°	31′	(from fig. 8.2)
	03	48°	31′	(converted)
— ayanamsa	00	23°	15′	(from fig. 5.2)
	03	25°	16′	(sidereal position ♂ 25°♊16′)[22]

17. The zodiac sign Pisces (♓) is converted to the number 12. When 30°00′ is transferred from the sign and the *ayanamsa* is subtracted, the position's sign automatically reverts to the previous sign in this circular cycle which is Aquarius (♒) or 11.

18. The zodiac sign Virgo (♍) is converted to the number 06. When 30°00′ is transferred from the sign and the *ayanamsa* is subtracted, the position's sign automatically reverts to the previous sign in this circular cycle, which is Leo (♌) or 05.

19. The zodiac sign Taurus (♉) is converted to the number 02. When 30°00′ is transferred from the sign and the *ayanamsa* is subtracted, the position's sign automatically reverts to the previous sign in this circular cycle, which is Aries (♈) or 01.

20. The zodiac sign Virgo (♍) is converted to the number 06. When 30°00′ is transferred from the sign and the *ayanamsa* is subtracted, the position's sign automatically reverts to the previous sign in this circular cycle, which is Leo (♌) or 05.

21. The zodiac sign Cancer (♋) is converted to the number 04. When 30°00′ is transferred from the sign and the *ayanamsa* is subtracted, the position's sign automatically reverts to the previous sign in this circular cycle, which is Gemini (♊) or 03.

22. Ibid.

Jupiter (♃ 25°♉36′)	02	25°	36′	*(from fig. 8.2)*
− *ayanamsa*	00	23°	15′	*(from fig. 5.2)*
	02	02°	21′	*(sidereal position* ♃ 02°♉21′*)*
Saturn (♄ 01°♓25′)	12	01°	25′	*(from fig. 8.2)*
	11	31°	25′	*(converted)*
− *ayanamsa*	00	23°	15′	*(from fig. 5.2)*
	11	08°	10′	*(sidereal position* ♄ 08°♒10′*)*[23]
Moon's North Node (☊ 29°♊40′)	03	29°	40′	*(from fig. 8.2)*
− *ayanamsa*	00	23°	15′	*(from fig. 5.2)*
	03	06°	25′	*(sidereal position* ☊ 06°♊25′*)*
Moon's South Node (☋ 29°♐40′)	09	29°	40′	*(from fig. 8.2)*
− *ayanamsa*	00	23°	15′	*(from fig. 5.2)*
	09	06°	25′	*(sidereal position* ☋ 06°♐25′*)*

The differences between Peter's Western (tropical) positions and Vedic (sidereal) positions can be quickly referenced by looking at the table in fig. 5.5:

FIGURE 5.5. PETER C.'S TROPICAL AND SIDEREAL PLANETARY POSITIONS.

ASCENDANT AND PLANETS IN CHART	POSITION IN WESTERN (TROPICAL) NATAL HOROSCOPE (FROM FIG. 8.3)	MINUS AYANAMSA FOR THE BIRTH YEAR 1964 (FIG. 5.2)	POSITION IN VEDIC (SIDEREAL) NATAL HOROSCOPE*
Ascendant (AS)	02°♓49′	23°15′	09°♒34′
Sun (☉)	04°♍41′	23°15′	11°♌26′
Moon (☽)	03°♉38′	23°15′	10°♈23′
Mercury (☿)	14°♍36′℞**	23°15′	21°♌21′℞
Venus (♀)	18°♋53′	23°15′	25°♊38′
Mars (♂)	18°♋31′	23°15′	25°♊16′
Jupiter (♃)	25°♉36′	23°15′	02°♉21′
Saturn (♄)	01°♓25′℞	23°15′	08°♒10′℞
Moon's North Node (☊)	29°♊40′℞	23°15′	06°♊25′℞
Moon's South Node (☋)	29°♐40′℞	23°15′	06°♐25′℞

* See fig. 5.3 for the English and Vedic names for the symbols used to represent the zodiac signs in this chart.
** ℞ indicates that the planet is in retrograde motion.

23. The zodiac sign Pisces (♓) is converted to the number 12. When 30°00′ is transferred from the sign and the *ayanamsa* is subtracted, the position's sign automatically reverts to the previous sign in this circular cycle, which is Aquarius (♒) or 11.

The critical data listed in the fourth column of figs. 5.4 and 5.5 are used to develop many portions of a *jataka* (natal) personality profile, including the construction and delineation of either a *rasicakra* (sign chart) or a *bhavacakra* (house chart), as well as subordinate *sodasavargas* (divisional charts) that are detailed later in this chapter.

STEP TWO: CONSTRUCTING AND INTERPRETING A NATAL HOROSCOPE

Now that the Vedic (sidereal) Ascendant, planetary, and node positions have been established, the Vedic natal horoscope can be constructed. The first and most relevant of the many *sodasavargas* (divisional charts) used in the *jataka* (natal) personality profile is executed in modern-day India in one of two optional ways: as a *rasicakra* (sign chart) or as a *bhavacakra* (house chart). Only one of these charts is needed or executed by an astrologer for a *jataka* (natal) personality profile. The preference for one over the other is subjective; it depends strictly upon where and by whom the practitioner was taught, not on the quality of information that can be derived from either source.

Constructing the *Rasicakra*

The Kerala-style (southern Indian) *rasicakra* (sign chart) places the twelve *rasis* (zodiac signs) in a clockwise fashion beginning with Aries (♈), which is designated as 1, ending with Pisces, which is designated as 12, and following the same order shown in fig. 5.3 (third column). These numbers are placed in the twelve boxes as designated in fig. 5.6, below. No matter whose chart is being constructed, these zodiac sign positions remain static in the *rasicakra* construction method. Symbols for the individual planets are never used by Vedic astrologers; rather, the names of the planets are generally written out in Sanskrit. Symbols are used here simply to facilitate comparisons between this type of Vedic chart and those executed by Western, Judaic, or Arabian practitioners.

Next, the sidereal position of the individual's Ascendant (as determined in "Step One: Establishing the Positions of the Planets," page 144) is marked by placing a diagonal line through the box—or position—that represents the Ascendant's zodiac sign. For example, Alice's Ascendant (AS 08°♑52′ in fig. 5.4, fourth column) is indicated in fig. 5.7 by a diagonal line in the box marked "10," because 10 represents the zodiac sign Capricorn (♑). Then proceed to place the planets into the numbered boxes. For each planet, locate the sign number (third column, fig. 5.3) that corresponds to the zodiac sign in planet's sidereal position (fourth column, fig. 5.4). Next, place the planet's symbol in the relevant numbered box as shown in fig. 5.7.

Beginning with box 1 in fig. 5.7, Jupiter (♃ 17°♈47′ in fig. 5.4, fourth column) is placed in box 1 (fig. 5.7), which represents the zodiac sign Aries (♈). Venus (♀ 29°♉26′ in fig. 5.4, fourth column) is placed in box 2 (fig. 5.7), which represents

FIGURE 5.6. THE KERALA-STYLE *RASICAKRA*.

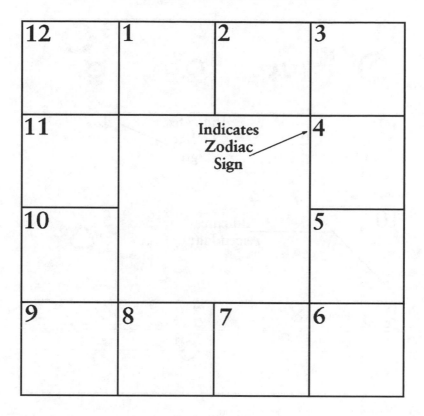

the zodiac sign Taurus (♉). The Sun (☉ 01°♊50′ in fig. 5.4, fourth column) and Mercury (☿ 10°♊23′ in fig. 5.4, fourth column) are both placed in box 3 (fig. 5.7), which represents the zodiac sign Gemini (♊). The Moon's South Node (☋ 00°♌18′ in fig. 5.4, fourth column) is placed in box 5 (fig. 5.7), which represents the zodiac sign Leo (♌). Saturn (♄ 15°♍07′, in fig. 5.4, fourth column) is placed in box 6 (fig. 5.7), which represents the zodiac sign Virgo (♍). Mars (♂ 08°♎19′ in fig. 5.4, fourth column) is placed in box 7 (fig. 5.7), which represents the zodiac sign Libra (♎). The Moon's North Node (☊ 00°♒18′ in fig. 5.4, fourth column) is placed in box 11 (fig. 5.7), which represents the zodiac sign Aquarius (♒). And the Moon (☽ 18°♓23′ in fig. 5.4, fourth column) is placed in box 12 (fig. 5.7), which represents the zodiac sign Pisces (♓).

Because none of the planetary positions in fig. 5.4 (fourth column) occupy the zodiac signs Cancer (♋, box 4 in fig. 5.7), Scorpio (♏, box 8 in fig. 5.7), Sagittarius (♐, box 9 in fig. 5.7), or Capricorn (♑, box 10 in fig. 5.7), these boxes—or positions—remain empty. The degrees and minutes of Alice's Ascendant, planetary, and node positions are kept as reference notes, as shown in fig. 5.4 (fourth column), but are not incorporated onto her *rasicakra* (fig. 5.7).

FIGURE 5.7. ALICE T.'S *RASICAKRA*.

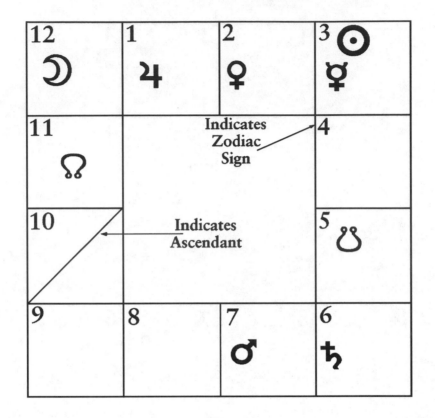

The same process is applied to Peter's Vedic positions as follows. His Ascendant (AS 09°≈34′ in fig. 5.5, fourth column) is indicated in fig. 5.8 by a diagonal line in box 11, which represents the zodiac sign Aquarius (≈). Beginning with box 1 in fig. 5.8, the Moon (☽ 10°♈23′ in fig. 5.5, fourth column) is placed in box 1 (fig. 5.8), which represents the zodiac sign Aries (♈). Jupiter (♃ 02°♉21′ in fig. 5.5, fourth column) is placed in box 2 (fig. 5.8), which represents the zodiac sign Taurus (♉). Venus (♀ 25°♊38′ in fig. 5.5, fourth column), Mars (♂ 25°♊16′ in fig. 5.5, fourth column), and the Moon's North Node (☊ 06°♊25′ in fig. 5.5, fourth column) are all placed in the box marked 3 (fig. 5.8), which represents the zodiac sign Gemini (♊). The Sun (☉ 11°♌26′ in fig. 5.5, fourth column) and Mercury (☿ 21°♌21′ in fig. 5.5, fourth column) are placed in box 5 (fig. 5.8), which represents the zodiac sign Leo (♌). The Moon's South Node (☋ 06°♐25′ in fig. 5.5, fourth column) is placed in box 9 (fig. 5.8), which represents the zodiac sign Sagittarius (♐). Saturn (♄ 08°≈10′ in fig. 5.5, fourth column) is placed in box 11 (fig. 5.8), which represents the position of the zodiac sign Aquarius (≈).

Because none of the planetary positions in fig. 5.5 (fourth column) occupy the zodiac signs Cancer (♓, box 4 in fig. 5.8), Virgo (♍, box 6 in fig. 5.8), Libra (♎, box

FIGURE 5.8. PETER C.'s RASICAKRA.

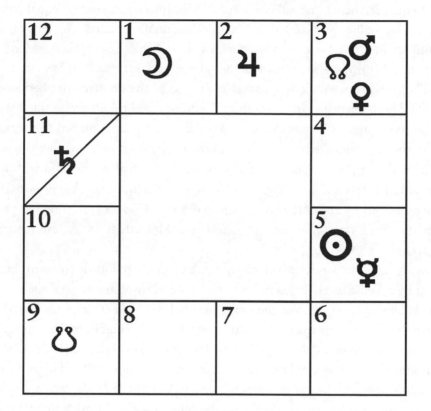

7 in fig. 5.8), Scorpio (♏, box 8 in fig. 5.8), Capricorn (♑, box 10 in fig. 5.8), or Pisces (♓, box 12 in fig. 5.8), these boxes—or positions—remain empty. Once again, the degrees and minutes of Peter's Ascendant, planetary, and node positions are kept as reference notes as shown in fig. 5.5 (fourth column), but are not incorporated onto his *rasicakra* (fig. 5.8).

Unlike the Western and Judaic chart systems, the visual presentation of the natal data in the *rasicakra* (such as those in figs. 5.7 and 5.8) is merely an outline from which the astrologer makes his or her delineation of the planets' positions. It is a facet that the Vedic system shares with Chinese and Tibetan documentation methods (see chapters 3 and 4).

Interpreting the Ascendant Position in a *Rasicakra*
Identifying the Ascendant's Naksatra

The Vedic *naksatras*[24] are closely related to other lunar mansion systems such as the Arabian *manazils*, Chinese *sieu*, and medieval European lunar mansions (see

---

24. Pronounced "nahk-sha-tra," this term means "constellation" or "lunar mansion."

chapter 2, "The Moon School"). But instead of subdividing the zodiac into twenty-eight equal segments, the *naksatras* are divided into twenty-seven equal segments plus an intercalary station[25] that is only occasionally applied. Ancient observers identified these fixed stars—or lunar mansions—as stopping points the Moon regularly passed as it traversed the arc of the sidereal zodiac thousands of years ago.

The *naksatras* provide a remarkable glimpse at the connectivity between religion and pure science in Indian culture. Vedic oral traditions narrate the tale of the Moon god, Soma, as he traveled from one *naksatra* (lunar mansion) to the next on his journey through the heavens. In Vedic astrology, each *naksatra* (fig. 5.9) is associated with a 13°20′ segment of the 360-degree sidereal zodiac, and with a fixed star within a given constellation. For example, the *naksatra* Asvini corresponds with 00°00′ to 13°20′ of the zodiac sign Aries (00°♈00′–13°♈20′ in fig. 5.9) and with the fixed stars Sharatan (β Aries) and Mesarthim (γ Aries) (chapter 2, fig. 2.1).

Every *naksatra* is not only ruled by a planet (fig. 5.9, fourth column), but governed by a Vedic deity (listed below). The general interpretation of each *naksatra* was documented in the five-thousand-year-old *Rig Veda* (one of the four Vedas) and in texts written by the sixth-century astrologer Varahamihira. In modern Vedic astrology, the *naksatras* are applied to the interpretation of the Ascendant, which is represented by a diagonal line in a *rasicakra* (figs. 5.7 and 5.8). To identify an Ascendant's *naksatra*, locate the person's exact Ascendant in degrees and minutes (figs. 5.4 and 5.5, fourth column). Find the general zodiac location in fig. 5.9 (third column). Then read across to the first and second columns to identify the Ascendant's *naksatra*.

For example, Alice's Ascendant (AS 08°♑52′ in fig. 5.4, fourth column; box 10 in fig. 5.7) occupies the twenty-first *naksatra*—the *naksatra* Uttarasadha (26°♐41′–10°♑00′ in fig. 5.9). Peter's Ascendant (AS 09°♒34′ in fig. 5.5, fourth column; box 11 in fig. 5.8) resides in the twenty-fourth *naksatra*—the *naksatra* Satabhisaj (06°♒41′–20°♒00′ in fig. 5.9).

The Ascendant's *naksatra* is then interpreted using the material that follows:

1. Asvini   *Deities:* the Asvins named Dasra and Nasatya, who are sons of the Sun.
                   Traits: well-dressed; good-looking; has many friends; has a positive outlook; determination; humility; is very moral.

---

25.   The *naksatra* Abhijit (pronounced "ab-he-jeet," which means "victorious") is placed by some practitioners between the twenty-first and twenty-second *naksatras*. It is intended to complement the twenty-eight parts of the lunar cycle applied by Chinese and Tibetan astrologers. Located between the *naksatras* Uttarasadha and Sravana, the *naksatra* Abhijit's fixed star is Vega (α Lyra).

FIGURE 5.9. THE *NAKSATRAS*.

NAKSATRA NUMBER	NAKSATRA NAME (TRANSLATION)	ZODIAC SIGN LOCATION IN DEGREES (°) AND MINUTES (′)	NAKSATRA PLANETARY RULER
1	Asvini (possessing horses)	00°♈00′–13°♈20′	Moon's South Node (☋)
2	Bharani (bearing)	13°♈21′–20°♈40′	Venus (♀)
3	Krttika (cutters)	26°♈41′–10°♉00′	Sun (☉)
4	Rohini (red one)	10°♉01′–23°♉20′	Moon (☽)
5	Mrgasiras (deer's head)	23°♉21′–06°♊40′	Mars (♂)
6	Ardra (moist one)	06°♊41′–20°♊00′	Moon's North Node (☊)
7	Punarvasu (two who are prosperous again)	20°♊01′–03°♋20′	Jupiter (♃)
8	Pusya (nourishment)	03°♋21′–16°♋40′	Saturn (♄)
9	Aslesa (embracing)	16°♋41′–00°♌00′	Mercury (☿)
10	Magha (increasing)	00°♌01′–13°♌20′	Moon's South Node (☋)
11	Purvaphalguni (former red one)	13°♌21′–26°♌40′	Venus (♀)
12	Uttaraphalguni (latter red one)	26°♌41′–10°♍00′	Sun (☉)
13	Hasta (hand)	10°♍01′–23°♍20′	Moon (☽)
14	Citra (many-colored)	23°♍21′–06°♎40′	Mars (♂)
15	Svati (independent)	06°♎41′–20°♎00′	Moon's North Node (☊)
16	Visakha (forked)	20°♎01′–03°♏20′	Jupiter (♃)
17	Anuradha (after Radha)	03°♏21′–16°♏40′	Saturn (♄)
18	Jyestha (eldest)	16°♏41′–00°♐00′	Mercury (☿)
19	Mula (root)	00°♐01′–13°♐20′	Moon's South Node (☋)
20	Purvasadha (former unconquered)	13°♐21′–26°♐40′	Venus (♀)
21	Uttarasadha (latter unconquered)	26°♐41′–10°♑00′	Sun (☉)
22	Sravana (hearing)	10°♑01′–23°♑20′	Moon (☽)
23	Sravistha (most famous)	23°♑21′–06°♒40′	Mars (♂)
24	Satabhisaj (possessing a hundred physicians)	06°♒41′–20°♒00′	Moon's North Node (☊)
25	Purvabhadrapada (former one who has lucky feet)	20°♒01′–03°♓20′	Jupiter (♃)
26	Uttarabhadrapada (latter one who has lucky feet)	03°♓21′–16°♓40′	Saturn (♄)
27	Revati (wealthy)	16°♓41′–30°♓00′	Mercury (☿)

2. Bharani   *Deity:* Yamaraj, the King of Dharma and the God of Death.
              Traits: brave; helpful; somewhat gullible; may suffer from others'
              jealousy; very sexually inclined; may have a small family.

3. Krttika   *Deity:* Agnidev, the God of Fire.
              Traits: very capable; heroic; has many leadership qualities; has
              high personal goals; succeeds on a material level.

4. Rohini

Deity: Lord Brahma, the Creator.
Traits: handsome; popular; professionally successful; has leadership potential; is very critical of other people.

5. Mrgasiras

Deity: Soma, the god of both the Sacred Drink and of the Moon.
Traits: physically beautiful; fond of creature comforts, the fine arts, and learning; close to his or her mother; may have been sickly as a child.

6. Ardra

Deity: Ancient texts stated that Ardra's ruler was Lord Rudra the Howler. But in later documents, Siva the Storm God was indicated. (Siva is one of the three supreme gods and is the regent of destruction, procreation, and transformation.)
Traits: physically strong; long-lived; ends up in an intellectually unstimulating position, becoming critical of others.

7. Punarvasu

Deity: Sri Aditi (Infinity), the wife of the ancient sage Kasyapa and mother of an important group of gods known as the Aditya (Bhaga, Aryaman, Mitra, and Indra).
Traits: generous; intelligent; wallows in self-doubts; changes residence often; has difficulty making a commitment to a relationship.

8. Pusya

Deity: Brhaspati, the priest of the gods and the God of the planet Jupiter (♃).
Traits: considerate; sincere; a good communicator; has a successful career; has a good family life.

9. Aslesa

Deities: the serpent gods Naga and Nagini.
Traits: energetic; needs direction; uncomfortable in the company of strangers; unkind to those who are not family members or trusted friends.

10. Magha

Deities: the Pitris, the deified ancestors.
Traits: highly intelligent; extremely successful; has the potential to acquire great wealth and happiness; sensual; religious; very popular; doesn't like many people.

11. Purva-phalguni

Deity: Bhaga, the Aditya (a son of the goddess Aditi and the ancient sage Kasyapa) who protects happiness in marriage.
Traits: energetic; healthy; generous; likes action; succeeds in positions of authority.

12. Uttara-phalguni

Deity: Aryaman, the Aditya (a son of the goddess Aditi and the ancient sage Kasyapa), who presides over hospitality.
Traits: handsome; intelligent; has a varied love life; has a high opinion of self; has the potential to become wealthy and to have a successful career.

13. Hasta

Deities: Suryadev the Sun God, and the life-giving god Savitr the Impeller.
Traits: adept at communication; enjoys travel and socializing; possesses an attractive disposition; is somewhat conservative in his or her actions.

14. Citra

Deity: Tvastr, the Heavenly Carpenter.
Traits: moves far from his or her birthplace; loves beautiful clothes; enjoys many diversified interests; can be condescending to others.

15. Svati

Deity: Vayu, the God of Wind and Breath.
Traits: kind; self-satisfied; lives far from his or her birthplace; takes his or her time executing any task.

16. Visakha

Deity: Indra, the Aditya (a son of the goddess Aditi and the ancient sage Kasyapa), who is the King of the Thirty-three Gods, and Agni, who is the God of the East and the God of Fire.
Traits: philosophic; knowledgeable; energetic; has little patience; may become wealthy.

17. Anuradha

Deity: Mitra, the Aditya (a son of the goddess Aditi and the ancient sage Kasyapa), who presides over friendship.
Traits: family-loving; shy in public; loves to travel; may live far from his or her birthplace; attractive; spiritual; suffers from occasional bouts of depression.

18. Jyestha

Deity: Indra, the Aditya (a son of the goddess Aditi and the ancient sage Kasyapa), who is the King of the Thirty-three Gods.
Traits: respectable; capable; acts and speaks well in public; others may look up to this person.

19. Mula

Deity: Nritta, the Goddess of Destruction, Corruption, and Decay.
Traits: handsome; intelligent; experiences occasional poor health; may vacillate from an intended goal; marriage causes problems.

20. Purvasadha   *Deities:* the Apahs, who are the Water Goddesses.
Traits: pleasant; social; does not have an advanced education; humble; kind; has many friends; has a large family.

21. Uttarasadha   *Deities:* a group of gods known as the Visvadevas, who are brothers. The group includes the ten gods Vasu (Good), Satya (Truth), Kratu (Power), Daksa (Skill), Kala (Time), Kama (Love), Dhrti (Constancy), Rocaka (Bright), Dhuri (Summit), and Dhvani (Sound). The group also includes two deified kings: Kuru, who is the ancestor of the Suryavamsa (the Sun's dynasty of kings), and Pururvas, who is the ancestor of the Candravamsa (the Moon's dynasty of kings). (See "The Times of Issuing-Forth, Continuance, and Destruction" in chapter 1.) Occasionally the deified king Madravas is also mentioned, but his origins are not well known.
Traits: intelligent; fun-loving; generous; destined for fame; must be aware of enemies.

22. Sravana   *Deity:* Sri Visnu, the God of Preservation and a member of the main triad that includes the Lords Brahma and Siva.
Traits: intelligent; educated; moves far from his or her birthplace; may become famous; encounters many enemies.

23. Sravistha   *Deities:* the Vasus, who include the gods Apa (Water), Dhruva (Pole Star), Soma (Moon), Dhara (Bearer), Anila (Wind), Anala (Fire), Pratyusa (Dawn), and Prabhasa (Light).
Traits: strong; has a powerful ego; occasionally generous; encounters many confrontations within marriage. (This same *naksatra* is popularly known as Dhanista in the West and by many Indian astrologers as well.)

24. Satabhisaj   *Deity:* Varuna, the God of the Ocean.
Traits: supportive of other people's work; has an unobtrusive nature; can possess a devious side.

25. Purva-   *Deity:* Ajaikapad, the one-footed goat, who is a member of Lord
bhadrapada[26]   Siva's entourage.
Traits: changes residence often; uniquely talented at achieving a given goal through hard work and ingenuity; sensual; philosophical; slightly nervous.

---

26. This station is sometimes called Purvaprosthapada.

26. Uttara-bhadrapada[27]	*Deity:* Ahirbudhnya, the Serpent of the Depths. *Traits:* eccentric; fickle; shy; well-spoken; wants to become rich; has many enemies.
27. Revati	*Deity:* Pushan the Nurturer, who is the protector of flocks and herds. *Traits:* handsome; brave; well mannered; sensual; very successful.

As mentioned earlier in this section, Alice's Ascendant (AS 08°♑52′ in fig. 5.4, fourth column) occupies the twenty-first *naksatra*—the *naksatra* Uttarasadha (26°♐41′–10°♑00′ in fig. 5.9, third column)—indicating she is intelligent, fun-loving, generous, and destined for fame. She must remain aware of her enemies.

Peter's Ascendant (AS 09°♒34′ in fig. 5.5, fourth column) resides in the twenty-fourth *naksatra*—the *naksatra* Satabhisaj (06°♒40′–20°♒00′ in fig. 5.9, third column)—which suggests that Peter is supportive of other people's work and has an unobtrusive nature. He can possess a devious side, however.

Interpreting the Planetary Positions in a *Rasicakra*

Remarkably similar to the delineation of the planets by sign, as employed in Western and Judaic astrology, the interpretation of the *rasicakra* is based upon a planet's position within a particular *rasi* (sign). For example, in Alice's *rasicakra* (fig. 5.7), the Moon (☽) is placed in box 12. According to the table in fig. 5.3, this number represents the zodiac sign Pisces (♓). Therefore an astrologer would read the interpretation for the Moon in Pisces, below. In Peter's *rasicakra* (fig. 5.8), the Moon (☽) is placed in box 1. According to the table in fig. 5.3, this number represents the zodiac sign Aries (♈). Therefore the astrologer would read the interpretation for the Moon in Aries, below. This same process is used to interpret the effects of the Sun (☉), Moon (☽), Mercury (☿), Venus (♀), Mars (♂), Jupiter (♃), and Saturn (♄). Surprisingly, there is no mention in any of the classic Vedic astrological texts of the influence that the Moon's North (☊) and South (☋) Nodes exert in the various zodiac signs. Thus, no delineations follow for their positions in a *rasicakra*.

Each astrologer assesses the position of a planet a little differently from any other. This subjectivity is primarily based on personal experience, client observation, and oral tradition rather than on any technical differences or flaws. The reading of any item of interpretative data must be assessed as merely a small portion of the larger whole, which includes the quality and strength of the planet's placement in the horoscope (see "Applying the *Shadbala*," page 230). More important, another

27. This station is sometimes called Uttaraprosthapada.

assessment formulates its results according to patterns of planetary combination that yield specific characteristics which have been passed down for centuries. Known as a *yoga*, each formula prescribes a personality type by combining planetary positions in specific houses along with the six *shadbala*. Very complex in their structure and delineation, these *yoga*-based characteristics appear most profound during fixed and predictable periods of the individual's life, which are discussed more thoroughly later in this chapter. Therefore the interpretative material below represents only a general understanding of what effect the individual planets have on a person's personality.

The Sun[28] (☉) in the Various Zodiac Signs[29]

The Sun's occupation of the individual zodiac signs produces an influence in a man or a woman as follows:

Aries (♈)	freedom-loving; natural-born leader; persistent; quick-witted; quick-tempered; has a forgiving nature
Taurus (♉)	self-reliant; cautious; fears pain; has extreme patience; furious when angered; loves nature and the arts; has psychic or healing talents; succeeds in executive positions or public service
Gemini (♊)	sensitive; intuitive; youthful-looking; active mind; easily influenced by kindness; quick and efficient in emergencies; needs to work independently on more than one project at a time; succeeds in writing, research, or investigation
Cancer (♋)	sensitive; changeable; fertile imagination; profoundly affected by surroundings; possesses dramatic flair; has many mood swings; craves kindness; fears ridicule; remembers everything
Leo (♌)	dramatic; outspoken; easy to anger and please; sports-minded; loves children; has many friends; is a natural-born leader; determined; independent
Virgo (♍)	frugal; practical; contemplative; industrious; youthful-looking; perfectionistic; desires wealth; worries; has a sharp temper, but abhors fighting; has a strong command of language; is able to learn quickly; has high endurance level

---

28. Vedic practitioners' name for the Sun is Surya.
29. To find the Vedic names for the various zodiac signs, refer to fig. 5.3, which gives both the English and Vedic names for each sign.

Libra (♎)   peace-loving; sensitive; neat; clean; profoundly affected by surroundings; needs harmony and balance; generally marries young[30]

Scorpio (♏)   shrewd; critical; skeptical; calculating; determined; tenacious; efficient; economical; may make trouble for others; fond of grandeur and luxury[31]

Sagittarius (♐)   generous; outspoken; self-reliant; perseverent; optimistic; energetic; loves the outdoors, active sports, and freedom; able to hone in and make a mark on a situation

Capricorn (♑)   practical; quiet; ambitious; opportunistic; has strong self-esteem; is often disappointed; suffers from bouts of gloom and depression

Aquarius (♒)   unobtrusive; determined; eccentric; has very strong likes and dislikes; is a faithful friend; is a humanitarian; slow to anger; easily influenced by kindness; suffers from feelings of rejection

Pisces (♓)   amiable; loving; secretive; lacks self-confidence; needs order; bestows kindness on defenseless animals, underdogs, and people in distress; feels protected by some unseen force of nature

The Moon[32] (☽) in the Various Zodiac Signs[33]

The Moon's occupation of the individual zodiac signs produces an influence in a man or a woman as follows:

Aries (♈)   highly imaginative; self-reliant; inventive; has a restless mind; quick-tempered; independent; carves a unique path; heads a major undertaking; reaches prominence

Taurus (♉)   conservative; determined; stubborn; driven by love, marriage, and friendship; finances aided by the opposite sex

Gemini (♊)   warm-hearted; humane; reserved; intellectual; dislikes arguments; sometimes drawn into embarrassing situations; gains much from books and science

---

30. According to Western astrologers, it is not uncommon for this person to marry more than once.
31. Some Western practitioners believe this person also does well as a surgeon, chemist, detective, peace officer, or contractor.
32. Vedic astrologers' name for the Moon is Candra.
33. To find the Vedic names for the various zodiac signs, refer to fig. 5.3.

Cancer (♋)   agreeable; sympathetic; follows the path of least resistance; travels; cooks; collects antiques; encounters great obstacles

Leo (♌)   self-confident; self-reliant; generous; meticulously dressed; well-mannered; popular with the opposite sex; free-spirited; loves sports

Virgo (♍)   highly intellectual; intuitive; unpretentious; quietly ambitious; a quick study; investigative; experiences frequent travel and changes; many friends among the opposite sex[34]

Libra (♎)   affectionate; social; very popular; fond of younger people; extremely affected by surroundings; loves romance, marriage, luxury, fine clothes, and the fine arts

Scorpio (♏)   vigorous; determined; abrupt; makes sacrifices for the right reasons; has problems with the opposite sex because of impulsiveness[35]

Sagittarius (♐)   restless; benevolent; quick-tempered; frequently moves from one place to another; enjoys outdoor sports; involved in religious, political, or educational reforms; experiences possible public notoriety

Capricorn (♑)   cold; calculating; cares little for others' feelings; comes to public attention, inspiring others for better or worse

Aquarius (♒)   active; unconventional; highly inventive; very independent; attracted to science, education, the occult, secret societies, and politics

Pisces (♓)   imaginative; kind; intuitive; psychic; literary; meets with many misfortunes and obstacles; loves beauty and luxury; has difficulty saving money or affording things; has trouble making emotional commitment in romance

---

34. This person is also said by some Western astrologers to have secret sorrows in marriage that cause stomach and intestinal distress.
35. According to some Western astrologers, this placement indicates that voyages and childbirth can be dangerous for this person.

Mercury[36] (☿) in the Various Zodiac Signs[37]

Mercury's occupation of the individual zodiac signs produces an influence on a man or a woman as follows:

Aries (♈)	impulsive; fast-talking; quick-thinking; antagonistic; prone to unconscious exaggeration; restless; indecisive
Taurus (♉)	diplomatic; strong likes and dislikes; fond of the opposite sex, pleasure, music, and art; obsessed with the acquisition of money and possessions
Gemini (♊)	unbiased; ingenious; detail-oriented; loves reading, traveling, observing, and learning; has a talent for law, public speaking, or business
Cancer (♋)	diplomatic; adaptable; restless; impressionable; loyal; enjoys family reunions, poetry, music, ocean voyages, and spiritual pursuits
Leo (♌)	ambitious; quick-tempered; has a heart of gold; a natural-born leader; progressive; fond of children, the arts, sports, fine food and drink[38]
Virgo (♍)	cautious; inventive; quiet; practical; possesses literary talent and powers of persuasion; communicative; organized; fond of literature, mathematics, the healing arts, investigation, and mystery
Libra (♎)	refined; broad-minded; quiet; dispassionate; fond of invention, music, and mathematics; able to draw comparisons
Scorpio (♏)	obstinate; sarcastic; positive; bold; inquisitive; appreciates various ideologies, psychologies, and mystical subjects; loves to socialize at parties and with the opposite sex; encounters many disappointments because of friends and relatives
Sagittarius (♐)	independent; rebellious; generous; rash and impulsive; wise and prophetic; appreciates nature, travel, change for its own sake, family, authority, and sports

---

36. Vedic practitioners' name for Mercury (☿) is Budha (Knower), which is different from Buddha (Enlightened).
37. To find the Vedic names for the various zodiac signs, refer to fig. 5.3.
38. According to some Western practitioners, this same person must take care not to overindulge in food or beverages that might adversely affect the heart.

Capricorn (♑)   critical; suspicious; fickle; discontented; strongly influenced by kindness; always busy; has many interests including literature, science, philosophy, and the occult[39]

Aquarius (♒)   observant; penetrating; keen judge of human nature; friends are intellectuals, eccentrics, and elders; talents center around mathematics, science, invention, politics, and systems analysis

Pisces (♓)   imaginative; impressionable; knowledge acquired by perception and intuition rather than by scholarship; changes occupations often; does well in nursing or healing professions[40]

Venus[41] (♀) in the Various Zodiac Signs[42]

Venus's occupation of the individual zodiac signs produces an influence on a man or a woman as follows:

Aries (♈)   very popular; generous; affectionate; appreciates recreation, the arts, entertainment, and the opposite sex; may marry very early or hastily, and will likely encounter an inharmonious relationship

Taurus (♉)   affectionate; has deep, enduring emotions; encounters delays in marriage; appreciates money, comfort, and pleasure; gains from profession and spirit

Gemini (♊)   inventive; intuitive; profits from writing, speaking, drama, art, music, travel, or entertainment; receives rewards from more than one source; falls in love many times; carries on two simultaneous love affairs, or marries more than once

Cancer (♋)   home-loving; domestically inclined; love of mother; possesses a sympathetic and mediumistic nature; has many clandestine love affairs; has an older or younger spouse; encounters marital problems caused by parents, money, or profession

Leo (♌)   freedom-loving; generous; naturally artistic, dramatic, or musically talented; has a strong social and romantic life; gains through investments, speculation, or inheritance

---

39. This is a position shared by many Western military leaders.
40. According to some Western astrologers, there is some indication of psychic or mediumistic ability, but this person's overly receptive nature may cause danger in these areas.
41. Vedic astrologers' name for Venus is Sukra.
42. To find the Vedic names for the various zodiac signs, refer to fig. 5.3.

Virgo (♍)   quiet; rarely expresses deep emotions; experiences disappoint-
                     ment or delays in romance; marries an employee, a co-worker,
                     a doctor, or an invalid; profits through spouse's or partner's
                     investments[43]

Libra (♎)   sympathetic; loving; marries well; profits through marriage or
                     partnership; has talented children; appreciates cultured amuse-
                     ments, social functions, and the friendship of philosophical or
                     literary people

Scorpio (♏)   passionate; affectionate; emotional; a spendthrift; gains from
                     things connected with water or the dead; encounters financial
                     troubles through legacy, gifts, or partnerships; experiences dis-
                     appointments or losses in courtship and marriage

Sagittarius (♐)   charitable; just; impressionable; loyal; appreciates beauty,
                     travel, romance, and the outdoors; respects literary and intel-
                     lectual work; gains from horses, shipping, travel, sports, specu-
                     lation, investment, legacy, and partnership; marries more than
                     once; potentially has a long-distance romance

Capricorn (♑)   trustworthy; responsible; gains favors from superiors; profits
                     from business, investments, stocks, shares, and executive posi-
                     tions; marries for professional, financial, or social reasons;
                     spouse may become disappointed, cold, or indifferent

Aquarius (♒)   amiable; sincere; appreciates life; has a diversified group of
                     friendships; has strong convictions; profits through corpora-
                     tions, partnerships, investments, or inheritance; has unusual
                     love affairs; marries late in life; marries an eccentric older or
                     younger person

Pisces (♓)   romantically fickle; charitable; moved to sympathy by the plight
                     of the underdog; appreciates the arts, beauty, luxury, and soci-
                     ety; financially profits through friends, artistic pursuits, or occu-
                     pations involving the beautification of the surroundings

---

43. Some Western practitioners believe this person does well in medical, agricultural, horticultural, or environmental fields.

Mars[44] (♂) in the Various Zodiac Signs[45]

Mars's occupation of the individual zodiac signs produces an influence in a man or a woman as follows:

Aries (♈)	adventurous; quarrelsome; self-assured; self-interested; forceful; impulsive; unable to keep secrets or conceal emotions[46]
Taurus (♉)	rash; audacious; causes harm to women, or is harmed by women; experiences property loss; encounters danger from adultery and wild animals; has violent tendencies
Gemini (♊)	cunning and mentally keen; has unfortunate travels; experiences sudden or unexpected financial losses
Cancer (♋)	fearless but changeable; lacks perseverance; nurses ill feelings for long periods
Leo (♌)	bold; an aggressive opponent; a forgiving friend; encounters victory from struggles; has powerful enemies
Virgo (♍)	has a strong interest in scientific or medical innovations; craves fame and power, but encounters downfalls, obstacles, reversals, and struggles of a bizarre nature; marries a person of lower social standing; loses friends through misunderstandings, serious quarrels, or death[47]
Libra (♎)	observant; perceptive; intuitive; romantically impulsive; has leadership skills; survives fierce competition; delays marriage because of an early heartbreak, or an early marriage breaks up in argument[48]
Scorpio (♏)	hardworking; inventive; selfish; vengeful; passionate; has a cold disregard for other people's feelings; is best suited for espionage or diplomatic work; has satisfying love affairs and a beneficial marriage

---

44. Vedic astrologers refer to Mars by two different names: Kuja or Mangala.
45. To find the Vedic names for the various zodiac signs, refer to fig. 5.3.
46. Some practitioners indicate that this person must take precautions around fires, avoid surgery, and quickly treat fevers or inflammations.
47. According to some practitioners, this position also indicates nervous or intestinal disorders.
48. This position also promises the subject highly intelligent children.

Sagittarius (♐)   enthusiastic; ambitious; speaks or acts impulsively; appreciates arguments, jokes, original ideas, outdoor sports, and adventure; marries more than once (and in one instance has concerns over a spouse's or child's health)

Capricorn (♑)   courageous; responsible; has powerful friends; has ambitions for both public life and wealth; thoroughly learns any subject; marries someone older or from a lower social caste early in life[49]

Aquarius (♒)   ambitious; independent; highly intelligent; a humanitarian; occasionally abrupt in speech or manners

Pisces (♓)   free-spending; indecisive; shy; bold if provoked; anxious to become rich; capable of quietly accomplishing a goal; has powerful friends; has romantic disappointments; has more than one marriage

Jupiter[50] (♃) in the Various Zodiac Signs[51]

Jupiter's occupation of the individual zodiac signs produces an influence on a man or a woman as follows:

Aries (♈)   has good fortune; successful enterprises; ambitious; has leadership qualities; frequently travels

Taurus (♉)   has dangerous relations with evil men; gains from women or profession; experiences ingratitude from friends; has a happy marriage

Gemini (♊)   receives help from powerful friends; has good fortune; encounters sudden reversals toward age forty-five; gains by negotiation; benefits from invention

Cancer (♋)   wealth derived from real estate; has powerful but inconsistent friends; wealth gained by popularity; prominence is poorly acquired[52]

---

49. Some practitioners indicate that this person's parents might divorce, or a parent might die prematurely, or the person might separate from his or her father over a disagreement. The person might be prone to broken ankles, knees, or legs.
50. Vedic practitioners refer to Jupiter as either Guru or Brhaspati.
51. To find the Vedic names for the various zodiac signs, refer to fig. 5.3.
52. Some astrologers add that this person encounters a peaceful, honorable death abroad, or far from his or her birthplace.

Leo (♌)   gains favors from powerful people; has a rich and good marriage; has wisdom, foresight, and willpower; has leadership qualities; has good fortune

Virgo (♍)   has a prosperous marriage; has mysterious good fortune; experiences danger or loss through secret means; has unforeseen gains

Libra (♎)   experiences a happy marriage; has many love affairs; gains support of superiors after some difficulty; receives help from influential women

Scorpio (♏)   has an unhappy marriage; experiences loss of inheritance; encounters danger through imprudence; is disgraced; has envious opponents; prominence is acquired by violent means

Sagittarius (♐)   has success with horses; has good fortune; is victorious over enemies; succeeds in all things

Capricorn (♑)   experiences delay of fortune; has an unsatisfactory marriage; has small ambitions; despotic; avaricious; has treacherous friends

Aquarius (♒)   marries an older person or marries later in life; gains fortune because of friends; is indifferent to ordinary life; has dangerous afflictions or quarrels

Pisces (♓)   possibly has two marriages; has scandals in marriage; encounters travel or financial adversities before the age of thirty; has increasing fortunes

Saturn[53] (♄) in the Various Zodiac Signs[54]

Saturn's occupation of the individual zodiac signs produces an influence on a man or a woman as follows:

Aries (♈)   ambitious; argumentative; driven by success; prospers through perseverance; first half of life is filled with obstacles; a jealous spouse makes marriage difficult

Taurus (♉)   short-tempered; hard to please; prudent; loves gardening; finds domestic life and relationships with kin difficult

---

53. Vedic practitioners' name for Saturn is Sani.
54. To find the Vedic names for the various zodiac signs, refer to fig. 5.3.

Gemini (♊)   observant; ingenious; well suited for a career in science, literature, or mathematics; finds relatives and home life troublesome

Cancer (♋)   dissatisfied with home; moves often; finds sorrow in parents, children, and domestic life

Leo (♌)   generous; quick-tempered; spiritual; encounters sorrows in romance and children; becomes ill if overworked; health affected by subordinates or inferiors who cause problems and psychic conditions

Virgo (♍)   cautious; quiet; worries; mistrusts many situations; investigates the mysterious; invests carefully; encounters marital or partnership troubles as well as serious obstacles during the first half of life

Libra (♎)   refined; has an aptitude for debate and controversy; finds sorrow at the loss of a deep attachment; reaches a high position and then falls to disgrace; delays marriage; women are the source of many problems

Scorpio (♏)   jealous; passionate; violent; shrewd; succeeds by persistence after overcoming many obstacles; faces sorrow in love affairs, secret alliances, intrigues, or domestic difficulties

Sagittarius (♐)   fearless; champions domestic or political advancements; has prophetic insights into the future welfare of civilization in general or into scientific breakthroughs; discovers that opposition creates resentment; pursues more than one career

Capricorn (♑)   melancholic; discontented; very anxious to succeed, ultimately does, then fails because of unreliable friends, inferior attachments, and an unsatisfactory marriage; suffers from chronic physical or mental illness

Aquarius (♒)   humane; a late bloomer; has a penetrating intellect; is able to express thoughts and feelings; succeeds in the arts and sciences; finds one true romantic tie that lasts

Pisces (♓)   indecisive; inspired; controlled by circumstances; is unlucky in romance, friendship, and marriage; is the source of his or her own demise due to emotions

As mentioned earlier in this section, in Alice's *rasicakra* (fig. 5.7), the Moon (☽) is placed in box 12, which represents the zodiac sign Pisces (♓). Using the material above, this indicates that Alice is imaginative, kind, intuitive, and psychic. She possesses literary talent. She encounters many misfortunes and obstacles and has difficulty saving money or affording things. She has trouble making an emotional commitment in romance. And she loves beauty and luxury.

In Peter's *rasicakra* (fig. 5.8), the Moon (☽) is placed in box 1, which represents the zodiac sign Aries (♈). Using the material above, this indicates that Peter is highly imaginative, self-reliant, and inventive. He has a restless mind and a quick temper. He exerts his independence and carves a unique path. Potentially he will head a major undertaking and reach prominence during his lifetime.

This same process is then used by the practitioner to interpret the effects of the Sun (☉), Mercury (☿), Venus (♀), Mars (♂), Jupiter (♃), and Saturn (♄) on both Alice's and Peter's personalities, using the material above. As mentioned earlier, once all the interpretative data derived from the *rasicakra* are gathered, they are synthesized with other factors such as the six *shadbala*, *yoga*, and additional charts such as the *bhavacakra* to formulate a complete personality profile.

Constructing the *Bhavacakra*

The second and most popular form of natal horoscope in Vedic astrology is the chart style used in northern India, which is called the *bhavacakra* (house chart). This horoscope closely resembles an early Greek chart structure called the Decussata chart, which was adapted from Arabian sources.[55] (The name *bhavacakra* is sometimes used to describe a supplementary chart that employs an alternate house system.)

The *bhavacakra* is divided into twelve *bhavas* (houses), most of which govern the same facets of life as those defined in Western, Judaic, and Chinese astrology, such as family, finances, marriage, and children. Other houses encompass segments that feature more prominently in Indian life, such as the role of karma in determining an individual's marriage prospects. The twelve *bhavas* and their Vedic names are as follows:

---

55. The Decussata chart was only one of the formats that applied a "quadrated circle" as a visual presentation of the horoscope's twelve houses. In these early Western versions, however, the Midheaven (House X) appeared in the top diamond, and the houses radiated in a counterclockwise fashion from the Ascendant, which was placed in the left full-diamond.

House I	House I or the Ascendant is generally called Lagna.[56] This house presides over an individual's appearance, character, temperament, and how he or she is perceived by other people. It also governs the brain and the head.
House II	Called Artha,[57] House II governs an individual's speech, familial wealth, learning, and the level of truthfulness the person conveys. (Sometimes, this house is also said to control dietary habits.) It also rules the right eye and the face.
House III	Called Bhratr,[58] House III presides over personal courage, the fulfillment of personal desires, dietary habits, creative talent and interests,[59] and the individual's relationship with siblings. It also rules the hands, arms, shoulders, right ear, and lungs.
House IV	Called Bandhu,[60] House IV governs a person's relationship with his or her mother, the family, domestic environment, real estate and real property,[61] the level of material comfort, and advanced education. It also presides over the heart, chest, and breasts.
House V	Called Putra,[62] House V presides over an individual's education. It governs children, creative work, speculation, level of intelligence, past-life karma, romances, and entertainment interests. This house also presides over the stomach and solar plexus.
House VI	Called Ari,[63] House VI rules the individual's work habits, desire to serve others, health, adversaries, employees, coworkers, obstacles, and litigation. This same house also governs the hips, navel, and lower back.

---

56. Pronounced "lahg-nah," this term literally means "that which meets one," and is generally considered to mean "ground zero," or the starting point from which a chart is read, but not necessarily House I. This house is alternately known as Tanu (the Body).

57. Pronounced "ar-thah," this term means "wealth."

58. Pronounced "brah-try," this term means "brothers."

59. These include music, dance, drama, film, photography, writing, and poetry.

60. Pronounced "bahn-dhoo," this term means "kin."

61. Cars, boats, and other major possessions fall under this heading.

62. Pronounced "poo-trah," this term means "sons."

63. Pronounced "ar-ee," this term means "enemy." This house is sometimes known as Vrana, which means "wounds."

House VII	Called Kalatra,[64] House VII governs a person's marriage, spouse, passions, business or legal partnerships, and homes in foreign places. It also rules the groin (including the kidneys, abdomen, and intestines) as well as the veins.
House VIII	Called Mrtyu,[65] House VIII presides over an individual's passions (both sexual and emotional), potential for accidents or chronic illness, obstacles, joint financial life, potential longevity, and unearned moneys such as insurance, inheritance, legacy, spouse's income, lotteries, and legal settlements.
House IX	Called Dharma,[66] House IX governs the person's general fortune or luck, his or her father, advanced education, religious or ideological beliefs, medicine, and foreign travel. It also rules the hips and thighs.
House X	Called Karma,[67] House X rules an individual's profession, social and public standing, business acumen, and his or her father's financial condition. It also governs the skeleton and knees.
House XI	Called Aya,[68] House XI governs a person's income from a profession or side ventures, friendships, fulfillment of goals and desires, and participation as a member of a community. It also rules the left ear, ankles, legs, and calves.
House XII	Called Vyaya,[69] House XII rules the person's spiritual nature, the things that an individual does not personally control, and financial expenditures. It also governs the feet and the left eye.

Roman numerals are used in the *bhavacakras* that follow (figs. 5.10 and 5.11) to make it easier to understand how the positions of the zodiac signs (in Arabic numbers) change in the various houses, depending upon the location of the Ascendant in the zodiac. However, this is not done by Vedic practitioners. Furthermore, symbols for the individual planets are never used by Vedic astrologers. The names of

---

64. Pronounced "kah-lah-trah," this term means "wife." Alternately, this house is known as Kama, which means "love."
65. Pronounced "mirt-you," this term means "death." Alternately, this house is known as Randhra, which means "vital points."
66. Used in this context, *dharma* refers to appropriate actions or the proper way.
67. In this context, *karma* refers to actions or work.
68. Pronounced "ah-yah," this term means "gain."
69. Pronounced "vay-yah-yah," this terms means "loss."

FIGURE 5.10. ALICE T.'S BHAVACAKRA.

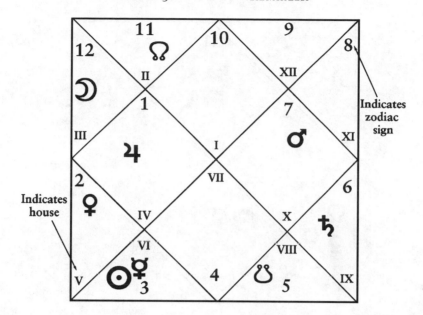

the planets are generally written out in Sanskrit. Symbols are used in this chart to facilitate comparisons between this type of Vedic chart and those executed by Western, Judaic, or Arabian practitioners.

The *bhavacakra*'s format places the number of the zodiac sign that represents the Ascendant or House I (figs. 5.4 and 5.5, fourth column) in the top diamond of the chart. For example, the diamond marked "I" in fig. 5.10 is the Ascendant or House I. The "10" in the same diamond designates the Ascendant's zodiac sign as Capricorn (♑, fig. 5.3, third column). The information for this placement is found in fig. 5.4 (fourth column). The *bhavacakra*'s Ascendant is interpreted in exactly the same manner as described in the section titled "Identifying the Ascendant's *Naksatra*," page 155.

Peter's Ascendant is placed in a similar manner. The diamond marked "I" in fig. 5.11 is his Ascendant (House I). The "11" in the same diamond designates the Ascendant's zodiac sign as Aquarius (♒, fig. 5.3, third column). The information for this placement is found in fig. 5.5 (fourth column). The *bhavacakra*'s Ascendant is interpreted in exactly the same manner as described in the section titled "Identifying the Ascendant's *Naksatra*," page 155.

The remaining house numbers and zodiac sign numbers are placed in sequential order around the frame in a counterclockwise fashion, as shown in both figs. 5.10 and 5.11. Then the planets are placed in the diamonds as each relates to the zodiac sign numbers. For example, beginning with Alice's *bhavacakra* (fig. 5.10), the Moon's North Node (☊ 00°♒18' in fig. 5.4, fourth column) is placed in the

FIGURE 5.11. PETER C.'S *BHAVACAKRA*.

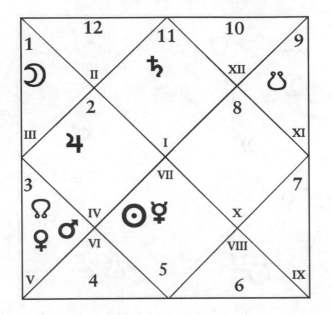

diamond marked "II" (House II) and "11" (because ♒ [Aquarius] is 11 in fig. 5.3). The Moon (☽ 18°♓23′ in fig. 5.4, fourth column) is placed in the diamond marked "III" (House III) and "12" (because ♓ [Pisces] is 12 in fig. 5.3). Jupiter (♃ 17°♈47′ in fig. 5.4, fourth column) is placed in the diamond marked "IV" (House IV) and "1" (because ♈ [Aries] is 1 in fig. 5.3). Venus (♀ 29°♉26′ in fig. 5.4, fourth column) is placed in the diamond marked "V" (House V) and "2" (because ♉ [Taurus] is 2 in fig. 5.3). The Sun (☉ 01°♊50′ in fig. 5.4, fourth column) and Mercury (☿ 10°♊23′ in fig. 5.4, fourth column) are both placed in the diamond marked "VI" (House VI) and "3" (because ♊ [Gemini] is 3 in fig. 5.3). The Moon's South Node (☋ 00°♌18′ in fig. 5.4, fourth column) is placed in the diamond marked "VIII" (House VIII) and "5" (because ♌ [Leo] is 5 in fig. 5.3). Saturn (♄ 15°♍07′ in fig. 5.4, fourth column) is placed in the diamond marked "IX" (House IX) and "6" (because ♍ [Virgo] is 6 in fig. 5.3). And Mars (♂ 08°♎19′ in fig. 5.4, fourth column) is placed in the diamond marked "X" (House X) and "7" (because ♎ [Libra] is 7 in fig. 5.3).

Because none of the planetary positions in fig. 5.4 (fourth column) occupy Houses I (diamond I in fig. 5.10), VII (diamond VII in fig. 5.10), XI (diamond XI in fig. 5.10), and XII (diamond XII in fig. 5.10), these diamonds—or houses—remain empty. The degrees and minutes of Alice's Ascendant, planetary, and node positions are kept for reference as shown in fig. 5.4 (fourth column), but are not incorporated onto her *bhavacakra* (fig. 5.10).

The same process is applied to Peter's Vedic positions as follows. In Peter's *bhavacakra* (fig. 5.11), Saturn (♄ 08°♒10′ in fig. 5.5, fourth column) is placed in the diamond marked "I" (Ascendant or House I) and "11" (because ♒ [Aquarius] is 11 in fig. 5.3). The Moon (☽ 10°♈23′ in fig. 5.5, fourth column) is placed in the diamond marked "III" (House III) and "1" (because ♈ [Aries] is 1 in fig. 5.3). Jupiter (♃ 02°♉21′ in fig. 5.5, fourth column) is placed in the diamond marked "IV" (House IV) and "2" (because ♉ [Taurus] is 2 in fig. 5.3). Venus (♀ 25°♊38′ in fig. 5.5, fourth column), Mars (♂ 25°♊16′ in fig. 5.5, fourth column), and the Moon's North Node (☊ 06°♊25′ in fig. 5.5, fourth column) are all placed in the diamond marked "V" (House V) and "3" (because ♊ [Gemini] is 3 in fig. 5.3). The Sun (☉ 11°♌26′ in fig. 5.5, fourth column) and Mercury (☿ 21°♌21′ in fig. 5.5, fourth column) are placed in the diamond marked "VII" (House VII) and "5" (because ♌ [Leo] is 5 in fig. 5.3). And the Moon's South Node (☋ 06°♐25′ in fig. 5.5, fourth column) is placed in the diamond marked "XI" (House XI) and "9" (because ♐ [Sagittarius] is 9 in fig. 5.3).

Because none of the planetary positions in fig. 5.5 (fourth column) occupy Houses II (diamond II in fig. 5.11), VI (diamond VI in fig. 5.11), VIII (diamond VIII in fig. 5.11), X (diamond X in fig. 5.11), and XII (diamond XII in fig. 5.11), these diamonds—or houses—remain empty. Once again, the degrees and minutes of Peter's Ascendant, planetary, and node positions are kept for reference as shown in fig. 5.5 (fourth column), but are not incorporated into the *bhavacakra* (fig. 5.11).

Unlike the Western and Judaic chart systems, the visual presentation of the natal data in the *bhavacakra* (figs. 5.10 and 5.11) is merely an outline from which the astrologer makes his or her delineation of the planets' positions. This characteristic is common to Chinese and Tibetan documentation methods (see chapters 3 and 4) and the Vedic *rasicakra* (see "Constructing the *Rasicakra*," page 152).

Interpreting the House Rulers in the *Bhavacakra*

Similar to the delineation of the planets by house, the influence exerted by a zodiac sign in a given house in a *bhavacakra* is also interpreted. This system is very similar to the method of house rulership interpretation used in both Western and Judaic astrology.

Using the table in fig. 5.3, the Vedic practitioner identifies the zodiac sign (first column) according to the Arabic figure (third column) placed in each house. For example, in Alice's *bhavacakra* (fig. 5.10), the houses are ruled by the zodiac signs as follows:

House I	is ruled by Capricorn (♑, 10 in fig. 5.10)
House II	is ruled by Aquarius (♒, 11 in fig. 5.10)

House III   is ruled by Pisces (♓, 12 in fig. 5.10)
House IV   is ruled by Aries (♈, 1 in fig. 5.10)
House V   is ruled by Taurus (♉, 2 in fig. 5.10)
House VI   is ruled by Gemini (♊, 3 in fig. 5.10)
House VII   is ruled by Cancer (♋, 4 in fig. 5.10)
House VIII   is ruled by Leo (♌, 5 in fig. 5.10)
House IX   is ruled by Virgo (♍, 6 in fig. 5.10)
House X   is ruled by Libra (♎, 7 in fig. 5.10)
House XI   is ruled by Scorpio (♏, 8 in fig. 5.10)
House XII   is ruled by Sagittarius (♐, 9 in fig. 5.10)

Similarly, in Peter's *bhavacakra* (fig. 5.11), the houses are ruled by the zodiac signs as follows:

House I   is ruled by Aquarius (♒, 11 in fig. 5.11)
House II   is ruled by Pisces (♓, 12 in fig. 5.11)
House III   is ruled by Aries (♈, 1 in fig. 5.11)
House IV   is ruled by Taurus (♉, 2 in fig. 5.11)
House V   is ruled by Gemini (♊, 3 in fig. 5.11)
House VI   is ruled by Cancer (♋, 4 in fig. 5.11)
House VII   is ruled by Leo (♌, 5 in fig. 5.11)
House VIII   is ruled by Virgo (♍, 6 in fig. 5.11)
House IX   is ruled by Libra (♎, 7 in fig. 5.11)
House X   is ruled by Scorpio (♏, 8 in fig. 5.11)
House XI   is ruled by Sagittarius (♐, 9 in fig. 5.11)
House XII   is ruled by Capricorn (♑, 10 in fig. 5.11)

The rulership of the *bhavas* (houses) by each of the *rasis* (signs), as shown above, is then interpreted according to the material below.

House I (The Ascendant) Rulers

House I presides over an individual's appearance, character, and temperament, and how he or she is perceived by other people. Therefore, the occupation of House I by a zodiac sign produces physical and personality traits in a man or woman as follows:

Aries (♈)   megalomaniacal; inconsistent; disorganized; reckless; decisive
                Physical traits: a ruddy complexion or a distinctive birthmark on the head or face

Taurus (♉)   materialistic; sensual; has a quick, violent temper; tactile; obstinate; artistic
                Physical traits: tends to be overweight

Gemini (♊)   secretive; communicative; has a literary or designerly talent; adaptable
Physical traits: retains youthful appearance

Cancer (♋)   detail-conscious; fears criticism; desires guidance; domestic
Physical traits: retains water; round-faced

Leo (♌)   exhibitionistic; a natural leader; irritability can turn into arrogance
Physical traits: tends toward baldness

Virgo (♍)   hypercritical; loves natural beauty; health- and hygiene-conscious
Physical traits: oval face; dark complexion

Libra (♎)   emotionally indiscriminate; superficial; altruistic; loves beauty and candy
Physical traits: attractive

Scorpio (♏)   magnetic; erotic; investigative; frank; fearless
Physical traits: square build; thick hair

Sagittarius (♐)   sociable; theatrical; active; trusting
Physical traits: tends to stamp or scrape feet

Capricorn (♑)   responsible; opportunistic; competitive
Physical traits: elongated face

Aquarius (♒)   highly opinionated; hates change, but makes alterations without remorse; mentally poised
Physical traits: square jaw; friendly face

Pisces (♓)   self-sacrificing; compassionate; ambivalent
Physical traits: small hands and feet

House II Rulers

House II governs an individual's speech, familial wealth, learning, and the level of truthfulness the person conveys. The occupation of House II by a zodiac sign produces personality traits in a man or a woman as follows:

Aries (♈)   spendthrift tendencies; potential desire to buy people's affections or loyalties; lawsuits over money; financial fluctuations

Taurus (♉)	stinginess; unwillingness to take financial risks; hard work or real-estate yields financial rewards
Gemini (♊)	bold financial approach; financial gains from business, writing, or teaching
Cancer (♋)	financial fluctuations; overspending; heavy debts
Leo (♌)	squanders money; lives beyond means; overly generous
Virgo (♍)	financial gains from literary profession; cautious spending; occasional financial difficulties
Libra (♎)	conscientious management of finances; financial rewards through art-related fields; interest in speculation
Scorpio (♏)	secretive about financial circumstances; financial gains from mysterious or secret sources
Sagittarius (♐)	financial gains from numerous sources; feels a need to impress others with money
Capricorn (♑)	cautious spending; selfishness over finances; gains from hard work and persistence
Aquarius (♒)	unexpected financial fluctuations; unconventional ways of spending and saving money
Pisces (♓)	shrewdness in financial management; irregular or illegal income

House III Rulers

House III presides over personal courage, the fulfillment of personal desires, dietary habits, creative talent and interests, and the individual's relationship with siblings. The occupation of House III by a zodiac sign produces personality traits in a man or woman as follows:

Aries (♈)	argumentative or violent communications; confrontational relations with siblings and neighbors; impulsive intellect
Taurus (♉)	taciturn; close or cordial relations with siblings and neighbors; slow, careful mentality
Gemini (♊)	obsessive desire to write and talk; communicative or gossipy with siblings and relations; curious and intellectual

Cancer (♋)   strong need to express feelings secretively or in a circumspect manner; emotional connection with siblings and neighbors; strong imagination

Leo (♌)   communicates as a direct expression of ego; strong interaction with siblings and neighbors; need to develop ideas

Virgo (♍)   communicates through writing or design; concise and abundant communication with siblings and neighbors; critical and analytical mentality

Libra (♎)   diplomatic and cordial communication; close, harmonic relations with siblings and neighbors; early education and subsequent mentality relies on social interaction

Scorpio (♏)   secret or sarcastic communication; intense power of concentration and observation; appreciation of siblings and neighbors

Sagittarius (♐)   spontaneous and frank communication; warm and friendly relations with siblings and neighbors; restless, curious mentality

Capricorn (♑)   limited communication skills; reluctance to express verbally; limited or delayed education; responsibility for or extremely close relations with siblings; stable and long relationships with neighbors; organized mentality

Aquarius (♒)   erratic communication skills; highly receptive to new concepts; easily self-taught; separation from siblings or neighbors

Pisces (♓)   overly emotional communications; emotional ties to siblings and neighbors; intuitive, but mentally lazy

House IV Rulers

House IV governs a person's relationships with his or her mother, the family, domestic environment, real estate and real property, the level of material comfort, and advanced education. The occupation of House IV by a zodiac sign produces personality traits in a man or woman as follows:

Aries (♈)   a domineering parent; confrontational or active home life

Taurus (♉)   sentimental attachment to home and family; strong ties to parents

Gemini (♊)   prefers to work at home; many changes of residence, or ownership of more than one residence at a time; may live with or near siblings as an adult; strong communication with parents

Cancer (♋)   strong emotional ties to home, family, and parents (especially to the mother); many changes of residence; prefers to work at home and live near the water

Leo (♌)   ego-oriented connection to home, family, and parents; prestige gained as a result of family or sibling assistance

Virgo (♍)   prefers to work at home; applies critical but constructive eye to home and family; compulsion for neatness at home; many changes of residence, or more than one residence at a time; good communications with parents

Libra (♎)   needs beauty and comfort at home; enjoys sociable and harmonious relations with family and parents;

Scorpio (♏)   a childhood trauma involving a family member or parent deeply affects home life as an adult; must control all aspects of home life

Sagittarius (♐)   home, family, and parents are closely linked to religion, education, or a foreign culture

Capricorn (♑)   heavy responsibilities or restrictions connected with home life or parents; few or no changes of residence; long and stable relations with family and parents

Aquarius (♒)   unusual situations surround childhood, parents, and domestic life; unexpected changes of residence; sudden separation from family or parents

Pisces (♓)   oversensitive to chaotic events surrounding home, family, or parents; possible literal or figurative abandonment as a child; deep connection with a highly religious or artistic parent

House V Rulers

House V presides over an individual's education. It governs children, creative work, speculation, level of intelligence, past-life karma, romances, and entertainment interests. The occupation of House V by a zodiac sign produces personality traits in a man or woman as follows:

Aries (♈) vivid imagination, but wasted energy; excessively romantic; attached to children; excessive with pleasures; attracted to competitive sports

Taurus (♉) highly artistic; attractive to the opposite sex; good luck; indulgent with pleasures; excellent rapport with children

Gemini (♊) creativity closely linked to communication; pleasures are intellectual; romantically attracted to intellectuals; possibly a twin or the parent of twins

Cancer (♋) love of the arts; underdisciplined creatively; strong emotional link to children; romantically sensitive and affectionate; pleasure from home or family activities

Leo (♌) significant creative urge; devotion to children; loyal lover; children may become artists, musicians, or actors; pleasure from entertaining or being entertained

Virgo (♍) creativity linked with an intellectual skill such as writing or acting; mentally stimulated by speculative activities; romantically attracted to intelligence and natural beauty; critical of mental accomplishments of both lovers and children

Libra (♎) creative talent for design, music, writing, or drawing; pleasure from luxury items; romantic but indecisive lovers; social rapport with children

Scorpio (♏) seeks attention for creativity; unusually close relationship with children; romantically attracted to intellectual or powerful people; secretive love affairs

Sagittarius (♐) vivid imagination and abundant creativity; warm and generous attachment to children; pleasure in merry amusements or risky sports

Capricorn (♑) creativity is frustrated by outside sources; serious responsibilities with children; romantically attracted to older people; overly cautious with speculations

Aquarius (♒) erratic or unusual love affairs; unusual or ingenious children; if female, has difficulty with conception or redirection of creative energies; if male, may sire but not raise children, or may raise adopted children; enjoys group entertainment

Pisces (♓)   secret love affairs or romantic deceptions; attracted to a person
                    from a minority group or one who works with the sea, medicine,
                    or feet; children (or lovers) are very creative; occasionally lucky
                    with speculative ventures; pleasure on or near the water

House VI Rulers

House VI rules the individual's work habits, desire to serve others, health,
adversaries, employees, co-workers, obstacles, and litigation. The occupation of
House VI by a zodiac sign produces personality and health traits in a man or
woman as follows:

Aries (♈)   energetic and enthusiastic worker; strong managerial skills;
                    prone to fevers, rash, high blood pressure, headaches, or stress-
                    related illnesses;

Taurus (♉)   prefers to work with a partner or many co-workers;[70] cannot
                    work when unappreciated or in uncomfortable places; takes
                    great care of pets; pursues health and fitness programs; may suf-
                    fer from weight gain

Gemini (♊)   keeps busy at work and on work in the home; can do more than
                    one job at a time; generates a lot of paperwork; enjoys owning
                    many pets; has respiratory or nervous complaints

Cancer (♋)   delicate health patterns, but few major illnesses; prefers to work
                    at home or in home-related jobs; strong emotional ties to em-
                    ployees or co-workers; inconsistent work habits; emotionally at-
                    tached to pets

Leo (♌)   needs personal pride from work; employees and co-workers are
                    of great personal concern; pets are treated like children; health
                    and fitness are of importance

Virgo (♍)   service-oriented worker who needs to be busy and get the job
                    done; detail-oriented; sends pet to obedience school; health
                    and fitness fanatic

Libra (♎)   dislikes working alone; diplomatic with employees and co-
                    workers; inefficient worker when not appreciated; prefers fancy
                    or exotic pets; reasonable health, but some bladder problems

---

70.   This attribute can turn into extreme laziness if the position is afflicted.

Scorpio (♏)   needs to manipulate and control his or her work environment; hates interference from employees or co-workers; excellent researcher; remarkable recuperative powers of physical health; prefers highly submissive pets

Sagittarius (♐)   strong need for independence in the workplace; unable to manage employees; overindulgence affects health; unable to discipline pets properly; relationships with those who work for or with them

Capricorn (♑)   heavy work responsibilities; very organized and structured work habits; best at working alone or with few co-workers; rarely ill, but diseases are chronic or long-term; loving, caring pet owner

Aquarius (♒)   need for independence in the workplace; self-employment preferred; sudden changes of employment; erratic health and nervous conditions; application of unusual health and fitness regimens

Pisces (♓)   works alone or in an isolated environment; has an unrealistic view of his or her job, or confused job assignments; suffers from lack of recognition for work done; secrecy or fraud might be connected to job; employee or co-worker scandals; hypochondria or undiagnosed illness; extreme drug sensitivity

House VII Rulers

House VII governs a person's marriage, spouse, passions, business or legal partnerships, and homes in foreign places. The occupation of House VII by a zodiac sign produces personality traits in a man or woman as follows:

Aries (♈)   need for a stimulating spouse or partner; potential for a domineering spouse or partner; attracted to open confrontation; if adversely aspected (see "Rating by *Drigbala*," page 234) or poorly positioned (see "Rating by *Sthanabala*," page 230), attracted to violence or arguments; loss of spouse or partner through accident

Taurus (♉)   need for constant interaction with others; prefers partnership to operating alone; stable, long-lasting, and happy marriage or partnership

Gemini (♊)   may have siblings or close relatives as business partners; possibly more than one marriage, or may not marry at all; spouse or partner might be in the teaching, writing, communications, publishing, or advertising industry

Cancer (♋)   close, caring relationship with partners or spouse; if male, may marry someone who strongly resembles his mother or is younger than himself; if female, may maintain a strong emotional connection to a dominating spouse

Leo (♌)   marriage or partnership positively satisfies ego; success comes from working closely with others

Virgo (♍)   constructively critical of spouse or partner; possible partnership with sibling or close relative from the maternal side; potential for more than one marriage

Libra (♎)   enjoys marriage, but may equate romance and charm with emotional commitment; may have difficulty deciding to settle down or form a lasting partnership

Scorpio (♏)   needs to control or manipulate marriage or partnership; attracts intellectual or powerful spouse or partners; secrecy or mystery attached to the relationship

Sagittarius (♐)   must have personal freedom within marriage or partnership; attracted to a spouse or partner who thinks and acts on a grand scale

Capricorn (♑)   possible marriage to an older person; stable and long-lasting marriage or partnership if it transpires after the age of twenty-seven; happily takes on the responsibilities of marriage or partnership

Aquarius (♒)   strong potential for more than one marriage, or may not marry at all; sudden or unexpected end to marriage or partnerships; unconventional marriage or spouse

Pisces (♓)   unrealistic expectations about a marriage or partnership; potential untimely loss of a partner or spouse to an inferior person; spouse or partner may be very artistic, from a minority group, or addicted to drugs or alcohol

House VIII Rulers

House VIII presides over an individual's passions (both sexual and emotional), potential for accidents or chronic illness, obstacles, joint financial life, potential longevity, and unearned moneys such as insurance, inheritance, legacy, spouse's income, lotteries, and legal settlements. The occupation of House VIII by a zodiac sign produces personality traits in a man or woman as follows:

Aries (♈)   resourceful and talented in the management of other people's money; connected in some way to fire insurance or other forms of insurance; denies the inevitability of death

Taurus (♉)   tends to conserve financial resources from partnership, marriage, or the assets of other people; may inherit money or artistic talent; takes the concept of death in stride

Gemini (♊)   strongly involved in stocks, taxes, insurance, and managing other people's money; indifferent to the concept of death

Cancer (♋)   strong potential for inheritance or legacy; too influenced by outside opinion to be a sound manager of other people's money; fears death

Leo (♌)   shrewdly manipulates financial resources and assets for both self and others; secretly fears death

Virgo (♍)   always seeking ways to improve financial resources; spouse or partner is somehow involved in investments, taxes, insurance, or the management of other people's money; is resigned to the concept of death

Libra (♎)   needs to give equal measure of assets in marriage or partnership; spouse's income comes from music, literature, fashion, design, or law; rationalizes the concept of death

Scorpio (♏)   secrecy or mystery attached to management of other people's money; mystery attached to inheritance; thoroughly researches all avenues before acting on taxes or insurance; fear of death is mixed with fascination

Sagittarius (♐)   spouse's or partner's income is derived from writing, advertising, broadcasting, art, religion, publishing, politics, foreign dealings, or education; not good at managing inheritances, legacies, or other people's money; cannot tolerate the thought of death

Capricorn (♑)   spouse or partner has few assets, or is unwilling to share them; inheritance or legacy might be small or bring more sorrow than happiness; manages other people's assets very responsibly; debt collection, insurance, and taxes are sources for legitimate concern; has a detached attitude toward death

Aquarius (♒)   sudden or unexpected changes surround inheritances and legacies as well as other people's money; develops ingenious or unorthodox (but not necessarily illegal) methods of tax reporting, insurance coverage, or debt recovery; has no interest in the afterlife

Pisces (♓)   has difficulty collecting on debts; distorts facts about taxes or insurance; deception may surround inheritance or legacy; depletion of spouse's or partner's assets; chaotic management of other people's money; fears death

House IX Rulers

House IX governs the person's general fortune or luck, his or her father, advanced education, religious or ideological beliefs, medicine, and foreign travel. The occupation of House IX by a zodiac sign produces personality traits in a man or woman as follows:

Aries (♈)   strong interest in sports, philosophy, religion, culture, foreign studies, or international trade; potential for fanaticism or unrealistic ideology; if adversely aspected (see "Rating by *Drigbala*," page 234) or poorly positioned (see "Rating by *Sthanabala*," page 230), potential for difficulties with higher education, judgments, or spouse's parents

Taurus (♉)   interest in culture, religion, philosophy, and academia; worldly self-image, even if he or she has never traveled; may develop idealistic or impractical ideologies; marriage to a foreigner; if adversely aspected (see "Rating by *Drigbala*," page 234) or poorly positioned (see "Rating by *Sthanabala*," page 230), antisocial or prejudiced

Gemini (♊)   interest in higher education, publishing, advertising, religion, travel, and anthropology; if adversely aspected (see "Rating by *Drigbala*," page 234) or poorly positioned (see "Rating by

Sthanabala," page 230), lacks patience or ability to pursue advanced education

Cancer (♋)	emotional connection to higher education, culture, publishing, religion, and politics; mother may be of foreign birth

Leo (♌)   needs to express ego through higher education, religion, publishing, culture, or politics; has strong ideological instincts; may live abroad; if adversely aspected (see "Rating by *Drigbala,*" page 234) or poorly positioned (see "Rating by *Sthanabala,*" page 230), morally righteous or superficially intellectual

Virgo (♍)   concerned with higher education, publishing, philosophy, religion, anthropology, and travel abroad; potential to earn an advanced degree abroad; if adversely aspected (see "Rating by *Drigbala,*" page 234) or poorly positioned (see "Rating by *Sthanabala,*" page 230), morally righteous, demagogic, or lacking in intellectual abilities

Libra (♎)   artistically, academically, or philosophically oriented; if adversely aspected (see "Rating by *Drigbala,*" page 234) or poorly positioned (see "Rating by *Sthanabala,*" page 230), antisocial or prejudiced; difficulty earning advanced degrees; overly idealistic about ideology

Scorpio (♏)   advanced education is equated with personal power or implied control; potential for fanatical religious or philosophical views; mystery attached to higher education, travel abroad, or spiritual pursuits

Sagittarius (♐)   a profound appreciation for knowledge and education; intellectual and spiritual curiosity; a strong attraction to travel; if adversely aspected (see "Rating by *Drigbala,*" page 234) or poorly positioned (see "Rating by *Sthanabala,*" page 230), mental laziness or difficulty connected to the pursuit of higher education; religious or philosophical fanaticism

Capricorn (♑)   higher education is best achieved later in life; obstacles limit the attainment or utilization of advanced training or education

Aquarius (♒)   higher education or advanced training is self-taught; sudden or unexpected disruptions in education or training; unorthodox religious beliefs or ideologies; unusual intellectual preferences

Pisces (♓)   highly developed intuition; strong interest in spiritualism and the occult; potential for ideological or religious disillusionment; secret or illegal dealings involving foreigners or business abroad; potential for fanatical or unrealistic ideals

House X Rulers

House X rules an individual's profession, social and public standing, business acumen, and father's financial condition. The occupation of House X by a zodiac sign produces personality traits in a man or woman as follows:

Aries (♈)   strong desire for self-employment; need for public attention; attraction to surgery, the military, promotion, building, manufacturing, and sports; if adversely aspected (see "Rating by *Drigbala*," page 234) or poorly positioned (see "Rating by *Sthanabala*," page 230), loss of mother or both parents through accident or poor relations with domineering parent

Taurus (♉)   the arts, finance, real estate, agriculture, architecture, landscaping, or conservation may be the chosen profession; a stable and sociable relationship with the mother or both parents

Gemini (♊)   communication, such as writing or public speaking, is central to the person's profession; mental or intellectual profession; potential for more than one career; if adversely aspected (see "Rating by *Drigbala*," page 234) or poorly positioned (see "Rating by *Sthanabala*," page 230), problems communicating with mother or both parents

Cancer (♋)   often the center of attention in chosen profession; deep emotional identification with profession; unusually close relationships with mother or both parents; potential to enter mother's or father's profession; potential career involves women, babies, housing, or food

Leo (♌)   ego and mode of self-expression are closely related to choice of profession; a parent is involved in career choice; seeks leadership or public role in profession; potentially self-employed

Virgo (♍)   desire to communicate or put into practice his or her ideas; potential for a career in writing, teaching, public speaking, or training; potential mental or intellectual profession; potential for more than one career in a lifetime; if adversely aspected (see "Rating by *Drigbala*," page 234) or poorly positioned (see "Rating by *Sthanabala*," page 230), communication problems with both parents or mother

Libra (♎︎)   attracts attention because of physical appearance, artistic talent, or social position; needs to find a balance between home and career; if adversely aspected (see "Rating by *Drigbala*," page 234) or poorly positioned (see "Rating by *Sthanabala*," page 230), sacrifices home for career, or professional interests for domestic life; tends to be antisocial with mother or both parents

Scorpio (♏︎)   a traumatic event that occurs during childhood instills a sense of having no control over circumstances; does not allow anyone to control his or her personal destiny; relinquishing control impedes growth; potential for a change of career late in life; attracts powerful friends; secrecy or mystery connected with profession, social status, or parents

Sagittarius (♐︎)   needs to exhibit intellect, artistic talent, or training; must teach what he or she knows; may become a promoter or agent; potential for public notice; if adversely aspected (see "Rating by *Drigbala*," page 234) or poorly positioned (see "Rating by *Sthanabala*," page 230), problems with mother or both parents; difficulty with promotion; untrained for assigned activity

Capricorn (♑︎)   needs profession that provides security or position of great authority; dedicated to hard work and perseverance; potential for abuse of power; limited relations or heavy responsibilities involving mother or both parents

Aquarius (♒︎)   actions attract public attention; unexpected and sudden career changes; unorthodox choice of profession; attraction to medicine, social organizations, fund raising, international finance, communication, or computers; sudden or unexpected separation from mother

Pisces (♓︎)   drawn to profession in the theater, art, medicine, or religion; danger of scandal by action or association; glamorous or mysterious public image; potentially abandoned (literally or figuratively) by mother or both parents; if adversely aspected (see "Rating by *Drigbala*," page 234) or poorly positioned (see "Rating by *Sthanabala*," page 230), fails to receive public recognition for work; potential career assisting the disabled, institutionalized, underprivileged, or minorities

House XI Rulers

House XI governs a person's income from a profession or side ventures, friendships, fulfillment of goals and desires, as well as participation as a member of a community. The occupation of House XI by a zodiac sign produces personality traits in a man or woman as follows:

Aries (♈)   strong attraction to friends who are soldiers, hunters, pioneers, sportsmen, inventors, and risk-takers; participation in clubs and fraternal organizations; equates happiness with activity; if adversely aspected (see "Rating by *Drigbala*," page 234) or poorly positioned (see "Rating by *Sthanabala*," page 230), argumentative social habits and antisocial behavior; never happy with what's at hand; many acquaintances but few friends, owing to lack of personal commitment

Taurus (♉)   stable and long-lasting friendships; may use friendships for personal gain; participates in clubs and worthwhile organizations; may marry a friend; remains friends with romantic partners after the affair ends; if adversely aspected (see "Rating by *Drigbala*," page 234) or poorly positioned (see "Rating by *Sthanabala*," page 230), antisocial; a social climber; victimized by mercenary friends

Gemini (♊)   fond of tossing ideas back and forth with friends; attracts friendships with educators, writers, computer specialists, and salespeople; many acquaintances, few real friends; takes an active role in fraternal associations and societies; close friendships with siblings; if adversely aspected (see "Rating by *Drigbala*," page 234) or poorly positioned (see "Rating by *Sthanabala*," page 230), involved in gossip or a victim of gossip

Cancer (♋)   strong emotional identification with friends; difficulty establishing commitments or long-range goals that involve friends or associates

Leo (♌)
ego and self-expression are strongly connected to friendships; excels at managing an organization, but may fail at maintaining personal affairs

Virgo (♍)
strong interchange of thoughts with friends; active participant in organizations and societies; friends may be associated with health and social services, or with the arts, writing, or design; few close friends but many acquaintances; accepts responsibility for friends; if adversely aspected (see "Rating by *Drigbala*," page 234) or poorly positioned (see "Rating by *Sthanabala*," page 230), critical of friends, antisocial

Libra (♎)
needs to balance friends and other areas of life such as the home; may marry a friend; may remain friends with ex-lovers; if adversely aspected (see "Rating by *Drigbala*," page 234) or poorly positioned (see "Rating by *Sthanabala*," page 230), antisocial; confrontational with friends

Scorpio (♏)
may make new friends in a new environment to improve life; may make friendships to improve social or professional status; potential for victimization by friends; secrecy or mystery associated with friendships or organizations

Sagittarius (♐)
makes more friends than he or she can afford time to have; attaches more importance to friendship than necessary; may perceive friendship where none exists; friends are intellectuals, actors, religious people, travelers, artists, and clerics

Capricorn (♑)
serious or heavy responsibilities associated with friendship; few friends, but very long-lasting friendships; most friends are older, or are acquired in older age; rarely joins organizations or societies; often feels friendless

Aquarius (♒)
erratic or unusual friendships; sudden or unexpected separation from friends; attraction to fraternal organizations; friends involved in unusual professions, highly technological fields, medicine, or communications

Pisces (♓)
either never content or makes the best of circumstances; falls in love with a friend; potential scandal connected with friends or organizations; friends may be involved in addictive habits or illegal activities; may be deceived or inspired by friends

House XII Rulers

House XII rules the person's spiritual nature, the things that an individual does not personally control, and financial expenditures. The occupation of House XII by a zodiac sign produces personality traits in a man or woman as follows:

Aries (♈)   activities go largely unnoticed; involved in investigations of the past or the occult; if adversely aspected (see "Rating by *Drigbala*," page 234) or poorly positioned (see "Rating by *Sthanabala*," page 230), deceived by spouse or partner; early death of spouse or partner by accident

Taurus (♉)   needs patient study and practical application of dream analysis or psychoanalysis; if adversely aspected (see "Rating by *Drigbala*," page 234) or poorly positioned (see "Rating by *Sthanabala*," page 230), refuses to progress by disconnecting from the past; threatens suicide or is victimized by potentially suicidal people

Gemini (♊)   prefers quiet surroundings in which to think and communicate; attracted to the subconscious and the psychic

Cancer (♋)   strong emotional attachment to psychology and the occult; potential of becoming a victim of the past; feels that there is loss associated with emotional commitment; clandestine or secret attachment

Leo (♌)   conceals true self and motivations from most people; conceals sorrow out of false pride

Virgo (♍)   acute self-knowledge; attracted to practical application of psychology and the occult; keeps many thoughts to himself or herself

Libra (♎)   extremely sensitive about relationships; a lack of self-confidence negatively affects the formation and maintenance of relationships; threatens suicide or falls victim to potentially suicidal people

Scorpio (♏)   conceals knowledge of psychology or the occult; participates in secret activities or societies; has an unconscious need to possess power

Sagittarius (♐)	unrealistic inability to worry or to have concern; receives help from unknown sources; intuitive; interested in the psychology and the occult
Capricorn (♑)	spends a great deal of time in solitude; has difficulty attaining true recognition, but may achieve success; victimized by unfounded fears and worries; strong interest in the psychic and the occult, but no desire to know the future
Aquarius (♒)	unconscious resentment of authority or convention; erratic sleep patterns; unexpected changes occur in partner's or spouse's employment; spouse may introduce unconventional health regimen; involvement in secret societies or a friend's secret activities; entrusts secrets to a friend
Pisces (♓)	strongly influenced by dreams, guilt, and the past; subconsciously vulnerable; potential for spiritual and intuitive development

Applying the above material to Alice's *bhavacakra* (fig. 5.10), House I's ruler (Capricorn [♑] or 10 in fig. 5.10) indicates that she is responsible, opportunistic, and competitive. Physically, it suggests that she has an elongated face.

House II's ruler (Aquarius [♒] or 11 in fig. 5.10) suggests that she experiences unexpected financial fluctuations and has unconventional spending and saving habits.

House III's ruler (Pisces [♓] or 12 in fig. 5.10) purports that she is overly emotional in her communications with others, and that she has emotional ties to siblings and neighbors. It also indicates that she is intuitive but mentally lazy.

House IV's ruler (Aries [♈] or 1 in fig. 5.10) suggests that she has a domineering parent. It also indicates that she has a confrontational or active home life.

House V's ruler (Taurus [♉] or 2 in fig. 5.10) indicates that she is highly artistic, attractive to the opposite sex, and experiences good luck. She might be indulgent with pleasures. And she has an excellent rapport with children.

House VI's ruler (Gemini [♊] or 3 in fig. 5.10) indicates that she keeps busy at work and on work in the home. She can do more than one job at a time, and generates a lot of paperwork. She enjoys owning many pets. She suffers, however, from respiratory or nervous complaints.

House VII's ruler (Cancer [♋] or 4 in fig. 5.10) suggests that she has a close, caring relationship with business partners or a spouse. She maintains a strong emotional connection to a dominating spouse.

House VIII's ruler (Leo [♌] or 5 in fig. 5.10) indicates that she shrewdly manipulates financial resources and assets for herself and others. She secretly fears death.

House IX's ruler (Virgo [♍] or 6 in fig. 5.10) indicates that she is concerned with higher education, publishing, philosophy, religion, anthropology, and travel abroad. She has the potential to earn an advanced degree abroad.

House X's ruler (Libra [♎] or 7 in fig. 5.10) suggests that she attracts attention because of her physical appearance, artistic talent, or social position. She needs to find a balance between home and career.

House XI's ruler (Scorpio [♏] or 8 in fig. 5.10) indicates that she may make new friends in a new environment to improve life. She may also make friendships to improve her social or professional status. She is potentially victimized by her friends. And there is an element of secrecy or mystery associated with some of her friendships or organizations.

And House XII's ruler (Sagittarius [♐] or 9 in fig. 5.10) suggests that she has an unrealistic inability to worry or to have concern. She receives help from unknown sources. She is intuitive and has an interest in psychology and the occult.

Similarly, applying the above material to Peter's *bhavacakra* (fig. 5.11), House I's ruler (Aquarius [♒] or 11 in fig. 5.11) indicates that he is highly opinionated and hates change, but makes alterations without remorse. He possesses mental poise. Physically, he has a square jaw and a friendly face.

House II's ruler (Pisces [♓] or 12 in fig. 5.11) suggests that he exerts shrewdness in financial management. He also has an irregular or illicit income.

House III's ruler (Aries [♈] or 1 in fig. 5.11) indicates that he is argumentative or communicates violently. He has confrontational relations with siblings and neighbors. And he has an impulsive intellect.

House IV's ruler (Taurus [♉] or 2 in fig. 5.11) suggests that he has a sentimental attachment to home and family. He also has strong ties to his parents.

House V's ruler (Gemini [♊] or 3 in fig. 5.11) indicates that his creativity is closely linked to communication, and that his pleasures are intellectual. He is romantically attracted to intellectuals. He is possibly a twin or the parent of twins.

House VI's ruler (Cancer [♋] or 4 in fig. 5.11) indicates that he has delicate health patterns but few major illnesses. He prefers to work at home or in home-related jobs. He has strong emotional ties to his employees or co-workers, and has inconsistent work habits. He is also emotionally attached to his pets.

House VII's ruler (Leo [♌] or 5 in fig. 5.11) suggests that marriage or another form of partnership satisfies his ego. His success comes from working closely with others.

House VIII's ruler (Virgo [♍] or 6 in fig. 5.11) indicates that he is continually seeking ways to improve his financial resources. His spouse or business partner is somehow involved in investments, taxes, insurance, or the management of other people's money. He is resigned to the concept of death.

House IX's ruler (Libra [♎] or 7 in fig. 5.11) indicates that he is artistically, academically, or philosophically oriented.

House X's ruler (Scorpio [♏] or 8 in fig. 5.11) suggests that a traumatic event that occurs during childhood instills in him a sense of having no control over circumstances. He does not allow anyone to control his personal destiny. For him, relinquishing control impedes growth. There is potential for a change of career late in life. He attracts powerful friends. There is secrecy or mystery connected with his profession, social status, or parents.

House XI's ruler (Sagittarius [♐] or 9 in fig. 5.11) suggests that he makes more friends than he can afford time to have and attaches more importance to friendship than necessary. He may perceive friendship where none exists. His friends are intellectuals, actors, religious people, travelers, artists, and clerics.

House XII's ruler (Capricorn [♑] or 10 in fig. 5.11) indicates that he spends a great deal of time in solitude. He has difficulty attaining true recognition, but may achieve success. He is victimized by unfounded fears and worries. He also has a strong interest in the psychic and the occult, but no desire to know the future.

This material is then blended with the synthesized delineation of the planetary positions within the zodiac signs (see "Interpreting the Planetary Positions in a *Rasicakra*," page 161) and within each house (see "Interpreting the Planetary Positions in a *Bhavacakra*," below) to create a complete composite. Frequently, practitioners will also incorporate the significance of the planetary ruler of a given house when it occupies another house. For instance, the planetary ruler of House VIII in Alice's *bhavacakra* (fig. 5.10) is the Sun (☉) (fig. 5.3) because Leo (5 in fig. 5.10) is governed by that planet. However, the Sun (☉) itself occupies House VI. Therefore, a practitioner would delineate the placement of House VIII's ruler in House VI. It would take volumes to thoroughly explain these complex relationships and their significance. It should be noted, however, that in a formal reading, these data would be included in the practitioner's assessment.

Interpreting the Planetary Positions in a *Bhavacakra*

Similar to the delineation of the planets by sign employed in the interpretation of the *rasicakra* (see "Interpreting the Planetary Positions in a *Rasicakra*," page 161), the delineation of the planets by house is based upon a planet's position within a particular *bhava* (house). This system is very similar to the method of interpretation used in Western and Judaic astrology.

In Alice's *bhavacakra* (fig. 5.10), the Moon (☽) is placed in the diamond marked "III," representing House III, which presides over personal courage, the fulfillment of personal desires, dietary habits, creative talent and interests,[71] and the individual's relationship with siblings. Therefore the astrologer would read the interpretation for the Moon in House III, page 199.

In Peter's *bhavacakra* (fig. 5.11), the Moon (☽) is also placed in the diamond marked "III," which represents House III. Therefore the astrologer would, again, read the interpretation for the Moon in House III, page 199. This same process is used to interpret the effects of the Sun (☉), the Moon (☽), Mercury (☿), Venus (♀), Mars (♂), Jupiter (♃), and Saturn (♄). Unlike the delineation of the *rasicakra*, the Moon's North (☊) and South (☋) Nodes are also interpreted in a *bhavacakra*.

The interpretation and synthesis of each position varies from practitioner to practitioner and from region to region. Consequently the characteristics mentioned below are more generalized than those expressed by Vedic practitioners during a consultation. This material does, however, provide a reasonable foundation for comparison with other astrological traditions such as Western (chapter 8) and Judaic (chapter 7).

The Sun[72] (☉) in the Various Houses

House I	irritable; lacks self-confidence; appears proud and confident; is a natural leader; achieves recognition; is close to his or her father
House II	enjoys financial benefits; works hard to acquire wealth; is interested in learning and knowledge
House III	has a strong relationship with siblings; extremely ambitious; strong-willed; fulfills personal desires; has a strong interest in music, dance, writing, and drama
House IV	experiences problems with real estate; has difficulties in obtaining an advanced educational degree
House V	enjoys speculation; has a strong interest in painting and handicrafts; has an interest in religious rituals; has the potential to parent male children; keen intellect; past life bestows a political career in the present; benefits from father

---

71. These include music, dance, drama, film, photography, writing, and poetry.
72. The Sun is called Surya in Vedic astrology.

House VI	strong health; defeats enemies easily; gains recognition; conducts service-oriented work; difficulties with father during childhood
House VII	has a strong desire for marriage; is preoccupied with spouse or partner; has marital problems or delays in marriage; has potential for insufficient dowry, religious differences, or social differences connected with marriage
House VIII	experiences difficulties with government or authority figures; intuitive; has low self-confidence; has a strong interest in astrology and metaphysics; father dies early or suffers a great deal
House IX	enjoys travel; has a strong interest in religion and philosophy; may change from the family's religion; has a successful and long-lived father
House X	has professional success; is a natural leader; gains fame; provides good deeds for the community; has a powerful father
House XI	acquires wealth from hobbies or freelance work; has many male friends; leadership ability grows with age; fulfills personal desires and goals; has a strong relationship with powerful friends
House XII	lacks self-confidence and assertiveness; potentially becomes imprisoned; has difficulties achieving success; needs seclusion and contemplation; suffers because of his or her father

The Moon[73] (☽) in the Various Houses

House I	self-indulgent; overly objective; emotional; gains fame; intellectual
House II	has a retentive memory; derives financial gains through women or the public; well educated; wealthy, although wealth fluctuates; has happy family life
House III	fulfills strong desires; has many siblings; has happy relations with siblings; may become a musician, dancer, writer, or actor; has an unhappy life[74]

---

73. The Moon is called Candra in Vedic astrology.
74. In a woman's or the mother's chart, it indicates that the person encounters many troubles.

House IV	has a close relationship with his or her mother; lives in comfortable surroundings; happy; has many female friends
House V	is passionate about ideologies; devoted and moral; mentally brilliant; a quick study; has painting or crafts talent; past-life karma affords benefits from women, especially his or her mother; gains from speculation
House VI	lacks peace of mind; excels at attending to details; has poor health during childhood; has a talent for medicine, health, or food-service occupation; attracts jealous people
House VII	has a happy and strong marriage; has a nurturing spouse who is ingenious or famous; has a passionate marriage
House VIII	lacks peace of mind; lacks luck; has many illnesses during childhood, or chronic illness as an adult; intuitive; derives financial gains from spouse or legacy; encounters problems with women; has talent in astrology or metaphysics
House IX	strong religious and philosophical beliefs; happy; remarkably lucky; achieves advanced education; has problems that are easily solved; travels abroad; benefits from his or her mother, who is long-lived
House X	achieves success; enters an artistic profession; has more than one career; achieves fame; has a high-profile career or achievements; has a powerful mother
House XI	gains great wealth from hobbies or freelance work; sociable; easily fulfills goals; lives according to personal dreams or visions; has continuous opportunities
House XII	experiences an unhappy and sickly childhood; encounters emotional suffering and distress; plagued by fears; has difficulties gaining recognition

Mercury[75] (☿) in the Various Houses

House I	excels at writing; communicative; highly intelligent; has a youthful appearance

---

75. Mercury is called Budha (Knower), as opposed to Buddha (Enlightened), in Vedic astrology.

House II	has a strong imagination; excels at writing, especially poetry
House III	has publishing talent; has good business sense; fulfills desires
House IV	encounters fortunate conclusions to events; intelligent; communicative
House V	is objective; is a highly intellectual thinker; past-life karma bestows literary talent; has painting or craft talent; children bring happiness
House VI	works as a writer or in the publishing industry; has debating talent; has a speech impediment or difficulties in childhood; strong self-expression
House VII	has an intelligent but emotionally detached spouse; has a low sex drive; succeeds in writing or communication
House VIII	financial gains are derived from legacy, lottery, or insurance; lacks peace of mind; communicates well
House IX	has scholarly comprehension of religion or philosophy; cultured
House X	succeeds in the publishing or communications industries; has business talent
House XI	gains wealth and success from hobbies or freelance work; fulfills personal desires; has many friends
House XII	holds on to material wealth; has difficulties with education; lacks confidence

Venus[76] (♀) in the Various Houses

House I	passionate; healthy; happy; artistic; overindulges in sweets
House II	gains wealth easily; has a happy domestic life; truthful; well-spoken
House III	artistic; possesses *joie de vivre*; fulfills personal goals; has strong desires
House IV	has a forgiving nature; the conclusion of events is peaceful; lucky in love; lives in a materially beautiful environment

---

76.   Venus is called Sukra in Vedic astrology.

House V   wealthy; comfortable; past-life karma bestows artistic talent; optimistic; has romantic happiness

House VI   works in the arts; excels in detail work; has difficulties with romance; succeeds in employment

House VII   compassionate; passionate; has a romantic marriage; has an artistic spouse

House VIII   financial gains are derived through inheritance or legacy; has difficulties in romance; psychic; has problems achieving happiness; dies a peaceful death

House IX   derives happiness from religion or philosophy; generally fortunate; artistic; has spiritual spouse from a foreign land; has abundant wealth

House X   achieves professional success, fame, and honor; enters a performing-arts profession; does very well with the public

House XI   has fortunate opportunities; gains wealth from hobbies or freelance work; fulfills goals and desires; has artistic goals; has artistic friends

House XII   encounters difficulties with women and romance; has a strong sexual appetite; spends money entertaining guests; encounters spiritual evolution through contemplation

Mars[77] (♂) in the Various Houses

House I   ambitious; aggressive; competitive; succeeds in sports; quick-tempered; marriage harmed by karma; accident-prone

House II   financially aggressive; has marital and familial difficulties; earns illicit or immoral money; has difficulties with early education

House III   encounters conflicts with siblings; succeeds through concentration; has intense desires; has mechanical talent

House IV   marriage harmed by karma; generally unhappy; has conflicts with mother; conclusions to events are tense or violent

---

77.   Mars is called Kuja in Vedic astrology.

House V	past-life karma bestows talent in sports or politics; has technical talent; does not perform good deeds
House VI	excels in technical skills; defeats enemies; has a strong sex drive
House VII	marital conflicts and confrontations; passionate; marriage is harmed by karma; succeeds in business
House VIII	encounters difficulties with legacies and property; marriage is harmed by karma; experiences an accidental death; experiences conflicts over joint finances
House IX	has conflicts with religious or spiritual teachers; has unhappy travels abroad; ambitious; has a strong interest in religion; suffers because of his or her father
House X	has professional success in technical fields; is ruthless in business; encounters conflicts with parents; is tyrannical in professional life
House XI	has conflicts with oldest sibling and friends; gains wealth from hobbies or freelance work; fulfills desires
House XII	is a spendthrift; marriage is harmed by karma; lacks assertiveness; has problems in foreign lands; has a strong sex drive

Jupiter[78] (♃) in the Various Houses

House I	remarkably lucky; famous; protected from harm; long-lived; spiritual; has a fortunate marriage
House II	wealthy; imaginative; has a happy education; truthful; has a strong memory; acquires money through moral acts
House III	succeeds through will and energy; has many siblings; motivated; has artistic talent; fulfills desires without effort
House IV	has many material comforts; successful; inherits wealth; encounters fortunate conclusions to events; experiences happiness with his or her mother
House V	encounters happiness from children; gains through speculation; wealthy; intelligent; past-life karma bestows remarkable luck

78. Jupiter is called Guru in Vedic astrology.

House VI   has few children; is well liked by co-workers and employees; has difficulties with religion; has defective luck

House VII   has a happy marriage to a spiritual spouse; passionate; succeeds in business; surpasses parents in achievement

House VIII   has a very long life; gains from legacies, inheritance, insurance, or lotteries; derives financial gains from spouse; dies peacefully; encounters conflicts with religious teachers

House IX   is very fortunate with spiritual teachers; solves problems quickly; takes spiritual or religious pilgrimages; wise; has legal talent

House X   succeeds professionally; wealthy; famous; performs good deeds; professional life elevates the public consciousness; has good relations with his or her parents

House XI   oldest sibling is fortunate; derives wealth from freelance work and hobbies; experiences limitless money-making opportunities; fulfills spiritual goals

House XII   has difficulties with spiritual or religious teachers; stockpiles and retains wealth; enjoys meditation and contemplation; has difficulties with educational institutions; experiences many sexual pleasures.

Saturn[79] *(♄) in the Various Houses*

House I   humble; self-critical; serious; limits his or her own talents; has an unhappy childhood; lacks self-confidence; patient; responsible

House II   has a limited imagination; has an unhappy family life; has difficulties earning money; poorly educated

House III   has few siblings; lacks motivation; does not easily fulfill desires; executes tasks, but receives no help

House IV   encounters unhappy conclusions to events; depressed; experiences major fluctuations in home life; suffers because of his or her mother; has difficulty with advanced education

---

79.   Saturn is called Sani in Vedic astrology.

House V	logical; overly serious; encounters difficulties because of children; past-life karma bestows responsibility and humility; experiences loss through speculation; has a depressed mentality; frustrated by nonthinking people
House VI	has difficulties with bosses or co-workers; has a remarkable ability to defeat enemies; rises to the top of his or her profession
House VII	has an unfortunate marriage; experiences major fluctuations in married life; is either frigid or sexually indulgent
House VIII	experiences many hardships; has a very long life; has difficulties acquiring wealth; derives no money from inheritance, lotteries, legacies, or insurance
House IX	encounters difficulties during long journeys; experiences difficulties with his or her father; lacks religious or philosophical faith
House X	has a strong desire to influence people; experiences major professional fluctuations; has natural leadership ability
House XI	fulfills personal goals through hard work; achieves wealth later in life; succeeds in side ventures concerning buildings or construction
House XII	encounters professional fluctuations; lacks sexual happiness; has problems concerning discipline and patience

The Moon's North Node[80] (☊) in the Various Houses

House I	has an eccentric nature; experiences a possible divorce followed by remarriage; craves power and wealth; power increases during the forty-second year of life
House II	loquacious; addictive tendencies; lacks marital fidelity; craves wealth
House III	succeeds professionally in music, drama, dance, writing, or the arts; encounters marital or familial strife; desires to communicate
House IV	has too much faith in other people; experiences difficulties with a domineering mother; encounters dramatic endings, changes, and removals

---

80. This node, treated as a planet, is called Rahu in Vedic astrology.

House V   experiences stormy emotions associated with romance; has difficulties with children; fulfills desires through manipulation; power increases during the forty-second year of life

House VI   has a strong constitution; defeats enemies; works hard; has difficulties with employees or co-workers

House VII   stoic; has an unfaithful and domineering or manipulative spouse; encounters marital difficulties

House VIII   has criminal tendencies; separated from family and friends

House IX   has anarchistic and criminal tendencies; craves philosophic or religious knowledge; gains power and wealth; power increases during the forty-second year of life

House X   professional success achieved in the fields of social work, philosophy, or the arts; supports parents early in life; takes spiritual pilgrimages

House XI   gains power and success from hobbies or freelance work, but setbacks do occur; experiences abundant opportunities; has a domineering or manipulative eldest sibling; fulfills very intense goals and desires

House XII   experiences troubles in romance; hungers for spiritual evolution; is a spendthrift; incurs many debts

The Moon's South Node[81] (☋) in the Various Houses

House I   experiences marital difficulties; has a short life span; introvertive; spiritual

House II   encounters confrontations with spouse; has limited finances and few possessions; tends to lie

House III   eccentric; easily fulfills desires; experiences suffering caused by siblings

House IV   has problems with home and mother; has difficulties with higher education

House V   has few children; has introspective children; past-life karma bestows psychic ability

---

81.   This node, treated as a planet, is called Ketu in Vedic astrology.

House VI   experiences problems with employees or co-workers; has a strong constitution; easily defeats enemies

House VII   has a strange spouse; marriage fluctuates

House VIII   experiences an unhappy home life; separated from friends; has a chronic illness

House IX   encounters business and travel problems; lacks interest in religion; his or her father may suffer from alcoholism

House X   has professional success; fulfills professional ambitions

House XI   derives wealth from hobbies or freelance work; attracts unusual friends

House XII   has romantic and sexual problems; highly intuitive; unable to accumulate money.

As mentioned earlier in this section, in Alice's *bhavacakra* (fig. 5.10), the Moon (☽) is placed in the diamond marked "III" (House III) and "12" (Pisces [♓] in fig. 5.3). Using the interpretative material above, the Moon's placement in House III indicates that Alice fulfills her strong desires. She may have many siblings with whom she has happy relations. She may become a musician, dancer, writer, or actor. She has many troubles throughout her life, however. Employing the delineation material found in the section titled "Interpreting the Planetary Positions in a *Rasicakra*" (page 161), the Moon's position in the zodiac sign Pisces (♓, or 12 in fig. 5.10) further indicates that Alice is imaginative, kind, intuitive, and psychic. She has literary talent and loves both beauty and luxury. She encounters many misfortunes and obstacles, has difficulty saving money or affording things, and has trouble making an emotional commitment in romance. The practitioner then synthesizes these two interpretations during a consultation.

In Peter's *bhavacakra* (fig. 5.11), the Moon (☽) is also placed in the diamond marked "III" (House III). But the sign indicated in the diamond is 1 (Aries [♈] in fig. 5.3). Using the interpretative material above, the Moon's placement in House III indicates that Peter fulfills his strong desires. He may have many siblings with whom he has happy relations. He may become a musician, dancer, writer, or actor. Overall, however, he has an unhappy life. Employing the delineation material found in the section entitled "Interpreting the Planetary Positions in a Rasicakra," page 161, the Moon's position in the zodiac sign Aries (♈, or 1 in fig. 5.11) further indicates that Peter is highly imaginative, self-reliant, and inventive. He has a restless mind and a quick temper. He exerts his independence and carves a unique path. Potentially he might head a major undertaking, and could reach prominence during his lifetime. The practitioner then synthesizes these two interpretations during a consultation to derive a final analysis.

This same process is then used by the practitioner to interpret the effects of the Sun (☉), Mercury (☿), Venus (♀), Mars (♂), Jupiter (♃), Saturn (♄), the Moon's North Node (☊), and the Moon's South Node (☋) on both Alice's and Peter's personalities, using the material in the manner described above. In this manner, the significance of the planets' locations—both by house and by zodiac sign—is synthesized into one segment of a personality profile which includes the delineation of the six *shadbala*, *yoga*, and additional charts as mentioned earlier.

STEP THREE: CONSTRUCTING AND INTERPRETING THE NAVAMSACAKRA

Unlike any other form of astrology, the Vedic tradition employs the delineation of more than one chart in the development of a personality profile. As mentioned at the beginning of this chapter, there are four additional *sodasavargas* (divisional charts) that are commonly constructed to accompany either the *rasicakra* (sign chart) or *bhavacakra* (house chart) in a *jataka* (natal) personality profile. The

FIGURE 5.12. TABLE OF NAVAMSA SIGNS.

ZODIAC SIGN LOCATION IN DEGREES (°) AND MINUTES (')	PLANETARY RULER OF ZODIAC SIGN (SYMBOL)	NAVAMSA SIGN NUMBER (ZODIAC SIGN AND SYMBOL)	NAVAMSA PLANETARY RULER (SYMBOL)
00°♈00'–03°♈20'	Mars (♂)	1 (Aries, ♈)	Mars (♂)
03°♈21'–06°♈40'	Mars (♂)	2 (Taurus, ♉)	Venus (♀)
06°♈41'–10°♈00'	Mars (♂)	3 (Gemini, ♊)	Mercury (☿)
10°♈01'–13°♈20'	Mars (♂)	4 (Cancer, ♋)	Moon (☽)
13°♈21'–16°♈40'	Mars (♂)	5 (Leo, ♌)	Sun (☉)
16°♈41'–20°♈00'	Mars (♂)	6 (Virgo, ♍)	Mercury (☿)
20°♈01'–23°♈20'	Mars (♂)	7 (Libra, ♎)	Venus (♀)
23°♈21'–26°♈40'	Mars (♂)	8 (Scorpio, ♏)	Mars (♂)
26°♈41'–30°♈00'	Mars (♂)	9 (Sagittarius, ♐)	Jupiter (♃)
00°♉00'–03°♉20'	Venus (♀)	10 (Capricorn, ♑)	Saturn (♄)
03°♉21'–06°♉40'	Venus (♀)	11 (Aquarius, ♒)	Saturn (♄)
06°♉41'–10°♉00'	Venus (♀)	12 (Pisces, ♓)	Jupiter (♃)
10°♉01'–13°♉20'	Venus (♀)	1 (Aries, ♈)	Mars (♂)
13°♉21'–16°♉40'	Venus (♀)	2 (Taurus, ♉)	Venus (♀)
16°♉41'–20°♉00'	Venus (♀)	3 (Gemini, ♊)	Mercury (☿)
20°♉01'–23°♉20'	Venus (♀)	4 (Cancer, ♋)	Moon (☽)
23°♉21'–26°♉40'	Venus (♀)	5 (Leo, ♌)	Sun (☉)
26°♉41'–30°♉00'	Venus (♀)	6 (Virgo, ♍)	Mercury (☿)

first of these is the *navamsacakra* (ninth-sign chart), which is a *sodasavarga* (divisional chart) that indicates an individual's ultimate direction in life and is also used to determine the outcome of marriage. The chart is constructed by converting the Vedic (sidereal) positions of the Ascendant, the planets, and the nodes (figs. 5.4 and 5.5, fourth column) into *navamsa* signs (fig. 5.12, third column), which are divided into increments of 03°20′ each. This is executed by locating the range of degrees and minutes that the Ascendant, planet, or node occupies in a zodiac sign (figs. 5.4 or 5.5, fourth column) in the first column of fig. 5.12.

As mentioned earlier in this chapter, Vedic practitioners do not use symbols to represent the zodiac signs in their charts. Each of the twelve zodiac signs is simply represented by the sign's numeric position (fig. 5.3, third column). Therefore, the *navamsa* number (fig. 5.12, third column) represents a zodiac sign that is designated in parentheses in fig. 5.12.

For example, the sidereal position of Alice's Ascendant (08°♑52′ in fig. 5.4, fourth column) is located between 06°♑40′ and 10°♑00′ (fig. 5.12, first column). Reading across, the *navamsa* sign—*navamsa* 12—is identified (fig. 5.12, third col-

Zodiac Sign Location in Degrees (°) and Minutes (′)	Planetary Ruler of Zodiac Sign (Symbol)	Navamsa Sign Number (Zodiac Sign and Symbol)	Navamsa Planetary Ruler (Symbol)
00°♊00′–03°♊20′	Mercury (☿)	7 (Libra, ♎)	Venus (♀)
03°♊21′–06°♊40′	Mercury (☿)	8 (Scorpio, ♏)	Mars (♂)
06°♊41′–10°♊00′	Mercury (☿)	9 (Sagittarius, ♐)	Jupiter (♃)
10°♊01′–13°♊20′	Mercury (☿)	10 (Capricorn, ♑)	Saturn (♄)
13°♊21′–16°♊40′	Mercury (☿)	11 (Aquarius, ♒)	Saturn (♄)
16°♊41′–20°♊00′	Mercury (☿)	12 (Pisces, ♓)	Jupiter (♃)
20°♊01′–23°♊20′	Mercury (☿)	1 (Aries, ♈)	Mars (♂)
23°♊21′–26°♊40′	Mercury (☿)	2 (Taurus, ♉)	Venus (♀)
26°♊41′–30°♊00′	Mercury (☿)	3 (Gemini, ♊)	Mercury (☿)
00°♋00′–03°♋20′	Moon (☽)	4 (Cancer, ♋)	Moon (☽)
03°♋21′–06°♋40′	Moon (☽)	5 (Leo, ♌)	Sun (☉)
06°♋41′–10°♋00′	Moon (☽)	6 (Virgo, ♍)	Mercury (☿)
10°♋01′–13°♋20′	Moon (☽)	7 (Libra, ♎)	Venus (♀)
13°♋21′–16°♋40′	Moon (☽)	8 (Scorpio, ♏)	Mars (♂)
16°♋41′–20°♋00′	Moon (☽)	9 (Sagittarius, ♐)	Jupiter (♃)
20°♋01′–23°♋20′	Moon (☽)	10 (Capricorn, ♑)	Saturn (♄)
23°♋21′–26°♋40′	Moon (☽)	11 (Aquarius, ♒)	Saturn (♄)
26°♋41′–30°♋00′	Moon (☽)	12 (Pisces, ♓)	Jupiter (♃)
00°♌00′–03°♌20′	Sun (☉)	1 (Aries, ♈)	Mars (♂)

umn), which means that the *navamsa* sign for Alice's sidereal Ascendant is Pisces (12 in fig. 5.3). The same procedure is then applied to the positions of the Sun (☉), the Moon (☽), Mercury (☿), Mars (♂), Venus (♀), Jupiter (♃), Saturn (♄), the Moon's North Node (☊), and the Moon's South Node (☋). The resulting information is kept in reference notes such as the table shown in fig. 5.13.

Zodiac Sign Location in Degrees (°) and Minutes (')	Planetary Ruler of Zodiac Sign (Symbol)	Navamsa Sign Number (Zodiac Sign and Symbol)	Navamsa Planetary Ruler (Symbol)
03°♌21'–06°♌40'	Sun (☉)	2 (Taurus, ♉)	Venus (♀)
06°♌41'–10°♌00'	Sun (☉)	3 (Gemini, ♊)	Mercury (☿)
10°♌01'–13°♌20'	Sun (☉)	4 (Cancer, ♋)	Moon (☽)
13°♌21'–16°♌40'	Sun (☉)	5 (Leo, ♌)	Sun (☉)
16°♌41'–20°♌00'	Sun (☉)	6 (Virgo, ♍)	Mercury (☿)
20°♌01'–23°♌20'	Sun (☉)	7 (Libra, ♎)	Venus (♀)
23°♌21'–26°♌40'	Sun (☉)	8 (Scorpio, ♏)	Mars (♂)
26°♌41'–30°♌00'	Sun (☉)	9 (Sagittarius, ♐)	Jupiter (♃)
00°♍00'–03°♍20'	Mercury (☿)	10 (Capricorn, ♑)	Saturn (♄)
03°♍21'–06°♍40'	Mercury (☿)	11 (Aquarius, ♒)	Saturn (♄)
06°♍41'–10°♍00'	Mercury (☿)	12 (Pisces, ♓)	Jupiter (♃)
10°♍01'–13°♍20'	Mercury (☿)	1 (Aries, ♈)	Mars (♂)
13°♍21'–16°♍40'	Mercury (☿)	2 (Taurus, ♉)	Venus (♀)
16°♍41'–20°♍00'	Mercury (☿)	3 (Gemini, ♊)	Mercury (☿)
20°♍01'–23°♍20'	Mercury (☿)	4 (Cancer, ♋)	Moon (☽)
23°♍21'–26°♍40'	Mercury (☿)	5 (Leo, ♌)	Sun (☉)
26°♍41'–30°♍00'	Mercury (☿)	6 (Virgo, ♍)	Mercury (☿)
00°♎00'–03°♎20'	Venus (♀)	7 (Libra, ♎)	Venus (♀)
03°♎21'–06°♎40'	Venus (♀)	8 (Scorpio, ♏)	Mars (♂)
06°♎41'–10°♎00'	Venus (♀)	9 (Sagittarius, ♐)	Jupiter (♃)
10°♎01'–13°♎20'	Venus (♀)	10 (Capricorn, ♑)	Saturn (♄)
13°♎21'–16°♎40'	Venus (♀)	11 (Aquarius, ♒)	Saturn (♄)
16°♎41'–20°♎00'	Venus (♀)	12 (Pisces, ♓)	Jupiter (♃)
20°♎01'–23°♎20'	Venus (♀)	1 (Aries, ♈)	Mars (♂)
23°♎21'–26°♎40'	Venus (♀)	2 (Taurus, ♉)	Venus (♀)
26°♎41'–30°♎00'	Venus (♀)	3 (Gemini, ♊)	Mercury (☿)
00°♏00'–03°♏20'	Mars (♂)	4 (Cancer, ♋)	Moon (☽)
03°♏21'–06°♏40'	Mars (♂)	5 (Leo, ♌)	Sun (☉)
06°♏41'–10°♏00'	Mars (♂)	6 (Virgo, ♍)	Mercury (☿)
10°♏01'–13°♏20'	Mars (♂)	7 (Libra, ♎)	Venus (♀)
13°♏21'–16°♏40'	Mars (♂)	8 (Scorpio, ♏)	Mars (♂)
16°♏41'–20°♏00'	Mars (♂)	9 (Sagittarius, ♐)	Jupiter (♃)

Zodiac Sign Location in Degrees (°) and Minutes (′)	Planetary Ruler of Zodiac Sign (Symbol)	Navamsa Sign Number (Zodiac Sign and Symbol)	Navamsa Planetary Ruler (Symbol)
20°♏01′–23°♏20′	Mars (♂)	10 (Capricorn, ♑)	Saturn (♄)
23°♏21′–26°♏40′	Mars (♂)	11 (Aquarius, ♒)	Saturn (♄)
26°♏41′–30°♏00′	Mars (♂)	12 (Pisces, ♓)	Jupiter (♃)
00°♐00′–03°♐20′	Jupiter (♃)	1 (Aries, ♈)	Mars (♂)
03°♐21′–06°♐40′	Jupiter (♃)	2 (Taurus, ♉)	Venus (♀)
06°♐41′–10°♐00′	Jupiter (♃)	3 (Gemini, ♊)	Mercury (☿)
10°♐01′–13°♐20′	Jupiter (♃)	4 (Cancer, ♋)	Moon (☽)
13°♐21′–16°♐40′	Jupiter (♃)	5 (Leo, ♌)	Sun (☉)
16°♐41′–20°♐00′	Jupiter (♃)	6 (Virgo, ♍)	Mercury (☿)
20°♐01′–23°♐20′	Jupiter (♃)	7 (Libra, ♎)	Venus (♀)
23°♐21′–26°♐40′	Jupiter (♃)	8 (Scorpio, ♏)	Mars (♂)
26°♐41′–30°♐00′	Jupiter (♃)	9 (Sagittarius, ♐)	Jupiter (♃)
00°♑00′–03°♑20′	Saturn (♄)	10 (Capricorn, ♑)	Saturn (♄)
03°♑21′–06°♑40′	Saturn (♄)	11 (Aquarius, ♒)	Saturn (♄)
06°♑41′–10°♑00′	Saturn (♄)	12 (Pisces, ♓)	Jupiter (♃)
10°♑01′–13°♑20′	Saturn (♄)	1 (Aries, ♈)	Mars (♂)
13°♑21′–16°♑40′	Saturn (♄)	2 (Taurus, ♉)	Venus (♀)
16°♑41′–20°♑00′	Saturn (♄)	3 (Gemini, ♊)	Mercury (☿)
20°♑01′–23°♑20′	Saturn (♄)	4 (Cancer, ♋)	Moon (☽)
23°♑21′–26°♑40′	Saturn (♄)	5 (Leo, ♌)	Sun (☉)
26°♑41′–30°♑00′	Saturn (♄)	6 (Virgo, ♍)	Mercury (☿)
00°♒00′–03°♒20′	Saturn (♄)	7 (Libra, ♎)	Venus (♀)
03°♒21′–06°♒40′	Saturn (♄)	8 (Scorpio, ♏)	Mars (♂)
06°♒41′–10°♒00′	Saturn (♄)	9 (Sagittarius, ♐)	Jupiter (♃)
10°♒01′–13°♒20′	Saturn (♄)	10 (Capricorn, ♑)	Saturn (♄)
13°♒21′–16°♒40′	Saturn (♄)	11 (Aquarius, ♒)	Saturn (♄)
16°♒41′–20°♒00′	Saturn (♄)	12 (Pisces, ♓)	Jupiter (♃)
20°♒01′–23°♒20′	Saturn (♄)	1 (Aries, ♈)	Mars (♂)
23°♒21′–26°♒40′	Saturn (♄)	2 (Taurus, ♉)	Venus (♀)
26°♒41′–30°♒00′	Saturn (♄)	3 (Gemini, ♊)	Mercury (☿)
00°♓00′–03°♓20′	Jupiter (♃)	4 (Cancer, ♋)	Moon (☽)
03°♓21′–06°♓40′	Jupiter (♃)	5 (Leo, ♌)	Sun (☉)
06°♓41′–10°♓00′	Jupiter (♃)	6 (Virgo, ♍)	Mercury (☿)
10°♓01′–13°♓20′	Jupiter (♃)	7 (Libra, ♎)	Venus (♀)
13°♓21′–16°♓40′	Jupiter (♃)	8 (Scorpio, ♏)	Mars (♂)
16°♓41′–20°♓00′	Jupiter (♃)	9 (Sagittarius, ♐)	Jupiter (♃)
20°♓01′–23°♓20′	Jupiter (♃)	10 (Capricorn, ♑)	Saturn (♄)
23°♓21′–26°♓40′	Jupiter (♃)	11 (Aquarius, ♒)	Saturn (♄)
26°♓41′–30°♓00′	Jupiter (♃)	12 (Pisces, ♓)	Jupiter (♃)

FIGURE 5.13. ALICE T.'s NAVAMSA SIGNS.

ELEMENT IN CHART (FROM FIG. 5.4)	POSITION IN VEDIC (SIDEREAL) NATAL HOROSCOPE (FROM FIG. 5.4)	ZODIAC SIGN LOCATION IN DEGREES (°) AND MINUTES (') (FROM FIG. 5.12)	PLANETARY RULER OF ZODIAC SIGN (FROM FIG. 5.12)	NAVAMSA SIGN NUMBER (SIGN) (FROM FIG. 5.12)	PLANETARY RULER OF NAVAMSA (FROM FIG. 5.12)
Ascendant (AS)	08°♑52'	06°♑41'–10°♑00'	Saturn (♄)	12 (Pisces, ♓)	Jupiter (♃)
Sun (☉)	01°♊50'	00°♊00'–03°♊20'	Mercury (☿)	7 (Libra, ♎)	Jupiter (♃)
Moon (☽)	18°♓23'	16°♓41'–20°♓00'	Jupiter (♃)	9 (Sagittarius, ♐)	Jupiter (♃)
Mercury (☿)	10°♊23'	10°♊01'–13°♊20'	Mercury (☿)	10 (Capricorn, ♑)	Saturn (♄)
Venus (♀)	29°♉26'	26°♉41'–30°♉00'	Venus (♀)	6 (Virgo, ♍)	Mercury (☿)
Mars (♂)	08°♎19'	06°♎41'–10°♎00'	Venus (♀)	9 (Sagittarius, ♐)	Jupiter (♃)
Jupiter (♃)	17°♈47'	16°♈41'–20°♈00'	Mars (♂)	6 (Virgo, ♍)	Mercury (☿)
Saturn (♄)	15°♍07'	13°♍21'–16°♍40'	Mercury (☿)	2 (Taurus, ♉)	Venus (♀)
Moon's North Node (☊)	00°♒18'ʀ	00°♒00'–03°♒20'	Saturn (♄)	7 (Libra, ♎)	Venus (♀)
Moon's South Node (☋)	00°♌18'ʀ	00°♌00'–03°♌20'	Sun (☉)	1 (Aries, ♈)	Mars (♂)

The sidereal position of Peter's Ascendant (09°♒34' in fig. 5.5, fourth column) is located between 06°♒40' and 10°♒00' (fig. 5.12, first column). Reading across, the *navamsa* sign—*navamsa* 9—is identified (fig. 5.12, third column), which means that the *navamsa* sign for Peter's sidereal Ascendant is Sagittarius (9 in fig. 5.3). The same procedure is then applied to the positions of the Sun (☉), the Moon (☽), Mercury (☿), Mars (♂), Venus (♀), Jupiter (♃), Saturn (♄), the Moon's North Node (☊), and the Moon's South Node (☋). The resulting information is kept in reference notes such as the table shown in fig. 5.14.

The derived *navamsa* signs (figs. 5.13 and 5.14) are then placed onto either a *rasicakra*-style or *bhavacakra*-style chart. For the sake of space, only the construction of a *rasicakra*-style *navamsacakra* will be shown in this section.[82]

This chart is created in the same manner as a *rasicakra* (see "Constructing the *Rasicakra*," page 152). For example, in Alice's *navamsacakra* (fig. 5.15), her Ascendant (AS *navamsa* 12 in fig. 5.13, fourth column) is indicated by a diagonal line in the box marked "12," which represents *navamsa* 12 (Pisces [♓] in fig. 5.13). Beginning with the box marked "1" in fig. 5.15, the Moon's South Node (☋ 00°♌18' in fig. 5.4, fourth column) is placed in that box, which represents *navamsa* 1 (Aries [♈] in fig. 5.13). Saturn (♄ 15°♍07' in fig. 5.4, fourth column) is placed in the box

---

82. To create a *bhavacakra*-style *navamsacakra*, follow the placement procedure outlined in the section titled "Constructing the *Bhavacakra*," page 000.

FIGURE 5.14. PETER C.'S *NAVAMSA* SIGNS.

ELEMENT IN CHART (FROM FIG. 5.5)	POSITION IN VEDIC (SIDEREAL) NATAL HOROSCOPE (FROM FIG. 5.5)	ZODIAC SIGN LOCATION IN DEGREES (°) AND MINUTES (') (FROM FIG. 5.12)	PLANETARY RULER OF ZODIAC SIGN (FROM FIG. 5.12)	NAVAMSA SIGN NUMBER (SIGN) (FROM FIG. 5.12)	PLANETARY RULER OF NAVAMSA
Ascendant (AS)	09°♒34′	06°♒41′–10°♒00′	Saturn (♄)	9 (Sagittarius, ♐)	Saturn (♄)
Sun (☉)	11°♌26′	10°♌01′–13°♌20′	Sun (☉)	4 (Cancer, ♋)	Mercury (☿)
Moon (☽)	10°♈23′	10°♈01′–13°♈20′	Mars (♂)	4 (Cancer, ♋)	Mercury (☿)
Mercury (☿)	21°♌21′ʀ	20°♌01′–23°♌20′	Sun (☉)	7 (Libra, ♎)	Venus (♀)
Venus (♀)	25°♊38′	23°♊21′–26°♊40′	Mercury (☿)	2 (Taurus, ♉)	Venus (♀)
Mars (♂)	25°♊16′	23°♊21′–26°♊40′	Mercury (☿)	2 (Taurus, ♉)	Venus (♀)
Jupiter (♃)	02°♉21′	00°♉00′–03°♉20′	Venus (♀)	10 (Capricorn, ♑)	Saturn (♄)
Saturn (♄)	08°♒10′ʀ	10°♒01′–13°♒20′	Saturn (♄)	10 (Capricorn, ♑)	Jupiter (♃)
Moon's North Node (☊)	06°♊25′ʀ	03°♊21′–06°♊40′	Mercury (☿)	8 (Scorpio, ♏)	Mars (♂)
Moon's South Node (☋)	06°♐25′ʀ	03°♐21′–06°♐40′	Jupiter (♃)	2 (Taurus, ♉)	Venus (♀)

marked "2" in fig. 5.15, which represents *navamsa* 2 (Taurus [♉] in fig. 5.13). Jupiter (♃ 17°♈47′ in fig. 5.4, fourth column) and Venus (♀ 29°♉26′ in fig. 5.4, fourth column) are placed in the box marked "6" in fig. 5.15, which represents *navamsa* 6 (Virgo [♍] in fig. 5.13). The Moon's North Node (☊ 00°♒18′ in fig. 5.4, fourth column) is placed in the box marked "7" in fig. 5.15, which represents *navamsa* 7 (Libra [♎] in fig. 5.13). The Sun (☉ 01°♊50′ in fig. 5.4, fourth column), Mars (♂ 08°♎19′ in fig. 5.4, fourth column), and the Moon (☽ 18°♓23′ in fig. 5.4, fourth column) are placed in the box marked "9" in fig. 5.15, which represents *navamsa* 9 (Sagittarius [♐] in fig. 5.13). And Mercury (☿ 10°♊23′ in fig. 5.4, fourth column) is placed in the box marked "3" in fig. 5.15, which represents *navamsa* 10 (Gemini [♊] in fig. 5.13).

Because none of the planetary positions in fig. 5.4 (fourth column) occupies *navamsa* 3 (box 3 in fig. 5.15), *navamsa* 4 (box 4), *navamsa* 5 (box 5), *navamsa* 8 (box 8), *navamsa* 11 (box 11), and *navamsa* 12 (box 12), these boxes—or positions—remain empty.

The same process is applied to Peter's *navamsa*-sign positions as follows. Peter's Ascendant (AS 09°♒34′ in fig. 5.5, fourth column) is indicated in fig. 5.16 by a diagonal line in the box marked "9," which represents *navamsa* 9 (Sagittarius [♐] in fig. 5.14). Beginning with the box marked "2" in fig. 5.16, Venus (♀ 25°♊38′ in fig. 5.5, fourth column), Mars (♂ 25°♊16′ in fig. 5.5, fourth column), and the Moon's South Node (☋ 06°♐25′ in fig. 5.5, fourth column) are placed in that box, which

FIGURE 5.15. ALICE T.'S *RASICAKRA-STYLE NAVAMSACAKRA.*

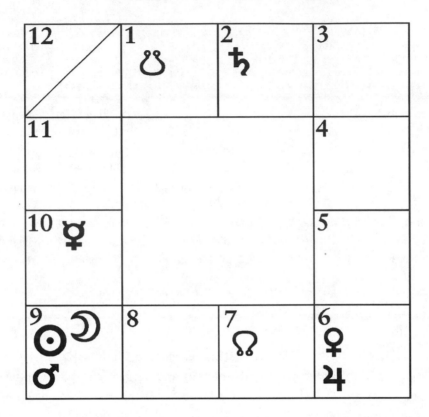

represents *navamsa* 2 (Taurus [♉] in fig. 5.14). The Sun (☉ 11°♌26′ in fig. 5.5, fourth column) and the Moon (☽ 10°♈23′ in fig. 5.5, fourth column) are placed in the box marked "4" in fig. 5.16, which represents *navamsa* 4 (Cancer [♋] in fig. 5.14). Mercury (☿ 21°♌21′ in fig. 5.5, fourth column) is placed in the box marked "7" in fig. 5.16, which represents *navamsa* 7 (Libra [♎] in fig. 5.13). The Moon's North Node (☊ 06°♊25′ in fig. 5.5, fourth column) is placed in the box marked "8" in fig. 5.16, which represents *navamsa* 8 (Scorpio [♏] in fig. 5.14). Saturn (♄ 08°♒10′ in fig. 5.5, fourth column) and Jupiter (♃ 02°♉21′ in fig. 5.5, fourth column) are placed in the box marked "10" in fig. 5.16, which represents *navamsa* 10 (Capricorn [♑] in fig. 5.14).

Because none of the planetary positions in fig. 5.5 (fourth column) occupies *navamsa* 1 (box 1), *navamsa* 3 (box 3), *navamsa* 5 (box 5), *navamsa* 6 (box 6), *navamsa* 9 (box 9), *navamsa* 11 (box 11), or *navamsa* 12 (box 12), these boxes—or positions—remain empty.

As mentioned earlier, the *navamsacakra* is a *sodasavarga* (divisional chart) that indicates an individual's ultimate direction in life and is also used to determine the outcome of marriage. And the planetary positions in the *rasicakra*-style *navam-*

FIGURE 5.16. PETER C.'S *RASICAKRA-STYLE NAVAMSACAKRA.*

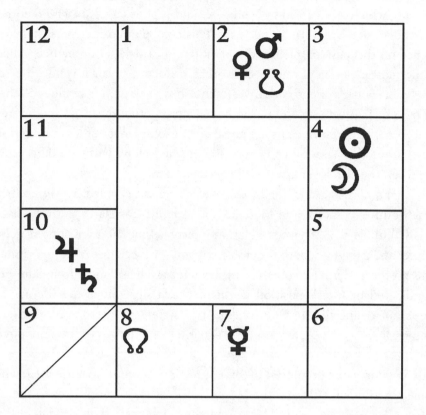

sacakra are interpreted by the exact same method as the *rasicakra* itself[83] (see "Interpreting the Planetary Positions in a *Rasicakra*," page 161), which concentrates on the interpretation of planetary positions based on the zodiac sign each entity occupies. It also focuses on the individual's dominant interests, which are evidenced by the occupation of a *navamsa* sign by more than one planet, or by a planet that exerts a strong influence in the person's life, which will be discussed later in this chapter.

In Alice's *navamsacakra* (fig. 5.15), *navamsa* 9 is occupied by the Sun (☉), the Moon (☽), and Mars (♂). *Navamsa* 9 correlates to the zodiac sign Sagittarius (♐) in fig. 5.13. This combination indicates that Alice is able to hone in and make a mark on a situation because of the Sun's influence. Involvement in religious, political, or educational reforms as well as possible public notoriety are evidenced by the Moon's occupation of the position. Mars's influence on the position indicates that Alice marries more than once (and in one instance has concerns over the spouse's or a child's health).

---

83. The *bhavacakra*-style *navamsacakra* is interpreted by the exact same method as the *bhavacakra* (see "Interpreting the Planetary Positions in a *Bhavacakra*," page 197).

A secondary point of interest in this *navamsacakra* (fig. 5.15) occurs in *navamsa* 6, which is occupied by Venus (♀) and Jupiter (♃). *Navamsa* 6 correlates to the zodiac sign Virgo (♍) in fig. 5.13. This combination indicates that Venus's influence on this position creates disappointment or delays in romance. Alice potentially marries an employee, a co-worker, a doctor, or an invalid. She profits through her spouse's or partner's investments, however. Jupiter's influence changes some of Venus's prognostications, producing a prosperous marriage and mysterious good fortune. Unforeseen gains are possible, but so is danger or loss through secret means. Naturally, many other factors are weighed along with the data provided above when the astrologer assesses the *navamsacakra*.

In Peter's *navamsacakra* (fig. 5.16), *navamsa* 2 is occupied by Venus (♀), the Moon's South Node (☋), and Mars (♂). *Navamsa* 2 correlates to the zodiac sign Taurus (♉) in fig. 5.14. This combination indicates that Peter encounters delays in marriage, and gains from both his profession and spirit because of Venus's influence on this position. Harm to women or by women as well as danger from adultery are also indicated by Mars's position in this *navamsa* sign. Since the Moon's South Node is not delineated in the *rasicakra*-style system of interpretation, there are no details given as to its effect on Peter's marital experiences or ultimate direction in life.

A secondary point of interest in this *navamsacakra* occurs in *navamsa* 4, which is occupied by the Sun (☉) and the Moon (☽). *Navamsa* 4 correlates to the zodiac sign Cancer (♋) in fig. 5.14. This combination indicates that ultimately Peter is sensitive, changeable, and has a fertile imagination. He is profoundly affected by surroundings and possesses dramatic flair. He has many mood swings, craves kindness, and fears ridicule. He remembers everything. According to the Moon's influence on this position, Peter is also agreeable, sympathetic, and follows the path of least resistance. He travels, cooks, collects antiques, and encounters great obstacles.

STEP FOUR: CONSTRUCTING THE *HORACAKRA*, *DREKKANACAKRA*, AND *SAPTAMSACAKRA*

As mentioned at the beginning of this chapter, Vedic astrologers commonly construct more than just a *rasicakra* (sign chart) or *bhavacakra* (house chart) when creating an individual's *jataka* (natal) profile. The *navamsacakra* discussed earlier and the *candralagna*, which will be covered later in this chapter, are two common ancillary charts developed by Vedic practitioners. However, there are three additional *sodasavargas* (divisional charts, as in fig. 5.1) that are also regularly consulted by astrologers: the *horacakra*, the *drekkanacakra*, and the *saptamsacakra*.

FIGURE 5.17. TABLE OF *HORA* POSITIONS.

Zodiac Sign Location in Degrees (°) and Minutes (′)	Hora Planet	Zodiac Sign Location in Degrees (°) and Minutes (′)	Hora Planet
00°♈00′–15°♈00′	Sun (☉)	00°♎00′–15°♎00′	Sun (☉)
15°♈01′–30°♈00′	Moon (☽)	15°♎01′–30°♎00′	Moon (☽)
00°♉00′–15°♉00′	Moon (☽)	00°♏00′–15°♏00′	Moon (☽)
15°♉01′–30°♉00′	Sun (☉)	15°♏01′–30°♏00′	Sun (☉)
00°♊00′–15°♊00′	Sun (☉)	00°♐00′–15°♐00′	Sun (☉)
15°♊01′–30°♊00′	Moon (☽)	15°♐01′–30°♐00′	Moon (☽)
00°♋00′–15°♋00′	Moon (☽)	00°♑00′–15°♑00′	Moon (☽)
15°♋01′–30°♋00′	Sun (☉)	15°♑01′–30°♑00′	Sun (☉)
00°♌00′–15°♌00′	Sun (☉)	00°♒00′–15°♒00′	Sun (☉)
15°♌01′–30°♌00′	Moon (☽)	15°♒01′–30°♒00′	Moon (☽)
00°♍00′–15°♍00′	Moon (☽)	00°♓00′–15°♓00′	Moon (☽)
15°♍01′–30°♍00′	Sun (☉)	15°♓01′–30°♓00′	Sun (☉)

The interpretation of these *sodasavargas* is very extensive and would require many more chapters to cover in full detail. The general structure of each type is defined here, however, to provide a moderate sample of the intricacy of this particular tradition.

Constructing the *Horacakra*

The *horacakra* (half-sign chart) reviews the strength of six planets: the Sun (☉), the Moon (☽), Venus (♀), Mars (♂), Jupiter (♃), and Saturn (♄). This information is employed to determine an individual's ability to acquire wealth. The *horacakra* is not displayed in chart form like the *rasicakra*, *bhavacakra*, or *navamsacakra*. Instead, the data is recorded in the astrologer's reference notes.

The *horacakra* is constructed by converting the Vedic (sidereal) positions of the Sun (☉), the Moon (☽), Venus (♀), Mars (♂), Jupiter (♃), and Saturn (♄) (figs. 5.4 and 5.5, fourth column) into *hora* signs (fig. 5.17, second column), which are divided into increments of 15°00′ each. This is executed by locating the range of degrees and minutes in which each planet (fig. 5.4 or 5.5, fourth column) resides in the first column of fig. 5.17.

As mentioned earlier, Vedic practitioners do not write symbols for each of the planets. The Sun (☉) and the Moon (☽) are simply written down in Sanskrit by the astrologer. For comparison with the other traditions, however, the symbols of these planets are used throughout this section.

FIGURE 5.18. ALICE T.'s HORACAKRA.

ELEMENT IN CHART (FROM FIG. 5.4)	POSITION IN VEDIC (SIDEREAL) NATAL HOROSCOPE (FROM FIG. 5.4)	ZODIAC SIGN LOCATION IN DEGREES (°) AND MINUTES (') (FROM FIG. 5.17)	HORA SIGN (FROM FIG. 5.17)
Ascendant (AS)	08°♑52′	NOT USED	NOT USED
Sun (☉)	01°♊50′	00°♊00′–15°♊00′	Sun (☉)
Moon (☽)	18°♓23′	15°♓01′–30°♓00′	Sun (☉)
Mercury (☿)	10°♊23′	NOT USED	NOT USED
Venus (♀)	29°♉26′	15°♉01′–30°♉00′	Sun (☉)
Mars (♂)	08°♎19′	00°♎00′–15°♎00′	Sun (☉)
Jupiter (♃)	17°♈47′	15°♈01′–30°♈00′	Moon (☽)
Saturn (♄)	15°♍07′	15°♍01′–30°♍00′	Sun (☉)
Moon's North Node (☊)	00°♒18′ʀ	NOT USED	NOT USED
Moon's South Node (☋)	00°♌18′ʀ	NOT USED	NOT USED

For example, Alice's Sun (☉ 01°♊50′ in fig. 5.4, fourth column), Moon (☽ 18°♓23′ in fig. 5.4, fourth column), Venus (♀ 29°♉26′ in fig. 5.4, fourth column), and Mars (♂ 08°♎19′ in fig. 5.4, fourth column) are in the Sun's *hora* (00°♎01′–15°♎00′ in fig. 5.17). Jupiter (♃ 17°♈47′ in fig. 5.4, fourth column) is in the Moon's *hora* (15°♈01′–30°♈00′ in fig. 5.17). And Saturn (♄ 15°♍07′ in fig. 5.4, fourth column) is in the Sun's *hora* (15°♍01′–30°♍00′ in fig. 5.17). These data would be documented as shown in fig. 5.18, below.

The same process is applied to Peter's planetary positions. Peter's Sun (☉ 11°♌26′ in fig. 5.5, fourth column) and Moon (☽ 10°♈23′ in fig. 5.5, fourth column) are in the Sun's *hora* (00°♈00′–15°♈00′ in fig. 5.17). Venus (♀ 25°♊38′ in fig. 5.5, fourth column), Mars (♂ 25°♊16′ in fig. 5.5, fourth column) and Jupiter (♃ 02°♉21′ in fig. 5.5, fourth column) are in the Moon's *hora* (00°♉00′–15°♉00′ in fig. 5.17). And Saturn (♄ 08°♒10′ in fig. 5.5, fourth column) is in the Sun's *hora* (00°♒00′–15°♒00′ in fig. 5.17).

Once again, the resulting data are not placed in a chart or other visual display. Instead, they are simply written into the astrologer's notes as shown in fig. 5.19, below.

When this information has been gathered (figs. 5.18 and 5.19), the Sun (☉), the Moon (☽), Venus (♀), Mars (♂), Jupiter (♃), and Saturn (♄) are compared to the Sun's and Moon's *horas*. If the Sun (☉), Mars (♂), or Jupiter (♃) is within the Sun's *hora*, the characteristics and strengths of the specific planet are enhanced. But if the Sun (☉), Mars (♂), or Jupiter (♃) is within the Moon's *hora*, there is no intensified influence. The same theory applies if the Moon (☽), Venus

FIGURE 5.19. PETER C.'S HORACAKRA.

ASCENDANT AND PLANETS IN CHART (FROM FIG. 5.5)	POSITION IN VEDIC (SIDEREAL) NATAL HOROSCOPE (FROM FIG. 5.5)	ZODIAC SIGN LOCATION IN DEGREES (°) AND MINUTES (') (FROM FIG. 5.17)	HORA SIGN (FROM FIG. 5.17)
Ascendant (AS)	09°♒34'	NOT USED	NOT USED
Sun (☉)	11°♌26'	00°♌00'–15°♌00'	Sun (☉)
Moon (☽)	10°♈23'	00°♈00'–15°♈00'	Sun (☉)
Mercury (☿)	21°♌21'ʀ	NOT USED	NOT USED
Venus (♀)	25°♊38'	15°♊01'–30°♊00'	Moon (☽)
Mars (♂)	25°♊16'	00°♊00'–15°♊00'	Moon (☽)
Jupiter (♃)	02°♉21'	00°♉00'–15°♉00'	Moon (☽)
Saturn (♄)	08°♒10'ʀ	00°♒00'–15°♒00'	Sun (☉)
Moon's North Node (☊)	06°♊25'ʀ	NOT USED	NOT USED
Moon's South Node (☋)	06°♐25'ʀ	NOT USED	NOT USED

(♀), or Saturn (♄) is within the Moon's *hora*.[84] But if the Moon (☽), Venus (♀), or Saturn (♄) is within the Sun's *hora*, there is no intensified influence.

For example, Alice's Sun (☉ 01°♊51' in fig. 5.4, fourth column) and Mars (♂ 08°♎19' in fig. 5.4, fourth column) fall within the Sun's *hora* (fig. 5.18). Therefore these two planets would be more thoroughly analyzed by a practitioner.

Peter's Sun (☉ 11°♌26' in fig. 5.5, fourth column) falls within the Sun's *hora* (fig. 5.18). And Peter's Venus (♀ 25°♊38' in fig. 5.5, fourth column) falls within the Moon's *hora* (fig. 5.18). Again, these two planets would be more thoroughly analyzed by a practitioner.

As mentioned at the beginning of this section, the interpretation of the *horacakra* is very extensive and would require many more chapters to cover in full detail. Its general structure has been provided here, however, to demonstrate the intricacy of Vedic personality profile development.

Constructing the *Drekkanacakra*

The *drekkanacakra* (third-sign chart) is a *sodasavarga* (divisional chart) that designates the person's relationships with his or her siblings and the type of effort he or she makes to fulfill personal desires. It is a commonly applied ancillary chart just like the *horacakra*, and is used in conjunction with either a *rasicakra* or *bhavacakra* in a *jataka* (natal) personality profile.

---

84. In this system, the Ascendant (AS), Mercury (☿), the Moon's North Node (☊), and the Moon's South Node (☋) are neutral entities, and as such they are not studied.

FIGURE 5.20. TABLE OF DREKKANA SIGNS.

Zodiac Sign Location in Degrees (°) and Minutes (′)	Drekkana Sign (Symbol)	Drekkana Sign Element	Zodiac Sign Location in Degrees (°) and Minutes (′)	Drekkana Sign (Symbol)	Drekkana Sign Element
00°♈00′–10°♈00′	Aries (♈)	fire	00°♎00′–10°♎00′	Libra (♎)	air
10°♈01′–20°♈00′	Leo (♌)	fire	10°♎01′–20°♎00′	Aquarius (♒)	air
20°♈01′–30°♈00′	Sagittarius (♐)	fire	20°♎01′–30°♎00′	Gemini (♊)	air
00°♉00′–10°♉00′	Taurus (♉)	earth	00°♏00′–10°♏00′	Scorpio (♏)	water
10°♉01′–20°♉00′	Virgo (♍)	earth	10°♏01′–20°♏00′	Pisces (♓)	water
20°♉01′–30°♉00′	Capricorn (♑)	earth	20°♏01′–30°♏00′	Cancer (♋)	water
00°♊00′–10°♊00′	Gemini (♊)	air	00°♐00′–10°♐00′	Sagittarius (♐)	fire
10°♊01′–20°♊00′	Libra (♎)	air	10°♐01′–20°♐00′	Aries (♈)	fire
20°♊01′–30°♊00′	Aquarius (♒)	air	20°♐01′–30°♐00′	Leo (♌)	fire
00°♋00′–10°♋00′	Cancer (♋)	water	00°♑00′–10°♑00′	Capricorn (♑)	earth
10°♋01′–20°♋00′	Scorpio (♏)	water	10°♑01′–20°♑00′	Taurus (♉)	earth
20°♋01′–30°♋00′	Pisces (♓)	water	20°♑01′–30°♑00′	Virgo (♍)	earth
00°♌00′–10°♌00′	Leo (♌)	fire	00°♒00′–10°♒00′	Aquarius (♒)	air
10°♌01′–20°♌00′	Sagittarius (♐)	fire	10°♒01′–20°♒00′	Gemini (♊)	air
20°♌01′–30°♌00′	Aries (♈)	fire	20°♒01′–30°♒00′	Libra (♎)	air
00°♍00′–10°♍00′	Virgo (♍)	earth	00°♓00′–10°♓00′	Pisces (♓)	water
10°♍01′–20°♍00′	Capricorn (♑)	earth	10°♓01′–20°♓00′	Cancer (♋)	water
20°♍01′–30°♍00′	Taurus (♉)	earth	20°♓01′–30°♓00′	Scorpio (♏)	water

Divided into increments of 10°00′ each (just like the Judaic decanates [see "Delineating the Ascendant" in chapter 7] and the Western decanates), the *drekkana* are interpreted according to the ruling element (fire, earth, air, or water) and subsidiary influence represented by the *drekkana*'s ruling sign as shown in fig. 5.20. The *drekkana*'s four ruling elements are identical to those found in Western (see "Analyzing the Predominant Features" in chapter 8), Arabian, and Judaic traditions; and are similar to the five *hsing* (elements) that are critical ingredients in both Chinese (see "Locating and Interpreting the Birth *Gen*" in chapter 3) and Tibetan (see "Reviewing the Sign's Forces" in chapter 4) astrology.

The *drekkanacakra* is constructed by converting the Vedic (sidereal) positions of the Ascendant, planets, and nodes (figs. 5.4 and 5.5, fourth column) into *drekkana* signs (fig. 5.20, second column). This is executed by locating the range of degrees and minutes of a planet's position (fig. 5.4 or 5.5, fourth column) in the first column of fig. 5.20. Both the *drekkana*'s ruling sign (fig. 5.20, second column) and element (fig. 5.20, third column) are also noted for future reference.

For example, Alice's Ascendant (AS 08°♑52′ in fig. 5.4, fourth column) occupies the *drekkana* sign Capricorn (♑, 00°♑00′–10°♑00′ in fig. 5.20). The Sun

(☉ 01°♊50′ in fig. 5.4, fourth column) occupies the *drekkana* sign Gemini (♊, 00°♊00′–10°♊00′ in fig. 5.20). The Moon (☽ 18°♓23′ in fig. 5.4, fourth column) occupies the *drekkana* sign Cancer (♋) (10°♓01′–20°♓00′ in fig. 5.20). Mercury (☿ 10°♊23′ in fig. 5.4, fourth column) occupies the *drekkana* sign Libra (♎, 10°♊01′–20°♊00′ in fig. 5.20). Venus (♀ 29°♉26′ in fig. 5.4, fourth column) occupies the *drekkana* sign Capricorn (♑, 20°♉01′–30°♉00′ in fig. 5.20). Mars (♂ 08°♎19′ in fig. 5.4, fourth column) occupies the *drekkana* sign Libra (♎, 00° ♎00′–10°♎00′ in fig. 5.20). Jupiter (♃ 17°♈47′ in fig. 5.4, fourth column) occupies the *drekkana* sign Leo (♌, 00°♈00′–10°♈00′ in fig. 5.20). Saturn (♄ 15°♍07′ in fig. 5.4, fourth column) occupies the *drekkana* sign Capricorn (♑, 10°♍01′–20°♍00′ in fig. 5.20). The Moon's North Node (☊ 00°♒18′ in fig. 5.4, fourth column) occupies the *drekkana* sign Aquarius (♒, 00°♒00′–10°♒00′ in fig. 5.20). And the Moon's South Node (☋ 00°♌18′ in fig. 5.4, fourth column) occupies the *drekkana* sign Leo (♌, 00°♌00′–10°♌00′ in fig. 5.20). This information is then documented as shown in fig. 5.21, below.

The same process is applied to Peter's Vedic positions. In Peter's *drekkanacakra* (fig. 5.22), Peter's Ascendant (AS 09°♒34′ in fig. 5.5, fourth column) occupies the *drekkana* sign Aquarius (♒, 00°♒00′–10°♒00′ in fig. 5.20). The Sun (☉ 11°♌26′ in fig. 5.5, fourth column) occupies the *drekkana* sign Sagittarius (♐, 10°♌01′–20°♌00′ in fig. 5.20). The Moon (☽ 10°♈23′ in fig. 5.5, fourth column) occupies the *drekkana* sign Leo (♌, 10°♈01′–20°♈00′ in fig. 5.20). Mercury (☿ 21°♌21′ in

FIGURE 5.21. ALICE T.'s DREKKANACAKRA.

ELEMENT IN CHART (FROM FIG. 5.4)	POSITION IN VEDIC (SIDEREAL) NATAL HOROSCOPE (FROM FIG. 5.4)	ZODIAC SIGN LOCATION IN DEGREES (°) AND MINUTES (′) (FROM FIG. 5.20)	DREKKANA SIGN (SYMBOL) (FROM FIG. 5.20)	DREKKANA ELEMENT (FROM FIG. 5.20)
Ascendant (AS)	08°♑52′	00°♑00′–10°♑00′	Capricorn (♑)	earth
Sun (☉)	01°♊50′	00°♊00′–10°♊00′	Gemini (♊)	air
Moon (☽)	18°♓23′	10°♓01′–20°♓00′	Cancer (♋)	water
Mercury (☿)	10°♊23′	10°♊01′–20°♊00′	Libra (♎)	air
Venus (♀)	29°♉26′	20°♉01′–30°♉00′	Capricorn (♑)	earth
Mars (♂)	08°♎19′	00°♎00′–10°♎00′	Libra (♎)	air
Jupiter (♃)	17°♈47′	10°♈01′–20°♈00′	Leo (♌)	fire
Saturn (♄)	15°♍07′	10°♍01′–20°♍00′	Capricorn (♑)	earth
Moon's North Node (☊)	00°♒18′ʀ	00°♒00′–10°♒00′	Aquarius (♒)	air
Moon's South Node (☋)	00°♌18′ʀ	00°♌00′–10°♌00′	Leo (♌)	fire

FIGURE 5.22. PETER C.'S DREKKANACAKRA.

ELEMENT IN CHART (FROM FIG. 5.5)	POSITION IN VEDIC (SIDEREAL) NATAL HOROSCOPE (FROM FIG. 5.5)	ZODIAC SIGN LOCATION IN DEGREES (°) AND MINUTES (') (FROM FIG. 5.20)	DREKKANA SIGN (SYMBOL) (FROM FIG. 5.20)	DREKKANA ELEMENT (FROM FIG. 5.20)
Ascendant (AS)	09°♒34′	00°♒00′–10°♒00′	Aquarius (♒)	air
Sun (☉)	11°♌26′	10°♌01′–20°♌00′	Sagittarius (♐)	fire
Moon (☽)	10°♈23′	10°♈01′–20°♈00′	Leo (♌)	fire
Mercury (☿)	21°♌21′ʀ	20°♌01′–30°♌00′	Aries (♈)	fire
Venus (♀)	25°♊38′	20°♊01′–30°♊00′	Aquarius (♒)	air
Mars (♂)	25°♊16′	20°♊01′–30°♊00′	Aquarius (♒)	air
Jupiter (♃)	02°♉21′	00°♉00′–10°♉00′	Taurus (♉)	earth
Saturn (♄)	08°♒10′ʀ	00°♒00′–10°♒00′	Aquarius (♒)	air
Moon's North Node (☊)	06°♊25′ʀ	00°♊00′–10°♊00′	Gemini (♊)	air
Moon's South Node (☋)	06°♐25′ʀ	00°♐00′–10°♐00′	Sagittarius (♐)	fire

fig. 5.5, fourth column) occupies the *drekkana* sign Aries (♈, 20°♌01′–30°♌00′ in fig. 5.20). Venus (♀ 25°♊38′ in fig. 5.5, fourth column) occupies the *drekkana* sign Aquarius (♒, 20°♊01′–30°♊00′ in fig. 5.20). Mars (♂ 25°♊16′ in fig. 5.5, fourth column) occupies the *drekkana* sign Aquarius (♒, 20°♊01′–30°♊00′ in fig. 5.20). Jupiter (♃ 02°♉21′ in fig. 5.5, fourth column) occupies the *drekkana* sign Taurus (♉, 00°♉00′–10°♉00′ in fig. 5.20). Saturn (♄ 08°♒10′ in fig. 5.5, fourth column) occupies the *drekkana* sign Aquarius (♒, 00°♒00′–10°♒00′ in fig. 5.20). The Moon's North Node (☊ 06°♊25′ in fig. 5.5, fourth column) occupies the *drekkana* sign Gemini (♊, 00°♒00′–10°♒00′ in fig. 5.20). The Moon's South Node (☋ 06°♐25′ in fig. 5.5, fourth column) occupies the *drekkana* sign Sagittarius (♐, 00°♐00′–10°♐00′ in fig. 5.20).

The resulting data in figs. 5.21 and 5.22 would not be placed in a chart or other visual display. Instead they are simply written into the astrologer's notes, as shown in the examples of Alice's (fig. 5.21) and Peter's (fig. 5.22) *drekkanacakras*. As mentioned at the beginning of this section, the interpretation of the *drekkanacakra* is very extensive. However, its general structure has been provided above to demonstrate the complexity of *jataka* (natal) personality profile development.

Constructing the *Saptamsacakra*

The *saptamsacakra* (seventh-sign chart) is a *sodasavarga* (divisional chart) that determines an individual's potential for offspring. It is a commonly applied ancillary chart, just like the *horacakra* and *drekkanacakra* that are used in conjunction with either a *rasicakra* or *bhavacakra* in a *jataka* (natal) personality profile.

FIGURE 5.23. TABLE OF *SAPTAMSA* SIGNS.

ZODIAC SIGN LOCATION IN DEGREES (°) AND MINUTES (')	SAPTAMSA SIGN (SYMBOL)	ZODIAC SIGN LOCATION IN DEGREES (°) AND MINUTES (')	SAPTAMSA SIGN (SYMBOL)
00°♈00'–04°♈17'	Aries (♈)	25°♊43'–30°♊00'	Sagittarius (♐)
04°♈18'–08°♈34'	Taurus (♉)	00°♋00'–04°♋17'	Capricorn (♑)
08°♈35'–12°♈51'	Gemini (♊)	04°♋18'–08°♋34'	Aquarius (♒)
12°♈52'–17°♈08'	Cancer (♋)	08°♋35'–12°♋51'	Pisces (♓)
17°♈09'–21°♈25'	Leo (♌)	12°♋52'–17°♋08'	Aries (♈)
21°♈26'–25°♈42'	Virgo (♍)	17°♋09'–21°♋25'	Taurus (♉)
25°♈43'–30°♈00'	Libra (♎)	21°♋26'–25°♋42'	Gemini (♊)
00°♉00'–04°♉17'	Scorpio (♏)	25°♋43'–30°♋00'	Cancer (♋)
04°♉18'–08°♉34'	Sagittarius (♐)	00°♌00'–04°♌17'	Leo (♌)
08°♉35'–12°♉51'	Capricorn (♑)	04°♌18'–08°♌34'	Virgo (♍)
12°♉52'–17°♉08'	Aquarius (♒)	08°♌35'–12°♌51'	Libra (♎)
17°♉09'–21°♉25'	Pisces (♓)	12°♌52'–17°♌08'	Scorpio (♏)
21°♉26'–25°♉42'	Aries (♈)	17°♌09'–21°♌25'	Sagittarius (♐)
25°♉43'–30°♉00'	Taurus (♉)	21°♌26'–25°♌42'	Capricorn (♑)
00°♊00'–04°♊17'	Gemini (♊)	25°♌43'–30°♌00'	Aquarius (♒)
04°♊18'–08°♊34'	Cancer (♋)	00°♍00'–04°♍17'	Pisces (♓)
08°♊35'–12°♊51'	Leo (♌)	04°♍18'–08°♍34'	Aries (♈)
12°♊52'–17°♊08'	Virgo (♍)	08°♍35'–12°♍51'	Taurus (♉)
17°♊09'–21°♊25'	Libra (♎)	12°♍52'–17°♍08'	Gemini (♊)
21°♊26'–25°♊42'	Scorpio (♏)	17°♍09'–21°♍25'	Cancer (♋)

The *saptamsacakra* is constructed by converting the Vedic (sidereal) positions of the Ascendant, planets, and nodes (figs. 5.4 and 5.5, fourth column) into *saptamsa* signs, which are divided into increments of 04°17' each (fig. 5.23, second and fourth columns). This is executed by locating the range of degrees and minutes in which these positions (fig. 5.4 or 5.5, fourth column) reside (fig. 5.23, first and third columns).

For example, Alice's Ascendant (AS 08°♑52' in fig. 5.4, fourth column) occupies the *saptamsa* sign Virgo (♍, 08°♑35'–12°♑51' in fig. 5.23). The Sun (☉ 01° ♊50' in fig. 5.4, fourth column) occupies the *saptamsa* sign Gemini (♊, 00° ♊00'–04°♊17' in fig. 5.23). The Moon (☽ 18°♓23' in fig. 5.4, fourth column) occupies the *saptamsa* sign Capricorn (♑, 17°♓09'–21°♓25' in fig. 5.23). Mercury (☿ 10°♊23' in fig. 5.4, fourth column) occupies the *saptamsa* sign Leo (♌, 08°♊35'–12°♊51' in fig. 5.23). Venus (♀ 29°♉26' in fig. 5.4, fourth column) occupies the *saptamsa* sign Taurus (♉, 25°♉43'–30°♉00' in fig. 5.23). Mars (♂ 08°♎19' in fig. 5.4, fourth column) occupies the *saptamsa* sign Scorpio (♏, 04° ♎18'–08°♎34' in fig. 5.23). Jupiter (♃ 17°♈47' in fig. 5.4, fourth column)

FIGURE 5.23. TABLE OF SAPTAMSA SIGNS (CONTINUED).

Zodiac Sign Location in Degrees (°) and Minutes (′)	Saptamsa Sign (Symbol)	Zodiac Sign Location in Degrees (°) and Minutes (′)	Saptamsa Sign (Symbol)
21°♍26′–25°♍42′	Leo (♌)	25°♐43′–30°♐00′	Gemini (♊)
25°♍43′–30°♍00′	Virgo (♍)	00°♑00′–04°♑17′	Cancer (♋)
00°♎00′–04°♎17′	Libra (♎)	04°♑18′–08°♑34′	Leo (♌)
04°♎18′–08°♎34′	Scorpio (♏)	08°♑35′–12°♑51′	Virgo (♍)
08°♎35′–12°♎51′	Sagittarius (♐)	12°♑52′–17°♑08′	Libra (♎)
12°♎52′–17°♎08′	Capricorn (♑)	17°♑09′–21°♑25′	Scorpio (♏)
17°♎09′–21°♎25′	Aquarius (♒)	21°♑26′–25°♑42′	Sagittarius (♐)
21°♎26′–25°♎42′	Pisces (♓)	25°♑43′–30°♑00′	Capricorn (♑)
25°♎43′–30°♎00′	Aries (♈)	00°♒00′–04°♒17′	Aquarius (♒)
00°♏00′–04°♏17′	Taurus (♉)	04°♒18′–08°♒34′	Pisces (♓)
04°♏18′–08°♏34′	Gemini (♊)	08°♒35′–12°♒51′	Aries (♈)
08°♏35′–12°♏51′	Cancer (♋)	12°♒52′–17°♒08′	Taurus (♉)
12°♏52′–17°♏08′	Leo (♌)	17°♒09′–21°♒25′	Gemini (♊)
17°♏09′–21°♏25′	Virgo (♍)	21°♒26′–25°♒42′	Cancer (♋)
21°♏26′–25°♏42′	Libra (♎)	25°♒43′–30°♒00′	Leo (♌)
25°♏43′–30°♏00′	Scorpio (♏)	00°♓00′–04°♓17′	Virgo (♍)
00°♐00′–04°♐17′	Sagittarius (♐)	04°♓18′–08°♓34′	Libra (♎)
04°♐18′–08°♐34′	Capricorn (♑)	08°♓35′–12°♓51′	Scorpio (♏)
08°♐35′–12°♐51′	Aquarius (♒)	12°♓52′–17°♓08′	Sagittarius (♐)
12°♐52′–17°♐08′	Pisces (♓)	17°♓09′–21°♓25′	Capricorn (♑)
17°♐09′–21°♐25′	Aries (♈)	21°♓26′–25°♓42′	Aquarius (♒)
21°♐26′–25°♐42′	Taurus (♉)	25°♓43′–30°♓00′	Pisces (♓)

occupies the *saptamsa* sign Leo (♌, 17°♈09′–21°♈25′ in fig. 5.23). Saturn (♄ 15°♍07′ in fig. 5.4, fourth column) occupies the *saptamsa* sign Gemini (♊, 12°♍52′–17°♍08′ in fig. 5.23). The Moon's North Node (☊ 00°♒18′ in fig. 5.4, fourth column) occupies the *saptamsa* sign Aquarius (♒, 00°♒00′–04°♒17′ in fig. 5.23). And the Moon's South Node (☋ 00°♌18′ in fig. 5.4, fourth column) occupies the *saptamsa* sign Leo (♌, 00°♌00′–04°♌17′ in fig. 5.23). The information is then documented as shown in fig. 5.24.

The same process is applied to Peter's Vedic positions. Peter's Ascendant (AS 09°♒34′ in fig. 5.5, fourth column) occupies the *saptamsa* sign Aries (♈, 08°♒35′–12°♒51′ in fig. 5.23). The Sun (☉ 11°♌26′ in fig. 5.5, fourth column) occupies the *saptamsa* sign Libra (♎, 08°♌35′–12°♌51′ in fig. 5.23). The Moon (☽ 10°♈23′ in fig. 5.5, fourth column) occupies the *saptamsa* sign Gemini (♊, 08°♈35′–12°♈51′ in fig. 5.23). Mercury (☿ 21°♌21′ in fig. 5.5, fourth column) occupies the *saptamsa* sign Sagittarius (♐, 17°♌09′–21°♌25′ in fig. 5.23). Venus (♀ 25°

FIGURE 5.24. ALICE T.'s SAPTAMSACAKRA.

Element in Chart (FROM FIG. 5.4)	Position in Vedic (Sidereal) Natal Horoscope (FROM FIG. 5.4)	Zodiac Sign Location in Degrees (°) and Minutes (') (FROM FIG. 5.23)	Saptamsa Sign (Symbol) (FROM FIG. 5.23)
Ascendant (AS)	08°♑52'	08°♑35'–12°♑51'	Virgo (♍)
Sun (☉)	01°♊50'	00°♊00'–04°♊17'	Gemini (♊)
Moon (☽)	18°♓23'	17°♓19'–21°♓25'	Capricorn (♑)
Mercury (☿)	10°♊23'	08°♊35'–12°♊51'	Leo (♌)
Venus (♀)	29°♉26'	25°♉43'–30°♉00'	Taurus (♉)
Mars (♂)	08°♎19'	04°♎18'–08°♎34'	Scorpio (♏)
Jupiter (♃)	17°♈47'	17°♈19'–21°♈25'	Leo (♌)
Saturns (♄)	15°♍07'	12°♍52'–17°♍08'	Gemini (♊)
Moon's North Node (☊)	00°♒18'ʀ	00°♒00'–04°♒17'	Aquarius (♒)
Moon's South Node (☋)	00°♌18'ʀ	00°♌00'–04°♌17'	Leo (♌)

♊38' in fig. 5.5, fourth column) occupies the *saptamsa* sign Scorpio (♏, 21° ♊26'–25°♊42' in fig. 5.23). Mars (♂ 25°♊16' in fig. 5.5, fourth column) occupies the *saptamsa* sign Scorpio (♏, 25°♊43'–30°♊00' in fig. 5.23). Jupiter (♃ 02°♉21' in fig. 5.5, fourth column) occupies the *saptamsa* sign Scorpio (♏, 00°♉00'–04° ♉17' in fig. 5.23). Saturn (♄ 08°♒10' in fig. 5.5, fourth column) occupies the *saptamsa* sign Pisces (♓, 04°♒18'–08°♒34' in fig. 5.23). The Moon's North Node (☊ 06°♊25' in fig. 5.5, fourth column) occupies the *saptamsa* sign Cancer (♋, 04° ♒18'–08°♒34' in fig. 5.23). The Moon's South Node (☋ 06°♐25' in fig. 5.5, fourth column) occupies the *saptamsa* sign Capricorn (♑, 04°♐18'–08°♐34' in fig. 5.23). The data are then recorded as shown in fig. 5.25.

The *saptamsacakra* data are not placed in a chart or other visual display. Instead they are simply written into the astrologer's notes as shown in figs. 5.24 and 5.25. As mentioned earlier, the interpretation of the *saptamsacakra* is very extensive. But its construction has been provided here to demonstrate the Vedic tradition's complexity.

Once the *rasicakra* or *bhavacakra, navamsacakra, horacakra, drekkanacakra,* and *saptamsacakra* have been constructed, an ancillary chart called a *candralagna* (moon chart) is commonly developed and employed as part of the retinue of astrological data that is analyzed. Although it is not a *sodasavarga,* the *candralagna* is considered to be a critical source of information: a mirror image of the prognostications that are derived from the *rasicakra* or *bhavacakra.*

FIGURE 5.25. PETER C.'S SAPTAMSACAKRA.

ELEMENT IN CHART (FROM FIG. 5.5)	POSITION IN VEDIC (SIDEREAL) NATAL HOROSCOPE (FROM FIG. 5.5)	ZODIAC SIGN LOCATION IN DEGREES (°) AND MINUTES (′) (FROM FIG. 5.23)	SAPTAMSA SIGN (SYMBOL) (FROM FIG. 5.23)
Ascendant (AS)	09°♒34′	08°♒35′–12°♒51′	Aries (♈)
Sun (☉)	11°♌26′	08°♌35′–12°♌51′	Libra (♎)
Moon (☽)	10°♈23′	08°♈35′–12°♈51′	Gemini (♊)
Mercury (☿)	21°♌21′℞	17°♌09′–21°♌25′	Libra (♎)
Venus (♀)	25°♊38′	21°♊26′–25°♊42′	Scorpio (♏)
Mars (♂)	25°♊16′	21°♊26′–25°♊42′	Scorpio (♏)
Jupiter (♃)	02°♉21′	00°♉00′–04°♉17′	Scorpio (♏)
Saturn (♄)	08°♒10′℞	04°♒18′–08°♒34′	Aries (♈)
Moon's North Node (☊)	06°♊25′℞	04°♊18′–08°♊34′	Cancer (♋)
Moon's South Node (☋)	06°♐25′℞	04°♐18′–08°♐34′	Capricorn (♑)

STEP FIVE: CONSTRUCTING THE CANDRALAGNA[85] (MOON CHART)

As mentioned at the beginning of this chapter, the *candralagna* is a specialized chart that serves as a visual comparative to the prognostications of either the *rasicakra* (sign chart) or *bhavacakra* (house chart), providing additional confirmation of the person's dominant characteristics and qualities. The *candralagna* can also aid in uncovering otherwise unforeseen facets in the individual's personality. Vedic astrologers refer to this secondary *sodasavarga* primarily when creating a woman's personality profile. Since the Moon (Candra) is feminine and represents the woman and the mother, the *candralagna* is also consulted to assess a woman's physical health, emotional makeup, and ability to bear children. This chart is delineated in exactly the same fashion as the *bhavacakra*.

The *candralagna* is constructed in the same manner as either the *rasicakra* (see "Constructing the *Rasicakra*," page 152) or the *bhavacakra* (see "Constructing the *Bhavacakra*," page 172). For the sake of space, only the construction of a *bhavacakra*-style *candralagna* will be shown in this section.

In this charting method, the Moon is always placed in House I. Roman numerals are used in the *candralagnas* that follow (figs. 5.26 and 5.27) to make it easier to understand how the positions of the zodiac signs change, depending upon the Moon's location in the zodiac. This is not done by Vedic practitioners, however. Furthermore, symbols for the individual planets are never used by Vedic astrologers. The names of the planets are generally written out in Sanskrit. Symbols

85. Pronounced "chahn-drah-lahg-nah," meaning "Moon as Ascendant."

are used in this section to facilitate comparisons between this type of Vedic chart and those executed by Western, Judaic, or Arabian practitioners.

Physically, the *candralagna*'s format places the number of the zodiac sign that represents the Moon (figs. 5.4 and 5.5, fourth column) in House I, which is the top diamond of the chart. For example, the diamond marked "I" in fig. 5.26, below, is the "Moon as Ascendant" or House I. The "12" in the same diamond designates that the Moon's zodiac sign is Pisces (♓, fig. 5.3, third column). The information for this placement is found in fig. 5.4 (fourth column). And the *candralagna*'s Moon is interpreted as if it were an Ascendant, using the same process that is described in the section titled "Identifying the Ascendant's *Naksatra*."

Similarly, the diamond marked "I" in fig. 5.27, below, is the "Moon as Ascendant" or House I. (Naturally, this means that the Ascendant itself is not used in this particular type of chart.) The "1" in the same diamond designates that the Moon occupies the zodiac sign is Aries (♈, fig. 5.3, third column). The information for this placement is found in fig. 5.5 (fourth column). Again, the *candralagna*'s Moon is interpreted as if it were an Ascendant (see "Identifying the Ascendant's *Naksatra*," page 155).

FIGURE 5.26. ALICE T.'S CANDRALAGNA.

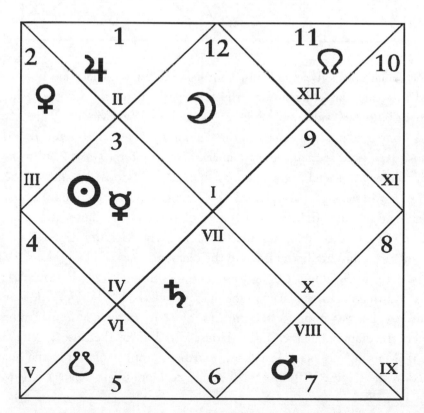

FIGURE 5.27. PETER C.'S *CANDRALAGNA*.

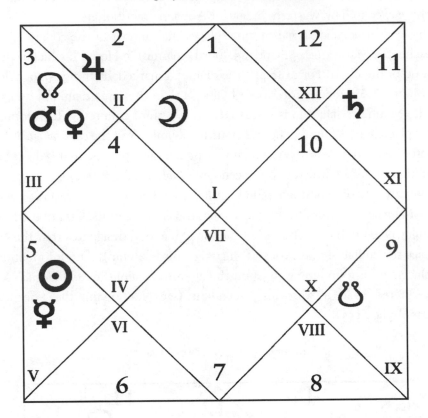

The remaining house numbers (II through XII) and zodiac sign numbers are placed in sequential order around the frame in a counterclockwise fashion, as shown in both figs. 5.26 and 5.27. For example, Alice's Moon (☽ 18°♓23′ in fig. 5.4, fourth column) is placed in the diamond marked "I" (House I) and "12" (because ♓, Pisces is 12 in fig. 5.3) in fig. 5.26. Jupiter (♃ 17°♈47′ in fig. 5.4, fourth column) is placed in the diamond marked "II" (House II) and "1" (because ♈, Aries is 1 in fig. 5.3). Venus (♀ 29°♉26′ in fig. 5.4, fourth column) is placed in the diamond marked "III" (House III) and "2" (because ♉, Taurus is 2 in fig. 5.3). The Sun (☉ 01°♊50′ in fig. 5.4, fourth column) and Mercury (☿ 10°♊23′ in fig. 5.4, fourth column) are both placed in the diamond marked "IV" (House IV) and "3" (because ♊, Gemini is 3 in fig. 5.3). The Moon's South Node (☋ 00°♌18′ in fig. 5.4, fourth column) is placed in the diamond marked "VI" (House VI) and "5" (because ♌, Leo is 5 in fig. 5.3). Saturn (♄ 15°♍07′ in fig. 5.4, fourth column) is placed in the diamond marked "VII" (House VII) and "6" (because ♍, Virgo is 6 in fig. 5.3). Mars (♂ 08°♎19′ in fig. 5.4, fourth column) is placed in the diamond marked "VIII" (House VIII) and "7" (because ♎, Libra is 7 in fig. 5.3). The Moon's

North Node (☊ 00°♒18′ in fig. 5.4, fourth column) is placed in the diamond marked "XII" (House XII) and "11" (because ♒, Aquarius is 11 in fig. 5.3).

Because none of the planetary positions in fig. 5.4 (fourth column) occupy the zodiac signs Cancer (4 in fig. 5.26), Scorpio (8 in fig. 5.26), Sagittarius (9 in fig. 5.26), and Capricorn (10 in fig. 5.26), those diamonds—or houses—remain empty. The degrees and minutes of Alice's "Moon as Ascendant," planetary, and node positions are kept for reference as shown in fig. 5.4 (fourth column), but are not incorporated into her *candralagna* (fig. 5.26).

The same process is applied to Peter's Vedic positions. Peter's Moon (☽ 10° ♈23′ in fig. 5.5, fourth column) is placed in the diamond marked "I" (House I) and "1" (because ♈, Aries is 1 in fig. 5.3). Jupiter (♃ 02°♉21′ in fig. 5.5, fourth column) is placed in the diamond marked "II" (House II) and "2" (because ♉, Taurus is 2 in fig. 5.3). Venus (♀ 25°♊38′ in fig. 5.5, fourth column), Mars (♂ 25°♊16′ in fig. 5.5, fourth column), and the Moon's North Node (☊ 06°♊25′ in fig. 5.5, fourth column) are all placed in the diamond marked "III" (House III) and "3" (because ♊, Gemini is 3 in fig. 5.3). The Sun (☉ 11°♌26′ in fig. 5.5, fourth column) and Mercury (☿ 21°♌21′ in fig. 5.5, fourth column) are placed in the diamond marked "V" (House V) and "5" (because ♌, Leo is 5 in fig. 5.3). The Moon's South Node (☋ 06°♐25′ in fig. 5.5, fourth column) is placed in the diamond marked "IX" (House IX) and "9" (because ♐, Sagittarius is 9 in fig. 5.3). And Saturn (♄ 08°♒10′ in fig. 5.5, fourth column) is placed in the diamond marked "XI" (House XI) and "11" (because ♒, Aquarius is 11 in fig. 5.3).

Because none of the planetary positions in fig. 5.5 (fourth column) occupies the zodiac signs Cancer (4 in fig. 5.27), Virgo (6 in fig. 5.27), Libra (7 in fig. 5.27), Scorpio (8 in fig. 5.27), Capricorn (10 in fig. 5.27), and Pisces (12 in fig. 5.27), these diamonds—or houses—remain empty. The degrees and minutes of Peter's "Moon as Ascendant," planetary, and node positions are kept for reference as shown in fig. 5.5 (fourth column), but are not incorporated into his *candralagna* (fig. 5.27).

The same form of house and zodiac sign interpretation that is used to delineate the *bhavacakra* (see "Interpreting the Planetary Positions in a *Bhavacakra,*" page 197) is employed to delineate the *bhavacakra*-style *candralagna*. And, as mentioned earlier, special attention is paid to dominant characteristics or qualities that also predominate in Alice's and Peter's *bhavacakras*. The astrologer would also focus on Alice's *candralagna* with regard to her physical health, emotional makeup, and ability to bear children.

Within every successive level of distillation, a Vedic astrologer hones the final synthesis of an individual's personality as revealed by the *sodasavargas* (divisional charts). But this represents only a small portion of the analytic procedure employed in the assessment of a *jataka* (natal) personality profile. The practitioner also reviews the qualities of the planets that appear in a person's horoscope according to properties called *shadbala*.

Step Six: Applying the Shadbala

Besides the construction and interpretation of a variety of *sodasavargas* (divisional charts) and a *candralagna*, a Vedic astrologer assesses the strengths and weaknesses of the signs and planetary positions within an individual's *rasicakra* (sign chart) or *bhavacakra* (house chart) according to a series of reviews that are collectively called *shadbala*. Each type of *shadbala* is separately tallied according to a complex rating system that aids the astrologer in determining the type of power an individual receives from his or her relationship with the various planets. The procedure simply enhances what has already been derived from the delineation of the Ascendant, planet, and lunar node positions as outlined earlier in this chapter.

This section will not detail how the *shadbala* are finally tallied; the scoring system is far more complex than could be adequately documented in a single volume. And the interpretation of these *shadbala* would require many more chapters to cover in full detail. The general structure of each type of *shadbala* is defined here, however, to provide a moderate example of the intricacy of the Vedic tradition.

There are six *shadbala* (sources) from which a planet draws its strength: the *sthanabala*, *drigbala*, *naisargikabala*, *chestabala*, *dikbala*, and *kalabala*. None of the resulting information is placed in a formal chart structure like the *rasicakra* or *bhavacakra*; rather, the scores from each rating method are simply written down in the astrologer's interpretation notes for final tallying.

Rating by *Sthanabala*

The first *shadbala*, called *sthanabala*, rates a planet's strength based upon its position within a given house or zodiac sign and its compatibility with other planets and *navamsa* signs (see "Step Three: Constructing and Interpreting the *Navamsacakra*," page 208). There are five ways in which a planet achieves strength and, thus, importance in an individual's horoscope: *ucca*, *mulatrikona*, *swakshetra*, friendship, or if it occupies a house that is a *trikona* or *kendra* house. These assessment methods are very similar to the review of planetary dignities and debilities conducted by many modern-day Western astrologers.

Sthanabala *by* Ucca

If a planet is in *ucca* (exalted position),[86] it reaches its highest potency, exerting its most positive qualities through the individual. This occurs for each planet in a specific sign and degree as shown below:

Sun (☉)	10°♈00' (10°00' Aries)[87]
Moon (☽)	03°♉00' (03°00' Taurus)
Mercury (☿)	15°♍00' (15°00' Virgo)
Venus (♀)	27°♓00' (27°00' Pisces)
Mars (♂)	28°♑00' (28°00' Capricorn)
Jupiter (♃)	05°♋00' (05°00' Cancer)[88]
Saturn (♄)	20°♎00' (20°00' Libra)[89]
Moon's North Node (☊)	00°♉00'–30°♉00' (00°00'–30°00' Taurus)[90]
Moon's South Node (☋)	00°♏00'–30°♏00' (00°00'–30°00' Scorpio)[91]

Using the Vedic (sidereal) positions for both Alice's (fig. 5.4, fourth column) and Peter's (fig. 5.5, fourth column) planets and nodes, the practitioner would compare each position to the list above. However, none of their planets or nodes is in *ucca*.

In Western astrology, if a planet is positioned at one of these critical points, it is considered to be in an exalted or dignified state, and the astrologer would pay special attention to its delineation.

Sthanabala *by* Mulatrikona

If a planet is in its *mulatrikona*,[92] it's in a potent state, exhibiting the planet's positive qualities through the individual. This occurs for each planet in a specific sign and degree as shown below:

Sun (☉)	01°♌00'–20°♌00' (01°00'–20°00' Leo)
Moon (☽)	03°♉00'–30°♉00' (03°00'–30°00' Taurus)
Mercury (☿)	16°♍00'–20°♍00' (16°00'–20°00' Virgo)
Venus (♀)	01°♎00'–05°♎00' (01°00'–05°00' Libra)
Mars (♂)	01°♈00'–12°♈00' (01°00'–12°00' Aries)
Jupiter (♃)	01°♐00'–10°♐00' (01°00'–10°00' Sagittarius)

---

86. Pronounced "ooch-chah."
87. Western astrologers identify the Sun's position to be 19°♈00'.
88. Western astrologers designate Jupiter's position to be 15°♋00'.
89. Western astrologers identify Saturn's position to be 21°♎00'.
90. Western astrologers indicate the Moon's North Node position to be 03°♊00'.
91. Western astrologers indicate the Moon's South Node position to be 03°♐00'.
92. Pronounced, "moo-lah-tree-koh-nah," meaning "root triangle."

Saturn (♄)   01°♒00'–20°♒00' (01°00'–20°00' Aquarius)[93]

Moon's North Node (☊)   00°♊00'–30°♊00' (00°00'–30°00' Gemini)

                                00°♍00'–30°♍00' (00°00'–30°00' Virgo)[94]

Moon's South Node (☋)   00°♐00'–30°♐00' (00°00'–30°00' Sagittarius)

                                00°♓00'–30°♓00' (00°00'–30°00' Pisces)[95]

Using the Vedic (sidereal) positions for both Alice's (fig. 5.4, fourth column) and Peter's (fig. 5.5, fourth column) planets and nodes, the practitioner would compare each position to the list above. None of Alice's planets or nodes is in *mulatrikona*. However, Peter's Sun (☉ 11°♌26' in fig. 5.5, fourth column), Moon's South Node (☋ 06°♐25' in fig. 5.5, fourth column), and Saturn (♄ 08°♒10' in fig. 5.5, fourth column) are all in *mulatrikona*.

This assessment method is similar to the application of critical degrees (see chapter 3, note 16, page 107) in Western astrology. However, Vedic practitioners attribute a broader range of degrees and minutes in which a planetary position can exert a greater influence than do their Western counterparts.

Sthanabala *by* Swakshetra

In comparison to the heightened levels of potency a planet reaches in its *ucca* or *mulatrikona*, the same planet exerts 75 percent of its potency in its *swakshetra* (sign of rulership). The planetary rulerships follow the same pattern used by ancient Western astrologers as well as Arabian and Judaic practitioners. The rulerships are as follows:

Sun (☉)	rules Leo (♌)
Moon (☽)	rules Cancer (♋)
Mercury (☿)	rules both Gemini (♊) and Virgo (♍)
Venus (♀)	rules both Taurus (♉) and Libra (♎)
Mars (♂)	rules both Aries (♈) and Scorpio (♏)
Jupiter (♃)	rules both Sagittarius (♐) and Pisces (♓)
Saturn (♄)	rules both Capricorn (♑) and Aquarius (♒)

Using the Vedic (sidereal) positions for both Alice's (fig. 5.4, fourth column) and Peter's (fig. 5.5, fourth column) planets and nodes, the practitioner would compare each position to the list above. Alice's Venus (♀ 29°♉26' in fig. 5.4, fourth column) and Mercury (☿ 10°♊23' in fig. 5.4, fourth column) are both

93. There seems to be some discrepancy as to the exact degrees in which this condition occurs. Author Valerie J. Roebuck defined the Moon's *mulatrikona* as occurring between 04°♉00'–30°♉00'; Mercury's *mulatrikona* between 26°♍00'–30°♍00'; Jupiter's *mulatrikona* between 00°♐00'–05°♐00'; Venus's *mulatrikona* between 00°♎00'–20°♎00'; and Saturn's *mulatrikona* between 00°♒00'–20°♒00'.

94. This secondary indication is believed to be the node's "home," while the first indication is believed to be its true *mulatrikona*.

95. Ibid.

in *swakshetra*. Peter's Sun (☉ 11°♌26′ in fig. 5.5, fourth column) and Saturn (♄ 08°♒10′ in fig. 5.5, fourth column) are both in *swakshetra*.

Sthanabala *by Occupation of a "Friend's" Sign*

A planet exerts 62.5 percent of its potency when it occupies a zodiac sign that is ruled by a "friend." This is unique to Vedic astrology. There is no parallel process found in Western, Arabian, Judaic, or Chinese astrology. It is very similar, however, to the designation of interrelationships between zodiac signs found in Tibetan astrology (see "Determining the Individual's Animal Sign" in chapter 4). This occurs in the following positions:

Sun (☉) or Mars (♂)	occupies the zodiac signs Cancer (♋), Sagittarius (♐), or Pisces (♓)
Moon (☽)	occupies Leo (♌), Gemini (♊), or Virgo (♍)
Mercury (☿)	occupies Leo (♌), Taurus (♉), or Libra (♎)
Venus (♀)	occupies Gemini (♊), Virgo (♍), Capricorn (♑), or Aquarius (♒)
Jupiter (♃)	occupies Leo (♌), Cancer (♋), Aries (♈), or Scorpio (♏)
Saturn (♄)	occupies Taurus (♉), Scorpio (♏), Gemini (♊), or Virgo (♍).

Using the Vedic (sidereal) positions for both Alice's (fig. 5.4, fourth column) and Peter's (fig. 5.5, fourth column) planets and nodes, the practitioner compares each position to the list above. Alice's Jupiter (♃ 17°♈47′ in fig. 5.4, fourth column) occupies the "friend" sign Aries (♈); and her Saturn (♄ 15°♍07′ in fig. 5.4, fourth column) occupies the "friend" sign Virgo (♍). Peter's Venus (♀ 25°♊38′ in fig. 5.5, fourth column) occupies the "friend" sign Gemini (♊); and his Mercury (☿ 21°♌21′ in fig. 5.5, fourth column) occupies the "friend" sign Leo (♌).

Sthanabala *by Occupation of a* Trikona *or* Kendra *House*

A planet exerts 50 percent of its potency if it's positioned in a house that is designated to be *trikona* or *kendra*. Vedic practitioners originally based this hierarchy on the nature of the house rulers. The *trikona* (Houses V and IX) are scored as being most auspicious, while the *kendra* (Houses I, IV, VII, and X) are scored a little lower on the rating system, but are still considered to be auspicious. This rating system closely resembles the angular, succedent, and cadent houses applied by Western astrologers (see "Step Eight: Analyzing the Houses" in chapter 8).[96]

96. According to Western astrologers, a planet is accidentally dignified or strengthened if it occupies an angular house (Houses I, IV, VII, or X); the planet is neutral if it occupies a succedent house (Houses II, V, VIII, or XI); and the planet is accidentally debilitated or weakened if it occupies a cadent house (Houses III, VI, IX, or XII).

Using Alice's (fig. 5.10) and Peter's (fig. 5.11) *bhavacakras* (house charts), the practitioner would look for planets occupying the *trikona* and *kendra* houses described above. Consequently, Alice's Venus (♀) occupies the *trikona* house, House V (fig. 5.10); and her Saturn (♄) occupies the *trikona* house, House IX (fig. 5.10). Alice's Jupiter (♃) occupies the *kendra* house, House IV (fig. 5.10); and her Mars (♂) occupies the *kendra* house, House X (fig. 5.10). Therefore, prognostications of these four planets would be considered auspicious.

Peter's Venus (♀), Mars (♂), and Moon's North Node (☊) occupy the *trikona* House V (fig. 5.11). His Jupiter (♃) occupies the *kendra* House IV (fig. 5.11); his Saturn (♄) occupies the *kendra* House I (fig. 5.11); and his Sun (☉) occupies the *kendra* House VII (fig. 5.11). Therefore, prognostications of these six planets would be considered auspicious.

Furthermore, planets located in *upachaya* houses (Houses III, VI, X, and XI) are considered to be influential, producing growth (especially House X) or difficulty (especially House VI) for an individual. Planets in *dusthana* houses (Houses VI, VIII, and XII) generally cause adversity.

The final assessment and interpretation of *sthanabala* is an intricate process that would require many chapters to cover in full detail. The general structure of each type of *sthanabala* is defined here, however, for reference when comparing this tradition to other forms of astrology.

Rating by *Drigbala*

The second *shadbala* is *drigbala*, which rates the difference in degrees and minutes between a specific planet and a planet that is either naturally benefic or is deemed benefic to the individual's Ascendant. (The degrees of difference between two planets form what is commonly called an angle or aspect in Vedic, Arabian, Judaic, and Western astrology.) Using a table similar to the one shown in fig. 5.28, the astrologer scores each aspect for its positive or negative potency.

Much like the process used by Western (see "Step Seven: Locating the Planetary Aspects" in chapter 8), Arabian, and Judaic astrologers as well as by some Chinese practitioners to assess the aspects or angles formed between the planets, the angle formed between a specific planet and a benefic or malefic planet is scored for the potency of the angle (60°00′ difference, 90°00′ difference, 120° difference, or 180° difference) and whether the influence exerted by the angle is positive (benefic), neutral, or negative (malefic).

The final assessment and interpretation of the *drigbala* score is an intricate process that would require more space to cover in full detail. But the general struc-

FIGURE 5.28. TABLE OF BENEFIC QUALITIES.

PLANET	QUALITY OR NATURE	BENEFIC ASCENDANT POSITIONS IN THE ZODIAC SIGNS
Sun (☉)	malefic	Aries (♈), Taurus (♉), Leo (♌), Scorpio (♏), Sagittarius (♐), Aquarius (♒)
Moon (☽)	waxing: benefic; waning: malefic	Scorpio (♏), Pisces (♓)
Mercury (☿)	neutral	Taurus (♉), Libra (♎), Capricorn (♑)
Venus (♀)	benefic	Gemini (♊), Virgo (♍), Libra (♎), Capricorn (♑), Aquarius (♒)
Mars (♂)	malefic	Aries (♈), Taurus (♉), Cancer (♋), Leo (♌), Libra (♎), Sagittarius (♐), Aquarius (♒), Pisces (♓)
Jupiter (♃)	benefic	Aries (♈), Cancer (♋), Scorpio (♏)
Saturn (♄)	malefic	Taurus (♉), Gemini (♊), Libra (♎), Capricorn (♑), Aquarius (♒)

ture of *drigbala* is defined here for reference when comparing this tradition to other forms of astrology.

Rating by *Naisargikabala*

The third *shadbala* is *naisargikabala*, which assigns each planet's natural strengths to a specific numeric score as shown in fig. 5.29. This mandatory score is added onto each planet's tally, affecting the final tally and overall *shadbala* interpretation.

The information derived from this specific procedure does not change from individual to individual. It cannot be interpreted solely on its own merits, and affects only the final outcome of the entire *shadbala* assessment. There is no parallel process used by Western, Arabian, Judaic, Chinese, or Tibetan practitioners in the assessment of a planet's influence.

FIGURE 5.29. TABLE OF NATURAL PLANETARY STRENGTHS.

STRENGTH SCORE	PLANET
1	Moon's North Node (☊)
1	Moon's South Node (☋)
2	Sun (☉)
3	Moon (☽)
4	Venus (♀)
5	Jupiter (♃)
6	Mercury (☿)
7	Mars (♂)
8	Saturn (♄)

Rating by *Chestabala*

The fourth *shadbala* is *chestabala,* which determines the potency of the Sun's or Moon's motion. This score is added onto the Sun's and Moon's individual tallies, but does not offer any insights solely on its own merits. Like the *naisargikabala,* the *chestabala* affects only the final tally and overall *shadbala* interpretation. The *chestabala* rating system is simple. If the Sun (☉) or the Moon (☽) is placed in one of the zodiac's northern latitudes (i.e., the zodiac signs Capricorn [♑], Aquarius [♒], Pisces [♓], Aries [♈], Taurus [♉], and Gemini [♊]), it is given a bonus score.

For example, Alice's Sun (☉ 01°♊50′ in fig. 5.4, fourth column) is in the northern latitude zodiac sign of Gemini (♊); and her Moon (☽ 18°♓23′ in fig. 5.4, fourth column) is in the northern latitude zodiac sign of Pisces (♊). Therefore, both planets would receive a bonus score. Peter's Moon (☽ 10°♈23′ in fig. 5.5) is in the northern latitude zodiac sign of Aries (♈). Therefore, his Moon would receive a bonus score.

Once again, there is no parallel assessment found in any of the other astrological traditions. Like *nasargikabala, chestabala* is unique to Vedic astrology.

Rating by *Dikbala*

The fifth *shadbala* is *dikbala,* which determines the planet's potency based upon its direction. The information derived from this specific procedure cannot be interpreted solely on its own merits, and its score affects only the final outcome of the entire *shadbala* assessment. A "bonus" score is given to a planet if it occupies a *kendra* house (see "Rating by *Sthanabala,*" page 230) as shown below:

Mercury (☿)	occupies House I
Jupiter (♃)	occupies House I
Moon (☽)	occupies House IV
Venus (♀)	occupies House IV
Saturn (♄)	occupies House VII
Sun (☉)	occupies House X
Mars (♂)	occupies House X

Using Alice's (fig. 5.10) and Peter's (fig. 5.11) *bhavacakras* (house charts), the practitioner would look for the specific planets occupying the *kendra* houses described above. Alice's Mars (♂) occupies the *kendra* House X (fig. 5.10). Therefore, an additional score would be added to her final *shadbala* tally. None of Peter's planets, on the other hand, occupies a *kendra* house, and therefore his *shadbala*'s final tally would not be affected by this procedure.

Although *dikbala* conceptually has much in common with the rating of the planets used in a *sthanabala* assessment of a planet by its occupation of a *trikona* or *kendra* house (see "*Sthanabala* by Occupation of a *Trikona* or *Kendra* House," page 233)—as well as with the Western application of angular, succedent, and cadent houses—this particular method is unique to the Vedic tradition.

Rating by *Kalabala*

The sixth *shadbala* is *kalabala*, which determines a planet's strength based upon the time of the individual's birth. This rating system is also unique to the Vedic tradition. According to practitioners, certain planets exert more influence on a chart cast for a daytime birth, while others have a greater effect on a nocturnal chart.

The Sun (☉), Venus (♀), and Jupiter (♃) are stronger in the chart of a person born between sunrise and sunset. The Moon (☽), Mars (♂), and Saturn (♄) are more potent in the chart of person born between sunset and sunrise. Mercury (☿) is powerful no matter what time the individual was born.

The information derived from this specific procedure cannot be interpreted solely on its own merits, and its score affects only the final outcome of the entire *shadbala* assessment. A "bonus" score is given to a planet if it occupies the time slots mentioned above. For example, the Moon (☽), Mars (♂), and Saturn (♄) would score higher in this procedure because both Alice and Peter were born at night (see the introduction to Part Two). Mercury (☿) receives a mandatory bonus score in both *shadbala* tallies, as mentioned earlier.

Once totaled, the scores of the six *shadbala* demonstrated in this section determine which facets of an individual's chart contain potent positive elements and which areas need to be carefully monitored or redirected throughout the person's life. As mentioned throughout this section, the final assessment and interpretation of the *shadbala* scores is an intricate process that would require many more chapters to cover in full detail. The general structures have only been defined here for reference when comparing this tradition to other forms of astrology.

STEP SEVEN: IDENTIFYING THE YOGA

The practitioner then proceeds to assess the data derived from these varied sources, looking for *yogas* (unions), which consist of planetary combinations or relationships that are said to consistently form specific personality types. As with the *shadbala*, it would take more space than is available in this book to detail the many *yogas* that exist in the body of Vedic astrological knowledge. However, to give you an idea of the process and resulting delineations, here are a few selected examples of potential patterns practitioners look for in a *bhavacakra*:

ruchaka-yoga	*Description:* Mars (♂) occupies Capricorn (10), Aries (1), or Scorpio (8) in Houses I, IV, VII, or X. *Traits:* assertive; aggressive; adventurous; pursues fame or infamy.
bhadra-yoga	*Description:* Mercury (☿) occupies Virgo (6) or Gemini (3) in Houses I, IV, VII, or X. *Traits:* intelligent; curious; sensual; generous; attains professional or financial success.
hamsa-yoga	*Description:* Jupiter (♃) occupies Cancer (3), Sagittarius (9), or Pisces (12) in Houses I, IV, VII, or X. *Traits:* generous; graceful; domineering; philosophical.
malavya-yoga	*Description:* Venus (♀) occupies Taurus (2) or Libra (7) in Houses I, IV, VII, or X. *Traits:* attractive; creative; sensual. Sex overrides all other aspects of life if positioned in House VII.
sasa-yoga	*Description:* Saturn (♄) occupies Libra (7), Capricorn (10), or Aquarius (11) in Houses I, IV, VII, or X. *Traits:* directed; ambitious; long-lived; very intelligent; ruthlessly pursues financial success.
kesari-yoga	*Description:* Moon (☽) and Jupiter (♃) occupy the same house or are 4, 7, or 10 houses apart. *Traits:* intelligent; passionate; ferociously destroys his or her enemies.
kalasarpa-yoga	*Description:* All planets in the *bhavacakra* occupy houses between the Moon's North (☊) and South (☋) Nodes. *Traits:* cursed by events that occurred during a previous life.
raj-yoga[97]	*Description:* Three planets occupy the same zodiac sign that each rules. For example, if Mercury (☿) occupies Virgo (6) or Gemini (3), Jupiter (♃) occupies Sagittarius (9) or Pisces (12), and Saturn (♄) occupies Capricorn (10) or Aquarius (11) in the same chart, this pattern exists. *Traits:* extremely powerful and successful.
dhana-yoga	*Description:* The planetary ruler of House I, II, V, IX, or XI occupies one of these same houses.

---

97. This is only one of the many hundreds of *raj-yogas* (royal combinations) that were described by ancient astrologers.

Traits: produces wealth in the areas represented by the occupied house.

Peter's *bhavacakra* (fig. 5.11) exhibits the *sasa-yoga* because Saturn (♄) occupies Aquarius (11) in House I. This suggests that he is directed, ambitious, very intelligent, and will live for a long time. He ruthlessly pursues financial success.

In Alice's *bhavacakra* (fig. 5.10), the planetary ruler (see "*Sthanabala by Swakshetra,*" page 232) of Houses I and II (♄, Saturn) occupies House IX and the planetary ruler of House V (♀, Venus) occupies the house that it rules. According to practitioners, this is a *dhana-yoga*. Using the house descriptions presented in the section "Constructing the *Bhavacakra,*" this *yoga* indicates that she will become wealthy because of her general fortune or luck, her father, advanced education, religious or ideological beliefs, medicine, or foreign travel (ruled by House IX); or through creative work, speculation, intellect, or entertainment interests (ruled by House V) (see "Constructing the *Bhavacakra,*" page 172).

As mentioned earlier, the definitions and delineations of all the *yogas* would be too difficult to cover in this volume. Much of the material has only been passed on through oral tradition from practitioner to practitioner. But this overview gives you an idea of how Vedic astrologers establish a foundation from which all the elements of a personality profile are ultimately viewed.

STEP EIGHT: CREATING A VEDIC PERSONALITY PROFILE

When the practitioner has constructed the essential *sodasavargas* and ancillary charts needed to develop the *jataka* (natal) personality profile, he or she proceeds to the intricate job of identifying the applicative *yoga* and interpreting the various pieces of cross-referenced data. In this section, a general delineation of a few of the charts will be presented to give you an idea of how the process unfolds. The sampling of data that will be interpreted below includes the *bhavacakra* (see "Constructing the *Bhavacakra,*" page 172) according to the house rulers and planetary positions by both zodiac sign and house, the Ascendant's *naksatra* (see "Identifying the Ascendant's *Naksatra,*" page 155), and the *navamsacakra* (see "Constructing and Interpreting the *Navamsacakra,*" page 208). This material would then be compiled along with the *shadbala* ratings (see "Applying the *Shadbala,*" page 230).

Alice T.'s Personality Profile

It is initially determined by the astrologer that Alice's *bhavacakra* displays a *dhana-yoga* (see "Identifying the *Yoga,*" page 237) because the planetary ruler (see "*Sthanabala by Swakshetra,*" page 232) of Houses I and II (♄, Saturn) occupies House IX and the planetary ruler of House V (♀, Venus) occupies the house that it rules. Using the house descriptions presented in the section "Constructing the *Bhava-cakra*," this *yoga* indicates that she will become wealthy because of her general fortune or luck, her father, advanced education, religious or ideological beliefs, medicine, or foreign travel (ruled by House IX); or through creative work, speculation, intellect, or entertainment interests (ruled by House V).

The practitioner then proceeds to confirm or enhance this overall profile. Beginning with the identification of the Ascendant's *naksatra* (see "Identifying the Ascendant's *Naksatra*"), Alice's Ascendant (AS 08°♑51′ in fig. 5.4, fourth column) occupies the twenty-first *naksatra*—the *naksatra* Uttarasadha (26°♐41′– 10°♑00′ in fig. 5.9, third column), indicating she is intelligent, fun-loving, generous, and destined for fame. She must, however, be aware of her enemies (see "Identifying the Ascendant's *Naksatra*"). The Ascendant or House I's ruler (Capricorn (♑) or 10 in fig. 5.10) in Alice's *bhavacakra* (fig. 5.10) indicates that she is responsible, opportunistic, and competitive. Physically it suggests that she has an elongated face (see "Interpreting the House Rulers in the *Bhavacakra*").

House II's ruler (Aquarius [♒] or 11 in fig. 5.10) suggests that she experiences unexpected financial fluctuations and has unconventional ways of spending and saving money (see "Interpreting the House Rulers in the *Bhavacakra*"). The Moon's North Node (☊ in fig. 5.10) resides in House II, indicating that she is talkative and has an addictive personality. She may lack marital fidelity and may crave wealth (see "The Moon's North Node in the Various Houses").

House III's ruler (Pisces [♓] or 12 in fig. 5.10) purports that she is overly emotional in her communications with others. She also has emotional ties to siblings and neighbors. It also indicates that she is intuitive, but mentally lazy (see "Interpreting the House Rulers in the *Bhavacakra*"). The Moon (☽ in fig. 5.10) resides in House III, suggesting that she fulfills strong personal desires, yet has troubles throughout her life. It further indicates that she has happy relationships with her siblings. She also has the talent to become a musician, dancer, writer, or actor (see "The Moon in the Various Houses").

House IV's ruler (Aries [♈] or 1 in fig. 5.10) suggests that she has a domineering parent. It also indicates that she has a confrontational or active home life (see "Interpreting the House Rulers in the *Bhavacakra*"). Jupiter (♃ in fig. 5.10) is positioned in House IV, indicating general success and the acquisition of many material comforts. She inherits wealth, encounters fortunate conclusions to events, and experiences happiness with her mother (see "Jupiter in the Various Houses").

House V's ruler (Taurus [♉] or 2 in fig. 5.10) indicates that she is highly artistic, attractive to the opposite sex, and experiences good luck. She might be indulgent with pleasures. And she has an excellent rapport with children (see "Interpreting the House Rulers in the *Bhavacakra*"). Venus (♀ in fig. 5.10) is placed in House V, which indicates that she becomes wealthy, comfortable, and achieves romantic happiness. Her past-life karma gives her artistic talent (see "Venus in the Various Houses").

House VI's ruler (Gemini [♊] or 3 in fig. 5.10) indicates that she keeps busy at work and on work in the home. She can do more than one job at a time, and generates a lot of paperwork. She enjoys owning many pets. However, she suffers from respiratory or nervous complaints (see "Interpreting the House Rulers in the *Bhavacakra*"). The Sun (☉ in fig. 5.10), occupies House VI, indicating that she has strong health and defeats her enemies easily. She gains recognition for her work, but has difficulties with her father during childhood (see "The Sun in the Various Houses"). Mercury (☿ in fig. 5.10) is located in Alice's House VI, indicating that she may work as a writer or in the publishing industry. She has a talent for debate, even though she had a speech impediment or had many difficulties when she was a child (see "Mercury in the Various Houses").

House VII's ruler (Cancer [♋] or 4 in fig. 5.10) suggests that she has a close, caring relationship with business partners or a spouse. She maintains a strong emotional connection to a domineering spouse (see "Interpreting the House Rulers in the *Bhavacakra*").

House VIII's ruler (Leo [♌] or 5 in fig. 5.10) indicates that she shrewdly manipulates financial resources and assets for herself and others. She secretly fears death (see "Interpreting the House Rulers in the *Bhavacakra*"). The Moon's South Node (☋ in fig. 5.10) occupies House VIII, indicating that she encounters unhappiness in her home life, separation from friends, and chronic illness (see "The Moon's South Node in the Various Houses").

House IX's ruler (Virgo [♍] or 6 in fig. 5.10) indicates that she is concerned with higher education, publishing, philosophy, religion, anthropology, and travel abroad. She has the potential to earn an advanced degree abroad (see "Interpreting the House Rulers in the *Bhavacakra*"). In Alice's chart, Saturn (♄ in fig. 5.10) occupies House IX, indicating that she encounters difficulties during long journeys and in experiences with her father. It also indicates that she lacks religious or philosophic faith (see "Saturn in the Various Houses").

House X's ruler (Libra [♎] or 7 in fig. 5.10) suggests that she attracts attention because of her physical appearance, artistic talent, or social position. She needs to find a balance between home and career (see "Interpreting the House Rulers in the *Bhavacakra*"). Mars (♂ in fig. 5.10) resides in Alice's House X, which suggests that she achieves professional success in technical fields such as design or architecture.

She is ruthless in business and tyrannical in her professional life. This position also suggests that she experiences conflicts with her parents (see "Mars in the Various Houses").

House XI's ruler (Scorpio [♏] or 8 in fig. 5.10) indicates that she may make new friends in a new environment to improve life. She may also make friendships to enhance her social or professional status. There is a potential that she may be victimized by her friends. And there is an element of secrecy or mystery associated with some of her friendships or with organizations she belongs to (see "Interpreting the House Rulers in the *Bhavacakra*").

House XII's ruler (Sagittarius [♐] or 9 in fig. 5.10) suggests that she has an unrealistic inability to worry or to have concern. She receives help from unknown sources. She is intuitive and has an interest in psychology and the occult (see "Interpreting the House Rulers in the *Bhavacakra*").

As mentioned earlier, the above material would also be synthesized along with delineations of each planetary position according to the zodiac sign occupied (see "Constructing the *Rasicakra*") during a consultation. Then the practitioner would add the prognostications disclosed in the final tallying of the *shadbala* (see "Applying the *Shadbala*") and the delineation of ancillary *sodasavargas* such as the *navamsacakra*.

In Alice's *navamsacakra* (see "Constructing the *Navamsacakra*"), *navamsa* 9 is occupied by the Sun (☉), the Moon (☽), and Mars (♂) (fig. 5.15). As mentioned earlier, this *navamsa* sign correlates to the zodiac sign Sagittarius (♐, fig. 5.13), indicating that Alice is able to hone in and make a mark on a situation because of the Sun's influence in this zodiac sign (see "The Sun in the Various Zodiac Signs"). Involvement in religious, political, or educational reforms, as well as possible public notoriety, are evidenced by the Moon's occupation of the zodiac sign (see "The Moon in the Various Zodiac Signs"). Mars's influence indicates that Alice marries more than once (and in one instance has concerns over her spouse's or child's health) (see "Mars in the Various Zodiac Signs").

A secondary point of interest in her *navamsacakra* occurs in *navamsa* 6, which is occupied by Venus and Jupiter (♀ and ♃, fig. 5.15). This *navamsa* sign correlates to the zodiac sign Virgo (♍, fig. 5.13), and the combination indicates that Venus's influence creates disappointment or delays in romance. Alice potentially marries an employee, a co-worker, a doctor, or an invalid. However, she profits through her spouse's or partner's investments (see "Venus in the Various Zodiac Signs"). Jupiter's influence changes some of Venus's prognostications, producing a prosperous marriage and mysterious good fortune. Unforeseen gains are possible, but so is danger or loss through secret means (see "Jupiter in the Various Zodiac Signs").

Peter C.'s Personality Profile

The astrologer initially determines that Peter's *bhavacakra* (fig. 5.11) exhibits the *sasa-yoga* because Saturn (♄) occupies Aquarius (11) in House I. This suggests that he is directed, ambitious, very intelligent, and will live for a long time. He ruthlessly pursues financial success.

As in Alice's profile, the practitioner then proceeds to confirm or enhance this overall prognostication. For example, Peter's Ascendant (AS 09°♒34' in fig. 5.5, fourth column) resides in the twenty-fourth *naksatra*—the *naksatra* Satabhisaj (06°♒40'–20°♒00' in fig. 5.9, third column)—which suggests that he is supportive of other people's work and has an unobtrusive nature. He can possess a devious side, however, (see "Identifying the Ascendant's *Naksatra*"). The Ascendant or House I's ruler (Aquarius [♒] or 11 in fig. 5.11) indicates that Peter is highly opinionated and hates change, but makes alterations without remorse. He possesses mental poise. Physically, he has a square jaw and a friendly face (see "Interpreting the House Rulers in the Bhavacakra"). Saturn (♄ in fig. 5.11) in Peter's chart resides in House I, suggesting that he is humble, patient, responsible, self-critical, and serious. He sometimes limits his own talents because he lacks self-confidence, and had an unhappy childhood (see "Saturn in the Various Houses").

House II's ruler (Pisces [♓] or 12 in fig. 5.11) suggests that he exerts shrewdness in financial management. He also has an irregular income or illicit income (see "Interpreting the House Rulers in the *Bhavacakra*").

House III's ruler (Aries [♈] or 1 in fig. 5.11) indicates that he is argumentative or communicates violently. He has confrontational relations with siblings and neighbors. And he has an impulsive intellect (see "Interpreting the House Rulers in the *Bhavacakra*"). The Moon (☽ in fig. 5.11) resides in House III, suggesting that Peter fulfills strong personal desires, yet has an unhappy life. It also indicates that he has happy relationships with his siblings. He also has the talent to become a musician, dancer, writer, or actor (see "The Moon in the Various Houses").

House IV's ruler (Taurus [♉] or 2 in fig. 5.11) suggests that he has a sentimental attachment to home and family. He also has strong ties to his parents (see "Interpreting the House Rulers in the *Bhavacakra*"). Jupiter (♃ in fig. 5.11) is positioned in House IV, instilling general success and the acquisition of many material comforts. He inherits wealth, encounters fortunate conclusions to events, and experiences happiness with his mother (see "Jupiter in the Various Houses").

House V's ruler (Gemini [♊] or 3 in fig. 5.11) indicates that his creativity is closely linked to communication, and that his pleasures are intellectual. He is romantically attracted to intellectuals. He is possibly a twin or the parent of twins (see "Interpreting the House Rulers in the *Bhavacakra*"). Venus (♀ in fig. 5.11) occupies House V, indicating that he becomes wealthy, comfortable, and achieves romantic happiness. His past-life karma gives him artistic talent (see "Venus in the Various Houses"). Peter's Mars (♂ in fig. 5.11) also occupies House V, which indicates that a past life bestows on him talent in sports or politics. He also has technical talent in design or architecture. It additionally suggests that he does not perform good deeds (see "Mars in the Various Houses"). In Peter's chart, the Moon's North Node (☊ in fig. 5.11) is placed in House V, suggesting that there are stormy emotions associated with romance and difficulties with children. Peter fulfills his desires through manipulation, and his power increases during his forty-second year (see "The Moon's North Node in the Various Houses").

House VI's ruler (Cancer [♋] or 4 in fig. 5.11) indicates that he has delicate health patterns but few major illnesses. He prefers to work at home or in home-related jobs. He has strong emotional ties to his employees or co-workers, and has inconsistent work habits. He is also emotionally attached to his pets (see "Interpreting the House Rulers in the *Bhavacakra*").

House VII's ruler (Leo [♌] or 5 in fig. 5.11) suggests that marriage or another form of partnership positively satisfies his ego. His success comes from working closely with others (see "Interpreting the House Rulers in the *Bhavacakra*"). The Sun (☉ in fig. 5.11) is in House VII, suggesting that he has a strong desire for marriage and is preoccupied with his wife or partner. Marriage may be delayed because of an insufficient dowry or religious or social differences (see "The Sun in the Various Houses"). Peter's Mercury (☿ in fig. 5.11) is placed in House VII, signifying that he marries an intelligent but emotionally detached wife. He achieves success in writing or communication (see "Mercury in the Various Houses").

House VIII's ruler (Virgo [♍] or 6 in fig. 5.11) indicates that he is always seeking ways to improve his financial resources. His spouse or business partner is somehow involved in investments, taxes, insurance, or the management of other people's money. He is resigned to the concept of death (see "Interpreting the House Rulers in the *Bhavacakra*").

House IX's ruler (Libra [♎] or 7 in fig. 5.11) indicates that he is artistically, academically, or philosophically oriented (see "Interpreting the House Rulers in the *Bhavacakra*").

House X's ruler (Scorpio [♏] or 8 in fig. 5.11) suggests that a traumatic event that occurs during childhood instills in him a sense of having no control over circumstances. He does not allow anyone to control his personal destiny. For him, relinquishing control impedes growth. There is potential for a change of career late in life. He attracts powerful friends. Secrecy or mystery is connected with his profession, social status, or parents (see "Interpreting the House Rulers in the *Bhavacakra*").

House XI's ruler (Sagittarius [♐] or 9 in fig. 5.11) suggests that he makes more friends than he can afford time to have, and attaches more importance to friendship than necessary. He may perceive friendship where none exists. His friends are intellectuals, actors, religious people, travelers, artists, and clerics (see "Interpreting the House Rulers in the *Bhavacakra*"). In Peter's chart, the Moon's South Node (☋ in fig. 5.11) is in House XI, suggesting that he acquires wealth through hobbies or freelance work, and attracts unusual friends (see "The Moon's South Node in the Various Houses").

House XII's ruler (Capricorn [♑] or 10 in fig. 5.11) indicates that he spends a great deal of time in solitude. He has difficulty attaining true recognition, but may achieve success. He is victimized by unfounded fears and worries. And he has a strong interest in the psychic and the occult, but no desire to know the future (see "Interpreting the House Rulers in the *Bhavacakra*").

As mentioned earlier, the above material would also be synthesized along with delineations of each planetary position during a consultation according to the zodiac sign occupied (see "Constructing the *Rasicakra*"). Then the practitioner would add the prognostications disclosed in the final tallying of the *shadbala* (see "Applying the *Shadbala*") and the delineation of ancillary *sodasavargas* such as the *navamsacakra*.

In Peter's *navamsacakra* (see "Constructing the *Navamsacakra*"), *navamsa* 2 is occupied by Venus, the Moon's South Node, and Mars (♀, ☋, and ♂, fig. 5.16). This *navamsa* sign correlates to the zodiac sign Taurus (♉, fig. 5.14). The combination indicates that Peter encounters delays in marriage, and gains from both his profession and spirit because of Venus's influence (see "Venus in the Various Zodiac Signs"). Harm to women or by women as well as danger from adultery are also indicated by Mars's position (see "Mars in the Various Zodiac Signs"). Since the Moon's South Node is not delineated in the *rasicakra*-style system of interpretation, there are no details given as to its effect on Peter's marital life or ultimate direction in life.

A secondary point of interest in this *navamsacakra* occurs in *navamsa* 4, which is occupied by the Sun and the Moon (☉, ☽, fig. 5.16). *Navamsa* 4 correlates to the zodiac sign Cancer (♋, fig. 5.14). This combination indicates that ultimately Peter is sensitive, changeable, and has a fertile imagination. He is profoundly affected by his surroundings and possesses dramatic flair. He has many mood swings, craves kindness, and fears ridicule. He remembers everything. According to the Moon's influence on this position, Peter is also agreeable, sympathetic, and follows the path of least resistance. He travels, cooks, collects antiques, and encounters great obstacles.

Although pinpointing the periods in which events occur or change is not generally considered to be part of natal astrology, there is form of predictive astrology that is ordinarily incorporated into the delineation of a *jataka* (natal)

personality profile. This personal chronology is called a *vimsottari dasa*. It is a valuable tool that not only times events. The *vimsottari dasa* aids practitioners in determining at what age and for how long the general characteristics disclosed in the person's *yoga* and supporting planetary as well as house-ruler delineations will appear most profound.

STEP NINE: CREATING AND INTERPRETING THE *Vimsottari Dasa*
Constructing the *Vimsottari Dasa*

According to Vedic astrologers, a person passes through a complete sequence of planetary influences in his or her lifetime. That entire cycle is equal to 120°00′ of the 360°00′ sidereal zodiac (or 120 years). This hypothetical life span was developed by ancient scholars and will very likely include the death of the body prior to its cyclical completion. Called the *vimsottari dasa*,[98] this timeline is divided into nine *dasas* (time periods) of 13.33°00′ each. The *dasa* is subdivided into nine *bhukti* of 01.48°00′ each, and is further segmented into eighty-one *antardasa* of 0.1644°00′ each.

Every *dasa*, *bhukti*, or *antardasa* represents an event or change in a person's life corresponding to a year, month, or day. The *vimsottari dasa* is perhaps the most difficult portion of Vedic chart delineation because it contains so many interpretative intricacies. But it is also the point at which this particular tradition delves deeper than Western natal astrologers ever do into the timing of critical events, or than Chinese and Tibetan practitioners execute on the occasion of an individual's birth. It is, however, similar to the Chinese ten-year fate cycles (see "Locating and Interpreting the Birth *Miao*" in chapter 3) and the Tibetan *bap-par* (see "Locating the *Bap-Par*" in chapter 4) in its purpose and incorporation into the overall personality profile.

There are many *dasa* systems employed by Indian practitioners. One of the easiest methods for calculating individual events is to construct a type of *dasa* chart called a *naksatradasa* (lunar-mansion time period). Identifying the *naksatra* position (fig. 5.9) of an individual's Moon (☽, figs. 5.4 or 5.5, fourth column), the *naksatra*'s allotted time period is calculated against the individual's birth date to determine how long the Moon traveled through that *naksatra* before the person was born. Then the time between the birth date and the entry of the Moon into the next *naksatra* is determined. The data in fig. 5.30 is used to identify the specific *naksatra*, the Moon's location in degrees and minutes in the zodiac, the number of years a particular *naksatra* influences a person's life, and the resulting *dasa*'s respective planetary ruler.

---

98. Pronounced "vim-shot-tah-ree dah-sha," meaning "120-system period."

FIGURE 5.30. THE *NAKSATRA* PLANETARY PERIODS.

Naksatra Number	Naksatra Name	Zodiac Sign Location in Degrees (°) and Minutes (′)	Dasa Rulership in Years	Dasa Planetary Ruler
1	Asvini	00°♈00′–13°♈20′	7	Moon's South Node (☋)
2	Bharani	13°♈21′–26°♈40′	20	Venus (♀)
3	Krttika	26°♈41′–10°♉00′	6	Sun (☉)
4	Rohini	10°♉01′–23°♉20′	10	Moon (☽)
5	Mrgasiras	23°♉21′–06°♊40′	7	Mars (♂)
6	Ardra	06°♊41′–20°♊00′	18	Moon's North Node (☊)
7	Punarvasu	20°♊01′–03°♋20′	16	Jupiter (♃)
8	Pusya	03°♋21′–16°♋40′	19	Saturn (♄)
9	Aslesa	16°♋41′–30°♋00′	17	Mercury (☿)
10	Magha	00°♌00′–13°♌20′	7	Moon's South Node (☋)
11	Purvaphalguni	13°♌21′–26°♌40′	20	Venus (♀)
12	Uttaraphalguni	26°♌41′–10°♍00′	6	Sun (☉)
13	Hasta	10°♍01′–23°♍20′	10	Moon (☽)
14	Citra	23°♍21′–06°♎40′	7	Mars (♂)
15	Svati	06°♎41′–20°♎00′	18	Moon's North Node (☊)
16	Visakha	20°♎01′ 03°♏20′	16	Jupiter (♃)
17	Anuradha	03°♏21′–16°♏40′	19	Saturn (♄)
18	Jyestha	16°♏41′–30°♏00′	17	Mercury (☿)
19	Mula	00°♐00′–13°♐20′	7	Moon's South Node (☋)
20	Purvasadha	13°♐21′–26°♐40′	20	Venus (♀)
21	Uttarasadha	26°♐41′–10°♑00′	6	Sun (☉)
22	Sravana	10°♑01′–23°♑20′	10	Moon (☽)
23	Sravistha	23°♑21′–06°♒40′	7	Mars (♂)
24	Satabhisaj	06°♒41′–20°♒00′	18	Moon's North Node (☊)
25	Purvabhadrapada	20°♒01′–03°♓20′	16	Jupiter (♃)
26	Uttarabhadrapada	03°♓21′–16°♓40′	19	Saturn (♄)
27	Revati	16°♓41′–30°♓00′	17	Mercury (☿)

For example, Alice T.'s Moon (☽ 18°♓23′ in fig. 5.4, fourth column) is in the *naksatra* Revati (16°♓41′–00°♈00′ in fig. 5.30) which is ruled by Mercury (☿, fig. 5.30, fifth column) and therefore represents the Mercury *dasa*. According to fig. 5.30, the entire *naksatra* Revati is 13°20′ in length (or 00°800′), spanning a period of seventeen years. The difference between Alice's Moon position (☽ 18° ♓23′ in fig. 5.4, fourth column) and the *naksatra* Revati's last degree (16° ♓41′–00°♈00′ in fig. 5.30) is 11°37′ (or 00°697′, which is derived by subtracting 18°♓23′ from 00°♈00′). The fractionalized portion of difference is multiplied by the total years that the given *naksatra* rules the period. In this case, the *naksatra* Revati rules for seventeen years. Therefore, 00°697′ out of this *naksatra*'s total

13°20′ (or 00°800′) is multiplied by the *naksatra*'s time period (seventeen years in fig. 5.30, fifth column). The total is converted to a decimalized figure and multiplied by the number of days in a year (365.25 days). The final result is the remaining days in the given *naksatra*'s time period at the moment of the individual's birth as follows:

00°697′/00°800′ × 17 years = 00°11,849′/00°800′ = 14.8112 × 365.25 days = 5409.79 days or 14 years, 296 days

This means that there were 14 years and 296 days left in Mercury *dasa* (*naksatra* Revati, fig. 5.30, fifth column) when Alice was born. Therefore, the first major *dasa* of her life lasted from June 15, 1952, to April 5, 1966. The remaining *dasas* would then be calculated by following the sequential order of the *naksatra* periods, following the data and sequential order shown in fig. 5.30.

Since Alice was born while the Moon was in the *naksatra* Revati (the twenty-seventh *naksatra*), the next *dasa* that governs events in her life is the first *naksatra*, Asvini. According to fig. 5.30, this *dasa* is ruled by the Moon's South Node (☋, fifth column), lasting for seven years (fourth column) from April 6, 1966, to April 5, 1973. The remaining *naksatras* that would influence her life occur in the following sequential and chronological order. The next *dasa* that governs events in her life is the second *naksatra*, Bharani. According to fig. 5.30, this *dasa* is ruled by Venus (♀, fifth column), lasting for twenty years (fourth column) from April 6, 1973, to April 5, 1993. The next *dasa* that governs events in her life is the third *naksatra*, Krttika. According to fig. 5.30, this *dasa* is ruled by the Sun (☉, fifth column), lasting for six years (fourth column) from April 6, 1993, to April 5, 1999. The next *dasa* that governs events in her life is the fourth *naksatra*, Rohini. According to fig. 5.30, this *dasa* is ruled by the Moon (☽, fifth column), lasting for ten years (fourth column) from April 6, 1999, to April 5, 2010. The next *dasa* that governs events in her life is the fifth *naksatra*, Mrgasiras. According to fig. 5.30, this *dasa* is ruled by Mars (♂, fifth column), lasting for seven years (fourth column) from April 6, 2010, to April 5, 2017. The next *dasa* that governs events in her life is the sixth *naksatra*, Ardra. According to fig. 5.30, this *dasa* is ruled by the Moon's North Node (☊, fifth column), lasting for eighteen years (fourth column) from April 6, 2017, to April 5, 2035. The next *dasa* that governs events in her life is the seventh *naksatra*, Punarvasu. According to fig. 5.30, this *dasa* is ruled by Jupiter (♃, fifth column), lasting for sixteen years (fourth column) from April 6, 2035, to April 5, 2051. The next *dasa* that governs events in her life is the eighth *naksatra*, Pusya. According to fig. 5.30, this *dasa* is ruled by Saturn (♄, fifth column), lasting for nineteen years (fourth column) from April 6, 2051, to April 5, 2070. The last *dasa* that governs events in her 120-year life is the ninth *naksatra*, Aslesa. According to fig. 5.30, this *dasa* is ruled by Mercury ($\female$, fifth column), lasting for seventeen years (fourth column) from April 6, 2070, to April 5, 2087.

This information is documented as demonstrated in fig. 5.31. Alice's entire 120-year life span of *naksatras* is recorded by the astrologer in his or her interpretation notes. There is no formal visual display created for this chronology.

The same procedure is applied to Peter C., whose Moon ($\leftmoon$ 10°$\aries$23′ in fig. 5.5, fourth column) is in the *naksatra* Asvini (00°$\aries$00′–13°$\aries$20′ in fig. 5.30) which is ruled by the Moon's South Node ($\mho$, fig. 5.30, fifth column) and therefore represents the Moon's South Node *dasa*. According to fig. 5.30, the *naksatra* Asvini is 13°20′ in length (or 00°800′), spanning a period of seven years. The difference between Peter's Moon position ($\leftmoon$ 10°$\aries$23′ in fig. 5.5, fourth column) and the *naksatra* Asvini's last degree (00°$\aries$00′–13°$\aries$20′ in fig. 5.30) is 03°03′ (or 00°183′, which is derived by subtracting 10°$\aries$23′ from 13°$\aries$20′). The fractionalized portion of difference is multiplied by the total years that the given *naksatra* rules the period. In this case, the *naksatra* rules for seven years. Therefore, 00°183′ out of the *naksatra*'s total 13°20′ (00°800′) is multiplied by the *naksatra*'s time period (seven

FIGURE 5.31. ALICE T.'S NAKSATRADASA.

Naksatra Number	Naksatra Name	Dasa Rulership in Years	Chronological Dates When This Influence Occurs	Dasa Planetary Ruler (Symbol)
27	Revati	17	Jan. 15, 1952–Apr. 5, 1966 (birth to 14.8 years old)	Mercury ($\female$)
1	Asvini	7	Apr. 6, 1966–Apr. 5, 1973 (14.81 years old to 21.81 years old)	Moon's South Node ($\mho$)
2	Bharani	20	Apr. 6, 1973–Apr. 5, 1993 (21.81 years old to 41.81 years old)	Venus ($\female$)
3	Krttika	6	Apr. 6, 1993–Apr. 5, 1999 (41.81 years old to 47.81 years old)	Sun ($\odot$)
4	Rohini	10	Apr. 6, 1999–Apr. 5, 2010 (47.81 years old to 57.81 years old)	Moon ($\leftmoon$)
5	Mrgasiras	7	Apr. 6, 2010–Apr. 5, 2017 (57.81 years old to 64.81 years old)	Mars ($\male$)
6	Ardra	18	Apr. 6, 2017–Apr. 5, 2035 (64.81 years old to 82.81 years old)	Moon's North Node (Ω)
7	Punarvasu	16	Apr. 6, 2035–Apr. 5, 2051 (82.81 years old to 98.81 years old)	Jupiter ($\jupiter$)
8	Pusya	19	Apr. 6, 2051–Apr. 5, 2070 (98.81 years old to 117.81 years old)	Saturn ($\saturn$)
9	Aslesa	17	Apr. 6, 2070–Apr. 5, 2087 (117.81 years old to 134.81 years old)	Mercury ($\female$)

years in fig. 5.30, fifth column). The total is converted to a decimal and multiplied by the number of days in a year (365.25 days). The final result is the remaining days in the *naksatra*'s time period at the moment of the individual's birth as follows:

$$00°183'/00°800' \times 7 \text{ years} = 00°1281'/00°800' = 1.60125 \times 365.25 \text{ days} = 1 \text{ year, } 219.61 \text{ days}$$

This means that 1 year and 219.61 days were left in the Moon's South Node *dasa* (fig. 5.30, fifth column) when Peter was born. Consequently, the first major *dasa* of his life lasted from August 27, 1964 (his birth date) to January 19, 1966. The next *dasa* that governs events in his life is the second *naksatra*, Bharani. According to fig. 5.30, this *dasa* is ruled by Venus (♀, fifth column), lasting for twenty years (fourth column) from January 20, 1966, to January 19, 1986. The next *dasa* that governs events in his life is the third *naksatra*, Krttika. According to fig. 5.30, this *dasa* is ruled by the Sun (☉, fifth column), lasting for six years (fourth column) from January 20, 1986, to January 19, 1992. The next *dasa* that governs events in his life is the fourth *naksatra*, Rohini. According to fig. 5.30, this *dasa* is ruled by the Moon (☽, fifth column), lasting for ten years (fourth column) from January 20, 1992, to January 19, 2002. The next *dasa* that governs events in his life is the fifth *naksatra*, Mrgasiras. According to fig. 5.30, this *dasa* is ruled by Mars (♂, fifth column), lasting for seven years (fourth column) from January 20, 2002 to January 19, 2009. The next *dasa* that governs events in his life is the sixth *naksatra*, Ardra. According to fig. 5.30, this *dasa* is ruled by the Moon's North Node (☊, fifth column), lasting for eighteen years (fourth column) from January 20, 2009, to January 19, 2027. The next *dasa* that governs events in his life is the seventh *naksatra*, Punarvasu. According to fig. 5.30, this *dasa* is ruled by Jupiter (♃, fifth column), lasting for sixteen years (fourth column) from January 20, 2027, to January 19, 2043. The next *dasa* that governs events in his life is the eighth *naksatra*, Pusya. According to fig. 5.30, this *dasa* is ruled by Saturn (♄, fifth column), lasting for nineteen years (fourth column) from January 20, 2043, to January 19, 2062. The next *dasa* that governs events in his life is the ninth *naksatra*, Aslesa. According to fig. 5.30, this *dasa* is ruled by Mercury (☿, fifth column), lasting for seventeen years (fourth column) from January 20, 2062, to January 19, 2079. The last *dasa* that governs events in his 120-year life is the tenth *naksatra*, Magha. According to fig. 5.30, this *dasa* is ruled by the Moon's South Node (☋, fifth column), lasting for seven years (fourth column) from January 20, 2079, to January 19, 2086.

This information is documented as demonstrated in fig. 5.32. Peter's entire 120-year life span is recorded by the astrologer in his or her interpretation notes. There is no formal visual display created for this chronology.

FIGURE 5.32. PETER C.'s NAKSATRADASA.

NAKSATRA NUMBER	NAKSATRA NAME	DASA RULERSHIP IN YEARS	CHRONOLOGICAL DATES WHEN THIS INFLUENCE OCCURS	DASA PLANETARY RULER (SYMBOL)
1	Asvini	7	Aug. 27, 1964–Jan. 19, 1966 (birth to 1.33 years old)	Moon's South Node (☋)
2	Bharani	20	Jan. 20, 1966–Jan. 19, 1986 (1.33 years old to 20.33 years old)	Venus (♀)
3	Krttika	6	Jan. 20, 1986–Jan. 19, 1992 (20.33 years old to 26.33 years old)	Sun (☉)
4	Rohini	10	Jan. 20, 1992–Jan. 19, 2002 (26.33 years old to 36.33 years old)	Moon (☽)
5	Mrgasiras	7	Jan. 20, 2002–Jan. 19, 2009 (36.33 years old to 43.33 years old)	Mars (♂)
6	Ardra	18	Jan. 20, 2009–Jan. 19, 2027 (43.33 years old to 61.33 years old)	Moon's North Node (☊)
7	Punarvasu	16	Jan. 20, 2027–Jan. 19, 2043 (61.33 years old to 77.33 years old)	Jupiter (♃)
8	Pusya	19	Jan. 20, 2043–Jan. 19, 2062 (77.33 years old to 96.33 years old)	Saturn (♄)
9	Aslesa	17	Jan. 20, 2062–Jan. 19, 2079 (96.33 years old to 113.33 years old)	Mercury (☿)
10	Magha	7	Jan. 20, 2079–Jan. 19, 2086 (113.33 years old to 120.33 years old)	Moon's South Node (☋)

Interpreting the *Vimsottari Dasa*

The method used to delineate an individual's *vimsottari dasa* concentrates on the planetary ruler for each *dasa* (time period) in the person's life. A practitioner would interpret the individual's various *dasas* using the interpretative material below:

Moon's South Node (☋) New professional opportunities arise. spiritual advancement occurs. If adversely aspected (see "Rating by *Drigbala*") or poorly positioned (see "Rating by *Sthanabala*"), a dramatic loss in the house of the *bhavacakra* that the node occupies takes place (see "The Moon's South Node in the Various Houses"); unhappiness occurs; financial loss can happen; need for seclusion is great.

Venus (♀) Successful relationships with loved ones take place. Children are born. Social harmony exists. Travel and acquisition occur. If adversely aspected (see "Rating by *Drigbala*") or poorly positioned (see "Rating by *Sthanabala*") extravagance prevails, and there may be arguments with loved ones.

Sun (☉)

The activities of the house in the *bhavacakra* (see "The Sun in the Various Houses") or the zodiac sign in the *rasicakra* (see "The Sun in the Various Zodiac Signs") that the Sun occupies are accentuated. Life focuses on travel, finances, profession, education, and the acquisition of land. If adversely aspected (see "Rating by *Drigbala*") or poorly positioned (see "Rating by *Sthanabala*"), or if the Sun occupies House VI, VIII, or XII in the *bhavacakra*, it suggests vision or dental ailments, problems with authority figures or the father, difficulties with inheritance, or a loss of status.

Moon (☽)

Time to start a new business. Success is achieved in publishing. Harmony is attained in one's life. The mother, spouse, or children will also be fortunate. If adversely aspected (see "Rating by *Drigbala*") or poorly positioned (see "Rating by *Sthanabala*"), many emotional fluctuations occur; misunderstandings may be encountered with friends and family; or there will be an indecisive period in business.

Mars (♂)

Time to develop a new health and fitness regimen to bolster health. Travel, adventure, and action are all possible. Determination can be applied to any undertaking, and assistance from friends is beneficial. If adversely aspected (see "Rating by *Drigbala*") or poorly positioned (see "Rating by *Sthanabala*"), it is a very restless period; marital discord occurs, there may be changes of residence or profession, or arguments with friends.

Moon's North Node (☊)

Success, wealth, and travel occur. If adversely aspected (see "Rating by *Drigbala*") or poorly positioned (see "Rating by *Sthanabala*"), many professional setbacks occur, as well as the potential for divorce or for separation from friends.

Jupiter (♃)

A very fortunate and prosperous period. Marriage, children, or professional success occurs. Interest in philosophy, religion, or the law arises during this period. If adversely aspected (see "Rating by *Drigbala*") or poorly positioned (see "Rating by *Sthanabala*"), greed, indolence, extravagance, or lost opportunities prevail.

Saturn (♄)

Success earned by hard work and persistence is harvested. Prosperous conclusions to events that were begun in another period also occur if the person continues to work hard and exercise patience. If adversely aspected (see "Rating by *Drigbala*") or poorly positioned (see "Rating by *Sthanabala*"), uncontrollable obstacles, illness, depression, and loneliness prevail.

Mercury (☿)   Success in business. Time to begin a writing or communications career, or return to school for an advanced educational degree. Changes of residence or profession may occur.

For example, a practitioner would determine that during Alice's Mercury *dasa* (June 15, 1952, to April 5, 1966), she achieves success in business. It's a time to begin a writing or communications career, or return to school for an advanced educational degree. Changes of residence or profession occur during this time. During her Moon's South Node *dasa* (April 6, 1966, to April 5, 1973), new professional opportunities arise and spiritual advancement occurs. Since this node is poorly positioned (see "Rating by *Sthanabala*"), she experiences marital difficulties and a shortened life span. She is introvertive and spiritual. Unhappiness occurs, financial loss can happen, and the need for seclusion is great. During her Venus *dasa* (April 6, 1973, to April 5, 1993), successful relationships with loved ones take place, children are born, and social harmony exists. She travels and makes acquisitions. During her Sun's *dasa* (April 6, 1993, to April 5, 1999), her work habits, desire to serve others, health, adversaries, employees, co-workers, obstacles, and litigation are accentuated. Alice's life focuses on travel, finances, profession, education, and the acquisition of land. This occurs because the Sun occupies House VI in her *bhavacakra* (see "Constructing the *Bhavacakra*"). The Sun's placement also suggests that vision or dental ailments exist, and that she has problems with authority figures or her father. There are difficulties with inheritance, or a possible loss of status. Around the time of her Moon *dasa* (April 6, 1999, to April 5, 2010), it is time to start a new business. Success is achieved in publishing, and harmony is attained in her life. Alice's mother, husband, or children will also be fortunate. During her Mars *dasa* (April 6, 2010, to April 5, 2017), it is time to develop a new health and fitness regimen to bolster her health. Travel, adventure, and action are all possible. Determination can be applied to any undertaking, and assistance from friends is beneficial. The practitioner would continue in this same manner to determine the direction of her life during her Moon's North Node *dasa* (April 6, 2017, to April 5, 2035), her Jupiter *dasa* (April 6, 2035, to April 5, 2051), her Saturn *dasa* (April 6, 2051, to April 5, 2070), and her second Mercury *dasa* (April 6, 2070, to April 5, 2087), which all occur after the age of seventy.

A practitioner would determine that during Peter's Moon's South Node *dasa*

(August 27, 1964, to January 19, 1966), he attained spiritual advancement. During his Venus *dasa* (January 20, 1966 to January 19, 1986), he had successful relationships with loved ones and social harmony. Travel and acquisition were also prognosticated. Around the time of his Sun *dasa* (January 20, 1986, to January 19, 1992), the Sun's placement in his *bhavacakra* (see "The Sun in the Various Houses") is accentuated. This suggests that his education, children, creative work, speculation, level of intelligence, past-life karma, romances, and entertainment interests are highlighted (see "Constructing the *Bhavacakra*"). His Moon *dasa* (January 20, 1992, to January 19, 2002) marks a good time to start a new business, achieve success in publishing, and attain harmony in his life. His mother, wife, or children will also be fortunate. His Mars *dasa* (January 20, 2002, to January 19, 2009) heralds a time to develop a new health and fitness regimen to bolster his health. Travel, adventure, and action are all possible. Determination can be applied to any undertaking, and assistance from friends is beneficial. During his Moon's North Node *dasa* (January 20, 2009, to January 19, 2027), success, wealth, and travel are possible. The Jupiter *dasa* (January 20, 2027, to January 19, 2043) of Peter's life is a very fortunate and prosperous period. Professional success and an interest in philosophy, religion, or the law occur during this period. The practitioner would continue in this same manner to determine the direction of his life during his Saturn *dasa* (January 20, 2043, to January 19, 2062); his Mercury *dasa* (January 20, 2062, to January 19, 2079); and his Moon's South Node *dasa* (January 20, 2079, to January 19, 2086).

Vedic astrology provides a roadmap to the strengths and weaknesses inherent in an individual. Attributing spiritual and physical abilities to past-life karma, relationships with family, friends, spouse, or partners, as well as celestially prescribed professional, marital, or social destiny.

Ultimately, the information derived from this complex astrological system is used to achieve enlightenment, freeing the individual from karmic debt and the compulsions represented by relationships among the various planets. A Western adept of Vedic astrology, Linda Johnsen, describes the application of astrology in India: "People don't just go to a *jysotishi* [astrologer] to see what's going to happen—if something untoward is predicted. They want to know what they can do about it. Sometimes the answer is nothing, but in most cases *jyostishis* will prescribe chanting *mantras* and *stotras,* giving charitable gifts, taking pilgrimages, etc. to help the individual redirect the course of his or her negative karma and/or enhance their positive karma."

As mentioned at the beginning of this chapter, this Moon-school tradition also embraces many facets of Vedic religious dogma, including beliefs about the planets and their associated deities. Even though Tibetan astrology was greatly influenced by this spiritual side of the Vedic tradition, only the mathematical and scientific aspects exerted any significant influence upon Chinese astrology. The same holds true of Vedic astrology's effect upon the structure of Arabian astrology.

Casting Lots

CALCULATION OF THE ARABIAN PARTS

Arabian astrology (also known as Tajika) is a Sun-school discipline that was practiced throughout the Egyptian, Persian, and Muslim empires. It shares the same mathematical complexity found in the Vedic, Judaic, and Western traditions. Just like its Sun-school counterparts (the Judaic and Western traditions), it applies the tropical zodiac. Arabian astrology is secular in its general focus, just like Western and Chinese astrology. In fact, the revival of the Parts' use among some modern Western astrologers is easy to comprehend since an individual's financial prospects, sex life, and social status are the primary concerns of the Arabian tradition.[1]

Although at one point this tradition employed a version of the lunar mansions, called the *manazils*, that are similar to the Chinese *sieu* and the Vedic *naksatras* (see "The Moon School" in chapter 2), their application in Arabian delineation is generally unknown. What is known is that much of modern-day Western astrology was adapted from early Arabian methods. However, a unique portion of Arabian astrology was not wholly embraced by the knowledge-hungry Western astrological community during the Renaissance. The corollary points known as the "fates of the houses" or the Arabian Parts whose origins can be traced to an ancient Western astrological method were not generally incorporated into post-Renaissance Western astrological procedures, with the exception of the Part of Fortune.

The Arabian Parts were originally based on a series of Western astrological

---

1.   During the past few decades, some modern Western astrologers have even introduced a number of contemporary variations, replacing Parts that were not adequately documented or do not fulfill contemporary needs.

equations called the Seven Lots, which were developed by the ancient Greeks.[2] The Lots were believed to mirror or enhance the delineation of the planetary positions in a natal horoscope. Each Lot pinpointed a specific location between the positions of the Ascendant (cusp of House I) and a given planet along the 360°00' circle of the zodiac. For example, the Lot of Fortune represented a point between the Ascendant's and the Moon's positions on the zodiac. This was disclosed by adding the Ascendant's and Moon's positions and subtracting the Sun's position from the sum. (The Lots of Necessity, Eros, Daimon, Audacity, Nemesis, and Victory followed the same pattern, determining the midpoint between the Ascendant and Saturn, Venus, Mercury, the Sun, Mars, and Jupiter.) More than forty of these equations were developed over the next three centuries by both Greek and Egyptian astrologers.

Based on this mathematical theory, Arabian practitioners developed an initial ninety-seven corollary points from the original seven. That number gradually increased to over 143 Arabian Parts by the eleventh century. Although most of the Parts focus on the Ascendant's relationship with planets, house cusps, or nodes, there are some that centralize on the relationship between two Parts.

Ancient astrologers believed each of the Arabian Parts[3] enabled them to refine a natal delineation, answer horary questions, and verify planetary indicators in an individual's horoscope. This concept of verification or elaboration upon what is found in a natal chart appears to be unique to both Arabian astrology and the Vedic tradition, which employs one or more divisional charts (*sodasavargas*) to determine the significance or veracity of information disclosed by either a *rasicakra* (sign chart) or a *bhavacakra* (house chart).

The two main causes for the Parts' initial demise were the mass destruction of Arabian scholarly texts by Christian armies during the Crusades, and the complexity of the calculations. Arabian astrology was deemed heretical by medieval European theologians and nobles who fervently set out to eradicate any interest in non-Christian scholarship. The works of Arabian astrologers such as Albumazar and Al'biruni survived only as excerpts in books published by the first-century Egyptian astrologer Claudius Ptolemy, the eleventh-century Judaic astrologer Abraham ben Meir ibn Ezra, and the thirteenth-century Italian astrologer Guido Bonatti. Tragically, the existing method used to calculate and interpret most of the Arabian Parts is only partial, and the procedures applied to other Parts have completely disappeared.

---

2.   The early Western astrological traditions include Chaldean, Babylonian, Greek, Egyptian, and Roman.
3.   These corollary points are sometimes called Arabian Directions or Arabian Points.

According to Bonatti, the Arabian Parts are subdivided into three major categories: the planetary Arabian Parts, the house Arabian Parts, and the horary Arabian Parts. For the sake of space, the following chapter covers only the calculation and interpretation of the planetary and house Arabian Parts. The horary Arabian Parts, which concentrate on such obscurities as the success of wheat harvests or the outcome of battle, are too numerous to mention here. Furthermore, the documentation of these Parts is somewhat sketchy in surviving texts such as Bonatti's *Liber Astronomiae* and Ptolemy's *Tetrabiblos*.

This chapter begins by constructing a natal horoscope that is almost identical to a Western natal chart and outlining the general process employed in the calculation of the Arabian Parts. It then details the specific methods for calculating and interpreting thirty-seven Arabian Parts, which are divided into two groups: planetary Arabian Parts, which are similar to the original Seven Lots, and house Arabian Parts, which are subdivided into twelve groups.

AN OVERVIEW OF ARABIAN PART CALCULATION AND INTERPRETATION

Unlike the Judaic and Western natal charts presented in chapters 7 and 8, ancient Arabian natal horoscopes were constructed according to the tropical zodiac, using the Equal House system.[4] Some modern Western astrologers, however, use the data accumulated from conventional tropical-zodiac natal horoscopes created according to the Placidus system, such as those found in chapter 8, figs. 8.2 and 8.3. For the sake of simplicity and comparison with the other traditions presented in this book, data derived from Western natal horoscopes will be employed in the calculations made throughout this chapter. Step-by-step details on the calculation and construction of a tropical-zodiac Western natal horoscope can be found in chapter 8. For convenience, these same charts are presented as figs. 6.1 and 6.2.

Each natal horoscope represents the 360°00' circle of the zodiac. In the Equal House system, this circle is divided into twelve segments of 30°00' each, which are called houses. However, in other house-division systems such as the Placidus

---

4. The Equal House system places every house cusp exactly one zodiac sign (or 30°00') from the Ascendant's position expressed in degrees and minutes. In other words, if the Ascendant is situated at 01°♒57', the cusp of House II is located 30°00' or one zodiac sign away from the Ascendant (01°♓57') as determined in the calculation below:

Ascendant (01°♒57')	11	01°	57'	
+ one zodiac sign	01	00°	00'	
House II cusp	12	01°	57'	(01°♓57')

(Note: For an explanation of the numeric positions for various zodiac signs, see page 261.)

Houses III through XII would continue through the sequential order of the zodiac. Thus, the cusp of House III occupies 01°♈57', the cusp of House IV resides at 01°♉57', and so forth.

FIGURE 6.1. ALICE T.'s WESTERN NATAL HOROSCOPE.

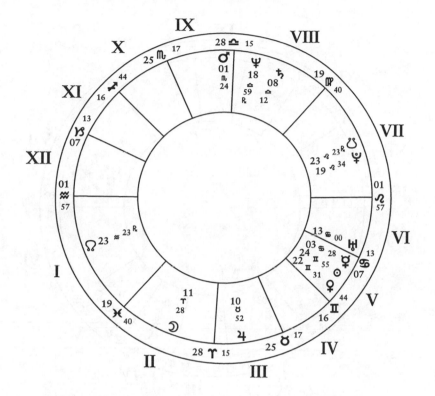

method that is employed by most Western astrologers (see introduction to chapter 8), these twelve unequal segments can vary in size from 15°00′ to 45°00′. Each house is believed to govern a specific facet of an individual's life, as shown below:

House I   personality
House II   finances
House III   mental pursuits and siblings
House IV   home, family, and father
House V   creativity, children, and speculation
House VI   health, employment, and employees
House VII   marriage and partnerships
House VIII   legacies, other people's money, and death
House IX   journeys, religion, and higher education
House X   professional and social standing
House XI   friends and freelance income
House XII   personal limitations

This house identification system is identical to the one used in Judaic and Western astrology, and varies only slightly from the house systems applied in the Vedic (see "Constructing the *Bhavacakra*" in chapter 5) and Chinese (see chapter 3,

FIGURE 6.2. PETER C.'s WESTERN NATAL HOROSCOPE.

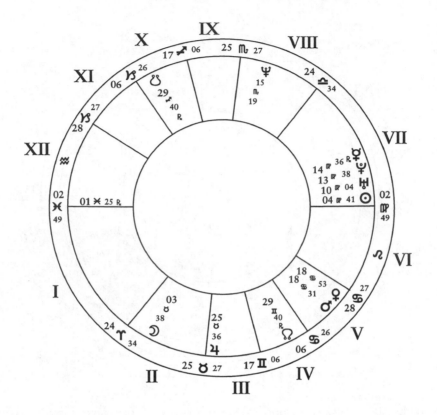

fig. 3.10) traditions. This system is frequently referenced throughout the interpretations of the Arabian Parts.

Because each house is apportioned a certain number of degrees and minutes out of the total 360°00' zodiac circle, the beginning of each house is identified in the outer ring of a natal horoscope by degrees, the symbol of the zodiac sign (which follows the sequential order shown on page 261), and minutes. For example, in Alice's natal chart (fig. 6.1), House I or the Ascendant begins at 01°♒57' (one degree, fifty-seven minutes in the zodiac sign Aquarius). Moving counterclockwise, House II begins at 19°♓40' (nineteen degrees, forty minutes in the zodiac sign Pisces). Continuing in a counterclockwise fashion throughout the remaining ten houses, House III begins at 28°♈16' (twenty-eight degrees, sixteen minutes in the zodiac sign Aries). House IV begins at 25°♉17' (twenty-five degrees, seventeen minutes in the zodiac sign Taurus). House V begins at 16°♊44' (sixteen degrees, forty-four minutes in the zodiac sign Gemini). House VI begins at 07°♋13' (seven degrees, thirteen minutes in the zodiac sign Cancer). House VII begins at 01°♌57' (one degree, fifty-seven minutes in the zodiac sign Leo). House VIII begins at 19° ♍40' (nineteen degrees, forty minutes in the zodiac sign Virgo). House IX begins at

28°♎16′ (twenty-eight degrees, sixteen minutes in the zodiac sign Libra). House X begins at 25°♏17′ (twenty-five degrees, seventeen minutes in the zodiac sign Scorpio). House XI begins at 16°♐44′ (sixteen degrees, forty-four minutes in the zodiac sign Sagittarius). And House XII begins at 07°♑13′ (seven degrees, thirteen minutes in the zodiac sign Capricorn).

All twelve zodiac signs must be placed in the outer ring of the horoscope. However, there are instances when one or two zodiac signs might not be positioned in the twelve house cusps. For example, two zodiac signs are missing from the sequence in Peter's chart (fig. 6.2): Leo (♌), which should appear between Cancer (♋, House VI in fig. 6.2) and Virgo (♍, House VII in fig. 6.2); and Aquarius (♒), which should appear between Capricorn (♑, House XII in fig. 6.2) and Pisces (♓, House I in fig. 6.2). These are called "intercepted signs" because each has been overtaken since more than one house-cusp position is assigned to the same zodiac sign. This occurs at various points in the Table of Houses and after the house positions have been adjusted to reflect the actual time and place of a given birth.

Nevertheless, these intercepted zodiac signs must be taken into consideration during the delineation process. So each zodiac sign is placed in the outer ring between the cusps where each zodiac sign should have appeared. Therefore, the symbol for Leo (♌) is placed between House VI (28°♋27′ in fig. 6.2) and House VII (02°♍49′ in fig. 6.2); the sign for Aquarius (♒) is placed between House XII (28°♑27′ in fig. 6.2) and House I (02°♓49′ in fig. 6.2).

To facilitate the addition and subtraction of planetary, house, and node positions from the Ascendant's position, the zodiac sign associated with each position is converted to a number in the same fashion as shown in chapter 5 (fig. 5.3, third column), in which each of the twelve zodiac signs is simply represented by the sign's numeric position in the zodiac's sequential order. For convenience, this information is detailed below:

Aries (♈)	is designated as 1.
Taurus (♉)	is designated as 2.
Gemini (♊)	is designated as 3.
Cancer (♋)	is designated as 4.
Leo (♌)	is designated as 5.
Virgo (♍)	is designated as 6.
Libra (♎)	is designated as 7.
Scorpio (♏)	is designated as 8.
Sagittarius (♐)	is designated as 9.
Capricorn (♑)	is designated as 10.
Aquarius (♒)	is designated as 11.
Pisces (♓)	is designated as 12.

There are no formal charts, grids, or other visual aids constructed for the Arabian Parts. Instead, astrologers simply make notes of each Part's position for incorporation into the individual's chart delineation.

Calculating an Arabian Part

Generally speaking, an Arabian Part is calculated by adding a planetary position's sign number (see above), degrees, and minutes to the Ascendant position's zodiac sign number (see above), degrees, and minutes, and subtracting another planetary position's sign number (see above), degrees, and minutes. For example, to find Alice's Part of Fortune, the Moon (☽ 11°♈28′ in fig. 6.1) is added to her Ascendant (01°♒57′ in fig. 6.1, House I) and then the Sun is subtracted (☉ 24° ♊55′ in fig. 6.1) from this figure by converting the zodiac signs to sign numbers (see above) and adding the sign numbers, degrees, and minutes in the following fashion:

Ascendant (01°♒57′)	11	01°	57′	*(from fig. 6.1, House I)*
+ Moon (☽ 11°♈28′)	01	11°	28′	*(from fig. 6.1)*
	12	12°	85′	*(signs, degrees, and minutes)*

Each zodiac sign equals 30°00′[5] of the zodiac's 360°00′ circle; this is an important fact to remember when doing these calculations. An Arabian Part—which is the result of the subtraction of the next planetary position's sign, degrees, and minutes—must be in positive integers. In order to achieve this, it frequently becomes necessary to transfer one sign's worth of degrees (30°00′) from the planetary position's zodiac sign to the planetary position's degrees. For example, the sum above can be written down as follows to facilitate the next step in the calculation:

	11	42°	85′	*(converted sum from above)*

The converted sum can then be used to complete the equation as follows:

	11	42°	85′	*(converted sum from above)*
− Sun (☉ 24°♊55′)	03	24°	55′	*(from fig. 6.1)*
	08	18°	30′	*(18°♏ 30′ Part of Fortune)*

The remainder's zodiac sign number is then converted back into a sign symbol (see above) and written down with the degrees and minutes in the astrologer's notes as 18°♏ 30′.

---

5. This figure is read as "thirty degrees, zero minutes." The zodiac sign's maximum degrees, 30°00′, can also be represented as 29°60′ in a calculation, since 01°00′ is equal to 00°60′.

Positioning and Interpreting an Arabian Part

The placement of an Arabian Part in the natal horoscope is determined by the house it occupies. For example, Alice's Part of Fortune (18°♏ 30′, above) is placed in her House IX, which begins at 28°♎16′ (fig. 6.1) and ends at 25°♏ 17′: a house that occupies 27°01′ of the total 360°00′ horoscope. (The zodiac sign Libra [♎] ends with 30°♎00′ within this house because all zodiac signs are only apportioned 30°00′ within the zodiac circle. The zodiac sign Scorpio [♏] begins at 00°♏00′ and ends in this house at 25°♏17′, which is the beginning of House X. Since 18°30′ comes before 25°17′ in numeric order, the Part of Fortune is positioned in House IX.)

Once an Arabian Part is calculated and positioned in a house in the individual's horoscope, it is delineated according to the house it occupies, the condition of the house planetary ruler, or the angle (aspect) it forms with another planet (see "Delineating Planetary Aspects" in chapter 8), depending upon the specific Part.

THE PLANETARY ARABIAN PARTS

Since the extra-Saturnian planets (Uranus [♅], Neptune [♆], and Pluto [♇]) were unknown to ancient Arabian astrologers and astronomers, there are only seven planetary Arabian Parts. The calculation and interpretation of two of these will be presented in this section. They are the Part of Fortune (Part of the Moon [☽]), and the Part of the Spirit (Part of the Sun [☉]). The remaining planetary Arabian Parts—the Part of Love and Concord (Part of Venus [♀]),[6] Part of Happiness (Part of Jupiter[♃]),[7] Part of Daring (Part of Mars [♂]),[8] Part of Heaviness

---

6. According to modern astrologers, issues about love are best disclosed by Parts associated with House VII, which are discussed later in this chapter. The Part of Love and Concord (Part of Venus [♀]) influences the person's desires for love, concord, and physical pleasures. The Part is derived by adding the Ascendant's position to Venus's position and subtracting the Sun's position from the sum. An early version, documented by Bonatti, subtracts the Arabian Part of the Future (*Pars Futurorum*) from the Part of Fortune (see "The Part of Fortune," page 264) rather than the Sun's position, which is used by modern Western astrologers to derive this same projection.

7. According to modern astrologers, issues about happiness and achievement are best disclosed by Parts associated with Houses IX and XI, which are discussed later in this chapter. The Part of Happiness (Part of Jupiter [♃]) influences the person's potential for happiness, to receive assistance, and to achieve honor. (This Part is called the Part of Increase by Nicholas deVore in his *Encyclopedia of Astrology* [1947]). It is derived by adding the Ascendant's position to Jupiter's position and subtracting the Sun's position from the sum. Although modern Western astrologers subtract the Sun's position to derive this Part, Bonatti indicated that the practitioner should subtract the Arabian Part of the Future (*Pars Futurorum*). However, this early version required additional calculation and fell into disuse.

8. According to modern astrologers, issues about intellect and mental pursuits are best disclosed by Parts associated with Houses III or IX, which are discussed later in this chapter. The Part of Daring (Part of Mars [♂]) influences the person's mental keenness, impulsiveness, and daring. (This Part is called the Part of Passion by Nicholas deVore). It's derived by adding the Ascendant's position to Mars's position and subtracting the Sun's position from the sum. An alternate method used by Bonatti subtracts the Part of Fortune (see "The Part of Fortune," page 264) rather than the Sun's position, which is used by modern Western astrologers to derive this Part.

•

(Part of Saturn[♄]),[9] and Part of Ordinary Intellect (Part of Mercury [☿])[10]—are not delineated by modern astrologers and there is little information given as to their delineation by ancient Arabian practitioners. Therefore, they will not be discussed in this section.

The planetary Arabian Parts are generally plotted by adding the specific planet's position to the Ascendant's position and subtracting a luminary's position (either the Sun [☉] or the Moon [☽]). As mentioned earlier, an Arabian Part can be delineated in one of three ways: according to the house it occupies, the condition of the house planetary ruler, or the angle (aspect) it forms with another planet (see "Delineating Planetary Aspects" in chapter 8). No set rule for interpretation was ever established in either the ancient or modern system of the Arabian Parts.

The Part of Fortune

The Part of Fortune (Part of the Moon [☽]) indicates the person's chances for worldly success, and is the most popular of the Arabian Parts, even in modern times.[11] Equally distant in longitude (degrees and minutes) from the Ascendant as the Moon (☽) is from the Sun(☉), the Part is derived by adding the Ascendant's position in degrees and minutes to the Moon's position in degrees and minutes and subtracting the Sun's position in degrees and minutes from the sum.

Alice T.:

Ascendant (01°♒57')	11	01°	57'	(from fig. 6.1, House I)
+ Moon (☽ 11°♈28')	01	11°	28'	(from fig. 6.1)
	12	12°	85'	(signs, degrees, and minutes)
	11	42°	85'	(converted sum from above)
− Sun (☉ 24°♊55')	03	24°	55'	(from fig. 6.1)
	08	18°	30'	(18°♏ 30' Part of Fortune)

---

9. According to modern astrologers, issues about intellect and mental pursuits are best disclosed by Parts associated with Houses III or IX, which are discussed later in this chapter. The Part of Heaviness (Part of Saturn [♄]) influences the person's memory, philosophic attitude, and relationship to the Earth and its by-products. (Nicholas deVore calls this the Part of Fatality.) The Part is derived by adding the Ascendant's position to Saturn's position and subtracting the Sun's position from the sum. According to Bonatti's translations, an alternate way to derive this Part is to subtract the Part of Fortune (see "The Part of Fortune," above) instead of the Sun's position from the sum.

10. According to modern astrologers, issues about intellect and mental pursuits are best disclosed by Parts associated with Houses III or IX, which are discussed later in this chapter. The Part of Ordinary Intellect (Part of Mercury [☿]) influences the person's ability to reason, negotiate, and write, as well as his or her interest in the sciences. (This is called the Part of Commerce in Nicholas deVore's *Encyclopedia of Astrology*.) The Part is derived by adding the Ascendant's position to Mercury's position and subtracting the Sun's position from the sum. Bonatti's treatise applied an earlier method that subtracts the Part of Fortune (see "The Part of Fortune," above) from the Part of the Future (*Pars Futurorum*) to derive this Part, rather than the Sun's position, which is employed by modern Western astrologers.

11. The Part of Fortune is sometimes used to verify the Moon's particular phase at the time of the person's birth. If the Part occupies the Ascendant (House I), it's a New Moon. If the Part occupies House VII, it's a Full Moon. If the Part occupies House X, there's a fourth-quarter Moon. And if the Part occupies House IV, there's a second-quarter Moon. In some forms of Western astrology, the Moon's phase at the time of birth increases or decreases its influence on the individual's emotional makeup.

Peter C.:

Ascendant (02°♓49′)	12	02°	49′	(*from fig. 6.2, House I*)
+ Moon (☽ 03°♉38′)	02	03°	38′	(*from fig. 6.2*)
	14	05°	87′	(*signs, degrees, and minutes*)
	13	35°	87′	(*converted sum from above*)
− Sun (☉ 04°♍41′)	06	04°	41′	(*from fig. 6.2*)
	07	31°	46′	(*remainder*)
	08	01°	46′	(01°♏ 46′ *Part of Fortune*)[12]

Ptolemy delineated the Part by consulting its planetary ruler, noting that "Saturn [traditional ruler of both Capricorn and Aquarius] will affect the acquirement of wealth by means of buildings, agriculture, or navigation; Jupiter [traditional ruler of both Sagittarius and Pisces], by holding some government position, or office of trust, or by the priesthood; Mars [traditional ruler of both Aries and Scorpio], by the army or military command; Venus [traditional ruler of both Taurus and Libra] by means of friends, by the dowry of wives, or by other gifts proceeding from women; and Mercury [traditional ruler of both Gemini and Virgo] by the sciences and by trade."[13] But he did not mention how the Sun [traditional ruler of Leo] and the Moon [traditional ruler of Cancer] affect the individual when ruling this Part. Since Alice's (18°♏30′) and Peter's (01°♏46′) Parts of Fortune are situated in Scorpio, which is ruled by Mars, both reap their fortunes through the army or military command according to Ptolemy's method.

In modern practice, this particular Part is interpreted according to its placement in an individual's horoscope (see "Positioning and Interpreting an Arabian Part," page 263). For example, as discussed earlier in this chapter, Alice's Part of Fortune (18°♏30′) occupies House IX in her natal horoscope because it is situated between House IX (28°♎15′) and House X (25°♏17′) in numeric order (see "Positioning and Interpreting an Arabian Part"). And Peter's Part of Fortune (01° ♏46′) occupies House VIII in his natal horoscope because it is situated between House VIII (24°♎34′) and House IX (25°♏27′) in numeric order (see "Positioning and Interpreting an Arabian Part").

Based on their understanding of this Part, modern Western astrologers Llewellyn George and Press Roberts delineated the Part of Fortune's influence by

---

12. This remainder needed to be converted by adding one full sign (30°00′) to the remainder's sign number since the degrees in the resulting Part must be less than 30°00′.

13. J. M. Ashmand's translation of Ptolemy's *Tetrabiblos*, Chapter II ("The Fortune of Wealth") of Book IV, appears to apply the traditional rulerships of the signs. Pluto [♇], Neptune [♆], and Uranus [♅] had not been discovered in Ptolemy's day. Consequently, Mars ruled both Scorpio and Aries, Saturn ruled both Capricorn and Aquarius, and Jupiter ruled both Pisces and Sagittarius.

the house it occupies in the person's chart. According to them, an individual would have a propensity to prosper as follows:

House I	from one's own industry, especially if the Part is aspected (see "Locating Planetary Aspects" in chapter 8) with Jupiter (♃) or Venus (♀)
House II	through property, employment, and business
House III	from writings, publishing, and advertising, brethren, and short journeys
House IV	through treasure, metals, minerals, and land (this is also a sign of a stable patrimony)
House V	through speculation, children, young people, and ambassadors, and the person's children also prosper
House VI	from prosperous aunts, uncles, employees, small animals, and service industries including health
House VII	through conquest, partnerships, marriage, and bargains
House VIII	from inheritance, other people's money, and the dead
House IX	through churches, educational properties, foreigners, inventions, the occult, and books
House X	from business assets, while honors and promotions come from lucky events and situations
House XI	through friends in high places
House XII	from secret, unexpected, or quiet sources (naturally, if this Part forms a square [90°00′ distance, ±06°00′] or an opposition [180°00′ distance, ±06°00′] with another planet [see "Locating Planetary Aspects" in chapter 8], the person suffers losses in the same areas)

Alice's Part of Fortune (18°♏ 30′) occupies House IX in her natal horoscope (see fig. 6.1), she reaps good fortune through churches, educational properties, foreigners, inventions, the occult, and books. Because Peter's Part of Fortune (01°♏ 46′) occupies House VIII in his natal horoscope (see fig. 6.2), his fortunes come from inheritance, from other people's money, and from the dead.

The Part of Spirit

Bonatti noted that the Part of Fortune's direct complement is the Part of Spirit (Part of the Sun [☉]), which influences the person's spiritual or intangible world. Like day and night, the equation for the Part of Spirit is the Part of Fortune's opposite. This Part is derived by adding the Ascendant's position to the Sun's position and subtracting the Moon's position from the sum. Then it is interpreted by the house it occupies in the individual's horoscope (see "Positioning and Interpreting an Arabian Part," page 263).

Alice T.:

Ascendant (01°♒57')	11	01°	57'	(from fig. 6.1, House I)
+ Sun (☉ 24°♊55')	03	24°	55'	(from fig. 6.1)
	14	25°	112'	(signs, degrees, and minutes)
− Moon (☽ 11°♈28')	01	11°	28'	(from fig. 6.1)
	13	14°	84'	(remainder)
	01	15°	24'	(15°♈24' Part of Spirit)[14]

Peter C.:

Ascendant (02°♓49')	12	02°	49'	(from fig. 6.2, House I)
+ Sun (☉ 04°♍41')	06	04°	41'	(from fig. 6.2)
	18	06°	90'	(signs, degrees, and minutes)
− Moon (☽ 03°♉38')	02	03°	38'	(from fig. 6.2)
	16	03°	52'	(remainder)
	04	03°	52'	(03°♋52' Part of Spirit)[15]

If this Part is situated in Houses I, II, III, or XII, the person is a self-starter. If it is positioned in Houses IV, V, VI, or VII, he or she is dependent on the leadership and actions of others. If it occupies Houses VIII, IX, X, or XI, he or she is obsessed with the desire for physical or intellectual achievement.

For example, Alice's Part of Spirit (15°♈24') is situated in her House II (see "Positioning and Interpreting an Arabian Part," page 263), indicating that she is a self-starter. Peter's Part of Spirit (03°♋52') occupies House IV (see "Positioning and Interpreting an Arabian Part"), suggesting that he is dependent on the leadership and actions of others.

---

14. This remainder needed to be converted for two reasons: First, the sign number in the remainder exceeds the total number of zodiac signs (12). Therefore, 12 is subtracted from the remainder (13) to derive the final sign number, 1. Second, and similarly, the number of minutes in the remainder (84') exceeds 59'. Since 60' equal 01°, 60' are subtracted from the total minutes in the remainder (84') and 01° is added to the number of degrees in the remainder (14°), increasing the degrees to 15°.

15. This remainder needed to be converted because the sign number in the remainder exceeds the total number of zodiac signs (12). Therefore, 12 is subtracted from the remainder (16) to derive the final sign number, 4.

THE HOUSE ARABIAN PARTS

Unlike the planetary Arabian Parts in the previous section, the majority of Arabian Parts relate to the horoscope's twelve houses (see "An Overview of Arabian Part Calculation and Interpretation," page 258). Astrologers rarely calculate all of the house Arabian Parts, which are grouped according to their association with a specific house throughout this section. In fact, practitioners usually select only a few house Arabian Parts to calculate and interpret if there is special interest expressed in a particular facet of life such as finances, marriage, or profession. The house Arabian Parts are also employed if verification or enhancement of a planetary or house delineation is needed while developing a personality profile from a natal horoscope.

The calculation and interpretation of each house Arabian Part pertaining to House I activities (specifically, personality) will be covered in the section titled "Parts Associated with House I." These have names such as the Part of Life, Root of Life, Part of Aptness, Part of Understanding, and Part of Durability. House Arabian Parts pertaining to House II activities (specifically, finances) will be covered in the section titled "Part Associated with the House II." These have names such as the Part of Goods, Part of Moneylenders, Part of Happiness, and Part of Collection. The same holds true for the house Arabian Parts associated with Houses III through XII.

The house Arabian Parts are generally plotted by the same method as the planetary Arabian Parts: by adding the specific planet's position to the Ascendant's position and subtracting another planet's position. As mentioned earlier, an Arabian Part can be delineated in one of three ways: according to the house it occupies, to the condition of the house planetary ruler, or to the angle (or aspect) it forms with another planet (see "Delineating Planetary Aspects" in chapter 8). No set rule for interpretation was ever established in either the ancient or modern system of the Arabian Parts.

Parts Associated with House I

Five house Arabian Parts used by ancient astrologers correspond to House I (the Ascendant) in a person's horoscope: the Part of Life, Root of Life (*Pars Hyleg*),[16]

---

16. The Pars Hyleg, or *radix vitae* (root of life), was reportedly used during the time of the ninth-century astrologer Albumazar. It signifies the disposition of the person's whole physical, spiritual, and emotional being. No particular delineation was narrated by Bonatti in his treatise, but he did note that the calculation is the reverse of the Part of Life. It is derived by adding the Ascendant's position to the position of the Full Moon that immediately precedes the birth and subtracting the Moon's position from the sum. Albumazar applied this Part in a manner similar to the Almochoden (also called Alcohoden) as an indication of the person's propensity for good health and

Part of Aptness, Part of Understanding, and Part of Durability. Each Part analyzes a facet of the person's personality as it is perceived by the outside world. The methods for calculating and delineating four of these Parts are included in this section. These are the Part of Life, Part of Aptness, Part of Understanding, and Part of Durability.

The Part of Life

The most important of the five house Arabian Parts associated with House I is the Part of Life, which signifies the person's general emotional state or attitude toward life. The Part is derived by adding the Ascendant's position to the Moon's position and subtracting from the sum the position of the Full Moon that immediately precedes the subject's birth.[17] The Part is then interpreted according to the house it occupies in the horoscope (see "Positioning and Interpreting an Arabian Part," page 263).

Alice T.:

Ascendant (01°♒57')	11	01°	57'	(from fig. 6.1, House I)
+ Moon (☽ 11°♈28')	01	11°	28'	(from fig. 6.1)
	12	12°	85'	(signs, degrees, and minutes)
	11	42°	85'	(converted sum from above)
Full Moon (June 6, 1952)				
– (☽ 22°♏25')	08	22°	25'	(from an ephemeris)
	03	20°	60'	(remainder)
	03	21°	00'	(21°♊00', Part of Life)[18]

Peter C.:

Ascendant (02°♓49')	12	02°	49'	(from fig. 6.2, House I)
+ Moon (☽ 03°♉38')	02	03°	38'	(from fig. 6.2)
	14	05°	87'	(signs, degrees, and minutes)
	13	35°	87'	(converted sum from above)

---

longevity. The Almochoden occurs when a planet is positioned in one of the hylegical degrees—places that induce the most beneficial influence on longevity in any chart. These places include: 05°00'–25°00' below the Ascendant (House I cusp); 05°00'–25°00' above the Descendant (House VII cusp); or in the area lying from 05°00' below the House IX cusp to 25°00' above the House XI cusp.

17. According to Bonatti, an earlier method subtracted Saturn's position from Jupiter's position rather than applying the Moon at birth and the preceding Full Moon shown in this example.

18. This remainder needed to be converted because the number of minutes in the remainder (68') exceeds 59'. Since 60' equal 01°, 60' are subtracted from the total minutes in the remainder (68'), and 01° is added to the number of degrees in the remainder (20°), increasing the degrees to 21°.

Full Moon (August 26, 1964)

− (☽ 09°♈24′)	01	09°	24′	*(from an ephemeris)*
	12	24°	63′	*(remainder)*
	12	25°	03′	*(25°♓03′, Part of Life)*[19]

Ptolemy and Bonatti said little about this Part's delineation. But Western astrologers like Press Roberts appear to have interpreted the Part's influence by the house it occupies (see "Positioning and Interpreting an Arabian Part," page 263) according to the material below:

House I	emotionally self-sufficient and self-contained
House II	emotionally dependent upon financial security
House III	communicative about his or her feelings
House IV	dependent upon domestic security
House V	emotionally dependent upon love and pleasure
House VI	needs to serve or assist other people
House VII	emotionally dependent upon having a spouse or partner
House VIII	somewhat morbid, and driven by thoughts about the dead and death
House IX	spiritually and intellectually driven
House X	driven by work and achievement
House XI	emotionally dependent on friends and associates
House XII	secretive about his or her true feelings

Alice's Part of Life (21°♊00′) resides in House V (see "Positioning and Interpreting an Arabian Part," page 263). Therefore, she is emotionally dependent upon love and the pursuit of pleasure. In direct contrast, Peter's Part of Life (25°♓03′) is positioned in his House I (see "Positioning and Interpreting an Arabian Part"), indicating that he is emotionally self-contained and self-sufficient.

Some practitioners also believed that if the Part forms an aspect (see "Delineat-

---

19. This remainder needed to be converted because the number of minutes in the remainder (63′) exceeds 59′. Since 60′ equal 01°, 60′ are subtracted from the total minutes in the remainder (63′), and 01° is added to the number of degrees in the remainder (24°), increasing the degrees to 25°.

ing Planetary Aspects" in Chapter 8) with Venus (♀), Jupiter (♃), or the Sun (☉) as each is positioned in a given chart, the person has a very positive outlook. For example, Peter's Part (25°♓03′) forms a sextile[20] to Jupiter (♃ 25°♉36′ in fig. 6.2); and Alice's Part (21°♊00′) forms a conjunction to both the Sun (☉ 24°♊55′ in fig. 6.1) and Venus (♀ 22°♊31′ in fig. 6.1).[21] If it forms an aspect (see "Locating Planetary Aspects" in chapter 8) with Mars (♂) in a chart, the person has an angry nature. If it forms an aspect (see "Delineating Planetary Aspects" in Chapter 8) with Uranus (♅) in a chart, the person encounters radical and unexpected changes of attitude. If the Part forms an aspect (see "Delineating Planetary Aspects" in Chapter 8) with Mercury (☿) or Neptune (♆) in a chart, the person encounters many mental or emotional changes. For example, Alice's Part (21°♊00′) forms a trine[22] to Neptune (♆ 18°♎59′ in fig. 6.1), indicating that such changes are possible.

---

20. The distance between Peter's Part of Life (25°♓03′) and Jupiter (♃ 25°♉36′) is determined by subtracting the two positions as shown below:

Jupiter (♃ 25°♉36′)	14	25°	36′	*(12 signs are added to facilitate calculation)*
− Part of Life (25°♓03′)	12	25°	03′
	02	00°	33′	*(remainder)*

The two zodiac signs of difference are then converted into degrees (°) by multiplying 2 by 30°00′ (the complete distance of a zodiac sign) and adding the result to the existing degrees. Thus, the distance between the Part and the planet is 60°33′, forming a sextile (60°00′ distance, ±06°00′).

21. The distance between Alice's Part of Life (21°♊31′) and the Sun (☉ 24°♊55′) is determined by subtracting the two positions as shown below:

Sun (☉ 24°♊55′)	03	24°	55′
− Part of Life (21°♊00′)	03	21°	00′
	00	03°	55′

Thus, the distance between the Part and the planet forms a conjunction (00°00′ distance, ±06°00′) because the distance is 03°55′. Similarly, the distance between the Part and Venus is determined by subtracting the positions as shown below:

Venus (♀ 22°♊31′)	03	22°	31′
− Part of Life (21°♊00′)	03	21°	00′
	00	01°	31′

Thus, the distance between the Part and the planet forms a conjunction (00°00′ distance, ±06°00′) because the distance is 01°31′.

22. The distance between Alice's Part of Life (21°♊31′) and Neptune (♆ 18°♎59′) is determined by subtracting the two positions as shown below:

Neptune (♆ 18°♎59′)	07	18°	59′
− Part of Life (21°♊00′)	03	21°	00′
	03	27°	59′

The three zodiac signs of difference are then converted into degrees by multiplying 3 by 30°00′ (the complete distance of a zodiac sign) and adding the result to the existing degrees. Thus, the distance between the Part and the planet is 117°59′, forming a trine (120°00′ or 240°00′ distance, ±06°00′).

The Part of Aptness

The Arabian Part of Aptness influences the person's ability to act appropriately at any given moment. The Part is derived by adding the Ascendant's position to Mercury's position and subtracting Saturn's position from the sum. The Part is then interpreted according to the house it occupies (see "Positioning and Interpreting an Arabian Part," page 263).

Alice T.:

Ascendant (01°♒57')	11	01°	57'	(from fig. 6.1, House I)
+ Mercury (☿ 03°♋28')	04	03°	28'	(from fig. 6.1)
	15	04°	85'	(signs, degrees, and minutes)
	14	34°	85'	(converted sum from above)
− Saturn (♄ 08°♎12')	07	08°	12'	(from fig. 6.1)
	07	26°	73'	(remainder)
	07	27°	13'	(27°♎13', Part of Aptness)[23]

Peter C.:

Ascendant (02°♓49')	12	02°	49'	(from fig. 6.2, House I)
+ Mercury (☿ 14°♍36')	06	14°	36'	(from fig. 6.2)
	18	16°	85'	(signs, degrees, and minutes)
− Saturn (♄ 01°♓25')	12	01°	25'	(from fig. 6.2)
	06	15°	60'	(remainder)
	06	16°	00'	(16°♍00', Part of Aptness)[24]

Western astrologers delineate the Part's influence by the house it occupies (see "Positioning and Interpreting an Arabian Part," page 263) according to the material below:

House I   tends to follow his or her own values uncompromisingly, succeeding in any project he or she finishes

House II   succeeds as a leader or CEO, placing others before oneself

House III   use of practical application leads to achievement

---

23. This remainder needed to be converted because the number of minutes (') in the remainder (73') exceeds 59'. Since 60' equal 01°, 60' are subtracted from the total minutes in the remainder (73') and 01° is added to the number of degrees in the remainder (26°), increasing the degrees to 27°.

24. This remainder needed to be converted because the number of minutes in the remainder (60') exceeds 59'. Since 60' equal 01°, 60' are subtracted from the total minutes in the remainder (60'), and 01° is added to the number of degrees in the remainder (15°), increasing the degrees to 16°.

House IV	goals that encompass a broad range of interest and participation are achieved
House V	creativity and ability to inspire others are the keys to success
House VI	succeeds by serving others
House VII	able to make the most out of the least
House VIII	he or she serves as the spokesperson for others' ideas
House IX	the application of traditional family and national values, especially religion, leads to success
House X	acts well as the administrator or executor for a group
House XI	acts as the *vox populi* (voice of the people)
House XII	responds to a holistic view of humanity, and is most effective when working in an organized fashion

Alice's Part of Aptness (27°♎13′) occupies House VIII (see "Positioning and Interpreting an Arabian Part," page 263), which suggests that she serves as the spokesperson for others' ideas. Peter's Part of Aptness (16°♍00′) is positioned in House VII (see "Positioning and Interpreting an Arabian Part"), which indicates that he has the ability to make the most out of the least.

The Part of Understanding

The Arabian Part of Understanding focuses on the person's inherent wisdom, concentrating on reason, imagination, and speech. The Part is derived by adding the Ascendant's position to Mars's position and subtracting Mercury's position from the sum.[25] The Part is then interpreted according to the aspects (see "Locating Planetary Aspects" in chapter 8) it forms with various planets in the individual's horoscope.

Alice T.:

Ascendant (01°♒57′)	11	01°	57′	*(from fig. 6.1, House I)*
+ Mars (♂ 01°♏24′)	08	01°	24′	*(from fig. 6.1)*
	19	02°	81′	*(signs, degrees, and minutes)*

25. According to Bonatti, an earlier method applied a reverse calculation for a person born during the daytime hours, using this equation only for individuals born during the night. However, modern Western astrologers commonly apply the equation shown in the above examples for all subjects.

	18	32°	81′	*(converted sum from above)*
— Mercury (☿ 03°♋28′)	04	03°	28′	*(from fig. 6.1)*
	14	29°	53′	*(remainder)*
	02	29°	53′	*(29°♉53′, Part of Understanding)*[26]

Peter C.:

Ascendant (02°♓49′)	12	02°	49′	*(from fig. 6.2, House I)*
+ Mars (♂ 18°♋31′)	04	18°	31′	*(from fig. 6.2)*
	16	20°	80′	*(signs, degrees, and minutes)*
— Mercury (☿ 14°♍36′)	06	14°	36′	*(from fig. 6.2)*
	10	06°	44′	*(06°♑44′, Part of Understanding)*

Arabian astrologers such as Albumazar believed that the person in question would be rational, understanding, knowledgeable, thoughtful, and well-spoken if this Part were to form a conjunct (00°00′ distance, ±06°00′) aspect to the Ascendant's ruling planet[27] or form any type of aspect (see "Locating Planetary Aspects" in chapter 8) with the house planetary ruler physically occupied by the Part (see "The Part of Fortune," page 264). If Mercury (☿) forms a trine (120°00′ or 240°00′ distance, ±06°00′), sextile (60°00′ distance, ±06°00′), or even a square (90°00′ distance, ±06°00′) aspect with reception[28] (see "Delineating Planetary Aspects" in chapter 8) with this Part, the person is more emotional or subjective. If Mars (♂) forms the same type of aspects, however, the person will be wise, sharp-minded, and able to learn quickly and retain information that he or she has learned.

If this Part forms a conjunct (00°00′ distance, ±06°00′) aspect to the Sun (☉)

---

26. This remainder needed to be converted because the sign number in the remainder exceeds the total number of zodiac signs (12). Therefore, 12 is subtracted from the remainder (14) to derive the final sign number, 2.

27. Arabian astrologers applied the same planetary rulerships to the zodiac signs as their Vedic counterparts:

Sun (☉)	rules Leo (♌)
Moon (☽)	rules Cancer (♋)
Mercury (☿)	rules both Gemini (♊) and Virgo (♍)
Venus (♀)	rules both Taurus (♉) and Libra (♎)
Mars (♂)	rules both Aries (♈) and Scorpio (♏)
Jupiter (♃)	rules both Sagittarius (♐) and Pisces (♓)
Saturn (♄)	rules both Capricorn (♑) and Aquarius (♒)

28. When a planet is received by the dispositor (the ruler of the sign it occupies), it is in reception. For example, if the Sun (☉) enters House V, which is ruled by Gemini (♊), it is received by the house's dispositor, Mercury (☿), which is the planetary ruler of Gemini (see preceding footnote). If two planets enter zodiac signs that are planetary rulers of those zodiac signs, both entities are in mutual reception. For example, if the Sun enters House V, which is ruled by Gemini, while Mercury enters House VII, ruled by Leo (♌), both planets would be in mutual reception because the Sun rules the zodiac sign Leo, and Mercury rules the zodiac sign Gemini. Similarly, when a planet forms an aspect (see "Delineating the Planetary Aspects" in chapter 8) with a faster-moving planet, it is in reception. If, for example, the slower-orbiting planet Saturn (♄) forms an aspect with the faster-orbiting planet Mercury (☿), Saturn is in reception of the aspect.

or Jupiter (♃), the person is objective. If it forms a trine (120°00′ or 240°00′ distance, ±06°00′) or sextile (60°00′ distance, ±06°00′) aspect (see "Delineating Planetary Aspects" in Chapter 8) with Venus (♀), he or she is optimistic. If the Part forms any aspect (see "Delineating Planetary Aspects" in chapter 8) with Saturn (♄), however, then the individual easily becomes depressed. In Peter's case, the Part of Understanding (06°♑44′) forms a sextile (60°00′ distance, ±06°00′) aspect (see "Delineating Planetary Aspects" in Chapter 8) with Saturn (♄ 01°♓25′ in fig. 6.2), suggesting that he is optimistic.[29]

If the Sun (☉) or Jupiter (♃) forms an opposing (180°00′ distance, ±06°00′) or square (90°00′ distance, ±06°00′) aspect (see "Delineating Planetary Aspects" in Chapter 8) with the Part, confusion prevails in the afflicted house in the horoscope. If this Part forms an aspect with Mercury (☿) (see "Delineating Planetary Aspects" in chapter 8), the person is more emotional or subjective.[30] (This condition is exacerbated if the Part forms an aspect with the Moon [☽]. This is the case with Peter's Part of Understanding (06°♑44′), which forms a trine (120°00′ or 240°00′ distance, ±06°00′) aspect with the Moon (☽ 03°♉38′ in fig. 6.2).[31]

None of these conditions exist with Alice's Part of Understanding, so the Part would not be considered in a full interpretation of her House I. Consequently, the practitioner would learn nothing from the application of this Part, simply because none of the above conditions exist.

The Part of Durability

The Part of Durability indicates the condition of the person's whole being, including physical appearance. However, Albumazar apparently placed a great deal of

---

29. The distance between Peter's Part of Understanding (06°♑44′) and Saturn (♄ 01°♓25′) is determined by subtracting the two positions as shown below:

Saturn (♄ 01°♓25′)	12	01°	25′	
	11	30°	85′	(converted)
− Part of Understanding (06°♑44′)	10	06°	44′	
	01	24°	41′	

The one zodiac sign of difference is then converted into degrees by multiplying 1 by 30°00′ (the complete distance of a zodiac sign) and adding the result to the existing degrees. Thus, the distance between the Part and the planet is 54°41′, forming a sextile (60°00′ distance, ±06°00′).

30. Modern Western astrologers have added Neptune (♆) and Uranus (♅) to the possible pairings.

31. The distance between Peter's Part of Understanding (06°♑44′) and the Moon (☽ 03°♉38′) is determined by subtracting the two positions as shown below:

Part of Understanding (06°♑44′)	10	06°	44′
− Moon (☽ 03°♉38′)	02	03°	38′
	08	03°	06′

The eight zodiac signs of difference are then converted into degrees by multiplying 8 by 30°00′ (the complete distance of a zodiac sign) and adding the result to the existing degrees. Thus, the distance between the Part and the planet is 243°06′, forming a trine (120°00′ or 240°00′ distance, ±06°00′).

confidence in this part to disclose other facets of the person's life. As Bonatti documented: "[Albumazar] said if you desire to know the durability of anything, for instance the life of the person, from a question or a revolution or from whatever other method you desire to know his [or her] durability or death, whether the matter is known or unknown, manifest or occult, look to this part." The Part is derived by adding the Ascendant's position to the Part of Fortune and subtracting the Part of Spirit. The Part is then interpreted according to the house it occupies in the horoscope (see "Positioning and Interpreting an Arabian Part," page 263).

Alice T.:

Ascendant (01°♒57')	11	01°	57'	(from fig. 6.1, House I)
+ Part of Fortune (18°♏30')	08	18°	30'	(from "The Part of Fortune")
	19	19°	87'	(signs, degrees, and minutes)
− Part of Spirit (15°♈24')	01	15°	24'	(from "The Part of Spirit")
	18	04°	63'	(remainder)
	06	05°	03'	(05°♍03', Part of Durability)[32]

Peter C.:

Ascendant (02°♓49')	12	02°	49'	(from fig. 6.2, House I)
+ Part of Fortune (01°♏46')	08	01°	46'	(from "The Part of Fortune")
	20	03°	95'	(signs, degrees, and minutes)
	19	33°	95'	(converted from above)
− Part of Spirit (04°♋08')	04	04°	08'	(from "The Part of Spirit")
	15	29°	87'	(remainder)
	04	00°	27'	(00°♋27', Part of Durability)[33]

According to some practitioners, if the Part of Durability forms a conjunct (00°00' distance, ±06°00') aspect to the Part of the Mother (see "The Part of the Mother," page 325) in the individual's horoscope, the person will be like his or her

---

32. This remainder needed to be converted for two reasons: First, because the sign number in the remainder exceeds the total number of zodiac signs (12), that number is subtracted from the remainder (18) to derive the final sign number, 6. Second, the number of minutes in the remainder (63') exceeds 59'. Since 60' equal 01°, 60' are subtracted from the total minutes in the remainder (63') and 01° is added to the number of degrees in the remainder (04°), increasing the degrees to 05°.

33. This remainder needed to be converted for three reasons: First, because the sign number in the remainder exceeds the total number of zodiac signs (12), that number is subtracted from the remainder (15) to derive the final sign number, 3. Second, the number of minutes in the remainder (87') exceeds 59'. Since 60' equal 01°, 60' are subtracted from the total minutes in the remainder (87') and 01° is added to the number of degrees in the remainder (29°), increasing the degrees to 30°. Third, because the number of degrees in the remainder (30°) now exceeds 29°, this figure must also be converted. Since 30° equal one full zodiac sign, 30° are subtracted from the total degrees in the remainder (30°) and one sign is added to the sign number in the remainder (3), increasing the sign number to 4.

mother and will live at home with her. If this Part forms an aspect (see "Delineating Planetary Aspects" in chapter 8) with the planetary ruler of the house (see "The Part of Fortune," page 264) the Part occupies; is accidentally exalted;[34] is dignified;[35] or forms a conjunct (oo°oo′ distance, ±o6°oo′) aspect to the Ascendant's planetary ruler or the planetary ruler (see "The Part of Fortune") of an angular house (especially Houses I or X, but also Houses IV or VII), the person will find profits in journeys, longevity, and security in health and physical matters, and will be endowed with physical beauty. However, if the Part forms an adverse aspect such as a square (90°oo′ distance, ±o6°oo′) or opposition (180°oo′ distance, ±o6°oo′) (see "Delineating Planetary Aspects" in chapter 8) in an angular house (Houses I, IV, VII, or X), the person will experience the "durability" of a secure existence coupled with sadness and terror. For instance, Peter's Part of Durability (oo°♋27′) is positioned in House IV and Alice's Part of Durability (o5°♍o3′) occupies House VII (see "Positioning and Interpreting an Arabian Part," page 263), suggesting that both people experience the "durability" of a secure existence coupled with sadness and terror. If the Part occupies a cadent house (Houses III, VI, IX, or XII), changes of residence, destruction of hopes and dreams, and general insecurity are implied for the person. If the Part occupies a succedent house (especially Houses II or VIII, but also Houses V or XI), the person's "durability" is always uncertain and in doubt.

Parts Associated with House II

The acquisition and accumulation of possessions was of immense interest to the patrons of the Arabian astrologers who developed the Part of Goods, Part of Moneylenders,[36] Part of Happiness,[37] and Part of Collection as well as innumerable horary parts to prognosticate the outcome of planted crops, the exchange of merchandise, and the accumulation of wealth. Albumazar documented a number of

---

34. A planet is accidentally exalted when it occupies the Midheaven (House X) or the Ascendant (House I).
35. A planet is dignified if it occupies an angular house (Houses I, IV, VII, or X), the zodiac sign that it naturally rules (see note 27, page 274), or an exalted position (see below), or if it forms a favorable aspect such as a trine (120°oo′ or 240°oo′ distance, ±o6°oo′), sextile (60°oo′ distance, ±o6°oo′), or conjunction (oo°oo′ distance, ±o6°oo′) (see "Delineating Planetary Aspects" in chapter 8). Some practitioners consider a planet to be dignified if it occupies the same sign, degrees, and minutes as either Jupiter (♃) or Venus (♀).
    A planet is exalted when it occupies a specific degree or is within ±o3°oo′: for example, if the Sun occupies 19°♈oo′; the Moon occupies o3°♉oo′; Mercury occupies 15°♍oo′; Venus occupies 27°♓oo′; Mars occupies 28°♑oo′; Jupiter occupies 15°♋oo′; Saturn occupies 21°♎oo′; Uranus occupies oo°♒oo′–30°♒oo′ or oo°♏oo′–30°♏oo′; Neptune occupies oo°♌oo′–30°♌oo′; Pluto occupies oo°♓oo′–30°♓oo′; the Moon's North Node is o3°♊oo′; and the Moon's South Node is o3°♐oo′.
36. The Part of Moneylenders indicates the increase of personal wealth due to the involvement of usury and moneylending. According to Bonatti, the Part is derived by adding the Ascendant's position to Saturn's position and subtracting Mercury's position from the sum. Its delineation was not documented in any detail, however.
37. The Part of Happiness indicates an individual's potential for material happiness and is derived from adding the Ascendant's position to Saturn's position and subtracting Jupiter's position from the sum for a daytime horoscope, reversing the order in a nighttime chart. But its delineation was not described in any detail.

Arabian Parts that relate to the acquisition, possession, and distribution of material wealth. (However, Bonatti's treatise cites only the Part of Collection, Part of Moneylenders, and Part of Happiness.) Modern-day Western astrologers even developed another Part—the Part of Sorrow—to determine the person's weakest areas for material attainment. The methods for calculating and delineating three of these Parts are included in this section. These are the Part of Goods, the Part of Collection, and the modern-day Part of Sorrow.

The Part of Goods

The Arabian Part of Goods is considered to be the strongest indicator of a person's material wealth. The Part is derived by adding the Ascendant's position to the cusp of House II and subtracting the planetary ruler of House II's position from the sum. The Part is then interpreted according to the house it occupies in the horoscope (see "Positioning and Interpreting an Arabian Part," page 263).

Alice T.:

Ascendant (01°♒57′)	11	01°	57′	(from fig. 6.1, House I)
+ House II cusp (19°♓40′)	12	19°	40′	(from fig. 6.1, House II)
	23	20°	97′	(signs, degrees, and minutes)
− Jupiter (♄ 10°♉52′)	02	10°	52′	(from fig. 6.1)[38]
	21	10°	45′	(remainder)
	09	10°	45′	(10°♐45′, Part of Goods)[39]

Peter C.:

Ascendant (02°♓49′)	12	02°	49′	(from fig. 6.2, House I)
+ House II cusp (24°♈34′)	01	24°	34′	(from fig. 6.2, House II)
	13	26°	83′	(signs, degrees, and minutes)
− Mars (♂ 18°♋31′)	04	18°	31′	(from fig. 6.2)[40]
	09	08°	52′	(08°♐52′, Part of Goods)

The house in which this Part is positioned (see "Positioning and Interpreting an Arabian Part," page 263) determines the particular type of business, investment, or pursuit that produces the individual's material wealth. The delineations are exactly

---

38.   The planetary ruler of the house is determined by the zodiac sign occupying the house cusp on the horoscope's outer circle. The planetary ruler of the zodiac sign then becomes the planetary ruler of the house (see note 27, page 274).

39.   This remainder needed to be converted because the sign number in the remainder exceeds the total number of zodiac signs (12). Therefore, 12 is subtracted from the remainder (21) to derive the final sign number, 9.

40.   See note 27, page 274, to determine House II's planetary ruler.

the same as those applied to the Part of Fortune (see "The Part of Fortune," page 264) shown below:

House I   from one's own industry, especially if the Part is aspected (see "Delineating Planetary Aspects" in Chapter 8) with Jupiter (♃) or Venus (♀)

House II   through property, employment, and business

House III   from writings, publishing, and advertising; through brethren and short journeys

House IV   through treasure, metals, minerals, or land (this is also a sign of a stable patrimony)

House V   through speculation, children, young people, and ambassadors (the person's children also prosper)

House VI   derived from prosperous aunts, uncles, employees, small animals, and service industries including health

House VII   through conquest, partnerships, marriage, and bargains

House VIII   from inheritance, other people's money, and from the dead

House IX   through churches, educational properties, foreigners, inventions, the occult, and books

House X   from business assets, while honors and promotions come from lucky events and situations

House XI   through friends in high places

House XII   from secret, unexpected, or quiet sources (Naturally, if this Part forms a square [90°00′ distance] or an opposing [180°00′ distance] aspect with another planet [see "Delineating Planetary Aspects" in chapter 8], the person suffers losses in the same areas.)

In Alice's case, her Part of Goods (10°♐45′) is situated in House X (see "Positioning and Interpreting an Arabian Part," page 263), indicating that her material wealth comes from business assets. Peter's Part of Goods (08°♐52′), on the other hand, is positioned in House IX (see "Positioning and Interpreting an Arabian Part"), suggesting that he gains material wealth through churches, educational properties, foreigners, inventions, the occult, and books.

Additionally, if this Part forms a trine (120°00′ or 240°00′ distance, ±06°00′), a sextile (60°00′ distance, ±06°00′), or a conjunct aspect (00°00′ distance, ±06°00′) (see "Delineating Planetary Aspects" in chapter 8) with Mercury (☿), the person gains wealth from books, printing, writing, and communications. If the Part forms a trine, sextile, or conjunct aspect (see "Delineating Planetary Aspects" in Chapter 8) with the Moon (☽), it signifies gains from restaurants. This is the case with Alice's Part of Goods (10°♐45′), which forms a trine[41] with the Moon (☽ 11°☽28′ in fig. 6.1).

If it forms a trine (120°00′ or 240°00′ distance, ±06°00′), sextile (60°00′ distance, ±06°00′), or conjunct aspect (00°00′ distance, ±06°00′) (see "Delineating Planetary Aspects" in Chapter 8) with Jupiter (♃), this indicates gains from science, travel, or medicine. If it forms a trine, sextile, or conjunct aspect (see "Delineating Planetary Aspects" in chapter 8) with Mars (♂), this yields gains from design, building, and management. If the Part forms a trine, sextile, or conjunct aspect (see "Delineating Planetary Aspects" in chapter 8) with Saturn (♄), gains are found in land, mineral rights, mining, real estate, and other earth-oriented properties. If this part forms a trine, sextile, or conjunct aspect (see "Delineating Planetary Aspects" in chapter 8) with Venus (♀), gains are found in jewelry, clothing, artwork, and other aesthetic pleasures. If this Part forms a trine, sextile, or conjunct aspect (see "Delineating Planetary Aspects" in chapter 8) with Mercury (☿), the person gains wealth from books, printing, writing, and communications. If the Part forms a trine, sextile, or conjunct aspect (see "Delineating Planetary Aspects" in chapter 8) with the Sun (☉), it indicates gains from the theater or the healing professions.

Western astrologers have added modern planetary formations to this delineation. If the Part forms a trine (120°00′ or 240°00′ distance, ±06°00′), sextile (60°00′ distance, ±06°00′), or conjunct aspect (00°00′ distance, ±06°00′) with Uranus (♅), it indicates gains from electronics. If the Part forms a trine, sextile, or conjunct aspect with Neptune (♆), it foretells of gains from liquids and from the sea. If the Part forms a trine, sextile, or conjunct aspect with Pluto (♇), it yields gains from munitions or psychoanalysis.

---

41. The distance between Alice's Part of Goods (10°♐45′) and the Moon (☽ 11°♈28′) is determined by subtracting the two positions as shown below:

Part of Goods (10°♐45′)	09	10°	45′
	08	40°	45′ (converted)
− Moon (☽ 11°♈28′)	01	11°	28′
	07	29°	17′

The seven zodiac signs of difference are then converted into degrees by multiplying 7 by 30°00′ (the complete distance of a zodiac sign) and adding the result to the existing degrees. Thus, the distance between the Part and the planet is 239°17′, forming a trine (120°00′ or 240°00′ distance, ±06°00′).

The Part of Collection

The Part of Collection is an indicator of the person's ability to accumulate unexpected wealth by recovering things he or she has lost or discovering things that were abandoned or discarded. The Part is derived by two different means. If the person was born during the daytime, the Part is calculated by adding the Ascendant's position to Mercury's position and then subtracting Venus's position from the sum. If the person was born at night, the Part is calculated by adding the Ascendant's position to Venus's position and then subtracting Mercury's position from the sum. Both Alice and Peter were born at night. Therefore, the examples below will employ the nighttime equation. The Part is then interpreted by the aspect (see "Locating Planetary Aspects" in chapter 8) it forms with either the planetary ruler of a house in the individual's horoscope or with either the Sun or the Moon.

Alice T.:

Ascendant (01°♒57′)	11	01°	57′	*(from fig. 6.1, House I)*
+ Venus (♀ 22°♊31′)	03	22°	31′	*(from fig. 6.1)*
	14	23°	88′	*(signs, degrees, and minutes)*
− Mercury (☿ 03°♋28′)	04	03°	28′	*(from fig. 6.1)*
	10	20°	60′	*(remainder)*
	10	21°	00′	(21°♑00′, *Part of Collection*)[42]

Peter C.:

Ascendant (02°♓49′)	12	02°	49′	*(from fig. 6.2, House I)*
+ Venus (♀ 18°♋53′)	04	18°	53′	*(from fig. 6.2)*
	16	20°	102′	*(signs, degrees, and minutes)*
− Mercury (☿ 14°♍36′)	04	14°	36′	*(from fig. 6.2)*
	12	06°	66′	*(remainder)*
	12	07°	06′	(07°♓06′, *Part of Collection*)[43]

If the Part forms a trine (120°00′ or 240°00′ distance, ±06°00′), sextile (60°00′ distance, ±06°00′), or conjunct aspect (00°00′ distance, ±06°00′) (see "Delineating Planetary Aspects" in chapter 8) with the planetary ruler of the zodiac sign[44] that the Part occupies; or if either the Sun (☉) or the Moon (☽) forms a trine

---

42. This remainder needed to be converted because the remainder (60′) exceeds 59′. Since 60′ equal 01°, 60′ is subtracted from the total minutes in the remainder (60′) and 01° is added to the number of degrees in the remainder (20°), increasing the degrees to 21°.

43. The number of minutes in the remainder (149′) exceeds 59′. Since 60′ equal 01°, 60′ are subtracted twice from the total minutes in the remainder (66′) and 01° is added to the number of degrees in the remainder (06°), increasing the degrees to 07°.

44. See note 27, page 274.

(120°00′ or 240°00′ distance, ±06°00′), sextile (60°00′ distance, ±06°00′), or conjunct (00°00′ distance, ±06°00′) aspect with the Part, but is not combust,[45] the person will accidentally discover things while walking down a road, beach, riverbank, or path; by digging up or encountering a fallen, escaped, concealed, or forgotten item. Neither Alice's nor Peter's Part forms any of these aspects. Therefore, no further prognostications are made by the practitioner using this material.

The Part of Sorrow

Western astrologers developed a direct opposite to the Part of Fortune, called the Arabian Part of Sorrow, which indicates the person's material misfortune. The Part is derived by adding the Ascendant's position to the Part of Fortune's position and subtracting Neptune's position from the sum. The resulting part is read as a mirror image of the Part of Fortune's indications.

Alice T.:

Ascendant (01°♒57′)	11	01°	57′	(from fig. 6.1, House I)
+ Part of Fortune (18°♏30′)	08	18°	30′	(from "The Part of Fortune")
	19	19°	87′	(signs, degrees, and minutes)
− Neptune (♆ 18°♎59′)	07	18°	59′	(from fig. 6.1)
	12	01°	28′	(01°♓28′, Part of Sorrow)

Peter C.:

Ascendant (02°♓49′)	12	02°	49′	(from fig. 6.2, House I)
+ Part of Fortune (01°♏46′)	08	01°	46′	(from "The Part of Fortune")
	20	03°	95′	(signs, degrees, and minutes)
	19	33°	95′	(converted from above)
− Neptune (♆ 15°♏19′)	08	15°	19′	(from fig. 6.2)
	11	18°	76′	(remainder)
	11	19°	16′	(19°♒16′, Part of Sorrow)[46]

As mentioned earlier, the delineations are the exact opposites of those applied to the Part of Fortune (see "The Part of Fortune," page 264). The individual is likely to experience loss and sorrow in the following ways:

---

45. When Mercury passes between the Sun and Earth while simultaneously occupying the same zodiac sign, degrees and minutes as the Sun ±08°30′, Mercury's nature becomes temporarily weakened, creating an inferior conjunction. The same transformation affects the planet Venus as it passes through an identical course. Conversely, if either Mercury or Venus forms a conjunction with the Sun while passing the Earth's opposing path, its nature is strengthened. This modification is commonly referred to as a combust. Arabian astrologers believed that when a planet conjuncts the Sun within a 00°17′ orb of influence, an extreme version of combustion occurs, called *cazimi*.

46. This remainder needed to be converted because the remainder (76′) exceeds 59′. Since 60′ equal 01°, 60′ are subtracted from the total minutes in the remainder (76′) and 01° is added to the number of degrees in the remainder (18°), increasing the degrees to 19°.

House I	through his or her own industry
House II	through property, employment, and business
House III	from writings, publishing, and advertising, brethren (i.e., siblings and close relatives), and short journeys
House IV	through treasure, metals, minerals, land
House V	through speculation, children, young people, and ambassadors; also, the person's children experience sorrow
House VI	derived from prosperous aunts, uncles, employees, small animals, and service industries including health
House VII	through conquest, partnerships, marriage, and bargains
House VIII	from inheritance, other people's money, and the dead
House IX	through churches, educational properties, foreigners, inventions, the occult, and books
House X	from business assets
House XI	through friends in high places
House XII	from secret, unexpected, or quiet sources

Because her Part of Sorrow (01°♓ 28′) is situated in House I, Alice experiences material loss and sorrow through her own industry. Peter's Part of Sorrow (19° ♒ 16′) resides in House XII, indicating loss and sorrow from secret, unexpected, or quiet sources. (See "Positioning and Interpreting an Arabian Part.")

Additionally, some practitioners believe that if the Part forms a square (90°00′ distance, ±06°00′) or opposing (180°00′ distance, ±06°00′) aspect (see "Delineating Planetary Aspects" in chapter 8) with Neptune (Ψ), a wrong committed against that individual resurfaces. An example of this is Peter's Part of Sorrow (19° ♒ 16′), which forms a square aspect with Neptune (Ψ 15°♏ 18′ in fig. 6.2), making him vulnerable to a past wrong.[47]

---

47. The distance between Peter's Part of Sorrow (19°♒16′) and Neptune (Ψ 15°♏18′) is determined by subtracting the two positions as shown below:

Part of Sorrow (19°♒16′)	11	19°	16′
	11	18°	76′ (converted)
− Neptune (Ψ 15°♏18′)	08	15°	18′
	03	03°	58′

The three zodiac signs of difference are then converted into degrees by multiplying 3 by 30°00′ (the complete distance of a zodiac sign) and adding the result to the existing degrees. Thus, the distance between the Part and the planet is 93°58′, forming a square (90°00′ distance, ±06°00′).

If the Part forms a square (90°00′ distance, ±06°00′) or opposing (180°00′ distance, ±06°00′) aspect (see "Delineating Planetary Aspects" in chapter 8) with the Sun (☉), it indicates that the person's lack of confidence causes failure. If the Part forms a square or opposing aspect (see "Delineating Planetary Aspects" in chapter 8) with the Moon (☽), it creates emotional frustrations. If it forms a square or opposing aspect (see "Delineating Planetary Aspects" in chapter 8) with Mercury (☿), it creates worries and anxieties over petty details. If it forms a square or opposing aspect (see "Delineating Planetary Aspects" in chapter 8) with either Venus (♀) or Jupiter (♃), it causes physical distress. If it forms a square or opposing aspect (see "Delineating Planetary Aspects" in chapter 8) with either Mars (♂) or Saturn (♄), it causes the person to become self-destructive. If it forms a square or opposing aspect (see "Delineating Planetary Aspects" in chapter 8), with Uranus (♅), it instigates fits of temper and aggressive behavior. If it forms a square or opposing aspect (see "Delineating Planetary Aspects" in chapter 8) with Pluto (♇), it compacts and explodes repressed emotions at the wrong times. Alice's Part does not form any aspects. Therefore, no additional prognostications would be made using this material.

Parts Associated with House III

Although House III oversees communications, mentality, and short trips, as well as the person's brothers, sisters, and other close relatives within the sphere of Western astrology, Arabian practitioners concentrated their efforts on delineations concerning "brethren." The Arabian Part of Brethren, Part of the Number of Brothers,[48] Part of the Number of Brethren,[49] and Part of the Death of Brothers and Sisters[50] attest to the overriding concern for family security based on the number and condition of an individual's siblings, grandparents, aunts, uncles, and close cousins. Modern Western astrologers developed the Part of Love of Brethren, reflecting their culture's concern for strong communicative ties among siblings and close relatives. This section presents the construction and interpretation of only two of these Parts: the Part of Brethren and the Part of Love of Brethren.

---

48.   Bonatti mentioned the Part of the Number of Brothers (*Pars de Numero Fratrum*), which derives the number of siblings born by adding the Ascendant's position to Mercury's position and subtracting Saturn's position from the sum. However, this Part appears to be redundant and its delineation was not thoroughly documented, so it is not explained in this section.

49.   The Part of the Number of Brethren was employed by Arabian astrologers. However, the Part seems to be redundant in that the same information is derived from the Part of Brethren, so it is not included in this section. The Part of the Number of Brethren is derived by adding the Ascendant's position to Mercury's position and subtracting Saturn's position from the sum. If this Part occupies a fertile or fruitful sign such as Cancer (♋), Scorpio (♏), or Pisces (♓), the person will have many siblings.

50.   The Part of the Death of Brothers and Sisters is derived by adding the Ascendant's position to the Sun's position and subtracting the Midheaven (House X) from the sum. Neither Bonatti nor Ptolemy explained how to delineate this Part, however, so it is not executed in this section.

The Part of Brethren

The Arabian Part of Brethren—a term that encompasses both siblings and close relatives such as aunts, uncles, and first cousins—indicates the person's relationship to those family members. Commonly known as the Arabian Part of Brothers and Sisters, the Part is derived by adding the Ascendant's position to Saturn's position and subtracting Jupiter's position from the sum.[51] The Part is interpreted by reviewing the zodiac sign that it occupies, and its distance from its planetary ruler.

Alice T.:

Ascendant (01°♒57')	11	01°	57'	*(from fig. 6.1, House I)*
+ Saturn (♄ 08°♎12')	07	08°	12'	*(from fig. 6.1)*
	18	09°	69'	*(signs, degrees, and minutes)*
	17	39°	69'	*(converted from above)*
− Jupiter (♃ 10°♉52')	02	10°	52'	*(from fig. 6.1)*
	15	29°	17'	*(remainder)*
	03	29°	17'	*(29°♊17', Part of Brethren)*[52]

Peter C.:

Ascendant (02°♓49')	12	02°	49'	*(from fig. 6.2, House I)*
+ Saturn (♄ 01°♓25')	12	01°	25'	*(from fig. 6.2)*
	24	03°	74'	*(signs, degrees, and minutes)*
	23	33°	74'	*(converted from above)*
− Jupiter (♃ 25°♉36')	02	25°	36'	*(from fig. 6.2)*
	21	08°	38'	*(remainder)*
	09	08°	38'	*(08°♐38', Part of Brethren)*[53]

If the Part resides in the zodiac signs Gemini (♊), Virgo (♍), Sagittarius (♐), or Pisces (♓), the person potentially has many siblings or close relatives. No matter which sign the Part occupies, however, the number of signs between the Part of Brethren and the Part's ruler is generally used to indicate how many siblings an individual might have.

---

51. Some modern Western astrologers prefer to use this particular calculation for nighttime horoscopes and reverse the calculation for daytime charts. In Bonatti's era, however, the same calculation was used for both types of horoscopes.

52. This remainder needed to be converted because the sign number in the remainder exceeds the total number of zodiac signs (12). Therefore, that number is subtracted from the remainder (15) to derive the final sign number, 3.

53. This remainder needed to be converted because the sign number in the remainder exceeds the total number of zodiac signs (12). Therefore, that number is subtracted from the remainder (21) to derive the final sign number, 9.

For example, Alice has one sign between the Part of Brethren (29°♊17′) and the Part's planetary ruler,[54] Mercury (☿03°♋28′ in fig. 6.1). Therefore she has one sibling (which, in fact, she does). Peter, however, has four signs between the Part of Brethren (08°♐38′) and the Part's planetary ruler,[55] Jupiter (♃ 25°♉36′ in fig. 6.2). This indicates that he has four siblings (which he does). Furthermore, if the Part of Brethren is positioned in Houses III, I, IV, or VII, respectively, the person also encounters close psychic ties with siblings or other close relatives.

The Part of Love of Brethren

Western astrologers developed the Arabian Part of Love of Brethren, which identifies the person's sense of familial duty toward siblings or close relatives. This Part is derived by adding the Ascendant's position to Saturn's position and subtracting the Sun's position from the sum. (It is identical to the equation used to derive the Part of Heaviness; see "The Planetary Arabian Parts," page 263.) It is only interpreted if the Part forms an aspect with another planet.

Alice T.:

Ascendant (01°♒57′)	11	01°	57′	(from fig. 6.1, House I)
+ Saturn (♄ 08°♎12′)	07	08°	12′	(from fig. 6.1)
	18	09°	69′	(signs, degrees, and minutes)
	17	39°	69′	(converted from above)
− Sun (☉ 24°♊55′)	03	24°	55′	(from fig. 6.1)
	14	15°	14′	(remainder)
	02	15°	14′	(15°♉14′, Part of Brethren)[56]

Peter C.:

Ascendant (02°♓49′)	12	02°	49′	(from fig. 6.2, House I)
+ Saturn (♄ 01°♓25′)	12	01°	25′	(from fig. 6.2)
	24	03°	74′	(signs, degrees, and minutes)
	23	33°	74′	(converted from above)
− Sun (☉ 04°♍41′)	06	04°	41′	(from fig. 6.2)
	17	29°	33′	(remainder)
	05	29°	33′	(29°♌33′, Part of Brethren)[57]

---

54. See note 27, page 274.
55. Ibid.
56. This remainder needed to be converted because the sign number in the remainder exceeds the total number of zodiac signs (12). Therefore, that number is subtracted from the remainder (14) to derive the final sign number, 2.
57. This remainder needed to be converted because the sign number in the remainder exceeds the total number of zodiac signs (12). Therefore, 12 is subtracted from the remainder (21) to derive the final sign number, 9.

Western astrologers believe that if the Part of Love of Brethren forms a square (90°00′ distance, ±06°00′) or opposing (180°00′ distance, ±06°00′) aspect (see "Delineating Planetary Aspects" in chapter 8) with any planet, the person cares very little about his or her siblings. For example, Alice's Part (15°♉14′) forms a square to Pluto (♇ 19°♌34′ in fig. 6.1).[58] Similarly, Peter's Part (29°♌33′) forms a square to Jupiter (♃ 25°♉36′ in fig. 6.2).[59] This suggests that neither person cares about his or her siblings.

However, if the Part is favorably aspected by a trine (90°00′ distance, ±06°00′), sextile (60°00′ distance, ±06°00′), or conjunction (0°00′ distance, ±06°00′) aspect (see "Delineating Planetary Aspects" in chapter 8) with any planet, the person's sentiments and bonds toward siblings are strong and long-lasting. For example, Alice's Part (15°♉14′) forms a sextile to Uranus (♅ 13°♋00′ in fig. 6.1)[60] and a conjunction to Jupiter (♃ 10°♉52′ in fig. 6.1).[61] Because a sextile aspect

---

58.   The distance between Alice's Part (15°♉14′) and Pluto (♇ 19°♌34′) is determined by subtracting the two positions as shown below:

Pluto (♇ 19°♌34′)	05	19°	34′
− Part of Love of Brethren (15°♉14′)	02	15°	14′
	03	04°	20′

The three zodiac signs of difference are then converted into degrees by multiplying 3 by 30°00′ (the complete distance of a zodiac sign) and adding the result to the existing degrees. Thus the distance between the Part and the planet is 94°20′, forming a square (90°00′ distance, +06°00′).

59.   The distance between Peter's Part (29°♌33′) and Jupiter (♃ 25°♉36′) is determined by subtracting the two positions as shown below:

Part of Love of Brethren (29°♌33′)	05	29°	33′	
	05	28°	93′	*(converted)*
− Jupiter (♃ 25°♉36′)	02	25°	36′	
	03	03°	57′	

The three zodiac signs of difference are then converted into degrees by multiplying 3 by 30°00′ (the complete distance of a zodiac sign) and adding the result to the existing degrees. Thus the distance between the Part and the planet is 93°57′, forming a square (90°00′ distance, ±06°00′).

60.   The distance between Alice's Part (15°♉14′) and Uranus (♅ 13°♋00′) is determined by subtracting the two positions as shown below:

Uranus (♅ 13°♋00′)	04	13°	00′	
	03	42°	60′	*(converted)*
− Part of Love of Brethren (15°♉14′)	02	15°	14′	
	01	27°	46′	

The one zodiac sign of difference is then converted into 30°00′ (the complete distance of a zodiac sign) and the result added to the existing degrees. Thus the distance between the Part and the planet is 57°46′, forming a sextile (60°00′ distance, ±06°00′).

61.   The distance between Alice's Part (15°♉14′) and Jupiter (♃ 10°♉52′) is determined by subtracting the two positions as shown below:

Part of Love of Brethren (15°♉14′)	02	15°	14′	
	02	14°	74′	*(converted)*
− Jupiter (♃ 10°♉52′)	02	10°	52′	
	00	04°	22′	

Thus the distance between the Part and the planet is 04°22′, forming a conjunction (0°00′ distance, ±06°00′).

exerts less influence than a square aspect, this prognostication would not override the affect of Pluto on the Part as mentioned in the previous paragraph.

Parts Associated with House IV

The condition of an individual's father and his ancestors, the person's inheritance, and the outcome of harvests were considerable House IV concerns to Arabian astrologers. This particular house was of paramount importance because early opportunities and skills were basically passed down or bequeathed by the person's father or ancestors. Questions of heredity were often resolved by astrologers who cast the Part of the Father, the Part of the Grandfather,[62] the Part of Ancestors,[63] and the Part of Inheritance and Possessions. But since House IV also presides over land, mineral rights, and mining interests that were largely inherited, the Part of Fortune in Husbandry is also included in this category. This section presents the construction and interpretation of three of these Parts: the Part of the Father, the Part of Inheritance and Possessions, and the Part of Fortune in Husbandry.

The Part of the Father

The Arabian Part of the Father corresponds to the person's father. This Part is derived by adding the Ascendant's position to the Sun's position and subtracting Saturn's position from the sum. It is only interpreted if the Part forms an aspect with another planet.

Alice T.:

Ascendant (01°♒57')	11	01°	57'	(from fig. 6.1, House I)
+ Sun (☉ 24°♊55')	03	24°	55'	(from fig. 6.1)
	14	25°	112'	(signs, degrees, and minutes)
− Saturn (♄ 08°♎12')	07	08°	12'	(from fig. 6.1)
	07	17°	100'	(remainder)
	07	18°	40'	(18°♎40', Part of the Father)[64]

---

62. This Part is derived by adding the Ascendant's position to the ruler of the house that the Sun occupies and subtracting Saturn's position from the sum. It was apparently delineated in the same manner as the Part of the Father. It cannot be confirmed, however, so this Part is not detailed in this section.

63. The Part of Ancestors categorized an individual within the realms of nobility (noble parents and honest ancestors) or lower castes (poor or ignorant parents). The Part is derived by adding the Ascendant's position to Saturn's position and subtracting Mars's position from the sum. Then the number of degrees Saturn has completed in the natal sign as well as the cusp of the house Saturn occupies are added to the sum. If the Part occupies an angular house such as Houses I, IV, VII, or X, the person comes from noble stock; if the Part is located in a cadent house such as Houses III, VI, IX, or XII, the person is the product of "low-quality" parents or education. This Part obviously fell into disuse over the centuries and its interpretation is unknown, so it is not included in this section.

64. This remainder needed to be converted because the remainder (100') exceeds 59'. Since 60' equal 01°, 60' is subtracted from the total minutes in the remainder (100') and 01° is added to the number of degrees in the remainder (17°), increasing the degrees to 18°.

Peter C.:

Ascendant (02°♓49′)	12	02°	49′	(from fig. 6.2, House I)
+ Sun (☉ 04°♍41′)	06	04°	41′	(from fig. 6.2)
	18	06°	90′	(signs, degrees, and minutes)
− Saturn (♄ 01°♓25′)	12	01°	25′	(from fig. 6.2)
	06	05°	65′	(remainder)
	06	06°	05′	(06°♍05′, Part of the Father)[65]

According to the Arabian astrologer Albumazar, the Part of the Father is delineated by reviewing its relationship to specific planets. If this Part forms a square (90°00′ distance, ±06°00′) or opposing (180°00′ distance, ±06°00′) aspect (see "Delineating Planetary Aspects" in chapter 8) with Saturn (♄), Mercury (☿), or Mars (♂), the person fails to communicate with his or her father. If the Part forms a trine (120°00′ or 240°00′ distance, ±06°00′), sextile (60°00′ distance, ±06°00′), square (90°00′ distance, ±06°00′), opposing (180°00′ distance, ±06°00′), or conjunct (00°00′ distance, ±06°00′) aspect (see "Delineating Planetary Aspects" in chapter 8) with the Sun (☉), Jupiter (♃), or Uranus (♅), it indicates that the individual's father exerts a strong influence on the person. (This is a positive influence if the aspect is a trine, sextile, or conjunct aspect; it is a negative influence is the aspect is a square or opposing aspect.) Both are the case with Alice's Part of the Father (18°♎40′), which squares Uranus (♅ 13°♋00′ in fig. 6.1)[66] and trines the Sun (☉ 24°♊55′ in fig. 6.1).[67] Similarly, Peter's Part of

---

65. This remainder needed to be converted because the remainder (65′) exceeds 59′. Since 60′ equal 01°, 60′ is subtracted from the total minutes in the remainder (65′) and 01° is added to the number of degrees in the remainder (05°), increasing the degrees to 06°.

66. The distance between Alice's Part (18°♎40′) and Uranus (♅ 13°♋00′) is determined by subtracting the two positions as shown below:

Part of the Father (18°♎40′)	07	18°	40′
− Uranus (♅ 13°♋00′)	04	13°	00′
	03	05°	40′

The three zodiac signs of difference are then converted into degrees (°) by multiplying 3 by 30°00′ (the complete distance of a zodiac sign) and adding the result to the existing degrees. Thus, the distance between the Part and the planet is 95°40′, forming a square (90°00′ distance, ±06°00′).

67. The distance between Alice's Part (18°♎40′) and the Sun (☉ 24°♊55′) is determined by subtracting the two positions as shown below:

Part of the Father (18°♎40′)	07	18°	40′	
	06	47°	100′	(converted)
− Sun (☉ 24°♊55′)	03	24°	55′	
	03	23°	45′	

The three zodiac signs of difference are then converted into degrees by multiplying 3 by 30°00′ (the complete distance of a zodiac sign) and adding the result to the existing degrees. Thus the distance between the Part and the planet is 113°45′, forming a trine (120°00′ distance, ±06°00′).

the Father (06°♍05′) forms a conjunction to the Sun (☉ 04°♍41′ in fig. 6.2).[68]

If the Part of the Father forms a trine (120°00′ or 240°00′ distance, ±06°00′), sextile (60°00′ distance, ±06°00′), square (90°00′ distance, ±06°00′), opposing (180°00′ distance, ±06°00′), or conjunct (00°00′ distance, ±06°00′) aspect (see "Delineating Planetary Aspects" in chapter 8) with the Moon (☽) or Venus (♀), it indicates that the individual's mother exerts a strong influence on the person. (This is a positive influence if the aspect is a trine, sextile, or conjunct aspect; it is a negative influence if the aspect is a square or opposing aspect.) This is the case with Peter's Part of the Father (06°♍05′), which trines the Moon (☽ 03°♉38′ in fig. 6.2),[69] suggesting that despite a strong paternal influence, his mother also affects his life.

The Part of Inheritances and Possessions

The Arabian Part of Inheritances and Possessions indicates what the person may materially or financially receive from his or her family or ancestors. The Part is derived by adding the Ascendant's position to the Moon's position and subtracting Saturn's position from the sum. This particular Part is interpreted according to its placement in an individual's horoscope (see "Positioning and Interpreting an Arabian Part," page 263).

Alice T.:

Ascendant (01°♒57′)	11	01°	57′	(from fig. 6.1, House I)
+ Moon (☽ 11°♈28′)	01	11°	28′	(from fig. 6.1)
	12	12°	85′	(signs, degrees, and minutes)

---

68. The distance between Peter's Part (06°♍05′) and the Sun (☉ 04°♍41′) is determined by subtracting the two positions as shown below:

Part of the Father (06°♍05′)	06	06°	05′
	06	05°	65′ (converted)
− Sun (☉ 04°♍41′)	06	04°	41′
	00	01°	24′

Thus the distance between the Part and the planet is 01°24′, forming a conjunction (00°00′ distance, ±06°00′).

69. The distance between Peter's Part (06°♍05′) and the Moon (☽ 03°♉38′) is determined by subtracting the two positions as shown below:

Part of the Father (06°♍05′)	06	06°	05′
	06	05°	65′ (converted)
− Moon (☽ 03°♉38′)	02	03°	38′
	04	02°	27′

The four zodiac signs of difference are then converted into degrees by multiplying 4 by 30°00′ (the complete distance of a zodiac sign) and adding the result to the existing degrees. Thus the distance between the Part and the planet is 122°27′, forming a trine (120°00′ distance, ±06°00′).

− Saturn (♄ 08°♎12′)	07	08°	12′	(*from fig. 6.1*)
	05	04°	73′	(*remainder*)
	05	05°	13′	(05°♌13′, *Part of Inheritances and Possessions*)[70]

Peter C.:

Ascendant (02°♓49′)	12	02°	49′	(*from fig. 6.2, House I*)
+ Moon (☽ 03°♉38′)	02	03°	38′	(*from fig. 6.2*)
	14	05°	87′	(*signs, degrees, and minutes*)
− Saturn (♄ 01°♓25′)	12	01°	25′	(*from fig. 6.2*)
	02	04°	62′	(*remainder*)
	02	05°	02′	(05°♉02′, *Part of Inheritances and Possessions*)[71]

Modern Western astrologers delineate the Part's influence by the house it occupies (see "Positioning and Interpreting an Arabian Part") according to the material below:

House I   self-sufficient, inheriting little from others

House II   from money or farm products

House III   from writings, books, or other communications (it is also possible the person will inherit from a sibling or close relative)

House IV   through lands, mineral rights, mining interests, or household goods (it is also possible the person will inherit from a parent)

House V   through works of art or music

House VI   because of his or her service to other people

House VII   from spouse or partners

House VIII   from his or her ancestors

House IX   may not inherit possessions, but does learn from and is inspired by others

---

70. This remainder needed to be converted because the remainder (73′) exceeds 59′. Since 60′ equal 01°, 60′ is subtracted from the total minutes in the remainder (73′) and 01° is added to the number of degrees in the remainder (04°), increasing the degrees to 05°.

71. This remainder needed to be converted because the remainder (62′) exceeds 59′. Since 60′ equal 01°, 60′ is subtracted from the total minutes in the remainder (62′) and 01° is added to the number of degrees in the remainder (04°), increasing the degrees to 05°.

House X   from entrepreneurial ventures or favors from government officials

House XI   money through scientifically oriented materials or from large corporations

House XII   from secret sources or through research and investigation

According to this method, Alice's Part of Inheritance and Possessions (05°♌13′) is in House VII (see "Positioning and Interpreting an Arabian Part"), indicating that she might inherit wealth from a spouse or business partner. Peter's Part (05°♌02′), is placed in House II (see "Positioning and Interpreting an Arabian Part"), indicating that he inherits from money or farm products.

If the Part forms a trine (120°00′ or 240°00′ distance, ±06°00′), sextile (60°00′ distance, ±06°00′), or conjunct (00°00′ distance, ±06°00′) aspect (see "Delineating Planetary Aspects" in chapter 8) with Jupiter (♃), the person knows how to gain property from others.

Modern Western astrologers have incorporated the use of Uranus (♅), Neptune (♆), and Pluto (♇) in the delineation of this Part. Consequently, if the Part forms a trine (120°00′ or 240°00′ distance, ±06°00′), sextile (60°00′ distance, ±06°00′), or conjunct (00°00′ distance, ±06°00′) aspect (see "Delineating Planetary Aspects" in chapter 8) with Uranus (♅), Mars (♂), or Neptune (♆), the person receives unexpected gains of possessions from others. If the Part forms a square (90°00′ distance, ±06°00′) or opposing (180°00′ distance, ±06°00′) aspect (see "Delineating Planetary Aspects" in chapter 8) with those same planets, however, losses will be incurred. Alice's Part (05°♌13′) which is located in her House VII (fig. 6.1) squares Mars (♂ 01°♏24′ in fig. 6.1),[72] making the losses of inheritance or possessions possible. If the Part forms a trine, sextile, square, opposing, or conjunct aspect (see "Delineating Planetary Aspects" in chapter 8) with Pluto (♇), the person is obsessed with financial possessions, investments, or acquisitions. Peter's

---

72.   The distance between Alice's Part (05°♌13′) and Mars (♂ 01°♏24′) is determined by subtracting the two positions as shown below:

Mars (♂ 01°♏24′)	08	01°	24′
	07	31°	24′ (converted)
Part of Inheritances			
− and Possessions (05°♌13′)	05	05°	13′
	02	26°	11′

The two zodiac signs of difference are then converted into degrees by multiplying 2 by 30°00′ (the complete distance of a zodiac sign) and adding the result to the existing degrees. Thus the distance between the Part and the planet is 86°11′, forming a square (90°00′ distance, ±06°00′).

Part does not form any of these aspects. Therefore, no additional prognostications would be made.

The Part of Fortune in Husbandry

In modern Western astrological interpretation, the Arabian Part of Fortune in Husbandry not only indicates the person's ability to reap abundance from the land; it also prognosticates the general domestic environment and the person's ability to deal with household issues. This Part is derived by adding the Ascendant's position to Saturn's position and subtracting Venus's position from the sum. The Part's delineation is based upon its position in the horoscope (see "Positioning and Interpreting an Arabian Part"), the Part's planetary ruler,[73] and the aspects it forms (see "Delineating Planetary Aspects" in chapter 8).

Alice T.:

Ascendant (01°♒57')	11	01°	57'	(from fig. 6.1, House I)
+ Saturn (♄ 14°♍08')	06	14°	08'	(from fig. 6.1)
	17	15°	65'	(signs, degrees, and minutes)
	16	45°	65'	(converted)
− Venus (♀ 22°♊31')	03	22°	31'	(from fig. 6.1)
	13	23°	34'	(remainder)
	01	23°	34'	(22°♈31', Part of Fortune in Husbandry)[74]

Peter C.:

Ascendant (02°♓49')	12	02°	49'	(from fig. 6.2, House I)
+ Saturn (♄ 01°♓25')	12	01°	25'	(from fig. 6.2)
	24	03°	74'	(signs, degrees, and minutes)
	23	33°	74'	(converted)
− Venus (♀ 18°♋53')	04	18°	53'	(from fig. 6.2)
	19	15°	21'	(remainder)
	07	15°	21'	(15°♎21', Part of Fortune in Husbandry)[75]

---

73. See note 27, page 274.

74. This remainder needed to be converted because the sign number in the remainder exceeds the total number of zodiac signs (12); therefore, that number is subtracted from the remainder (13) to derive the final sign number, 1.

75. This remainder needed to be converted because the sign number in the remainder exceeds the total number of zodiac signs (12); therefore, that number is subtracted from the remainder (19) to derive the final sign number, 7.

If the Part forms a trine (120°00′ or 240°00′ distance, ±06°00′), sextile (60°00′ distance, ±06°00′), or conjunct (00°00′ distance, ±06°00′) aspect (see "Delineating Planetary Aspects" in chapter 8) with the Sun (☉), Venus (♀), or Jupiter (♃), the person has help with all household matters. Some modern Western astrologers have also cited Neptune (♆) as exerting a similar influence when aspected with this Part. An example of this can be seen with Alice's Part (22°♈31′), which sextiles both the Sun (☉ 24°♊55′ in fig. 6.1)[76] and Venus (♀ 24°♊31′ in fig. 6.1),[77] indicating that she receives a great deal of help with all household matters.

If it forms a square (90°00′ distance, ±06°00′) or opposing (180°00′ distance, ±06°00′) aspect (see "Delineating Planetary Aspects" in chapter 8) with Mars (♂), the person finds that home and hearth are sources of irritation. Some modern Western astrologers have also cited Pluto (♇) as exerting a similar influence when aspected with this Part.

If the Part forms a square (90°00′ distance, ±06°00′) or opposing (180°00′ distance, ±06°00′) aspect (see "Delineating Planetary Aspects" in chapter 8) with the Moon (☽), Mercury (☿), or Saturn (♄), the person is the perpetrator of household upsets. Some modern Western astrologers have also cited Uranus (♅) as exerting a similar influence when aspected with this Part.

If none of these aspects is formed, the practitioner would not make a prognostication using this Part. Such is the case with Peter's Part (15°♎21′).

Parts Associated with House V

Arabian astrologers divined the Part of Children, the Part of Female Children, and the Part of Male Children to determine an individual's potential to produce progeny and to indicate the number of children a person might parent, as well as

---

76.   The distance between Alice's Part (22°♈31′) and the Sun (☉ 24°♊55′) is determined by subtracting the two positions as shown below:

Sun (☉ 24°♊55′)	03	24°	55′
− Part of Fortune in Husbandry (22°♈31′)	01	22°	31′
	02	02°	24′

The two zodiac signs of difference are then converted into degrees by multiplying 2 by 30°00′ (the complete distance of a zodiac sign) and adding the result to the existing degrees. Thus the distance between the Part and the planet is 62°24′, forming a sextile (60°00′ distance, ±06°00′).

77.   The distance between Alice's Part (22°♈31′) and Venus (♀ 24°♊31′) is determined by subtracting the two positions as shown below:

Venus (♀ 24°♊31′)	03	24°	31′
− Part of Fortune in Husbandry (22°♈31′)	01	22°	31′
	02	02°	00′

The two zodiac signs of difference are then converted into degrees by multiplying 2 by 30°00′ (the complete distance of a zodiac sign) and adding the result to the existing degrees. Thus the distance between the Part and the planet is 62°00′, forming a sextile (60°00′ distance, ±06°00′).

what gender they might be. The calculation and interpretation of all three of these Parts will be presented in this section.

Basically, all three Parts are interpreted in a similar manner to the method used in the Part of Brethren (see "The Part of Brethren," page 285). In this instance, however, it means that if any of these Parts occupies the zodiac signs Cancer (♋), Scorpio (♏), or Pisces (♓), the individual may have many children. How many off-spring depends on the number of zodiac signs positioned between the Part and the Part's planetary ruler.[78]

The Part of Children

Used to determine the number of progeny an individual might have, the Arabian Part of Children is derived by adding the Ascendant's position to Jupiter's position and subtracting Saturn's position. According to the Arabian astrologer Albumazar, if the Part resides in the zodiac signs Cancer (♋), Scorpio (♏), or Pisces (♓), the person potentially has many children. No matter which zodiac sign the Part occupies, however, the number of signs between the Part of Children and the Part's planetary ruler[79] is generally used to indicate how many children an individual might have.

Alice T.:

Ascendant (01°♒57')	11	01°	57'	(from fig. 6.1, House I)
+ Jupiter (♃ 10°♉52')	02	10°	52'	(from fig. 6.1)
	13	11°	109'	(signs, degrees, and minutes)
	12	41°	109'	(converted)
− Saturn (♄ 08°♎12')	07	08°	12'	(from fig. 6.1)
	05	33°	97'	(remainder)
	06	04°	37'	(04°♍37', Part of Children)[80]

Peter C.:

Ascendant (02°♓49')	12	02°	49'	(from fig. 6.2, House I)
+ Jupiter (♃ 25°♉38')	02	25°	38'	(from fig. 6.2)
	14	27°	87'	(signs, degrees, and minutes)

---

78. See note 27, page 274.
79. Ibid.
80. This remainder needed to be converted because the number of minutes in the remainder (97') exceeds 30'. Since 30° equal 1 sign, 30° are subtracted from the total degrees in the remainder (34°) and 1 sign is added to the number of signs in the remainder (5), increasing the signs to 6.

— Saturn (♄ 01°♓25')	12	01°	25'	(from fig. 6.2)
	02	26°	62'	(remainder)
	02	27°	02'	(27°♉02', Part of Children)[81]

Alice's Part (04°♍37') is not in one of the zodiac signs that promises many children (Cancer [♋], Scorpio [♏], or Pisces [♓]). The Part's planetary ruler,[82] Mercury (☿ 03°♋28' in fig. 6.1), is positioned 61°09'[83] or two zodiac signs plus 01°09' away from the Part. This suggests that she might have two children.

Peter's Part of Children (27°♉02') is also not in one of the zodiac signs that promises many children. And the Part's planetary ruler,[84] Venus (♀ 22°♊31' in fig. 6.2),[85] is situated one zodiac sign away from the Part, indicating that he might have one child.

The Part of Female Children

The Arabian Part of Female Children is derived by adding the Ascendant's position to Venus's position and subtracting the Moon's position. And as mentioned earlier, this Part is delineated in the same manner as the Part of Children, above.

Alice T.:

Ascendant (01°♒57')	11	01°	57'	(from fig. 6.1, House I)
+ Venus (♀ 22°♊31')	03	22°	31'	(from fig. 6.1)
	14	23°	88'	(signs, degrees, and minutes)

---

81. This remainder needed to be converted because the number of minutes in the remainder (62') exceeds 59'. Since 60' equal 01°, 60' are subtracted from the total minutes in the remainder (62') and 01° is added to the number of degrees in the remainder (26°), increasing the degrees to 27°.

82. See note 27, page 274.

83. The distance between Alice's Part (04°♍37') and Mercury (☿ 03°♋28') is determined by subtracting the two positions as shown below:

Part of Children (04°♍37')	06	04°	37'
— Mercury (☿ 03°♋28')	04	03°	28'
	02	01°	09'

The two zodiac signs of difference are then converted into degrees by multiplying 2 by 30°00' (the complete distance of a zodiac sign) and adding the result to the existing degrees. Thus the distance between the Part and the planet is 61°09'.

84. See note 27, page 274.

85. The distance between Peter's Part (27°♉02') and Venus (♀ 22°♊31') is determined by subtracting the two positions as shown below:

Venus (♀ 22°♊31')	03	22°	31'
	02	52°	31'	(converted)
— Part of Children (27°♉02')	02	27°	02'
	00	25°	29'

Thus the distance between the Part and the planet is 25°29'.

− Moon (☽ 11°♈28′)	01	11°	28′	(from fig. 6.1)
	13	12°	60′	(remainder)
	01	13°	00′	(13°♈00′, Part of Female Children)[86]

Peter C.:

Ascendant (02°♓49′)	12	02°	49′	(from fig. 6.2, House I)
+ Venus (♀ 18°♋53′)	04	18°	53′	(from fig. 6.2)
	16	20°	102′	(signs, degrees, and minutes)
− Moon (☽ 03°♉38′)	02	03°	38′	(from fig. 6.2)
	14	17°	64′	(remainder)
	02	18°	04′	(18°♉04′, Part of Female Children)[87]

Alice's Part of Female Children (13°♈00′) is situated in Aries (♈), which is not one of the zodiac signs that promises many children (Cancer [♋], Scorpio [♏], or Pisces [♓]). However, the Part's planetary ruler,[88] Mars (♂ 01°♏24′ in fig. 6.1), is positioned 198°24′[89] or six zodiac signs and 18°24′ away from the Part, suggesting that she might have six daughters even though her Part of Children (above) indicates that she will only have two children. In this scenario, the practitioner would rely on the prognostication of the Part of Children.

Peter's Part (18°♉04′) is situated in Taurus (♉), which is not one of the zodiac signs that promises many children (Cancer [♋], Scorpio [♏], or Pisces [♓]). However, the Part's planetary ruler,[90] Venus (♀ 18°♋53′ in fig. 6.2), is positioned

---

86. This remainder needed to be converted for two reasons: First, because the sign number in the remainder exceeds the total number of zodiac signs (12), that number is subtracted from the remainder (13) to derive the final sign number, 1. Second, the number of minutes in the remainder (60′) exceeds 59′. Since 60′ equal 01°, 60′ are subtracted from the total minutes in the remainder (64′) and 01° is added to the number of degrees in the remainder (17°), increasing the degrees to 18°.

87. This remainder needed to be converted because the sign number in the remainder exceeds the total number of zodiac signs (12). Therefore, 12 is subtracted from the remainder (13) to derive the final sign number, 1.

88. See note 27, page 274.

89. The distance between Alice's Part (13°♈00′) and Mars (♂01°♏24′) is determined by subtracting the two positions as shown below:

Mars (♂ 01°♏24′)	08	01°	24′
	07	31°	24′ (converted)
− Part of Female Children (13°♈00′)	01	13°	00′
	06	18°	24′

The six zodiac signs of difference are then converted into degrees by multiplying 6 by 30°00′ (the complete distance of a zodiac sign) and adding the result to the existing degrees. Thus the distance between the Part and the planet is 198°24′.

90. See note 27, page 274.

60°49′[91] or two zodiac signs, 00°49′ away from the Part, suggesting that he might have two daughters even though his Part of Children (above) indicates that he will only have one child. In this scenario, the practitioner would rely on the prognostication of the Part of Children.

The Part of Male Children

The Arabian Part of Male Children is derived by adding the Ascendant's position to Jupiter's position and subtracting the Moon's position. And as mentioned earlier, this Part is delineated in the same manner as both the Part of Children and the Part of Female Children, above.

Alice T.:

Ascendant (01°♒57′)	11	01°	57′	*(from fig. 6.1, House I)*
+ Jupiter (♃ 10°♉52′)	02	10°	52′	*(from fig. 6.1)*
	13	11°	109′	*(signs, degrees, and minutes)*
− Moon (☽ 11°♈28′)	01	11°	28′	*(from fig. 6.1)*
	12	00°	81′	*(remainder)*
	12	01°	21′	*(01°♓21′, Part of Male Children)[92]*

Peter C.:

Ascendant (02°♓49′)	12	02°	49′	*(from fig. 6.2, House I)*
+ Jupiter (♃ 25°♉38′)	02	25°	38′	*(from fig. 6.2)*
	14	27°	87′	*(signs, degrees, and minutes)*
− Moon (☽ 03°♉38′)	02	03°	38′	*(from fig. 6.2)*
	12	24°	49′	*(24°♓49′, Part of Male Children)*

Alice's Part of Male Children (01°♓21′) is situated in Pisces (♓), which is one of the zodiac signs that promises many children (Cancer [♋], Scorpio [♏], or Pisces [♓]). The Part's traditional planetary ruler,[93] Jupiter (♃ 10°♉52′ in fig. 6.1), is po-

---

91. The distance between Peter's Part (18°♉04′) and Venus (♀ 18°♋53′) is determined by subtracting the two positions as shown below:

Venus (♀ 18°♋53′)	04	18°	53′
− Part of Female Children (18°♉04′)	02	18°	04′
	02	00°	49′

The two zodiac signs of difference are then converted into degrees by multiplying 2 by 30°00′ (the complete distance of a zodiac sign) and adding the result to the existing degrees. Thus the distance between the Part and the planet is 60°49′.

92. This remainder needed to be converted because the number of minutes (′) in the remainder (81′) exceeds 59′. Since 60′ equal 01°, 60′ are subtracted from the total minutes in the remainder (81′) and 01° is added to the number of degrees in the remainder (00°), increasing the degrees to 01°.

93. See note 27, page 274.

sitioned 69°31′[94] or two zodiac signs plus 09°31′ away from the Part, suggesting that she might have two sons, which essentially coincides with her Part of Children (page 295).

Peter's Part (24°♓49′) is also situated in Pisces (♓), which is one of the zodiac signs that promises many children (Cancer [♋], Scorpio [♏], or Pisces [♓]). The Part's traditional planetary ruler,[95] Jupiter (♃ 25°♉36′ in fig. 6.1), is positioned 60°47′[96] or two zodiac signs plus 00°47′ away from the Part, suggesting that he might have two sons. In this scenario, the practitioner would rely on the prognostication of the Part of Children, which suggests that Peter will have only one child, and would not make a suggestion as to the gender of that child.

Parts Associated with House VI

Concern for the person's physical health was only a portion of the Arabian astrologers' analysis of House VI matters. The individual's ability to serve the spiritual realm, to provide aid to people in need, and to gain from a support network of servants or employees are some of the other concerns addressed. The Arabian Part of Infirmity,[97] Part of Servants, and Part of Slavery and Bondage were the primary sources for this valuable information. Modern Western astrologers modified the Part of Infirmity, renaming it the Part of Sickness.

This section will include the calculation and interpretation of three of these Parts: the Part of Sickness, Part of Servants, and Part of Slavery and Bondage.

---

94.   The distance between Alice's Part (01°♓21′) and Jupiter (♃ 10°♉52′) is determined by subtracting the two positions as shown below:

Jupiter (♃ 10°♉52′)	02	10°	52′	
	14	10°	52′	(12 signs added to facilitate calculation)
− Part of Male Children (01°♓21′)	12	01°	21′	
	02	09°	31′	

The two zodiac signs of difference are then converted into degrees by multiplying 2 by 30°00′ (the complete distance of a zodiac sign) and adding the result to the existing degrees. Thus the distance between the Part and the planet is 69°31′.

95.   See note 27, page 274.

96.   The distance between Peter's Part (24°♓49′) and Jupiter (♃ 25°♉36′) is determined by subtracting the two positions as shown below:

Jupiter (♃ 25°♉36′)	02	25°	36′	
	14	24°	96′	(12 signs added to facilitate calculation)
− Part of Male Children (25°♓49′)	12	24°	49′	
	02	00°	47′	

The two zodiac signs of difference are then converted into degrees by multiplying 2 by 30°00′ (the complete distance of a zodiac sign) and adding the result to the existing degrees. Thus the distance between the Part and the planet is 60°47′.

97.   The Part is derived by adding the Ascendant's position to Mars's position and subtracting Mercury's position. No specific details were ever given as to how the Part is delineated, so the Part is not presented in this section.

The Part of Sickness

The Arabian Part of Sickness signifies the person's physical weak point. The Part is derived by adding the Ascendant's position to Mars's position and subtracting Saturn's position. The Part is then interpreted by the house it occupies in the horoscope (see "Positioning and Interpreting an Arabian Part," page 263).

Alice T.:

Ascendant (01°♒57')	11	01°	57'	(*from fig. 6.1, House I*)
+ Mars (♂ 01°♏24')	08	01°	24'	(*from fig. 6.1*)
	19	02°	81'	(*signs, degrees, and minutes*)
	18	32°	81'	(*converted*)
− Saturn (♄ 08°♎12')	07	08°	12'	(*from fig. 6.1*)
	11	24°	69'	(*remainder*)
	11	25°	09'	(25°♒09', *Part of Sickness*)[98]

Peter C.:

Ascendant (02°♓49')	12	02°	49'	(*from fig. 6.2, House I*)
+ Mars (♂ 18°♋31')	04	18°	31'	(*from fig. 6.2*)
	16	20°	80'	(*signs, degrees, and minutes*)
− Saturn (♄ 08°♎12')	07	08°	12'	(*from fig. 6.2*)
	09	12°	68'	(*remainder*)
	09	13°	08'	(13°♐08', *Part of Sickness*)[99]

Since each house in the horoscope rules a particular portion of the body, as described by Ptolemy in his treatise *Tetrabiblos*, Western astrologers generally delineate the Part's influence by the house it occupies (see "Positioning and Interpreting an Arabian Part") according to the material below:

House I   head and face

House II   throat and ears

House III   shoulders, arms, hands, lungs, collar bones, and nervous system

House IV   breast, stomach, and digestive system

---

98. This remainder needed to be converted because the number of minutes in the remainder (69') exceeds 59'. Since 60' equal 01°, 60' are subtracted from the total minutes in the remainder (69') and 01° is added to the number of degrees in the remainder (24°), increasing the degrees to 25°.

99. This remainder needed to be converted because the number of minutes in the remainder (68') exceeds 59°. Since 60' equal 01°, 60' are subtracted from the total minutes in the remainder (68') and 01° is added to the number of degrees in the remainder (12°), increasing the degrees to 13°.

House V	heart and back
House VI	solar plexus and bowels
House VII	kidneys, ovaries, and lower back
House VIII	muscles, bladder, and genitals
House IX	liver and thighs
House X	knees
House XI	ankles
House XII	feet

Alice's Part of Sickness (25°♒︎09′) occupies House I (see "Positioning and Interpreting an Arabian Part") which indicates that diseases and illnesses might center on her head and face. Peter's Part (13°♐08′) occupies House IX (see "Positioning and Interpreting an Arabian Part") as well, which indicates that diseases and illnesses might center on his liver and thighs.

Furthermore, some modern Western astrologers believe that if this Part forms a square (90°00′ distance, ±06°00′) or opposing (180°00′ distance, ±06°00′) aspect (see "Delineating Planetary Aspects" in chapter 8) with the Moon (☽) or Neptune (♆), the person may have a sensitive stomach. If the Part forms a square or opposing aspect (see "Delineating Planetary Aspects" in chapter 8) with Saturn (♄), the person is apt to catch colds and chills. If it forms a square or opposing aspect (see "Delineating Planetary Aspects" in chapter 8) with Venus (♀) or Jupiter (♃), overindulgence is the cause of illness. If this Part forms a square or opposing aspect (see "Delineating Planetary Aspects" in chapter 8) with Uranus (♅) or Mars (♂), the person is accident-prone. If the Part forms a square or opposing aspect with Mercury (☿), the person suffers from anxiety and tension, which, in turn, cause illness. And if the Part forms a square or opposing aspect (see "Delineating Planetary Aspects" in chapter 8) with Pluto (♇), the person's illnesses could become complicated. None of these aspects are formed by Alice's or Peter's Parts. Therefore, no prognostications would be made using this material.

The Part of Servants

In earlier times, the Arabian Part of Servants indicated an individual's ability to hire and direct servants. But in this modern era, the ability to manage the physical world depends on an individual's relationships with employees or co-workers. Consequently, this Part has been transformed by modern Western astrologers into a

Part that signifies this relationship. The Part is derived by adding the Ascendant's position to the Moon's position and subtracting Mercury's position from the sum. It is delineated in a very unique manner: this Part's effect is only encountered for a few days at a time, activated by the passage of certain planets over the Part's position. It is also delineated if the Part forms an aspect (see "Delineating Planetary Aspects" in chapter 8) with certain planets.

Alice T.:

Ascendant (01°♒57′)	11	01°	57′	*(from fig. 6.1, House I)*
+ Moon (☽ 11°♈28′)	01	11°	28′	*(from fig. 6.1)*
	12	12°	85′	*(signs, degrees, and minutes)*
− Mercury (☿ 03°♋28′)	04	03°	28′	*(from fig. 6.1)*
	08	09°	57′	(09°♏57′, *Part of Servants*)

Peter C.:

Ascendant (02°♓49′)	12	02°	49′	*(from fig. 6.2, House I)*
+ Moon (☽ 03°♉38′)	02	03°	38′	*(from fig. 6.2)*
	14	05°	87′	*(signs, degrees, and minutes)*
	13	35°	87′	*(converted)*
− Mercury (☿ 14°♍36′)	06	14°	36′	*(from fig. 6.2)*
	07	21°	51′	(21°♎51′, *Part of Servants*)

If the Moon (☽) transits (passes by) the zodiac sign, degrees, and minutes occupied by the Part of Servants during the Moon's monthly orbit through the zodiac signs, it brings positive emotional concerns over employees. For example, if the Moon occupies 09°♏00′ (±01°00′) during a day or two in a given month, Alice's Part of Servants (09°♏57′) will stimulate positive emotional concerns. Similarly, if the Moon occupies 21°♎00′ (±01°00′) during a day or two in a given month, Peter's Part of Servants (21°♎51′) will stimulate positive emotional concerns.

If Mercury (☿), Uranus (♅), or Neptune (♆) transits the zodiac sign, degrees, and minutes occupied by the Part of Servants (±01°00′) during the planet's orbit through the zodiac signs, subordinates or co-workers have the upper hand in the relationship with the individual.

If the Part of Servants forms a trine (120°00′ or 240°00′ distance, ±06°00′), sextile (60°00′ distance, ±06°00′), or conjunct (00°00′ distance, ±06°00′) aspect (see "Delineating Planetary Aspects" in chapter 8) with the Sun (☉), Venus (♀), or Saturn (♄) in a person's natal horoscope, the person forms positive relationships with co-workers and subordinates. If Jupiter (♃) forms a trine (120°00′ or 240°00′ distance, ±06°00′), sextile (60°00′ distance, ±06°00′), or conjunct (00°00′ distance, ±06°00′) aspect (see "Delineating Planetary Aspects" in chapter 8) with this Part, the person is too generous and forgiving, causing a poor working relationship with employees or subordinates. None of the above aspects are formed with either Alice's or Peter's Parts, so the practitioner would make no further prognostications using this Part.

The Part of Slavery and Bondage

In contrast to the Part of Servants, the Arabian Part of Slavery and Bondage indicates whom or what an individual serves. The Part is derived by adding the Ascendant's position to the Moon's position and subtracting the planetary ruler[100] of the zodiac sign that the Moon occupies from the sum.[101] The Part is then interpreted by the house it occupies in the horoscope (see "Positioning and Interpreting an Arabian Part," page 263).

Alice T.:

Ascendant (01°♒57′)	11	01°	57′	(from fig. 6.1, House I)
+ Moon (☽ 11°♈28′)	01	11°	28′	(from fig. 6.1)
	12	12°	85′	(signs, degrees, and minutes)
− Mars (♂ 01°♏24′)	08	01°	24′	(from fig. 6.1)[102]
	04	11°	61′	(remainder)
	04	12°	01′	(12°♋01′, Part of Slavery and Bondage)[103]

Peter C.:

Ascendant (02°♓49′)	12	02°	49′	(from fig. 6.2, House I)
+ Moon (☽ 03°♉38′)	02	03°	38′	(from fig. 6.2)
	14	05°	87′	(signs, degrees, and minutes)
	13	35°	87′	(converted)
− Venus (♀ 18°♋53′)	04	18°	53′	(from fig. 6.2)[104]
	09	17°	34′	(17°♐34′, Part of Slavery and Bondage)

100. See note 27, page 274.
101. According to Arabian astrologers, this calculation should only be used if the person was born at night; the Sun's position should replace the Moon's position in a daytime horoscope.
102. Mars (♂) is the planetary ruler of the zodiac sign Aries (♈), which the Moon occupies in Alice's horoscope (see note 27, page 274).
103. This remainder needed to be converted because the number of minutes in the remainder (61′) exceeds 59′. Since 60′ equal 01°, 60′ are subtracted from the total minutes in the remainder (61′) and 01° is added to the number of degrees in the remainder (11°), increasing the degrees to 12°.
104. Venus (♀) is the planetary ruler of the zodiac sign Taurus (♉), which the Moon occupies in Peter's horoscope (see note 27, page 274).

Both ancient Arabian and modern Western astrologers delineate the Part's influence by the house it occupies (see "Positioning and Interpreting an Arabian Part") according to the material below:

House I	serves his or her own interests
House II	is spiritually bonded to his or her money or possessions
House III	is enslaved by his or her own senses
House IV	is a slave to the keeping and improvement of the home and domestic environment
House V	is enslaved by the pursuit of romantic, creative, and pleasurable goals, or is obsessed with the happiness of his or her children
House VI	is a workaholic
House VII	is spiritually bonded to a spouse or business partners
House VIII	is enslaved by the pursuit and fulfillment of sexual pleasure
House IX	serves only the improvement of his or her own intellect or spiritual being
House X	is enslaved by the quest for fame, honor, and power
House XI	is spiritually bonded to his or her friends and acquaintances
House XII	is enslaved by karmic debts and secret desires

Alice's Part of Slavery and Bondage (12°♋01') is located in House VI (see "Positioning and Interpreting an Arabian Part"), suggests that she is a workaholic. Situated in House X (see "Positioning and Interpreting an Arabian Part"), Peter's Part (17°♐34') indicates that he is enslaved by the quest for fame, honor, and power.

Parts Associated with House VII

Both men and women have been known to pursue the bonds of marriage with the daring and cunning of conquerors or hunters, or have found themselves ensnared in it like prey. Arabian astrologers developed Parts that not only determined the chase and the conquest, but the outcome as well. Numerous Parts, such as the Part of Men's Marriages, the Part of Luxury and Fornication of Men, the Part of the Marriage of Women, the Part of Pleasure and Amusements, the Part of Religion and the Honesty of Women, the Part of Marriage of Men and Women, the Part of the Marriage Hour, the Part of Intelligence and Ease of Marriage, the Part of Fathers-in-Law, and the Part of Discord and Controversy, used by ancient Arabian astrologers, are obsolete.[105] Each has been refined or completely replaced by versions more conducive to modern life over the centuries, such as the Part of Plays, the Part of Desire and Sexual Attraction, the Part of Sex, and the Part of Marriage. The construction and interpretation of these four Parts and of the Part of Discord and Controversy are documented in this section.

The Part of Plays

Modern Western astrologers developed the Arabian Part of Plays as an updated version of the Arabian Part of Pleasure and Amusements[106] to determine the person's approach to romance and the pursuit of sensual pleasure. This Part is derived by adding the Ascendant's position to Venus's position and subtracting Mars's position. The Part is interpreted by the house (see "Positioning and Interpreting an Arabian Part") and the zodiac sign it occupies.

Alice T.:

Ascendant (01°♒57')	11	01°	57'	(from fig. 6.1, House I)
+ Venus (♀ 22°31')	03	22°	31'	(from fig. 6.1)
	14	23°	88'	(signs, degrees, and minutes)
− Mars (♂ 01°♏24')	08	01°	24'	(from fig. 6.1)
	06	22°	64'	(remainder)
	06	23°	04'	(23°♍04', Part of Plays)[107]

Peter C.:

Ascendant (02°♓49')	12	02°	49'	(from fig. 6.2, House I)
+ Venus (♀ 18°♋53')	04	18°	53'	(from fig. 6.2)
	16	20°	102'	(signs, degrees, and minutes)
− Mars (♂ 18°♋31')	04	18°	31'	(from fig. 6.2)
	12	02°	71'	(remainder)
	12	03°	01'	(03°♓01', Part of Plays)

---

105. The formulas for these arcane Arabian Parts are detailed in Robert Zoller's book, *The Arabian Parts in Astrology: A Lost Key to Prediction* (Rochester, Vt.: Inner Traditions International, 1980).

106. The Arabian Part of Pleasure and Amusements is derived by adding the Ascendant's position to Venus's position and subtracting the cusp of House VII. There was no documentation as to its interpretation given by Bonatti, therefore, it is assumed that this information has disappeared.

107. This remainder needed to be converted because the number of minutes in the remainder (64') exceeds 59'. Since 60' equal 01°, 60' are subtracted from the total minutes in the remainder (64') and 01° is added to the number of degrees in the remainder (22°), increasing the degrees to 23°.

Alice's Part (23°♍04′) is situated in House VIII (see "Positioning and Interpreting an Arabian Part"), indicating that she is attracted to people who either handle other people's money or have inherited a legacy and are born under the zodiac sign Virgo (♍) (see "The Sun in the Various Zodiac Signs" in chapter 5). Peter's Part (03°♓01′) occupies House I (see "Positioning and Interpreting an Arabian Part"), suggesting that he is attracted to people who focus on their own personality and are born under the zodiac sign Pisces (♓) (see "The Sun in the Various Zodiac Signs" in chapter 5).

If the Part of Plays forms an aspect (see "Delineating Planetary Aspects" in chapter 8) with Mars (♂), Uranus (♅), or Pluto (♇), the person is overwhelmed by romantic encounters. If the Part of Plays forms an aspect (see "Delineating Planetary Aspects" in chapter 8) with Saturn (♄), the person's romantic life is stifled in some way. Peter's Part (03°♓01′) forms a conjunction with Saturn (♄ 01°♓25′ in fig. 6.2).[108] If this Part forms an aspect of any type (see "Delineating Planetary Aspects" in chapter 8) with Jupiter (♃), Venus (♀), the Sun (☉), Mercury (☿), or Neptune (♆), he or she possesses remarkable romantic energy. An example can be seen with Alice's Part (23°♍04′) which forms a square with both the Sun (☉ 24° ♊55′ in fig. 6-1)[109] and Venus (♀ 22°♊31′ in fig. 6.1).[110]

---

108. The distance between Peter's Part (03°♓01′) and Saturn (♄ 01°♓25′) is determined by subtracting the two positions as shown below:

Part of Plays (03°♓01′)	12	03°	01′	
	12	02°	61′	(converted)
− Saturn (♄ 01°♓25′)	12	01°	25′	
	00	01°	36′	

Thus the distance between the Part and the planet is 01°36′.

109. The distance between Alice's Part (23°♍04′) and the Sun (☉ 24°♊55′) is determined by subtracting the two positions as shown below:

Part of Plays (23°♍04′)	06	23°	04′	
	05	52°	64′	(converted)
− Sun (☉ 24°♊55′)	03	24°	55′	
	02	28°	09′	

The two zodiac signs of difference are then converted into degrees by multiplying 2 by 30°00′ (the complete distance of a zodiac sign) and adding the result to the existing degrees. Thus the distance between the Part and the planet is 88°09′, forming a square (90°00 distance, ±06°00′).

110. The distance between Alice's Part (23°♍04′) and Venus (♀ 22°♊31′) is determined by subtracting the two positions as shown below:

Part of Plays (23°♍04′)	06	23°	04′	
	05	52°	64′	(converted)
− Venus (♀ 22°♊31′)	03	22°	31′	
	02	30°	33′	

The two zodiac signs of difference are then converted into degrees by multiplying 2 by 30°00′ (the complete distance of a zodiac sign) and adding the result to the existing degrees. Thus the distance between the Part and the planet is 90°33′, forming a square (90°00 distance, ±06°00′).

Peter's Part (03°♓01′) forms an opposition with the Sun (☉ 04°♍41′ in fig. 6.2).[111] Thus, both people would be deemed to possess remarkable romantic energy.

The Part of Desire and Sexual Attraction

Another modern variation, the Arabian Part of Desire and Sexual Attraction, prognosticates what type of person the individual in question finds sexually attractive. If the individual is born during the night, the Part is derived by adding the Ascendant's position to House V's planetary ruler[112] and subtracting the cusp of House V from the sum. If the individual is born during the daytime, the Part is derived by adding the Ascendant's position to the cusp of House V and subtracting House V's planetary ruler from the sum. In either case, this Part is interpreted by the zodiac sign it occupies, indicating the character traits of the person that attracts the individual in question (see "The Sun in the Various Zodiac Signs" in chapter 5).

Both Alice and Peter were born during the night. Therefore the two examples below demonstrate the calculation of a nighttime Part of Desire and Sexual Attraction.

Alice T.:

Ascendant (01°♒57′)	11	01°	57′	(from fig. 6.1, House I)
+ Mercury (☿ 03°♋28′)	04	03°	28′	(from fig. 6.1)[113]
	15	04°	85′	(signs, degrees, and minutes)
	14	34°	85′	(converted)
− House V cusp (16°♊44′)	03	16°	44′	(from fig. 6.1)
	11	18°	41′	(18°♒41′, Part of Desire and Sexual Attraction)

---

111.   The distance between Peter's Part (03°♓01′) and the Sun (☉ 04°♍41′) is determined by subtracting the two positions as shown below:

Part of Plays (03°♓01′)	12	03°	01′	
	11	32°	61′	(converted)
− Sun (☉ 04°♍41′)	06	04°	41′	
	05	28°	20′	

The two zodiac signs of difference are then converted into degrees (°) by multiplying 5 by 30°00′ (the complete distance of a zodiac sign) and adding the result to the existing degrees. Thus, the distance between the Part and the planet is 178°20′, forming an opposition (180°00 distance, ±06°00′).

112.   See note 27, page 274.

113.   Mercury (☿) is the planetary ruler of the zodiac sign Gemini (♊), which governs House V in Alice's horoscope (see note 27, page 274).

Peter C.:

Ascendant (02°♓49′)	12	02°	49′	(*from fig. 6.2, House I*)
+ Moon (☽ 03°♉38′)	02	03°	38′	(*from fig. 6.2*)[114]
	14	05°	87′	(*signs, degrees, and minutes*)
	13	35°	87′	(*converted*)
− House V cusp (06°♋26′)	04	06°	26′	(*from fig. 6.2*)
	09	29°	61′	(*remainder*)
	10	00°	01′	(10°♑01′, *Part of Desire and Sexual Attraction*)[115]

Alice's Part (18°♒41′) occupies the zodiac sign Aquarius (♒). Since the Sun exerts a strong influence on the personality of an individual, you can refer to the delineation of the Sun in a zodiac sign to disclose the necessary information (see "The Sun in the Various Zodiac Signs" in chapter 5). In this case, Aquarius (♒) indicates that Alice is attracted to an unobtrusive, determined, eccentric person who has very strong likes and dislikes. This person is also a faithful friend and a humanitarian who is slow to anger, easily influenced by kindness, and suffers from feelings of rejection.

Peter's Part (00°♑01′) occupies the zodiac sign Capricorn (♑), indicating that he is attracted to a practical, quiet, ambitious, opportunistic person who has strong self-esteem. This person is often disappointed and suffers from bouts of gloom and depression.

The Part of Sex

Another modern variation, the Arabian Part of Sex, signifies the quality of the person's sexual drive. The Part is derived by adding the Ascendant's position to Pluto's position and subtracting Venus's position from the sum. Modern Western astrologers delineate the Part's influence by the house it occupies (see "Positioning and Interpreting an Arabian Part").

Alice T.:

Ascendant (01°♒57′)	11	01°	57′	(*from fig. 6.1, House I*)
+ Pluto (♇ 19°♌34′)	05	19°	34′	(*from fig. 6.1*)
	16	20°	91′	(*signs, degrees, and minutes*)

---

114.   The Moon (☽) is the planetary ruler of the zodiac sign Cancer (♋), which governs House V in Peter's horoscope (see note 27, page 000).

115.   This remainder needed to be converted because the number of minutes in the remainder (61′) exceeds 59′. Since 60′ equal 01°, 60′ are subtracted from the total minutes in the remainder (61′) and 01° is added to the number of degrees in the remainder (29°), increasing the degrees to 30°. The number of degrees in the remainder now exceeds 29°, so 30° is subtracted from the converted degrees (30°) and one full sign (30°00′) is added to the remainder's sign number (09), increasing it to 10.

	15	50°	91'	(*converted*)
− Venus (♀ 22°♊31')	03	22°	31'	(*from fig. 6.1*)
	12	28°	60'	(*remainder*)
	12	29°	00'	(29°♓00', *Part of Sex*)[116]

Peter C.:

Ascendant (02°♓49')	12	02°	49'	(*from fig. 6.2, House I*)
+ Pluto (♇ 13°♍38')	05	19°	34'	(*from fig. 6.2*)
	17	21°	83'	(*signs, degrees, and minutes*)
− Venus (♀ 18°♋53')	04	18°	53'	(*from fig. 6.2*)
	13	03°	30'	(*remainder*)
	01	03°	30'	(03°♈30', *Part of Sex*)[117]

Modern Western astrologers delineate the Part's influence by the house it occupies (see "Positioning and Interpreting an Arabian Part"), reflecting concerns similar to those determined by ancient Parts such as the Part of Luxury and Fornication of Men,[118] as shown in the material below:

House I   autoerotic

House II   sensually driven

House III   mentally preoccupied with sex

House IV   seeks sexual security

House V   seeks sexual pleasure

House VI   strongly fears sexually transmitted diseases and other sexual complications

House VII   bases every relationship on sex

House VIII   sexually curious

House IX   daydreams about sex

---

116.   This remainder needed to be converted because the number of minutes in the remainder (61') exceeds 59'. Since 60' equal 01°, 60' are subtracted from the total minutes in the remainder (60') and 01° is added to the number of degrees in the remainder (28°), increasing the degrees to 29°.

117.   This remainder needed to be converted because the sign number in the remainder exceeds the total number of zodiac signs (12). Therefore, 12 is subtracted from the remainder (13) to derive the final sign number, 1.

118.   This Part was derived by adding the Ascendant's position to Venus's position and subtracting Saturn's position from the sum. The Part was sometimes called the Part of Marriage of Men and Women. Bonatti did not document its delineation, however, so it was not included in this section.

House X	needs to be dominant in any sexual relationship
House XI	desires group sex
House XII	subconsciously fears sex

Alice's Part (29°♓00′) occupies House II (see "Positioning and Interpreting an Arabian Part"), indicating that she is sensually driven. Peter's Part (03°♈30′) occupies House I (see "Positioning and Interpreting an Arabian Part"), indicating that he is autoerotic.

The Part of Discord and Controversy

Modified by modern Western astrologers to include the planets Uranus (♅), Neptune (♆), and Pluto (♇) in its delineation, the Arabian Part of Discord and Controversy signifies the person's potential for encountering difficulties in communications with his or her spouse. The Part is derived by adding the Ascendant's position to Jupiter's position and subtracting Mars's position from the sum. This Part is delineated by the aspects it forms with other planets (see "Delineating Planetary Aspects" in chapter 8).

Alice T.:

Ascendant (01°≈57′)	11	01°	57′	(from fig. 6.1, House I)
+ Jupiter (♃ 10°♉52′)	02	10°	52′	(from fig. 6.1)
	13	11°	109′	(signs, degrees, and minutes)
− Mars (♂ 01°♏24′)	08	01°	24′	(from fig. 6.1)
	05	10°	85′	(remainder)
	05	11°	25′	(11°♌25′, Part of Discord and Controversy)[119]

Peter C.:

Ascendant (02°♓49′)	12	02°	49′	(from fig. 6.2, House I)
+ Jupiter (♃ 25°♉36′)	02	25°	36′	(from fig. 6.2)
	14	27°	85′	(signs, degrees, and minutes)
− Mars (♂ 18°♋31′)	04	18°	31′	(from fig. 6.2)
	10	09°	54′	(09°♑54′, Part of Discord and Controversy)

---

119. This remainder needed to be converted because the number of minutes in the remainder (61′) exceeds 59′. Since 60′ equal 01°, 60′ are subtracted from the total minutes in the remainder (85′) and 01° is added to the number of degrees in the remainder (10°), increasing the degrees to 11°.

If the Part of Discord and Controversy forms a square (90°00′ distance, ±06°00′) or opposing (180°00′ distance, ±06°00′) aspect (see "Delineating Planetary Aspects" in chapter 8) with Venus (♀) or the Moon (☽), the person encounters strife with a woman or a small child. If the Part forms a square or opposing aspect (see "Delineating Planetary Aspects" in chapter 8) with Mercury (☿), Mars (♂), or Uranus (♅), the person is the target of vindictive actions. If the Part forms a square or opposing aspect (see "Delineating Planetary Aspects" in chapter 8) with Pluto (♇), other people direct their deep discontent toward the person. If the Part forms a square or opposing aspect (see "Delineating Planetary Aspects" in chapter 8) with Jupiter (♃), the Sun (☉), or Saturn (♄), the person encounters many quarrels and arguments that lead to separation or divorce. If the Part forms a square or opposing aspect (see "Delineating Planetary Aspects" in chapter 8) with Neptune (♆), hidden plots and confusion are targeted at the person, who won't discover them until it's too late. Neither Alice's nor Peter's Parts form any of the above aspects. Therefore, this part would not be included in any prognostication.

The Part of Marriage

The modern version of the Arabian Part of Marriage of Men and Women is simply called the Part of Marriage, signifying the person's potential for marital happiness. The Part is derived by adding the Ascendant's position to the cusp of House VII and subtracting Venus's position from the sum. And like the Part of Discord and Controversy, this Part is delineated by the aspects it forms with other planets (see "Delineating Planetary Aspects" in chapter 8).

Alice T.:

Ascendant (01°♒57′)	11	01°	57′	(*from fig. 6.1, House I*)
+ House VII cusp (01°♌57′)	05	01°	57′	(*from fig. 6.1*)
	16	02°	114′	(*signs, degrees, and minutes*)
	15	32°	114′	(*converted*)
− Venus (♀ 22°♊31′)	03	22°	31′	(*from fig. 6.1*)
	12	10°	83′	(*remainder*)
	12	11°	23′	(11°♓23′, *Part of Marriage*)[120]

---

120. This remainder needed to be converted because the number of minutes in the remainder (83′) exceeds 59′. Since 60′ equal 01°, 60′ are subtracted from the total minutes in the remainder (83′) and 01° is added to the number of degrees in the remainder (10°), increasing the degrees to 11°.

Peter C.:

Ascendant (02°♓49′)	12	02°	49′	*(from fig. 6.2, House I)*
+ House VII cusp (02°♍49′)	06	02°	49′	*(from fig. 6.2)*
	18	04°	98′	*(signs, degrees, and minutes)*
	17	34°	98′	*(converted)*
− Venus (♀ 18°♋53′)	04	18°	53′	*(from fig. 6.2)*
	13	16°	45′	*(remainder)*
	01	16°	45′	(16°♈45′, *Part of Marriage*)[121]

If the Part of Marriage forms a trine (120°00′ or 240°00′ distance, ±06°00′), sextile (60°00′ distance, ±06°00′), or conjunct (00°00′ distance, ±06°00′) aspect (see "Delineating Planetary Aspects" in chapter 8) with the Sun (☉), the person is proud of his or her marriage. If the Part forms a trine, sextile, or conjunct aspect (see "Delineating Planetary Aspects" in chapter 8) with the Moon (☽), Venus (♀), or Jupiter (♃), then the marriage itself is successful. For example, Alice's Part of Marriage (11°♓23′) forms a sextile with Jupiter (♃ 10°♉52′ in fig. 6.1), suggesting that she has a successful union.[122]

If the Part forms a square (90°00′ distance, ±06°00′) or opposing (180°00′ distance, ±06°00′) aspect (see "Delineating Planetary Aspects" in chapter 8) with Mercury (☿), Mars (♂), Uranus (♅), or Pluto (♇), it suggests that the person has unfounded fears that his or her marriage will end. Peter's Part (16°♈45′) forms a square aspect with Mars (♂ 18°♋31′ in fig. 6.2), indicating that this is one of his concerns.[123]

---

121.   This remainder needed to be converted because the sign number in the remainder exceeds the total number of zodiac signs (12). Therefore, 12 is subtracted from the remainder (13) to derive the final sign number, 1.

122.   The distance between Alice's Part (11°♓23′) and Jupiter (♃ 10°♉52′) is determined by subtracting the two positions as shown below:

Jupiter (♃ 10°♉52′)	02	10°	52′	
	14	10°	52′	*(12 signs added to facilitate calculation)*
	13	40°	52′	*(converted)*
− Part of Marriage (11°♓23′)	12	11°	23′	
	01	29°	29′	

The one zodiac sign of difference is then converted into 30°00′ (the complete distance of a zodiac sign) and added to the existing degrees. Thus the distance between the Part and the planet is 59°29′, forming a sextile (60°00 distance, ±06°00′).

123.   The distance between Peter's Part (16°♈45′) and Mars (♂ 18°♋31′) is determined by subtracting the two positions as shown below:

Mars (♂ 18°♋31′)	04	18°	31′	
	04	17°	91′	*(converted)*
− Part of Marriage (16°♈45′)	01	16°	45′	
	03	01°	46′	

The three zodiac signs of difference are then converted into degrees by multiplying 3 by 30°00′ (the complete distance of a zodiac sign) and adding the result to the existing degrees. Thus the distance between the Part and the planet is 94°46′, forming a square (90°00 distance, ±06°00′).

If the Part forms a square (90°00′ distance, ±06°00′) or opposing (180°00′ distance, ±06°00′) aspect (see "Delineating Planetary Aspects" in chapter 8) with Saturn (♄), it portends marriage to, and eventual separation from, a cold-hearted spouse. If it forms a trine (120°00′ or 240°00′ distance, ±06°00′), sextile (60°00′ distance, ±06°00′), or conjunct (00°00′ distance, ±06°00′) aspect (see "Delineating Planetary Aspects" in chapter 8) with Neptune (♆), the marriage has a more optimistic bearing filled with strong memories of the good times that propel the couple through dark periods. If the Part does not form any of the above aspects with other planets, the practitioner would not make any prognostications using this part.

Parts Associated with House VIII

The timing and conditions of a person's death were studied by Arabian astrologers who observed the motion of an afflicted or malefic planet that they called the Anareta (Destroyer). If Mars (♂) or Saturn (♄) in the natal horoscope forms a conjunct, square, or opposing aspect to a transiting Almochoden,[124] the Sun (☉), the Moon (☽), or Mercury (☿), death is said to be imminent. Ptolemy also suggested that if the Ascendant, the Ascendant's ruler, the Sun, or the Moon occupies one of the *azemene*[125] degrees, the person will be born with a lifelong infirmity or terminal disease. Many of the ancient Arabian Parts associated with House VIII are almost too detailed in their approach to this subject, as evidenced by their names. For example, the Part of the Killing Planet,[126] the Part of the Year of Death,[127] the Part of the Heavy Planet,[128] and the Part of Occupation, Severity, and Destruction[129] were all employed in an attempt to determine the exact moment and happenstance of the person's death. In this section, only the calculation and interpretation of the Part of Death will be presented.

---

124.   The Almochoden is a planet that is positioned in one of the beneficial hylegical degrees: 05°00′–25°00′ below the Ascendant (House I); 05°00′–25°00′ above the Descendant (House VII); or in the area lying 05°00′ below House IX's cusp to 25°00′ above House XI's cusp.

125.   The *azemene* degrees are 06°♉00′–10°♉00′; 09°♋00′–13°♋00′; 18°♌00′, 27°♌00′, and 28°♌00′; 19°♏00′ and 28°♏00′; 01°♐00′, 07°♐00′–08°♐00′, and 18°♐00′–19°♐00′; 26°♑00′–29°♑00′; and 18°♒00′–19°♒00′.

126.   The Part is derived by adding the Ascendant's position to the Ascendant's ruler and subtracting the Moon. Its influence is similar to the Anareta. Bonatti did not detail its interpretation, however, so it is not included in this section.

127.   According to Bonatti, this Part was closely observed in progressed horoscopes if the Part formed an aspect with Saturn, the Ascendant, and the "lord of the house of conjunction or prevention which preceded the nativity, question, or revolution." Its delineation was not detailed, however, so it is not included in this section.

128.   The Part is calculated in the same way as the Part of Ancestors, but delineated for the potential of inherited illness that would cause the person's demise. The Part is derived by adding the Ascendant's position to Saturn's position and subtracting Mars's position from the sum. Bonatti, did not detail the Part's delineation, however, so it is not included in this section.

129.   This Part is derived by adding the Ascendant's position to Saturn's position and subtracting Mercury's position. Bonatti did not sufficiently document the Part's delineation, however, so it is not included in this section.

The Part of Death

The Arabian Part of Death signifies the conditions of a person's death, the person's preoccupation with life and death, and how prone the person is to accidents or violent crimes. According to modern Western astrologers, the Part is derived by adding the Ascendant's position to the cusp of House VIII and subtracting the Moon's position from the sum.[130] The Part is delineated by the aspects it forms with other planets (see "Delineating Planetary Aspects" in chapter 8).

Alice T.:

Ascendant (01°♒57′)	11	01°	57′	(from fig. 6.1, House I)
+ House VIII cusp (19°♍40′)	06	19°	40′	(from fig. 6.1)
	17	20°	97′	(signs, degrees, and minutes)
− Moon (☽ 11°♈28′)	01	11°	28′	(from fig. 6.1)
	16	09°	69′	(remainder)
	04	10°	09′	(10°♋09′, Part of Death)[131]

Peter C.:

Ascendant (02°♓49′)	12	02°	49′	(from fig. 6.2, House I)
+ House VIII cusp (24°♎34′)	07	24°	34′	(from fig. 6.2)
	19	26°	83′	(signs, degrees, and minutes)
− Moon (☽ 03°♉38′)	02	03°	38′	(from fig. 6.2)
	17	23°	45′	(remainder)
	05	23°	45′	(23°♌45′, Part of Death)[132]

If the Part of Death forms an aspect of any type (see chapter 8, "Delineating Planetary Aspects" in chapter 8) with Mars (♂), the person should take great precautions around firearms, fire, machinery, and general accidents. If the Part forms an aspect of any type (see "Delineating Planetary Aspects" in chapter 8) to the Sun (☉), it usually increases the desire for life. If it forms an aspect of any

---

130.   Ancient Arabian astrologers subtracted the cusp of House VIII from the Moon's position, added Saturn's position and the cusp of the house Saturn occupies to extract the same part. The equation used in the examples shown is, however, most commonly employed by contemporary practitioners.

131.   This remainder needed to be converted for two reasons: First, because the sign number in the remainder exceeds the total number of zodiac signs (12), that number is subtracted from the remainder (16) to derive the final sign number, 4. Second, it needed to be converted because the number of minutes in the remainder (69′) exceeds 59′. Since 60′ equal 01°, 60′ are subtracted from the total minutes in the remainder (69′) and 01° is added to the number of degrees in the remainder (09°), increasing the degrees to 10°.

132.   This remainder needed to be converted because the sign number in the remainder exceeds the total number of zodiac signs (12). Therefore, 12 is subtracted from the remainder (17) to derive the final sign number, 5.

type (see "Delineating Planetary Aspects" in chapter 8) to the Moon (☽), Neptune (♆), Pluto (♇), or Saturn (♄), the person is obsessed with death or health. This is the case with Alice, whose Part (10°♋09′) squares the Moon (☽ 11°♈28′ in fig. 6.1).[133] And if the Part forms an aspect of any type (see "Delineating Planetary Aspects" in chapter 8) with Uranus (♅), Jupiter (♃), or Venus (♀), the person is predisposed to carelessness. Peter's part does not form any of the above aspects. Therefore, no additional prognostications would be made using this material.

Parts Associated with House IX

Arabian astrologers developed a number of Parts that pertain to House IX matters, such as an individual's spiritual and philosophic leanings as well as the potential for long-distance journeys. Modern Western astrologers apply a few of these Parts, such as the Part of Faith, the Part of Journeys by Water, and the Part of Travels by Land. The calculation and interpretation of these three Parts are detailed in this section. But Arabian Parts such as the Part of Oration,[134] the Part of Wisdom,[135] the Part of Histories and Science,[136] and the Part of Rumors[137] have fallen into disuse over time and will not be explained here.

The Part of Faith

The person's belief system is the subject of the Arabian Part of Faith (Religion). This Part is derived by adding the Ascendant's position to Mercury's position and subtracting the Moon's position from the sum. The Part is delineated according to the house it occupies (see "Positioning and Interpreting an Arabian Part").

---

133. The distance between Alice's Part (10°♋09′) and the Moon (☽ 11°♈28′) is determined by subtracting the two positions as shown below:

Part of Death (10°♋09′)	04	10°	09′	
	03	39°	69′	(converted)
− Moon (☽ 11°♈28′)	01	11°	28′	
	02	28°	41′	

The two zodiac signs of difference are then converted into degrees by multiplying 2 by 30°00′ (the complete distance of a zodiac sign) and adding the result to the existing degrees. Thus the distance between the Part and the planet is 88°41′, forming a square (90°00′ distance, ±06°00′).

134. The Part is derived by adding the Ascendant's position to Saturn's position and subtracting the Moon's position. Bonatti did not adequately describe this Part's delineation.

135. The Part is derived by adding Mercury's position to Saturn's position and subtracting Jupiter's position. Bonatti did not describe the Part's interpretation.

136. The Part is derived by adding the Ascendant's position to the Sun's position and subtracting Jupiter's position. Bonatti did not disclose the Part's interpretation.

137. The Part is derived by adding the Ascendant's position to Mercury's position and subtracting the Moon's position. Again, Bonatti did not disclose the Part's delineation.

Alice T.:

Ascendant (01°≈57')	11	01°	57'	(from fig. 6.1, House I)
+ Mercury (☿ 03°♋28')	04	03°	28'	(from fig. 6.1)
	15	04°	85'	(signs, degrees, and minutes)
	14	34°	85'	(converted)
− Moon (☽ 11°♈28')	01	11°	28'	(from fig. 6.1)
	13	23°	57'	(remainder)
	01	23°	57'	(23°♈57', Part of Faith)

Peter C.:

Ascendant (02°♓49')	12	02°	49'	(from fig. 6.2, House I)
+ Mercury (☿ 14°♍36')	06	14°	36'	(from fig. 6.2)
	18	16°	85'	(signs, degrees, and minutes)
− Moon (☽ 03°♉38')	02	03°	38'	(from fig. 6.2)
	16	13°	47'	(remainder)
	04	13°	47'	(13°♋47', Part of Faith)[138]

Bonatti did not document the Part of Faith's delineation, but modern Western practitioners interpret it according to the Part's occupation of a particular house in the horoscope (see "Positioning and Interpreting an Arabian Part") based on the material below:

House I	believes in his or her own ideals
House II	has periods of spiritual and mental instability
House III	shares the beliefs of his or her siblings and close relatives
House IV	is resigned to following stronger forces
House V	is aware of stronger forces, but does not take a subservient position
House VI	chooses to serve stronger forces willingly
House VII	encounters periods of spiritual and mental instability
House VIII	embraces his or her beliefs with hope and optimism
House IX	strongly believes in the religion in which he or she was raised

---

138. This remainder needed to be converted because the sign number in the remainder (16) exceeds the total number of zodiac signs (12). So the latter is subtracted from the remainder (16) to derive the final sign number, 4.

House X	strongly believes in his or her profession
House XI	has blind faith in his or her friends and also has unrealistic hopes
House XII	is an escapist who believes in his or her dreams

Alice's Part of Faith (23°♈57′) is placed in House II (see "Positioning and Interpreting an Arabian Part"), which signifies that she has periods of spiritual and mental instability. Peter's Part (13°♋47′), however, is situated House V (see "Positioning and Interpreting an Arabian Part"), which indicates that he recognizes the existence of stronger forces but does not take a subservient position.

The Part of Journeys by Water

Travel-oriented Arabian Parts are generally consulted to determine the probability of the safe passage of a person to his or her destination. For instance, the Arabian Part of Journeys by Water is derived by adding the Ascendant's position to 15°00′ Cancer (15°♋00′) and subtracting Saturn's position from the sum. The Part is delineated by the aspects it forms with other planets (see "Delineating Planetary Aspects" in chapter 8).

Alice T.:

Ascendant (01°♒57′)	11	01°	57′	(from fig. 6.1, House I)
+ 15°♋00′	04	15°	00′	(from the above formula)
	15	16°	57′	(signs, degrees, and minutes)
− Saturn (♄ 08°♎12′)	07	08°	12′	(from fig. 6.1)
	08	08°	45′	(08°♏45′, Part of Journeys by Water)

Peter C.:

Ascendant (02°♓49′)	12	02°	49′	(from fig. 6.2, House I)
+ 15°♋00′	04	15°	00′	(from the above formula)
	16	17°	49′	(signs, degrees, and minutes)
− Saturn (♄ 01°♓25′)	12	01°	25′	(from fig. 6.2)
	04	16°	24′	(16°♋24′, Part of Journeys by Water)

If the Part of Journeys by Water forms a trine, sextile, or conjunct aspect (see "Delineating Planetary Aspects" in chapter 8) with the Sun (☉), Moon (☽), Mercury (☿), Venus (♀), or Jupiter (♃), the person has a pleasant voyage. For example, Alice's Part (08°♏45′) forms a trine aspect with Mercury (☿ 03°♋28′ in fig.

6.1)[139] and a sextile aspect with Jupiter (♃ 10°♉52′ in fig. 6.1).[140] Peter's Part (16°♋24′) forms a sextile aspect with Mercury (☿ 14°♋36′ in fig. 6.2),[141] and a conjunct aspect with Venus (♀ 18°♋53′ in fig. 6.2), indicating that both experience pleasant voyages.[142]

If this Part forms a square (90°00′ distance, ±06°00′) or opposing (180°00′ distance, ±06°00′) aspect (see "Locating Planetary Aspects" in chapter 8) with Mars (♂), Saturn (♄), Uranus (♅), or Pluto (♇), the person encounters complications along the way. If the Part does not form any of the above aspects, the practitioner does not make a prognostication based on this Part.

The Part of Travel by Land

Similarly, the Arabian Part of Travel by Land highlights long-distance overland journeys. This Part is derived by adding the Ascendant's position to the cusp of

---

139. The distance between Alice's Part (08°♏45′) and Mercury (☿ 03°♋28′) is determined by subtracting the two positions as shown below:

Part of Journeys by Water (08°♏45′)	08	08°	45′
− Mercury (☿ 03°♋28′)	04	03°	28′
	04	05°	17′

The four zodiac signs of difference are then converted into degrees by multiplying 4 by 30°00′ (the complete distance of a zodiac sign) and adding the result to the existing degrees. Thus the distance between the Part and the planet is 125°17′, forming a trine (120°00′ or 240°00′ distance, ±06°00′).

140. The distance between Alice's Part (08°♓45′) and Jupiter (♃ 10°♉52′) is determined by subtracting the two positions as shown below:

Jupiter (♃ 10°♉52′)	02	10°	52′
	14	10°	52′ (12 signs added to facilitate calculation)
−Part of Journeys by Water (08°♓45′)	12	08°	45′
	02	02°	07′

The two zodiac signs of difference are then converted into degrees by multiplying 2 by 30°00′ (the complete distance of a zodiac sign) and adding the result to the existing degrees. Thus the distance between the Part and the planet is 62°07′, forming a sextile (60°00′ distance, ±06°00′).

141. The distance between Peter's Part (16°♋24′) and Mercury (☿ 14°♍36′) is determined by subtracting the two positions as shown below:

Mercury (☿ 14°♍36′)	06	14°	36′
	05	44°	36′ (converted)
− Part of Journeys by Water (16°♋24′)	04	16°	24′
	01	28°	12′

The one zodiac sign of difference is then converted into 30°00′ (the complete distance of a zodiac sign) and added to the existing degrees. Thus the distance between the Part and the planet is 58°12′, forming a sextile (60°00′ distance, ±06°00′).

142. The distance between Peter's Part (16°♋24′) and Venus (♀ 18°♋53′) is determined by subtracting the two positions as shown below:

Venus (♀ 18°♋53′)	04	18°	53′
− Part of Journeys by Water (16°♋24′)	04	16°	24′
	00	02°	29′

Thus the distance between the Part and the planet is 02°29′, forming a conjunction (00°00′ distance, ±06°00′).

House IX and subtracting the ruler of House IX's position from the sum. Like its counterpart (the Part of Journeys by Water), the Part is delineated by the aspects it forms with other planets (see "Delineating Planetary Aspects" in chapter 8).

Alice T.:

Ascendant (01°♒57′)	11	01°	57′	*(from fig. 6.1, House I)*
+ House IX cusp (28°♎15′)	07	28°	15′	*(from fig. 6.1)*
	18	29°	72′	*(signs, degrees, and minutes)*
− Venus (♀ 22°♊31′)	03	22°	31′	*(from fig. 6.1)*[143]
	15	07°	41′	*(remainder)*
	03	07°	41′	(07°♊41′, *Part of Travel by Land)*[144]

Peter C.:

Ascendant (02°♓49′)	12	02°	49′	*(from fig. 6.2, House I)*
+ House IX cusp (25°♏27′)	08	25°	27′	*(from fig. 6.2)*
	20	27°	76′	*(signs, degrees, and minutes)*
− Mars (♂ 18°♋31′)	04	18°	31′	*(from fig. 6.2)*[145]
	16	09°	45′	*(remainder)*
	04	09°	45′	(09°♋45′, *Part of Travel by Land)*[146]

If the Part of Travel by Land forms a trine (120°00′ or 240°00′ distance, ±06°00′), sextile (60°00′ distance, ±06°00′), or conjunct (00°00′ distance, ±06°00′) aspect (see "Delineating Planetary Aspects" in chapter 8) with the Sun (☉), Moon (☽), Mercury (☿), Venus (♀), or Jupiter (♃), the person has a pleasant overland journey.

If this Part forms a square (90°00′ distance, ±06°00′) or opposing (180°00′ distance, ±06°00′) aspect (see "Delineating Planetary Aspects" in chapter 8) with Mars (♂), Saturn (♄), Uranus (♅), or Pluto (♇), the person encounters complications along the way. Since Alice's and Peter's Parts do not form any of the above aspects, the practitioner does not make a prognostication based on this Part.

---

143. See note 27, page 274.
144. This remainder needed to be converted because the sign number in the remainder exceeds the total number of zodiac signs (12). Therefore, 12 is subtracted from the remainder (15) to derive the final sign number, 3.
145. See note 27, page 274.
146. This remainder needed to be converted because the sign number in the remainder exceeds the total number of zodiac signs (12). Therefore, 12 is subtracted from the remainder (16) to derive the final sign number, 4.

Parts Associated with House X

An individual's career is the modern-day focus of the Arabian Parts relating to House X. Astrologers such as Ptolemy, Albumazar, Al'biruni, and Bonatti, however, concentrated their efforts on the development and use of Arabian Parts that related to higher levels of authority. But the viability of Parts such as the Part of Kingship and Kings, the Part of Kingship and Victory, the Part of Nobility and Honor, the Part of Soldiers and Ministers, the Part of Tradesmen, and the Part of Work and of Necessary and Absolute Things has dwindled over time and will not be explicated here.[147]

Nonetheless, certain Arabian Parts still appear to shed light on some House X matters such as the Part of Honor, the Part of Sudden Advancement, the Part of Magistery and Profession, and the Part of Merchandise. House X is also the realm of the individual's mother, and the Arabian Part of the Mother focuses on this critical parental relationship.

The Part of Honor

The Arabian Part of Honor is a refined version of the Arabian Part of Nobility and Honor,[148] which signifies how an individual achieves professional fame or honors. If the individual was born during the day, the Part is derived by adding the Ascendant's position to 19°00′ Aries (19°♈00′) and subtracting the Sun's position from the sum. Both Alice and Peter were born at night, so the equations shown below reflect the following nocturnal method. For an individual who was born at night, 03°00′ Taurus (03°♉00′) replaces 19°♈00′ in the aforementioned calculation. In both cases, the part is delineated according to the house it occupies in the horoscope (see "Positioning and Interpreting an Arabian Part").

Alice T.:

Ascendant (01°♒57′)	11	01°	57′	(from fig. 6.1, House I)
+ (03°♉00′)	02	03°	00′	(from the formula above)
	13	04°	57′	(signs, degrees, and minutes)
	12	34°	57′	(converted)
− Sun (☉ 24°♊55′)	03	24°	55′	(from fig. 6.1)
	09	10°	02′	(10°♐02′, Part of Honor)

Peter C.:

Ascendant (02°♓49′)	12	02°	49′	(*from fig. 6.2, House I*)
+ (03°♉00′)	02	03°	00′	(*from the formula above*)
	14	05°	49′	(*signs, degrees, and minutes*)
− Sun (☉ 04°♍41′)	06	04°	41′	(*from fig. 6.2*)
	08	01°	08′	(01°♏08′, *Part of Honor*)

Bonatti did not document how ancient Arabian astrologers delineated the Part of Honor. But modern Western practitioners interpret the Part according to the house it occupies in the horoscope (see "Positioning and Interpreting an Arabian Part") using the material below:

House I   achieves fame because he or she is a self-starter

House II   honors come through finance or farming

House III   fame comes through travel or writing

House IV   honors come through public service

House V   honors come through the fine arts, theater, or the education of children

House VI   fame comes through military service or clerical work

House VII   honors are achieved in politics or sales

House VIII   honors come through medicine or surgery

House IX   fame comes through higher education or religion

House X   honors come through administration or government

House XI   honors come through science or large corporations

House XII   fame comes through research and investigation

Alice's Part of Honor (10°♐02′) is situated in House IX (see "Positioning and Interpreting an Arabian Part"), indicating that her fame comes through administration or government. Peter's Part (01°♏08′) occupies House VIII (see "Positioning and Interpreting an Arabian Part"), which prognosticates that his honors come through medicine or surgery.

The Part of Sudden Advancement

A similar variation is the Arabian Part of Sudden Advancement, which focuses on a person's ability to climb the promotion ladder and to excel based on a particular skill or talent. The Part is derived by adding the Ascendant's position to the Part of Fortune (see "The Part of Fortune," page 264) and subtracting Saturn's position from the sum. (If Saturn conjuncts the Sun [see "Delineating Planetary Aspects" in chapter 8] in the person's natal horoscope, however, then Jupiter's position is substituted. In his *Encyclopedia of Astrology*, Nicholas deVore mentions another variation which replaces the Part of Fortune with the Sun's position.) The Part is delineated according to the house it occupies in the horoscope (see "Positioning and Interpreting an Arabian Part"), using the same material employed in the interpretation of the Part of Honor (see "The Part of Honor," page 320).

Alice T.:

Ascendant (01°♒57')	11	01°	57'	*(from fig. 6.1, House I)*
+ Part of Fortune (18°♏30')	08	18°	30'	*(from "The Part of Fortune")*
	19	19°	87'	*(signs, degrees, and minutes)*
− Saturn (♄ 08°♎12')	07	08°	12'	*(from fig. 6.1)*
	12	11°	75'	*(remainder)*
	12	12°	15'	*(12°♓15', Part of Sudden Advancement)*[149]

Peter C.:

Ascendant (02°♓49')	12	02°	49'	*(from fig. 6.2, House I)*
+ Part of Fortune (01°♏46')	08	01°	46'	*(from "The Part of Fortune")*
	20	03°	95'	*(signs, degrees, and minutes)*
− Saturn (♄ 01°♓25')	12	01°	25'	*(from fig. 6.2)*
	08	02°	70'	*(remainder)*
	08	03°	10'	*(03°♏10', Part of Sudden Advancement)*[150]

Alice's Part of Sudden Advancement (12°♓15') occupies House I (see "Positioning and Interpreting an Arabian Part"), which indicates she achieves fame

---

149.   This remainder needed to be converted because the number of minutes in the remainder (75') exceeds 59'. Since 60' equal 01°, 60' are subtracted from the total minutes in the remainder (75') and 01° is added to the number of degrees in the remainder (11°), increasing the degrees to 12°.

150.   This remainder needed to be converted because the number of minutes in the remainder (70') exceeds 59'. Since 60' equal 01°, 60' are subtracted from the total minutes in the remainder (70°) and 01° is added to the number of degrees in the remainder (02°), increasing the degrees to 03°.

because she is a self-starter. Peter's Part (03°♏ 10′) occupies House VIII (see "Positioning and Interpreting an Arabian Part"), indicating his advancement occurs through medicine or surgery.

The Part of Magistery and Profession

Another variation, called the Arabian Part of Magistery and Profession, signifies the person's potential professional interests, including the ability to acquire a political position.[151] It is derived by adding the Ascendant's position to the Moon's position and subtracting Saturn's position from the sum. (This equation is identical to the one used to derive the Part of Inheritances and Possessions, page 290.) Like the Part of Sudden Advancement and the Part of Honor, this Part is delineated according to the house it occupies in the horoscope (see "Positioning and Interpreting an Arabian Part"), using the same material employed in the interpretation of the Part of Honor (see "The Part of Honor," page 320).

Alice T.:

Ascendant (01°♒ 57′)	11	01°	57′	(from fig. 6.1, House I)
+ Moon (☽ 11°♈ 28′)	01	11°	28′	(from fig. 6.1)
	12	12°	85′	(signs, degrees, and minutes)
− Saturn (♄ 08°♎ 12′)	07	08°	12′	(from fig. 6.1)
	05	04°	73′	(remainder)
	05	05°	13′	(05°♌ 13′, Part of Magistery and Profession)[152]

Peter C.:

Ascendant (02°♓ 49′)	12	02°	49′	(from fig. 6.2, House I)
+ Moon (☽ 03°♉ 38′)	02	03°	38′	(from fig. 6.2)
	14	05°	87′	(signs, degrees, and minutes)
− Saturn (♄ 01°♓ 25′)	12	01°	25′	(from fig. 6.2)
	02	04°	62′	(remainder)
	02	05°	02′	(05°♉ 02′, Part of Magistery and Profession)[153]

---

151. The Part of Magistery and Profession was sometimes called the Part of Kings and What the Native Does.

152. This remainder needed to be converted because the number of minutes in the remainder (73′) exceeds 59′. Since 60′ equal 01°, 60′ are subtracted from the total minutes in the remainder (73′) and 01° is added to the number of degrees in the remainder (04°), increasing the degrees to 05°.

153. This remainder needed to be converted because the number of minutes in the remainder (62′) exceeds 59′. Since 60′ equal 01°, 60′ are subtracted from the total minutes in the remainder (62′) and 01° is added to the number of degrees in the remainder (04°), increasing the degrees to 05°.

Alice's Part of Magistery and Profession (05°♌13') occupies House VII (see "Positioning and Interpreting an Arabian Part"), indicating that she has an aptitude for politics or sales. Peter's Part (05°♉02') occupies House II (see "Positioning and Interpreting an Arabian Part"), signifying a strong talent for finance or farming.

The Part of Merchandise

The Arabian Part of Merchandise[154] prognosticates the person's potential for promoting ideas or goods. The Part is derived from exactly the same calculation used for the Part of Durability (see "The Part of Durability," page 275). Like the preceding Parts related to House X, this Part is delineated according to the house it occupies in the horoscope (see "Positioning and Interpreting an Arabian Part").

Alice T.:

Ascendant (01°♒57')	11	01°	57'	(from fig. 6.1, House I)
+ Part of Fortune (18°♏30')	08	18°	30'	(from "The Part of Fortune")
	19	19°	87'	(signs, degrees, and minutes)
− Part of Spirit (15°♈24')	01	15°	24'	(from "The Part of Spirit")
	18	04°	63'	(remainder)
	06	05°	03'	(05°♍03', Part of Merchandise)[155]

Peter C.:

Ascendant (02°♓49')	12	02°	49'	(from fig. 6.2, House I)
+ Part of Fortune (01°♏46')	08	01°	46'	(from "The Part of Fortune")
	20	03°	95'	(signs, degrees, and minutes)
	19	33°	95'	(converted)
− Part of Spirit (04°♋08')	04	04°	08'	(from "The Part of Spirit")
	15	29°	87'	(remainder)
	04	00°	27'	(00°♋27', Part of Merchandise)[156]

---

154.   An alternate name for this Part is the Part of Trade, Buying, and Selling.

155.   This remainder needed to be converted because the sign number in the remainder exceeds the total number of zodiac signs (12); the latter number is subtracted from the remainder (18) to derive the final sign number, 6. This remainder also needed to be converted because the number of minutes in the remainder (63') exceeds 59'. Since 60' equal 01°, 60' are subtracted from the total minutes in the remainder (63') and 01° is added to the number of degrees in the remainder (04°), increasing the degrees to 05°.

156.   This remainder needed to be converted for three reasons. First, because the sign number in the remainder exceeds the total number of zodiac signs (12), the latter number is subtracted from the remainder (15) to derive the final sign number, 3. Second, the number of minutes in the remainder (87') exceeds 59'. Since 60' equal 01°, 60' are subtracted from the total minutes in the remainder (87') and 01° is added to the number of degrees in the remainder (29°), increasing the degrees to 30°. Finally, because the number of degrees in the remainder (30°) now exceeds 29°, this figure must also be converted. Since 30° equal one full zodiac sign, 30° are subtracted from the total degrees in the remainder (30°) and one sign is added to the sign number in the remainder (3), increasing the sign number to 4.

The Part of Merchandise is delineated according to the house it occupies (see "Positioning and Interpreting an Arabian Part") to discover where a person's sales aptitude lies using the material below:

House I   the person sells himself or herself best[157]

House II   farm products and banking or financial services

House III   writing, advertising, or transportation

House IV   domestic services or real estate

House V   amusements, theatrical or speculative entertainment, fashions and accessories

House VI   photography, medical services or supplies, or food

House VII   stocks, bonds, or antiques

House VIII   wines, spirits, and appliances

House IX   books, magazines, newspapers, and educational equipment

House X   corporate instruments and businesses

House XI   electronics and animals

House XII   shoes, musical instruments, and woolens

Alice's Part of Merchandise (05°♍03′) occupies House VII (see "Positioning and Interpreting an Arabian Part"), signifying her ability to promote stocks, bonds, or antiques. Peter's Part (00°♋27′) occupies House IV (see "Positioning and Interpreting an Arabian Part"), indicating that he can promote domestic services and real estate.

The Part of the Mother

House X is also the realm of the mother. The Arabian Part of the Mother focuses on this maternal relationship. This Part is derived by adding the Ascendant's position to the Moon's position and subtracting Venus's position from the sum. The Part is delineated according the aspects it forms with other planets (see "Delineating Planetary Aspects" in chapter 8).

---

157.   This is considered to be a fortuitous indicator for entertainers.

Alice T.:

Ascendant (01°♒57′)	11	01°	57′	(from fig. 6.1, House I)
+ Moon (☽ 11°♈28′)	01	11°	28′	(from fig. 6.1)
	12	12°	85′	(signs, degrees, and minutes)
	11	42°	85′	(converted)
− Venus (♀ 22°♊31′)	03	22°	31′	(from fig. 6.1)
	08	20°	54′	(20°♏54′, Part of the Mother)

Peter C.:

Ascendant (02°♓49′)	12	02°	49′	(from fig. 6.2, House I)
+ Moon (☽ 03°♉38′)	02	03°	38′	(from fig. 6.2)
	14	05°	87′	(signs, degrees, and minutes)
	13	35°	87′	(converted)
− Venus (♀ 18°♋53′)	04	18°	53′	(from fig. 6.2)
	11	17°	34′	(17°♒34′, Part of the Mother)

If the Part of the Mother forms an aspect of any type (see "Delineating Planetary Aspects" in chapter 8) with the Sun (☉), the Moon (☽), Venus (♀), Jupiter (♃), or Mercury (☿), the person has strong bonds with his or her mother. The positive or negative nature of this aspect depends on the sort formed.

If this Part forms an aspect of any type (see "Locating Planetary Aspects" in chapter 8) with Mars (♂) or Saturn (♄), the person has more affinity with his or her father. According to modern Western astrologers, if the Part forms an aspect of any type (see "Delineating Planetary Aspects" in chapter 8) with Uranus (♅), Neptune (♆), or Pluto (♇), the person is free of his or her mother's influence, but might become too dependent upon the opinions and support of friends and associates. The positive or negative nature of this aspect depends on the type formed. For example, Alice's Part of the Mother (20°♏54′) squares Pluto (♇ 19°♌34′ in fig. 6.1),[158] indicating a negative maternal influence. Since Peter's Part does not form any of these aspects, the practitioner would not make any prognostications using this Part. The alleged nurturing aspects of friendship might have been the reason why some modern Western astrologers such as Nicholas deVore also delineated the

---

158.   The distance between Alice's Part (20°♏54′) and Pluto (♇ 19°♌34′) is determined by subtracting the two positions as shown below:

Part of the Mother (20°♏54′)	08	20°	54′
− Pluto (♇ 19°♌34′)	05	19°	34′
	03	01°	20′

The three zodiac signs of difference are then converted into degrees by multiplying 3 by 30°00′ (the complete distance of a zodiac sign) and adding the result to the existing degrees. Thus, the distance between the Part and the planet is 91°20′, forming a square (90°00′ distance, ±06°00′).

same Part to determine the individual's relationship with friends, using the same process and calling it the Part of Friends.

Parts Associated with House XI

There are ten ancient Arabian Parts that pertain to House XI matters such as friendships, acquaintanceships, and the fulfillment of material desires: the Part of Excellence, the Part of Concupiscence and Zeal, the Part of the Native Among Men, the Part of the Agreement of Friends, the Part of Friends, the Part of Fertility and Abundance, the Part of Felicity, the Part of Necessity, the Part of the Goodness of the Soul, and the Part of Praise and Gratitude.[159] Modern Western astrologers don't appear to apply these particular Arabian Parts, but it can be safely assumed that the system used to delineate the Part of the Mother (see "The Part of the Mother," above) was adapted to the interpretation of these Parts. In this section, however, only the calculation and interpretation of a modern variation called the Part of Friends and Mother will be presented.

The Part of Friends and Mother

The only Arabian Part with House XI associations that appears to be employed by modern Western astrologers is the Arabian Part of Friends and Mother, which signifies the person's relationship to friends, associates, and mother. This part is derived by adding the Ascendant's position to the Moon's position and subtracting Uranus's position from the sum. It is interpreted if it forms an aspect (see "Delineating Planetary Aspects" in chapter 8) with another planet.

Alice T.:

Ascendant (01°♒57′)	11	01°	57′	(from fig. 6.1, House I)
+ Moon (☽ 11°♈28′)	01	11°	28′	(from fig. 6.1)
	12	12°	85′	(signs, degrees, and minutes)
	11	42°	85′	(converted)
− Uranus (♅ 13°♋00′)	04	13°	00′	(from fig. 6.1)
	07	29°	85′	(remainder)
	08	00°	25′	(00°♏25′, Part of Friends and Mother)[160]

---

159. The formulas for these arcane Arabian Parts are detailed in Robert Zoller's book, *The Arabian Parts in Astrology: A Lost Key to Prediction* (Rochester, Vt.: Inner Traditions International, 1980).

160. This remainder needed to be converted for two reasons. The number of minutes in the remainder (85′) exceeds 59′. Since 60′ equal 01°, 60′ are subtracted from the total minutes in the remainder (85′) and 01° is added to the number of degrees in the remainder (29°), increasing the degrees to 30°. Because the number of degrees (°) in the remainder (30°) now exceeds 29°, this figure must also be converted. Since 30° equal one full zodiac sign, 30° are subtracted from the total degrees in the remainder (30°) and one sign is added to the sign number in the remainder (7), increasing the sign number to 8.

Peter C.:

Ascendant (02°♓49')	12	02°	49'	(*from fig. 6.2, House I*)
+ Moon (☽ 03°♉38')	02	03°	38'	(*from fig. 6.2*)
	14	05°	87'	(*signs, degrees, and minutes*)
	13	35°	87'	(*converted*)
− Uranus (♅ 10°♍04')	06	10°	04'	(*from fig. 6.2*)
	07	25°	83'	(*remainder*)
	07	26°	23'	(26°♎23', *Part of Friends and Mother*)[161]

If the Part of Friends and Mother forms an aspect of any type (see "Delineating Planetary Aspects" in chapter 8) with the Sun (☉), the Moon (☽), Venus (♀), Jupiter (♃), or Mercury (☿), the person has strong bonds with his or her friends. The positive or negative nature of this aspect depends on the type formed. For example, Alice's Part (00°♏25') forms a trine to Mercury (☿ 03°♋28' in fig. 6.1), indicating that the bonds of friendship are both strong and positive.[162]

If this Part forms an aspect of any type (see "Delineating Planetary Aspects" in chapter 8) with Mars (♂) or Saturn (♄), the person has more affinity with his or her male friends. For example, Alice's Part (00°♏25') conjuncts Mars (♂ 01°♏24' in fig. 6.1), suggesting that she is more comfortable with her male friends.[163]

According to modern Western astrologers, if the Part forms an aspect of any type (see "Delineating Planetary Aspects" in chapter 8) with Uranus (♅), Neptune (♆), or Pluto (♇), the person is free of his or her friends' influence. If, however, none of the above aspects are formed with the Part, as in Peter's case, the practitioner would not make any prognostication using this particular Part.

---

161. This remainder needed to be converted because the number of minutes in the remainder (83') exceeds 59'. Since 60' equal 01°, 60' are subtracted from the total minutes in the remainder (83') and 01° is added to the number of degrees in the remainder (25°), increasing the degrees to 26°.

162. The distance between Alice's Part (00°♏25') and Mercury (☿ 03°♋28') is determined by subtracting the two positions as shown below:

Part of Friends and Mother (00°♏25')	08	00°	25'
	07	29°	85'	(*converted*)
− Mercury (☿ 03°♋28')	04	03°	28'
	03	26°	57'

The three zodiac signs of difference are then converted into degrees (°) by multiplying 3 by 30°00' (the complete distance of a zodiac sign) and adding the result to the existing degrees. Thus, the distance between the Part and the planet is 126°57', forming a trine (120°00' distance, ±06°00').

163. This aspect is formed because the distance between Alice's Part (00°♏25') and Mars (♂ 01°♏24' in fig. 6.1) within the same sign is only 00°59'.

Parts Associated with House XII

An individual's private and public enemies are the focus of the parts relating to House XII matters. Ancient astrologers cast the Arabian Part of Secret Enemies[164] and the Part of the Perilous and Most Dangerous Year. However, modern Western astrologers have replaced the former with a variation called the Part of Private Enemies. This Part and the Part of the Perilous and Most Dangerous Year will be explained here.

The Part of Private Enemies

The Part of Private Enemies prognosticates the reasons why an individual encounters personal opposition. The Part is derived by adding the Ascendant's position to the cusp of House XII and subtracting House XII's planetary ruler.[165] The Part is delineated according to the house it occupies in the horoscope (see "Positioning and Interpreting an Arabian Part").

Alice T.:

Ascendant (01°♒57′)	11	01°	57′	(*from fig. 6.1, House I*)
+ House XII cusp (07°♑13′)	10	07°	13′	(*from fig. 6.1*)
	21	08°	70′	(*signs, degrees, and minutes*)
− Saturn (♄ 08°♎12′)	07	08°	12′	(*from fig. 6.1*)[166]
	14	00°	58′	(*remainder*)
	02	00°	58′	(00°♉58′, *Part of Private Enemies*)[167]

Peter C.:

Ascendant (02°♓49′)	12	02°	49′	(*from fig. 6.2, House I*)
+ House XII cusp (28°♑27′)	10	28°	27′	(*from fig. 6.2*)
	22	30°	76′	(*signs, degrees, and minutes*)
− Saturn (♄ 01°♓25′)	12	01°	25′	(*from fig. 6.2*)[168]
	10	29°	51′	(29°♑51′, *Part of Private Enemies*)

---

164. The Part of Secret Enemies is derived by adding the Ascendant's position to Saturn's position and subtracting Mars's position from the sum. But Bonatti did not adequately describe its delineation.
165. See note 27, page 274.
166. Ibid.
167. This remainder needed to be converted because the sign number in the remainder exceeds the total number of zodiac signs (12). Therefore, 12 is subtracted from the remainder (20) to derive the final sign number, 8.
168. See note 27, page 274.

The Part of Private Enemies is delineated according to the house it occupies (see "Positioning and Interpreting an Arabian Part"). The particulars of personal strife are prognosticated using the material below:

House I	personality clashes
House II	the person's jealous nature
House III	a lack of communication
House IV	the person is a threat to someone else's security
House V	pride stands in the way
House VI	the person is considered to be a bore
House VII	the person's fickleness and inability to commit to a relationship
House VIII	the person is too moody
House IX	a lack of education and a desire to communicate with educated people
House X	a difference in social classes between the individual and the people he or she wishes to meet
House XI	a lack of mutual associations or friendships
House XII	the person's reclusive nature

Alice's Part of Private Enemies (00°♉58′) is situated in House II (see "Positioning and Interpreting an Arabian Part"), indicating that she is a threat to someone else's security. Peter's Part (29°♑51′) is posited in House XII (see "Positioning and Interpreting an Arabian Part"), which signifies that he has a reclusive nature.

The Part of the Perilous and Most Dangerous Year

Similarly, the Arabian Part of the Perilous and Most Dangerous Year determines an individual's weak point in social relationships. This particular Part is derived by adding the Ascendant's position to House VIII's ruler and subtracting Saturn's position from the sum. The Part is delineated according to the house it occupies in the horoscope (see "Positioning and Interpreting an Arabian Part").

Alice T.:

Ascendant (01°♒57')	11	01°	57'	*(from fig. 6.1, House I)*
+ Mercury (☿ 03°♋28')	04	03°	28'	*(from fig. 6.1)* [169]
	15	04°	85'	*(signs, degrees, and minutes)*
	14	34°	85'	*(converted)*
− Saturn (♄ 08°♎12')	07	08°	12'	*from fig. 6.1)*
	07	26°	73'	*(remainder)*
	07	27°	13'	*(27°♎13', Part of the Perilous and Most Dangerous Year)* [170]

Peter C.:

Ascendant (02°♓49')	12	02°	49'	*(from fig. 6.2, House I)*
+ Venus (♀ 18°♋53')	04	18°	53'	*(from fig. 6.2)* [171]
	16	20°	102'	*(signs, degrees, and minutes)*
− Saturn (♄ 01°♓25')	12	01°	25'	*(from fig. 6.2)*
	04	19°	77'	*(remainder)*
	04	20°	17'	*(20°♋17', Part of the Perilous and Most Dangerous Year)* [172]

The Part of the Perilous and Most Dangerous Year is delineated according to the house it occupies (see "Positioning and Interpreting an Arabian Part") to describe the individual using the material below:

House I   overconfident

House II   too materialistic

House III   gossipy

House IV   obsessed with security

House V   too concerned with love affairs and children

House VI   a workaholic

169. See note 27, page 274.

170. This remainder needed to be converted because the number of minutes in the remainder (73') exceeds 59'. Since 60' equal 01°, 60' are subtracted from the total minutes in the remainder (73') and 01° is added to the number of degrees in the remainder (26°), increasing the degrees to 27°.

171. See note 27, page 274.

172. This remainder also needed to be converted because the number of minutes (') in the remainder (77') exceeds 59'. Since 60' equal 01°, 60' are subtracted from the total minutes in the remainder (77') and 01° is added to the number of degrees in the remainder (19°), increasing the degrees to 20°.

House VII	too concerned with marital or partnership matters or public affairs
House VIII	obsessed with sex and spouse's or partner's money or taxes
House IX	a religious or philosophical fanatic or a constant traveler
House X	obsessed with the pursuit of fame, fortune, and power
House IX	too concerned with unreliable friends and associates
House XII	ignores secret enemies who are the cause of social discredit

Alice's Part (27°♎13′) occupies House VIII (see "Positioning and Interpreting an Arabian Part"), which indicates that she is obsessed with sex and her husband's or partner's money or taxes. Peter's Part (20°♋17′) occupies House V (see "Positioning and Interpreting an Arabian Part"), which indicates that he is too concerned with love affairs and children.

The desire to know the future in detail was an obsession in ancient Arabian culture—so much so that it drove the tenth-century Arabian astrologer and historian Abu'l'rayhan Muhammad ibn Ahmad Al'biruni to scorn his peers publicly for their seemingly endless desire to create a Part for nearly every human activity. He claimed that the increased dependence upon the Arabian Parts to predict daily life reduced the science of astrology to a superficial level on a par with divinatory oracles such as crow auguries.

The views of ancient Arabian astrologers who spent their lives predicting the outcome of future earthly events for their affluent clients were also strongly contested by the Judaic astrologer Abraham ben Meir ibn Ezra, who called astrology a "sublime science," pointing out that it had survived centuries of the rigorous Talmudic debates that began before the sixth century B.C., echoing Al'biruni's scorn for these diviners.

The
Way to Go

Judaic Chart Construction

CHAPTER

7

Judaic astrology is a Sun-school tradition that embraces attributes of both the Sun-school and Moon-school systems. Discussed in numerous Tractates of the Talmud (the written embodiment of Jewish civil and religious law), this form of astrology incorporates a Sun-school belief in "free will," but is not as secularly oriented as Western or Arabian astrology. Natal horoscopes erected in this tradition are calculated according to the tropical zodiac, which was probably adopted from the Chaldeans and Babylonians.

But this same astrological system also applies physical aspects normally associated with the Moon school. For example, the Jewish calendar is a luni-solar system that applies the nineteen-year Metonic Cycle developed by the ancient Greeks to its calculation of lunar months and intercalary months. This format is almost identical to the Chinese, Tibetan, and Vedic calendars. The system divides the year into twelve lunar months plus an intercalary month to rectify the annual period with the Sun's apparent 365-day journey, and begins with the traditional year of Creation, 3761 B.C. But unlike the Chinese year, which begins with the second New Moon after the winter solstice, the Jewish ecclesiastical year begins with the first New Moon after the vernal equinox, while the civil year begins with the first New Moon following the autumnal equinox.

The poles that form the Earth's north-south axis move along an elliptical path, completing a 360°00′ cycle every 25,920 years. Vedic, Chinese, Tibetan, and Judaic astrologers call this cyclical phenomenon the "Great Year." This vast segment of time is divided into twelve precessional ages of 2,160 years each, which are sometimes called Astrological Ages or, in Judaic astrology, Prophetic Ages. These eras

333

serve as the basis for determining the ever-changing placement of the vernal equinox in both Vedic and Judaic astrology (see "Pole to Pole" in chapter 2). At the turn of each age, the vernal equinox appears to have moved by one full constellation (zodiac sign) along the ecliptic. This is noted in the names of the three ages that have passed during recorded history: the Age of Taurus (c. 4159 B.C. to 2001 B.C.), the Age of Aries (c. 2001 B.C. to 159 B.C.), and the current Age of Pisces (c. 159 B.C. to A.D. 2001).[1]

Unlike other Sun-school forms of astrology, the Judaic tradition focuses on the individual as an interactive entity, just as do Chinese, Tibetan, and Vedic astrologies. How the person is perceived and interacts with his or her family, spouse, neighbors, friends, and community are the focal points of the Judaic astrologer's delineation. The spiritual guidance derived from an analysis of a Judaic natal horoscope can be directed to aid the individual in living in accordance with Halachah (Jewish law), making it very similar to the practice of Vedic and Tibetan astrology.

The ancient names for the zodiac signs corresponded directly to the Hebrew terms for the twelve constellations (fig. 7.1), which the Talmud states were created by God along with a myriad of "hosts, legions, cohorts, files, and camps."[2]

FIGURE 7.1. HEBREW NAMES FOR THE CONSTELLATIONS.

CONSTELLATION (SYMBOL)	HEBREW ZODIAC SIGN	TRANSLATION
Aries (♈)	Taleh	prince
Taurus (♉)	Shor	heavenly bull
Gemini (♊)	Teomin	two figures
Cancer (♋)	Sarton	north gate of the Sun
Leo (♌)	Ari	lion
Virgo (♍)	Betulah	wife of Bel
Libra (♎)	Moznayim	chariot yoke
Scorpio (♏)	Akrab	stinger
Sagittarius (♐)	Kasshat	archery bow
Capricorn (♑)	Gedi	ibex or goat-fish
Aquarius (♒)	Deli	god of the storm
Pisces (♓)	Dagim	fish

1.   The actual entry date of the upcoming Age of Aquarius is debatable. According to Rabbi Joel C. Dobin, however, this event took place when Jupiter (♃) and Saturn (♄) formed a conjunct aspect (see "Delineating Planetary Aspects" in chapter 8) in Libra on December 31, 1980. Other scholars calculate that the Prophetic Age actually changes during the next Jupiter-Saturn conjunction, in 2001.

2.   These military terms were used in a celestial reference that was directly attributed to God in a Talmudic text, Berachoth 32b: "Twelve constellations have I created in the firmament and for each constellation I have created thirty hosts, and for each host I have created thirty legions, and for each legion I have created thirty files, and for each file I have created thirty cohorts, and for each cohort I have created thirty camps, and in each camp I have suspended three hundred and sixty-five thousand stars, in accordance with the days of the solar year."

References in both the Torah[3] and the Talmud to the Chaldeans (an archaic term for "astrologers") confirm Judaic astrology's Mesopotamian roots. And many scholars have cited the obvious connections between the descriptions of the twelve sons of Jacob in the Torah (fig. 7.2) and characteristics assigned to the twelve zodiac signs used in Judaic astrology.

There are also allusions in the Torah to a connection between the zodiac signs and the archangels Raphael, Gabriel, Michael, Haniel, Ma'admiel, Zidkiel, and Zophkiel.[4] Furthermore, the Talmud frequently refers to the planetary influences on the days and hours of the week. For example, in Shabbath 156a, the effect of a day's planetary ruler upon an individual's personality at birth was discussed in detail. An individual born on a Sunday (ruled by the Sun [☉]) is "wholly good or wholly bad." A person born on a Monday (ruled by the Moon [☽]) is bad-tempered. Someone born on a Tuesday (ruled by Mars [♂]) is wealthy and lustful. An individual born on a Wednesday (ruled by Mercury [☿]) possesses a retentive memory and is generally wise. A person born on a Thursday (ruled by Jupiter [♃]) is benevolent. If someone is born on a Friday (ruled by Venus [♀]) he or she is active and eager to follow the axioms of Judaic law. However, a person born on the

FIGURE 7.2. THE SONS OF JACOB AND BIBLICAL REFERENCES TO THE ZODIAC SIGNS.

CONSTELLATION (SYMBOL)	HEBREW ZODIAC SIGN	BIBLICAL TEXT REFERENCE	NAME OF JACOB'S SON
Aries (♈)	Taleh	Genesis 49:27; Deuteronomy 33:12	Benjamin
Taurus (♉)	Shor	Genesis 49:2–4; Deuteronomy 33:6	Reuben
Gemini (♊)	Teomin	Genesis 49:5–7	Simon
Cancer (♋)	Sarton	Genesis 49:5 7; Deuteronomy 33:8–11	Levi
Leo (♌)	Ari	Genesis 49:8–12; Deuteronomy 33:7	Judah
Virgo (♍)	Betulah	Genesis 49:13; Deuteronomy 33:18–19	Zebulun
Libra (♎)	Moznayim	Genesis 49:14–15; Deuteronomy 33:18–19	Issachar
Scorpio (♏)	Akrab	Genesis 49:16–18; Deuteronomy 33:22	Dan
Sagittarius (♐)	Kasshat	Genesis 49:19; Deuteronomy 33:20	Gad
Capricorn (♑)	Gedi	Genesis 49:20; Deuteronomy 33:24–25	Asher
Aquarius (♒)	Deli	Genesis 49:21; Deuteronomy 33:23	Naphtali
Pisces (♓)	Dagim	Genesis 49:22–26; Deuteronomy 33:13–17	Joseph

3. The Torah is the name given to the five books of the Bible said to have been written by Moses and known as the Pentateuch: Genesis, Exodus, Leviticus, Numbers, and Deuteronomy. The remaining books are the Nevi'im (the writings of the prophets), the Ketuvim (the Hagiogrypha, which includes Psalms, Proverbs, the Song of Songs, and the stories of Job, Esther, Daniel, Ruth, and Ezra), and others.

4. For a thorough explanation of the Talmudic association between the zodiac signs and the archangels, refer to chapter 20 of Rabbi Joel C. Dobin's book, *The Astrological Secrets of the Hebrew Sages: To Rule Both Day and Night* (Rochester, Vt.: Inner Traditions International, 1977).

Sabbath which is Saturday (ruled by Saturn [♄]) will die on a Sabbath day because his or her birth profaned the sanctity of the day by forcing the mother and midwife to attend to the work of childbirth instead of the observation of the Sabbath.[5]

Prior to the eleventh century A.D., this particular form of astrology had much in common with Arabian astrology and early forms of Western astrology (Greek, Egyptian, Chaldean, and Babylonian). Ancient Judaic practitioners enhanced their prognostications by casting and delineating many of the Arabian Parts (see chapter 6), based on a system documented by the Arabian astrologer Albumazar, which was adapted from a form of Greek celestial divination. The Arabian Parts were, however, condemned by the Judaic astrologer, Abraham ben Meir ibn Ezra, in his eleventh-century treatise *The Beginning of Wisdom*. Ibn Ezra claimed that the Arabian Parts were a form of celestial divination that deviated from Judaic astrology's higher purpose, and they fell into disuse. This opinion was shared by a number of Talmudic scholars. Consequently, the chart structure of Judaic astrology drew upon other influences and evolved into a system that is nearly identical to the form of astrology practiced by Western astrologers, as will be seen throughout this chapter.

CONSTRUCTING AND INTERPRETING A JUDAIC NATAL HOROSCOPE

Since Judaic astrology is firmly based in the same Babylonian and Chaldean roots as its Western counterpart, it's no wonder that modern Judaic practitioners calculate an individual's natal horoscope according to a tropical zodiac method that closely emulates modern Western procedures. The only subtle difference is that many Judaic practitioners apply the Meridian[6] house system instead of the highly popular Placidus house system employed by their Western counterparts. But the interpretations and insights derived from the resulting chart are often influenced by Talmudic writings, providing insight into the Jewish cultural framework itself.

Constructing a Judaic Natal Horoscope

To construct a Judaic natal chart, follow the calculation and construction instructions described in chapter 8. But instead of using *Dalton's Table of Houses* (a Placidus house system) to determine the house locations, apply the American Federation of Astrologers' *Tables of Diurnal Planetary Motion* (a Meridian house system), which differs slightly in the organization of house cusps. This is the only

---

5.   The planets Uranus (♅), Neptune (♆), and Pluto (♇) were not included in this discourse because they were not discovered until 1781, 1846, and 1930, respectively.

6.   This house system is a slight variation on Placidus house division (invented by either the seventeenth-century astrologer Placidus di Tito or the eighth-century Arabian astrologer ben Djabir [see chapter 8]), and is based on a theory presented by the seventeenth-century German astronomer Johannes Kepler.

variation between the two systems, which can be seen by comparing the Meridian charts below (figs. 7.3 and 7.4) with figs. 8.1 and 8.2.

If the individual's actual birth time is not known, use the Talmudic "first hour" (6:00 A.M. or 06:00:00) as the local time instead of the 12:00 P.M. (12:00:00) default that is usually applied by modern Western astrologers.

Delineating the Ascendant

As in modern Western and Vedic astrology, the Ascendant (House I) and its decanates (subdivisions of the Ascendant that comprise 10°00′ each) are the keys to uncovering an individual's personality. In Judaic astrology, this house is interpreted in the same manner as in Western astrology. Modern Judaic practitioners have elaborated on the characteristics described in both the Talmud and the Torah, refining the prognostications by further analyzing the Ascendant's general characteristics as well as the attributes of the Ascendant's specific decanate, as shown below:

FIGURE 7.3. ALICE T.'S JUDAIC NATAL CHART.

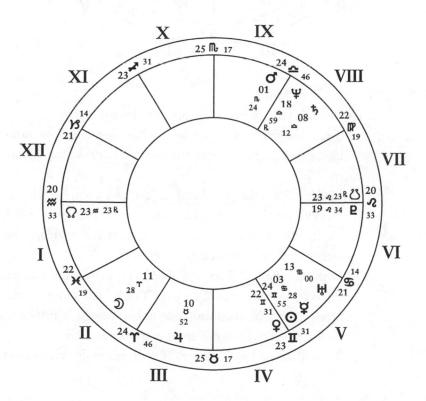

FIGURE 7.4. PETER C.'s JUDAIC NATAL CHART.

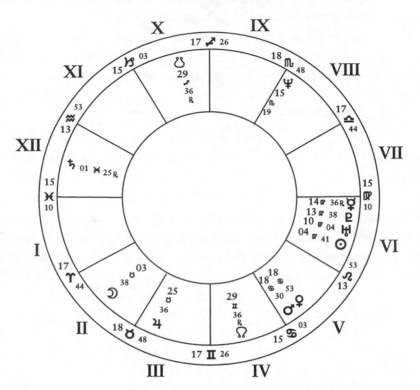

Aries (♈)[7]   Ruled by Mars (♂)

Talmudic description: a "shedder of blood[8]

Torah description: (Genesis 49:27) "Benjamin is a ravenous wolf, in the morning devouring the prey, and at evening dividing the spoil."

Modern delineation: hot-headed; just; talkative; health concerns center around the equilibrium, ears, brain, eyes, nose, and teeth; suited to be a "king" who practices justice, a military leader, surgeon, butcher, or traveler

First decanate (00°♈00′–10°♈00′): hates evil; has many friends

Second Decanate: (10°♈01′–20°♈00′): has many enemies; is prone to fits of uncontrollable anger; has high principles and strong breeding; comprehends matters perfectly

Third decanate (20°♈01′–30°♈00′): generally lives in isolation

---

7. The Hebrew name for each of the zodiac signs can be found in fig. 7.1.

8. Within the same passage in Shabbath 156a, however, another Rabbi suggested that the person born under this influence is a cupper (a person who practices the ancient healing technique of increasing the blood supply to a particular area of the body by placing a heated glass "cup" over the area to create suction), a butcher, or a circumciser.

Taurus (♉)	**Ruled by Venus (♀)**

Talmudic description: a wealthy person with lax morals

Torah description: (Genesis 49:3–4) "Reuben, you are my first-born, my might, and the first fruits of my strength, preeminent in pride and preeminent in power. Unstable as water, you shall not have preeminence because you went up to your father's bed; then you defiled it—you went up to my couch!"

Modern delineation: speaks incoherently; lacks education or knowledge; contrary attitude; lustful; overindulgent; health concerns center around the neck and throat; prone to goiter; suited to be an entertainer, a sensualist, or a procurer

First decanate (00°♉00'–10°♉00'): hedonistic; noble; has many friends

Second decanate (10°♉01'–20°♉00'): intelligent; possesses a generous nature

Third decanate (20°♉01'–30°♉00'): has little luck attracting the opposite sex; tends to overwork

Gemini (♊)	**Ruled by Mercury (♀)**

Talmudic description: a wise person with a long memory

Torah description: (Genesis 49:5–7) "Simeon and Levi are brothers; weapons of violence are their swords. O my soul, come not into their council; O my spirit, be not joined to their company; for in their anger they slay men, and in their wantonness they hamstring oxen. Cursed be their anger, for it is fierce; and their wrath, for it is cruel! I will divide them in Jacob and scatter them in Israel."

Modern delineation: truthful; skilled; ideologically moderate; health concerns center around arms, hands, shoulders, the lymph nodes or lymphatic system, and blood vessels; suited to be a "king," hero, magnate, magician, sorcerer, or an intricate craftsperson

First decanate (00°♊00'–10°♊00'): tends to overwork; patient; has little luck in attracting the opposite sex

Second decanate (10°♊01'–20°♊00'): associates with noble people; well-bred; well-spoken

Third decanate (20°♊01'–30°♊00'): tells lies; tends toward improper use of language; extremely sexual

Cancer (♋)	**Ruled by the Moon (☽)**

Talmudic description: a secretive person who "will be ailing, will build and destroy and again destroy and build, will eat and drink not of his own . . . and if he should venture to steal he will succeed"

Torah description: (Genesis 49:5–7) same as "Gemini," above

Modern delineation: highly respected; has hearing or speech impediment; loves mankind; health concerns center around the breasts, ribs, spleen, lungs, and the area surrounding the heart; suited to be a wanderer, repulsive to other people, or a plebeian

First decanate (00°♋00'–10°♋00'): many friends; good-natured; resorts to fraud when deemed necessary

Second decanate (10°♋01'–20°♋00'): loved by man and beast

Third decanate (20°♋01'–30°♋00'): suffers alone; physically strong, but prone to heart attacks

Leo (♌)

Ruled by the Sun (☉)

Talmudic description: a good, distinguished, and handsome provider whose secrets will be revealed . . . "and if he should venture to steal he will not succeed"

Torah description: (Genesis 49:8–12) "Judah, your brothers shall praise you; your hand shall be on the neck of your enemies; your father's sons shall bow down before you. Judah is a whelp; from the prey, my son, you have gone up. He stooped down, he crouched as a lion, and as a lioness; who dares rouse him up? The scepter shall not depart from Judah, nor the ruler's staff from between his feet, until he comes to whom it belongs; and to him shall be the obedience of the peoples. Binding his foal to the vine and his ass's colt to the choice vine, he washes his garments in wine and his vesture in the blood of grapes; his eyes shall be red with wine, and his teeth white with milk."

Modern delineation: educated; self-reliant; clever; generous; tyrannical in speech; melancholic; lustful; gluttonous; health concerns center around the heart, chest, upper stomach, diaphragm, back, and loins; suited to be a "king," noble person, jeweler, or tradesperson

First decanate (00°♌00'–10°♌00'): well-known in public

Second decanate (10°♌01'–20°♌00'): magnanimous; possesses physical presence and charisma; honored by the public

Third decanate (20°♌01'–30°♌00'): powerful speaking voice;

attracted to the opposite sex; possesses many friends and enemies; plagued by many illnesses

Virgo (♍)

Also ruled by Mercury (☿)
Talmudic description: a wise person with a long memory
Torah description: (Genesis 49:13) "Zebulon shall dwell at the
shore of the sea; he shall become a haven for ships, and his bor-
der shall be at Sidon."
Modern delineation: educated; intelligent; health concerns center around the stomach, intestines, and diaphragm; prone to
melancholia; suited to be a writer, mathematician, imperson-
ator, or sage
First decanate (00°♍00'–10°♍00'): kindhearted; potentially
impotent; has writing or mathematical talent
Second decanate (10°♍01'–20°♍00'): charming; magnanimous; desirous of compliments; candid
Third decanate (20°♍01'–30°♍00'): humble; wise; very intelligent and well educated

Libra (♎)

Also ruled by Venus (♀)
Talmudic description: a wealthy person with lax morals
Torah description: (Genesis 49:14–15) "Issachar is a strong ass,
crouching between the sheepfolds; he saw that a resting place
was good, and that the land was pleasant; so he bowed his
shoulder to bear, and became a slave at forced labor."
Modern delineation: attracted to the opposite sex; predatory; reliable; noble; health concerns center around the appendix,
lower intestines, and colon; suited to be a singer, mathematician, businessperson, merchant, or food and drink purveyor
First decanate (00°♎00'–10°♎00'): humble; refined; tends
toward overwork
Second decanate (10°♎01'–20°♎00'): sociable; liberal
Third decanate (20°♎01'–30°♎00'): well-known; respected

Scorpio (♏)

Also ruled by Mars (♂)
Talmudic description: a "shedder of blood"
Torah description: (Genesis 49:16–18) "Dan shall judge his people as one of the tribes of Israel. Dan shall be a serpent in the
way, a viper by the path, that bites the horse's heels so that his
rider falls backward. I wait for thy salvation, O Lord."

Modern delineation: generous; refined; reliable; astute; melancholic; if adversely aspected, can be destructive, unreliable, and deceitful; health concerns center around the reproductive organs; suited to be a judge or a worthless person
First decanate (00°♏00'–10°♏00'): educated; sensible; flippant
Second decanate (10°♏01'–20°♏00'): talkative; well-bred
Third decanate (20°♏01'–30°♏00'): fond of both sexes; suffers from feelings of dejection

Sagittarius (♐)   Ruled by Jupiter (♃)
Talmudic description: a righteous person who is charitable
Torah description: (Genesis 49:19) "Raiders shall raid Gad, but he shall raid at their heels."
Modern delineation: generous; agile; happy-go-lucky; potentially sly; inconsistent; health concerns center around the larynx and testicles or ovaries; suited to be a judge, philosopher, archer, philanthropist, dream interpreter, or "servant of God"
First decanate (00°♐00'–10°♐00'): righteous
Second decanate (10°♐01'–20°♐00'): just; overindulgent
Third decanate (20°♐01'–30°♐00'): helpful; modest

Capricorn (♑)   Ruled by Saturn (♄)
Talmudic description: a person whose plans are frustrated[9]
Torah description: (Genesis 49:20) "Asher's food shall be rich, and he shall yield royal dainties."
Modern delineation: lacks energy; addicted to sex; educated; deceitful; downfall caused by the opposite sex; health concerns center around the heart, chest, or external genitalia; suited to be a farmer, sailor, intermediary, or shepherd
First decanate (00°♑00'–10°♑00'): intelligent; magnanimous; generous
Second decanate (10°♑01'–20°♑00'): evil intention concealed by ingratiating attitude; irascible
Third decanate (20°♑01'–30°♑00'): shuns evil; extreme sexual addiction; sociable; refined

Aquarius (♒)   Also ruled by Saturn (♄)
Talmudic description: another person whose plans are frustrated (see "Capricorn," above)

---

9. Some scholars believe that the translation actually means that plans or plots against the person are frustrated.

Torah description: (Genesis 49:21) "Naphtali is a hind let loose, that bears comely fawns."

Modern delineation: magnanimous; self-praising; driven to acquire wealth; health concerns center around the legs; downcast, suffers from depression; suited to be a tanner, a sailor, or unemployed

First decanate (00°♒00′–10°♒00′): gregarious; refined

Second decanate (10°♒01′–20°♒00′): grief throughout life

Third decanate (20°♒01′–30°♒00′): overly fond of the opposite sex

Pisces (♓)

Also ruled by Jupiter (♃)

Talmudic description: a righteous person who is charitable

Torah description: (Genesis 49:22–26) "Joseph is a fruitful bough, a fruitful bough by spring; his branches run over the wall. The archers fiercely attacked him, shot at him, and harassed him sorely; yet his bow remained unmoved, his arms were made agile by the hands of the Mighty One of Jacob (by the name of the Shepherd, Rock of Israel), by the God of your father who will help you, by God Almighty who will bless you with blessings of heaven above, blessings of the deep that couches beneath, blessings of the breasts and of the womb. The blessings of your father are mighty beyond the blessings of the eternal mountains, the bounties of the everlasting hills; may they be on the head of Joseph, and on the brow of him who was separate from his brothers."

Modern delineation: irritable; polite; deceitful; freely consumes food, drink, and sleep; health concerns center around the feet and toes; suited to be a fisherman or an outcast

First decanate (00°♓00′–10°♓00′): beautifully proportioned physique and face

Second decanate (10°♓01′–20°♓00′): hostile; prepossessing appearance

Third decanate (20°♓01′–30°♓00′): frequently ill

Based on the above material, we can see in Alice's chart that her Ascendant resides in Aquarius (AS 20°♒33′ in fig. 7.3), indicating that she is magnanimous, self-praising, and driven to acquire wealth. Talmudic references indicate that she is either a person whose plans are frustrated or a person whose enemies' plans against her are thwarted. She does, however, suffer from bouts of depression and problems with her legs. Placed in the third decanate (20°♒01′–30°♒00′), her Ascendant also suggests that she is overly fond of the opposite sex (see "Aquarius," page 342).

Peter's Ascendant resides in Pisces (AS 15°♓10′ in fig. 7.4), suggesting that he is irritable but polite, and is potentially deceitful. Talmudic references describe him as a righteous person who is charitable. Placed in the second decanate (10°♓01′–20°♓00′), his Ascendant also suggests that he is hostile and has a pre-possessing appearance. He has no difficulties freely consuming food and drink; and he also enjoys sleeping for long periods. His main health concerns center around his feet and toes (see "Pisces," page 343).

Creating a Judaic Personality Profile

As mentioned earlier, factors other than the delineation of the Ascendant and its decanate that are used in the creation of a Judaic personality profile are so similar to the present-day Western and Vedic astrological systems outlined in chapters 8 and 5, respectively, that there is no need to duplicate the material here. This delineation information includes the sections on house rulerships ("Interpreting the House Rulers in the *Bhavacakra*" in chapter 5), planetary positions interpreted by both house and sign ("Delineating Planetary Positions by House and by Sign" in chapter 8), and the angles formed between the planets ("Delineating Planetary Aspects" in chapter 8).

On a superficial level, the casting and interpretation of a Judaic natal horoscope may not portray its religious or cultural significance outside of the Ascendant's interpretation, as one might suspect. As Rabbi Joel C. Dobin points out in his discussion of astrology, however, this tradition can play an obvious role in orthodox Jewish life:

"When an orthodox person is gravely ill, his or her nearest male relative will go to the synagogue on a morning on which the Torah is publicly read. The relative will ask to be called on to say the reading of the Scripture, he will ask that the reader say those special prayers which will 'add a name' to the Hebrew name of the sick one. . . . [Thus] the giving or taking of a new name indicates the necessity of a new natal chart for the symbolic new birth."

According to Rabbi Dobin, this name-changing ceremony stems directly from the Midrash Rabbah[10] in which "Rabbi Samuel ben Isaac commented that Abram said: 'My planetary fate oppresses me and declares 'Abram cannot beget a child.'

---

10.   A collection of moral and ethical commentaries on individual biblical verses that dates back to the sixth century.

Said the Holy One, Blessed Be He to him: 'Let it be even as thy words; Abram and Sarai cannot beget, but Abraham and Sarah can beget.' " A simple name change solved the couple's problem. Thus, the choice to instigate an individual's rebirth in order to redirect early natal prognostications is an affirmation of the power of planetary influences upon a person's life without denying the individual's free will.

A point that has been sorely contested by Christian theologians including Saint Augustine and Saint Thomas Aquinas, free will has been pitted against astrology in Western civilization both before and after the celestial science was banned by the Catholic Church at the Ecumenical Council of Nicea in A.D. 325. Religious fervor was later coupled with linear logic and scientific reasoning during the Renaissance to quash the practice of astrology, even though it was applied by physicians and other medical professionals until the late nineteenth century.

During the Victorian era, tales of the mystical Orient and other exotic lands rekindled interest in astrology throughout the western hemisphere. This is because it had never dwindled in Asian cultures, and four centuries of refined logic and un-yielding religious dogma still could not answer such simple questions as "Who am I?" and "Why am I here?"

What was resurrected during the nineteenth century was a homogenized version of the Western tradition that had been detailed by the Egyptian astrologer Claudius Ptolemy in the first century A.D. Synthesized and promoted in Great Britain by James Wilson and Raphael, and in the United States by the founder of the Theosophical Society, Madame Blavatsky, Western astrology shares more in common with the other secular tradition, Arabian astrology. But unlike the other forms of astrology described in this volume, the psyche plays a critical role in the interpretation of the modern Western natal horoscope, as you will see in the next chapter.

The
Lords of Nativity
WESTERN CHART CONSTRUCTION

estern astrology belongs to the "Sun school." It is an egocentric tradition with interpretations concentrating primarily on the physical realities of an individual's life: health, love, money, domestic life, social standing, and career. Claudius Ptolemy, a first-century A.D. Egyptian astrologer, is largely responsible for the development of the modern Western astrological system, whose ancestors include traditions created by the Chaldeans, Babylonians, and Greeks, as well as the Egyptians. Ptolemy's particular method employed simple mathematical calculations, requiring very little data to construct and delineate an individual's chart. Since then, many chart-construction techniques have been developed by Western astrologers following in Ptolemy's footsteps or seeking to refute his theories.

The most commonly applied systems in the United States, Europe, and most of the western hemisphere, the Western astrological tradition employs the tropical zodiac, assigning each zodiac sign to a planetary ruler (in contrast to the constellational rulers applied in the sidereal zodiac). The Sun, the Moon, eight planets, and two Moon's Nodes are positioned on a chart according to the Placidus house system, which is a time-oriented method of dividing the 360°00′ of a chart's circle into twelve unequal segments called houses. Although this system is conceptually identical to the fate houses found in Chinese, Tibetan, Vedic, Arabian, and Judaic astrologies, the manner in which the houses are divided according the Placidus method does not evenly apportion the same number of degrees to each house: one house may be 27°00′ in distance, while the next may be 34°00′. This particular method was developed in the seventeenth century by the Italian astrologer Placidus di Tito and was based on a set of eighth-century calculations created by the Arabian astrologer ben Djabir. And it is by no means the only method employed by modern Western astrologers.

Although there are now a handful of computer programs available that calculate Western-style natal charts and planetary transits, many professional European and North American astrologers still prefer to construct a subject's chart manually, to ensure accuracy. Even astrologers who never intend to hand-calculate entire charts should understand the formulae, as slight variations or errors can and do occur in astrological software.

This chapter provides a concise and usable primer on the development of a natal personality profile by focusing on the construction and interpretation of the horoscope. This process includes calculating house locations and planetary positions; determining the formation of aspects (angles of difference) between various planets; analyzing the finished horoscope's overall shape; interpreting planetary positions by zodiac sign, by zodiac house, and by the position of each house's ruling planet; and delineating the additional influence of any aspects.

REQUIRED REFERENCE MATERIALS
FOR HOROSCOPE CALCULATION

There are three phases to Western horoscope construction: determination of the chart's house divisions; location of the planets' exact positions at the time and place of birth; and identification of major aspects. Besides gathering the person's date, time, and place of birth, three reference texts are necessary: a gazetteer, atlas, or almanac that gives the exact geographical latitude and longitude for many of the world's cities; an ephemeris of planetary positions and sidereal times[1] for each day of a given year; and a Table of Houses established for all sidereal times and geographic latitudes in the northern or southern hemisphere, depending on where the person was born.

The precise geographical longitude and latitude of a person's place of birth can be found for most major cities in any volume of the *World Almanac* or *Information Please Almanac* at the local library. Other locations can be found in standard astronomical, geographical, and navigational reference works such as *The Cambridge World Gazetteer*, *Rand McNally's World Atlas*, *Longitudes and Latitudes Throughout the World* by Eugene Dernay, and *Longitudes and Latitudes in the United States*, also compiled by Eugene Dernay. In the case of very small towns and outlying areas, the exact geographical longitude and latitude can usually be found by contacting the local or state geographic survey office.

---

1. Sidereal time computes the duration of travel that specific fixed stars take to pass over predetermined points on the Earth into twenty-four sidereal hours, which are not equal to standard clock hours.

Published annually, ephemerides are essential to astrologers, astronomers, and navigators, who use them to calculate the exact position of a planet at any given time, as well as local sidereal time. The degrees of each planetary position differ from one emphemeris to another. One popular ephemeris used by Western astrologers, *Raphael's Astronomical Ephemeris of the Planets' Places*, has been published continuously by W. Foulsham & Co., Ltd., since 1821, and includes Tables of Houses for London, Liverpool, and New York. Another popular version is the Rosicrucian Fellowship's *Simplified Scientific Ephemeris of the Planets' Places*. Yet another is the *New American Ephemeris*, published by Astro Computing Service. To look up the data for any given birthdate, simply open an ephemeris for the year in question; turn to the month in which the birth occurred, and make notes of the planetary, nodal, declination, and sidereal information for both the date of birth and the following day, as shown below. The ephemeris data used to create Alice's and Peter's charts (fig. 8.1 and 8.2) follow for quick reference:

Alice T.: 1952 ephemeris for June 15 and 16
(calculated for mean noon at Greenwich, England)

LONGITUDE OF THE PLANETS AND SIDEREAL TIME

Day	☉	☽	♀	☿	♂	♃
15	24°♊18′	05°♈35′	21°♊44′	02°♋05′	01°♏24′	10°♉52′
16	26°♊06′	22°♈42′	24°♊01′	06°♋07′	01°♏26′	10°♉58′

Day	♄	♅	♆	♇	☊	SIDEREAL TIME
15	08°♎12′	13°♋00′	18°♎59′ʀ	19°♌34′	23°♒23′	05:34:51
16	08°♎12′	13°♋02′	18°♎58′ʀ	19°♌34′	24°♒35′	05:38:47

New Moon: June 22 (☽ 00°♋51′); Full Moon: June 8 (☽ 17°♐21′)

DECLINATION OF THE PLANETS

Day	☉	☽	♀	☿	♂	♃
15	23°N19′	03°N59′	23°N14′	25°N03′	12°S56′	14°N03′
16	23°N24′	10°N04′	23°N27′	25°N05′	13°S03′	14°N10′

Day	♄	♅	♆	♇
15	00°S55′	23°N11′	05°N52′	23°N33′
16	00°S56′	23°N10′	05°N52′	23°N33′

Peter C.: 1964 ephemeris for August 27 and 28
(calculated for mean noon at Greenwich, England)

Longitude of the Planets and Sidereal Time

Day	☉	☽	♀	☿	♂	♃
27	03° ♍ 44′	22° ♈ 06′	17° ♋ 57′	13° ♍ 52′ʀ	17° ♋ 53′	25° ♉ 36′
28	05° ♍ 36′	14° ♉ 43′	19° ♋ 47′	12° ♍ 26′ʀ	19° ♋ 08′	25° ♉ 38′

Day	♄	♅	♆	♇	☊	Sidereal Time
27	01° ♓ 25′ʀ	10° ♍ 04′	15° ♏ 19′	13° ♍ 38′	29° ♊ 40′ʀ	10:16:25
28	01° ♓ 21′ʀ	10° ♍ 07′	15° ♏ 20′	13° ♍ 38′	29° ♊ 42′ʀ	10:20:58

New Moon: August 7 (☽ 03° ♌ 33′); Full Moon: June 23 (☽ 27° ♒ 12′)

Declination of the Planets

Day	☉	☽	♀	☿	♂	♃
27	10°N08′	03°N27′	19°N10′	01°N33′	22°N57′	18°N03′
28	09°N47′	08°N49′	19°N08′	01°N52′	22°N52′	18°N03′

Day	♄	♅	♆	♇
27	12°S33′	08°N32′	14°N45′	19°N00′
28	12°S35′	08°N32′	14°N45′	19°N00′

Tables of Houses aid astrologers in establishing the house cusps only for the Ascendant (House I), House II, House III, House X, House XI, and House XII of a chart. (Houses IV through IX are determined manually, as you will see later in this chapter.) This data doesn't vary on an annual or daily basis like the ephemeris, but the material is divided by degrees of geographic latitude and by intervals of time that are four minutes (00:04:00) in duration. The most popular version is *Dalton's Tables of Houses*, which situates the house according to the Placidus house system. However, the Table of Houses published in *Raphael's Astronomical Ephemeris of the Planets' Places* and the American Federation of Astrologers' *Table of Diurnal Planetary Motion* are also very common sources. To look up the data for any given birth date, simply open the Table of Houses to the nearest geographical latitude to the birthplace latitude; cross-reference to both the earlier and later published Sidereal Times (see Step Three, page 357); and make note of the house locations for Houses I, II, III, XI, and XII for both published times as shown below. The Tables of Houses used to create Alice's and Peter's charts (figs. 8.1 and 8.2) follow for quick reference:

Alice T.: Table of Houses for Latitudes 41°00′N to 42°00′N

SIDEREAL TIME: 15:30:35					SIDEREAL TIME: 15:34:42					
LATITUDE	XI	XII	I	II	III	XI	XII	I	II	III
41°00′N	16°♐36′	07°♑24′	02°♒17′	19°♓18′	27°♈48′	17°♐36′	08°♑18′	03°♒34′	20°♓48′	29°♈00′
42°00′N	16°♐24′	06°♑48′	01°♒26′	19°♓06′	28°♈00′	17°♐18′	07°♑48′	02°♒43′	20°♓36′	29°♈12′

Peter C.: Table of Houses for Latitudes 43°00′N to 44°00′N

SIDEREAL TIME: 16:54:52					SIDEREAL TIME: 16:59:11					
LATITUDE	XI	XII	I	II	III	XI	XII	I	II	III
43°00′N	05°♑18′	27°♑54′	01°♓10′	20°♈12′	22°♉06′	06°♑18′	29°♑06′	02°♓58′	21°♈48′	23°♉18′
44°00′N	05°♑00′	27°♑18′	00°♓32′	20°♈30′	22°♉24′	06°♑00′	28°♑30′	02°♓21′54″	22°♈10′	23°♉30′

With birth data, reference books, and a calculator in hand, the Western astrologer then proceeds to calculate an individual's natal chart.

In both the Table of Houses and the ephemeris, symbols are used to designate the zodiac signs. These are the same symbols that have been used throughout this book, but for quick reference the zodiac signs, their symbols, and their numeric position (which will be used in many of the calculations in this chapter) are presented below:

01	Aries	(♈)
02	Taurus	(♉)
03	Gemini	(♊)
04	Cancer	(♋)
05	Leo	(♌)
06	Virgo	(♍)
07	Libra	(♎)
08	Scorpio	(♏)
09	Sagittarius	(♐)
10	Capricorn	(♑)
11	Aquarius	(♒)
12	Pisces	(♓)

Similarly, symbols are used to designate the planets and the Moon's nodes:

The Sun	☉
The Moon	☽
Mercury	☿
Venus	♀

Mars	♂
Jupiter	♃
Saturn	♄
Uranus	♅
Neptune	♆
Pluto	♇
Moon's North Node	☊
Moon's South Node	☋

ESTABLISHING HOUSE POSITIONS
Step One: Determining Local Mean Time

Once the reference books and birth data have been gathered, the first step in chart construction is the conversion of the person's birth time to local mean time. The basis for all western astrological time orientation is Greenwich Mean Time (GMT) or Universal Time (UT), which represents the time at the Prime Meridian (00°00′ longitude), located in Greenwich, England. GMT is the standard applied in navigation, astronomy, and international communications. Fueled by a desire to unify the way in which various parts of the world tell time for trade and shipping purposes, standard time zones were established around the world during the nineteenth century. All time zones are measured from starting and ending points expressed in degrees and minutes of geographic longitude east or west of the Prime Meridian (00°00′ longitude). Time zones are additionally expressed in the hours, minutes, and seconds (plus or minus) of twenty-four-hour marine time that a given time zone differs from the Prime Meridian's Greenwich Mean Time.

For example, the United States is divided into five major time zones, occupying 15°00′ of geographic longitude each. The Eastern Standard Time zone (EST) extends from 67°30′W[2] to 82°30′W (with its center at 75°00′W) and is 05:00:00 less than GMT.[3] The Central Standard Time zone (CST) spans 82°30′W to 97°30′W (with its center at 90°00′W) and is 06:00:00 hours less than GMT. Rocky Mountain Standard Time (MST) occupies 97°30′W to 112°30′W (with its center at 105°00′W) and is 07:00:00 hours less than GMT. The Pacific Standard Time zone (PST) stretches from 112°30′W to 127°30′W (with its center at 120°00′W) and is 08:00:00 hours less than GMT. And the Alaska-Hawaii Standard Time zone (AST/HST) extends from 141°00′W to 157°30′W (with its center at 150°00′W) and is 10:00:00 hours less than GMT.[4]

---

2. This is read as 67 degrees, 30 minutes longitude west of the Prime Meridian.
3. This is read as 5 hours, 0 minutes, 0 seconds less than Greenwich Mean Time.
4. Yukon Standard Time (YST) occupies a small segment of southeastern Alaska and the Canadian Yukon,

Greenwich Mean Time (GMT) is applied throughout the British Isles from 10°30′W to 02°00E (with its center at 00°00′), plus all of Portugal. Unlike the fixed longitudinal parameters employed in the computation of time in North America and the British Isles, the Central European Standard Time (CEST) zone spans from Spain to Poland and from Sweden and Norway to France and Italy, following the contour of national boundaries (although the zone's center is generally perceived to be 15°00′E). It is 01:00:00 hour more than GMT. The Eastern European Standard Time (EEST) zone includes Finland, Greece, Romania, Bulgaria, Egypt, the Sudan, South Africa, and the Near East with the exception of Turkey. This time zone also follows national boundaries rather than fixed longitudinal parameters. This zone's center is also generally perceived to be situated at 15°00′E. It is 02:00:00 hours more than GMT. Russian Standard Time (RST) (or Baghdad Time) is applied in Turkey, the Balkan States, Russia, Ukraine, Saudi Arabia, Iran, and Iraq. Following national boundaries instead of fixed longitudinal parameters, this zone's center is generally perceived to be situated at 30°00′E, and is 03:00:00 more than GMT.

India Time (INT) is specific to India, Sri Lanka, Nepal, and East Kazakhstan. Following national boundaries instead of fixed longitudinal parameters, this zone's center is generally perceived to be situated at 53°30′E, and is 05:30:00 hours more than GMT.[5] China Coast Time (CCT) is applied throughout China, Xizang (Tibet), Manchuria, the Philippines, western Australia[6] and portions of Siberia.[7] Following national boundaries instead of fixed longitudinal parameters, this zone's center is generally perceived to be situated at 70°00′E, and is 08:00:00 hours more than GMT. Japan Time (JST) is employed throughout Japan. Following national boundaries instead of fixed longitudinal parameters, this zone's center is generally perceived to be situated at 93°30′E, and is 09:00:00 hours more than GMT. New Zealand Time (NZT) is specifically employed in New Zealand. Following national

---

extending from 127°30′W westward to the Pacific Coast, and is 09:00:00 hours less than GMT. Bering Standard Time stretches along Alaska's far northwestern coast as well as the Aleutian Islands from 157°30′W to 172°30′W, and is 11:00:00 hours less than GMT. Atlantic Standard Time stretches eastward through New Brunswick, Labrador, Nova Scotia, and Prince Edward Island, extending from 52°30′W to 67°30′W, and is 04:00:00 hours less than GMT. And Newfoundland Time extends across the province of Newfoundland, and is 03:30:00 hours less than GMT.

5. Pakistan has its own time zone, which is 05:00:00 more than GMT. Bangladesh has its own time zone, which is 06:00:00 more than GMT.

6. In Australia, this is called Australian Western Standard Time (AWST). Additionally, Australian Central Standard Time (ACST) is 09:30:00 more than GMT and Australia Eastern Standard Time (AEST) is 10:00:00 more than GMT.

7. In Siberia, this zone used to be called USSR Time Zone 7 (UZ7).

boundaries instead of fixed longitudinal parameters, this zone's center is generally perceived to be situated at 115°00'E, and is 12:00:00 hours more than GMT.

In order to establish the most accurate birth time for a person, the time found on a birth certificate or other birth record needs to be converted to local mean time (LMT) by determining the degrees and minutes of difference between the birthplace's longitude and the time zone's center, multiplying the difference by four minutes (00:04:00) and then adding or subtracting the total minutes to the time of birth. (If the person was born east of the time zone's center, these minutes are added. If the birth took place west of the time zone's center, the minutes are subtracted.) Furthermore, if the birth took place during Daylight Savings Time (DST),[8] the LMT needs to be adjusted further by subtracting 1 hour (01:00:00) from the LMT to derive the adjusted LMT, which is also called "standard LMT."

Alice T.: June 15, 1952, Chicago, IL (longitude 87°39'W) at 10:45 P.M. CDT[9] (22:45:00 in 24-hour marine time). The Central Time Zone's center is 90°00'W.
Step 1, Calculation 1:

Central time zone center	90°00'W	*(see time zones above)*
	89°60'W	*(converted)*[10]
− Longitude of Chicago, IL	87°39'W	*(found in an atlas)*
	02°21'	*(or 2.35° difference)*[11]
×	00:04:00	*(see explanation above)*
	00:09:24	*(result)*
+ Actual birth time	22:45:00	*(from birth record)*[12]
	22:54:24	*(LMT [local mean time])*
− DST adjustment	01:00:00	*(see explanation above)*[13]
	21:54:24	*(standard LMT)*[14]

---

8. Calculated by subtracting 01:00:00 from a given standard zone time during the summer growing and harvesting months (with the exception of a few places in British Columbia, Canada, and portions of South America), daylight savings time (DST) occurs between late March and early October worldwide. During the First and Second World Wars, a similar daylight savings time (DST) adjustment, called war time, was enforced year-round. This took place during the period from March 31 to October 27, 1918; March 30 to October 26, 1919; and February 9, 1942, to September 30, 1945.

9. Central Daylight Time.

10. To facilitate calculation, 01° is converted to 60' and added to the existing minutes.

11. To facilitate calculation, 21' is divided by 60' to derive a decimalized figure.

12. The marine-time (24-hour clock) version of the birth time is employed in this instance to facilitate calculation. Because the birth took place east of the time zone's center (90°00'W), the minutes (00:09:24) are added to the birth time.

13. Since the birth time was recorded in Daylight Savings Time (DST), LMT must be decreased by 1 hour (01:00:00) to derive standard LMT, which is used in the remaining calculations.

14. This result is also called adjusted LMT.

Peter C.: August 27, 1964, Syracuse, NY (longitude 76°08′W) at 7:45 P.M. EDT[15] (19:45:00 in 24-hour marine time). The Eastern Time Zone's center is 75°00′W.

Step 1, Calculation 1:

Longitude of Syracuse, NY	76°08′W	*(found in an atlas)*
− Eastern time zone center	75°00′W	*(see time zones above)*
	01°08′	*(or 1.13° difference)*[16]
×	00:04:00	*(see explanation above)*
	00:04:32	*(result)*
− Actual birth time	19:45:00	*(from birth record)*[17]
	19:40:28	*(LMT [local mean time])*
− DST adjustment	01:00:00	*(see explanation above)*[18]
	18:40:28	*(standard LMT)*[19]

If the person's actual birth time is not known, Western astrologers usually calculate the natal chart based on a birth time of 12:00 P.M. (12:00:00), unlike Judaic astrologers, who apply 06:00 A.M. (06:00:00) for this same purpose. This generalization does not provide an accurate placement of the Ascendant and the houses, but it does serve as a starting point from which an experienced astrologer can then incrementally work to find interpretative clues that aid in ascertaining a closer approximation of the actual birth.

Step Two: Determining Local Sidereal Time

Once the adjusted or standard local mean time (LMT) is calculated, it is necessary to convert this figure into sidereal time. Sidereal time is based on the same principle as the sidereal zodiac (see "Pole to Pole: The Tropical and Sidereal Zodiacs" in chapter 2), breaking up the Sun's apparent passage over the vernal equinox (00° ♈00′ [00°00′ Aries]) into sidereal hours, minutes, and seconds instead. Although it's based on an identical 24-hour cycle, a sidereal day is 3 hours, 55.91 minutes of clock time (00:03:55.91) shorter than the average calendar days, as sidereal hours, minutes, and seconds are shorter than clock hours, minutes, and seconds. Ephemerides are used to find the Sidereal Time at noon for any given day.[20]

---

15.   Eastern Daylight Time.

16.   To facilitate calculation, 08′ is divided by 60′ to derive a decimalized figure.

17.   The marine-time version of the birth time is employed in this instance to facilitate calculation. Because the birth took place west of the time zone's center (75°00′W), the minutes (00:04:32) are subtracted from the birth time: 19:45:00 − 00:04:32 = 19:40:28.

18.   Since the birth time was recorded in Daylight Savings Time (DST), LMT must be decreased by 1 hour (01:00:00) to derive standard LMT, which is used in the remaining calculations.

19.   This result is also called adjusted LMT.

20.   There are, however, some ephemerides that calculate sidereal time from midnight rather than noon, such as *The New American Ephemeris*. In cases where the published time is set at midnight (12:00 A.M. or 00:00:00), 12:02:00 must be added to the published time before converting the given LMT into actual sidereal time.

Just like local mean time (LMT), the sidereal time must be adjusted to reflect the exact hours, minutes, and seconds of sidereal time of the person's birth. To achieve this, one of two calculations must be made, depending on the time of day the person was born. If the individual was born after 12:00 P.M. (noon), the standard LMT (local mean time) from above[21] is added to the published sidereal time for the person's birth. If the individual was born before 12:00 P.M., the standard LMT (local mean time) from above is subtracted from 12:00 P.M. (12:00:00). The difference is then subtracted from the published sidereal time for the person's birth.[22]

Alice T.: June 15, 1952, at 10:45 P.M. CDT,[23] (22:45:00 in 24-hour marine time).
Step 2, Calculation 1:

Sidereal time (6/15/52)	05:34:51	*(found in an ephemeris)*[24]
+ Standard LMT	09:54:24	*(Step 1, Calculation 1)*[25]
	14:88:75	*(LST [local sidereal time])*

Peter C.: August 27, 1964, at 7:45 P.M. EDT[26] (19:45:00 in 24-hour marine time).
Step 2, Calculation 1:

Sidereal time (8/27/64)	10:16:25	*(found in an ephemeris)*[27]
+ Standard LMT	06:40:28	*(Step 1, Calculation 1)*[28]
	16:56:53	*(LST [local sidereal time])*

Next, the interval between the previous noon and the actual birth time is converted to a decimal figure, multiplied by 10 seconds per hour, and added to the LST (local sidereal time) as shown below:

---

21. If marine time is employed in these calculations, 12 hours (12:00:00) are subtracted from the standard LMT to reflect the actual hours that occur after 12:00 P.M.
22. For a birth that occurs prior to 12:00 P.M. (12:00:00), an additional calculation needs to be made. The individual's birth LMT needs to be subtracted from noon (12:00:00). For example, if the person was born on January 1, 1997, at 03:54:24 A.M. (03:54:24), this LMT would be subtracted from 12:00:00, resulting in a difference of 08:05:36. The remainder would then be subtracted from the published sidereal time (18:44:42) to find the adjusted sidereal time of 10:39:06.
23. Central Daylight Time.
24. This information can also be found on page 348.
25. Twelve hours are subtracted from the marine time to reflect the actual hours between noon and the birth time.
26. Eastern Daylight Time.
27. This information can also be found on page 349.
28. Twelve hours (12:00:00) are subtracted from the marine time to reflect the actual hours between noon and the birth time.

Alice T.: June 15, 1952, at 10:45 P.M. CDT[29] (22:45:00 in 24-hour marine time).
Step 2, Calculation 2:

Standard LMT	09:54:24	*(Step 1, Calculation 1)*[30]
	09.9:00:00	*(converted)*[31]
×	00:00:10	*(see explanation above)*
	00:00:99	*(adjustment)*
+ LST	14:88:75	*(Step 2, Calculation 1)*
	14:88:174	*(hours, minutes, and seconds)*
	15:30:54	*(adjusted LST)*

Peter C.: August 27, 1964, at 7:45 P.M. EDT[32] (19:45:00 in 24-hour marine time).
Step 2, Calculation 2:

Standard LMT	06:40:28	*(Step 1, Calculation 1)*[33]
	06.7:00:00	*(converted)*[34]
×	00:00:10	*(see explanation above)*
	00:00:67	*(adjustment)*
+ LST	16:56:53	*(Step 2, Calculation 1)*
	16:56:120	*(total)*[35]
	16:58:00	*(adjusted LST)*

Finally, the adjusted LST (local sidereal time) is corrected for its true geographic longitude. This is accomplished by multiplying the longitudinal degrees and minutes of the person's birth location by 4 minutes (04:00:00), then converting the resulting minutes and seconds into hours, minutes, and seconds by dividing the total by 60 minutes (00:60:00). The converted total is then multiplied by 10 seconds (00:00:10). The resulting seconds are added to the adjusted LST if the person was born west of the Prime Meridian (00°00′ geographical longitude). If, however, the person was born east of the Prime Meridian, the resulting seconds are subtracted from the adjusted LST.

---

29. Central Daylight Time.
30. Twelve hours (12:00:00) are subtracted from the marine time to reflect the actual hours between noon and the birth time.
31. The 54 minutes in the standard LMT are converted by dividing 54 by 60 to derive a decimalized figure.
32. Eastern Daylight Time.
33. Twelve hours are subtracted from the marine time to reflect the actual hours between noon and the birth time.
34. The 40 minutes in the standard LMT are converted by dividing 40 by 60 and rounding the remainder to a single decimalized figure.
35. Because 60 seconds (00:00:60) equals 1 minute (00:01:00), 60 seconds are subtracted from the existing seconds and 1 minute is added to the existing minutes.

Alice T.: Chicago, IL (longitude 87°39′W)
Step 2, Calculation 3:

Longitude of Chicago	87°39′	(*found in an atlas*)
	87.65°	(*converted*)[36]
×	00:04:00	(*see explanation above*)
	00:350.6:00	(*total minutes*)
	05.83:00:00	(*converted*)[37]
×	00:00:10	(*see explanation above*)
	00:00:58	(*total seconds*)
+ Adjusted LST	15:30:54	(*Step 2, Calculation 2*)
	15:30:112	(*hours, minutes, seconds*)
	15:31:52	(*LST [local sidereal time]*)[38]

Peter C.: Syracuse, NY (longitude 76°08′W)
Step 2, Calculation 3:

Longitude of Syracuse	76°08′	(*found in an atlas*)
	76.13°	(*converted*)[39]
×	00:04:00	(*see explanation above*)
	00:304.52:00	(*total minutes*)
	05.06:00:00	(*converted*)[40]
×	00:00:10	(*see explanation above*)
	00:00:50	(*total seconds*)
+ Adjusted LST	16:58:00	(*Step 2, Calculation 2*)
	16:58:50	(*LST [Local Sidereal Time]*)

Step Three: Interpolating the Placement of the Houses

As mentioned earlier in this chapter, the house locations published in a Table of Houses are listed only for the Ascendant (House I), House II, House III, House X, House XI, and House XII. In this same table, the sidereal times from 00:00:00 to 24:00:00 are listed in increments of 00:04:20 each, and only a limited number of geographical latitudes are displayed. Consequently, the material presented must be adjusted to reflect the actual longitude and latitude of the birthplace before it is applied to an individual's horoscope.

---

36. To facilitate calculation, 39′ is divided by 60′ to derive a decimalized figure.
37. To facilitate calculation, 350.6 minutes are divided by 60 minutes to derive 5.83 hours.
38. Because 60 seconds (00:00:60) equals 1 minute (00:01:00), 60 seconds is subtracted from 112 seconds in the sum and 1 minute is added to 30 minutes.
39. To facilitate calculation, 08′ is divided by 60′ to derive a decimalized figure.
40. To facilitate calculation, 304.52 minutes are divided by 60 minutes to derive a decimalized figure.

Interpolating Longitudinal Placement

Using a Table of Houses, find the two Sidereal Times that the LST (Local Sidereal Time) derived from Step 2, Calculation 2 falls between, and calculate the difference between these two times as demonstrated below:

Alice T.: 15:31:52 LST
Step 3, Calculation 1:

Later published ST	15:34:42	(*from Table of Houses*)[41]
− Earlier published ST	15:30:35	(*from Table of Houses*)
	00:04:07	(*or 247 seconds*)

Peter C.: 16:58:50 LST
Step 3, Calculation 1:

Later published ST	16:59:11	(*from Table of Houses*)
	16:58:71	(*converted*)[42]
− Earlier published ST	16:54:52	(*from Table of Houses*)
	00:04:19	(*or 259 seconds*)

Using the Table of Houses, locate the nearest latitude to the birthplace latitude and read across to identify House I (Ascendant) associated with both the earlier and later published sidereal times from Step 3, Calculation 1. Then determine the difference in zodiac signs, degrees, and minutes between those two positions.

Alice T.: Chicago, IL (latitude 41°51′N, found in an atlas)
Step 3, Calculation 2:

Later House I (Ascendant)
    (Latitude 42°00′N,
    Sidereal time 15:34:42)[43]

(02°♒43′)	11	02°	43′	(*from Table of Houses*)[44]

Earlier House I (Ascendant)
    (Latitude 42°00′N,
    Sidereal time 15:30:55:)[45]

− (01°♒26′)	11	01°	26′	(*from Table of Houses*)
	00	01°	17′	(*or 00°00′4620″*)

---

41. This information is also found on page 350.
42. To facilitate calculation, 1 hour is converted to 60 minutes and added to the existing minutes.
43. See the Table of Houses data on page 350.
44. To facilitate calculation, the zodiac sign associated with each position is converted to a number, as shown in "Required Materials for Horoscope Calculation," page 347. In this case, ♒ = 11.
45. See the Table of Houses data on page 350.

Peter C.: Syracuse, NY (latitude 43°03′N, found in an atlas)
Step 3, Calculation 2:
Later House I (Ascendant)
   (Latitude 44°00′N,
   Sidereal time 16:59:11)

(02°♓21′ 54″)	12	02°	21.9′	*(from Table of Houses)*[46]
	12	01°	81.9′	*(converted)*[47]

Earlier House I (Ascendant)
   (Latitude 44°00′N,
   Sidereal time 16:54:52)

− (00°♓32′)	12	00°	32′	*(from Table of Houses)*
	00	01°	49.9′	*(or 00°00′6594″)*

By dividing the difference between the earlier and later published Ascendants by the difference between the earlier and later published sidereal times, the longitudinal equivalent of one sidereal second is determined.

Alice T.:
Step 3, Calculation 3:

Difference between Ascendants	4620″	*(Step 3, Calculation 2)*
÷ Difference between STs	00:00:247	*(Step 3, Calculation 1)*
	18:70″	*(longitudinal equivalent)*

Peter C.:
Step 3, Calculation 3:

Difference between Ascendants	6594″	*(Step 3, Calculation 2)*
÷ Difference between STs	00:00:259	*(Step 3, Calculation 1)*
	25.46″	*(longitudinal equivalent)*

Next, the earlier published sidereal time is subtracted from Alice's LST (local sidereal time) to determine the interval between the two periods.

Alice T.:
Step 3, Calculation 4:

Adjusted LST	15:31:52	*(Step 2, Calculation 3)*
− Earlier published ST	15:30:35	*(from Table of Houses)*
	00:01:17	*(interval)*

---

46. To facilitate calculation, the zodiac sign associated with each position is converted to a number as shown in "Required Materials for Horoscope Calculation," page 347. In this case, ♓ = 12.
47. To facilitate calculation, 01° is converted to 60′ and added to the existing minutes.

Peter C.:
Step 3, Calculation 4:

LST	16:58:50	*(Step 2, Calculation 2)*
	16:57:110	*(converted)* [48]
−Earlier published ST	16:54:52	*(from Table of Houses)*
	00:03:58	*(interval)*

This interval is then multiplied by the longitudinal equivalent determined in Step 3, Calculation 3:

Alice T.:
Step 3, Calculation 5:

Interval	00:01:17	*(Step 3, Calculation 4)*
	00:00:77	*(converted)* [49]
× Longitudinal equivalent	00°00′18.7″	*(Step 3, Calculation 3)*
	00°00′1439.9″	*(total)* [50]
	00°23′59.4″	*(converted)* [51]
	00°24′	*(longitudinal interval)*

Peter C.:
Step 3, Calculation 5:

Interval	00:03:58	*(Step 3, Calculation 4)*
	00:00:238	*(converted)* [52]
× Longitudinal equivalent	00°00′25.46″	*(Step 3, Calculation 3)*
	00°00′6060″	*(total)*
	01°41′	*(longitudinal interval)* [53]

Using only the degrees and minutes from Step 3, Calculation 5, the longitudinal interval is added to the earlier published Ascendant to determine the interpolated Ascendant:

---

48. To facilitate calculation, 1 hour is converted to 60 minutes and added to the existing minutes.
49. To facilitate calculation, 1 minute is converted to 60 seconds and added to the existing seconds.
50. Because 60″ equals 1′, the resulting 1439.9″ are divided by 60″.
51. This figure is then rounded out to the nearest whole minute.
52. To facilitate calculation, the minutes are converted to seconds by multiplying the minutes by 60 and adding those seconds to the existing sounds.
53. Because 60″ equals 1′, the resulting 6060″ are divided by 60″.

Alice T.:
Step 3, Calculation 6:

Longitudinal interval	00	00°	24′	(Step 3, Calculation 5)
+ Earlier Ascendant (01°♒26′)	11	01°	26′	(from Table of Houses)[54]
	11	01°	50′	(interpolated Ascendant, 01°♒50′)

Peter C.:
Step 3, Calculation 6:

Longitudinal interval	00	01°	41′	(Step 3, Calculation 5)
+ Earlier Ascendant (00°♓32′)	12	00°	32′	(from Table of Houses)[55]
	12	01°	73′	(total)[56]
	12	02°	13′	(interpolated Ascendant, 02°♓13′)

Interpolating Latitudinal Placement

To get a completely accurate Ascendant, the geographical latitude must also be adjusted, using procedures similar to those described in the previous section. To begin, find the difference between the birthplace latitude and the published latitude by subtracting the degrees and minutes as shown below:

Alice T.: Chicago, IL (latitude 41°51′N)
Step 3, Calculation 7:

Published latitude	42°00′N	(found in Table of Houses)
	41°60′	(converted)[57]
−Birthplace latitude	41°51′N	(found in an atlas)
	00°09′N	(latitudinal difference)

Peter C.: Syracuse, NY (latitude 43°03′N)
Step 3, Calculation 7:

Published latitude	44°00′N	(found in Table of Houses)
	43°60′	(converted)[58]
− Birthplace latitude	43°03′N	(found in an atlas)
	00°57′	(latitudinal difference)

---

54. This information can also be found on page 350.
55. Ibid.
56. Because 60′ equals 01°, 60′ is subtracted from the existing minutes and 01° is added to the existing degrees.
57. To facilitate calculation, 01° is changed into 60′ and added into the existing minutes.
58. To facilitate calculation, 01° is changed into 60′ and added into the existing minutes.

Next, the difference between the published Ascendants (House I) that are greater and lesser than the birth latitude is determined by subtracting the degrees and minutes as shown below, using the earlier published sidereal time from Step 3, Calculation 4:

Alice T.: Chicago, IL (latitude 41°51′N)
Step 3, Calculation 8:
Ascendant (latitude 41°00′)

(02°♒17′)	11	02°	17′	*(found in Table of Houses)*[59]
	11	01°	77′	*(converted)*[60]

Ascendant (latitude 42°00′)

− (01°♒26′)	11	01°	26′	*(found in Table of Houses)*[61]
	00	00°	51′	*(Ascendant difference)*

Peter C.: Syracuse, NY (latitude 43°03′N)
Step 3, Calculation 8:
Ascendant (latitude 43°00′N)

(01°♓10′)	12	01°	10′	*(found in Table of Houses)*[62]
	12	00°	70′	*(converted)*[63]

Ascendant (latitude 44°00′)

− (00°♓32′)	12	00°	32′	*(found in Table of Houses)*[64]
	00	00°	38′	*(Ascendant difference)*

The interval needed to adjust the Ascendant is derived by multiplying the latitudinal difference (Step 3, Calculation 7) by the Ascendant difference (Step 3, Calculation 8), as shown below:

Alice T.:
Step 3, Calculation 9:

Latitudinal difference	00°09′	*(Step 3, Calculation 7)*
× Ascendant difference	00°51′	*(Step 3, Calculation 8)*
	459	*(total seconds)*[65]
	07′39″	*(interval)*

---

59. This information can also be found on page 350.
60. To facilitate calculation, 01° is changed into 60′ and added into the existing minutes.
61. This information can also be found on page 350.
62. Ibid.
63. To facilitate calculation, 01° is changed into 60′ and added into the existing minutes.
64. This information can also be found on page 350.
65. To facilitate the next calculation, divide this total by 60, noting that the remainder is used as minutes and seconds instead of hours and minutes.

Peter C.:
Step 3, Calculation 9:

Latitudinal difference	00°57′	(*Step 3, Calculation 7*)
× Ascendant difference	00°38′	(*Step 3, Calculation 8*)
	2166	(*total seconds*)[66]
	36′06″	(*interval*)

Finally, only the minutes of this interval are added to the longitudinally interpolated Ascendant (Step 3, Calculation 6) as shown below:

Alice T.
Step 3, Calculation 10:

Longitudinally interpolated Ascendant (01°♒50′)	11	01°	50′	(*Step 3, Calculation 6*)
+ Latitudinal interval	00	00°	07′	(*Step 3, Calculation 9*)
	11	01°	57′	(01°♒57′, *interpolated Ascendant*)

Peter T.
Step 3, Calculation 10:

Longitudinally interpolated Ascendant (02°♓13′)	12	02°	13′	(*Step 3, Calculation 6*)
+ Latitudinal interval	00	00°	36′	(*Step 3, Calculation 9*)
	12	02°	49′	(02°♓49′, *interpolated Ascendant*)

Rectifying the Remaining House Positions

The procedures found in Step 3, Calculations 1 through 10, are then used to interpolate the positions for Houses II, III, X, XI, and XII found in the row associated with the earlier published Ascendant. For reference, these interpolated positions are as follows:

Alice T.:

Ascendant (House I)	01°♒57′	(01°57′ *Aquarius*)
House II	19°♓40′	(19°40′ *Pisces*)
House III	28°♈15′	(28°15′ *Aries*)
House X	25°♏17′	(25°17′ *Scorpio*)
House XI	16°♐44′	(16°44′ *Sagittarius*)
House XII	07°♑13′	(07°13′ *Capricorn*)

---

66. Ibid.

FIGURE 8.1. ALICE T.'s NATAL CHART.

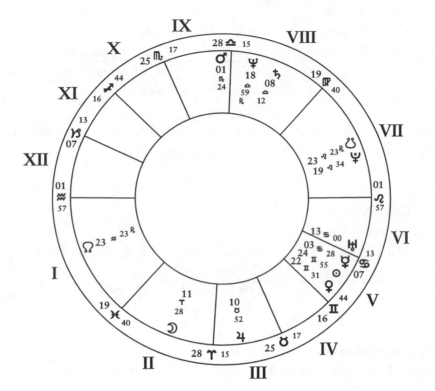

Peter C.:

Ascendant (House I)	02°♓49′	(02° 49′ Pisces)
House II	24°♈34′	(24° 34′ Aries)
House III	25°♉27′	(25° 27′ Taurus)
House X	17°♐06′	(17° 06′ Sagittarius)
House XI	06°♑26′	(06° 26′ Capricorn)
House XII	28°♑27′	(28° 27′ Capricorn)

Expressed in degrees and minutes as shown above, each house cusp is placed on the outer ring of Alice's and Peter's charts, as seen in figs. 8.1 and 8.2, next to its corresponding house using the traditional symbols for the zodiac signs as also shown above. The additional houses are then incorporated by following the rule of opposites, matching degrees and minutes from one side of the chart to the other. The opposite of each zodiac sign is as follows:

Aries (♈)	opposes Libra (♎)
Taurus (♉)	opposes Scorpio (♏)
Gemini (♊)	opposes Sagittarius (♐)
Cancer (♋)	opposes Capricorn (♑)

FIGURE 8.2. PETER C.'S NATAL CHART.

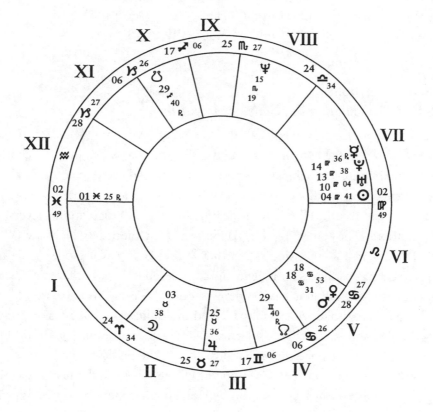

Leo (♌)   opposes Aquarius (♒)
Virgo (♍)   opposes Pisces (♓)

Thus, the remaining houses in both charts would be filled in with the information below:

Alice T.:

Ascendant (House I):	01°♒57'	House VII:	01°♌57'
House II:	19°♓40'	House VIII:	19°♍40'
House III:	28°♈15'	House IX:	28°♎15'
House X:	25°♏17'	House IV:	25°♉17'
House XI:	16°♐44'	House V:	16°♊44'
House XII:	07°♑13'	House VI:	07°♋13'

Peter C.:

Ascendant (House I):	02°♓49'	House VII:	02°♍49'
House II:	24°♈34'	House VIII:	24°♎34'
House III:	25°♉27'	House IX:	25°♏27'

House X:	17°♐06′	House IV:	17°♊06′
House XI:	06°♑26′	House V:	06°♋26′
House XII:	28°♑27′	House VI:	28°♋27′

Planetary Positions
Step Four: Calculating the Constant Logarithm

Before the positions of the Sun (☉), the Moon (☽), Mercury (☿), Venus (♀), and Mars (♂) listed in the ephemeris for a given day can be placed into the chart, the degrees and minutes of each planet's position must be adjusted to accommodate for the difference between the planetary positions found in an ephemeris (based upon GMT) and the true LMT (local mean time in Step 1, Calculation 1) version of those positions. The planets Jupiter (♃), Saturn (♄), Uranus (♅), Neptune (♆) and Pluto (♇), as well as the Moon's North (☊) and South (☋) Nodes, only move 00°01′ to 00°02′ per day, so it is generally considered unnecessary to convert their positions, since the difference is less than 00°00′01″ per day in each case.

The mathematical device used to convert multiplication and division problems into addition and subtraction problems, called a proportional logarithm, is employed to simplify the necessary equations. To find the proportional logarithm that reflects the difference between GMT and LMT, the Noon Mark must be located. If the person is born after 12:00 P.M., this temporal point is identified by multiplying 4 minutes (00:04:00) for each degree that is situated west of the Prime Meridian (00°00′ geographical longitude) (see Step 4, Calculation 1, below) and subtracting the result from the GMT; by multiplying 4 minutes (00:04:00) for each degree that is situated east of the Prime Meridian (00°00′ geographical longitude) (see Step 4, Calculation 1, below) and adding the result from the GMT. For example, Alice was born in Chicago, which is 87°39′ west of the Prime Meridian. Because this location is west of 00°00′ geographical latitude (the Prime Meridian), the derived hours, minutes, and seconds are then subtracted from 12:00 P.M. GMT (Greenwich Mean Time). Peter was born in Syracuse, which is 76°08′ west of the Prime Meridian. Since this location is west of Greenwich, England, the derived hours, minutes, and seconds are also subtracted from 12:00 P.M. GMT.

Alice T.: Chicago, IL (Longitude 87°39′W)
Step 4, Calculation 1:

Chicago (87°39′W)	87°39′	(found in an atlas)
	87.65°	(converted)[67]
×	00:04:00	(see explanation above)
	00:350.6:00	(total minutes)
	05:50:24	(difference between GMT and LMT)[68]

Step 4, Calculation 2:

12:00:00 P.M. GMT	11:59:60	(noon at Prime Meridian)[69]
− GMT to LMT difference	05:50:24	(Step 4, Calculation 1)
	06:09:36	(Noon Mark)

Peter C.: Syracuse, NY (longitude 76°08′W)
Step 4, Calculation 1:

Syracuse (76°08′W)	76°08′	(found in an atlas)
	76.13°	(converted)[70]
×	00:04:00	(see explanation above)
	00:304.52:00	(total minutes)
	05:04:31	(difference between GMT and LMT)[71]

Step 4, Calculation 2:

12:00:00 P.M. GMT	11:59:60	(noon at Prime Meridian)[72]
− GMT to LMT difference	05:04:31	(Step 4, Calculation 1)
	06:55:29	(Noon Mark)

Since Alice's and Peter's respective standard LMTs (standard local mean time from Step 1, Calculation 1) are closer to the Noon Mark of the next day,[73] the interval between the birth time and midnight (12:00 A.M.) must be determined and added to the Noon Mark as demonstrated below:

---

67. To facilitate calculation, 39′ is divided by 60′ to convert the minutes into a decimal figure.
68. By dividing 00:350.6:00 by 60 minutes, the hours, minutes, and seconds of time can be derived as shown.
69. To facilitate calculation, 1 hour (01:00:00) is converted to 60 minutes (00:60:00) and 1 minute (00:01:00) is converted to 60 seconds.
70. To facilitate calculation, 08′ is divided by 60′ to convert the minutes into a decimalized figure.
71. By dividing 00:350.6:00 by 60 minutes, the hours, minutes, and seconds of time can be derived as shown.
72. To facilitate calculation, 1 hour (01:00:00) is converted to 60 minutes (00:60:00) and 1 minute (00:01:00) is converted to 60 seconds (00:00:60).
73. Since Alice was born at 21:54:24 (09:54:24 P.M.) LMT, her birth time is 08:15:12 from 06:09:36 (Noon Mark of the next day), but is 15:44:48 from 06:09:36 (Noon Mark of the same day). Therefore, it's closer to the next day's Noon Mark.

Alice T.:

Step 4, Calculation 3:

12:00:00 A.M.	11:59:60	(midnight at Prime Meridian)[74]
− Standard LMT	09:54:24	(Step 1, Calculation 1)[75]
	02:05:36	(LMT interval)

Step 4, Calculation 4:

Noon Mark	06:09:36	(Step 4, Calculation 2)
+ Interval	02:05:36	(Step 4, Calculation 3)
	08:14:72	(sum)
	08:15:12	(interval)[76]

Peter C.:

Step 4, Calculation 3:

12:00:00 A.M.	11:59:60	(midnight at Prime Meridian)[77]
− Standard LMT	06:40:28	(Step 1, Calculation 1)[78]
	05:19:32	(LMT interval)

Step 4, Calculation 4:

Noon Mark	06:55:29	(Step 4, Calculation 2)
+ Interval	05:19:32	(Step 4, Calculation 3)
	11:74:61	(sum)
	12:15:01	(interval)[79]

If either person had been born before noon, the astrologer would have executed Step 4, Calculations 1 and 2. Then the resulting Noon Mark (Step 4, Calculation 2) would have been subtracted from the standard LMT (Step 1, Calculation 1).

The resulting interval in either case is then converted into a proportional loga-

---

74.   Clock time instead of marine time is used to make this particular calculation. To facilitate calculation, 1 hour (01:00:00) is converted to 60 minutes (00:60:00) and 1 minute (00:01:00) is converted to 60 seconds (00:00:60).
75.   Clock time instead of marine time is used to make this particular calculation. Consequently, 12 hours are subtracted from the marine time to reflect the actual hours between noon and the birth time.
76.   Because 00:00:60 equals 00:01:00, 60 seconds is subtracted from 72 seconds and 1 minute is added to the existing minutes.
77.   Clock time instead of marine time is used to make this particular calculation. To facilitate calculation, 1 hour (01:00:00) is converted to 60 minutes (00:60:00) and 1 minute (00:01:00) is converted to 60 seconds (00:00:60).
78.   Clock time instead of marine time is used to make this particular calculation. Consequently, 12 hours are subtracted from the marine time to reflect the actual hours between noon and the birth time.
79.   Because 00:00:60 equals 00:01:00, 60 seconds are subtracted from 60 seconds and 1 minute is added to the existing minutes. Then 60 minutes are subtracted from 74 minutes and 1 hour is added to the existing hours.

THE LORDS OF NATIVITY

rithm by referring to fig. 8.3. For example, Alice's interval (08:15:12 in Step 4, Calculation 4) is converted to log 0.4638 by locating the hours and minutes in fig. 8.3. Peter's interval (12:15:00 in Step 4, Calculation 4) translates into log 0.2921 using the same table. Each proportional logarithm is called the chart's constant logarithm. As mentioned at the beginning of this section, these logarithms will then be used to adjust the positions of the Sun (☉), the Moon (☽), Mercury (☿), Venus (♀), and Mars (♂).

Step Five: Calculating the Daily Motion of the Planets

The apparent positions of the Sun (☉), the Moon (☽), Mercury (☿), Venus (♀), and Mars (♂) in relation to the Earth change at varying rates from day to day, and this information is published in an ephemeris. However, since each published position is calculated for its position at the Prime Meridian (00°00′ geographical longitude) at noon, the daily motion for each of these planets must adjusted using the constant logarithm to render its exact location at the time and place of birth. As mentioned at the beginning of this section, the planets Jupiter (♃), Saturn (♄), Uranus (♅), Neptune (♆), and Pluto (♇) as well as the Moon's North (☊) and South (☋) Nodes only move 00°01′ to 00°02′ per day, so it is generally considered to be unnecessary to convert their positions, since the difference is less than 00°00′01″ per day in each case.

First, the given planet's position on the person's birth date is subtracted from its position on the following day as both are published in the ephemeris. The remainder is the planet's daily motion as calculated for 12:00:00 P.M. This figure is then converted into a proportional logarithm using fig. 8.3 as shown below:

Alice T.: June 15, 1952
Step 5, Calculation 1:
Sun (☉):

June 16 (26°♊06′)	03	26°	06′	(from an ephemeris)[80]
	03	25°	66′	(converted)[81]
− June 15 (24°♊18′)	03	24°	18′	(from an ephemeris)[82]
	00	01°	48′	(daily motion)
	log. 1.1249			(converted using fig. 8.3)

---

80. This information is also found on page 348.
81. To facilitate calculation, 01° is converted to 60′ and added to the existing minutes.
82. This information is also found on page 348.

FIGURE 8.3. TABLE OF PROPORTIONAL LOGARITHMS.

Degrees or Hours and Minutes	00° (or hours)	01° (or hours)	02° (or hours)	03° (or hours)	04° (or hours)	05° (or hours)	06° (or hours)
00′	3.1584	1.3802	1.0792	0.9031	0.7781	0.6812	0.6021
01′	3.1584	1.3730	1.0756	0.9007	0.7763	0.6798	0.6009
02′	2.8573	1.3660	1.0720	0.8983	0.7745	0.6784	0.5997
03′	2.6812	1.3590	1.0685	0.8959	0.7728	0.6769	0.5985
04′	2.5563	1.3522	1.0649	0.8935	0.7710	0.6755	0.5973
05′	2.4594	1.3454	1.0614	0.8912	0.7692	0.6741	0.5961
06′	2.3802	1.3388	1.0580	0.8888	0.7674	0.6726	0.5949
07′	2.3133	1.3323	1.0546	0.8865	0.7657	0.6712	0.5937
08′	2.2553	1.3258	1.0511	0.8842	0.7639	0.6698	0.5925
09′	2.2041	1.3195	1.0478	0.8819	0.7622	0.6684	0.5913
10′	2.1584	1.3133	1.0444	0.8796	0.7604	0.6670	0.5902
11′	2.1170	1.3071	1.0411	0.8773	0.7587	0.6656	0.5890
12′	2.0792	1.3010	1.0378	0.8751	0.7570	0.6642	0.5878
13′	2.0444	1.2950	1.0345	0.8728	0.7552	0.6628	0.5866
14′	2.0122	1.2891	1.0313	0.8706	0.7535	0.6614	0.5855
15′	1.9823	1.2833	1.0280	0.8683	0.7518	0.6600	0.5843
16′	1.9542	1.2775	1.0248	0.8661	0.7501	0.6587	0.5832
17′	1.9279	1.2719	1.0216	0.8639	0.7484	0.6573	0.5820
18′	1.9031	1.2663	1.0185	0.8617	0.7467	0.6559	0.5809
19′	1.8796	1.2607	1.0153	0.8595	0.7451	0.6546	0.5797
20′	1.8573	1.2553	1.0122	0.8573	0.7434	0.6532	0.5786
21′	1.8361	1.2499	1.0091	0.8552	0.7417	0.6519	0.5774
22′	1.8159	1.2445	1.0061	0.8530	0.7401	0.6505	0.5763
23′	1.7966	1.2393	1.0030	0.8509	0.7384	0.6492	0.5752
24′	1.7781	1.2341	1.0000	0.8487	0.7368	0.6478	0.5740
25′	1.7604	1.2289	0.9970	0.8466	0.7351	0.6465	0.5729
26′	1.7434	1.2239	0.9940	0.8445	0.7335	0.6451	0.5718
27′	1.7270	1.2188	0.9910	0.8424	0.7318	0.6438	0.5706
28′	1.7112	1.2139	0.9881	0.8403	0.7302	0.6425	0.5692
29′	1.6960	1.2090	0.9852	0.8382	0.7286	0.6412	0.5684
30′	1.6812	1.2041	0.9823	0.8361	0.7270	0.6398	0.5673
31′	1.6670	1.1993	0.9794	0.8341	0.7254	0.6385	0.5662
32′	1.6532	1.1946	0.9765	0.8321	0.7238	0.6372	0.5651
33′	1.6398	1.1899	0.9737	0.8300	0.7222	0.6359	0.5640
34′	1.6269	1.1852	0.9708	0.8279	0.7206	0.6346	0.5629
35′	1.6143	1.1806	0.9680	0.8259	0.7190	0.6333	0.5618
36′	1.6021	1.1761	0.9652	0.8239	0.7174	0.6320	0.5607
37′	1.5902	1.1716	0.9625	0.8219	0.7159	0.6307	0.5596
38′	1.5786	1.1671	0.9597	0.8199	0.7143	0.6294	0.5585
39′	1.5673	1.1627	0.9570	0.8179	0.7128	0.6282	0.5574

Degrees or Hours and Minutes	00° (or hours)	01° (or hours)	02° (or hours)	03° (or hours)	04° (or hours)	05° (or hours)	06° (or hours)
40'	1.5563	1.1584	0.9542	0.8159	0.7112	0.6269	0.5563
41'	1.5456	1.1540	0.9515	0.8140	0.7097	0.6256	0.5552
42'	1.5351	1.1498	0.9488	0.8120	0.7081	0.6243	0.5541
43'	1.5249	1.1455	0.9462	0.8101	0.7066	0.6231	0.5531
44'	1.5149	1.1413	0.9435	0.8081	0.7050	0.6218	0.5520
45'	1.5051	1.1372	0.9409	0.8062	0.7035	0.6205	0.5509
46'	1.4956	1.1331	0.9383	0.8043	0.7020	0.6193	0.5498
47'	1.4863	1.1290	0.9356	0.8023	0.7005	0.6180	0.5488
48'	1.4771	1.1249	0.9330	0.8004	0.6990	0.6168	0.5477
49'	1.4682	1.1209	0.9305	0.7985	0.6975	0.6155	0.5466
50'	1.4594	1.1170	0.9279	0.7966	0.6960	0.6143	0.5456
51'	1.4508	1.1130	0.9254	0.7947	0.6945	0.6131	0.5445
52'	1.4424	1.1091	0.9228	0.7929	0.6930	0.6118	0.5435
53'	1.4341	1.1053	0.9203	0.7910	0.6915	0.6106	0.5424
54'	1.4260	1.1015	0.9178	0.7891	0.6900	0.6094	0.5414
55'	1.4180	1.0977	0.9153	0.7873	0.6885	0.6081	0.5403
56'	1.4102	1.0939	0.9128	0.7854	0.6871	0.6069	0.5393
57'	1.4025	1.0902	0.9104	0.7836	0.6856	0.6057	0.5382
58'	1.3949	1.0865	0.9079	0.7818	0.6841	0.6045	0.5372
59'	1.3875	1.0828	0.9055	0.7800	0.6827	0.6033	0.5361

Degrees or Hours and Minutes	07° (or hours)	08° (or hours)	09° (or hours)	10° (or hours)	11° (or hours)	12° (or hours)	13° (or hours)
00'	0.5351	0.4771	0.4260	0.3802	0.3388	0.3010	0.2663
01'	0.5341	0.4762	0.4252	0.3795	0.3382	0.3004	0.2657
02'	0.5330	0.4753	0.4244	0.3788	0.3375	0.2998	0.2652
03'	0.5320	0.4744	0.4236	0.3780	0.3368	0.2992	0.2646
04'	0.5310	0.4735	0.4228	0.3773	0.3362	0.2986	0.2641
05'	0.5300	0.4726	0.4220	0.3766	0.3355	0.2980	0.2635
06'	0.5289	0.4717	0.4212	0.3759	0.3349	0.2974	0.2629
07'	0.5279	0.4708	0.4204	0.3752	0.3342	0.2968	0.2624
08'	0.5269	0.4699	0.4196	0.3745	0.3336	0.2962	0.2618
09'	0.5259	0.4690	0.4188	0.3738	0.3329	0.2956	0.2613
10'	0.5249	0.4682	0.4180	0.3730	0.3323	0.2950	0.2607
11'	0.5239	0.4673	0.4172	0.3723	0.3316	0.2945	0.2602
12'	0.5229	0.4664	0.4164	0.3716	0.3310	0.2938	0.2596
13'	0.5219	0.4655	0.4156	0.3709	0.3303	0.2933	0.2591
14'	0.5209	0.4646	0.4149	0.3702	0.3297	0.2927	0.2585
15'	0.5199	0.4638	0.4141	0.3695	0.3291	0.2921	0.2580
16'	0.5189	0.4629	0.4133	0.3688	0.3284	0.2915	0.2575

Degrees or Hours and Minutes	07° (or hours)	08° (or hours)	09° (or hours)	10° (or hours)	11° (or hours)	12° (or hours)	13° (or hours)
17'	0.5179	0.4620	0.4125	0.3681	0.3278	0.2909	0.2569
18'	0.5169	0.4611	0.4117	0.3674	0.3271	0.2903	0.2564
19'	0.5159	0.4603	0.4109	0.3667	0.3265	0.2897	0.2558
20'	0.5149	0.4594	0.4102	0.3660	0.3258	0.2891	0.2553
21'	0.5139	0.4585	0.4094	0.3653	0.3252	0.2885	0.2547
22'	0.5129	0.4577	0.4086	0.3646	0.3246	0.2880	0.2542
23'	0.5120	0.4568	0.4079	0.3639	0.3239	0.2874	0.2536
24'	0.5110	0.4559	0.4071	0.3632	0.3233	0.2868	0.2531
25'	0.5100	0.4551	0.4063	0.3625	0.3227	0.2862	0.2526
26'	0.5090	0.4542	0.4055	0.3618	0.3220	0.2856	0.2520
27'	0.5081	0.4534	0.4048	0.3611	0.3214	0.2850	0.2515
28'	0.5071	0.4525	0.4040	0.3604	0.3208	0.2845	0.2509
29'	0.5061	0.4516	0.4032	0.3597	0.3201	0.2839	0.2504
30'	0.5051	0.4508	0.4025	0.3590	0.3195	0.2833	0.2499
31'	0.5042	0.4499	0.4017	0.3583	0.3189	0.2827	0.2493
32'	0.5032	0.4491	0.4010	0.3577	0.3183	0.2821	0.2488
33'	0.5034	0.4482	0.4002	0.3570	0.3176	0.2816	0.2483
34'	0.5013	0.4474	0.3995	0.3563	0.3170	0.2810	0.2477
35'	0.5003	0.4466	0.3987	0.3556	0.3164	0.2804	0.2473
36'	0.4994	0.4457	0.3979	0.3549	0.3157	0.2798	0.2467
37'	0.4984	0.4449	0.3972	0.3542	0.3151	0.2793	0.2461
38'	0.4975	0.4440	0.3964	0.3535	0.3145	0.2787	0.2456
39'	0.4965	0.4432	0.3957	0.3529	0.3139	0.2781	0.2451
40'	0.4956	0.4424	0.3949	0.3522	0.3133	0.2775	0.2445
41'	0.4947	0.4415	0.3942	0.3515	0.3126	0.2770	0.2440
42'	0.4937	0.4407	0.3934	0.3508	0.3120	0.2764	0.2435
43'	0.4928	0.4399	0.3927	0.3501	0.3114	0.2758	0.2430
44'	0.4918	0.4390	0.3919	0.3495	0.3108	0.2753	0.2424
45'	0.4909	0.4382	0.3912	0.3488	0.3102	0.2747	0.2419
46'	0.4900	0.4374	0.3905	0.3481	0.3096	0.2741	0.2414
47'	0.4890	0.4365	0.3897	0.3475	0.3089	0.2736	0.2409
48'	0.4881	0.4357	0.3890	0.3468	0.3083	0.2730	0.2403
49'	0.4872	0.4349	0.3882	0.3461	0.3077	0.2724	0.2398
50'	0.4863	0.4341	0.3875	0.3455	0.3071	0.2719	0.2393
51'	0.4853	0.4333	0.3868	0.3448	0.3065	0.2713	0.2388
52'	0.4844	0.4324	0.3860	0.3441	0.3059	0.2707	0.2382
53'	0.4835	0.4316	0.3853	0.3435	0.3053	0.2702	0.2377
54'	0.4826	0.4308	0.3846	0.3428	0.3047	0.2696	0.2372
55'	0.4817	0.4300	0.3838	0.3421	0.3041	0.2691	0.2367
56'	0.4808	0.4292	0.3831	0.3415	0.3035	0.2685	0.2362
57'	0.4799	0.4284	0.3824	0.3408	0.3028	0.2679	0.2356

Degrees or Hours and Minutes	07° (or hours)	08° (or hours)	09° (or hours)	10° (or hours)	11° (or hours)	12° (or hours)	13° (or hours)
58'	0.4789	0.4276	0.3817	0.3401	0.3022	0.2674	0.2351
59'	0.4780	0.4268	0.3809	0.3395	0.3016	0.2668	0.2346

Degrees or Hours and Minutes	14° (or hours)	15° (or hours)	16° (or hours)	17° (or hours)	18° (or hours)	19° (or hours)	20° (or hours)
00'	0.2341	0.2041	0.1761	0.1498	0.1249	0.1015	0.0792
01'	0.2336	0.2036	0.1756	0.1493	0.1245	0.1011	0.0788
02'	0.2330	0.2032	0.1752	0.1489	0.1241	0.1007	0.0785
03'	0.2325	0.2027	0.1747	0.1485	0.1237	0.1003	0.0781
04'	0.2320	0.2022	0.1743	0.1481	0.1234	0.0999	0.0777
05'	0.2315	0.2017	0.1738	0.1476	0.1229	0.0996	0.0774
06'	0.2310	0.2012	0.1734	0.1472	0.1225	0.0992	0.0770
07'	0.2305	0.2008	0.1729	0.1468	0.1221	0.0988	0.0766
08'	0.2300	0.2003	0.1725	0.1464	0.1217	0.0984	0.0763
09'	0.2295	0.1998	0.1720	0.1460	0.1213	0.0980	0.0759
10'	0.2289	0.1993	0.1716	0.1455	0.1209	0.0977	0.0756
11'	0.2284	0.1989	0.1711	0.1451	0.1205	0.0973	0.0752
12'	0.2279	0.1984	0.1707	0.1447	0.1201	0.0969	0.0749
13'	0.2274	0.1979	0.1702	0.1443	0.1197	0.0965	0.0745
14'	0.2269	0.1974	0.1698	0.1438	0.1193	0.0962	0.0742
15'	0.2264	0.1969	0.1694	0.1434	0.1189	0.0958	0.0738
16'	0.2259	0.1965	0.1689	0.1430	0.1185	0.0954	0.0734
17'	0.2254	0.1960	0.1685	0.1426	0.1182	0.0950	0.0731
18'	0.2249	0.1955	0.1680	0.1422	0.1178	0.0947	0.0727
19'	0.2244	0.1950	0.1676	0.1417	0.1174	0.0943	0.0724
20'	0.2239	0.1946	0.1671	0.1413	0.1170	0.0939	0.0720
21'	0.2234	0.1941	0.1667	0.1409	0.1166	0.0935	0.0717
22'	0.2229	0.1936	0.1663	0.1405	0.1162	0.0932	0.0713
23'	0.2223	0.1932	0.1658	0.1401	0.1158	0.0928	0.0709
24'	0.2218	0.1927	0.1654	0.1397	0.1154	0.0924	0.0706
25'	0.2213	0.1922	0.1649	0.1393	0.1150	0.0920	0.0702
26'	0.2208	0.1917	0.1645	0.1388	0.1146	0.0917	0.0699
27'	0.2203	0.1913	0.1640	0.1384	0.1142	0.0913	0.0695
28'	0.2198	0.1908	0.1636	0.1380	0.1138	0.0909	0.0692
29'	0.2193	0.1903	0.1632	0.1376	0.1134	0.0905	0.0688
30'	0.2188	0.1899	0.1627	0.1372	0.1130	0.0902	0.0685
31'	0.2183	0.1894	0.1623	0.1368	0.1126	0.0898	0.0681
32'	0.2178	0.1890	0.1619	0.1363	0.1123	0.0894	0.0678
33'	0.2173	0.1885	0.1614	0.1359	0.1120	0.0891	0.0674
34'	0.2168	0.1880	0.1610	0.1355	0.1115	0.0887	0.0670

Degrees or Hours and Minutes	14° (or hours)	15° (or hours)	16° (or hours)	17° (or hours)	18° (or hours)	19° (or hours)	20° (or hours)
35'	0.2164	0.1875	0.1605	0.1351	0.1111	0.0883	0.0667
36'	0.2159	0.1871	0.1601	0.1347	0.1107	0.0880	0.0664
37'	0.2154	0.1866	0.1597	0.1343	0.1103	0.0876	0.0660
38'	0.2149	0.1862	0.1592	0.1339	0.1099	0.0872	0.0656
39'	0.2144	0.1857	0.1588	0.1335	0.1095	0.0868	0.0653
40'	0.2139	0.1852	0.1584	0.1331	0.1092	0.0865	0.0649
41'	0.2134	0.1848	0.1579	0.1327	0.1088	0.0861	0.0646
42'	0.2129	0.1843	0.1575	0.1322	0.1084	0.0857	0.0642
43'	0.2124	0.1838	0.1571	0.1318	0.1080	0.0854	0.6039
44'	0.2119	0.1834	0.1566	0.1314	0.1076	0.0850	0.0635
45'	0.2114	0.1829	0.1562	0.1310	0.1072	0.0846	0.0632
46'	0.2109	0.1825	0.1558	0.1306	0.1068	0.0843	0.0629
47'	0.2104	0.1820	0.1553	0.1302	0.1064	0.0839	0.0625
48'	0.2099	0.1816	0.1549	0.1298	0.1061	0.0835	0.6021
49'	0.2095	0.1811	0.1545	0.1294	0.1057	0.0832	0.0618
50'	0.2090	0.1806	0.1540	0.1290	0.1053	0.0828	0.0614
51'	0.2085	0.1802	0.1536	0.1286	0.1049	0.0824	0.0611
52'	0.2080	0.1797	0.1532	0.1282	0.1045	0.0821	0.0608
53'	0.2075	0.1793	0.1528	0.1278	0.1041	0.0817	0.0604
54'	0.2070	0.1788	0.1523	0.1274	0.1037	0.0814	0.0601
55'	0.2065	0.1784	0.1519	0.1270	0.1034	0.0810	0.0597
56'	0.2061	0.1779	0.1515	0.1266	0.1030	0.0806	0.0594
57'	0.2056	0.1774	0.1510	0.1261	0.1026	0.0803	0.0590
58'	0.2051	0.1770	0.1506	0.1257	0.1022	0.0799	0.0587
59'	0.2046	0.1765	0.1502	0.1253	0.1018	0.0795	0.0583

Degrees or Hours and Minutes	21° (or hours)	22° (or hours)	23° (or hours)	Degrees or Hours and Minutes	21° (or hours)	22° (or hours)	23° (or hours)
00'	0.0580	0.0378	0.0185	31'	0.0474	0.0277	0.0088
01'	0.0577	0.0375	0.0182	32'	0.0471	0.0274	0.0085
02'	0.0573	0.0371	0.0179	33'	0.0468	0.0271	0.0082
03'	0.0570	0.0368	0.0175	34'	0.0464	0.0267	0.0079
04'	0.0566	0.0364	0.0172	35'	0.0461	0.0264	0.0076
05'	0.0563	0.0361	0.0169	36'	0.0458	0.0261	0.0073
06'	0.0559	0.0358	0.0166	37'	0.0454	0.0258	0.0070
07'	0.0556	0.0355	0.0163	38'	0.0451	0.0255	0.0067
08'	0.0552	0.0352	0.0160	39'	0.0448	0.0251	0.0064
09'	0.0549	0.0348	0.0157	40'	0.0444	0.0248	0.0061
10'	0.0546	0.0345	0.0153	41'	0.0441	0.0245	0.0058

Degrees or Hours and Minutes	21° (or hours)	22° (or hours)	23° (or hours)	Degrees or Hours and Minutes	21° (or hours)	22° (or hours)	23° (or hours)
11′	0.0542	0.0342	0.0150	42′	0.0437	0.0242	0.0055
12′	0.0539	0.0339	0.0147	43′	0.0434	0.0239	0.0052
13′	0.0535	0.0335	0.0144	44′	0.0431	0.0235	0.0048
14′	0.0532	0.0332	0.0141	45′	0.0428	0.0232	0.0045
15′	0.0529	0.0329	0.0138	46′	0.0424	0.0229	0.0042
16′	0.0525	0.0326	0.0135	47′	0.0421	0.0226	0.0039
17′	0.0522	0.0322	0.0132	48′	0.0418	0.0223	0.0036
18′	0.0518	0.0319	0.0129	49′	0.0414	0.0220	0.0033
19′	0.0515	0.0316	0.0125	50′	0.0411	0.0216	0.0030
20′	0.0511	0.0313	0.0122	51′	0.0408	0.0213	0.0027
21′	0.0508	0.0309	0.0119	52′	0.0404	0.0210	0.0024
22′	0.0505	0.0306	0.0116	53′	0.0401	0.0207	0.0021
23′	0.0501	0.0303	0.0113	54′	0.0398	0.0204	0.0018
24′	0.0498	0.0300	0.0110	55′	0.0394	0.0201	0.0015
25′	0.0495	0.0296	0.0107	56′	0.0391	0.0197	0.0012
26′	0.0491	0.0292	0.0104	57′	0.0388	0.0194	0.0009
27′	0.0488	0.0290	0.0101	58′	0.0384	0.0191	0.0006
28′	0.0485	0.0287	0.0098	59′	0.0381	0.0188	0.0003
29′	0.0481	0.0283	0.0094				
30′	0.0478	0.0280	0.0091				

Moon (☽):

June 16 (22°♈42′)	01	22°	42′	*(from an ephemeris)*[83]
− June 15 (05°♈35′)	01	05°	35′	*(from an ephemeris)*[84]
	00	17°	07′	*(daily motion)*
	log. 0.1468			*(converted using fig. 8.3)*

Mercury (☿):

June 16 (06°♋07′)	04	06°	07′	*(from an ephemeris)*[85]
− June 15 (02°♋05′)	04	02°	05′	*(from an ephemeris)*[86]
	00	04°	02′	*(daily motion)*
	log. 0.7745			*(converted using fig. 8.3)*

83. Ibid.
84. Ibid.
85. Ibid.
86. Ibid.

Venus (♀):

June 16 (24°♊01′)	03	24°	01′	*(from an ephemeris)*[87]
	03	23°	61′	*(converted)*[88]
− June 15 (21°♊44′)	03	21°	44′	*(from an ephemeris)*[89]
	00	02°	17′	*(daily motion)*
	log. 1.0216			*(converted using fig. 8.3)*

Mars (♂):

June 16 (01°♏26′)	08	01°	26′	*(from an ephemeris)*[90]
− June 15 (01°♏24′)	08	01°	24′	*(from an ephemeris)*[91]
	00	00°	02′	*(daily motion)*
	log. 2.8573			*(converted using fig. 8.3)*

Peter C.:
Step 5, Calculation 1:
Sun (☉):

August 28 (05°♍36′)	06	05°	36′	*(from an ephemeris)*[92]
	06	04°	96′	*(converted)*[93]
− August 27 (03°♍44′)	06	03°	44′	*(from an ephemeris)*[94]
	00	01°	52′	*(daily motion)*
	log. 1.1091			*(converted using fig. 8.3)*

Moon (☽):

August 28 (14°♉43′)	02	14°	43′	*(from an ephemeris)*[95]
	01	44°	43′	*(converted)*[96]
− August 27 (22°♈06′)	01	22°	06′	*(from an ephemeris)*[97]
	00	22°	37′	*(daily motion)*
	log. 0.0258			*(converted using fig. 8.3)*

---

87. Ibid.
88. To facilitate calculation, 01° is converted to 60′ and added to the existing minutes.
89. This information is also found on page 348.
90. Ibid.
91. Ibid.
92. This information is also found on page 349.
93. To facilitate calculation, 01° is converted to 60′ and added to the existing minutes.
94. This information is also found on page 349.
95. Ibid.
96. To facilitate calculation, one full sign is converted to 30° and added to the existing degrees.
97. This information is also found on page 349.

Mercury (☿):

August 27 (13°♍52')	06	13°	52'	(from an ephemeris)[98]
— August 28 (12°♍26')	06	12°	26'	(from an ephemeris)[99]
	00	01°	26'	(daily motion)
	log. 1.2239			(converted using fig. 8.3)

Venus (♀):

August 28 (19°♋47')	04	19°	47'	(from an ephemeris)[100]
	04	18°	107'	(converted)[101]
— August 27 (17°♋57')	04	17°	057'	(from an ephemeris)[102]
	00	01°	050'	(daily motion)
	log. 1.1170			(converted using fig. 8.3)

Mars (♂):

August 28 (19°♋08')	04	19°	08'	(from an ephemeris)[103]
	04	18°	68'	(converted)[104]
— August 27 (17°♋53')	04	17°	53'	(from an ephemeris)[105]
	00	01°	15'	(daily motion)
	log. 1.2833			(converted using fig. 8.3)

The proportional logarithms of the given planet's daily motion and the chart's constant logarithm are then added together. The resulting logarithm is then converted to the nearest degrees and minutes by referring to the same table.

Alice T.:

Step 5, Calculation 2:

(All conversions from logarithm to degrees and minutes are derived from fig. 8.3.)

---

98.   This information is also found on page 349. During this period, Mercury (☿) was moving in an apparent reverse motion or retrograde along the ecliptic. Therefore, the August 28 position is subtracted from the August 27 position to derive daily motion.

99.   This information is also found on page 349.

100.   Ibid.

101.   To facilitate calculation, 01° is converted to 60' and added to the existing minutes.

102.   This information is also found on page 349.

103.   Ibid.

104.   To facilitate calculation, 01° is converted to 60' and added to the existing minutes.

105.   This information is also found on page 349.

Sun (☉):

Logarithm	0.4638	*(Step 4, Calculation 4)*
+ Daily motion	1.1249	*(Step 5, Calculation 1)*
	1.5877	*(total motion)*
	1.5902	*(nearest logarithm in fig. 8.3)*
	00°37′	*(converted from logarithm)*[106]

Moon (☽):

Logarithm	0.4638	*(Step 4, Calculation 4)*
+ Daily motion	0.1468	*(Step 5, Calculation 1)*
	0.6106	*(total motion)*
	0.6106	*(nearest logarithm in fig. 8.3)*
	05°53′	*(converted from logarithm)*

Mercury (☿):

Logarithm	0.4638	*(Step 4, Calculation 4)*
+ Daily motion	0.7745	*(Step 5, Calculation 1)*
	1.2383	*(total motion)*
	1.2393	*(nearest logarithm in fig. 8.3)*
	01°23′	*(converted from logarithm)*

Venus (♀):

Logarithm	0.4638	*(Step 4, Calculation 4)*
+ Daily motion	1.0216	*(Step 5, Calculation 1)*
	1.4854	*(total motion)*
	1.4863	*(nearest logarithm in fig. 8.3)*
	00°47′	*(converted from logarithm)*

Mars (♂):

Logarithm	0.4638	*(Step 4, Calculation 4)*
+ Daily motion	2.8573	*(Step 5, Calculation 1)*
	3.3211	*(total motion)*
	3.1584	*(nearest logarithm in fig. 8.3)*
	00°00′	*(converted from logarithm)*

---

106.   By locating the logarithm in fig. 8.3, the degrees (column head) and minutes (row head) can be identified.

Peter C.:
Step 5, Calculation 2:
Sun (☉):

Logarithm	0.2921	*(Step 4, Calculation 4)*
+ Daily motion	1.1091	*(Step 5, Calculation 1)*
	1.4012	*(total motion)*
	1.4025	*(nearest logarithm in fig. 8.3)*
	00°57′	*(converted from logarithm)*

Moon (☽):

Logarithm	0.2921	*(Step 4, Calculation 4)*
+ Daily motion	0.0258	*(Step 5, Calculation 1)*
	0.3179	*(total motion)*
	0.3183	*(nearest logarithm in fig. 8.3)*
	11°32′	*(converted from logarithm)*

Mercury (☿):

Logarithm	0.2921	*(Step 4, Calculation 4)*
+ Daily motion	1.2239	*(Step 5, Calculation 1)*
	1.5160	*(total motion)*
	1.5149	*(nearest logarithm in fig. 8.3)*
	00°44′	*(converted from logarithm)*

Venus (♀):

Logarithm	0.2921	*(Step 4, Calculation 4)*
+ Daily motion	1.1170	*(Step 5, Calculation 1)*
	1.4091	*(total motion)*
	1.4102	*(nearest logarithm in fig. 8.3)*
	00°56′	*(converted from logarithm)*

Mars (♂):

Logarithm	0.2921	*(Step 4, Calculation 4)*
+ Daily motion	1.2833	*(Step 5, Calculation 1)*
	1.5754	*(total motion)*
	1.5786	*(nearest logarithm in fig. 8.3)*
	00°38′	*(converted from logarithm)*

These converted degrees and minutes of total motion are finally added to the planetary positions published in the ephemeris for the date of the person's birth.

Alice T.:
Step 5, Calculation 3:
Sun (☉):

June 15 (24°♊18')	03	24°	18'	*(from an ephemeris)*
+ Log 1.5902	00	00°	37'	*(Step 5, Calculation 2)*
	03	24°	55'	*(actual position, 24°♊55')*

Moon (☽):

June 15 (05°♈35')	01	05°	35'	*(from an ephemeris)*
+ Log 0.6106	00	05°	53'	*(Step 5, Calculation 2)*
	01	10°	88'	*(total)* [107]
	01	11°	28'	*(actual position, 11°♈28')*

Mercury (☿):

June 15 (02°♋05')	04	02°	05'	*(from an ephemeris)*
+ Log 1.2393	00	01°	23'	*(Step 5, Calculation 2)*
	04	03°	28'	*(actual position, 03°♋28')*

Venus (♀):

June 15 (21°♊44')	03	21°	44'	*(from an ephemeris)*
+ Log 1.4863	00	00°	47'	*(Step 5, Calculation 2)*
	03	21°	91'	*(total)* [108]
	03	22°	31'	*(actual position, 22°♊31')*

Mars (♂):

June 15 (01°♏24')	08	01°	24'	*(from an ephemeris)*
+ Log 3.1584	00	00°	00'	*(Step 5, Calculation 2)*
	08	01°	24'	*(actual position, 01°♏24')*

Peter C.:
Step 5, Calculation 3:
Sun (☉):

August 27 (03°♍44')	06	03°	44'	*(from an ephemeris)*
+ Log 1.4025	00	00°	57'	*(Step 5, Calculation 2)*
	06	03°	101'	*(total)* [109]
	06	04°	41'	*(actual position, 04°♍41')*

---

107. Because 60' equals 01°, 60' is subtracted from 88', and 01° is added to the existing degrees.
108. Because 60' equals 01°, 60' is subtracted from 91', and 01° is added to the existing degrees.
109. Because 30° equals one full sign, 30° is subtracted from 33° and one sign is added to the existing signs.

Moon (☽):

August 27 (22°♈06')	01	22°	06'	*(from an ephemeris)*
+ Log 0.3183	00	11°	32'	*(Step 5, Calculation 2)*
	01	33°	38'	*(total)*[110]
	02	03°	38'	*(actual position, 03°♉38')*

Mercury (☿):

August 27 (13°♍52')	06	13°	52'	*(from an ephemeris)*
+ Log 1.5149	00	00°	44'	*(Step 5, Calculation 2)*
	06	13°	96'	*(total)*[111]
	06	14°	36'	*(actual position, 14°♍36')*

Venus (♀):

August 27 (17°♋57')	04	17°	57'	*(from an ephemeris)*
+ Log 1.4102	00	00°	56'	*(Step 5, Calculation 2)*
	04	17°	113'	*(total)*[112]
	04	18°	53'	*(actual position, 18°♋53')*

Mars (♂):

August 27 (17°♋53')	04	17°	53'	*(from an ephemeris)*
+ Log 1.5786	00	00°	38'	*(Step 5, Calculation 2)*
	04	17°	91'	*(total)*[113]
	04	18°	31'	*(actual position, 18°♋31')*

Step Six: Placing the Planets and Nodes in the Horoscope

The adjusted planetary positions for the Sun (☉), the Moon (☽), Mercury (☿), Venus (♀), and Mars (♂) from Step 5, Calculation 3 are gathered together along with the published positions for Jupiter (♃), Saturn (♄), Uranus (♅), Neptune (♆), and Pluto (♇) as well as the Moon's North Node (☊), which are located in the ephemeris and in the excerpt from the ephemeris that appears earlier in this chapter. (The Moon's South Node [☋] is calculated according to the instructions on page 386.) Using the order of the houses derived in the section titled "Rectifying the Remaining House Positions," the planetary positions and nodes are grouped according zodiac sign, degrees, and minutes as seen in the lists below:

---

110. Because 60' equals 01°, 60' is subtracted from 91' and 01° is added to the existing degrees.
111. Because 60' equals 01°, 60' is subtracted from 96' and 01° is added to the existing degrees.
112. Because 60' equals 01°, 60' is subtracted from 113', and 01° is added to the existing degrees.
113. Because 60' equals 01°, 60' is subtracted from 91', and 01° is added to the existing degrees.

Alice T.:

House I:

   (01°♒57′)   ("*Rectifying the Remaining House Positions*")

   ☊ 23°♒23′   (*from an ephemeris*)[114]

House II:

   (19°♓40′)   ("*Rectifying the Remaining House Positions*")

   ☽ 11°♈28′   (*Step 5, Calculation 3*)[115]

House III:

   (28°♈15′)   ("*Rectifying the Remaining House Positions*")

   ♃ 10°♉52′   (*from an ephemeris*)[116]

House IV:

   (25°♉17′)   ("*Rectifying the Remaining House Positions*")

No planets or nodes are located in the zodiac sign Taurus (♉) between the degrees 25°17′ and 30°00′, or in the zodiac sign Gemini (♊) between the degrees 00°00′ and 16°43′.

House V:

   (16°♊44′)   ("*Rectifying the Remaining House Positions*")

   ♀ 22°♊31′   (*Step 5, Calculation 3*)

   ☉ 24°♊55′   (*Step 5, Calculation 3*)

   ☿ 03°♋28′   (*Step 5, Calculation 3*)[117]

House VI:

   (07°♋13′)   ("*Rectifying the Remaining House Positions*")

   ♅ 13°♋00′   (*from an ephemeris*)

---

114. ☊ 23°♒23′ is placed in House I because this house begins at 01°♒57′. It includes the zodiac sign of Aquarius (♒) from 01°♒57′ through 29°♒59′. It also includes the zodiac sign of Pisces (♓) from 00°♓00′ through 19°♓39′.

115. ☽ 11°♈28′ is placed in House II because this house begins at 19°♓40′. It includes the zodiac sign of Pisces (♓) from 19°♓40′ through 29°♓59′. It also includes the zodiac sign of Aries (♈) from 00°♈00′ through 28°♓15′.

116. Jupiter (♃) is placed in House III because 10°♉52′ numerically precedes House IV's 25°♉17′.

117. Mercury (☿) is placed in House V because 03°♋28′ numerically precedes House VI's 07°♋13′.

House VII:

(01°♌57')   (*"Rectifying the Remaining House Positions"*)

♀ 19°♌34'   (*from an ephemeris*)

House VIII:

(19°♍40')   (*"Rectifying the Remaining House Positions"*)

♄ 08°♎12'   (*from an ephemeris*)[118]

♆ 18°♎59'   (*from an ephemeris*)[119]

House IX:

(28°♎15')   (*"Rectifying the Remaining House Positions"*)

♂ 01°♏24'   (*Step 5, Calculation 3*)[120]

House X:

(25°♏17')   (*"Rectifying the Remaining House Positions"*)

No planets or nodes are located in the zodiac sign Scorpio (♏) between the degrees 25°17' and 30°00', or in the zodiac sign Sagittarius (♐) between the degrees 00°00' and 16°43'.

House XI:

(16°♐44')   (*"Rectifying the Remaining House Positions"*)

No planets or nodes are located in the zodiac sign Sagittarius (♐) between the degrees 16°44' and 30°00', or in the zodiac sign Capricorn (♑) between the degrees 00°00' and 07°13'.

House XII:

(07°♑13')   (*"Rectifying the Remaining House Positions"*)

No planets or nodes are located in the zodiac sign Capricorn (♑) between the degrees 07°13' and 30°00', or in the zodiac sign Aquarius (♒) between the degrees 00°00' and 01°57'.

---

118.   Saturn (♄) is placed in House VIII because 08°♎12' numerically precedes House VI's 28°♎15'.
119.   Neptune (♆) is placed in House VIII because 18°♎59' numerically precedes House VI's 28°♎15'.
120.   Mars (♂) is placed in House IX because 01°♏24' numerically precedes House X's 25°♏17'.

Peter C.:

House I:

(02°♓49')   *("Rectifying the Remaining House Positions")*

No planets or nodes are located in the zodiac sign Pisces (♓) between the degrees 02°49' and 30°00' or in the zodiac sign Aries (♈) between the degrees 00°00' and 24°34'.

House II:

(24°♈34')   *("Rectifying the Remaining House Positions")*

☽ 03°♉38'   *(Step 5, Calculation 3)*[121]

House III:

(25°♉27')   *("Rectifying the Remaining House Positions")*

♃ 25°♉36'   *(from an ephemeris)*

House IV:

(17°♊06')   *("Rectifying the Remaining House Positions")*

☊ 29°♊40'   *(from an ephemeris)*

House V:

(06°♋26')   *("Rectifying the Remaining House Positions")*

♂ 18°♋31'   *(Step 5, Calculation 3)*

♀ 18°♋53'   *(Step 5, Calculation 3)*

House VI:

(28°♋27')   *("Rectifying the Remaining House Positions")*

No planets or nodes are located in the zodiac sign Cancer (♋) between the degrees 27°28' and 30°00', the entire zodiac sign Leo (00°♌00'–30°♌00'), or in the zodiac sign Virgo (♍) between the degrees 00°00' and 02°49'.

House VII:

(02°♍49')   *("Rectifying the Remaining House Positions")*

☉ 04°♍41'   *(Step 5, Calculation 3)*

♅ 10°♍04'   *(from an ephemeris)*

---

121.   The Moon (☽) is placed in House II because 03°♉38' numerically precedes House X's 25°♉27'.

♇ 13°♍38'   *(from an ephemeris)*
☿ 14°♍36'   *(Step 5, Calculation 3)*

House VIII:
(24°♎34')   *("Rectifying the Remaining House Positions")*
♆ 15°♏19'   *(from an ephemeris)* [122]

House IX:
(25°♏27')   *("Rectifying the Remaining House Positions")*
No planets or nodes are located in the zodiac sign Scorpio (♏) between the degrees 25°27' and 30°00', or in the zodiac sign Sagittarius (♐) between the degrees 00°00' and 17°06'.

House X:
(17°♐06')   *("Rectifying the Remaining House Positions")*
No planets or nodes are located in the zodiac sign Sagittarius (♐) between the degrees 17°06' and 30°00', or in the zodiac sign Capricorn (♑) between the degrees 00°00' and 06°26'.

House XI:
(06°♑26')   *("Rectifying the Remaining House Positions")*
No planets or nodes are located in the zodiac sign Capricorn (♑) between the degrees 06°26' and 27°28'.

House XII:
(28°♑27')   *("Rectifying the Remaining House Positions")*
♄ 01°♓25'   *(from an ephemeris)* [123]

The planets and the Moon's North Node (☊) shown in the above lists are then entered using each planet's symbol, degrees, zodiac sign's symbol, and minutes as shown above into the twelve interior segments of the chart (figs. 8.1 and 8.2) in exactly the same order as shown above.

---

122. Neptune (♆) is placed in House VIII because 15°♏19' numerically precedes House IX's 25°♏27'.
123. Saturn (♄) is placed in House XII because 01°♓25' numerically precedes House I's 02°♓49'.

Intercepted signs.   The order in which the zodiac signs appear in any horoscope must follow the sequential order shown on page 000. All twelve zodiac signs must be placed in the outer ring of the horoscope. There are instances, however, when one or two zodiac signs might not be placed in the twelve house cusps. For example, two zodiac signs are missing from the sequence in Peter's chart (fig. 8.2): Leo (♌), which should appear between Cancer (♋, House VI in fig. 8.2) and Virgo (♍, House VII in fig. 8.2); and Aquarius (♒), which should appear between Capricorn (♑, House XII in fig. 8.2) and Pisces (♓, House I in fig. 8.2). These are called intercepted signs because each has been overtaken since more than one house cusp position is assigned to the same zodiac sign. This occurs at various points in the Table of Houses and after the house positions have been adjusted to reflect the actual time and place of a given birth.

Nevertheless, these intercepted zodiac signs must be taken into consideration during the delineation process. So each zodiac sign is placed in the outer ring between the cusps where each zodiac sign should have appeared. Therefore, the symbol for Leo (♌) is placed between House VI (28°♋27′ in fig. 8.2) and House VII (02°♍49′ in fig. 8.2); the sign for Aquarius (♒) is placed between House XII (28°♑27′ in fig. 8.2) and House I (02°♓49′ in fig. 8.2).

The Moon's South Node: The Moon's South Node (☋) is always the exact opposite of the Moon's North Node (☊), so this position is entered in the house directly opposite the Moon's North Node (☊) in the opposite zodiac sign, but exactly the same degrees (°) and minutes (′). For example, Alice's North Node occupies 23°23′ Aquarius (☊23°♒23′ in the ephemeris). Therefore, her South Node is 23°23′ Leo (☋ 23°♌23′) (see list of opposite zodiac signs on page 000). Since this Node occurs after 01°♌57′ (House VII in fig. 8.1) and before 19°40′ (House VIII in Fig. 8.1), her South Node (☋) is placed in House VII (fig. 8.1). Similarly, Peter's North Node occupies 29°40′ Gemini (☊29°♊40′ in the ephemeris). Therefore, his South Node is 29°40′ Sagittarius (☋ 29°♐40′). Since this Node occurs after 17°♐06′ (House X in fig. 8.2) and before 06°♑26′ (House XI in fig. 8.2), his South Node (☋) is placed in House X (Fig. 8.2).

The interpretation of the zodiac signs that occupy the various houses and all of the planetary and nodal positions will be discussed in the sections titled "Reviewing the Moon's Nodes and the Part of Fortune," "Delineating the House Rulerships," and "Delineating Planetary Positions by House and by Sign," which appear later in this chapter.

Step Seven: Locating Planetary Aspects and Constructing an Aspectarian

The arc of a horoscope is divided into 360 increments of 01°00' each. The longi-tudinal distance between two points on astronomical and astrological charts is expressed in degrees, minutes, and sometimes seconds of arc. In astrology, this dis-tance determines the formation of an aspect and the location of a corollary point such as an Arabian Part.

An aspect can be visualized as follows: Draw a line from the position of a planet or node to the center of the chart (figs. 8.1 and 8.2), which represents the Earth's position. Next, draw a corresponding line from the chart's center to another planet or node. The resulting arc between the two lines is called an angle or aspect, and is measured in degrees. This relationship can also be seen by applying the following calculation to any pair of planets or nodes in a chart:

Step 7, Calculation 1:

Mars (σ 01°♏24')	08	01°	24'	(fig. 8.1)
	07	30°	84'	(converted)[124]
− Sun (☉ 24°♊55')	03	24°	55'	(fig. 8.1)
	04	06°	29'	(difference)[125]
		126°		(aspect or angle)

Western, Arabian, Tibetan, Vedic, and some Chinese astrological methods con-centrate on the location and interpretation of five major types of aspects: conjunc-tion (00°00' difference, ±08°00'), sextile (60°00' difference, ±08°00'), square or quartile (90°00' difference, ±08°00'), trine (120°00' difference, ±08°00'), and opposition (180°00' difference, ±08°00').

Conjunction. A conjunction (σ) occurs when two planets occupy the exact same zodiac sign, degrees, and minutes in a chart, allowing for a variance of ±08°00', which is also called an 08°00' orb of influence. In other words, if the difference be-tween the two locations is between 00°00' and 08°00', a conjunction (σ) is formed. An example of this occurs between Alice's Sun (☉) and Mercury (☿):

---

124.   To facilitate calculation, one full zodiac sign is converted to 30° and added to the existing degrees. Then 01° is converted to 60' and added to the exiting minutes.
125.   The four signs of difference are converted to degrees by multiplying 4 times 30° (120°). The minutes of difference are generally not represented in the final result.

Mercury (☿ 03°♋28′)	04	03°	28′	*(from fig. 8.1)*
	03	32°	88′	*(converted)* [126]
− Sun (☉ 24°♊55′)	03	24°	55′	*(from fig. 8.1)*
	00	08°	33′	*(difference)*
		08°		*(angle or aspect)* [127]

This aspect would be designated as a conjunction (☌) within an 08°00′ orb of influence. It is notated as ☉ ☌ ☿.

A conjunction (☌) [128] is interpreted as a variable aspect. It is usually considered to be very favorable unless the aspect is formed between certain planets in which the influence is deemed to be very adverse. One group of inauspicious conjunctions combines the Moon (☽) with the Sun (☉), Uranus (♅), or Neptune (♆). These are notated as follows:

☽ ☌ ☉   or   ☉ ☌ ☽

☽ ☌ ♅   or   ♅ ☌ ☽

☽ ☌ ♆   or   ♆ ☌ ☽

A second group of inauspicious conjunctions occurs if Mercury (☿), Venus (♀), or Mars (♂) conjuncts with Uranus (♅) or Neptune (♆). These are notated as follows:

☿ ☌ ♅   or   ♅ ☌ ☿

☿ ☌ ♆   or   ♆ ☌ ☿

♀ ☌ ♅   or   ♅ ☌ ♀

♀ ☌ ♆   or   ♆ ☌ ♀

♂ ☌ ♅   or   ♂ ☌ ♅

♂ ☌ ♆   or   ♂ ☌ ♆

Sextile.   A sextile (✶) takes place when two planets are positioned approximately two zodiac signs or 60°00′ (which equals one sixth of the 360°00′ zodiac, thus the name sextile) apart from each other within an 08°00′ orb of influence. In other words, if the difference is between 52°00′ and 68°00′, the planets form a sextile aspect. An example of this occurs between Peter's Mercury (☿) and Mars (♂):

---

126.   To facilitate calculation, one full zodiac sign is converted to 30° and added to the existing degrees. Then 01° is converted to 60′ and added to the existing minutes.

127.   The minutes of difference are not generally represented in the final result.

128.   Conjunctions (☌) are also the focus of two other celestial events, a *synodic period* and a *combust*. The recurring period between two successive conjunctions of two planets is called a synodic period. For example, the planets Saturn (♄) and Uranus (♅) form a recurring conjunction (♄ ☌ ♅) every 45 years, 132.5 days. The time between each event is the synodic period for the Uranus-Saturn conjunction. This period's orb of influence ranges from 00°00′ to 06°00′ in a natal chart, and from 00°00′ to 02°00′ in a progressed chart. The planets Mercury (☿) and Venus (♀) form a conjunction to the Sun (☿ ☌ ☉ or ♀ ☌ ☉) more frequently. When either planet forms a conjunction with the Sun, it creates a special relationship, called a combust.

Mercury (☿ 14°♍36′)	06	14°	36′	(fig. 8.2)
	05	44°	36′	(converted) [129]
— Mars (♂ 18°♋31′)	04	18°	31′	(fig. 8.2)
	01	26°	05′	(difference)
		56°		(angle or aspect) [130]

Because the difference falls within 52°00′ and 68°00′, a sextile is formed within a 04°00′ orb of influence. It is notated as ♂ ✶ ☿. A sextile is always interpreted as a mildly auspicious aspect.

Square. A square (□) occurs when two planets are positioned approximately three signs or 90°00′ apart from each other within an 08°00′ orb of influence. In other words, if the difference is between 82°00′ and 98°00′, the planets form a square aspect. An example of this occurs between Alice's Moon (☽) and Mercury (☿):

Mercury (☿ 03°♋28′)	04	03°	28′	(fig. 8.1)
	03	33°	28′	(converted) [131]
— Moon (☽ 11°♈28′)	01	11°	28′	(fig. 8.1)
	02	22°	00′	(difference) [132]
		82°		(angle or aspect)

Because the difference falls within 82°00′ and 98°00′, a square is formed within an 08°00′ orb of influence. It is notated as ☉ □ ☿. A square is always interpreted as an adverse influence on the planets involved.

Trine. A trine (△) occurs when two planets are positioned approximately four signs (120°00′) apart from each other within an 08°00′ orb of influence. In other words, if the difference is between 112°00′ and 128°00′, the planets form a trine. An example of this occurs between Peter's Sun (☉) and Moon (☽):

---

129. To facilitate calculation, one full zodiac sign is converted to 30° and added to the existing degrees. Then 01° is converted to 60′ and added to the existing minutes.

130. One full zodiac sign is converted to 30° and added to the existing degrees. The minutes of difference are not generally represented in the final result.

131. To facilitate calculation, one full zodiac sign is converted to 30° and added to the existing degrees.

132. The two signs of difference are converted to degrees by multiplying 2 times 30° (60°) and added to the existing degrees. The minutes of difference are not generally represented in the final result.

Sun (☉ 04°♍41′)	06	04° 41′	(fig. 8.2)
− Moon (☽ 03°♉28′)	02	03° 38′	(fig. 8.2)
	04	01° 13′	(difference)[133]
		121°	(angle or aspect)

Because the difference falls within 112°00′ and 128°00′, a trine is formed within a 01°00′ orb of influence. It is notated as ☉ △ ☽. A trine is always interpreted as a very favorable influence on the planets involved.

Opposition. An opposition (☍) takes place when two planets are approximately six signs or 180°00′ apart from each other in a chart within an 08°00′ orb of influence. In other words, if the difference is between 172°00′ and 188°00′, the planets form an opposition. An example of this occurs between Alice's Moon (☽) and Neptune (♆):

Neptune (♆ 18°♎39′)	07	18° 39′	(fig. 8.1)
− Moon (☽ 11°♈28′)	01	11° 28′	(fig. 8.1)
	06	07° 11′	(difference)[134]
		187°	(angle or aspect)

Because the difference falls within 172°00′ and 188°00′, an opposition is formed within a 07°00′ orb of influence. It is notated as ☽ ☍ ♆. An opposition is always interpreted as an extremely adverse influence on the planets involved.

Parallels. Mundane parallels (//), parallels (//), and rapt parallels (⫻) are interpreted as conjunctions (☌), even though these particular designations do not create true angular relationships. For example, a mundane parallel occurs when two planets are equally distant from the cusps of Houses I, IV, VII, or X. When this happens, each entity involved in forming the mundane parallel is said to be in *antiscia*. An instance of this phenomenon appears in Alice's chart. Pluto (♇ 19°♌34′ in fig. 8.1) occupies House VII (01°♌57′ in fig. 8.1). The distance between the planet and the house cusp is calculated as follows:

133. The four signs of difference are converted to degrees by multiplying 4 times 30° (120°) and added the existing degrees. The minutes of difference are not generally represented in the final result.
134. The six signs of difference are converted to degrees by multiplying 6 times 30° (180°) and added the existing degrees. The minutes of difference are not generally represented in the final result.

Pluto (♇ 19°♌34′)	05	19°	34′	(fig. 8.1)
	15	18°	94′	(converted)
— House VII (01°♌57′)	05	01°	57′	(fig. 8.1)
	00	17°	37′	(difference)

Similarly, Uranus (♅ 13°♋00′ in fig. 8.1) is 18°57′ House VII (01°♌57′ in fig. 8.1). The distance between the planet and the house cusp is calculated as follows:

House VII (01°♌57′)	05	01°	57′	(fig. 8.1)
	04	31°	57′	(converted)
— Uranus (♅ 13°♋00′)	04	13°	00′	(fig. 8.1)
	00	18°	57′	(difference)

These two planets form a mundane parallel (//) of equal distance (17°37′ and 18°57′, above) within a 01°20′ orb of influence, which is determined by subtracting the two differences as shown below:

Uranus difference	00	18°	57′	(from above calculation)
— Pluto difference	00	17°	37′	(from above calculation)
	00	01°	20′	(difference)

This parallel is notated as "Uranus parallels Pluto" (♅ // ♇), and is delineated just like a conjunction (☌).

A parallel (//), on the other hand, is formed by two planets that are equally distant from the celestial equator and have the same north or south declination. This type of parallel is notated with the same symbol used to designate a mundane parallel (//) if the planets are in the same declination: both in the north or both in the south. If one planet is north and the other is south at the same point, however, it is called a *rapt parallel* and is notated with the symbol ⊬. To determine these types of parallels, refer to the declination table in the ephemeris for the birth date in question.[135] For example, according to the declination table in the ephemeris excerpt on page 348, on Alice's birth date (June 15, 1952), Venus (♀) was 23°18′N and the Sun (☉) was 23°21′N. This means that the two planets formed a parallel within a 00°03′ orb of influence which is notated as ♀ // ☉. If Venus (♀) had been 23°18′ S and the Sun (☉) was 23°21′N, the two planets would have formed a rapt parallel (⊬) which would have been notated as ♀ ⊬ ☉.

The easiest way to start this entire process is to look at each chart and

---

135.   This same information can be found on pages 348–49.

determine which planets appear to form a conjunction (☌), a sextile (⚹), a square (□), a trine (△), or an opposition (☍).[136] Then apply the calculation demonstrated in Step 7, Calculation 1, above, to verify the type of aspect and its orb of influence. When all the aspects of a chart have been identified by using the calculation above and notated as in the lists below, an Aspectarian (a grid that displays all of the aspects' relationships) is constructed for all major aspects such as those shown in figs. 8.4 and 8.5. The interpretation of these aspects will be discussed in the section titled "Delineating the Planetary Aspects," which appears later in this chapter.

Alice T. (all aspects formed in fig. 8.1 and presented in fig. 8.4):

☉ ☌ ☿   (*Sun conjuncts Mercury in House V*)
☉ ☌ ♀   (*Sun conjuncts Venus in House V*)
☉ △ ♂   (*Sun trines Mars in Houses V and IX*)
☉ △ ♆   (*Sun trines Neptune in Houses V and VIII*)
☉ ⚹ ♇   (*Sun sextiles Pluto in Houses V and VII*)
☽ □ ☿   (*Moon squares Mercury in Houses II and V*)
☽ ☍ ♄   (*Moon opposes Saturn in Houses II and VIII*)
☽ □ ♅   (*Moon squares Uranus in Houses II and VI*)
☽ ☍ ♆   (*Moon opposes Neptune in Houses II and VIII*)
☿ △ ♂   (*Mercury trines Mars in Houses V and IX*)
☿ □ ♄   (*Mercury squares Saturn in Houses V and VIII*)
♀ △ ♆   (*Venus trines Neptune in Houses V and VIII*)
♀ ⚹ ♇   (*Venus sextiles Pluto in Houses V and VII*)
♃ ⚹ ♅   (*Jupiter sextiles Uranus in Houses III and VI*)
♃ □ ♇   (*Jupiter squares Pluto in Houses III and VII*)
♄ □ ♅   (*Saturn squares Uranus in Houses VI and VIII*)
♆ □ ♅   (*Neptune squares Uranus in Houses VI and VIII*)
♇ ⚹ ♆   (*Pluto sextiles Neptune in Houses VII and VIII*)
♀ // ☉   (*Venus [23°18′N] parallels the Sun [23°21′N]*)
♅ // ☉   (*Uranus [23°10′N] parallels the Sun [23°21′N]*)
♅ // ♀   (*Uranus [23°10′N] parallels Venus [23°18′N]*)
♇ // ☉   (*Pluto [23°25′N] parallels the Sun [23°21′N]*)
♇ // ♀   (*Pluto [23°25′N] parallels Venus [23°18′N]*)
♇ // ♅   (*Pluto [23°25′N] parallels Uranus [23°10′N]*)

---

136. The Moon's North and South Nodes are not generally included in this assessment by most Western practitioners, although some astrologers do analyze the potential relationship between these nodes as well as the house cusps for later delineation.

FIGURE 8.4. ASPECTARIAN FOR ALICE T.'S CHART.

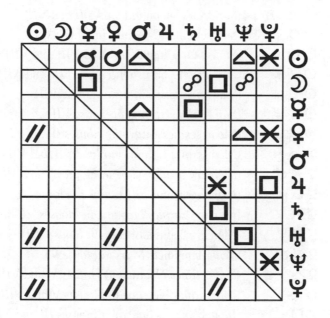

FIGURE 8.5. ASPECTARIAN FOR PETER C.'S CHART.

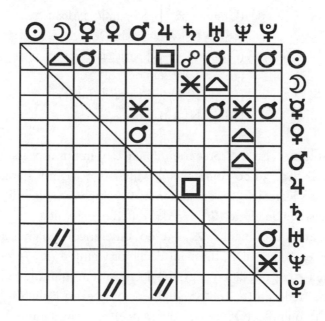

Peter C. (all aspects formed in fig. 8.2 and presented in fig. 8.5):

☉ △ ☽	(Sun trines Moon in Houses II and VII)
☉ ☌ ☿	(Sun conjuncts Mercury in House VII)
☉ □ ♃	(Sun squares Jupiter in Houses III and VII)
☉ ☍ ♄	(Sun opposes Saturn in Houses VII and XII)
☉ ☌ ♅	(Sun conjuncts Uranus in House VII)
☉ ☌ ♇	(Sun conjuncts Pluto in House VII)
☽ ⚹ ♄	(Moon sextiles Saturn in Houses II and XII)
☽ △ ♅	(Moon trines Uranus in Houses II and VII)
☿ ⚹ ♂	(Mercury sextiles Mars in Houses V and VII)
☿ ☌ ♅	(Mercury conjuncts Uranus in House V)
☿ ⚹ ♆	(Mercury sextiles Neptune in Houses VII and VIII)
☿ ☌ ♇	(Mercury conjuncts Pluto in House VII)
♀ ☌ ♂	(Venus conjuncts Mars in House V)
♀ △ ♆	(Venus trines Neptune in Houses V and VIII)
♂ △ ♆	(Mars trines Neptune in Houses V and VIII)
♃ □ ♄	(Jupiter squares Saturn in Houses III and XII)
♅ ☌ ♇	(Uranus conjuncts Pluto in House VII)
♇ ⚹ ♆	(Pluto sextiles Neptune in Houses VII and VIII)
♅ // ☽	(Uranus [08°28'N] parallels Moon [08°46'N] within 00°18')
♇ // ♀	(Pluto [18°57'N] parallels Venus [19°07'N] within 00°10')
♇ // ♃	(Pluto [18°57'N] parallels Jupiter [18°03'N] within 00°54')

Some astrologers also interpret the influence of minor aspects. These include the semi-sextile (⚺, 30°00' difference), which is a slightly harmonizing influence; the semi-square (∠, 45°00' difference), which is a slightly disintegrating influence; the sesquiquadrate (⚼, 135°00' difference), which is a slightly provoking influence; and the quincunx (⚻, 150°00' difference), which is a slightly indifferent influence. Additionally, the semi-decile or vigintile (⊥, 18°00' difference), the quindecile (✓, 24°00' difference), the decile or semi-quintile (⊥, 36°00' difference), and the tredecile (⨥, 108°00' difference) all exert a slightly positive influence. Both the quintile (**Q**, 72°00' difference) and the biquintile (±, 144°00' difference) play minor roles as strengthening influences.

FIGURE 8.6. HOUSES OF THE HOROSCOPE.

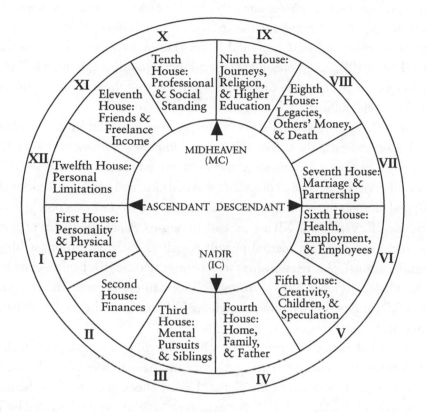

Once the required calculations, resulting data, representational horoscope (figs. 8.1 and 8.2), and Aspectarian (figs. 8.4 and 8.5) are completed, the material is ready for interpretation.

CHART INTERPRETATION

Step Eight: Analyzing the Houses

Bearing a remarkable resemblance to the Chinese fate houses (see "Locating and Interpreting the Birth *Miao*" in chapter 3) and the Vedic *bhavas* (see "Constructing the *Bhavacakra*" in chapter 5), the twelve houses of a Western horoscope (fig. 8.6) are segregated into three categories: angular, succedent, and cadent. This system is very similar to the Vedic *trikona* and *kendra* house designations (see "Rating by *Sthanabala*" in chapter 5). Not every chart displays an even distribution of planets throughout the houses, indicating a well-balanced, harmonic existence in which the person evenly distributes his or her attentions to every facet of life. A predominance of planets in a particular house or houses, therefore, focuses on the individual's critical interests.

The angular houses (House I, IV, VII, and X) are positioned closest to the chart's primary angles (Ascendant, Nadir, Descendant, and Midheaven)[137] as shown in fig. 8.6 and represent the individual's personality (House I); domestic situation including home, family, and father (House IV); marital and partnership status (House VII); and professional life and social standing (House X). Therefore, a predominance of planets in these houses signifies that the individual's life centers around personal fulfillment, home, marriage, and career.

Houses II, V, VIII, XI are the succedent houses. A preponderance of planets in those houses indicates the individual's interest in personal finances (House II); creative ability, prospects for offspring, and speculative interests (House V); ability to handle other people's money, comprehension of death, and receipt of legacies (House VIII); and relationships with friends and ability to earn freelance income (House XI).

Houses III, VI, IX, and XII are the cadent houses. A predominance of planets in those sectors signify that mental pursuits (such as early education, writing, and communications), plus relationships with siblings (House III); health, employment, and employees (House VI); journeys, religious interests, and higher education (House IX); and personal limitations (House XII) are the individual's primary areas of interest.

Indicated along the outer ring of the chart, the ruling zodiac sign for each house exerts either a positive or negative influence on the activities of the house it governs, just as the placement of the planets has an effect in each of the houses (see "Delineating House Rulerships"). For example, Alice's House IV is ruled by Taurus (25°♉17′ in fig. 8.1), House V is ruled by Gemini (16°♊44′ in fig. 8.1), and so forth.

Some practitioners also interpret the location of a given house's planetary ruler in the chart. Unlike the Vedic *swakshetra* (see "*Sthanabala* by *Swakshetra*" in chapter 5), Arabian planetary rulers, and Judaic planetary rulers, the modern Western rulerships are as follows:

Sun (☉)	rules Leo (♌)
Moon (☽)	rules Cancer (♋)
Mercury (☿)	rules both Gemini (♊) and Virgo (♍)
Mars (♂)	rules Aries (♈)
Jupiter (♃)	rules Sagittarius (♐)
Venus (♀)	rules both Taurus (♉) and Libra (♎)
Saturn (♄)	rules Capricorn (♑)
Uranus (♅)	rules Aquarius (♒)
Neptune (♆)	rules Pisces (♓)
Pluto (♇)	rules Scorpio (♏)

---

137.   The Midheaven is sometimes referred to as the Medium Coeli (MC).

Using Peter's chart to illustrate this point, Neptune (♆ 15°♏ 19′ in fig. 8.2) occupies House VIII, but this planet is also House I's planetary ruler because Neptune (♆) rules Pisces (♓, see above) which is House I's zodiac sign, Pisces (02° ♓ 49′ in fig. 8.2). Some practitioners interpret the significance of a house's planetary ruler when it resides in another house. For instance, an astrologer would determine the influence of House I's planetary ruler when it occupies House VIII in the above example.[138] Most practitioners, however, simply interpret the zodiac sign that occupies a particular house in a general natal consultation. The procedure employed in the delineation of house rulers appears later in this chapter (see "Delineating House Rulerships").

Step Nine: Assessing the Chart's Overall Shape

The distribution of the planets in a chart can shed light on the individual's overall personality. In his book, *Essentials of Astrological Analysis*, Western astrologer Marc Edmund Jones presented an interpretative method based on seven chart shapes: bowl, seesaw, splash, locomotive, bundle, bucket, and splay. These configurations are referred to as Jones's Patterns. Not every chart fits one of Jones's specific types perfectly, but used as a general template, Jones's chart-shape theory has proven useful in modern natal interpretation.

Bowl chart.   A bowl chart has all ten of its planets occupying 180°00′ or approximately six houses concentrated in one half of the chart (fig. 8.7). According to Jones, this configuration indicates that the individual is a self-contained person who concentrates his or her attentions only on the areas of life governed by houses occupied by planets, avoiding areas governed by unoccupied houses. For example, the person represented in fig. 8.7 focuses all of his or her attention on professional or social standing (House X); legal papers or other people's money (House VIII); education, religion, or long-distance travel (House IX); self-fulfillment (House I); and personal limitations (House XII). This same person is not concerned with his or her own finances (House II), intellectual pursuits (House III), home (House IV), children (House V), health (House VI), marriage (VII), friends (House XI), or any of the other factors governed by those empty houses. The leading planet (or the first planet in the cluster's sequential counterclockwise order) indicates the focal point of the person's attention. In this case, Mars (♂27° ♐ 38′ in fig. 8.7) is the lead planet, suggesting that the person is obsessed with the potential loss of a legacy or a spouse's income and assets, because it is House VIII that governs legacies and other people's money.

---

138.   For a list of these interpretations, see the chapter titled "Planetary House Rulers" in Llewellyn George's *The New A to Z Horoscope Maker and Delineator* (St. Paul, Minn.: Llewellyn Publications, 1994).

FIGURE 8.7. A BOWL CHART.

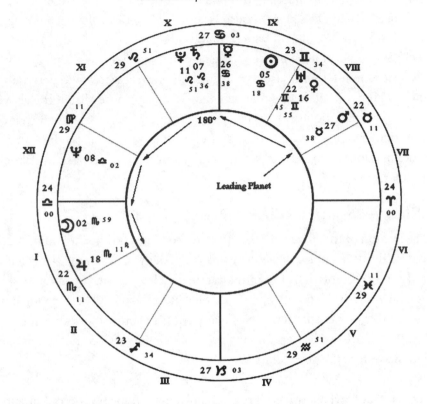

Bucket chart.   A bucket chart has nine out of ten planets clustered together on one side of the chart while one planet is positioned on the opposite side (fig. 8.8). This configuration indicates that the individual is pointed in one direction, represented by the solitary planet, making the person uncompromising about his or her goal or lifestyle. If the solitary planet (singleton) appears between Houses I through VI (below the horizon), the individual has a secret direction that he or she never reveals to others. If it appears between Houses VII through XII (above the horizon), the person's goal is obvious to everyone. (There doesn't need to be an opposing aspect for this shape to take effect, however.) For example, the singleton planet in fig. 8.8 is situated in House I, which indicates that the individual never reveals his or her goal to other people.

Bundle chart.   A bundle chart has all ten planets clustered within 120°00′ or approximately four houses of the horoscope (fig. 8.9). This indicates that the individual is solely concentrated on and limited to only one portion of his or her life. For example, a genius or savant may excel in a specific area of interest, but may find it difficult to socialize or communicate with friends, family, or business associates. This microcosmic view of life becomes the source of the person's problems. The

FIGURE 8.8. A BUCKET CHART.

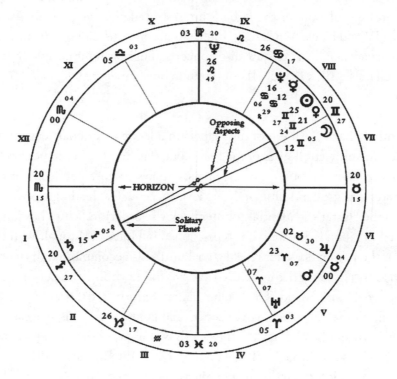

FIGURE 8.9. A BUNDLE CHART.

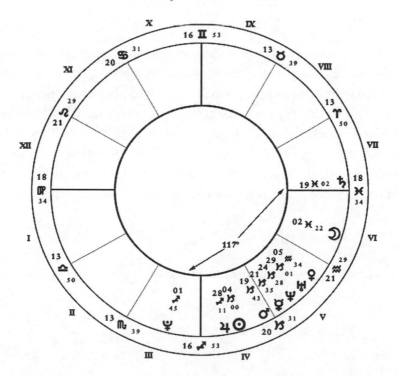

person represented in fig. 8.9 concentrates on home and children, the acquisition of land and speculation, or the father's interests and creative pursuits—which are all House IV and House V interests. Intellectual concerns, siblings, health, employment, marriage, and partners are also concerns, but play a minor role by comparison since Houses III, VI, and VII only contain one planet each.

Locomotive chart.   All ten of the planets in a locomotive chart occupy 240°00′ or approximately eight houses of the horoscope (fig. 8.10). The shape signifies that the individual is ambitious. He or she may seem slow to start a project, but will stick to the intended goal and ultimately achieve success. The leading planet (the first planet in the cluster's sequential counterclockwise order) indicates how and where his or her ambition is directed. If it is positioned in Houses I through VI (below the horizon), the person does not reveal a goal until it is accomplished. If the planet is positioned in Houses VII through XII (above the horizon), the person advertises his or her goal to the world. The leading planet, Saturn (♄ 01°♓25′ in fig. 8.10), is situated in House XII, which governs personal limitations. This suggests that the person advertises his or her goal to the world. Because there are an equal number of planets in Houses I through VI (below the horizon) and Houses VII through XII (above the horizon), the individual neither conceals nor advertises his or her goal. However, the leading planet's prognostication would take precedence.

Seesaw chart.   A seesaw chart has all ten planets situated in opposing houses (fig. 8.11). The shape indicates that the individual is always in conflict between the work that has to be done and the person's wishes or desires, making him or her very indecisive. This particular pattern has at least one opposition (see "Locating Planetary Aspects") such as the aspect formed between Saturn (♄ 28°♈19′ in fig. 8.11) in House XI and Neptune (♆ 28°♎09′ in fig. 8.11)[139] in House V within a 00°10′ orb of influence. (It is however, very common to find two oppositions in this pattern.) In fig. 8.11, the conflicts appear to center on the attention paid to children,

---

139.   This aspect is determined by subtracting the difference between the two planetary positions as shown below:

Neptune (♆ 28°♎19′)	07	28°	09′	(fig. 8.11)
	06	57°	69′	(converted)
− Saturn (♄ 28°♈19′)	01	28°	19′	(fig. 8.11)
	05	29°	50′	(total to be converted)
	179°	50′		(opposition)

FIGURE 8.10. A LOCOMOTIVE CHART.

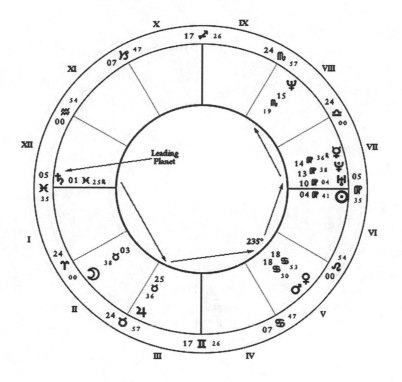

FIGURE 8.11. A SEESAW CHART.

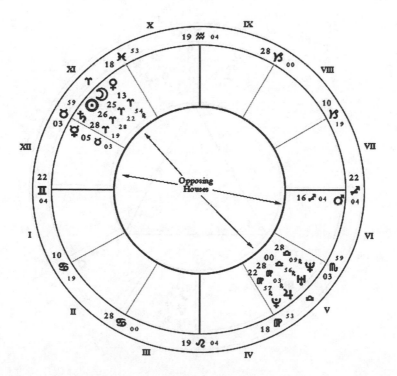

FIGURE 8.12. A SPLASH CHART.

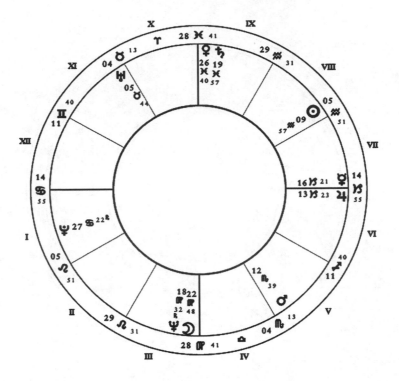

FIGURE 8.13. A SPLAY CHART.

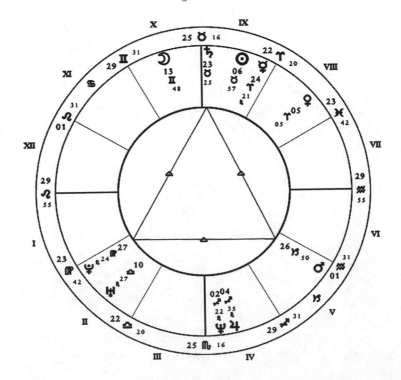

creativity, health, and employment, which are House V activities, versus time spent on House XI interests such as friends and associates.

Splash Chart. A splash or scatter chart has all ten planets scattered throughout the twelve houses (fig. 8.12). This configuration indicates that the person is interested in everything. The evolved version of this chart type desires to learn about the entire universe; the underdeveloped type becomes a dilettante who never completes anything and shows only a superificial interest in a everything. (This particular pattern is often mutated, containing one empty house, but never two consecutive empty houses.) In fig. 8.12, the individual seems to be interested in numerous pursuits, with the exception of anything to do with personal finances (House II), home (House IV), profession (House X), or personal limitations (House XII).

Splay chart. A splay chart contains an irregular flow of planets (fig. 8.13). According to Marc Edmund Jones, this shape indicates that the person is intensely independent, refusing to conform or to be categorized or criticized by others. The individual is often misunderstood by friends, family, and associates. This person tends to be a loner, and if Houses I, IV, VII, or X are stressed, he or she achieves notoriety or fame at some point. The emphasis in fig. 8.13 is on Houses II, IV, and IX, which suggests that the secret ambitions of this loner center on finances (House II), domestic life (House IV), and journeys, religion, or higher education (House IX).

Step Ten: Analyzing the Predominant Features
Elements

In Western astrology there are four influential elements or triplicities, so named because each encompasses three zodiac signs. These are fire, earth, water, and air. Developed in medieval Europe as a critical factor in medical diagnosis, each of the four elements coincides with the four humors or temperaments: choleric (fire), melancholic (earth), phlegmatic (water), and sanguine (air). If the planets in a chart occupy signs possessing a particular element, it appears to have a profound effect on the person's temperament.

Fire. The zodiac signs Aries (♈), Leo (♌), and Sagittarius (♐) are endowed with the nature of fire, highlighting activity and enthusiasm. Associated with a choleric temperament, a fire-oriented person is impulsive, rash, self-confident, and driven. This individual moves dynamically despite potential danger or remorse. According to ancient astrologers, Aries (♈) emulates the self-generating fire, while Leo (♌) expresses fire's ability to mold and form creatively. Sagittarius (♐) demonstrates the power of fire to burn passionately.

Earth.   The earth signs (Taurus [♉], Virgo [♍], and Capricorn [♑]) are associated with a melancholic temperament: a conservative, withdrawn, and constant (although nervous) nature. An earth-sign individual is practical, reserved, and reliable or miserly, materialistic, and rigid. Driven toward self-improvement as a means of self-expression, this person strives for rewards in the physical world. According to ancient practitioners, Taurus (♉) emulates the nature of the immovable Earth, while Capricorn (♑) expresses the power of the Earth as it moves upward, forming mountains. Virgo (♍) demonstrates the strength of the Earth's rhythmic motions as it reshapes itself through rare major shifts like earthquakes. For example, six out of ten planets[140] in Peter's horoscope (fig. 8.2) are situated in the earth signs Taurus (♉) and Virgo (♍), indicating an earth-dominated temperament.

Air.   The zodiac signs Gemini (♊), Libra (♎), and Aquarius (♒) are air signs. Mentally inclined, communicative, and somewhat restless or volatile, these signs are associated with a sanguine temperament: a tendency to intellectualize the material world; a desire for freedom and an optimistic nature. However, the person has difficulty maintaining an emotionally fulfilling relationship with another person. According to ancient practitioners, Gemini (♊) emulates the strength of the ocean winds, while Libra (♎) expresses the temperate nature of light breezes, and Aquarius (♒) demonstrates the power of thick, immovable air. For example, four out of ten planets[141] in Alice's horoscope (fig. 8.1) are located in the air signs Libra (♎) and Gemini (♊), indicating a air-dominated temperament.

Water.   Three signs are endowed with the natural characteristics of water: Cancer (♋), Scorpio (♏), and Pisces (♓). Sensitive, impressionable, and reflective, these signs are associated with the phlegmatic temperament: an emotional, confused, receptive, and self-protective nature. According to ancient practitioners, Cancer (♋) emulates the characteristics of changeable, moving water, while Scor-

---

140.   The Moon's North (☊) and South Nodes (☋) are not included in this process because they are not actual planets.
141.   Ibid.

pio (♏) expresses the obsessive nature of frozen water. And Pisces (♓) demonstrates the power of water vapors and fog.

Almost all charts demonstrate a balancing act of more than one elemental influence. Not every chart has an equal distribution of elements, however. Delineation of these qualities must weigh the predominant influence as it is tempered by any apparent subsidiary elements.

Qualities

The qualities or properties of the zodiac signs are subdivided into three categories: cardinal, fixed, and mutable (common). Each of the elements (fire, earth, air, and water) is represented in a specific quality type, as shown below:

Aries (♈)	cardinal fire sign
Taurus (♉)	fixed earth sign
Gemini (♊)	mutable air sign
Cancer (♋)	cardinal water sign
Leo (♌)	fixed fire sign
Virgo (♍)	mutable earth sign
Libra (♎)	cardinal air sign
Scorpio (♏)	fixed water sign
Sagittarius (♐)	mutable fire sign
Capricorn (♑)	cardinal earth sign
Aquarius (♒)	fixed air sign
Pisces (♓)	mutable water sign

A predominance of planets in one quality (cardinal, fixed, or mutable) is referred to as a cross. This phenomenon affects an individual's overall ability to relate to and interact with his or her immediate surroundings.

Cardinal cross. The zodiac signs Aries (♈), Cancer (♋), Libra (♎), and Capricorn (♑) are called the cardinal signs. A predominance of planets in cardinal signs is called a cardinal cross. Generally, if the predominance of planets is evenly distributed among the four cardinal signs mentioned above, this signifies that the person derives his or her personal values from external circumstances. In other words, this person adapts to the demands and expectations that either events or other people impose on a situation.

If most of the planets in a horoscope occupy Aries (♈), it indicates the subject's desire to conquer and absorb, and to fit everything into a mainstream view of life. Unfortunately, the person's motivation is very impetuous and perception is totally self-centered. Thus, every situation that is encountered directly has the ability to make or break this person.

If most of the planets in a horoscope occupy Cancer (♋), it indicates that the individual desires to know what everyone is thinking so he or she can react in a calculated manner. Consequently, this person can be somewhat emotionally indecisive if his or her surroundings have not been thoroughly assessed.

If most of the planets in a horoscope occupy Libra (♎), it indicates that the person absorbs the surrounding circumstances. His or her motivation is based on a strong desire to create harmony and balance in any situation.

If most of the planets in a horoscope occupy Capricorn (♑), it indicates the subject's desire to establish a rigid set of rules and regulations as a means for controlling every circumstance he or she encounters. The desire to lead others according to these self-created commandments often backfires, however, making the same individual a prisoner of self-inflicted strictures.

Cardinal grand cross. If four planets occupy cardinal signs (Aries [♈], Cancer [♋], Libra [♎], and Capricorn [♑]), and those planets form two oppositions (☍) and four squares (□) (see "Locating Planetary Aspects and Constructing an Aspectarian"), it is called a cardinal grand cross. This configuration signifies that the individual is a dynamic problem-solver who needs to be in a constant state of action or motion toward a particular objective. An excellent example of this is the cardinal grand cross appearing in Alice's chart (fig. 8.1). Two planets occupy the sign Libra (♎), two planets reside in Cancer (♋), and one planet occupies Aries (♈). The Moon (☽ 11°♈28′) forms an opposition to Neptune (♆ 18°♎59′) within a 07°31′ orb of influence.[142] It also forms an opposition to Saturn (♄ 08°♎12′) within a 03°16′ orb of influence;[143] a square to Mercury (☿ 03°♋28′) within an

---

142. This aspect is determined by subtracting the difference between the two planetary positions as shown below:

Neptune (♆ 18°♎59′)	07	18°	59′	(fig. 8.1)
− Moon (☽ 11°♈28′)	01	11°	28′	(fig. 8.1)
	06	07°	31′	(total to be converted)
		187°	31′	(opposition)

The total is then subtracted from 180°00′ to determine the orb of influence.

143. This aspect is determined by subtracting the difference between the two planetary positions as shown below:

Saturn (♄ 08°♎12′)	07	08°	12′	(fig. 8.1)
	06	37°	72′	(converted)
− Moon (☽ 11°♈28′)	01	11°	28′	(fig. 8.1)
	05	26°	44′	(total to be converted)
		176°	44′	(total)

The total is then subtracted from 180°00′ to determine the orb of influence.

08°00′ orb of influence;[144] and a square to Uranus (♅13°♋00′) within a 01°32′ orb of influence.[145] Mercury (☿ 03°♋28′) forms a square to Saturn (♄08°♎12′) within a 04°44′ orb of influence.[146] And Uranus (♅ 13°♋00′) forms a square to Neptune (♆ 18°♎59′) within a 05°59′ orb of influence.[147]

Fixed cross ("cross of crisis"). The zodiac signs Taurus (♉), Leo (♌), Scorpio (♏), and Aquarius (♒) are fixed signs. A predominance of planets in fixed signs indicates that the person is organized and resistant to change. Generally, if the predominance of planets is evenly distributed among the four fixed signs mentioned above, the individual is difficult to move or dissuade and requires a consistent daily routine. This person derives his or her personal values from the inner self. The subject is solely concerned with his or her internal dialogue and the demands of his or her unconscious mind, remaining totally unaffected by outside opinion or circumstances. There is a never-ending internal struggle to fuse the conscious and unconscious elements of self according to a very subjective view.

---

144. This aspect is determined by subtracting the difference between the two planetary positions as shown below:

Mercury (☿ 03°♋28′)	04	03°	28′	(fig. 8.1)
	03	33°	28′	(converted)
− Moon (☽ 11°♈28′)	01	11°	28′	(fig. 8.1)
	02	22°	00′	(total to be converted)
		82°	00′	(total)

The total is then subtracted from 90°00′ to determine the orb of influence.

145. This aspect is determined by subtracting the difference between the two planetary positions as shown below:

Uranus (♅ 13°♋00′)	04	13°	00′	(fig. 8.1)
	04	12°	60′	(converted)
− Moon (☽ 11°♈28′)	01	11°	28′	(fig. 8.1)
	03	01°	32′	(total to be converted)
		91°	32′	(total)

The total is then subtracted from 90°00′ to determine the orb of influence.

146. This aspect is determined by subtracting the difference between the two planetary positions as shown below:

Saturn (♄ 08°♎12′)	07	08°	12′	(fig. 8.1)
	07	07°	72′	(converted)
− Mercury (☿ 03°♋28′)	04	03°	28′	(fig. 8.1)
	03	04°	44′	(total to be converted)
		94°	44′	(total)

The total is then subtracted from 90°00′ to determine the orb of influence.

147. This aspect is determined by subtracting the difference between the two planetary positions as shown below:

Neptune (♆ 18°♎59′)	07	18°	59′	(fig. 8.1)
− Uranus (♅ 13°♋00′)	04	13°	00′	(fig. 8.1)
	03	05°	59′	(total to be converted)
		95°	59′	(total)

The total is then subtracted from 90°00′ to determine the orb of influence.

If most of the planets in a horoscope occupy Taurus (♉), it indicates that the person is persistent and stubborn when working on a single project, no matter how difficult the task. This "work" overtakes all other concerns, even if the battle and the war have been obviously lost.

If most of the planets in a horoscope occupy Leo (♌), it indicates that the individual has a strong need for material possessions and luxury, overcompensating for a subconscious insecurity about his or her standing in the world.

If most of the planets in a horoscope occupy Scorpio (♏), it indicates the individual's desire to dissect every nuance in both the unconscious and subconscious worlds. There is a constant need to analyze everything on an emotional-mental level from a highly subjective perspective.

If most of the planets in a horoscope occupy Aquarius (♒), it indicates the individual's desire to either tenaciously hold or remain completely detached from emotional situations based on his or her belief in a situation's intrinsic value.

Fixed grand cross.   If four planets occupy fixed signs (Taurus [♉], Leo [♌], Scorpio [♏], and Aquarius [♒]), and those planets form two oppositions (☍) and four squares (□) (see "Locating Planetary Aspects and Constructing an Aspectarian"), it is called a fixed grand cross. This formation signifies that the individual sets extremely high personal standards and goals. This person has a very rigid nature, but also possesses a great talent for delving deep into any investigation and has an understandable pride in his or her intellect.

Mutable cross (common cross).   The zodiac signs Gemini (♊), Virgo (♍), Sagittarius (♐), and Pisces (♓) are mutable (common) signs. Generally, a predominance of planets in mutable signs indicate that a person is endowed with the ability to adapt to his or her surroundings. This type of person can objectively learn and disseminate information. The appearance of a mutable cross in an individual's chart indicates that the individual is totally uninvolved with self-evaluation. He or she adapts to and restricts the absorption of external influences without fixed or directed reasoning.

If most of the planets in a horoscope occupy Gemini (♊), it indicates that the individual has a remarkable ability to collect and relate huge amounts of information. Sometimes this becomes unconscious, nonmalicious prying rather than investigation or mere curiosity.

If most of the planets in a horoscope occupy Virgo (♍), it indicates that the individual has an ability to analyze everything critically, from a totally objective vantage point. This includes self-analysis. Consequently, the individual seeks the purest essence in all things: the most chaste or the most excessive of every situation. An example of this formation occurs in Peter's chart (fig. 8.2), in which four planets occupy Virgo (♍) and one planet occupies Pisces (♓).

If most of the planets in a horoscope occupy Sagittarius (♐), it indicates that the individual desires to transmit dogmatic information without revision. This person is not willing to absorb any information or insight that would change an accepted mindset or curriculum.

If most of the planets in a horoscope occupy Pisces (♓), it indicates that the individual desires to place all people and events into a world he or she "feels." This person is incapable of analyzing a situation for its validity, because all of his or her energy is spent in this imagined world. Consequently, the individual tends to lose a realistic sense of self.

Mutable grand cross (common grand cross). If four planets occupy fixed signs (Gemini [♊], Virgo [♍], Sagittarius [♐], and Pisces [♓]) and those planets form two oppositions (☍) and four squares (□) (see "Locating Planetary Aspects and Constructing an Aspectarian"), it is called a mutable grand cross or a common grand cross. This formation signifies that the individual is high-strung and nervous. He or she has problems concentrating on any single subject, but always strives to know more about everything. This type of person can gather and disseminate massive amounts of information, but fails to remember or learn anything in depth.

Step Eleven: Reviewing the Moon's Nodes and the Part of Fortune

The Moon's North Node (☊) and South Node (☋) as well as the Arabian Part of Fortune (see "The Part of Fortune" in chapter 6) influence the luck factors in an individual's horoscope. Each entity is interpreted according to the house it occupies in the chart.

The Moon's North Node (☊)

The Moon's North Node (☊) is the point at which the Moon intersects the ecliptic while passing into a northern latitude. In a horoscope, this Node accentuates the individual's potential for financial gain, professional success, or the receipt of favors, and the vehicle(s) by which these opportunities are obtained. It takes nineteen years for the Moon's North Node (☊) to make its complete orbit through the zodiac. Ancient astrologers often referred to this designation as Caput Draconis (Dragon's Head), while Arabian practitioners called this position the Anahibazon. Vedic astrologers treat the Moon's North Node (☊) as a separate planet called Rahu. In Western astrology, the vehicle or area in which success or financial gain is found depends upon the house that the Moon's North Node (☊) occupies, as shown below:

House I	through the person's own strong, self-expressive personality
House II	through financial investments
House III	through mental pursuits such as writing or public speaking; through siblings
House IV	through home, family, or father[148]
House V	through creative ability, speculation, or children[149]
House VI	in the employment of others; through service to others; in health-related fields[150]
House VII	through a wise and wealthy business partner or spouse
House VIII	through legacies or inheritance[151]
House IX	through education, law, religion, or foreign affairs; or in foreign lands
House X	through profession or social standing;
House XI	through friends' and associates' aid; through freelance work or hobbies
House XII	through seclusion or by overcoming personal fears

For instance, Alice's Moon's North Node (☊ 23♒23 in fig. 8.1) is located in House I, suggesting that her potential for obtaining financial gain, professional success, or the receipt of favors centers on her strong, self-expressive personality. Peter's Moon's North Node (☊ 29♊40 in fig. 8.2) is located in House IV, indicating that his potential focuses on home, family, or father.

The Moon's South Node (☋)

Conversely, the Moon's South Node (☋) is the point at which the Moon intersects the ecliptic while passing into a southern latitude. In a horoscope, this Node accentuates the precise forms of chaos or problems a person encounters in life. Ancient astrologers often referred to it as Cauda Draconis (Dragon's Tail). Vedic astrologers treat the Moon's South Node (☋) as a separate planet called Ketu. In Western astrology, the vehicle or area in which problems arise depends upon the house that

---

148. This position also indicates a long and enjoyable life.
149. It also signifies a relatively disaster-free existence.
150. This position also indicates good health.
151. The position also indicates longevity.

the Moon's South Node (☋) occupies, as shown below. Note that these prognostications don't always directly relate to the nature of the given house (fig. 8.6), but are generally accepted and applied by modern-day practitioners.

House I	experiences many personal trials and tribulations including facial or eye injuries during a short life span
House II	encounters great financial misfortune, indebtedness, and financial worries
House III	has disputes with siblings and neighbors; has difficulties associated with mental pursuits such as writing
House IV	encounters family or domestic discord and land-based property losses
House V	experiences sudden loss of children, or is denied having children
House VI	has poor health, as well as illnesses caused by insect stings, reptile bites, or small animals
House VII	encounters sudden loss of spouse or business partner, or never forms a partnership of any kind; has many enemies and competitors (however, this same position also portends the death or destruction of those opponents)[152]
House VIII	encounters a sudden or violent death, as well as loss through the deception of others
House IX	has curious dreams and premonitions; has unfortunate voyages abroad
House X	encounters professional or occupational losses through deception or treachery, or through financial depressions, recessions, corporate takeovers, and stock failures
House XI	has bad friends and questionable associations; poor advice causes lost opportunities and quashed hopes
House XII	is the cause of his or her own undoing[153]

---

152.   It also indicates difficulties with a spouse or partner.
153.   This position also indicates that restrictions or imprisonment and harassment by secret enemies also affect the individual's health.

Alice's Moon's South Node (☋23°♌23 in fig. 8.1) is located in House VII, suggesting that she encounters the sudden loss of her spouse or business partner, or never forms a partnership of any kind. It also indicates that she has many enemies and competitors. (However, this same position also portends the death or destruction of those opponents.) Peter's Moon's South Node (☋29°♐40 in fig. 8.2) is located in House X, indicating that he encounters professional or occupational losses through deception or treachery, or through financial depressions, recessions, corporate takeovers, and stock failures.

The Arabian Part of Fortune

The Arabian Part of Fortune (Part of the Moon) indicates the person's chances for worldly success, and is the most popular of the Arabian Parts, even in modern times.[154] For details on the calculation and delineation of this Arabian Part, refer to the section titled "The Part of Fortune" in chapter 6.

Step Twelve: Delineating the House Rulerships

The zodiac sign occupying each house cusp in the outer ring of the horoscope dominates the activities of the entire house and is commonly referred to as the house ruler. For example, in Peter's chart (fig. 8.2), Pisces (♓) rules House I, Aries (♈) rules House II, Taurus (♉) rules House III, and so forth. While in Alice's chart (fig. 8.1), Aquarius (♒) rules House I, Pisces (♓) rules House II, Aries (♈) rules House III, and so on.

Each sign exerts a prescribed influence upon the individual's potential reaction to the events governed by the specific house. This system is identical to the procedures used by Vedic practitioners in the interpretation of a *bhavacakra* (house chart). In fact, the interpretative material used to delineate the house rulers is located in chapter 5 in the section titled "Interpreting the House Rulers in the *Bhavacakra*." Even if a particular house does not contain any planets or nodes, it is still affected by the zodiac sign that is its house ruler.

For example, in Alice's chart (fig. 8.1), Taurus rules House IV (25°♉17'). Using the interpretative material in the section titled "Interpreting the House Rulers in the *Bhavacakra*" in chapter 5, this rulership indicates that Alice has a sentimental attachment to home and family. She has strong ties to her parents (see "House IV Rulers" in chapter 5). In Peter's chart (fig. 8.2), Gemini rules House IV (17°♊06').

---

154.   The Part of Fortune is sometimes used to verify the Moon's particular phase at the time of the person's birth. If the Part occupies the Ascendant (House I), it's a New Moon. If the Part occupies House VII, it's a Full Moon. If the Part occupies House X, there's a fourth-quarter moon. And if the Part occupies House IV, there's a second-quarter moon. In some forms of Western astrology, the Moon's phase at the time of birth is considered to increase or decrease its influence on the individual's emotional makeup.

This rulership indicates that Peter prefers to work at home; experiences many changes of residence; may live near a sibling during his adult life; and has strong communication with his parents (see "House IV Rulers" in chapter 5). Following the above process, the practitioner delineates all twelve houses before proceeding to the interpretation of the planetary positions.

Step Thirteen: Delineating Planetary Positions by House and by Sign

Each planetary position in a chart is generally read in two ways: by the zodiac sign it occupies and by the house it attends. By assessing the house rulerships as shown in the previous section, along with the planets occupying those houses, an astrologer begins to synthesize the material into a complete delineation. Once again, the manner and content of interpretation is identical to the Vedic method. So refer to the section titled "Interpreting the Planetary Positions in a *Rasicakra*" in chapter 5 for a delineation of a planet's position by zodiac sign. Then refer to the material below to interpret the planetary position by the house it occupies and the ruler of that particular house (see "Interpreting the House Rulers in the *Bhavacakra*" in chapter 5).

For example, Peter's Sun (☉ 04°♍41′ in fig. 8.2) is located in the zodiac sign Virgo (♍) in House VII. The Sun (☉) in Virgo (♍) suggests that he is frugal, practical, contemplative, industrious, youthful-looking, and a perfectionist. He desires wealth, worries, and has a sharp temper, but abhors fighting. He has a strong command of language, is able to learn quickly, and has a high level of endurance (see "The Sun in the Various Zodiac Signs" in chapter 5).

Peter's Sun (☉ 04°♍41′ in fig. 8.2) is situated in House VII. Using the material below, this indicates that Peter has a strong desire for marriage or a strong partnership (see "The Sun in the Various Houses," below).

House VII's ruler (02°♍49′ in fig. 8.2)—Virgo (♍)—indicates that Peter is constructively critical of his spouse or business partner. He possibly establishes a business partnership with a sibling or close relative from the maternal side of his family. There is also potential for more than one marriage in Peter's life (see "House VII Rulers" in chapter 5).

The synthesis of these three elements is the heart of the astrologer's talent. No two practitioners blend the house ruler, planetary position by zodiac sign, and planetary position by house in precisely the same manner. Almost all Western astrologers agree, however, on what the individual positions represent. One way an astrologer might assess the above information is to say that Peter focuses a great deal of his energy on his marital relationship, seeking the perfect partner and the perfect situation. He brings practicality and frugality, as well as a strong desire and ability to work hard for a mutual goal, which usually entails the acquisition of wealth. He is constructively critical of his spouse, which may be the reason why there is potential for more than one marriage in Peter's life.

Each planet and node is delineated in this way, applying the material found in the section titled "Interpreting the Planetary Positions in a *Rasicakra*" in chapter 5, with the exception of Uranus (♅), Neptune (♆), and Pluto (♇), which appear in the material below. Because Uranus and Neptune weren't discovered until the late eighteenth and nineteenth centuries respectively, and Pluto was discovered in 1929, these planets were not incorporated into the astrological processes employed by Chinese, Tibetan, Vedic, Arabian, or Judaic practitioners. Also known as the "modern" or "extra-Saturnian" planets, they are unique to Western astrology. These data are combined with the interpretation of the planetary positions in the various houses, shown below. Then they are blended with the interpretation of the house rulers discussed in the previous section.

The Sun (☉) in the Various Houses

All the planets in our solar system revolve around the Sun, which is a fixed star that completes its cycle through the zodiac signs on an annual basis (365.25 days). Its apparent orbital path, called the ecliptic, begins at 00°00′ Aries (00°♈00′) and ends at 30°00′ Pisces (30°♓00′) on or around March 21, which is known as the vernal equinox. Its occupation of a particular house enhances its influence as follows:

House I	independent; extrovertive; egocentric; if adversely aspected,[155] frustrated over lack of independence
House II	reaps financial benefits; exploits situations to best financial advantage; if adversely aspected,[156] squanders money; has financial difficulties
House III	his or her personality shines through writing and communications; lords it over siblings; if adversely aspected,[157] has difficulties with writings and communications; has troubles with siblings or neighbors due to personality conflicts; is possibly an only child

---

155.   If a planet forms a square (☐) or opposition (☍) with any planet; if the Moon (☽) forms a conjunction (☌) or parallel (∥) with the Sun (☉), Uranus (♅), or Neptune (♆); or if Mercury (☿) or Venus (♀) forms a conjunction (☌) or parallel (∥) with Uranus (♅) or Neptune (♆) (see "Locating Planetary Aspects and Constructing an Aspectarian"), its influence is considered to be adversely aspected.
156.   Ibid.
157.   Ibid.

House IV	family and parents influence personality; if adversely aspected,[158] has personality conflicts in the home with family or with parents
House V	his or her personality shines through creativity, children, romance, or pleasures; if adversely aspected,[159] frustrated over children; abuses pleasures; is excessive[160]
House VI	gains through employees or co-workers; ambitions are limited to daily routine; if adversely aspected,[161] has personality conflicts with employees or co-workers; has health problems
House VII	has a strong desire for marriage or business partnership; if adversely aspected,[162] has difficulties relating to spouse or partners
House VIII	gains from death through legacy or inheritance; if adversely aspected,[163] experiences premature death of parent or spouse; has painful losses[164]
House IX	desires to elevate intellectual or spiritual plane; has success abroad or in relationships with foreigners; if adversely aspected,[165] has difficulties abroad or with foreigners; feels persecuted because of personal ideology or political leanings
House X	encounters professional and social success; if adversely aspected,[166] is ruthlessly ambitious
House XI	establishes friendships among powerful and influential people; if adversely aspected,[167] experiences loss of friendships
House XII	prevails over enemies; seeks to fulfill personal ideals; if adversely aspected,[168] finds that success is hard-won; has many trials and sacrifices

---

158. Ibid.
159. Ibid.
160. According to some astrologers, this person may unfortunately be denied children or has difficulty with childbirth if the Sun (☉) occupies a barren sign (Gemini (♊), Leo (♌), or Virgo (♍)).
161. See note 155, page 414.
162. Ibid.
163. Ibid.
164. Some astrologers believe that the person's forty-fifth year may be of critical importance. Heart trouble is also a concern throughout life. Fortunately, he or she becomes famous or is honored posthumously.
165. See note 155, page 414.
166. Ibid.
167. Ibid.
168. Ibid.

The Moon (☽) in the Various Houses

The Moon orbits around the Earth, completing its cycle through the zodiac signs in 29 days, 12 hours, and 44 minutes. (Many astrologers, however, use a cycle of 27 days, 7 hours, and 43 minutes or apply a 28-day period in chart construction.) This luminary's orbital cycle is segmented into four quarters or phases, called dichotomes or quadratures. Each quarter lasts about seven days. The Moon's influence on a particular house in a chart differs, depending on the gender of the individual. It is the only planet that has this overall gender-specific distinction. In numerous cultures the Moon has traditionally been associated with women, and its effect in a woman's chart is considered to be personal. But in a man's chart this influence might simply imply that a woman may somehow affect that particular area of life. Its occupation of a particular house enhances its influence as follows:

House I	*in a woman's chart:* has a strong, self-assertive personality; if adversely aspected,[169] has an overly-inflated ego *in a man's chart:* a woman is at the helm of every major decision; if adversely aspected, is a misogynist
House II	*in a woman's chart:* has considerable financial success; if adversely aspected,[170] possibly sells herself short financially *in a man's chart:* experiences financial gain through women; if adversely aspected, marries for money
House III	*in a woman's chart:* has success in studies; has favorable relations with sister; if adversely aspected,[171] has an intellectual rivalry with women; competes with sister *in a man's chart:* women provide positive influence on studies; if adversely aspected, intellectually rejects women
House IV	*in a woman's or a man's chart:* his or her mother is a strong influence; if adversely aspected,[172] rejects mother's influence; tends toward homosexuality
House V	*in a woman's or a man's chart:* lacks sexual inhibitions; has artistic and teaching talents; if adversely aspected,[173] has sexual or creative difficulties

---

169. Ibid.
170. Ibid.
171. Ibid.
172. Ibid.
173. Ibid.

House VI	*in a woman's chart:* experiences good health; has a strong sense of hierarchy in the work place; if adversely aspected,[174] has poor health *in a man's chart:* has a positive dependence on women in the workplace; if adversely aspected, views women as inferiors in the workplace[175]
House VII	*in a woman's or a man's chart:* encounters success through marriage and business partnerships with the opposite sex; if adversely aspected,[176] unable to comprehend spouse's or partner's needs[177]
House VIII	*in a woman's chart:* receives a positive maternal legacy; has an interest in the occult; bears many children; if adversely aspected,[178] rejects maternal legacy *in a man's chart:* encounters financial success through marriage; if adversely aspected, loses spouse's inheritance
House IX	*in a woman's chart:* has a talent for languages and education; loves to travel abroad; if adversely aspected,[179] escapes self through narcotics or alcohol *in a man's chart:* has a marriage or serious love relationship with a foreigner; if adversely aspected, escapes himself through the pursuit of unattainable women
House X	*in a woman's chart:* experiences professional success as well as fulfillment as a mother; if adversely aspected,[180] has unattainable professional aspirations *in a man's chart:* encounters professional success through a woman; if adversely aspected, perceives women as business or professional rivals

---

174. Ibid.

175. Some astrologers believe that as a child, this person might have been chronically ill or experienced a near-fatal accident, the part of the body afflicted with the illness or injury depending on the zodiac sign occupied. See footnote 217, page 422, for a list of body parts associated with the zodiac signs.

176. See note 155, page 414.

177. However, this location can indicate relationship problems with a loved one, spouse, or business partner as well as general unpopularity if adversely aspected. Some astrologers also say this position indicates the death of a partner. If the Moon (☽) forms any aspect with Uranus (♅) in the same chart, the subject is likely to marry suddenly, then fall in love with someone else later.

178. See note 155, page 414.

179. Ibid.

180. Ibid.

House XI   *in a woman's chart:* benefits from friendship; if adversely as-
                pected,[181] has disappointing friendships
                in a man's chart: establishes close friendships with women; if ad-
                versely aspected, has a bad attitude toward women stemming
                from poor relations with his mother

House XII   *in a woman's chart:* works well in seclusion; if adversely as-
                pected,[182] has overriding depression, frustration, and guilt
                in a man's chart: has secret but positive personal relation-
                ships with women; if adversely aspected, commits adultery;
                becomes involved with women without making an emotional
                commitment

Mercury (☿) in the Various Houses

Mercury is approximately 35,950,00 miles from the Sun, which it orbits at approximately 95,000 miles per hour, completing its cycle through the zodiac signs every
88 days. Its occupation of a particular house enhances its influence as follows:

House I   intelligent; critical; curious; intuitive; if adversely aspected,[183]
                argumentative; inconsistent

House II   encounters financial gains through shrewdness; has a flair for
                business; if adversely aspected,[184] opportunistic; behaves unethi-
                cally; steals

House III   has a talent for writing, communications, and public speaking;
                mentally adaptable; takes many short trips; has good relation-
                ships with siblings; if adversely aspected,[185] unchangeable; en-
                counters danger during short trips; has difficulties with siblings

House IV   has many changes of residence; has good relations with family;
                if adversely aspected,[186] encounters family intrigues; has overly
                elevated domestic expectations

---

181. Ibid.
182. Ibid.
183. Ibid.
184. Ibid.
185. Ibid.
186. Ibid.

House V	enjoys intellectual or artistic pursuits; has teaching talent; if adversely aspected,[187] is too talkative, is unstable
House VI	adapts to the workplace; profits from relations with employees and co-workers; if adversely aspected,[188] has nervous or respiratory ailments; experiences problems at work due to misjudgment
House VII	marriage choice is influenced by intellect; able to negotiate; takes advantage of opportunities offered through marriage or a business partnership; if adversely aspected,[189] has legal problems with marriage or partnership
House VIII	has an aptitude for astrology, psychoanalysis, or matters pertaining to death or inheritance; if adversely aspected,[190] has potential for death at an early age; experiences death of parents at an early age[191]
House IX	desires to live in foreign lands; studies languages; develops relations with foreigners; if adversely aspected,[192] has arguments over confused ideas; experiences losses in foreign lands or in relations with foreigners
House X	has success in intellectual, commercial or executive positions; has a desire for professional independence or mobility; finds success in literature, advertising, or speaking; if adversely aspected,[193] experiences professional losses due to misjudgment
House XI	has intellectual friends; has a harmonious marriage or partnership; if adversely aspected,[194] is ambivalent about marriage or entering into a partnership; has ambivalent friendships
House XII	is detached from reality; gains through research or investigation; if adversely aspected,[195] has mental illness during adolescence; is a victim or instigator of foul play

---

187. Ibid.
188. Ibid.
189. Ibid.
190. Ibid.
191. In a woman's chart, this also indicates financial troubles, worries, and quarrels with her business partner or spouse.
192. See note 155, page 414.
193. Ibid.
194. Ibid.
195. Ibid.

Venus (♀) in the Various Houses

The second planet of the solar system, Venus orbits the Sun at a distance of about 67,180,000 miles, completing its cycle through the zodiac signs every 224 days. Its occupation of a particular house enhances its influence as follows:

House I	fortunate; needs to be loved; self-interested; if adversely aspected,[196] overly sensitive; has frail health; emotionally frustrated
House II	makes money easily; works in the arts, jewelry trade, or fashion industry; luxury-loving; has a strong emotional link to his or her financial state; if adversely aspected,[197] encounters financial losses through loved ones or through natural circumstances
House III	has a strong attraction to learning; has amiable relations with siblings and neighbors; if adversely aspected,[198] frustrated over learning; has frustrating relations with siblings
House IV	has strong emotional ties to home and family; is fortunate in domestic matters or in real estate; if adversely aspected,[199] experiences painful separation from home or family; has losses in land or mines
House V	has strong attachment to children and romance; possesses strong creative ability; if adversely aspected,[200] fears sex or desires sexual deviation; emotionally frustrated over children
House VI	experiences good health; has amiable relations with employees and co-workers; possibly employed in a medical field or an artistic field; if adversely aspected,[201] is obsessed with health; disappointed with employees or co-workers
House VII	marriage or partnerships are positive emotional outlets and very fortunate; spouse or partner is amiable and sensitive; if adversely aspected, [202] experiences emotional disappointments connected with either marriage or partnerships[203]

---

196. Ibid.
197. Ibid.
198. Ibid.
199. Ibid.
200. Ibid.
201. Ibid.
201. Ibid.
202. Ibid.
203. Some practitioners believe this position foretells that he or she has a peaceful end.

House VIII   has fortunate gains through other people or inheritance; experiences death by natural causes; if adversely aspected,[204] has financial problems caused by the death of another person

House IX   experiences pleasant journeys to foreign lands; encounters romance with a foreigner or while living in foreign lands; emotional stimulation is found on an intellectual plane; if adversely aspected,[205] has a disappointing romance with a foreigner or while traveling abroad[206]

House X   prefers professional or social harmony; succeeds in any occupation dedicated to beautifying or harmonizing the immediate environment; if adversely aspected,[207] misses either professional or social opportunities because of involvement in his or her emotional life; or professional success overrides the person's love life or emotional happiness

House XI   encounters fortunate and amiable friendships; if adversely aspected,[208] experiences disappointment through friendships; has an unrealistic view of friends

House XII   conducts secret love relationships; idealizes love; has an unstable emotional life; if adversely aspected,[209] encounters unhappy love affairs; enjoys voluntary seclusion

Mars (♂) in the Various Houses

Sometimes called the Red Planet because of its unusual hue, Mars, the fourth planet of the solar system, orbits the Sun at a distance of about 141,500,000 miles, completing its cycle through the zodiac signs once every 1 year, 322 days, and reaching its minimum distance from the Earth every fifteen years. Its occupation of a particular house enhances its influence as follows:

House I   impulsive; ambitious; aggressive and competitive; succeeds in sports; if adversely aspected,[210] quick-tempered; behaves inconsistently

---

204.   See note 155, page 414.
205.   Ibid.
206.   This position also brightens the outlook of the entire chart, lightening disappointment and indicating a measure of good fortune.
207.   See note 155, page 414.
208.   Ibid.
209.   Ibid.
210.   Ibid.

House II   financially aggressive; desires to increase income and to spend it; if adversely aspected,[211] experiences financial loss through impulsiveness

House III   encounters social conflicts with siblings or neighbors due to domineering attitude; if adversely aspected,[212] experiences accidents that involve siblings or electricity

House IV   abused by parents or aggresses toward parents as a child; experiences increased activity halfway through life; if adversely aspected,[213] has violent parents; encounters accidents involving parents, home, or land

House V   has impetuous or violent love affairs; experiences danger through overindulgence; dominates children; if adversely aspected,[214] possible danger for children[215]

House VI   disputes with employees or co-workers, but not without profit; if adversely aspected,[216] has difficulties in the workplace; experiences danger due to surgery or acute illness[217]

House VII   behaves aggressively toward partner or spouse; if adversely aspected,[218] risks divorce or dissolution of partnership[219]

---

211. Ibid.
212. Ibid.
213. Ibid.
214. Ibid.
215. In a woman's chart, this position indicates that she might experience a dangerous pregnancy and delivery.
216. See note 155, page 414.
217. The person might also have surgery performed, leaving a scar on a part of the body ruled by the zodiac sign that Mars (♂) occupies. Aries (♈) rules the head and face. Taurus (♉) rules the neck, throat, and ears. Gemini (♊) rules the hands, arms, shoulders, collarbone, lungs and nervous system. Cancer (♋) rules the breast and stomach. Leo (♌) rules the heart, sides, and upper back. Virgo (♍) rules the solar plexus and bowels. Libra (♎) rules the kidneys, ovaries, and lower back. Scorpio (♏) rules the bladder and reproductive organs. Sagittarius (♐) rules the liver, hips, and thighs. Capricorn (♑) rules the knees. Aquarius (♒) rules the calves and ankles. Pisces (♓) rules the feet.
218. See note 155, page 414.
219. If Mars (♂) forms a sextile (✶) or trine (△) with any planet; or if it forms a conjunction (☌) or parallel (∦ or ∥) (see "Locating Planetary Aspects and Constructing an Aspectarian") with any planet except for Uranus (♅) or Neptune (♆), the person makes an auspicious marriage with an individual whose Sun (☉) is situated in Aries (♈). Thus many negative events are avoided. Some astrologers believe that in a woman's chart, this position portends that a critical accident or sudden death might befall her spouse. In a man's chart, it indicates that his spouse is likely to be very assertive and industrious.

House VIII	has disputes or troubles with legacies; has disputes with spouse over expenditures; if adversely aspected,[220] loses inheritance by contest or through excess[221]
House IX	has strong, aggressive political or religious beliefs; has problems with foreigners or travel abroad; if adversely aspected,[222] experiences accidents while traveling abroad; encounters mental conflicts[223]
House X	excessively ambitious; succeeds through courage and daring; if adversely aspected,[224] rash or violent behavior creates professional losses or rivalry
House XI	has a competitive attitude toward friends and associates; if adversely aspected,[225] encounters dangers caused by friends; experiences a sudden end to a friendship
House XII	has dangerous and violent enemies; has many unfortunate adventures and scandals; if adversely aspected,[226] has self-destructive or destructive tendencies; has fanatical tendencies[227]

Jupiter (♃) in the Various Houses

The fifth planet of the solar system, Jupiter orbits the Sun at a distance of about 483,300,000 miles, completing its cycle through the zodiac signs once every 11 years, 315 days. Its occupation of a particular house enhances its influence as follows:

220. See note 155, page 414.
221. Some practitioners also believe this position indicates that death comes quickly through a short sickness, shock, or an accident. If Mars (♂) is positioned in Cancer (♋), Scorpio (♏), or Pisces (♓), death by drowning is possible. If it is positioned in Gemini (♊), Aquarius (♒), or Libra (♎), death may occur through insanity or in an aerial accident. If it is positioned in Leo (♌), Sagittarius (♐), or Aries (♈), death is caused by fire, violence, or accident. If it is positioned in Taurus (♉), Virgo (♍), or Capricorn (♑), death occurs through disease or inflammation.
222. See note 155, page 414
223. If Mars (♂) forms a trine (△) or a sextile (⚹) with any planet, or if it forms a conjunction (☌) or parallel (// or #) with any planet except Uranus (♅) or Neptune (♆) (see "Locating Planetary Aspects and Constructing an Aspectarian"), the person could become a successful attorney or self-help advocate. If Mars (♂) forms a square (□) or opposition (☍) with any planet, the individual might become a religious fanatic, encounter disagreements with relatives, or suffer a violent death while traveling abroad.
224. See note 155, page 414.
225. Ibid.
226. Ibid.
227. According to some practitioners, death occurs in seclusion, while in restraint, or during imprisonment.

House I   logical; broad-minded; confident; optimistic; has executive talents; experiences good fortune; if adversely aspected,[228] excessive; lazy; unable to commit to anything

House II   financially successful in large, popular enterprises or the fields of government, law, insurance, banking, religion, science, education, literature, or commercial travel; if adversely aspected,[229] is a spendthrift; overly optimistic about speculative ventures or gambling

House III   experiences gains through advertising, publishing, writing, communications, public speaking, intellectual pursuits, or siblings; if adversely aspected,[230] is overly optimistic about communications

House IV   gains through land or father; succeeds close to home, birthplace, or family surroundings; if adversely aspected,[231] loses land through family and poor investment

House V   encounters good fortune or comfort through children; has pleasant love affairs; gains through teaching; if adversely aspected,[232] has no desire for serious romance; experiences financial problems through children[233]

House VI   experiences good health or medical treatment; is a positive healing source for others; succeeds in employment; if adversely aspected,[234] has problems with employees or co-workers; has difficulties with health

House VII   benefits from partnership or marriage; succeeds in lawsuits; if adversely aspected,[235] encounters financial losses through spouse or partners

---

228.   See note 155, page 414.
229.   Ibid.
230.   Ibid.
231.   Ibid.
232.   Ibid.
233.   For a woman, this location portends an attraction to a financially or socially secure person from a respectable profession, as well as the possibility of numerous children. For a man, this position promises success and gain through speculative enterprises such as stocks, bonds, securities, theatrical ventures, or amusements.
234.   See note 155, page 414.
235.   Ibid.

House VIII	gains through legacy, litigation, or other people's money; if adversely aspected,[236] loses lawsuits[237]
House IX	has profitable journeys abroad; has profitable relations with foreigners; succeeds through religious, educational, legal, philosophic, or philanthropic pursuits; if adversely aspected,[238] loses through foreigners; loses while traveling abroad; lacks mental application
House X	has a successful career; encounters many professional opportunities; receives honors and promotions; if adversely aspected,[239] loses business, professional, or social status
House XI	has fortunate friendships; makes friends with legislators, senators, judges, bankers, doctors, and professors; if adversely aspected,[240] experiences financial losses or disappointments through friends
House XII	succeeds around the age of forty or fifty; lives in seclusion and solitude; is protected during troubled times; if adversely aspected,[241] has difficulties with the law or finances; has a disregard for life or other people

Saturn (♄) in the Various Houses

The sixth planet of the solar system, Saturn orbits the Sun at a distance of about 886,000,000 miles, completing its cycle through the zodiac signs once every 28 years. Its occupation of a particular house enhances its influence as follows:

House I	lives a calculated, almost premeditated existence; is highly self-centered; if adversely aspected,[242] is introverted; does not enjoy life
House II	financial security is acquired through great effort and time; constantly frustrated over the acquisition or accumulation of money; if adversely aspected,[243] experiences self-denial; encounters serious financial loss

---

236. Ibid.
237. Happy dreams and a peaceful death are sometime indicated in this position.
238. See note 155, page 414.
239. Ibid.
240. Ibid.
241. Ibid.
242. Ibid.
243. Ibid.

House III   his or her communications are calculated; if adversely as-
                   pected,[244] has difficulty with education; has trouble with sib-
                   lings or neighbors

House IV   acquires land or property; has a strict upbringing; encounters
                   domestic frustration; if adversely aspected,[245] is orphaned or
                   otherwise deprived as a child; experiences discomfort at home

House V   disappointed in romance; encounters unhappiness through
                   children; does not enjoy amusements; if adversely aspected,[246]
                   is infertile; has a painful separation from children

House VI   has a cold demeanor toward employees and co-workers; ex-
                   presses a strong organizational ability in the workplace; if ad-
                   versely aspected,[247] is disappointed with employee or co-worker
                   relationships; is disappointed with daily routine

House VII   experiences difficulties or frustrations in marriage or partner-
                   ship; if adversely aspected,[248] encounters the end of a marriage
                   through separation, divorce, or death; experiences deprivation
                   while in a partnership

House VIII   lacks legacy or inheritance; desires to live "out of body"; if ad-
                   versely aspected,[249] encounters delays in the receipt of a legacy;
                   possibly loses a legacy

House IX   experiences trouble while traveling abroad; encounters prob-
                   lems while dealing with foreigners; has strong spiritual or reli-
                   gious development; if adversely aspected,[250] suffers while
                   traveling abroad; suffers through relations with foreigners; has
                   fanatical tendencies toward religion or ideology

House X   ambition and power drive the person's social or professional
                   success; if adversely aspected,[251] is ruthlessly ambitious; experi-
                   ences professional or social isolation

---

244. Ibid.
245. Ibid.
246. Ibid.
247. Ibid.
248. Ibid.
249. Ibid.
250. Ibid.
251. Ibid.

House XI   relations with associations and friends are calculated or cold; if adversely aspected,[252] has few friendships due to exclusive attitude

House XII   sacrifice and denial are overcome through his or her courage and reason; if adversely aspected,[253] has a persecution complex; encounters ideological crises

Uranus (♅) in the Various Zodiac Signs and Houses

The seventh planet in the solar system, Uranus was discovered by the British astronomer William Herschel in 1781 while he was conducting a telescopic survey of the sky. Consequently this planet was not incorporated into the astrological processes employed by Chinese, Tibetan, Vedic, Arabian, or Judaic astrologers. Its interpretation is unique to the modern Western tradition, and it was not delineated by western astrologers until the nineteenth and twentieth centuries. Orbiting the sun at a distance of 1,783,000,000 miles, it completes its cycle through the zodiac signs once every 84 years. Its occupation of a particular zodiac sign and house enhances its influence as follows:

Aries (♈)   independent; positive; verbally blunt or abrupt; has remarkable mental and physical energy; appreciates machinery, electrical devices, and travel

Taurus (♉)   determined; intuitive; resourceful; has a very jealous spouse; has numerous financial highs and lows

Gemini (♊)   versatile; eccentric; ingenious; has telepathic or clairvoyant faculties; appreciates new ideas, unusual studies, travel, and inventions; befriends literary and scientific people

Cancer (♋)   sensitive; patriotic; psychic; restless; cranky; loves home and children, but has many difficulties in those areas; has many original ideas

Leo (♌)   industrious; forceful; strongly believes in physical moderation; very rebellious; independent; intolerant of orders or contradictions; has strange likes and dislikes; has an unusual love life; suffers many estrangements[254]

---

252. Ibid.
253. Ibid.
254. Some astrologers add that this person's children might also cause sorrow. The sudden loss of a child is possible.

Virgo (♍)	independent; stubborn; eccentric; capable of great subtlety and originality; appreciates science; succeeds with the occult
Libra (♎)	ambitious; quick-tempered; charismatic; has strong artistic abilities; succeeds in a scientific, literary, artistic, or judicial profession; marries too quickly
Scorpio (♏)	persistent; bold; shrewd; secretive; has strong powers of concentration; has an unbreakable spirit; is outspoken; encounters altercations with others; pursues the study of self-advancement, drugless healing, the occult, or mechanics
Sagittarius (♐)	inventive; well-educated; freedom-loving; has dreams, visions, and premonitions; fascinated by science and travel
Capricorn (♑)	serious; conservative; profound; has a penetrating mind; very ambitious; has a remarkable talent for forecasting business trends and public tastes; succeeds in public office, systems analysis, or methodology
Aquarius (♒)	resourceful; freedom-loving; ingenious; humanitarian; has eccentric beliefs; loves things that are novel and unusual; succeeds in science, public life, social movements, or large corporations
Pisces (♓)	appreciates anything mysterious or psychic; farsighted; serious; has a pessimistic streak; succeeds in the research and development of chemical compounds, medications, and new forms of clinical treatment
House I	possesses strong convictions; demands recognition and independence; if adversely aspected,[255] behaves erratically; encounters obstacles that inhibit his or her personal freedom[256]
House II	frequently experiences sudden strokes of good fortune; earns income or invests in radical or new ways; if adversely aspected,[257] has sudden strokes of bad luck; makes poor financial decisions

---

255. See note 155, page 414.
256. Some astrologers indicate that to avoid physical injury, care should be taken by this person near lightning, electricity, machinery, explosives, and vehicles.
257. See note 155, page 414.

House III	is fortunate in mental pursuits; has diplomatic relations with siblings and neighbors; if adversely aspected,[258] experiences accidents while running errands; is separated from siblings[259]
House IV	encounters many changes of residence; has an unsettled home live unless family life is strongly promoted; if adversely aspected,[260] is suddenly separated from parents; has drastic changes in home life
House V	engages in impulsive or clandestine love affairs; believes in unconventional child-rearing; if adversely aspected,[261] his or her love affairs abruptly end; dangerous accidents happen to his or her children[262]
House VI	is manually dexterous; is recognized as a decision-maker in the workplace; if adversely aspected,[263] has a weak nervous system; is separated from or disagrees with employees or co-workers; has an unpredictable attitude in the workplace; experiences work- or tool-related accidents
House VII	has an unconventional marriage or partnership; if adversely aspected,[264] has an unstable marriage or partnerships; will potentially divorce or separate from spouse; has sudden or unexpected changes in relationships[265]
House VIII	receives an unexpected inheritance or legacy; encounters sudden financial changes through other people; is suddenly responsible for other people's money; if adversely aspected,[266] loses inheritance or legacy[267]

---

258. Ibid.
259. This position sometimes indicates that the person has a gift for clairvoyance.
260. See note 155, page 414.
261. Ibid.
262. Astrologers sometimes indicate that in this respect, children generally are a source of trouble, as are any forms of speculation. In a woman's chart, this sometimes indicates unexpected pregnancy or abortion.
263. See note 155, page 414.
264. Ibid.
265. This could also indicate a marriage to a genius if Uranus (♅) forms a sextile (⚹) or trine (△) aspect with any planet.
266. See note 155, page 414.
267. Some practitioners also suggest that this person experiences an unexpected or unusual death connected with electronics, vehicles, violence, or rare nervous disorders.

House IX   takes long journeys in foreign lands; has a linguistic talent; desires to learn and discover; if adversely aspected,[268] has accidents while traveling long distances; has mistaken or misunderstood ideals

House X   experiences unexpected or sudden professional or social success; able to capitalize on professional or social situations; if adversely aspected,[269] experiences erratic professional or social changes; miscalculates situations

House IX   makes friends with unusual or remarkable people; if adversely aspected,[270] experiences sudden estrangements from friends due to impetuousness

House XII   has a detached and original view of life; if adversely aspected,[271] has suicidal tendencies; experiences accidents during surgical procedures; believes in dangerous ideologies

Neptune (♆) in the Various Zodiac Signs and Houses

The eighth planet in our solar system, Neptune was discovered in 1846 by John C. Adams and Urbain J. J. Leverier, who individually calculated its mathematical position. It was eventually sighted that same year by Johann G. Galle. Like Uranus, this planet was not incorporated into the astrological processes employed by Chinese, Tibetan, Vedic, Arabian, or Judaic astrologers; its interpretation is unique to the modern Western tradition. Orbiting the sun at a distance of 2,793,000,000 miles, it completes its cycle through the zodiac signs once every 165 years. Neptune was not delineated by Western astrologers until the twentieth century. Its occupation of a particular zodiac sign and house enhances its influence as follows:

Aries (♈)   intensely emotional; joins secret societies; popularizes psychic research; travels abroad; attracted to new or original concepts concerning spiritual or physical healing and institutional reforms

Taurus (♉)   an unrepentant nonconformist; gains through speculation or secret organizations; attracted to the occult, ancient spiritual practices, scientific knowledge, and the arts; succeeds in marriage and friendship

---

268.   See note 155, page 414.
269.   Ibid.
270.   Ibid.
271.   Ibid.

Gemini (♊)	sensitive; genial; imaginative; highly impressionable; is well versed in the arts, philosophy, and the occult
Cancer (♋)	refined; idealistic; emotional; imaginative; endowed with psychic abilities; loves nature, science, home, and travel by water; experiences a change of residence that instigates an unusual occurrence
Leo (♌)	quiet; ambitious; charitable; loves the fine arts; has a keen intuition; has unusual sensations; engages in mysterious love affairs
Virgo (♍)	intelligent; reserved; has mathematical and psychic abilities; is fanatical about hygiene, health, or work; enjoys gardening and pets
Libra (♎)	compassionate; highly imaginative; loves the arts; enjoys friendship and marriage; attracted to the occult, magic, the cinema, and social equity
Scorpio (♏)	inventive; sensitive; secretive; interested in chemistry or science; has occult experiences
Sagittarius (♐)	ambitious; reverent; farsighted; travels a great deal; is endowed with prophetic visions about business, art, science, religion, foreign affairs, literature, or psychic research
Capricorn (♑)	cautious, yet fearless; has strong psychic powers; experiences bouts of depression; has family troubles during youth; benefits from the arts, corporations, and institutions
Aquarius (♒)	intuitive; perceptive; independent; has eccentric religious or scientific views; has an affinity for nature and for humanity
Pisces (♓)	quiet; serious; contemplative; has psychic abilities; has an inspirational nature; attracted to travel over water
House I	susceptible to surroundings; has artistic or psychic sensibility; if adversely aspected,[272] experiences identity crises
House II	encounters financial fluctuations; if adversely aspected, experiences chaotic financial states[273]

---

272. Ibid.

273. If the planet forms a conjunction (☌), sextile (⚹), trine (△), or parallel (∥ or ⚻) aspect (see "Locating Planetary Aspects and Constructing an Aspectarian"), this position promises financial success in speculation or investment.

House III	has a literary talent that blooms under a nom de plume; if adversely aspected,[274] is overly influenced by social surroundings; a sibling experiences mental illness
House IV	encounters many changes of residence; has a restless home or domestic life; if adversely aspected,[275] is unable to make a home anywhere; has a traumatic family life
House V	engages in unusual sexual experiences; has complicated relationships with children; if adversely aspected,[276] experiences deception in romance; has illegitimate children
House VI	is restless about daily routines; cleverly organizes work environment; if adversely aspected,[277] has infectious diseases; has chemical allergies; has skin or nervous diseases; experiences work constraints[278]
House VII	restlessness affects marriage or partnerships; if adversely aspected,[279] experiences deception or betrayal in marriage or partnership
House VIII	has a great talent at handling other people's money or inheritance; has acute psychological sensitivity; if adversely aspected,[280] loses legacy; encounters danger from water or infection[281]
House IX	travels abroad a great deal; has a strong desire to learn; if adversely aspected,[282] encounters danger on long journeys; has confused ideology
House X	has an unstable career or profession; if adversely aspected,[283] scandal or chaos surrounds the person's professional life[284]

---

274. See note 155, page 414.
275. Ibid.
276. Ibid.
277. Ibid.
278. Practitioners commonly advise people with this position to avoid narcotics and opiates at all costs. Similarly, food and clothing received from a sick person or someone who has undesirable habits should be avoided.
279. See note 155, page 414.
280. Ibid.
281. This position may foretell an unusual demise, possibly on the water or in conjunction with poisons, opiates, or anesthetics. If afflicted by the Moon, there is a danger of madness or total alienation.
282. See note 155, page 414.
283. Ibid.
284. According to some astrologers, it also indicates that one of the person's parents might die while he or she is a child, leaving an inheritance.

House XI   has friends who are disruptive influences; if adversely aspected,[285] has friends who are destructive influences

House XII   succeeds in spiritual or intellectual evolution; if adversely aspected,[286] experiences crisis over spiritual or intellectual development; encounters danger from epidemics

Pluto (♇ or ♇) in the Various Zodiac Signs and Houses

Pluto is the ninth planet in our solar system. It was discovered by Percival Lowell, who calculated its mathematical position in 1915, and sighted by Clyde W. Tombaugh, who first observed its movements in 1929. Consequently this planet was not incorporated into the astrological processes employed by Chinese, Tibetan, Vedic, Arabian, or Judaic astrologers; its interpretation is unique to the modern Western tradition, and it was not delineated by Western astrologers until the mid-twentieth century. Located 3,666,000,000 miles from the Sun, Pluto completes its orbital cycle through the zodiac signs once ever 248 years, and its occupation of a particular zodiac sign and house enhances its influence as follows:

Aries (♈)   has revolutionary and eccentric concepts about politics, society, the economy, or science

Taurus (♉)   tries to improve the general quality of life; develops new industrial, financial, and architectural inventions

Gemini (♊)   experiences breakthroughs in communications, transportation, and electronics; has a strong interest in regional or local traditions and in psychoanalytical investigations

Cancer (♋)   encounters dictatorships, racism, and the decentralization of traditions (including home and family); experiences the invention of labor-saving appliances and family planning methods

Leo (♌)   encounters an emphasis on leisure, entertainment, electronically oriented media, and the centralization of information, government, and administrative systems

Virgo (♍)   experiences increased computerization and specialization of work, as well as the advent of health, sanitation, and environmental improvements

---

285. See note 155, page 414.
286. Ibid.

Libra (♎)	encounters the reformation of sexual mores and gender-specific expectations, as well as the modification of laws and the application of new media
Scorpio (♏)	experiences increased military conflicts, extended human longevity, the use of biological warfare, and a possible breakthrough in psychic research
Sagittarius (♐)	experiences a global comprehension of ethnic diversity, desire to travel abroad; experiences a revival of religious consciousness; encounters educational or publishing innovations
Capricorn (♑)	experiences the instigation of rebellions against authority and government that lead to social and labor reforms
Aquarius (♒)	experiences an increased interest in social reforms, humanitarian reforms, electronics, or astronomy
Pisces (♓)	intensely interested in the fine arts, religion, philosophy, mystic arts, dreams, or the care of the mentally or physically afflicted
House I	desires dominance; if adversely aspected,[287] is power-hungry; has unexpressed psychological blocks
House II	experiences gains from speculation or inheritance; if adversely aspected,[288] encounters financial losses through risky or illegal ventures[289]
House III	attracted to psychoanalysis and criminology; dominates siblings; if adversely aspected,[290] encounters danger in social surroundings or while running errands
House IV	has a deep attachment to family and home; if adversely aspected,[291] experiences adversity in the parental home; unable to assert independence at home[292]

---

287. Ibid.
288. Ibid.
289. This location also indicates success in waste recycling, environmental clean-up, and sanitation businesses; occupations that deal with death such as funeral director, mortician, casket maker, or hearse driver; or investigative professions that delve into psychological motives, geology, or medical research.
290. See note 155, page 414.
291. Ibid.
292. This indication is even stronger if Pluto (♇) occupies Cancer (♋).

House V	obsessed with secret or complex love affairs; highly creative; if adversely aspected,[293] discovers that pleasures become vices; encounters dangers for his or her children; engages in destructive romances
House VI	dominates the workplace or daily routine; if adversely aspected,[294] experiences health risks in the workplace[295]
House VII	dominates the marriage or partnership; if adversely aspected,[296] self-destructive; has a destructive marriage or partnership[297]
House VIII	attracted to death and the concept of regeneration; experiences gains through inheritance or legacy; if adversely aspected,[298] encounters intrigues associated with legacy; may experience a mysterious death in a hidden place
House IX	fascinated with radical religious or philosophic beliefs; desires to develop radical ideologies; if adversely aspected,[299] influenced by dangerous ideologies; encounters danger through difficult situations in foreign places or with foreigners
House X	desires power; succeeds through unconventional means; if adversely aspected,[300] loses social or professional status; uses deception or illegal means to gain status or honor
House XI	establishes friendships based on psychological affinities; has secret friendships; if adversely aspected,[301] has destructive friendships or associations
House XII	intensely desires privacy and secretiveness; has a strong talent for psychological research; if adversely aspected,[302] tends to make enemies; instigates scandals or is the victim of scandals

---

293. See note 155, page 414.
294. Ibid.
295. He or she is susceptible to rare or unusual illnesses, particularly related to the bloodstream, and relies on unusual treatments for a cure.
296. See note 155, page 414.
297. If this position forms a trine ($\triangle$), sextile ($\ast$), or sometimes a conjunction (σ) or parallel (// or #) (see "Locating Planetary Aspects"), this same person dissolves the union and applies wisdom to the next relationship.
298. See note 155, page 414.
299. Ibid.
300. Ibid.
301. Ibid.
302. Ibid.

When all the planetary positions and house rulerships have been interpreted, the aspects (see "Locating Planetary Aspects and Constructing an Aspectarian") formed by the various planets are then delineated and incorporated into a synthesized interpretation.

Step Fourteen: Delineating Planetary Aspects

As mentioned earlier in this chapter, the aspects formed by planetary positions within a chart and recorded in an Aspectarian (figs. 8.4 and 8.5) are reviewed for the influences each might exert within the chart. (These include a conjunction [☌], an opposition [☍], a trine [△], a square [□], a sextile [⚹], and a parallel [//].) These aspects are generally interpreted as follows:

Aspects Formed with the Sun (☉)

Moon(☽) (☽△☉, ☽⚹☉)[303] strengthens the physical constitution; experiences success, promotion, and prosperity; gets help from influential people; profits from investments, speculation, and enterprise[304]

(☉□☽, ☉☍☽, ☉☌☽, ☉ // ☽) has financial problems; has a hard time keeping a job or saving money because overconfidence and ego lead to disappointment; has difficulty through women[305]

Mercury (☿)[306] (☉☌☿, ☉ // ☿) has a strong business aptitude; ambitious; intelligent; desires to observe and learn

303. As mentioned earlier in this chapter, this same interpretation would apply even if the planets were transposed. In other words, ☉△☽ and ☉⚹☽ would be delineated in the same manner as ☽△☉ and ☽⚹☉.
304. Combined with a trine (△), sextile (⚹), or conjunction (☌) with Jupiter (♃), it indicates wealth and a good marriage.
305. Ill health and a weak constitution are exacerbated into a long and serious illness if Saturn (♄) forms a square (□) or opposition (☍). A Sun-Moon conjunction (☉☌☽) is adverse if there is also a square (□) or opposition (☍) to Mars (♂), Uranus (♅), or Saturn (♄). Since this particular aspect occurs monthly, the person might experience depleted energy or indecisiveness at those times.
306. The maximum distance (elongation) between Mercury (☿) and the Sun (☉) is 28°00′. Since this distance is so narrow, Mercury (☿) cannot form a major angle other than a conjunction (☌) or parallel (//) to this planet. It can form a semi-sextile (⚺) or a semi-square (∠) to the Sun (☉), but these are rarely used by Western astrologers in chart interpretation.

Venus (♀)[307]   (☉ ☌ ♀, ☉ // ♀) receives financial gains from business, profession, speculation, or public occupation; creativity, popularity, and promotion; has musical, operatic, or artistic talent[308]

Mars (♂)   (☉ ☌ ♂, ☉ // ♂, ☉ △ ♂, ☉ ✶ ♂) improves health, vitality, determination, leadership ability, and confidence[309]

(☉ ☐ ♂, ☉ ☍ ♂) discovers that hasty behavior creates many highs and lows; encounters deaths, separations, litigation, and enmities that produce obstacles; encounters danger from accidents, fires, fevers, surgery, acute illness, cuts, burns, and scalds[310]

Jupiter (♃)   (☉ ☌ ♃, ☉ // ♃, ☉ △ ♃, ☉ ✶ ♃) improves chances for success and good fortune; experiences gains through influential friends, transportation, inventions, investment, large theatrical productions, sports, transportation, publishing, or electronics[311]

(☉ ☐ ♃, ☉ ☍ ♃) encounters financial losses by miscalculation, extravagance, or bad advice; has a weakened constitution later in life[312]

Saturn (♄)   (☉ ☌ ♄, ☉ // ♄, ☉ △ ♄, ☉ ✶ ♄) succeeds through personal efforts and a strong personality; experiences gains through mineral rights and mining, investments, or industry

---

307.   The maximum distance (elongation) between Venus (♀) and the Sun (☉) is 48°00′. Since this distance is so narrow, Venus (♀) cannot form a major angle other than a conjunction (☌) or parallel (//) to the Sun (☉). It can form a semi-sextile (⚺) or a semi-square (∠) to the Sun (☉), but these are rarely used by Western astrologers in chart interpretation.

308.   A conjunction (☌) indicates positive outcomes to love and marriage, even when there are negative aspects affecting those areas.

309.   If Mars (♂) or the Sun (☉) is in an air sign, it accentuates the intellect even further. Located in House I, IV, VII, or X, it positively emphasizes executive and leadership qualities.

310.   If Mars (♂) is in Capricorn (♑) or if the Sun (☉) is accidentally dignified it lightens this prognostication.

311.   This is considered to be especially true if Uranus (♅) forms a trine (△), sextile (✶), conjunction (☌), or parallel (//) in the same chart. In a woman's chart, this indicates a successful marriage or love affair. If Saturn (♄) forms a trine (△), sextile (✶), conjunction (☌), or parallel (//) in the same chart, there are gains from investment, inheritance, or gold. If Mars (♂) forms a trine (△), sextile (✶), conjunction (☌), or parallel (//) in the same chart, it is not good for saving money but does improve industrial success. If Venus (♀) forms a trine (△), sextile (✶), conjunction (☌), or parallel (//) in the same chart, however, it indicates good luck and gains from the arts, entertainment, and refinements. If Mercury (☿) forms a trine (△), sextile (✶), conjunction (☌), or parallel (//) in the same chart, it indicates gains through science, art, traveling, writings and publishing. If the Moon (☽) forms a trine (△), sextile (✶), conjunction (☌), or parallel (//) in the same chart, it improves any business dealings with the public or shipping.

312.   If the Moon (☽) forms a trine (△), sextile (✶), conjunction (☌), or parallel (//) in the same chart, it will lighten this indication, but the outcome remains the same. In a woman's chart, it signifies a good, but unlucky spouse.

(☉ □ ♄, ☉ ☍ ♄) has health and business problems; experiences disappointment and delays that spoil opportunities for success; experiences the death or estrangement of his or her father[313]

Uranus (♅)   (☉ ☌ ♅, ☉ // ♅, ☉ △ ♅, ☉ ✶ ♅) succeeds with inventions, public service, research, exploration, adventure, transportation, or electronics; improves longevity; benefits from the occult and astrology; marries early

(☉ □ ♅, ☉ ☍ ♅) has an unfortunate marriage; loses through friends, disasters, love affairs, partnerships, accidents involving machines, storms, or transportation

Neptune (♆)   (☉ ☌ ♆, ☉ // ♆, ☉ △ ♆, ☉ ✶ ♆) loves the arts and refined pleasures; receives benefits through mystical and spiritual subjects[314]

(☉ □ ♆, ☉ ☍ ♆) has lax or unconventional morals; has unusual romances; is a victim of scandal or fraud; has problems with children; experiences financial losses due to unsound speculation

Pluto (♇)   (☉ ☌ ♇, ☉ // ♇, ☉ △ ♇, ☉ ✶ ♇) has influence over other people; is able to modify self in order to attain personal goals[315]

(☉ □ ♇, ☉ ☍ ♇) ruthlessly dominates others; determined to attain goals and willing to use unethical means

Aspects Formed with the Moon (☽)

Sun (☉)   See "Aspects Formed with the Sun," page 436.

Mercury (☿)   (☿ ☌ ☽, ☿ // ☽, ☿ △ ☽, ☿ ✶ ☽) has a talent for speaking or writing;[316] has an interest in new ideas, art, music, literature, or travel

---

313. In a woman's chart, it signifies marital problems, no marriage, the husband's death, or marriage to a widower. If Saturn (♄) occupies Cancer (♋), Scorpio (♏), or Pisces (♓), the spouse has alcoholic tendencies or problems with drug addiction or infidelity.

314. If Mercury (☿) is situated close to the Ascendant (House I); located in House I, IV, VII, or X; or forms a trine (△), sextile (✶), conjunction (☌), or parallel (//) to the Sun (☉) or Neptune (♆) in the same chart, the person can inspire people through speaking or writing, and has a talent for playing stringed instruments.

315. If Pluto (♇) forms a conjunction (☌) or a parallel (//) with the Sun (☉), this drive may be overwhelming or used selfishly.

316. This is considered especially prevalent if either planet is positioned in Gemini (♊), Libra (♎), or Aquarius (♒).

(☿□☽,☿☍☽) anxious; worried; cynical; has occasional physical debilities; experiences business losses and legal problems

Venus (♀)

(♀☌☽,♀∥☽,♀△☽,♀⚹☽) appreciates the arts, literature, and social functions; is popular with the public and parents; encounters professional or social success; has a frugal nature; is financially successful[317]

(♀□☽,♀☍☽) his or her fickle nature creates romantic, marital, or partnership problems that lead to financial or property losses; suffers from scandal or slander, even if undeserved[318]

Mars (♂)

(♂☌☽,♂∥☽,♂△☽,♂⚹☽) strengthens the person's physical health; has increased energy and activity; experiences business and personal success due to hard work, common sense, and quick actions[319]

(♂□☽,♂☍☽) learns from experience that indiscreet words and actions create enemies; loses opportunities; has poor health that affects the head, eyes, breasts, stomach, or sex organs; is careless; has disregard for others, which precipitates criticism and scandals; sorrow stems from maternal sources[320]

Jupiter (♃)

(♃☌☽,♃∥☽,♃△☽,♃⚹☽) succeeds in literature, publishing, land, mineral rights and mining, education, religion, philosophy, spiritual affairs, the occult, or long journeys; experiences increased imagination and intuition; has improved chances for financial acquisition, marital happiness, good health, and gain from family or maternal sources

(♃□☽,♃☍☽) trusts the wrong people; discovers too late that deceptive actions create slander and false accusations; is predisposed to losses in speculation, gambling, and high-risk ventures; changes and travel are troublesome[321]

---

317. This aspect is beneficial if one of the planets is situated in House II, IV, or VII.
318. In a woman's chart, this indicates potential periodic health problems.
319. If legacies are indicated in the chart, this increases their potential, particularly if the source is maternal. This aspect also improves the house the Moon (☽) occupies, as well as House IV itself.
320. In a women's chart, poor health and menstrual cycles are also indicated. Care should be taken while boating or swimming.
321. In a woman's chart, this aspect is unfortunate for health. Problems center around the stomach, liver, or bloodstream. Tumors are also possible.

Saturn (♄)   (♄ ☌ ☽, ♄ // ☽, ♄ △ ☽, ♄ ✱ ☽) professional advancement occurs because of personal persistence; receives approval by those
in authority and by friends; lands, mineral rights and mining,
and agriculture are sources of profit[322]

(♄ ☐ ☽, ♄ ☍ ☽) is plagued by persecution, poverty, and
struggle; speculation, lands, agriculture, and gambling are
poor ventures; worry, anxiety, and despondency should be
mollified through exercise and activity rather than through
overindulgence[323]

Uranus (♅)   (♅ △ ☽, ♅ ✱ ☽) receives benefits from astrology and the occult; has an aptitude for healing and telepathy; benefits from
changes of residence and travel; learns that a strong imagination stimulates beneficial improvements, especially if it entails
electronics or computers

(♅ ☌ ☽, ♅ // ☽, ♅ ☐ ☽, ♅ ☍ ☽) experiences unlucky changes
of residence and journeys; the occult, the opposite sex, and unreliable friends cause great difficulties; has unusual likes and
dislikes; experiences mental disturbance, stomach distress, or
gastrointestinal problems

Neptune (♆)   (♆ △ ☽, ♆ ✱ ☽) has psychic ability; attracted to the mysterious, the occult, and psychic phenomena[324]

(♆ ☌ ☽, ♆ // ☽, ♆ ☐ ☽, ♆ ☍ ☽) attracted to unusual or unconventional people and things; has an eccentric nature[325]

Pluto (♇)   (♇ △ ☽, ♇ ✱ ☽) able to make the best of any situation; displays
great resilience and emotional sensitivity to people and conditions, providing a subtle form of inspiration in stressful times

---

322. If Jupiter (♃) forms a trine (△), sextile (✱), conjunction (☌), or parallel (//) in the same chart, wealth is possible; if the Sun (☉) forms a trine (△), sextile (✱), conjunction (☌), or parallel (//) in the same chart, professional prominence is probable.

323. If the Moon (☽) or Saturn (♄) is in Gemini (♊), Virgo (♍), Pisces (♓), or Sagittarius (♐), this person marries more than once. If not, he or she may not marry at all, or will not marry well. This aspect is tempered if the Sun (☉), Jupiter (♃), Mars (♂), or Venus (♀) forms a trine (△), sextile (✱), conjunction (☌), or parallel (//) in the same chart.

324. For men, this aspect improves the potential for making a good marriage. If Venus (♀) or Mercury (☿) forms a trine (△), sextile (✱), conjunction (☌), or parallel (//) in the same chart, art, music, singing, writing, speaking or acting that appeal to public tastes are favored, as are water-based activities (swimming, boating, shipping, etc.).

325. Indiscretion creates misfortune with the opposite sex and obstacles to marriage in a man's chart. Ill health is indicated, especially if the Moon (☽) or Neptune (♆) is in Cancer (♋), Scorpio (♏), or Pisces (♓). Physical disorders to the brain and nerves (Gemini [♊], Sagittarius [♐], Virgo [♍], or Pisces [♓]), glands (Taurus [♉], Leo [♌], Scorpio [♏], or Aquarius [♒]), and circulation (Aries [♈], Cancer [♋], Libra [♎], or Capricorn [♑]) are caused by an overreaction to surroundings.

(♆ ☌ ☽, ♆ // ☽, ♆ □ ☽, ♆ ☍ ☽) is prejudiced and overly sensitive; a severe, internalized emotional trauma periodically erupts into fits of violence, loss of self-control or self-discipline[326]

Aspects Formed with Mercury (☿)

Sun (☉) See "Aspects Formed with the Sun," page 436.

Moon (☽) See "Aspects Formed with the Moon," page 438.

Venus (♀)[327] (♀ ☌ ☿, ♀ // ☿) very attractive to and popular with the opposite sex; profits from speaking, writing, art, manual dexterity, or entertainment;[328] easily acquires money, property, and possessions; marriage occurs twice in a lifetime, or spouse is a cousin

Mars (♂) (♂ ☌ ☿, ♂ // ☿, ♂ △ ☿, ♂ ⚹ ☿) applies immense energy to music, design, art, chemistry, medicine, or engineering; educators, professionals, scientists, and literary people aid in personal development

(♂ □ ☿, ♂ ☍ ☿) extremely intelligent; sarcastic states caused by lack of sleep and rest, overwork, or boredom; experiences opposition from authority figures, parents, neighbors, and even employees; is accident- and addiction-prone

Jupiter (♃) (♃ ☌ ☿, ♃ // ☿, ♃ △ ☿, ♃ ⚹ ☿) experiences general success in the house Jupiter occupies,[329] especially in literature, science, profession, religion, or government; experiences both change and travel

(♃ □ ☿, ♃ ☍ ☿) encounters difficulties because of an incomplete education or unrealized accomplishments; has travel-related accidents; scandals, misfortune, change, and journeys are related to speculation, contracts, writings, foreign affairs, or religion

---

326. This conjunction (☌) also creates moodiness and depression.

327. The maximum distance (elongation) between Venus (♀) and Mercury (☿) is only 20°00′. Since this distance is so narrow, Venus (♀) cannot form a major angle other than a conjunction (☌) or parallel (//) to Mercury (☿).

328. If Mercury (☿) is more prominent, wordsmithing, advertising, publishing, design, and travel are favored. If Venus (♀) is more prominent, then look to the theater, the arts, fashion, and performing arts.

329. Refer to fig. 8.6 for a breakdown of areas ruled by each of the twelve houses.

Saturn (♄)   (♄ ☌ ☿, ♄ // ☿, ♄ △ ☿, ♄ ⚹ ☿) scientific literary, or intellectual pursuits are favored;[330] succeeds with large corporations because of natural diplomacy and determination

(♄ □ ☿, ♄ ☍ ☿) experiences delays, disappointments, and obstacles; has an incomplete education; experiences difficulty in reading; has a poorly developed retentive memory; encounters setbacks resulting from forged letters and others' miscommunications; the death, separation, or illness of a sibling or father causes sorrows and problems[331]

Uranus (♅)   (♅ △ ☿, ♅ ⚹ ☿) inspires invention and eccentricity; is fond of the occult and astrology; is talented in advertising, publishing, writing, invention, research, or exploration[332]

(♅ □ ☿, ♅ ☍ ☿, ♅ ☌ ☿, ♅ // ☿) unsuccessful in literary pursuits; receives public criticism in the media; experiences difficulty through societies, friends, and kin; subject to travel-related accidents

Neptune (♆)   (♆ △ ☿, ♆ ⚹ ☿) able to develop mediumistic and psychic qualities; attracted to psychic centers; has prophetic dreams; succeeds in unconventional healing or hydrotherapy; has good experiences associated with liquids, chemicals, drugs, the sea, hospitals, and private institutions[333]

(♆ □ ☿, ♆ ☍ ☿, ♆ ☌ ☿, ♆ // ☿) has a poor memory; experiences periods of mental aberration; is absentminded and restless; experiences changes, slander, and deception; encounters danger through drugs

Pluto (♇)   (♇ ☌ ☿, ♇ // ☿, ♇ △ ☿, ♇ ⚹ ☿) adaptable; persuasive; able to dominate others mentally[334]

(♇ □ ☿, ♇ ☍ ☿) impatient; cynical; potentially fanatical; obsessive; preoccupied with death

---

330.   This is especially true/strong if Mercury (☿) is in House I, III, or IX.

331.   This is also a bad aspect for the teeth, causing decay. Poor circulation or digestion can, however, be diverted by an improved diet and exercise.

332.   Literary, scientific, or artistic success is possible if Uranus (♅) or Mercury (☿) is in House I, III, or IX.

333.   This combination is particularly strong if Neptune (♆) or Mercury (☿) occupies House III or House IX. If Venus forms a trine (△), sextile (⚹), conjunction (☌), or parallel (//) in the same chart, the subject will have a remarkable faculty for music, poetry, art, literature, inspiration.

334.   A conjunction (☌) indicates self-centeredness and the abuse of this power.

Aspects Formed with Venus (♀)

Sun (☉)	See "Aspects Formed with the Sun," page 436.
Moon (☽)	See "Aspects Formed with the Moon," page 438.
Mercury (☿)	See "Aspects Formed with Mercury," page 441.

Mars (♂) (♂☌♀, ♂ // ♀, ♂△♀, ♂✶♀) gains through sports, design ability, or artistic talent; acquires money but does not accumulate it; strengthens potential of inheritance; strengthens potential for an early or sudden marriage[335]

(♂□♀, ♂☍♀) is careless and extravagant; loses through fire; problems stem from marriage, partnerships, or jealous friends[336]

Jupiter (♃) (♃☌♀, ♃ // ♀, ♃△♀, ♃✶♀) loves beauty, elegance, and expensive environs; enjoys doing charitable acts; succeeds in love, marriage, and finances

(♃□♀, ♃☍♀) loves beauty and refinement, but cannot afford to fulfill desires; careless; a spendthrift; encounters romantic or marital problems resulting from infidelity; loses property in floods

Saturn (♄) (♄☌♀, ♄ // ♀, ♄△♀, ♄✶♀) experiences success and fidelity in marriage and love; tends to save money; gains through elders, superiors, and investments

(♄□♀, ♄☍♀) experiences disappointments in marriage or love until twenty-eight years old; age, finances, or social status cause marital problems; experiences loss through theft or avarice; encounters misfortunes through elders, parents, or relatives

Uranus (♅) (♅△♀, ♅✶♀) has a magnetic personality; experiences good fortune in business; gains by unusual or unexpected circumstances; is favored by the opposite sex, artists, inventors, or unusual people

(♅☌♀, ♅ // ♀, ♅☍♀, ♅□♀) has trouble that involves the opposite sex, including jealousy during marriage or a love

---

335. If Saturn (♄) forms a trine (△), sextile (✶), conjunction (☌), or parallel (//) in the same chart, this person will also accumulate assets.

336. If Venus (♀) or Mars (♂) is in Cancer (♋), Scorpio (♏), or Pisces (♓), the individual likes to overindulge in extravagant tastes or excess emotions.

affair; hastiness leads to divorce; experiences losses through unexpected circumstances

Neptune (♆)   (♆△♀, ♆✶♀) loves beauty and the arts; benefits from friendships, associations, or mystical interests; gains from trusts, institutions, seaside resorts, shipping, or liquids[337]
(♆☌♀, ♆//♀, ♆☍♀, ♆□♀) encounters trouble in love or
marriage due to spouse's instability or deception;[338] experiences
danger from excess gratification, food poisoning, theft, financial
schemes, and misplaced trust

Pluto (♇)   (♇☌♀, ♇//♀, ♇△♀, ♇✶♀) is emotionally attached to those
in distress or who are in the underdog position[339]
(♇□♀, ♇☍♀) has a jealous, possessive nature that destroys
relationships; fears emotional rejection

Aspects Formed with Mars (♂)

Sun (☉)   See "Aspects Formed with the Sun," page 436.

Moon (☽)   See "Aspects Formed with the Moon," page 438.

Mercury (☿)   See "Aspects Formed with Mercury," page 441.

Venus (♀)   See "Aspects Formed with Venus," page 443.

Jupiter (♃)   (♃☌♂, ♃//♂, ♃△♂, ♃✶♂) confident; determined; able to
inspire others to achieve personal goals; always willing to help
those who help themselves[340]
(♃□♂, ♃☍♂) experiences religious or political problems;
has difficulties during foreign travels; has physical problems
such as fevers, blood or liver malfunctions; encounters financial
losses from speculation, fires, the treachery of others, impulsiveness, accidents, and extravagance[341]

---

337. Success as a film actor is also considered if Venus (♀) or Neptune (♆) are posited in House V.
338. This is considered to be especially true if the planets are posited in Houses V, VII, or XII.
339. A conjunction (☌) between these two planets also indicates a strong sex drive.
340. If legacies are indicated, this aspect strengthens the potential.
341. A square (□) or opposition (☍) with Uranus (♅) causes losses due to electricity, floods, explosions, or lightning.

Saturn (♄) (♄ ☌ ♂, ♄ // ♂, ♄ △ ♂, ♄ ✶ ♂) is overbearing and somewhat reckless; learns that sustained determination achieves goals; discovers that success is coupled with danger[342]

(♄ □ ♂, ♄ ☍ ♂) encounters opposition, obstacles, financial losses, and scandals caused by rash or vengeful actions; experiences danger through wars, accidents, revolutions, and riots; has marital or partnership troubles[343]

Uranus (♅) (♅ △ ♂, ♅ ✶ ♂) unique achievements and talents place the person in the limelight; the person always gets his or her own way; gains from travel, investigation, transportation, politics, psychology, or astrology

(♅ □ ♂, ♅ ☍ ♂, ♅ ☌ ♂, ♅ // ♂) has a rebellious or defiant spirit that creates unfortunate events including imprisonment, explosions, accidents with firearms or machinery, and encounters with violence

Neptune (♆) (♆ △ ♂, ♆ ✶ ♂) benefits from liquids, marine-oriented activities, drugs, chemicals, the occult, and medical institutions

(♆ □ ♂, ♆ ☍ ♂, ♆ ☌ ♂, ♆ // ♂) has problems with self-indulgent habits, the opposite sex, fraud, drugs, or poisons; is in danger on the water; suffers from hallucinations or mental derangements[344]

Pluto (♇) (♇ △ ♂, ♇ ✶ ♂, ♇ ☌ ♂, ♇ // ♂) goals are achieved through hard work, self-confidence, a competitive spirit, and by attacking spontaneously[345]

(♇ □ ♂, ♇ ☍ ♂) has problems living within the social norm; acts irrationally; has violent and sadistic tendencies

Aspects Formed with Jupiter (♃)

Sun (☉) See "Aspects Formed with the Sun," page 436.

Moon (☽) See "Aspects Formed with the Moon," page 438.

---

342. This is a favorable aspect for paternal legacy.
343. According to some astrologers, this is an unfortunate aspect that signifies the death or separation of parents as well as problems with legacies. If either planet forms a trine (△), sextile (✶), conjunction (☌), or parallel (//) in the same chart, these prognostications are lightened, but still signify problems.
344. If Mars (♂) or Neptune (♆) forms a trine (△), sextile (✶), conjunction (☌), or parallel (//) in the same chart, this position is positively modified.
345. If it forms a conjunction (☌), the person might be ruthless.

Mercury (☿)   See "Aspects Formed with Mercury," page 441.

Venus (♀)   See "Aspects Formed with Venus," page 443.

Mars (♂)   See "Aspects Formed with Mars," page 444.

Saturn (♄)   (♄ △ ♃, ♄ ✶ ♃, ♄ ☌ ♃, ♄ // ♃) has the power to overcome problems; experiences general prosperity and improved reputation; gains from publishing, politics, religion, foreign travel, science, or medicine[346]

(♄ □ ♃, ♄ ☍ ♃) experiences financial, professional, or business losses; encounters trouble through neighbors, companies, or the father; faces difficulties related to floods, earthquakes, epidemics, or dishonesty

Uranus (♅)   (♅ △ ♃, ♅ ✶ ♃, ♅ ☌ ♃, ♅ // ♃) encounters success and gains through legacy, foreign travel, publishing, religion, politics, academic institutions, invention, or transportation; has prophetic foresight

(♅ □ ♃, ♅ ☍ ♃) experiences unforeseen problems in travel, publishing, religion, politics, education, transportation, or with legacy; experiences delayed achievement of ambitions; encounters losses through natural disasters, friends, or national decrees

Neptune (♆)   (♆ △ ♃, ♆ ✶ ♃, ♆ ☌ ♃, ♆ // ♃) dreams, visions, and psychic experiences are favored; succeeds in secret societies; gains from the sea or large medical institutions; inspires others

(♆ □ ♃, ♆ ☍ ♃) encounters troubles through secret societies, psychic experiences, or religion; experiences losses due to fraud; encounters dangers at sea or through liquids, water, or chemicals; keeps sorrows a secret

Pluto (♇)   (♇ △ ♃, ♇ ✶ ♃, ♇ ☌ ♃, ♇ // ♃) has natural leadership and inspirational qualities[347]

(♇ □ ♃, ♇ ☍ ♃) has unrealistic expectations and a vacillating or destructive self-image

---

346.   According to some practitioners, if the planets occupy Cancer (♋), Libra (♎), Capricorn (♑), or Aries (♈) or are located in House I, IV, VIII, or X, the person beneficially works for the public; if posited in Taurus (♉), Leo (♌), Scorpio (♏), or Aquarius (♒), the individual is involved in important projects. If the planets occupy House IV or VIII, paternal legacies and finances are favored.

347.   Some astrologers believe that this conjunction (☌) indicates fame and recognition because of the person's qualities.

Aspects Formed with Saturn (♄)

Sun (☉)	See "Aspects Formed with the Sun," page 436.
Moon (☽)	See "Aspects Formed with the Moon," page 438.
Mercury (☿)	See "Aspects Formed with Mercury," page 441.
Venus (♀)	See "Aspects Formed with Venus," page 443.
Mars (♂)	See "Aspects Formed with Mars," page 444.
Jupiter (♃)	See "Aspects Formed with Jupiter," page 445.

Uranus (♅)   (♅ △ ♄, ♅ ✶ ♄, ♅ ☌ ♄, ♅ // ♄) has an increased ability to concentrate; succeeds because of determination and foresight[348]
(♅ □ ♄, ♅ ☍ ♄) has a destructive or rebellious nature; experiences misfortune by misdirection; a chronic or incurable illness might arise in a body part governed by the zodiac sign Saturn occupies;[349] experiences troubles associated with falls, falling objects, collisions, natural disasters, riots, or uprisings

Neptune (♆)   (♆ △ ♄, ♆ ✶ ♄, ♆ ☌ ♄, ♆ // ♄) succeeds through self-development, investigation, the occult, the sea, liquids, legacies, or the stock market
(♆ □ ♄, ♆ ☍ ♄) loses through bad timing, lack of action, treachery, or misunderstanding; experiences health problems due to poor dietary habits

Pluto (♇)   (♇ △ ♄, ♇ ✶ ♄, ♇ ☌ ♄, ♇ // ♄) is capable of enduring extreme austerity and exerting extreme self-discipline[350]
(♇ □ ♄, ♇ ☍ ♄) lust, jealousy, and domination are personal driving forces; the person might resort to self-exile; has destructive tendencies

---

348.   If the planets are situated in beneficial zodiac signs and form favorable aspects such as a trine (△) or sextile (✶), success is connected with railroads, electronics, inventions, steam, aluminum, platinum, lead, coal, or large public institutions. If the Sun (☉) or Moon (☽) form a trine (△) or sextile (✶), this formation improves longevity.

349.   Aries (♈) rules the head and face. Taurus (♉) rules the neck, throat and ears. Gemini (♊) rules the hands, arms, shoulders, collarbone, lungs, and nervous system. Cancer (♋) rules the breast and stomach. Leo (♌) rules the heart, sides, and upper back. Virgo (♍) rules the solar plexus and bowels. Libra (♎) rules the kidneys, ovaries, and lower back. Scorpio (♏) rules the bladder and reproductive organs. Sagittarius (♐) rules the liver, hips, and thighs. Capricorn (♑) rules the knees. Aquarius (♒) rules the calves and ankles. Pisces (♓) rules the feet.

350.   According to some astrologers, the conjunction also indicates a period of despondency associated with this person's frugal nature.

Aspects Formed with Uranus (♅)

Sun (☉)   See "Aspects Formed with the Sun," page 436.

Moon (☽)   See "Aspects Formed with the Moon," page 438.

Mercury (☿)   See "Aspects Formed with Mercury," page 441.

Venus (♀)   See "Aspects Formed with Venus," page 443.

Mars (♂)   See "Aspects Formed with Mars," page 444.

Jupiter (♃)   See "Aspects Formed with Jupiter," page 445.

Saturn (♄)   See "Aspects Formed with Saturn," page 447.

Neptune (♆)   (♆ △ ♅, ♆ ⚹ ♅, ♆ ☌ ♅, ♆ ∥ ♅) has unusual or unexpected likes and dislikes; attracted to psychic centers and unique occupations; success is closely linked to the occult, the sea, or large institutions
                   (♆ □ ♅, ♆ ☍ ♅) prognostication is similar to the above, but danger can occur because of extremes or poor selection of a close friend

Pluto (♇)   (♇ △ ♅, ♇ ⚹ ♅, ♇ ☌ ♅, ♇ ∥ ♅) succeeds in science or metaphysics; has rebellious tendencies
                   (♇ □ ♅, ♇ ☍ ♅) has an interest in mystery; possesses an intellectual nature

Aspects Formed with Neptune (♆)

Sun (☉)   See "Aspects Formed with the Sun," page 436.

Moon (☽)   See "Aspects Formed with the Moon," page 438.

Mercury (☿)   See "Aspects Formed with Mercury," page 441.

Venus (♀)   See "Aspects Formed with Venus," page 443.

Mars (♂)   See "Aspects Formed with Mars," page 444.

Jupiter (♃)   See "Aspects Formed with Jupiter," page 445.

Saturn (♄)   See "Aspects Formed with Saturn," page 447.

Uranus (♅)   See "Aspects Formed with Uranus," above.

Pluto (♇)   (♇△♆, ♇⚹♆, ♇☌♆, ♇∥♆) has spiritual tendencies; de-
                   sires justice
                   (♇□♆, ♇☍♆) encounters problems through spiritual beliefs

Aspects Formed with Pluto (♇)

Sun (☉)   See "Aspects Formed with the Sun," page 436.

Moon (☽)   See "Aspects Formed with the Moon," page 438.

Mercury (☿)   See "Aspects Formed with Mercury," page 441.

Venus (♀)   See "Aspects Formed with Venus," page 443.

Mars (♂)   See "Aspects Formed with Mars," page 444.

Jupiter (♃)   See "Aspects Formed with Jupiter," page 445.

Saturn (♄)   See "Aspects Formed with Saturn," page 447.

Uranus (♅)   See "Aspects Formed with Uranus," page 448.

Neptune (♆)   See "Aspects Formed with Neptune," page 448.

CREATING A WESTERN PERSONALITY PROFILE

A Western horoscope is delineated in a manner similar to the process used to interpret the Vedic *rasicakra* and *bhavacakra*, as well as Judaic natal horoscopes. This includes determining the influence of the zodiac signs in the individual houses, the positions of the planets in various zodiac signs and houses, and the aspects formed by those positions. The material is generally grouped on a subject-by-subject basis for final analysis and presentation.

Since most subjects focus their questions on specific portions of their lives, the vast amount of interpretative material is broken down into eleven major sections (see below) to aid the practitioner during a consultation. This is the juncture when the astrologer's true talent comes to the fore, assessing the pluses and minuses of the data and deriving an accurate appraisal. Interpretation is not simply a matter of tallying the planetary aspects and looking up their meanings. No planetary aspect or position exists in a vacuum. An individual aspect or position cannot be analyzed fully without looking at the cumulative influences of the other elements in an individual's chart, any more than a hand could be studied without some mention of the body as a whole and its influence upon the hand itself. The development of a proper personality profile involves the synthesis of the whole chart and the analysis of the varied influences on each other and on each facet of the individual's existence.

Practitioners commonly focus on the following sectors: individuality and personality; finances and legacies; home life; pleasure, creativity, and children; marriage and partnership; health and death; voyages and journeys; education and mentality; occupation; friends and associates; and personal limitations and restrictions.

To understand this process, a summarized delineation of Alice T.'s and Peter C.'s charts (figs. 8.1 and 8.2) follows. The process shown in each step is the general procedure used by all Western astrologers. There are additional features that are reviewed by some practitioners, such as the interpretation of a planetary house ruler (see "Analyzing the Houses") and the effect of a planet's retrograde motion on an individual's natal horoscope, which are not demonstrated here. It would take volumes to present all of the intricacies that can be synthesized into a western personality profile. The material below does, however, best exemplify the scope and complexity of profile development.

Step Fifteen: Individuality and Personality

A person's inherent qualities, tendencies, and latent powers including the ability to acquire self-knowledge are all considered part of one's individuality. To uncover this information, the practitioner reviews the chart's overall shape (see "Assessing the Chart's Overall Shape") and predominant features (see "Analyzing the Predominant Features"). Then the placement of the Moon's Nodes and the Arabian Part of Fortune are interpreted (see "Reviewing the Moon's Nodes and the Part of Fortune"). Next, the placement of the Sun (☉) and the Moon (☽)—which represent general character traits and emotional makeup respectively—are interpreted according to the zodiac sign and house these entities occupy in the horoscope (see "Delineating Planetary Positions by House and by Sign" in this chapter as well as "Interpreting the House Rulers in the *Bhavacakra*" and "Interpreting the Planetary Positions in a *Rasicakra*" in chapter 5). Then the zodiac sign that governs the Ascendant (House I), which represents the individual's personality, is interpreted (see "Delineating House Rulerships" in this chapter, as well as "Interpreting the House Rulers in the *Bhavacakra*" in chapter 5). Any planets that occupy House I are interpreted according to their placement by zodiac sign and by house (see "Delineating Planetary Positions by House and by Sign" in this chapter, as well as "Interpreting the Planetary Positions in a *Rasicakra*" in chapter 5). Aspects formed by the Sun (☉), the Moon (☽), and any of the planets occupying House I are then synthesized into the interpretation (see "Delineating Planetary Aspects").

Alice's Personality

Overall shape. The locomotive shape (see "Assessing the Chart's Overall Shape") of Alice's chart (fig. 8.1) indicates that she is ambitious. She may seem slow to start a project, but will stick to the intended goal and ultimately achieve success. The leading planet (the first planet in the cluster's sequential clockwise order) indicates how and where her ambition is directed. The Moon (☽ in fig. 8.1) is Alice's leading planet. Because it is situated in House II, it suggests that she wants to acquire and accumulate money (see fig. 8.6). But because the planet is positioned below the horoscope's horizon (between Houses I through VI), she doesn't publicly reveal that goal until it is accomplished.

Houses of the chart. Alice has six out of ten planets in succedent houses (Houses II, V, and VIII in fig. 8.1) that stress her focus on personal finances (House II); creativity, speculation, or children (House V); and legacies, death, and other people's money (House VIII) (see "Analyzing the Houses").

Predominant Features. Alice has four planets in air signs (Gemini [♊] and Libra [♎]); three planets in water signs (Scorpio [♏] and Cancer [♋]); two in fire signs (Leo [♌] and Aries [♈]); and one in an earth sign (Taurus [♉]; see "Analyzing the Predominant Features"). This configuration is dominated by air signs, which indicates that she is mentally inclined, communicative, and somewhat restless or volatile. She has a tendency to intellectualize the material world; a desire for freedom; difficulty in maintaining an emotionally fulfilling relationship with another person; and an optimistic nature.

She has five planets in cardinal signs (one planet in Aries [♈], two planets in Cancer [♋], and two planets in Libra [♎]; see "Analyzing the Predominant Features"). This predominance of cardinal signs indicates that she derives her personal values from external circumstances. In other words, she adapts to the demands and expectations that either events or other people impose on a situation.

The planets occupying these signs also form a cardinal grand cross, which means that the planets form two oppositions (☍) and four squares (□) (see "Locating Planetary Aspects and Constructing an Aspectarian"). The Moon (☽ 11°♈28′ in fig. 8.1) forms an opposition to Neptune (♆ 18°♎59′ in fig. 8.1) within a 07°31′ orb of influence.[351] The Moon (☽ 11°♈28′ in fig. 8.1) also forms an opposition

---

351.   This aspect is determined by subtracting the difference between the two planetary positions as shown below:

Neptune (♆ 18°♎59′)	07	18°	59′	*(fig. 8.1)*
− Moon (☽ 11°♈28′)	01	11°	28′	*(fig. 8.1)*
	06	07°	31′	*(total to be converted)*
		187°	31′	*(opposition)*

The total is then subtracted from 180°00′ to determine the orb of influence.

to Saturn (♄ 08°♎12′ in fig. 8.1) within a 03°16′ orb of influence.[352] The Moon (☽ 11°♈28′ in fig. 8.1) also forms a square to Mercury (☿ 03°♋28′ in fig. 8.1) within an 08°00′ orb of influence.[353] The Moon (☽ 11°♈28′ in fig. 8.1) also forms a square to Uranus (♅ 13°♋00′ in fig. 8.1) within a 01°32′ orb of influence.[354] Mercury (☿ 03°♋28′ in fig. 8.1) forms a square to Saturn (♄ 08°♎12′ in fig. 8.1) within a 04°44′ orb of influence.[355] And Uranus (♅ 13°♋00′ in fig. 8.1) forms a square to Neptune (♆ 18°♎59′ in fig. 8.1) within a 05°59′ orb of influence.[356] This cardinal grand cross signifies that Alice is a dynamic problem-solver who needs to

352. This aspect is determined by subtracting the difference between the two planetary positions as shown below:

Saturn (♄ 08°♎12′)	07	08°	12′	*(fig. 8.1)*
	06	37°	72′	*(converted)*
– Moon (☽ 11°♈28′)	01	11°	28′	*(fig. 8.1)*
	05	26°	44′	*(total to be converted)*
		176°	44′	*(total)*

The total is then subtracted from 180°00′ to determine the orb of influence.

353. This aspect is determined by subtracting the difference between the two planetary positions as shown below:

Mercury (☿ 03°♋28′)	04	03°	28′	*(fig. 8.1)*
	03	33°	28′	*(converted)*
– Moon (☽ 11°♈28′)	01	11°	28′	*(fig. 8.1)*
	02	22°	00′	*(total to be converted)*
		82°	00′	*(total)*

The total is then subtracted from 90°00′ to determine the orb of influence.

354. This aspect is determined by subtracting the difference between the two planetary positions as shown below:

Uranus (♅ 13°♋00′)	04	13°	00′	*(fig. 8.1)*
	04	12°	60′	*(converted)*
– Moon (☽ 11°♈28′)	01	11°	28′	*(fig. 8.1)*
	03	01°	32′	*(total to be converted)*
		91°	32′	*(total)*

The total is then subtracted from 90°00′ to determine the orb of influence.

355. This aspect is determined by subtracting the difference between the two planetary positions as shown below:

Saturn (♄ 08°♎12′)	07	08°	12′	*(fig. 8.1)*
	07	07°	72′	*(converted)*
– Mercury (☿ 03°♋28′)	04	03°	28′	*(fig. 8.1)*
	03	04°	44′	*(total to be converted)*
		94°	44′	*(total)*

The total is then subtracted from 90°00′ to determine the orb of influence.

356. This aspect is determined by subtracting the difference between the two planetary positions as shown below:

Neptune (♆ 18°♎59′)	07	18°	59′	*(fig. 8.1)*
– Uranus (♅ 13°♋00′)	04	13°	00′	*(fig. 8.1)*
	03	05°	59′	*(total to be converted)*
		95°	59′	*(total)*

The total is then subtracted from 90°00′ to determine the orb of influence.

be in a constant state of action or motion toward a particular objective (see "Analyzing the Predominant Features").

The Moon's Nodes and the Part of Fortune. The Moon's North Node in House I of Alice's chart (☊ 23°♒23' in fig. 8.1) signifies that the vehicle or area in which Alice finds success or financial gain is found in her strong, self-expressive personality (see "Reviewing the Moon's Nodes and the Part of Fortune").

The Moon's South Node in House VII of Alice's chart (☋ 23°♌23' in fig. 8.1) indicates that the precise form of chaos she encounters in life stems from the sudden loss of her spouse. She also has many enemies and competitors. This same position, however, also portends the death or destruction of those opponents (see "Reviewing the Moon's Nodes and the Part of Fortune").

Alice's Part of Fortune (18°♏30') occupies House IX (see "The Part of Fortune" in chapter 6), which signifies that she reaps good fortune through churches, educational properties, foreigners, inventions, the occult, and books.

The Sun (☉) and the Moon (☽): Alice's Sun is in Gemini (☉ 24°♊55' in fig. 8.1), indicating that she is sensitive, intuitive, and youthful-looking. She has an active mind and is easily influenced by kindness. She is quick and efficient in emergencies, and needs to work independently on more than one project at a time. She succeeds in writing, research, or investigation (see "Delineating Planetary Positions by House and by Sign" in this chapter as well as "Interpreting the Planetary Positions in a *Rasicakra*" in chapter 5).

Alice's Moon is in Aries (☽ 11°♈28' in fig. 8.1), indicating that she is highly imaginative, self-reliant, and inventive. She has a restless mind and is quick-tempered and independent. She carves a unique path. She heads a major undertaking and reaches prominence during her lifetime (see "Delineating Planetary Positions by House and by Sign" in this chapter as well as "Interpreting the Planetary Positions in a *Rasicakra*" in chapter 5).

The Ascendant (House I). House I in Alice's chart is ruled by Aquarius (01°♒57' in fig. 8.1), signifying that she is highly opinionated. She hates change, but makes alterations without remorse. She has mental poise. It also suggests that she has a square jaw and a friendly face (see "Delineating House Rulerships" in this chapter as well as "Interpreting the House Rulers in the *Bhavacakra*" in chapter 5).

Planets occupying House I and their aspects. There are no planets occupying House I in Alice's chart. Therefore, no prognostications are made using this particular portion of the process.

Peter's Personality

Overall shape. The locomotive shape (see "Assessing the Chart's Overall Shape") of Peter's chart (fig. 8.2) indicates that he is ambitious. He may seem slow to start a project, but will stick to the intended goal and ultimately achieve success. The leading planet (the first planet in the cluster's sequential clockwise order) indicates how and where his ambition is directed. The Moon (☽ in fig. 8.2) is Peter's leading planet. Because it is situated in House II, he wants to acquire and accumulate money (fig. 8.6). But because the planet is positioned below the horoscope's horizon (between Houses I through VI), he doesn't publicly reveal that goal until it is accomplished.

Houses of the chart. Peter has four out of ten planets in succedent houses (Houses II, V, and VIII in fig. 8.2) that stress his focus on personal finances (House II); creativity, speculation, or children (House V); and legacies, death, and other people's money (House VIII) (see "Analyzing the Houses"). He also has four out of ten planets in angular houses (Houses IV and VII), which equally stress his focus on home life (House IV) and marriage (House VII) (see "Analyzing the Houses").

Predominant Features. Peter has six planets in earth signs (Virgo [♍] and Taurus [♉]); and four planets in water signs (Scorpio [♏], Cancer [♋], and Pisces [♓]) (see "Analyzing the Predominant Features"). This indicates that he has a conservative, withdrawn, and steady (although nervous) nature. Peter is practical, reserved, and reliable or miserly, materialistic, and rigid. Driven toward self-improvement as a means of self-expression, he strives for rewards in the physical world.

With five planets in mutable signs (four planets in Virgo [♍] and one planet in Pisces [♓]) (see "Analyzing the Predominant Features"), this configuration indicates that Peter is endowed with the ability to adapt to his surroundings. He can objectively learn and disseminate facts. He is totally uninvolved with self-evaluation. He adapts to and restricts the absorption of external influences without fixed or directed reasoning (see "Delineating the Predominant Features").

Most of the planets occupy Virgo (♍), which indicates he has an ability to critically analyze everything from a totally objective vantage point. This includes self-analysis. Consequently, he seeks the purest essence in all things: the most chaste or most excessive of every situation (see "Delineating the Predominant Features").

The Moon's Nodes and the Part of Fortune. The Moon's North Node in House IV of Peter's chart (☊ 29°♊40′ in fig. 8.2) signifies that the vehicle or area in which Peter finds success or financial gain is in home, in family, or through his father. This position also indicates that he will have a long and enjoyable life (see "Reviewing the Moon's Nodes and the Part of Fortune").

The Moon's South Node in House X of Peter's chart (☋ 29°♐40′ in fig. 8.2) indicates that the precise form of chaos he encounters in life stems from professional or occupational losses through deception, treachery, or through financial depressions, recessions, corporate takeovers, and stock failures (see "Reviewing the Moon's Nodes and the Part of Fortune").

Peter's Part of Fortune (01°♏46′) occupies House VIII (see "The Part of Fortune" in chapter 6), which signifies that his fortunes come from inheritance, other people's money, and from the dead.

The Sun (☉) and the Moon (☽).   Peter's Sun is in Virgo (☉ 04°♍41′ in fig. 8.2), indicating that he is frugal, practical, contemplative, industrious, and youthful-looking. He is a perfectionist who worries, desires wealth, and has a sharp temper, but abhors fighting and has a strong command of language. He is able to learn quickly and has a high endurance level (see "Delineating Planetary Positions by House and by Sign" in this chapter as well as "Interpreting the Planetary Positions in a *Rasicakra*" in chapter 5).

Peter's Moon is in Taurus (☽ 03°♉38′ in fig. 8.2), indicating that he is conservative, determined, and stubborn. He is driven by love, marriage, and friendship. His finances are aided by the opposite sex (see "Delineating Planetary Positions by House and by Sign" in this chapter as well as "Interpreting the Planetary Positions in a *Rasicakra*" in chapter 5).

The Ascendant (House I).   House I in Peter's chart is ruled by Pisces (02°♓49′ in fig. 8.2), signifying that he is self-sacrificing, compassionate, and ambivalent. It also indicates that he might have small hands and feet (see "Delineating House Rulerships" in this chapter as well as "Interpreting the House Rulers in the *Bhavacakra*" in chapter 5).

Planets occupying House I and their aspects.   There are no planets occupying House I in Peter's chart. Therefore, no prognostications are made using this particular portion of the procedure.

Step Sixteen: Finances and Legacies

The ability to acquire and accumulate money, as well as the person's potential for receiving legacies, gifts, grants, and benefactions, is determined by delineating the zodiac signs that govern Houses II and VIII respectively (see "Delineating House Rulerships" in this chapter as well as "Interpreting the House Rulers in the

Bhavacakra" in chapter 5). Then, any planets that occupy Houses II and VIII are interpreted according to their placement by zodiac sign and by house (see "Delineating Planetary Positions by House and by Sign" in this chapter as well as "Interpreting the Planetary Positions in a *Rasicakra*" in chapter 5). Aspects formed by any of the planets occupying Houses II and VIII are then synthesized into the interpretation (see "Delineating Planetary Aspects").

Alice's Finances

Houses II and VIII.   House II in Alice's chart is ruled by Pisces (19°♓40′ in fig. 8.1), signifying that she exercises shrewdness in financial management and has an irregular or illegal income (see "Delineating House Rulerships" in this chapter as well as "Interpreting the House Rulers in the *Bhavacakra*" in chapter 5). House VIII in her chart is ruled by Virgo (19°♍40′ in fig. 8.1), which indicates that she is always seeking ways to improve her financial resources. Her spouse or business partner is somehow involved in investments, taxes, insurance, or the management of other people's money (see "Delineating House Rulerships" in this chapter as well as "Interpreting the House Rulers in the *Bhavacakra*" in chapter 5).

Planets occupying House II and their aspects.   Alice's Moon occupies House II (☽ 11°♈28′ in fig. 8.1), indicating that she has considerable financial success (see "Delineating Planetary Positions by House and by Sign"). Her Moon is in Aries (☽ 11°♈28′ in fig. 8.1), indicating that she is highly imaginative, self-reliant, and inventive. She has a restless mind and is quick-tempered and independent. She carves a unique path. She heads a major undertaking and reaches prominence during her lifetime (see "Delineating Planetary Positions by House and by Sign" in this chapter as well as "Interpreting the Planetary Positions in a *Rasicakra*" in chapter 5).

Alice's Moon (☽ 11°♈28′ in fig. 8.1) forms a square aspect (□) to Mercury (☿ 03°♋28′ in fig. 8.1) within an 08°00′ orb of influence (see "Locating Planetary Aspects and Constructing an Aspectarian").[357] This suggests that she is also anxious, worried, and cynical; and experiences business losses and legal problems (see "Delineating Planetary Aspects").

---

357.   This aspect is determined by subtracting the planets' positions as demonstrated below:

Mercury (☿ 03°♋28′)	04	03°	28′
	03	33°	28′
− Moon (☽ 11°♈28′)	01	11°	28′
	02	22°	00′	*(difference)*
		82°		*(angle or aspect)*

Her Moon (☽ 11°♈28′ in fig. 8.1) forms an opposition (☍) to Saturn (♄ 08° ♎12′ in fig. 8.1) within a 03°16′ orb of influence (see "Locating Planetary Aspects and Constructing an Aspectarian").[358] This indicates that she is plagued by persecution, poverty, and struggle. It also suggests that speculation, land, agriculture, and gambling are poor ventures (see "Delineating Planetary Aspects").

Her Moon (☽ 11°♈28′ in fig. 8.1) forms a square (□) to Uranus (♅ 13°♋00′ in fig. 8.1) within a 01°32′ orb of influence (see "Locating Planetary Aspects and Constructing an Aspectarian").[359] This indicates that she experiences unlucky changes of residence and journeys. The occult, the opposite sex, and unreliable friends cause great difficulties. She also has unusual likes and dislikes (see "Delineating Planetary Aspects"). An astrologer could interpret all of these factors as obstacles to her financial security.

Her Moon (☽ 11°♈28′ in fig. 8.1) forms an opposition (☍) to Neptune (♆ 18°♎59′ in fig. 8.1) within a 07°31′ orb of influence (see "Locating Planetary Aspects and Constructing an Aspectarian").[360] This indicates that she is attracted to unusual or unconventional people and things and has an eccentric nature (see "Delineating Planetary Aspects"). Once again, all of these factors could be interpreted as obstacles to her financial security by a practitioner.

Because the above aspects are considered to be adverse,[361] the practitioner would comment that she possibly sells herself short financially: an enhanced indication noted in the placement of the Moon in House II (see "Delineating Planetary Positions by House and by Sign" in this chapter as well as "Interpreting the Planetary Positions in a *Rasicakra*" in chapter 5).

Planets occupying House VIII and their aspects. Neptune occupies House VIII (♆ 18°♎59′ in fig. 8.1) in Alice's chart, indicating that she has a great talent for handling other people's money or inheritance (see "Delineating Planetary Positions by House and by Sign" in this chapter as well as "Interpreting the Planetary Positions in a *Rasicakra*" in chapter 5). Neptune in Libra (♆ 18°♎59′ in fig. 8.1) indicates that she is compassionate and highly imaginative, and that she enjoys friendship and marriage (see "Delineating Planetary Positions by House and by Sign" in this chapter as well as "Interpreting the Planetary Positions in a *Rasicakra*" in chapter 5). Some practitioners would assess that her talent for managing other people's money might be associated with her spouse's or a friend's finances.

---

358. This aspect is determined by subtracting the planets' positions as shown in note 357, above.
359. Ibid.
360. Ibid.
361. See note 155, page 414.

As mentioned earlier, her Moon (☽ 11°♈28' in fig. 8.1) forms an opposition (☍) to Neptune (♆ 18°♎59' in fig. 8.1) within a 07°31' orb of influence (see "Locating Planetary Aspects and Constructing an Aspectarian").362 This indicates that she is attracted to unusual or unconventional people and things and has an eccentric nature (see "Delineating Planetary Aspects"). Once again, all of these factors could be interpreted by a practitioner as obstacles to any legacies or inheritances.

The Sun (☉ 24°♊55' in fig. 8.1) forms a trine (△) to Neptune (♆ 18°♎59' in fig. 8.1) within a 05°56' orb of influence (see "Locating Planetary Aspects and Constructing an Aspectarian").363 This suggests that she receives benefits through mystical and spiritual subjects (see "Delineating Planetary Aspects").

Venus (♀ 22°♊31' in fig. 8.1) forms a trine (△) to Neptune (♆ 18°♎59' in fig. 8.1) within an 03°32' orb of influence (see "Locating Planetary Aspects and Constructing an Aspectarian").364 This suggests that she benefits from friendships, associations, or mystical interests. It also indicates that she gains from trusts, institutions, seaside resorts, shipping, or liquids (see "Delineating Planetary Aspects").

Uranus (♅ 13°♋00' in fig. 8.1) forms a square (□) to Neptune (♆ 18°♎59' in fig. 8.1) within a 05°59' orb of influence (see "Locating Planetary Aspects and Constructing an Aspectarian").365 This indicates that she has unusual or unexpected likes and dislikes. She is attracted to psychic centers and unique occupations. And her success is closely linked to the occult, the sea, or large institutions. But danger can occur because of extremes or poor selection of a close friend (see "Delineating Planetary Aspects"). Once again, all of these factors could be interpreted by a practitioner as obstacles to any legacies or inheritances.

Pluto (♇ 19°♌34' in fig. 8.1) forms a sextile (✶) to Neptune (♆ 18°♎59' in fig. 8.1) within a 00°35' orb of influence (see "Locating Planetary Aspects and Constructing an Aspectarian").366 This indicates that she desires justice (see "Delineating Planetary Aspects"). Some practitioners might suggest that she would choose to litigate in order to right any wrongs pertaining to inheritances or legacies.

Because two out of five aspects are considered to be adverse,367 the practitioner would further caution that she may encounter delays in receipt of legacies: an enhanced indication noted in the placement of Neptune in House VIII (see "Delineating Planetary Position by House and by Sign").

---

362. This aspect is determined by subtracting the planets' positions as shown in note 357, above.
363. Ibid.
364. Ibid.
365. Ibid.
366. Ibid.
367. See note 155, page 414.

Saturn occupies House VIII (♄ 08°♎12′ in fig. 8.1) in Alice's chart, indicating that she lacks legacy or inheritance (see "Delineating Planetary Positions by House and by Sign"). Saturn in Libra (♄ 08°♎12′ in fig. 8.1), indicates that women are the source of many of her problems (see "Delineating Planetary Positions by House and by Sign" in this chapter as well as "Interpreting the Planetary Positions in a *Rasicakra*" in chapter 5).

As mentioned earlier, her Moon (☽ 11°♈28′ in fig. 8.1) forms an opposition (☍) to Saturn (♄ 08°♎12′ in fig. 8.1) within a 03°16′ orb of influence (see "Locating Planetary Aspects and Constructing an Aspectarian").[368] This indicates that she is plagued by persecution, poverty, and struggle (see "Delineating Planetary Aspects").

Mercury (☿ 03°♋28′ in fig. 8.1) forms a square (□) to Saturn (♄ 08°♎12′ in fig. 8.1) within a 04°44′ orb of influence (see "Locating Planetary Aspects").[369] This indicates that she experiences delays, disappointments, and obstacles. And she encounters forged letters and miscommunications (see "Delineating Planetary Aspects").

Uranus (♅ 13°♋00′ in fig. 8.1) forms a square (□) to Saturn (♄ 08°♎12′ in fig. 8.1) within a 04°48′ orb of influence (see "Locating Planetary Aspects and Constructing an Aspectarian").[370] This indicates that she experiences misfortune by misdirection (see "Delineating Planetary Aspects").

Peter's Finances

Houses II and VIII. House II in Peter's chart is ruled by Aries (24°♈34′ in fig. 8.2), signifying that he has spendthrift tendencies. He potentially desires to buy people's affections or loyalties. He engages in lawsuits over money, and suffers more than one financial fluctuation (see "Delineating House Rulerships" in this chapter as well as "Interpreting the House Rulers in the *Bhavacakra*" in chapter 5). House VIII in his chart is ruled by Libra (24°♎34′ in fig. 8.2), which indicates that he needs to give an equal measure of assets in a marriage or partnership. His wife's income comes from music, literature, fashion, design, or law (see "Delineating House Rulerships" in this chapter as well as "Interpreting the House Rulers in the *Bhavacakra*" in chapter 5).

Planets Occupying House II and their aspects. Peter's Moon occupies House II (☽ 03°♉38′ in fig. 8.2), indicating that he experiences financial gain through

---

368. This aspect is determined by subtracting the planets' positions as shown in note 357, page 456.
369. Ibid.
370. Ibid.

women (see "Delineating Planetary Positions by House and by Sign"). His Moon is in Taurus (☽ 03°♉38′ in fig. 8.2), indicating that his finances are aided by the opposite sex (see "Delineating Planetary Positions by House and by Sign").

Peter's Moon (☽ 03°♉38′ in fig. 8.2) forms a trine (△) to the Sun (☉ 04°♍41′ in fig. 8.2) within a 01°03′ orb of influence (see "Locating Planetary Aspects and Constructing an Aspectarian").[371] This signifies success, promotion, and prosperity. He gets help from influential people and profits from investments, speculation, and his own enterprise (see "Delineating Planetary Aspects").

His Moon (☽ 03°♉38′ in fig. 8.2) forms a sextile (⚹) to Saturn (♄ 01°♓25′ in fig. 8.2) within a 02°13′ orb of influence (see "Locating Planetary Aspects and Constructing an Aspectarian").[372] This signifies that professional advancement is favored because of Peter's own persistence. Lands, mineral rights and mining, and agriculture are sources of profit (see "Delineating Planetary Aspects").

The Moon (☽ 03°♉38′ in fig. 8.2) forms a trine (△) to Uranus (♅ 10°♍04′ in fig. 8.2) within a 06°26′ orb of influence and forms a parallel (//) with a 00°18′ orb of influence (see "Locating Planetary Aspects and Constructing an Aspectarian").[373] Both aspects indicate that he receives benefits from astrology and the occult. He also benefits from changes of residence and travel. He discovers that a strong imagination stimulates beneficial improvements, especially if it entails electronics or computers (see "Delineating Planetary Aspects").

Planets Occupying House VIII and their aspects Neptune occupies House VIII (♆ 15°♏19′ in fig. 8.2) in Peter's chart, indicating that he has a great talent for handling other people's money or inheritances (see "Delineating Planetary Positions by House and by Sign" in this chapter as well as "Interpreting the Planetary Positions in a *Rasicakra*" in chapter 5). His Neptune is in Scorpio (♆ 15°♏19′ in fig. 8.2), indicating that he is inventive, sensitive, and secretive. It also suggests that he is interested in chemistry or silence (see "Delineating Planetary Positions by House and by Sign" in this chapter as well as "Interpreting the Planetary Positions in a *Rasicakra*" in chapter 5). Some practitioners would assess that his talent for managing other people's money or an inheritance might be positively associated with assets linked to science or chemistry.

Neptune (♆ 15°♏19′ in fig. 8.2) forms a sextile (⚹) to Mercury (☿ 14°♍36′ in fig. 8.2) within a 00°43′ orb of influence (see "Locating Planetary Aspects and

371. Ibid.
372. Ibid.
373. Ibid.

Constructing an Aspectarian").374 This indicates that he has good experiences associated with liquids, chemicals, drugs, the sea, hospitals, and private institutions (see "Delineating Planetary Aspects"). Once again, an inheritance or legacy could be associated with assets linked to science or chemistry.

Neptune (♆ 15°♍19′ in fig. 8.2) forms a trine (△) to Venus (♀ 18°♋53′ in fig. 8.2) within a 03°34′ orb of influence (see "Locating Planetary Aspects and Constructing an Aspectarian").375 This indicates that he gains from trusts, institutions, seaside resorts, shipping, or liquids (see "Delineating Planetary Aspects").

Peter's Neptune (♆ 15°♍19′ in fig. 8.2) forms a trine (△) to Mars (♂ 18°♋31′ in fig. 8.2) within a 03°12′ orb of influence (see "Locating Planetary Aspects and Constructing an Aspectarian").376 This also indicates that he benefits from liquids, marine-oriented activities, drugs, and chemicals, as well as the occult and medical institutions (see "Delineating Planetary Aspects").

Step Seventeen: Home Life

The home environs, family life, and general domestic situation are determined by delineating the zodiac signs that govern House IV (see "Delineating House Rulerships" in this chapter as well as "Interpreting the House Rulers in the *Bhavacakra*" in chapter 5). Then any planets that occupy House IV are interpreted according to their placement by zodiac sign and by house (see "Delineating Planetary Positions by House and by Sign" in this chapter as well as "Interpreting the Planetary Positions in a *Rasicakra*" in chapter 5). Aspects formed by any of the planets occupying House IV are also synthesized into the interpretation (see "Delineating Planetary Aspects").

Alice's Home Life

House IV.   House IV in Alice's chart is ruled by Taurus (25°♉17′ in fig. 8.1), signifying that she has a sentimental attachment to home and family. She also has very strong ties to her parents (see "Delineating House Rulerships" in this chapter as well as "Interpreting the House Rulers in the *Bhavacakra*" in chapter 5).

Planets occupying House IV and their aspects.   There are no planets occupying House IV in Alice's chart. Therefore, no prognostications are made using this particular portion of the process.

---

374.   Ibid.
375.   Ibid.
376.   Ibid.

Peter's Home Life

House IV.   House IV in Peter's chart is ruled by Gemini (17°♊08′ in fig. 8.2), signifying that he prefers to work at home. He may make many changes of residence,
or own more than one residence at a time. He may live with or near siblings as an
adult. And he has strong lines of communication with his parents (see "Delineating
House Rulerships" in this chapter as well as "Interpreting the House Rulers in the
Bhavacakra" in chapter 5).

Planets occupying House IV and their aspects.   There are no planets occupying
House IV in Peter's chart. Therefore, no prognostications are made using this particular portion of the process.

Step Eighteen: Pleasure, Creativity, and Children

An individual's interest in speculative ventures, romance, gambling, sports, and
pleasures are determined by delineating the zodiac signs that govern House V (see
"Delineating House Rulerships" in this chapter as well as "Interpreting the House
Rulers in the *Bhavacakra*" in chapter 5). Then any planets that occupy House V are
interpreted according to their placement by zodiac sign and by house (see "Delineating Planetary Positions by House and by Sign" in this chapter as well as "Interpreting the Planetary Positions in a *Rasicakra*" in chapter 5). Aspects formed by any
of the planets occupying House V are then synthesized into the interpretation (see
"Delineating Planetary Aspects").

Many astrologers review this same material as an indication of a person's
creativity. If the chart applies to a performing or visual artist, this area should definitely be taken into consideration along with the traditional occupational elements
(see "Step Twenty-three: Occupation and Professional Honors," page 484).

The promise of children in a person's chart is determined by delineating the zodiac sign that governs House V (see "Delineating House Rulerships" in this chapter
as well as "Interpreting the House Rulers in the *Bhavacakra*" in chapter 5). Then
any planets that occupy House V are interpreted according to their placement by
zodiac sign and by house (see "Delineating Planetary Positions by House and by
Sign" in this chapter as well as "Interpreting the Planetary Positions in a *Rasicakra*"
in chapter 5). Aspects formed by any of the planets occupying House V are also
synthesized into the interpretation (see "Delineating Planetary Aspects").

In general, if the Moon (☽) occupies Cancer (♋), Scorpio (♏), Pisces (♓), or
Taurus (♉), the chance for offspring is very strong. This is also the case if the Ascendant (House I) or Sun (☉) occupies one of those zodiac signs. If the Moon (☽)
occupies an angular house (House I, IV, VII, or X), it increases the number of chil-

dren the person might have. If the Sun (☉), Moon (☽), or Jupiter (♃) occupies Houses V or XI, there is the potential for offspring.

However, if Aries (♈), Gemini (♊), Leo (♌), Virgo (♍), Sagittarius (♐), or Aquarius (♒) rules those same houses, the individual may have few or no children. If a feminine zodiac sign such as Taurus (♉), Cancer (♋), Virgo (♍), Scorpio (♏), Capricorn (♑), or Pisces (♓) occupies House V, it indicates that most of the person's children will be female. The opposite applies in the case of a masculine zodiac sign (Aries [♈], Gemini [♊], Leo [♌], Libra [♎], Sagittarius [♐], or Aquarius [♒]) occupying that house.

Alice's Pleasure, Creativity, and Children

General indicators for children.   Alice's Sun (☉) occupies House V, so there is the potential for offspring. But Gemini (16°♊44′) rules the house, so she may have few or no children. Because Gemini (♊) is a masculine zodiac sign, if she has children, they will possibly be male (see above comments).

House V.   House V in Alice's chart is ruled by Gemini (61°♊44′ in fig. 8.1), signifying that her creativity is closely linked to communication. Her pleasures are intellectual. She is romantically attracted to intellectuals. She is possibly a twin or the parent of twins (see "Delineating House Rulerships" in this chapter as well as "Interpreting the House Rulers in the *Bhavacakra*" in chapter 5).

Planets occupying House V and their aspects.   Alice's Venus occupies this house (♀22°♊31′ in fig. 8.1), suggesting that she has a strong attachment to children and romance. She also possesses strong creative ability (see "Delineating Planetary Positions by House and by Sign" in this chapter as well as "Interpreting the Planetary Positions in a *Rasicakra*"). Venus is in Gemini (♀22°♊31′ in fig. 8.1), indicating that she is inventive and intuitive. She profits from writing, speaking, drama, art, music, travel, or entertainment. She receives rewards from more than one source and falls in love many times. She carries on two simultaneous love affairs or marries more than once (see "Delineating Planetary Positions by House and by Sign" in this chapter as well as "Interpreting the Planetary Positions in a *Rasicakra*" in chapter 5).

As noted earlier, Alice's Sun is in Gemini (☉ 24°♊55′ in fig. 8.1), indicating that she is sensitive, intuitive, and youthful-looking. She has an active mind and is easily influenced by kindness. She is quick and efficient in emergencies and needs to work independently on more than one project at a time. She succeeds in writing, research, or investigation (see "Delineating Planetary Positions by House and by Sign" in this chapter as well as "Interpreting the Planetary Positions in a *Rasicakra*" in chapter 5). The Sun's placement in House V (☉ 24°♊55′ in fig. 8.1) suggests that her personality shines through creativity, children, romance, or pleasures (see "Delineating Planetary Positions by House and by Sign").

Alice's Mercury also occupies this house (☿ 03°♋28′ in fig. 8.1), suggesting that she enjoys intellectual or artistic pursuits. She also has a talent for teaching (see "Delineating Planetary Positions by House and by Sign"). Mercury is in Cancer (☿ 03°♋28′ in fig. 8.1), indicating that she enjoys family reunions, poetry, music, ocean voyages, or spiritual pursuits as well (see "Delineating Planetary Positions by House and by Sign").

The Sun (☉ 24°♊55′ in fig. 8.1) forms a conjunction (☌) to Mercury (☿ 03° ♊28′ in fig. 8.1) within an 08°33′ orb of influence (see "Locating Planetary Aspects and Constructing an Aspectarian"),[377] which suggests that she is ambitious and intelligent, and desires to observe and learn (see "Delineating Planetary Aspects").

The Sun (☉ 24°♊55′ in fig. 8.1) forms a conjunction (☌) to Venus (♀ 22° ♊31′ in fig. 8.1) within a 02°24′ orb of influence as well as a parallel (∥) within a 00°04′ orb of influence (see "Locating Planetary Aspects and Constructing an Aspectarian"),[378] which both indicate that she possesses creativity, popularity, and promotion. She also has musical, operatic, or artistic talent (see "Delineating Planetary Aspects").

The Sun (☉ 24°♊55′ in fig. 8.1) forms a trine (△) to Mars (♂ 01°♏24′ in fig. 8.1) within a 06°29′ orb of influence (see "Locating Planetary Aspects and Constructing an Aspectarian"),[379] which indicates that she has vitality, determination, and confidence (see "Delineating Planetary Aspects").

The Sun (☉, declination 23°21′N in an ephemeris) forms a parallel (∥) to Uranus (♅, declination 23°10′N in an ephemeris) within a 00°11′ orb of influence (see "Locating Planetary Aspects and Constructing an Aspectarian")[380] which suggests that she succeeds with inventions, public service, research, exploration, adventure, transportation, or electronics.

The Sun (☉ 24°♊55′ in fig. 8.1) forms a trine (△) to Neptune (♆ 18°♎59′ in fig. 8.1) within a 05°56′ orb of influence (see "Locating Planetary Aspects and Constructing an Aspectarian"),[381] which suggests that she loves the arts and refined pleasures (see "Delineating Planetary Aspects").

---

377. This aspect is determined by subtracting the planets' positions as shown in note 357, above.
378. Ibid.
379. Ibid.
380. Ibid.
381. Ibid.

The Sun (☉ 24°♊55′ in fig. 8.1) forms a sextile (⚹) to Pluto (♇ 19°♌34′ in fig. 8.1) within a 05°21′ orb of influence, as well as a parallel (∥) within an 08°04′ orb of influence (see "Locating Planetary Aspects and Constructing an Aspectarian");[382] these combine to indicate that she has influence over other people (see "Delineating Planetary Aspects").

Mercury (☿ 03°♊28′ in fig. 8.1) forms a square (□) to the Moon (☽ 11°♈28′ in fig. 8.1) within an 08°00′ orb of influence (see "Locating Planetary Aspects and Constructing an Aspectarian"),[383] which indicates that she is anxious, worried, and cynical (see "Delineating Planetary Aspects").

Mercury (☿ 03°♋28′ in fig. 8.1) forms a trine (△) to Mars (♂ 01°♏24′ in fig. 8.1) within a 02°04′ orb of influence (see "Locating Planetary Aspects and Constructing an Aspectarian"),[384] which suggests that she applies immense energy to music, design, art, chemistry, medicine, or engineering. Educators, professionals, scientists, and literary people aid in personal development (see "Delineating Planetary Aspects").

Mercury (☿ 03°♋28′ in fig. 8.1) forms a square (□) to Saturn (♄ 08°♎12′ in fig. 8.1) within a 04°44′ orb of influence (see "Locating Planetary Aspects and Constructing an Aspectarian"),[385] which indicates that she experiences delays, disappointments, and obstacles. She encounters forged letters and miscommunications as well (see "Delineating Planetary Aspects").

Venus (♀ 22°♊31′ in fig. 8.1) forms a trine (△) to Neptune (♆ 18°♌59′ in fig. 8.1) within a 03°32′ orb of influence (see "Locating Planetary Aspects and Constructing an Aspectarian"),[386] which suggests that she loves beauty and the arts (see "Delineating Planetary Aspects").

Venus (♀ 22°♊31′ in fig. 8.1) forms a sextile (⚹) to Pluto (♇ 19°♌34′ in fig. 8.1) within a 02°57′ orb of influence (see "Locating Planetary Aspects and Constructing an Aspectarian"),[387] which indicates that she is emotionally attached to people in distress or who hold underdog positions (see "Delineating Planetary Aspects"). All of these aspects reflect in one way or another upon Alice's pleasure interests, creativity, and ability to have children, which the practitioner would synthesize into the main body of the interpretation.

---

382. Ibid.
383. Ibid.
384. Ibid.
385. Ibid.
386. Ibid.
387. Ibid.

Peter's Pleasure, Creativity, and Children

General Indicators for children.   Peter's Moon (☽) occupies Taurus (♉), so the chance for offspring is very strong. The Ascendant (House I) occupies Pisces (♓), which accentuates this prognostication. The feminine zodiac sign Cancer (♋) governs House V (06°♋26′ in fig. 8.2), which indicates that most of his children will be female. (See comments on pages 462–63.)

House V.   House V in Peter's chart is ruled by Cancer (06°♋26′ in fig. 8.2), signifying that he has a love of the arts, but is underdisciplined creatively. He has a strong emotional link to children. He is romantically sensitive and affectionate. His pleasures come from home or family activities (see "Delineating House Rulerships" in this chapter as well as "Interpreting the House Rulers in the *Bhavacakra*" in chapter 5).

Planets occupying House V and their aspects.   Peter's Mars occupies this house (♂ 18°♋31′ in fig. 8.2), indicating that he has impetuous or violent love affairs, experiences danger through overindulgence, and dominates his children (see "Delineating Planetary Positions by House and by Sign" in this chapter as well as "Interpreting the Planetary Positions in a *Rasicakra*" in chapter 5). Mars is in Cancer (♂ 18°♋31′ in fig. 8.2), which indicates that he is fearless, but changeable and lacking in perseverance. He also nurses ill feelings for long periods (see "Delineating Planetary Positions by House and by Sign" in this chapter as well as "Interpreting the Planetary Positions in a *Rasicakra*" in chapter 5).

Peter's Venus also occupies this house (♀ 18°♋53′ in fig. 8.2), which suggests that he has a strong attachment to children and romance. He also possesses strong creative ability (see "Delineating Planetary Positions by House and by Sign" in this chapter as well as "Interpreting the Planetary Positions in a *Rasicakra*" in chapter 5). Venus is in Cancer (♀ 18°♋53′ in fig. 8.2), which indicates that he is home-loving and domestically inclined. He has many clandestine love affairs and has an older or younger spouse (see "Delineating Planetary Positions by House and by Sign" in this chapter as well as "Interpreting the Planetary Positions in a *Rasicakra*" in chapter 5).

Mars (♂ 18°♋31′ in fig. 8.2) forms a conjunction (☌) to Venus (♀ 18°♋53′ in fig. 8.2) within a 00°22′ orb of influence (see "Locating Planetary Aspects and Constructing an Aspectarian"),[388] which suggests that Peter gains through sports, his design ability, or his artistic talent (see "Delineating Planetary Aspects").

Mars (♂ 18°♋31′ in fig. 8.2) forms a trine (△) to Neptune (♆ 15°♏19′ in

388.   Ibid.

fig. 8.2) within a 03°12′ orb of influence (see "Locating Planetary Aspects and Constructing an Aspectarian"),[389] which indicates that he benefits from liquids, marine-oriented activities, drugs, and chemicals, as well as the occult and medical institutions (see "Delineating Planetary Aspects").

Venus ($♀$ 18°$♋$53′ in fig. 8.2) forms a trine ($△$) to Neptune ($♆$ 15°$♏$19′ in fig. 8.2) within a 03°34′ orb of influence as well as a parallel ($//$) within a 00°10′ orb of influence (see "Locating Planetary Aspects and Constructing an Aspectarian"),[390] which suggests that he loves beauty and the arts. He also benefits from friendships, associations, or mystical interests (see "Delineating Planetary Aspects"). All of these aspects reflect in one way or another upon Peter's pleasure interests, creativity, and ability to have children, and the practitioner would synthesize all the aspects into the main body of the interpretation.

Step Nineteen: Marriage and Partnerships

A person's marital status and the condition of that union are determined by delineating the zodiac signs that govern House VII (see "Delineating House Rulerships" in this chapter as well as "Interpreting the House Rulers in the *Bhavacakra*" in chapter 5). Then any planets that occupy House VII are interpreted according to their placement by zodiac sign and by house (see "Delineating Planetary Positions by House and by Sign" in this chapter as well as "Interpreting the Planetary Positions in a *Rasicakra*" in chapter 5). Aspects formed by any of the planets occupying House VII are then interpreted and synthesized into the interpretation (see "Delineating Planetary Aspects").

Some practitioners additionally analyze the condition of the Moon ($☽$) and Venus ($♀$) in a man's chart (the Sun [$☉$] and Mars [$♂$] in a woman's chart) to determine how many marriages or serious love relationships an individual might have and what type of person attracts him or her. If the Moon ($☽$) in a man's chart (the Sun [$☉$] in a woman's chart) forms more than one aspect excluding parallels ($//$) (see "Locating Planetary Aspects and Constructing an Aspectarian"), the person will have a serious love relationship with, or will marry, more than one person in his or her life.

If the Moon ($☽$) in a man's chart (the Sun [$☉$] in a woman's chart) occupies House V or VII and does not form a square ($□$) or opposition ($☍$) to another planet (see "Locating Planetary Aspects and Constructing an Aspectarian"), the person finds a mate early in life. (This is especially true if it also occupies a fertile zodiac sign such as Cancer [$♋$], Scorpio [$♏$], Pisces [$♓$], or Taurus [$♉$].) If, however,

---

389. Ibid.
390. Ibid.

the Moon (☽) in a man's chart (the Sun [☉] in a woman's chart) forms a square (□) or opposition (☍) to Saturn (♄) (see "Locating Planetary Aspects and Constructing an Aspectarian"), or occupies a barren zodiac sign such as Aries (♈), Gemini (♊), Leo (♌), Virgo (♍), Sagittarius (♐), or Aquarius (♒) in House V or VII, the person may marry late in life or remain unattached.

A synastry of a couple's charts is occasionally constructed that visually displays the number of parallel zodiacal degrees or the lack of shared degrees between the two horoscopes. Some astrologers also prepare and delineate a composite horoscope composed of midpoints between the planetary positions in both charts.

House VII is also used to analyze an individual's relationship with business partners. The same procedures outlined above for the delineation of the house ruler, planets, and their aspects are used to determine the potential and outcome of these equally important relationships.

Alice's Marital Status

General indicators for marriage.   Alice's Sun (☉) forms five aspects excluding parallels (∥) (see fig. 8.4 and "Locating Planetary Aspects and Constructing an Aspectarian"). This indicates that she will have five serious love relationships or will marry more than once.

Alice's Mars is in Scorpio (♂ 01°♏24′ in fig. 8.1), which suggests that she is attracted to a hard-working, inventive, selfish, vengeful, and passionate person who has a cold disregard for other people's feelings. This individual is best suited for espionage or diplomatic work, and has satisfying love affairs and a beneficial marriage (see "Delineating Planetary Positions by House and by Sign"). Her Sun (☉ 24°♊55′ in fig. 8.1) occupies House V and does not form a square or opposition to another planet (see "Locating Planetary Aspects and Constructing an Aspectarian"). Therefore, she finds a mate early in life.[391]

House VII.   House VII in Alice's chart is ruled by Leo (01°♌57′ in fig. 8.1), signifying that marriage positively satisfies her ego (see "Delineating House Rulerships").

Planets occupying House VII and their aspects.   Alice's Pluto occupies this house (♇ 19°♌34′ in fig. 8.1), suggesting that she dominates the marriage (see "Delineating Planetary Positions by House and by Sign"). Pluto is in Leo (♇ 19°♌34′ in fig. 8.1), indicating that she encounters an emphasis on leisure, enter-

---

391.   There is a contradiction to this prognostication. The Sun (☉) occupies the barren zodiac sign Gemini (♊), which suggests that she might marry late in life or remain unattached. A practitioner might comment that she will not settle down with her first spouse or serious lover, but may do so later in life.

tainment, and electronically oriented media, as well as the centralization of information, government, and administrative systems (see "Delineating Planetary Positions by House and by Sign" in this chapter as well as "Interpreting the Planetary Positions in a *Rasicakra*" in chapter 5).

Pluto (♇ 19°♌34′ in fig. 8.1) forms a sextile (✶) to the Sun (☉ 24°♊55′ in fig. 8.1) within a 05°21′ orb of influence (see "Locating Planetary Aspects and Constructing an Aspectarian").[392] Pluto (♇, declination 23°33′N in an ephemeris) also forms a parallel to the Sun (☉, declination 23°19′N in an ephemeris) within a 00°14′ orb of influence (see "Locating Planetary Aspects and Constructing an Aspectarian").[393] Both aspects suggest that she has influence over other people, and that she is able to modify herself in order to attain her personal goals (see "Delineating Planetary Aspects").

Pluto (♇ 19°♌34′ in fig. 8.1) forms a sextile (✶) to Venus (♀ 22°♊31′ in fig. 8.1) within a 02°57′ orb of influence (see "Locating Planetary Aspects and Constructing an Aspectarian").[394] Pluto (♇, declination 23°33′N in an ephemeris) also forms a parallel (∥) to Venus (♀, declination 23°14′N in an ephemeris) within a 00°19′ orb of influence (see "Locating Planetary Aspects and Constructing an Aspectarian").[395] Both aspects suggests that she is emotionally attached to those in distress or in underdog positions (see "Delineating Planetary Aspects").

Pluto (♇ 19°♌34′ in fig. 8.1) forms a square (□) to Jupiter (♃ 10°♉52′ in fig. 8.1) within an 08°42′ orb of influence (see "Locating Planetary Aspects and Constructing an Aspectarian").[396] This suggests that she has unrealistic expectations and a vacillating or destructive self-image (see "Delineating Planetary Aspects").

Pluto (♇ 19°♌34′ in fig. 8.1) forms a sextile (✶) to Neptune (♆ 18°♎59′ in fig. 8.1) within a 00°35′ orb of influence (see "Locating Planetary Aspects and Constructing an Aspectarian").[397] This suggests that she has spiritual tendencies and desires justice (see "Delineating Planetary Aspects").

Pluto (♇, declination 23°33′N in an ephemeris) also forms a parallel (∥) to Uranus (♅, declination 23°11′N in an ephemeris) within a 00°22′ orb of influence (see "Locating Planetary Aspects and Constructing an Aspectarian").[398] This suggests that she has rebellious tendencies (see "Delineating Planetary Aspects"). All of the above aspects with Pluto would be factored into an assessment of Alice's marriage and her position in that relationship.

---

392. This aspect is determined by subtracting the planets' position as shown in note 357, page 456.
393. Ibid.
394. Ibid.
395. Ibid.
396. Ibid.
397. Ibid.
398. Ibid.

Peter's Marital Status

General indicators for marriage.   Peter's Moon (☽) forms three aspects excluding parallels (//) (see fig. 8.5 and "Locating Planetary Aspects"), indicating that he will have three serious love relationships or will marry more than once (see comments above).

Peter's Venus is in Cancer (♀ 18°♋53′ in fig. 8.2), which suggests that he is attracted to a home-loving, domestically inclined person who loves her mother. She possesses a sympathetic and mediumistic nature. She has many clandestine love affairs, has an older or younger spouse, and encounters marital problems due to parents, money, or profession (see "Delineating Planetary Positions by House and by Sign" in this chapter as well as "Interpreting the Planetary Positions in a *Rasicakra*" in chapter 5). Peter's Moon (☽) occupies the fertile zodiac sign Taurus (♉). This indicates that he will find a mate early in life.

House VII.   House VII in Peter's chart is ruled by Virgo (02°♍49′ in fig. 8.2), signifying that he is constructively critical of his spouse. He also has the potential for more than one marriage or serious love relationship (see "Delineating House Rulerships" in this chapter as well as "Interpreting the House Rulers in the *Bhavacakra*" in chapter 5).

Planets occupying House VII and their aspects.   Peter's Sun occupies this house (☉ 04°♍41′ in fig. 8.2). This indicates that he has a strong desire for marriage (see "Delineating Planetary Positions by House and by Sign" in this chapter as well as "Interpreting the Planetary Positions in a *Rasicakra*" in chapter 5). The Sun is in Virgo (☉ 04°♍41′ in fig. 8.2), suggesting that he is frugal, practical, contemplative, industrious, and youthful-looking. He is a perfectionist and desires wealth. He worries and has a sharp temper, but abhors fighting. He has a strong command of language and is able to learn quickly. He has a high endurance level (see "Delineating Planetary Positions by House and by Sign" in this chapter as well as "Interpreting the Planetary Positions in a *Rasicakra*" in chapter 5).

His Uranus occupies this house (♅ 10°♍04′ in fig. 8.2). This indicates that he has an unconventional marriage or serious love relationship (see "Delineating House Rulerships" in this chapter as well as "Interpreting the House Rulers in the *Bhavacakra*" in chapter 5). Uranus is in Virgo (♅ 10°♍04′ in fig. 8.2), suggesting that he is independent, stubborn, and eccentric. And he is capable of great subtlety and originality (see "Delineating Planetary Positions by House and by Sign" in this chapter as well as "Interpreting the Planetary Positions in a *Rasicakra*" in chapter 5).

Pluto occupies this house (♇ 13°♍38′ in fig. 8.2). This indicates that he dominates his marriage or serious love relationship (see "Delineating Planetary Positions by House and by Sign" in this chapter as well as "Interpreting the Planetary Positions in a *Rasicakra*" in chapter 5). Pluto is in Virgo (♇ 13°♍38′ in fig. 8.2), suggesting that he experiences increased computerization and specialization of work as well as the initialization of health, sanitation, and environmental improvements (see "Delineating Planetary Positions by House and by Sign" in this chapter as well as "Interpreting the Planetary Positions in a *Rasicakra*" in chapter 5).

Peter's Mercury also occupies this house (☿ 14°♍36′ in fig. 8.2). This indicates that his marriage choice is influenced by his intellect. He is able to negotiate, and takes advantage of opportunities offered through his marriage or serious love relationship (see "Delineating Planetary Positions by House and by Sign" in this chapter as well as "Interpreting the Planetary Positions in a *Rasicakra*" in chapter 5). Mercury is in Virgo (☿ 14°♍36′ in fig. 8.2), suggesting that he is cautious, inventive, quiet, and practical. He possesses powers of persuasion, and is communicative. He is also organized (see "Delineating Planetary Positions by House and by Sign" in this chapter as well as "Interpreting the Planetary Positions in a *Rasicakra*" in chapter 5).

Peter's Sun (☉ 04°♍41′ in fig. 8.2) forms a trine (△) to the Moon (☽ 03° ♉38′ in fig. 8.2) within a 01°03′ orb of influence (see "Locating Planetary Aspects and Constructing an Aspectarian").[399] This indicates that he finds success, promotion, and prosperity. He gets help from influential people (see "Delineating Planetary Aspects"). The practitioner might assess that success is due to his marriage.

Peter's Sun (☉ 04°♍41′ in fig. 8.2) forms a conjunction (☌) to Mercury (☿ 14°♍36′ in fig. 8.2) within a 09°55′ orb of influence (see "Locating Planetary Aspects and Constructing an Aspectarian").[400] This indicates that he is ambitious and intelligent, and desires to observe and learn (see "Delineating Planetary Aspects").

His Sun (☉ 04°♍41′ in fig. 8.2) forms a square (□) to Jupiter (♃ 25°♉36′ in Fig. 8-2) within a 09°05′ orb of influence (see "Locating Planetary Aspects and Constructing an Aspectarian").[401] This suggests that he encounters financial losses by miscalculation, extravagance, or bad advice (see "Delineating Planetary Aspects").

The Sun (☉ 04°♍41′ in fig. 8.2) forms an opposition (☍) to Saturn (♄ 01° ♓25′ in fig. 8.2) within a 03°16′ orb of influence (see "Locating Planetary Aspects and Constructing an Aspectarian").[402] This indicates that he experiences

---

399. Ibid.
400. Ibid. Not all practitioners believe that this aspect has any influence within the chart because it exceeds the general 08°00′ orb of influence.
401. Ibid. Not all practitioners believe that this aspect has any influence within the chart because it exceeds the general 08°00′ orb of influence.
402. Ibid.

disappointment and delays that spoil opportunities for success (see "Delineating Planetary Aspects").

Peter's Sun (☉ 04°♍41′ in fig. 8.2) forms a conjunction (☌) to Uranus (♅ 10°♍04′ in fig. 8.2) within a 05°23′ orb of influence (see "Locating Planetary Aspects and Constructing an Aspectarian").[403] This indicates the he marries early (see "Delineating Planetary Aspects").

His Sun (☉ 04°♍41′ in fig. 8.2) forms a conjunction (☌) to Pluto (♇ 13°♍38′ in fig. 8.2) within an 08°57′ orb of influence (see "Locating Planetary Aspects and Constructing an Aspectarian").[404] This suggests that he has influence over other people and is able to modify himself in order to attain personal goals (see "Delineating Planetary Aspects").

Peter's Uranus (♅ 10°♍04′ in fig. 8.2) forms a conjunction (☌) to Pluto (♇ 13°♍38′ in fig. 8.2) within a 03°34′ orb of influence (see "Locating Planetary Aspects and Constructing an Aspectarian").[405] This indicates that he has rebellious tendencies (see "Delineating Planetary Aspects").

Uranus (♅ 10°♍04′ in fig. 8.2) forms a trine (△) to the Moon (☽ 03°♉38′ in fig. 8.2) within a 06°26′ orb of influence (see "Locating Planetary Aspects and Constructing an Aspectarian").[406] This suggests that he benefits from changes of residence and travel. He also learns that a strong imagination stimulates beneficial improvements, especially if it entails electronics or computers (see "Delineating Planetary Aspects").

Peter's Uranus (♅ 10°♍04′ in fig. 8.2) forms a conjunction (☌) to Mercury (☿ 14°♍36′ in fig. 8.2) within a 04°32′ orb of influence (see "Locating Planetary Aspects and Constructing an Aspectarian").[407] This indicates that he is inspired to invent and to express his eccentricity (see "Delineating Planetary Aspects").

Peter's Pluto (♇ 13°♍38′ in fig. 8.2) forms a conjunction (☌) to Mercury (☿ 14°♍36′ in fig. 8.2) within a 00°52′ orb of influence (see "Locating Planetary Aspects and Constructing an Aspectarian").[408] This indicates that he is adaptable, persuasive, and able to dominate others mentally (see "Delineating Planetary Aspects").

Peter's Pluto (♇ 13°♍38′ in fig. 8.2) forms a sextile (✳) to Neptune (♆ 15° ♍19′ in fig. 8.2) within a 01°41′ orb of influence (see "Locating Planetary Aspects and Constructing an Aspectarian").[409] This suggests that he desires justice (see "Delineating Planetary Aspects").

---

403. Ibid.
404. Ibid.
405. Ibid.
406. Ibid.
407. Ibid.
408. Ibid.
409. Ibid.

Peter's Pluto (♇, declination 19°00′N in an ephemeris) forms a parallel (∥) to Venus (♀), declination 19°10′N in an ephemeris within a 00°10′ orb of influence (see "Locating Planetary Aspects and Constructing an Aspectarian").[410] This indicates that he is emotionally attached to those in distress or in underdog positions (see "Delineating Planetary Aspects").

Peter's Pluto (♇, declination 19°00′N in an ephemeris) forms a parallel (∥) to Jupiter (♃), declination 18°03′N in an ephemeris) within a 00°57′ orb of influence (see "Locating Planetary Aspects and Constructing an Aspectarian").[411] This indicates that he has natural leadership and inspirational qualities (see "Delineating Planetary Aspects").

Peter's Uranus (♅, declination 08°32′N in an ephemeris) forms a parallel (∥) to the Moon (☽), declination 06°08′N in an ephemeris) within a 02°24′ orb of influence (see "Locating Planetary Aspects and Constructing an Aspectarian").[412] This suggests that he experiences unlucky changes of residence and journeys. The occult, the opposite sex, and unreliable friends cause great difficulties. He has unusual likes and dislikes (see "Delineating Planetary Aspects").

Mercury (☿ 14°♍36′ in fig. 8.2) forms a sextile (⚹) to Mars (♂ 18°♋31′ in fig. 8.2) within a 03°55′ orb of influence (see "Locating Planetary Aspects and Constructing an Aspectarian").[413] This suggests that educators, professionals, scientists, and literary people aid in his personal development (see "Delineating Planetary Aspects").

Mercury (☿ 14°♍36′ in fig. 8.2) also forms a sextile (⚹) to Neptune (♆ 15° ♏ 19′ in fig. 8.2) within a 00°43′ orb of influence (see "Locating Planetary Aspects and Constructing an Aspectarian").[414] This indicates that he is attracted to psychic centers and has prophetic dreams (see "Delineating Planetary Aspects"). A practitioner might conclude that all these developmental events occur during his marriage.

Step Twenty: Health and Death

A person's overall health, attitude toward death, and eventual demise are determined by delineating the zodiac signs that govern Houses VI and VIII (see "Delineating House Rulerships" in this chapter as well as "Interpreting the House Rulers in the *Bhavacakra*" in chapter 5). Then any planets that occupy Houses VI and VIII are interpreted according to their placement by zodiac sign and by house (see

---

410. Ibid.
411. Ibid.
412. Ibid.
413. Ibid.
414. Ibid.

"Delineating Planetary Positions by House and by Sign" in this chapter as well as "Interpreting the Planetary Positions in a *Rasicakra*" in chapter 5). Aspects formed by any of the planets occupying House VIII are then synthesized into the interpretation (see "Delineating Planetary Aspects").

Death is treated as the termination of life in Western civilization. House VIII is sometimes consulted for the potential accidental or criminal events connected with the end of a person's life. Additionally, House VI is reviewed for indications of chronic or acute illness and the quality of the person's life.

Alice's Health and Attitude Toward Death

Houses VI and VIII.   House VI in Alice's chart is ruled by Cancer (07°♋13' in fig. 8.1), signifying that she has delicate health patterns but few major illnesses (see "Delineating House Rulerships" in this chapter as well as "Interpreting the House Rulers in the *Bhavacakra*" in chapter 5). House VIII in her chart is ruled by Virgo (19°♍40' in fig. 8.1) which indicates that she is resigned to the concept of death (see "Delineating House Rulerships" in this chapter as well as "Interpreting the House Rulers in the *Bhavacakra*" in chapter 5).

Planets Occupying House VI and Their Aspects.   Alice's Uranus is in Cancer (♅ 13°♋00' in fig. 8.1), which suggests that she is sensitive, restless, and cranky (see "Delineating Planetary Positions by House and by Sign" in this chapter as well as "Interpreting the Planetary Positions in a *Rasicakra*" in chapter 5). Her Uranus occupies House VI (♅ 13°♋00' in fig. 8.1), indicating that she has a weak nervous system (see "Delineating Planetary Positions by House and by Sign" in this chapter as well as "Interpreting the Planetary Positions in a *Rasicakra*" in chapter 5).

Uranus (♅ 13°♋00' in fig. 8.1) forms a square (□) to the Moon (☽ 11°♈28' in fig. 8.1) within a 01°32' orb of influence (see "Locating Planetary Aspects and Constructing an Aspectarian").[415] This suggests that she experiences mental disturbance, stomach distress, or gastrointestinal problems (see "Delineating Planetary Aspects").

Alice's Uranus (♅ 13°♋00' in fig. 8.1) forms a square (□) to Saturn (♄ 08° ♎12' in fig. 8.1) within a 04°48' orb of influence (see "Locating Planetary Aspects and Constructing an Aspectarian").[416] This suggests that worry, anxiety, and despondency should be mollified through exercise and activity rather than overindulgence (see "Delineating Planetary Aspects").

Uranus (♅ 13°♋00' in fig. 8.1) also forms a square (□) to Neptune (♆ 18°

---

415.   Ibid.
416.   Ibid.

♎ 59′ in fig. 8.1) within a 05°59′ orb of influence (see "Locating Planetary Aspects and Constructing an Aspectarian").⁴¹⁷ This suggests that she has unusual or unexpected likes and dislikes, but danger can occur because of extremes (see "Delineating Planetary Aspects").

Uranus (♅ 13°♋00′ in fig. 8.1) forms a sextile (⚹) to Jupiter (♃ 10°♉52′ in fig. 8.1) within a 02°08′ orb of influence (see "Locating Planetary Aspects and Constructing an Aspectarian").⁴¹⁸ This suggests that she experiences prophetic foresight (see "Delineating Planetary Aspects"). A practitioner might imply that Alice foresees or has premonitions of physical problems before they occur.

Uranus (♅, declination of 23°11′N in an ephemeris) forms a parallel (∥) to the Sun (☉, declination 23°19′N in an ephemeris) within a 00°08′ orb of influence (see "Locating Planetary Aspects and Constructing an Aspectarian").⁴¹⁹ This improves her longevity (see "Delineating Planetary Aspects").

Uranus (♅, declination 23°11′N in an ephemeris) forms a parallel (∥) to Venus (♀, declination 23°14′N in an ephemeris) within a 00°03′ orb of influence (see "Locating Planetary Aspects and Constructing an Aspectarian").⁴²⁰ This suggests that she experiences losses through unexpected circumstances (see "Delineating Planetary Aspects"). All of these aspects, which in one way or another reflect upon Alice's health, the practitioner would synthesize into the main body of the interpretation.

Planets occupying House VIII and their aspects.   Alice's Neptune occupies House VIII (♆ 18°♎59′ in fig. 8.1), indicating that she has acute psychological sensitivity (see "Delineating Planetary Positions by House and by Sign" in this chapter as well as "Interpreting the Planetary Positions in a *Rasicakra*" in chapter 5). Neptune is in Libra (♆ 18°♎59′ in fig. 8.1), which suggests that she is compassionate and highly imaginative (see "Delineating Planetary Positions by House and by Sign" in this chapter as well as "Interpreting the Planetary Positions in a *Rasicakra*" in chapter 5). Some practitioners might suggest that she is very sensitive in her attitude toward death.

Alice's Saturn occupies House VIII (♄ 08°♎12′ in fig. 8.1), indicating that she desires to live "out of body" (see "Delineating Planetary Positions by House and by Sign" in this chapter as well as "Interpreting the Planetary Positions in a *Rasicakra*" in chapter 5). Saturn is in Libra (♄ 08°♎12′ in fig. 8.1), which suggests that she finds sorrow at the loss of a deep attachment and that women are the source

417.   Ibid.
418.   Ibid.
419.   Ibid.
420.   Ibid.

of many problems (see "Delineating Planetary Positions by House and by Sign" in this chapter as well as "Interpreting the Planetary Positions in a *Rasicakra*" in chapter 5).

Neptune (♆ 18°♎59′ in fig. 8.1) forms a square (□) to Uranus (♅ 13°♋00′ in fig. 8.1) within a 05°59′ orb of influence (see "Locating Planetary Aspects and Constructing an Aspectarian").[421] This suggests that she has unusual or unexpected likes and dislikes. She is attracted to psychic centers, and unique occupations, but danger can occur because of extremes (see "Delineating Planetary Aspects").

Neptune (♆ 18°♎59′ in fig. 8.1) forms a trine (△) to the Sun (☉ 24°♊55′ in fig. 8.1) within a 05°56′ orb of influence (see "Locating Planetary Aspects and Constructing an Aspectarian").[422] This suggests that she receives benefits through mystical and spiritual subjects (see "Delineating Planetary Aspects").

Neptune (♆ 18°♎59′ in fig. 8.1) forms an opposition (☍) to the Moon (☽ 11° ♈28′ in fig. 8.1) within a 07°31′ orb of influence (see "Locating Planetary Aspects and Constructing an Aspectarian").[423] This suggests that she has an eccentric nature (see "Delineating Planetary Aspects").

Neptune (♆ 18°♎59′ in fig. 8.1) forms a trine (△) to Venus (♀ 22°♊31′ in fig. 8.1) within a 03°32′ orb of influence (see "Locating Planetary Aspects and Constructing an Aspectarian").[424] This suggests that she benefits from friendships, associations, or mystical interests (see "Delineating Planetary Aspects").

Neptune (♆ 18°♎59′ in fig. 8.1) also forms a sextile (✳) to Pluto (♇ 19°♌34′ in fig. 8.1) within a 00°35′ orb of influence (see "Locating Planetary Aspects and Constructing an Aspectarian").[425] This suggests that she has spiritual tendencies and desires justice (see "Delineating Planetary Aspects").

Saturn (♄ 08°♎12′ in fig. 8.1) forms an opposition (☍) to the Moon (☽ 11° ♈28′ in fig. 8.1) within a 03°16′ orb of influence (see "Locating Planetary Aspects and Constructing an Aspectarian").[426] This suggests that she is plagued by persecution, poverty, and struggle (see "Delineating Planetary Aspects").

Saturn (♄ 08°♎12′ in fig. 8.1) forms a square (□) to Mercury (☿ 03°♋28′ in fig. 8.1) within a 04°44′ orb of influence (see "Locating Planetary Aspects and Constructing an Aspectarian").[427] This suggests that the death, separation, or ill-

421. Ibid.
422. Ibid.
423. Ibid.
424. Ibid.
425. Ibid.
426. Ibid.
427. Ibid.

ness of a sibling or her father causes sorrows and problems (see "Delineating Planetary Aspects").

Saturn (♄ 08°♎12′ in fig. 8.1) forms a square (□) to Uranus (♅ 13°♋00′ in
fig. 8.1) within a 04°48′ orb of influence (see "Locating Planetary Aspects and
Constructing an Aspectarian").[428] This suggests that she has a destructive or rebellious nature. A chronic or incurable illness might arise in the kidneys, ovaries, or
lower back. And she experiences troubles associated with falls, falling objects, collisions, natural disasters, riots, or uprisings (see "Delineating Planetary Aspects").
All of these aspects, which in one way or another reflect upon Alice's attitude
toward death and her eventual demise, the practitioner would synthesize into the
main body of the interpretation.

Peter's Health and Attitude Toward Death

Houses VI and VIII.   House VI in Peter's chart is ruled by Cancer (28°♋27′ in
fig. 8.2), signifying that he has delicate health patterns but few major illnesses (see
"Delineating House Rulerships" in this chapter as well as "Interpreting House
Rulers in the *Bhavacakra*" in chapter 5). Because the zodiac sign Leo intercepts this
house (see "Placing the Planets and Nodes in the Horoscope"), it is also read as an
influence. This configuration suggests that health and fitness are of importance
(see "Delineating House Rulerships" in this chapter as well as "Interpreting the
House Rulers in the *Bhavacakra*" in chapter 5).

House VIII in Peter's chart is ruled by Libra (24°♎34′ in fig. 8.2). This indicates
that he rationalizes the concept of death (see "Delineating House Rulerships" in
this chapter as well as "Interpreting the House Rulers in the *Bhavacakra*" in chapter 5).

Planets occupying House VI and their aspects.   There are no planets occupying
House VI in Peter's chart. Therefore, no prognostications are made using this particular portion of the process.

Planets occupying House VIII and their aspects.   Peter's Neptune occupies
House VIII (♆ 15°♏19′ in fig. 8.2), indicating that he has acute psychological sensitivity (see "Delineating Planetary Positions by House and by Sign" in this chapter
as well as "Interpreting the Planetary Positions in a *Rasicakra*" in chapter 5). Neptune is in Scorpio (♆ 15°♏19′ in fig. 8.2), which suggests that he is sensitive and
secretive. He also has occult experiences (see "Delineating Planetary Positions by
House and by Sign" in this chapter as well as "Interpreting the Planetary Positions

---

428. Ibid.

in a *Rasicakra*" in chapter 5). Some practitioners might suggest that this oversensitivity affects his attitude toward death.

Neptune (♆ 15°♏19' in fig. 8.2) forms a sextile (⚹) to Mercury (☿ 14°♍36' in fig. 8.2) within a 00°43' orb of influence (see "Locating Planetary Aspects and Constructing an Aspectarian").[429] This suggests that he is attracted to psychic centers and has prophetic dreams. He succeeds in unconventional healing or hydrotherapy. He also has good experiences associated with liquids, chemicals, drugs, the sea, hospitals, and private institutions (see "Delineating Planetary Aspects").

Neptune (♆ 15°♏19' in fig. 8.2) forms a trine (△) to Venus (♀ 18°♋53' in fig. 8.2) within a 03°34' orb of influence (see "Locating Planetary Aspects and Constructing an Aspectarian").[430] This suggests that he benefits from friendships, associations, or mystical interests (see "Delineating Planetary Aspects").

Neptune (♆ 15°♏19' in fig. 8.2) forms a trine (△) to Mars (♂ 18°♋31' in fig. 8.2) within a 03°12' orb of influence (see "Locating Planetary Aspects and Constructing an Aspectarian").[431] This suggests that he benefits from liquids, marine-oriented activities, drugs, and chemicals, as well as the occult and medical institutions (see "Delineating Planetary Aspects").

Neptune (♆ 15°♏19' in fig. 8.2) forms a sextile (⚹) to Pluto (♇ 13°♍38' in fig. 8.2) within a 02°41' orb of influence (see "Locating Planetary Aspects and Constructing an Aspectarian").[432] This suggests that he has spiritual tendencies and desires justice (see "Delineating Planetary Aspects"). All of these aspects, which in one way or another reflect upon Peter's attitude toward death and his eventual demise, the practitioner would synthesize into the main body of the interpretation.

— ✳ —

In addition to House VIII, some astrologers study the Apheta's condition to determine the person's potential for longevity. According to ancient astrologers, a planet is called the Apheta[433] when it is positioned in one of the hylegical degrees: 05°00' to 25°00' below the Ascendant (House I); 05°00' to 25°00' above the Descendant (House VII); or in the area lying 05°00' below House IX's cusp to 25°00' above House XI's cusp. If the Apheta forms a conjunction (☌), square (□), or opposition (☍), the person's life and health may be jeopardized. A transiting planet that forms a conjunction (☌), square (□), or opposition (□) to the Apheta is

---

429. Ibid.
430. Ibid.
431. Ibid.
432. Ibid.
433. This position is also called the Prorogator (Giver of Life). Arabian astrologers referred to it as Almochoden or Alcohoden.

called the Anareta (Destroyer). According to ancient astrologers, this position marks the point in time and the condition of an individual's death. Other practitioners define the Anareta as the formation of a transiting square (□) or opposition (☍) between the position of Mars (♂) or Saturn (♄) in the natal chart and the Sun (☉), the Moon (☽), or Mercury (☿) during a selected time in the present or future.

Step Twenty-one: Voyages and Journeys

An individual's potential for traveling long distances, as well as the condition and outcome of short trips, is determined by delineating the zodiac signs that govern Houses IX and III respectively (see "Delineating House Rulerships" in this chapter as well as "Interpreting the House Rulers in the *Bhavacakra*" in chapter 5). Then any planets that occupy Houses IX and III are interpreted according to their placement by zodiac sign and by house (see "Delineating Planetary Positions by House and by Sign" in this chapter as well as "Interpreting the Planetary Positions in a *Rasicakra*" in chapter 5). Aspects formed by any of the planets occupying Houses IX and III are then interpreted and synthesized into the interpretation (see "Delineating Planetary Aspects").

Alice's Voyages and Journeys

Houses III and IX.   House III in Alice's chart is ruled by Aries (28°♈15′ in fig. 8.1), signifying that she has confrontational relations with neighbors (see "Delineating House Rulerships" in this chapter as well as "Interpreting the House Rulers in the *Bhavacakra*" in chapter 5). House IX in her chart is ruled by Libra (28°♎15′ in fig. 8.1), which indicates that she is antisocial or prejudiced (see "Delineating House Rulerships" in this chapter as well as "Interpreting the House Rulers in the *Bhavacakra*" in chapter 5). A practitioner might indicate that she has confrontations with neighbors when she's doing errands, and with friends on journeys.

Planets occupying House III and their aspects.   Alice's Jupiter occupies House III (♃ 10°♉52′ in fig. 8.1), which suggests that she experiences gains through publishing, writing, communications, and public speaking (see "Delineating Planetary Positions by House and by Sign" in this chapter as well as "Interpreting the Planetary Positions in a *Rasicakra*" in chapter 5). Her Jupiter occupies Taurus (♃ 10° ♉52′ in fig. 8.1), indicating that she has dangerous relations with evil men. She also gains from women or her profession (see "Delineating Planetary Positions by House and by Sign" in this chapter as well as "Interpreting the Planetary Positions in a *Rasicakra*" in chapter 5). A practitioner might suggest from this that she takes short trips for writing, publishing, communications, or public speaking. He or she might also add that Alice has dangerous relations with evil men during short trips or gains from women or her profession.

Jupiter (♃ 10°♉52′ in fig. 8.1) forms a sextile (⚹) to Uranus (♅ 13°♋00′ in fig. 8.1) within a 02°08′ orb of influence (see "Locating Planetary Aspects and Constructing an Aspectarian").[434] This suggests that Alice encounters success and gains through foreign travel or transportation (see "Delineating Planetary Aspects").

Jupiter (♃ 10°♉52′ in fig. 8.1) forms a square (□) to Pluto (♇ 19°♌34′ in fig. 8.1) within an 08°42′ orb of influence (see "Locating Planetary Aspects and Constructing an Aspectarian").[435] This suggests that she has unrealistic expectations and a vacillating or destructive self-image (see "Delineating Planetary Aspects"). All of these aspects, which in one way or another reflect upon Alice's short trips, the practitioner would synthesize into the main body of the interpretation.

Planets occupying House IX and their aspects. Alice's Mars occupies House IX (♂ 01°♏24′ in fig. 8.1), which suggests that she has problems with foreigners or foreign travel (see "Delineating Planetary Positions by House and by Sign" in this chapter as well as "Interpreting the Planetary Positions in a *Rasicakra*" in chapter 5). Her Mars occupies Libra (♂ 01°♏24′ in fig. 8.1), indicating that she has a cold disregard for other people's feelings. But she is best suited for espionage or diplomatic work (see "Delineating Planetary Positions by House and by Sign" in this chapter as well as "Interpreting the Planetary Positions in a *Rasicakra*" in chapter 5).

Mars (♂ 01°♏24′ in fig. 8.1) forms a trine (△) to the Sun (☉ 24°♊55′ in fig. 8.1) within a 06°29′ orb of influence (see "Locating Planetary Aspects and Constructing an Aspectarian").[436] This suggests that she improves in health, vitality, determination, leadership ability, and confidence (see "Delineating Planetary Positions by House and by Sign" in this chapter as well as "Interpreting the Planetary Positions in a *Rasicakra*" in chapter 5).

Mars (♂ 01°♏24′ in fig. 8.1) forms a trine (△) to Mercury (☿ 03°♋28′ in fig. 8.1) within a 02°24′ orb of influence (see "Locating Planetary Aspects and Constructing an Aspectarian").[437] This suggests that she applies immense energy to music, design, art, chemistry, medicine, or engineering. Educators, professionals, scientists, and literary people aid in her personal development (see "Delineating Planetary Positions by House and by Sign" in this chapter as well as "Interpreting

434. This aspect is determined by subtracting the planets' positions as shown in note 357, page 456.
435. Ibid.
436. Ibid.
437. Ibid.

the Planetary Position in a *Rasicakra*" in chapter 5). A practitioner might suggest that the above aspects primarily take place while Alice is on long journeys.

Peter's Voyage and Journeys

Houses III and IX.   House III in Peter's chart is ruled by Taurus (25°♉27′ in fig. 8.2), signifying that he is taciturn and has close or cordial relations with siblings and neighbors (see "Delineating House Rulerships" in this chapter as well as "Interpreting the House Rulers in the *Bhavacakra*" in chapter 5). A practitioner might say that he makes short trips to visit siblings and neighbors. House IX in his chart is ruled by Scorpio (25°♏27′ in fig. 8.2), which indicates that there is mystery attached to travel abroad (see "Delineating House Rulerships" in this chapter as well as "Interpreting the House Rulers in the *Bhavacakra*" in chapter 5).

Planets occupying House III and their aspects.   Peter's Jupiter occupies House III (♃ 25°♉36′ in fig. 8.2) which suggests that he experiences gains through publishing, writing, communications, and public speaking (see "Delineating Planetary Positions by House and by Sign" in this chapter as well as "Interpreting the Planetary Positions in a *Rasicakra*" in chapter 5). His Jupiter occupies Taurus (♃ 25° ♉36′ in fig. 8.2), indicating that he has dangerous relations with evil men. He also gains from women or his profession (see "Delineating Planetary Positions by House and by Sign" in this chapter as well as "Interpreting the Planetary Positions in a *Rasicakra*" in chapter 5). A practitioner might suggest from this that he takes short trips for writing, publishing, communications, or public speaking. He or she might also add that Peter has dangerous relations with evil men during short trips or gains from women or his profession.

Jupiter (♃ 25°♉36′ in fig. 8.2) forms a square (□) to the Sun (☉ 04°♍41′ in fig. 8.2) within a 09°05′ orb of influence (see "Locating Planetary Aspects and Constructing an Aspectarian").[438] This suggests that he encounters financial losses by miscalculation, extravagance, or bad advice (see "Delineating Planetary Aspects").

Jupiter (♃ 25°♉36′ in fig. 8.2) forms a square (□) to Saturn (♄ 01°♓25′ in fig. 8.2) within a 05°49′ orb of influence (see "Locating Planetary Aspects and Constructing an Aspectarian").[439] This suggests that he experiences difficulties related to floods, earthquakes, epidemics, or dishonesty (see "Delineating Planetary Aspects"). These aspects in one way or another reflect upon Peter's short trips, which the practitioner would synthesize into the main body of the interpretation.

---

438.   Ibid. However, not all practitioners would agree that this aspect is pertinent, because it exceeds the 08°00′ orb of influence that is generally accepted.

439.   Ibid. However, not all practitioners would agree that this aspect is pertinent because it exceeds the 08°00′ orb of influence that is generally accepted.

Planets occupying House IX and their aspects.   There are no planets occupying House IX in Peter's chart. Therefore, no prognostications are made using this particular portion of the process.

Step Twenty-two: Education and Mentality

A person's ability to learn and his or her general level of interest in education as well as intellectual interests and the individual's cognitive abilities are also determined by delineating the zodiac signs that govern House IX and III, respectively (see "Delineating House Rulerships"). Then any planets that occupy Houses IX and III are interpreted according to their placement by zodiac sign and by house (see "Delineating Planetary Positions by House and by Sign"). Aspects formed by any of the planets occupying Houses IX and III are then interpreted and synthesized into the interpretation (see "Delineating Planetary Aspects").

Alice's Education and Mentality

Houses III and IX.   House III in Alice's chart is ruled by Aries (28°♈15′ in fig. 8.1), signifying that she has argumentative or violent communications and an impulsive intellect (see "Delineating House Rulerships"). House IX in her chart is ruled by Libra (28°♎15′ in fig. 8.1), which indicates that she is artistically, academically, or philosophically oriented (see "Delineating House Rulerships" in this chapter as well as "Interpreting the House Rulers in the *Bhavacakra*" in chapter 5).

Planets occupying House III and their aspects.   Alice's Jupiter occupies House III (♃ 10°♉52′ in fig. 8.1), which suggests that she experiences gains through advertising, publishing, writing, communications, public speaking, and intellectual pursuits (see "Delineating Planetary Positions by House and by Sign" in this chapter as well as "Interpreting the Planetary Positions in a *Rasicakra*" in chapter 5). Her Jupiter occupies Taurus (♃ 10°♉52′ in fig. 8.1), indicating that she has dangerous relations with evil men, but gains from women or her profession (see "Delineating Planetary Positions by House and by Sign" in this chapter as well as "Interpreting the Planetary Positions in a *Rasicakra*" in chapter 5).

Jupiter (♃ 10°♉52′ in fig. 8.1) forms a sextile (⚹) to Uranus (♅ 13°♋00′ in fig. 8.1) within a 02°08′ orb of influence (see "Locating Planetary Aspects and Constructing an Aspectarian").[440] This suggests that she encounters success and gains through publishing or academic institutions, and has prophetic foresight (see "Delineating Planetary Aspects.").

Jupiter (♃ 10°♉52′ in fig. 8.1) forms a square (□) to Pluto (♇ 19°♌34′ in fig.

440.   Ibid.

8.1) within an 08°42′ orb of influence (see "Locating Planetary Aspects and Constructing an Aspectarian").[441] This suggests that she has unrealistic expectations and a vacillating or destructive self-image (see "Delineating Planetary Aspects"). All of these aspects in one way or another reflect upon Alice's mentality. A practitioner would synthesize these into the main body of the interpretation.

Planets occupying House IX and their aspects.   Alice's Mars occupies House IX (♂ 01°♏24′ in fig. 8.1), which suggests that she has strong, aggressive political or religious beliefs (see "Delineating Planetary Positions by House and by Sign" in this chapter as well as "Interpreting the Planetary Positions in a *Rasicakra*" in chapter 5). Her Mars occupies Scorpio (♂ 01°♏24′ in fig. 8.1), indicating that she is hardworking, inventive, selfish, vengeful, and passionate. She has a cold disregard for other people's feelings (see "Delincating Planetary Positions by House and by Sign" in this chapter as well as "Interpreting the Planetary Positions in a *Rasicakra*" in chapter 5).

Mars (♂ 01°♏24′ in fig. 8.1) forms a trine (△) to the Sun (☉ 24°♊55′ in fig. 8.1) within a 06°29′ orb of influence (see "Locating Planetary Aspects and Constructing an Aspectarian").[442] This suggests that she has vitality, determination, leadership ability, and confidence (see "Delineating Planetary Aspects").

Mars (♂ 01°♏24′ in fig. 8.1) forms a trine (△) to Mercury (☿ 03°♋28′ in fig. 8.1) within a 02°04′ orb of influence (see "Locating Planetary Aspects and Constructing an Aspectarian").[443] This suggests that she applies immense energy to music, design, art, chemistry, medicine, or engineering. Educators, professionals, scientists, and literary people aid in her personal development (see "Delineating Planetary Aspects"). All of the above aspects reflect in one way or another upon Alice's pursuit of a higher education; the practitioner would synthesize this information into the main body of the interpretation.

Peter's Education and Mentality

Houses III and IX.   House III in Peter's chart is ruled by Taurus (28°♉15′ in fig. 8.2), signifying that he is taciturn and slow. He has a careful mentality (see "Delineating House Rulerships" in this chapter as well as "Interpreting the House Rulers in the *Bhavacakra*" in chapter 5). House IX in his chart is ruled by Scorpio (25° ♏27′ in fig. 8.2), which indicates that he equates advanced education with personal power or implied control. He potentially has fanatical religious or philosophical views. There is mystery attached to his higher education or spiritual pursuits

---

441. Ibid.
442. Ibid.
443. Ibid.

(see "Delineating House Rulerships" in this chapter as well as "Interpreting the House Rulers in the *Bhavacakra*" in chapter 5).

Planets occupying House III and their aspects.   Peter's Jupiter occupies House III (♃ 10°♉52′ in fig. 8.2), which suggests that he experiences gains through publishing, writing, communications, and public speaking (see "Delineating Planetary Positions by House and by Sign" in this chapter as well as "Interpreting the Planetary Positions in a *Rasicakra*" in chapter 5). His Jupiter occupies Taurus (♃ 10° ♉52′ in fig. 8.2), indicating that he has dangerous relations with evil men. He also gains from women or his profession (see "Delineating Planetary Positions by House and by Sign" in this chapter as well as "Interpreting the Planetary Positions in a *Rasicakra*" in chapter 5).

Jupiter (♃ 25°♉36′ in fig. 8.2) forms a square (□) to the Sun (☉ 04°♍41′ in fig. 8.2) within a 09°05′ orb of influence (see "Locating Planetary Aspects and Constructing an Aspectarian").[444] This suggests that he encounters financial losses by miscalculation, extravagance, or bad advice (see "Delineating Planetary Aspects").

Jupiter (♃ 25°♉36′ in fig. 8.2) forms a square (□) to Saturn (♄ 01°♓25′ in fig. 8.2) within a 05°49′ orb of influence (see "Locating Planetary Aspects and Constructing an Aspectarian").[445] This suggests that he experiences difficulties related to floods, earthquakes, epidemics, or dishonesty (see "Delineating Planetary Aspects"). All of the above aspects reflect in one way or another upon Peter's mentality; the practitioner would synthesize this information into the main body of the interpretation.

Planets occupying house IX and their aspects.   There are no planets occupying House IX in Peter's chart. Therefore, no prognostications are made using this particular portion of the process.

Step Twenty-three: Occupation and Professional Honors

The ideal type of business, career, or employment for an individual, as well as the potential for receiving professional honors and awards, is determined by delineating the zodiac signs that govern Houses VI and X (see "Delineating House Rulerships" in this chapter as well as "Interpreting the House Rulers in the *Bhavacakra*" in chapter 5). Then any planets that occupy Houses VI and X are interpreted ac-

---

444.   Ibid. However, not all practitioners would agree this aspect is pertinent, because it exceeds the 08°00′ orb of influence that is generally accepted.
445.   Ibid.

cording to their placement by zodiac sign and by house (see "Delineating Planetary Positions by House and by Sign" in this chapter as well as "Interpreting the Planetary Positions in a *Rasicakra*" in chapter 5). Aspects formed by any of the planets occupying Houses VI and X are then synthesized into the interpretation (see "Delineating Planetary Aspects").

In astrology, the commercial world is divided into ten general professional divisions, each of which is ruled by a specific planet. So, according to some practitioners, it is advisable to look to the ruling planet (the planetary ruler of House I) (see "Delineating House Rulerships" in this chapter as well as "Interpreting the House Rulers in the *Bhavacakra*" in chapter 5) for vocational clues exhibited by that planet. The Moon (☽) governs common employments. Mercury (☿) rules schools, intellectual affairs, and publishing. Venus (♀) influences entertainment, art, and social functions. The Sun (☉) rules government employment. Mars (♂) influences manufacturing, building, and munitions. Jupiter (♃) controls religious, legal, publishing, and financial professions. Saturn (♄) rules mining, farming, and working with cement while Uranus (♅) controls railroads and the aerial and electronic industries. Neptune (♆) controls petroleum, other oils, and fishing. Pluto (♇) controls waste recycling and research work.

Alice's Occupation

General indications. House I in Alice's chart is ruled by Aquarius (♒), which is ruled by Uranus (♅) (see "Analyzing the Houses"). According to some practitioners, it suggests that she does well in employment in the railroad, aerial, or electronic industries (see comments above).

House VI. House VI in Alice's chart is ruled by Cancer (07°♋13′ in fig. 8.1), signifying that she prefers to work at home or in home-related jobs. She has strong emotional ties to employees or co-workers. She has inconsistent work habits (see "Delineating House Rulerships" in this chapter as well as "Interpreting the House Rulers in the *Bhavacakra*" in chapter 5).

Planets occupying House VI and their aspects. Alice's Uranus is in Cancer (♅ 13°♋00′ in fig. 8.1), which suggests that she is sensitive, psychic, restless, cranky, and has many original ideas (see "Delineating Planetary Positions by House and by Sign" in this chapter as well as "Interpreting the Planetary Positions in a *Rasicakra*" in chapter 5). Her Uranus occupies House VI (♅ 13°♋00′ in fig. 8.1), indicating that she is manually dexterous and recognized as a decision-maker in the workplace. She is separated from, or disagrees with, employees or co-workers. She has an unpredictable attitude in the workplace. She experiences work- or tool-related accidents (see "Delineating Planetary Positions by House and by Sign" in this chapter as well as "Interpreting the Planetary Positions in a *Rasicakra*" in chapter 5) because this planet forms three square aspects that affect the planet adversely, as shown below.[446]

Uranus (♅ 13°♋00′ in fig. 8.1) forms a square (□) to the Moon (☽ 11°♈28′ in fig. 8.1) within a 01°32′ orb of influence (see "Locating Planetary Aspects and Constructing an Aspectarian").[447] This suggests that she experiences unlucky changes of residence and journeys. She has unusual likes and dislikes (see "Delineating Planetary Aspects").

Alice's Uranus (♅ 13°♋00′ in fig. 8.1) forms a square (□) to Saturn (♄ 08° ♎12′ in fig. 8.1) within a 04°48′ orb of influence (see "Locating Planetary Aspects and Constructing an Aspectarian").[448] This suggests that she has a destructive or rebellious nature. She experiences misfortune by misdirection. And she experiences troubles associated with falls, falling objects, collisions, natural disasters, riots, or uprisings (see "Delineating Planetary Aspects").

Uranus (♅ 13°♋00′ in fig. 8.1) also forms a square (□) to Neptune (♆ 18° ♎59′ in fig. 8.1) within a 05°59′ orb of influence (see "Locating Planetary Aspects and Constructing an Aspectarian").[449] This suggests that she has unusual or unexpected likes and dislikes. She is attracted to psychic centers and unique occupations. Her success is closely linked to the occult, the sea, or large institutions, but danger can occur because of extremes or poor selection of a close friend (see "Delineating Planetary Aspects").

There are also three favorable aspects relating to this planet. Uranus (♅ 13° ♋00′ in fig. 8.1) forms a sextile (✶) to Jupiter (♃ 10°♉52′ in fig. 8.1) within a 02°08′ orb of influence (see "Locating Planetary Aspects and Constructing an Aspectarian").[450] This suggests that she experiences success and gains through publishing, religion, politics, academic institutions, invention, or transportation. She has prophetic foresight (see "Delineating Planetary Aspects").

Uranus (♅, declination 23°11′N in an ephemeris) forms a parallel (∥) to the Sun (☉, declination 23°19′N in an ephemeris) within a 00°08′ orb of influence (see "Locating Planetary Aspects and Constructing an Aspectarian").[451] This indicates that she succeeds with inventions, public service, research, exploration, adventure, transportation, or electronics (see "Delineating Planetary Aspects").

---

446. See note 155, page 414.
447. This aspect is determined by subtracting the planets' positions as shown in note 357, page 456.
448. Ibid.
449. Ibid.
450. Ibid.
451. Ibid.

Uranus (♅, declination 23°11′N in an ephemeris) forms a parallel (∥) to Venus (♀, declination 23°14′N in an ephemeris) within a 00°03′ orb of influence (see "Locating Planetary Aspects and Constructing an Aspectarian").[452] This suggests that she has trouble with the opposite sex, and experiences losses through unexpected circumstances (see "Delineating Planetary Positions by House and by Sign"). All of these aspects, which in one way or another reflect upon Alice's employment and relationship to employees, the practitioner would synthesize into the main body of the interpretation.

House X. House IV in Alice's chart is ruled by Scorpio (25°♏17′ in fig. 8.1), signifying that she does not allow anyone to control her personal destiny. There is potential for a change of career late in life. And secrecy or mystery is connected with profession, social status, or parents (see "Delineating House Rulerships" in this chapter as well as "Interpreting the House Rulers in the *Bhavacakra*" in chapter 5).

Planets occupying House X and their aspects. There are no planets occupying House X in Alice's chart. Therefore, no prognostications are made using this particular portion of the process.

Peter's Occupation

General Indications. House I in Peter's chart is ruled by Pisces (♓), which is ruled by Neptune (♆) (see "Analyzing the Houses"). According to some practitioners, it suggests that he does well in employment in the petroleum or other oil industries and the fishing industry (see comments on page 485).

House VI. House VI in Peter's chart is ruled by Cancer (28°♋27′ in fig. 8.2), signifying that he prefers to work at home or in home-related jobs. He has strong emotional ties to employees or co-workers. He has inconsistent work habits (see "Delineating House Rulerships" in this chapter as well as "Interpreting the House Rulers in the *Bhavacakra*" in chapter 5). Because the zodiac sign Leo is intercepted in this house (see "Placing the Planets and Nodes in the Horoscope"), this sign must also be delineated. Leo (♌ in fig. 8.2) indicates that Peter needs personal pride from work. Employees and co-workers are of great personal concern (see "Delineating House Rulerships" in this chapter as well as "Interpreting the House Rulers in the *Bhavacakra*" in chapter 5).

452. Ibid.

Planets Occupying House VI and Their Aspects.   There are no planets occupying House VI in Peter's chart. Therefore, no prognostications are made using this particular portion of the process.

House X.   House X in Peter's chart is ruled by Sagittarius (17°♐08' in fig. 8.2), signifying that he needs to exhibit his intellect, artistic talent, or training. He must teach what he knows. He may become a promoter or agent. And there is potential for public notice of his professional work (see "Delineating House Ruler-ships" in this chapter as well as "Interpreting the House Rulers in the *Bhavacakra*" in chapter 5).

Planets occupying House X and their aspects.   There are no planets occupying House X in Peter's chart. Therefore, no prognostications are made using this particular portion of the process.

Step Twenty-four: Friends and Associates

A person's ability to develop friendships and associations within a particular social sphere is determined by delineating the zodiac signs that govern House XI (see "Delineating House Rulerships" in this chapter as well as "Interpreting the House Rulers in the *Bhavacakra*" in chapter 5). Then any planets that occupy House XI are interpreted according to their placement by zodiac sign and by house (see "De-lineating Planetary Positions by House and by Sign" in this chapter as well as "In-terpreting the Planetary Positions in a *Rasicakra*" in chapter 5). Aspects formed by any of the planets occupying House XI are then interpreted and synthesized into the interpretation (see "Delineating Planetary Aspects").

Alice's Friends

House XI.   House XI in Alice's chart is ruled by Sagittarius (16°♐44' in fig. 8.1), signifying that she may make new friends in a new environment to improve life. She may make friendships to improve social or professional status. There is poten-tial for victimization by friends. There is secrecy or mystery associated with friend-ships or organizations (see "Delineating House Rulerships" in this chapter as well as "Interpreting the House Rulers in the *Bhavacakra*" in chapter 5).

Planets occupying House XI and their aspects.   There are no planets occupying House XI in Alice's chart. Therefore, no prognostications are made using this par-ticular portion of the process.

Peter's Friends

House XI. House XI in Peter's chart is ruled by Capricorn (06°♑26′ in fig. 8.2), signifying that he has serious or heavy responsibilities associated with friendship. He has few friends but very long-lasting friendships. Most of his friends are older than he, or he acquires them at an older age. He rarely joins organizations or societies. And he often feels friendless (see "Delineating House Rulerships" in this chapter as well as "Interpreting the House Rulers in the *Bhavacakra*" in chapter 5).

Planets occupying House XI and their aspects. There are no planets occupying House XI in Peter's chart. Therefore, no prognostications are made using this particular portion of the process.

Step Twenty-five: Personal Limitations and Restrictions

A person's potential limitations or personal restrictions are determined by delineating the zodiac signs that govern House XII (see "Delineating House Rulerships" in this chapter as well as "Interpreting the House rulers in the *Bhavacakra*" in chapter 5). Then any planets that occupy House XII are interpreted according to their placement by zodiac sign and by house (see "Delineating Planetary Positions by House and by Sign" in this chapter as well as "Interpreting the Planetary Positions in a *Rasicakra*" in chapter 5). Aspects formed by any of the planets occupying House XII are then interpreted and synthesized into the interpretation (see "Delineating Planetary Aspects").

Alice's Personal Limitations

House XII. House XII in Alice's chart is ruled by Capricorn (07°♑13′ in fig. 8.1), signifying that she spends a great deal of time in solitude. She has difficulty attaining true recognition, but may achieve success. She is victimized by unfounded fears and worries. She has a strong interest in the psychic and the occult, but no desire to know the future (see "Delineating House Rulerships" in this chapter as well as "Interpreting the House Rulers in the *Bhavacakra*" in chapter 5).

Planets occupying House XII and their aspects. There are no planets occupying House XII in Alice's chart. Therefore, no prognostications are made using this particular portion of the process.

Peter's Personal Limitations

House XII. House XII in Peter's chart is ruled by Capricorn (28°♑27′ in fig. 8.2), signifying that he spends a great deal of time in solitude. He has difficulty attaining true recognition, but may achieve success. He is victimized by unfounded fears and worries. He has a strong interest in the psychic and the occult, but no desire to know the future (see "Delineating House Rulerships" in this chapter as well as "Interpreting the House Rulers in the *Bhavacakra*" in chapter 5).

Because the zodiac sign Aquarius is intercepted in this house (see "Placing the Planets and Nodes in the Horoscope"), this sign must also be delineated. Aquarius (♒ in fig. 8.2) indicates that Peter harbors an unconscious resentment of authority or convention. He has erratic sleep patterns. Unexpected changes occur in his spouse's employment, and his spouse may introduce unconventional health regimens. He gets involved in secret societies or a friend's secret activities. And he entrusts secrets to a friend (see "Delineating House Rulerships" in this chapter as well as "Interpreting the House Rulers in the *Bhavacakra*" in chapter 5).

Planets occupying House XII and their aspects.   Peter's Saturn occupies House XII (♄ 01°♓28′ in fig. 8.2), indicating that he overcomes sacrifice and denial through courage and reason. He has a persecution complex and encounters ideological crises (see "Delineating Planetary Positions by House and by Sign" in this chapter as well as "Interpreting the Planetary Positions in a *Rasicakra*" in chapter 5). Saturn is in Pisces (♄ 01°♓28′ in fig. 8.2), which suggests that he is indecisive, inspired, and controlled by circumstance. He is the source of his own demise due to emotions (see "Delineating Planetary Positions by House and by Sign" in this chapter as well as "Interpreting the Planetary Positions in a *Rasicakra*" in chapter 5).

Saturn (♄ 01°♓25′ in fig. 8.2) forms an opposition (☍) to the Sun (☉ 04° ♍41′ in fig. 8.2) within a 03°16′ orb of influence (see "Locating Planetary Aspects and Constructing an Aspectarian").[453] This suggests that he experiences disappointment and delays that spoil opportunities for success. He experiences the death or estrangement of his father (see "Delineating Planetary Aspects").

Saturn (♄ 01°♓25′ in fig. 8.2) forms a sextile (⚹) to the Moon (☽ 03°♉38′ in fig. 8.2) within a 02°13′ orb of influence (see "Locating Planetary Aspects and Constructing an Aspectarian").[454] This suggests that professional advancement is likely because of his personal persistence. He receives approval by those in authority and by friends (see "Delineating Planetary Aspects").

Saturn (♄ 01°♓25′ in fig. 8.2) forms a square (□) to Jupiter (♃ 25°♉36′ in fig. 8.2) within a 05°49′ orb of influence (see "Locating Planetary Aspects and Constructing an Aspectarian").[455] This suggests that he encounters trouble through

---

453. Ibid.
454. Ibid.
455. Ibid.

neighbors, companies, or his father. He experiences difficulties related to floods, earthquakes, epidemics, or dishonesty (see "Delineating Planetary Positions by House and by Sign" in this chapter as well as "Interpreting the Planetary Positions in a *Rasicakra*" in chapter 5). All of these aspects, which in one way or another reflect upon Peter's personal limitations, the practitioner would synthesize into the main body of the interpretation.

It may seem obvious at this juncture that the Western interpretation of a natal chart concentrates on cause and effect—the influence of the planets as it affects the individual, and the individual's resultant choice of behavior—without fate or destiny dictating events. Besides working strictly within the present tense (i.e., the accumulation or dissemination of karmic debts or predestination in its purest sense is not considered in this form of interpretation), Western astrology views the impact of planetary motion as manifesting itself primarily in an individual's psychological profile and motivations: it is egocentric. Negative characteristics or prognostications are treated by the astrologer as critical areas for redirection. In other words, the Western astrologer's position is that of a counselor, revealing to the individual the forces that drive him or her, and presenting the individual with options that will potentially improve the outcome of potential events presented in the chart. This physical, self-examining reality, however, has little in common with the application of other astrologies around the world.

At this point, it should be obvious that each form of astrological interpretation (Chinese, Tibetan, Vedic, Arabian, Judaic, and Western) offers a unique twist on the behavioral, emotional, spiritual, and physical aspects of an individual's personality. As mentioned at the beginning of this book, this presentation is not meant to promote or diminish any astrological tradition. By highlighting both conspicuous and subtle differences in ideology and interpretation, the intent is to find the intrinsic value of each form so that it can be appropriately employed in the assessment of an individual personality. The best way to demonstrate how two or more astrologies can be applied in an interpretation is to present the personality profile of one individual derived from all six astrologies.

A Global Understanding

Written *in the* Stars

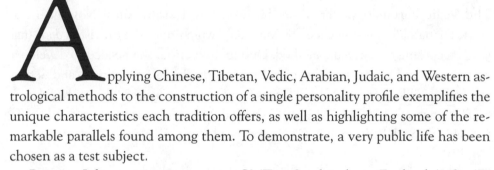

Applying Chinese, Tibetan, Vedic, Arabian, Judaic, and Western astrological methods to the construction of a single personality profile exemplifies the unique characteristics each tradition offers, as well as highlighting some of the remarkable parallels found among them. To demonstrate, a very public life has been chosen as a test subject.

Born on July 1, 1961, at 7:45 P.M. GMT in Sandringham, England (00°30′E/ 52°50′N), Lady Diana Frances Spencer became known to the world as Diana, Princess of Wales, when she married Great Britain's royal heir apparent, Charles, at twenty years of age. From her globally televised marriage until her tragic death in 1997, it appeared that every aspect of Diana's life was quickly converted to public knowledge. Her alleged fairytale-princess life, her complicated separation and divorce, and her death were all documented by the media in books and magazine articles and on television.

But how much of her life was "written in the stars" according to six of the world's major astrologies? A detailed profile based on all six traditions could fill volumes. Therefore, this chapter will focus solely on her personal chronology and essential interpretative highlights of her personality, finances, mentality, relationship to her siblings, domestic life, children, pursuit of pleasure and creativity, physical health, marital status, social and professional status, friends, and personal limitations.

DIANA'S PERSONAL CHRONOLOGIES

All six forms of astrology have something to divulge about Diana's character. But lifetime chronologies are unique to the Vedic and Chinese methods of astrology. Using the Vedic formula for the construction of a *naksatradasa* (a personal chronology based on the Moon's position at the person's birth) as outlined in chapter 5 (see "Constructing the *Vimsottari Dasa*") and combining it with the construction of the Chinese Ten-Year Fate Cycles outlined in chapter 3 (see "Locating and Interpreting the Birth *Miao*"), provides a chronological view into Diana's life. An example of how those two types of chronologies can be combined to create a more detailed picture of Diana's short life follows.

July 1961 to July 1963

The Vedic chronology.   From her birth on July 1, 1961, until November 20, 1961, Diana's life was influenced by Mars (♂), which rules the Sravistha *dasa* (fig. 5.30) according to the Vedic method. During this period, she needed to develop a new health and fitness regimen to bolster health. Travel, adventure, and action were all possible. Because Mars (♂) was poorly positioned (see "Rating by *Sthanabala*" in chapter 5), it was a very restless period. Marital discord occurred in her life (possibly through her parents). Changes of residence took place.

The Chinese chronology.   According to the Chinese fate cycles, Diana's life was affected by her parents' marriage since the *ti chih* (Terrestrial Branch) of her birth *miao* (month pillar)—*ti chih* VII (fig. 3.6)—occupied the seventh fate house (wives and concubines, in fig. 3.10) from her birth until July 1963. This period was influenced by the *hsing* (elements) that ruled her *miao ti chih* (VII, which is ruled by the fire *hsing* in figs. 3.9 and 3.2) and her *hua t'ien kan* (2, which is ruled by the wood *hsing* in figs. 3.13 and 3.1). The relationship between fire and wood is positive (fig. 3.14). This indicates that her emotional state was volatile and angry. She was dynamic but egotistical.

July 1963 to July 1983

The Chinese chronology.   Diana's second Chinese fate cycle (July 1963 to July 1973) was a period in which the *ti chih* (Terrestrial Branch) of her progressed *miao* (month pillar)—*ti chih* VIII—occupied the eighth fate house (sickness and distress, in fig. 3.10). It was during these formative years that her emotional torment affected her health, causing fits of depression and anxiety. This period was influenced by the *hsing* (elements) that ruled her *miao ti chih* (VIII, which is ruled by the metal *hsing* in fig. 3.2) and her *hua t'ien kan* (2, which is ruled by the wood *hsing* in figs.

3.13 and 3.1). The relationship between metal and wood is negative (fig. 3.14). This indicates that she was energetic and possessed the virtue of rectitude. Her emotional state was often anger and sadness. Her actions were guided by the passionate intensity of her feelings. Despite her physical problems, a determined and somewhat rigid, opinionated outlook guided her through both hard times and false starts while she maintained her self-confidence and compassion. In real life, Diana's parents divorced when she was eight years old, affecting her self-esteem.

During her third Chinese fate cycle (July 1973 to July 1983) the *ti chih* (Terrestrial Branch) her progressed *miao* (month pillar)—*ti chih* IX—occupied the ninth fate house (removal and change, in fig. 3.10). She traveled, experiencing many changes in her lifestyle under this influence. She was, in fact, sent to a Swiss finishing school during this period. She also met Prince Charles and married him (July 29, 1981), relocating to his home. Her marital problems, miscarriages, postpartum depressions, and eating disorders began during this time, which was influenced by the *hsing* (elements) that ruled her *miao ti chih* (IX, which is ruled by the metal *hsing* in fig. 3.2) and her *hua t'ien kan* (2, which is ruled by the wood *hsing* in figs. 3.13 and 3.1). As previously mentioned, the relationship between metal and wood is negative (fig. 3.14). This indicates that she was still energetic and possessed the virtue of rectitude. Again, her emotional state was filled with anger and sadness. Her actions were guided by her passionately intense feelings. A determined and somewhat rigid, opinionated outlook guided her through both hard times and false starts while she maintained her self-confidence and compassion.

The Vedic chronology. According to her Vedic chronology, the Moon's North Node (☊) influenced her Satabhisaj *dasa* (fig. 5.30), which lasted for eighteen years (November 21, 1961, to November 20, 1979). Success, wealth, and travel occurred. In real life, she attended a Swiss finishing school during this period.

Diana entered her Purvabhadrapada *dasa* on November 21, 1979. It was influenced by Jupiter (♃) (fig. 5.30). This period lasted for sixteen years, until November 20, 1995. Adversely aspected by its position at Diana's birth, Jupiter (♃) indicated that this otherwise very fortunate and prosperous period in which marriage, children, or professional success occurred was tainted by greed, indolence, extravagance, or lost opportunities. She met and married Prince Charles in 1981. And the Vedic prognostications for Diana's marriage (July 29, 1981) were not good. Her separation from Prince Charles in December 1995 opened a battery of accusations and media assaults about her extravagant habits during their marriage, which had lasted fourteen years.

July 1983 to August 1997

The Chinese chronology.   During Diana's fourth Chinese fate cycle (July 1983 to July 1993) the *ti chih* (Terrestrial Branch) of her progressed *miao* (month pillar)—*ti chih* X—occupied the tenth fate house (official, reward, and profession in fig. 3.10). Diana received considerable recognition and honors during this cycle. But her public image and social status were not only her profession, they were the cause of many problems. This period was influenced by the *hsing* (elements) that ruled her *miao ti chih* (X, which is ruled by the metal *hsing* in fig. 3.2) and her *hua t'ien kan* (2, which is ruled by the wood *hsing* in figs. 3.13 and 3.1). The relationship between metal and wood is negative (fig. 3.14). This indicates that she was energetic and possessed the virtue of rectitude. Her emotional state was filled with anger and sadness. And her actions were guided by her passionately intense feelings. Once again, a determined and somewhat rigid, opinionated outlook guided her through both hard times and false starts while she maintained her self-confidence and compassion.

During Diana's fifth Chinese fate cycle (July 1993 to July 2003) the *ti chih* (Terrestrial Branch) of her progressed *miao* (month pillar)—*ti chih* XI—occupied the eleventh fate house (good fortune, virtue, and opportunities, in fig. 3.10). Diana experienced a period of good fortune and abundant opportunities while this cycle influenced her life. This period was influenced by the hsing (elements) that ruled her *miao ti chih* (XI, which is ruled by the earth *hsing* in fig. 3.2) and her *hua t'ien kan* (2, which is ruled by the wood *hsing* in figs. 3.13 and 3.1). The relationship between earth and wood is negative (fig. 3.14). This indicates that she was prudent and yet she was filled with desire and anger. She had learned to move cautiously and shrewdly, measuring each action for its potential result. She still possessed self-confidence and compassion. And she still loved both nature and children. Progressive in outlook, she had learned to delegate, diversify, and organize in an executive manner, making her an ideal manager of large-scale projects which came to light after her separation from Charles in 1995 and eventual divorce in 1996.

The Vedic chronology.   According to her Vedic chronology, Saturn (♄) influenced her Uttarabhadrapada *dasa* (fig. 5.30) for nineteen years (November 21, 1995, to November 20, 2014). Although success was earned by hard work and persistence, Saturn's (♄) poor positioning (see "Rating by *Sthanabala*" in chapter 5) indicated that uncontrollable obstacles, illness, depression, and loneliness prevailed during this period. Diana's divorce from Prince Charles became official on August 9, 1996. And her difficult pregnancies, postpartum depression, eating disorders, and family strife were detailed in the media for public scrutiny which led to fits of depression until her death in 1997.

——— ✳ ———

As mentioned earlier, the data derived from these two forms of personal chronology are general and used only to time the course of events indicated by more specific astrological prognostications that follow. Each facet of Diana's life—her general personality, financial outlook, and ability to bear children, as well as her marriage, religious beliefs, and profession—is uncovered in a variety of ways by the different astrological traditions. Not all traditions appear in every section. For example, there is little or no mention of profession in Tibetan astrology, and higher education is not a concern in Arabian, Tibetan, or Chinese astrology.

A PUBLIC PRIVATE LIFE: DIANA'S PERSONALITY

The following section demonstrates how each tradition perceived the individuality and personality of this very public figure. With little disagreement among the methodologies, the profile of an independent person with ambition and determination appears. Her greatest financial successes came from legacies or inheritance; and her greatest struggles came from within, in the form of uncertainty, anxiety, and depression. Though she was concerned about self-improvement and self-preservation, and was very attached to home and children, she was also troubled and materialistic, and sought sexual gratification. This persona is disclosed from a synthesis of the prognostications that follow.

Western chart shape.   Diana's Western natal horoscope (fig. 9.1) formed a splay shape (see "Assessing the Chart's Overall Shape" in chapter 8). This suggests that she was intensely independent and refused to conform, or to be categorized or criticized by others.

Western houses of the chart.   Diana had six out of ten planets in succedent houses (Houses II, V, and VIII in fig. 9.1), which stressed her focus on personal finances (House II); creativity, speculation, and/or children (House V); legacies, death, and other people's money (House VIII) (see "Analyzing the Houses" in chapter 8).

Western predominance of elements.   Four out of ten planets in Diana's chart (fig. 9.1) were positioned in earth signs (see "Analyzing the Predominant Features" in chapter 8), while three planets occupied water signs, two planets resided in air signs, and one planet was situated in a fire sign. This predominance of earth signs suggests that she had a melancholic temperament: a conservative, withdrawn, and constant (although nervous) nature. She was primarily practical, reserved, and

FIGURE 9.1. DIANA SPENCER'S WESTERN NATAL CHART.

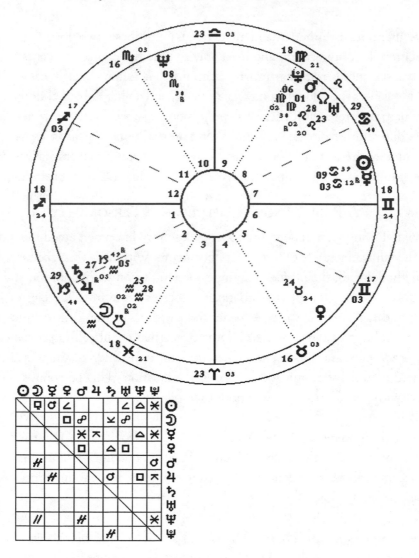

reliable or miserly, materialistic, and rigid. Driven toward self-improvement as a means of self-expression, she looked for rewards in the physical world. But this was tempered by a substantial water-sign influence that additionally indicated that she was sensitive, impressionable, and reflective, possessing an emotional, confused, receptive, and self-protective nature.

Western predominance of qualities. Five out of ten planets in Diana's chart (fig. 9.1) occupied the fixed signs of Aquarius (♒), Taurus (♉), Leo (♌), and Scorpio (♏), forming a "fixed cross" or a "cross of crisis" (see "Analyzing the Predominant Features" in chapter 8). This suggests that she was organized and resistant to change. She was difficult to move or dissuade, and required a consistent daily routine. Solely concerned with her internal dialogue and the demands of her unconscious mind, remaining totally unaffected by outside opinion or circumstances, Diana derived her personal values from her inner self. She fought a constant internal battle to fuse the conscious and unconscious elements of self according to her very subjective view.

Location of the Moon's North and South Nodes in the Western chart.   The Moon's North Node (☊ 28°♌02′ in fig. 9.1) was situated in House VIII of Diana's Western horoscope, which indicates that her potential for financial gain, professional success, and receipt of favors was closely linked to legacies or inheritance (see "Reviewing the Moon's Nodes and the Part of Fortune" in chapter 8).

Indicating the type of problems that occurred in Diana's life, the Moon's South Node (☋ 28°♒02′ in fig. 9.1) was situated in House II, which suggests that she encountered great financial misfortune, indebtedness, or financial worries (see "Reviewing the Moon's Nodes and the Part of Fortune" in chapter 8).

The Sun (☉) and the Moon (☽).   According to her Western horoscope, Diana's Sun is in Cancer (☉ 09°♋39′ in fig. 9.1), indicating that she was sensitive and changeable. She had a fertile imagination and was profoundly affected by her surroundings. (This point is a contradiction to the predominance of qualities mentioned above. In this case, a practitioner would rely primarily on the actual planetary positions rather than the analysis of predominant features.) Possessing dramatic flair and experiencing many mood swings, she craved kindness, feared ridicule, and remembered everything (see "Delineating Planetary Positions by House and by Sign" in chapter 8).

Diana's Moon is in Aquarius (☽ 25°♒02′ in fig. 9.1), indicating that she was active, unconventional, highly inventive, and very independent. She was attracted to science, education, the occult, secret societies, and politics (see "Delineating Planetary Positions by House and by Sign" in chapter 8).

The Arabian Part of Fortune and Part of Aptness.   Used in both Arabian and modern Western astrology, the Arabian Part of Fortune (see "The Part of Fortune" in chapter 6) indicates the type and quality of worldly success an individual might anticipate. Derived by adding the Western Ascendant's position (18°♐24′ in fig. 9.1) to the Moon's position (☽ 25°♒02′ in fig. 9.1) and subtracting the Sun's position (☉ 09°♋39′ in fig. 9.1) from the sum, Diana's Part of Fortune (03°♌46′) is situated in House VIII. This suggests that her worldly success was attributable to an inheritance or in some way to other people's money (such as her husband's).

FIGURE 9.2. DIANA SPENCER'S JUDAIC NATAL CHART.

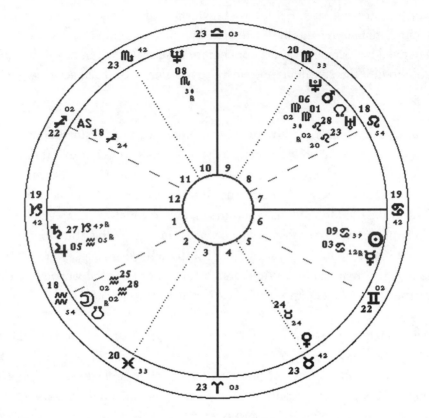

Despite this troubled persona, the Arabian Part of Aptness (see "Parts Associated with House I" in chapter 6) suggests that there was a productive side to the princess's character. The Part is derived by adding the Ascendant's position (18°♐24′ fig. 9.1) to Mercury's position (☿ 03°♋12′ fig. 9.1) and subtracting Saturn's position (♄ 27°♑49′ fig. 9.1) from the sum. Diana's Arabian Part of Aptness (23°♊47′) is positioned in House VII, which indicates she had the ability to make the most out of the least (see "The Part of Aptness" in chapter 6).

Western, Judaic, and Vedic Ascendants.   Diana's Western Ascendant (18°♐24′ in fig. 9.1) suggests that she was sociable, theatrical, active, and trusting. It also indicates that she tended to stamp or scrape her feet (see "Delineating the House Rulerships" in chapter 8).

Her Judaic Ascendant (19°♑42′ in fig. 9.2) suggests that she lacked energy. She was a sex addict whose downfall was caused by the opposite sex. She was educated but deceitful. Its placement in the second decanate (11°♑00′–20°♑00′) further indicates that her evil intentions were concealed by an ingratiating attitude. It also suggests that she was irascible (see "Delineating the Ascendant" in chapter 7).

FIGURE 9.3. DIANA SPENCER'S VEDIC NATAL CHART

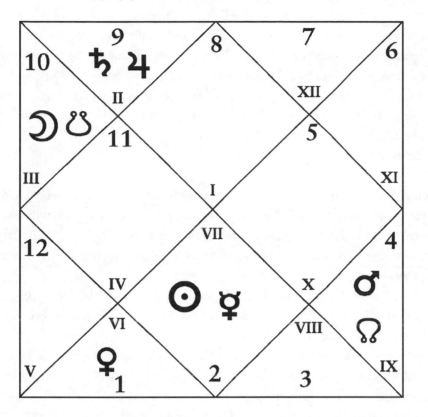

Her Vedic Ascendant (8°, ♏ [Scorpio] in fig. 9.3) is governed by the eighteenth *naksatra:* the *naksatra* Jyestha (16°♏ 40′–00°♐ 00′) (see "Identifying the Ascendant's *Naksatra*" in chapter 5). This placement indicates that she was respectable and capable. She acted and spoke well in public. Other people looked up to her. This Ascendant (25°♏ 11′ in fig. 9.3) is also ruled by the zodiac sign Scorpio (♏), which suggests that she was magnetic, erotic, investigative, frank, and fearless (see "Interpreting the House Rulers in the *Bhavacakra*" in chapter 5).

Planets in the Western chart's House I.   Saturn (♄ 27°♑ 49′ in fig. 9.1) occupies House I in Diana's Western horoscope, which suggests that she lived a calculated, almost premeditated existence. She was highly self-centered (see "Delineating Planetary Positions by House and by Sign" in chapter 8). The planet's placement in Capricorn also suggests that she was melancholic, discontented, very anxious to succeed, and ultimately successful. However, once success was hers, she lost much of it through unreliable friends, inferior attachments, and an unsatisfactory marriage. It also suggests that she suffered from chronic physical or mental illness (see "Delineating Planetary Positions by House and by Sign" in chapter 8).

Saturn ($\hbar$ 27°♑49′ in fig. 9.1) forms a trine to Venus (♀24°♉24′ in fig. 9.1) (see "Locating Planetary Aspects and Constructing an Aspectarian" in chapter 8), which suggests that she experienced success and fidelity in marriage and love. She also tended to save money and gained through elders, superiors, and investments (see "Delineating Planetary Aspects" in chapter 8). Saturn ($\hbar$ 27°♑49′ in fig. 9.1) also forms a conjunction to Jupiter (♃ 05°♒05′ in fig. 9.1), which suggests that she had the power to overcome problems. She experienced general prosperity and an improved reputation. She gained from publishing, politics, religion, foreign travel, science, or medicine.

Tibetan Year of Birth and Forces.   According to Tibetan astrology, Diana was born in an Ox year (1961), influenced by metal (fig. 4.1). This configuration suggests that she liked to sleep. She was also stubborn and disobedient. Although difficult to change, Diana was surprisingly agreeable when confronted. Somewhat slow and procrastinating, she also had an even temper.

A Tibetan practitioner would also review the four essential forces that guided Diana's overall personality. These are the *sok* (life force), *la* (spirit force), *lung ta* (luck force), and *wang* (power force). Her *sok* (life force) was governed by the earth element, which stabilized and strengthened her overall being (see "Determining the *Sok*" in chapter 4). Because her *sok* was ruled by the earth element, her *la* (spirit or emotional force) was governed by fire because fire is the "mother" of earth (see "Determining the *La*" in chapter 4). This suggests that she possessed a strong, fast-moving, and hot emotional makeup. Her *lung ta* (luck force) was governed by the harmonious relationship between the earth element of her *sok* and the metal element that rules the Ox Year's *lung ta* (see "Determining the *Lung Ta*" in chapter 4). Because the relationship of these two elements is very positive (fig. 4.3), Diana was graced with ample good fortune. Her *wang* (power force) was ruled by metal, which suggests that she overcame obstacles by applying strong, cutting, changeable, and direct energy to problems (see "Determining the *Wang*" in chapter 4).

FIGURE 9.4. DIANA SPENCER'S *SSU CHU* GRID.

5 (GUO T'IEN KAN FROM FIG. 3.17)	2 (HUA T'IEN KAN FROM FIG. 3.13)	I (MIAO T'IEN KAN FROM FIG. 3.6)	8 (GEN T'IEN KAN FROM FIG. 3.4)
III (GUO TI CHIH FROM FIG. 3.16)	II (HUA TI CHIH FROM FIG. 3.13)	VII (MIAO TI CHIH FROM FIG. 3.6)	II (GEN TI CHIH FROM FIG. 3.4)

Chinese Year of Birth and "Song of the Four Seasons."   According to the Ming Shu version of Chinese astrology, Diana was born in a Metal Ox year (1961) (see "Interpreting the *Ming Shu*" in chapter 3). This suggests that she was hardworking, stubborn, and even-tempered. Despite a plodding, deliberate outward persona, Diana was very intelligent, using quiet analysis, caution, tenacity, and steady motion before moving forward. Very attached to home, family, and children, she was a lover of the arts, but maintained a mental "stone wall." She preferred to fight rather than change her personal viewpoint. Her forceful personality was combined with a less than affectionate nature, making her almost militant about life, unable to accept failure or defeat.

Her *gen's* (year pillar) *ba tze* pair (8/II, fig. 9.4) indicates that she was influenced by the metal *hsing* that governs *t'ien kan* 8 (Celestial Stem). This suggests that she was energetic and possessed the essential virtue of rectitude. Her overall emotional state was filled with sadness. She was guided by her passionately intense feelings. Her determined and somewhat rigid, opinionated outlook guided her through hard times and false starts. Ultimately, however, she found success (see chapter 3, "Locating and Interpreting the Birth *Gen*"). The earth *hsing* governs *ti chih* II (Terrestrial Branch), which instilled prudence, faith, and desire into her persona. Practical, conservative, and reliable, she moved cautiously and shrewdly, measuring each action for its potential result. She also loved to delve deeply into any matter, seeking critical details as well as bits of trivia along the way.

Diana's *guo* (hour pillar) is used to determine her share of good fortune (see "Applying the Birth *Guo* with the 'Song of the Four Seasons' " in chapter 3, and fig. 9.4). Her *guo's ti chih*—*ti chih* II—is positioned in the emperor's hands in the summer season (fig. 3.18). This placement indicates that her quality of life improved when she left her place of birth. Business and trade were her primary sources for her fortune. Her beginnings were modest, compared to later years. Her family also enjoyed abundance.

THE NEED FOR SECURITY: DIANA'S FINANCIAL AND MATERIAL ASSETS

Western, Judaic, Arabian, and Vedic astrological data yield a great deal of information related to Diana's financial status and attitude toward material acquisition. A shrewd manipulator of funds, she had rather unconventional saving and spending habits. She experienced unexpected financial fluctuations throughout her life, but experienced general prosperity. Diana also had a need to impress others with her money, and regularly overspent (resulting in disputes with her husband). She had a strong potential for inheritance, for gains through litigation, and for receiving favors from powerful people. Her material misfortunes arose from marital problems, jealousy, indiscretions with friends, and mental or physical illness.

She also had unlucky friendships and journeys. And though she craved power, she suffered bizarre and unexpected losses, as shown in the delineations below.

Western, Judaic, and Vedic House II rulers.   House II (29°♑48′ in fig. 9.1) in Diana's Western natal chart, which is ruled by Capricorn (♑), indicates that she was cautious about spending: she displayed selfishness over her finances. She also gained from hard work and persistence (see "Delineating House Rulerships" in chapter 8). The zodiac sign Aquarius (♒) is also intercepted in House II (fig. 9.1), which suggests that she experienced unexpected financial fluctuations and engaged in unconventional ways of spending and saving money.

House II (18°♒54′ in fig. 9.2) in Diana's Judaic natal chart, however, suggests that she only experienced the Aquarian influences mentioned above. House II (10 in fig. 9.3) in Diana's Vedic natal chart, on the other hand, suggests that she gained financially from numerous sources. It also indicates that she needed to impress others with her money.

Western, Judaic, and Vedic House VIII rulers.   House VIII (29°♋48′ in fig. 9.1), which is ruled by Cancer (♋) in Diana's Western natal chart, indicates that Diana had a strong potential for inheritance or legacy. It also suggests, however, that she was too influenced by outside opinion to be a proficient manager of other people's money (see "Delineating House Rulerships" in chapter 8). The zodiac sign Leo (♌) is also intercepted in House VIII (fig. 9.1), which suggests that she was a shrewd manipulator of financial resources and assets, for herself and others.

House VIII (18°♌54′ in fig. 9.2), which is ruled by Leo (♌) in Diana's Judaic natal chart, however, suggests that she only experienced the Leonine influences mentioned above. House VIII (3 in fig. 9.3) in Diana's Vedic natal chart, on the other hand, suggests that she had a strong involvement in stocks, taxes, insurance, and managing other people's money.

The Arabian Part of Slavery and Bondage, Part of Inheritance and Possessions, and Part of Sorrow.   The Arabian Part of Slavery and Bondage (see "The Part of Slavery and Bondage" in chapter 6) indicates who or what an individual serves. The Part is derived by adding the Western Ascendant's position (18°♐24′ in fig. 9.1) to the Moon's position (☽ 25°♒02′ in fig. 9.1) and subtracting the planetary ruler of the zodiac sign that the Moon occupies from the sum (which in this case is Saturn [♄], the traditional ruler of that zodiac sign).[1] The final sum is Diana's Part

---

1.   See chapter 6, note 27, page 274.

of Slavery and Bondage (15°♑37′), which is situated in House I. This suggests that she served her own interests.

The Arabian Part of Inheritances and Possessions (see "The Part of Inheritances and Possessions" in chapter 6) indicates what the person may materially or financially receive from his or her family or ancestors. The Part is derived by adding the Western Ascendant's position (18°♐24′ in fig. 9.1) to the Moon's position (☽ 25°♒02′ in fig. 9.1) and subtracting Saturn's position (♄ 27°♑49′ in fig. 9.1) from the sum. The final sum is Diana's Part of Inheritances and Possessions (15°♑37′) which is situated in House I. This suggests that she was self-sufficient, inheriting little from others.

The Arabian Part of Sorrow (see "The Part of Sorrow" in Chapter 6) indicates the person's material misfortune. The Part is derived by adding the Western Ascendant's position (18°♐24′ in fig. 9.1) to the Part of Fortune's position (03°♌46′ from above) and subtracting Neptune's position (♆ 08°♏38′ in fig. 9.1) from the sum. Diana's Part of Sorrow (13°♍52′) is situated in House VIII. This suggests that her material misfortunes stemmed from from inheritance, from other people's money, and from the dead.

Planets in the Western and Judaic charts' House II.   Jupiter (♃ 05°♒05′ in fig. 9.1) occupied House II of Diana's natal chart, indicating that she was financially successful in large, popular enterprises or the fields of government, law, insurance, banking, religion, science, education, literature, or commercial travel. But this planet was also adversely aspected, suggesting that she was a spendthrift and was overly optimistic about speculative ventures or gambling (see "Delineating Planetary Positions by House and by Sign" in chapter 8). Her extravagant expenditures on clothes, hairdressers, and makeup were reputedly in excess of $250,000 per year, a figure that did not include day-to-day living expenses.

Jupiter (♃ 05°♒05′ in fig. 9.1) formed a conjunction to Saturn (♄ 27°♑49′ in fig. 9.1), suggesting that she had the power to overcome problems and experienced general prosperity and improved reputation. She gained from publishing, politics, religion, foreign travel, science, or medicine (see "Delineating Planetary Aspects" in chapter 8). However, Jupiter (♃ 05°♒05′ in fig. 9.1) formed a square to Neptune (♆ 08°♏38′ in fig. 9.1), which indicates that she encountered troubles through secret societies, psychic experiences, or religion. She also experienced losses due to fraud. Additionally, she encountered dangers at sea or through liquids, water, or chemicals. And she kept her sorrows a secret (see chapter 8, "Delineating Planetary Aspects").

As mentioned earlier, Diana's Moon is in Aquarius (☽ 25°♒02′ in fig. 9.1),

indicating that she was active, unconventional, highly inventive, and very independent. She was attracted to science, education, the occult, secret societies, and
politics (see "Delineating Planetary Positions by House and by Sign" in chapter 8).
It also occupies House II, which suggests that she had considerable financial success. Since it was also adversely aspected, she possibly sold herself short financially
(see "Delineating Planetary Positions by House and by Sign" in chapter 8).

The Moon (☽ 25°♒02′ in fig. 9.1) formed a square to Venus (♀ 24°♉24′ in fig.
9.1), suggesting that her fickle nature created romantic, marital, or partnership
problems that led to financial or property losses (see "Delineating Planetary Aspects" in chapter 8). The Moon (☽ 25°♒02′ in fig. 9.1) formed an opposition to
Mars (♂ 01°♍38′ in fig. 9.1), indicating that she learned from experience that indiscreet words and actions create enemies. She lost opportunities and was careless
(see "Delineating Planetary Aspects" in chapter 8). The Moon (☽ 25°♒02′ in fig.
9.1) formed an opposition to Uranus (♅ 23°♌20′ in fig. 9.1), indicating that she
experienced unlucky changes of residence and journeys. The occult, the opposite
sex, and unreliable friends caused great difficulties. She also had unusual likes and
dislikes (see "Delineating Planetary Aspects" in chapter 8).

The Moon (☽ 25°♒02′ in fig. 9.2) in Diana's Judaic chart had the same effect
mentioned above. The planetary aspects also formulated the same prognostications.

Planets in the Vedic chart's House II.   Saturn (♄ in fig. 9.3) occupied the zodiac
sign Sagittarius (9 in fig. 9.3) in Diana's Vedic chart, which suggests that the
princess was fearless and championed domestic or political advancements. She had
prophetic insights into the future welfare of civilization in general, or a scientific
breakthrough. She also discovered that opposition creates resentment; and she
pursued more than one career (see "Interpreting the Planetary Positions in a *Rasicakra*" in chapter 5). Its placement in House II indicates that she had a limited
imagination, an unhappy family life, difficulties earning money, and was poorly educated (see "Interpreting the Planetary Positions in a *Bhavacakra*" in chapter 5).

Jupiter (♃ in fig. 9.3) occupied the zodiac sign Sagittarius (9 in fig. 9.3) in
Diana's Vedic chart, suggesting that she had success with horses as well as good fortune. She was victorious over enemies and succeeded in all things (see "Interpreting the Planetary Positions in a *Rasicakra*" in chapter 5). Its placement in House II
indicated that she was wealthy, imaginative, and had a happy education. Diana was
truthful and had a strong memory. She acquired money through moral acts (see
"Interpreting the Planetary Positions in a *Bhavacakra*" in chapter 5).

Planets in the Western and Judaic charts' House VIII.   House VIII in both
Diana's Western and Judaic charts was occupied by Uranus (♅ 20°♌23′ in figs. 9.1

and 9.2), indicating that she gained through legacy, litigation, or other people's money. Since it was also adversely aspected, she also lost lawsuits (see "Delineating Planetary Positions by House and by Sign" in chapter 8). Uranus is in Leo (♅ 20°♌23′ in figs. 9.1 and 9.2), suggesting that she gained favors from powerful people. It is indicated that she had a rich and good marriage. She also possessed wisdom, foresight, willpower, leadership qualities, and good fortune.

As mentioned earlier, the Moon (☽ 25°♒02′ in figs. 9.1 and 9.2) formed an opposition to Uranus (♅ 23°♌20′ in figs. 9.1 and 9.2), indicating that she experienced unlucky changes of residence and journeys. The occult, the opposite sex, and unreliable friends caused great difficulties. She also had unusual likes and dislikes (see "Delineating Planetary Aspects" in chapter 8).

Venus (♀ 24°♉24′ in figs. 9.1 and 9.2) formed a square to Uranus (♅ 23°♌20′ in figs. 9.1 and 9.2), indicating that she had trouble with the opposite sex, including jealousy during marriage or a love affair. She experienced losses through unexpected circumstances (see "Delineating Planetary Aspects" in chapter 8).

The planet Pluto (♇ 06°♍02′ in figs. 9.1 and 9.2) occupied House VIII in both Diana's Western and Judaic charts. This suggests that she gained through inheritance or legacy (see "Delineating Planetary Positions by House and by Sign" in chapter 8).

Pluto (♇ 06°♍02′ in figs. 9.1 and 9.2) formed a sextile to the Sun (☉ 09°♋39′ in figs. 9.1 and 9.2), indicating that she had influence over other people and was able to modify herself in order to attain personal goals. Pluto (♇ 06°♍02′ in figs. 9.1 and 9.2) formed a sextile to Mercury (☿ 03°♋12′ in figs. 9.1 and 9.2), indicating that she was adaptable and persuasive (see "Delineating Planetary Aspects" in chapter 8).

The planet Pluto (♇ 06°♍02′ in figs. 9.1 and 9.2) formed a conjunction to Mars (♂ 01°♍38′ in figs. 9.1 and 9.2), indicating that her goals were achieved through hard work, self-confidence, and a competitive spirit, and by attacking spontaneously (see "Delineating Planetary Aspects" in chapter 8).

Mars (♂ 01°♍38′ in figs. 9.1 and 9.2) occupied House VIII in both Diana's Western and Judaic charts. This suggests that she had disputes or troubles with legacies. She also had disputes with her husband over expenditures. Since the planet was adversely aspected, she could have lost her inheritance by contest or through excess (see "Delineating Planetary Positions by House and by Sign" in chapter 8). Its placement in the zodiac sign Virgo suggests that she craved fame and power, but encountered downfalls, obstacles, reversals, and struggles of a bizarre nature (see "Delineating Planetary Positions by House and by Sign" in chapter 8).

As mentioned earlier, the Moon (☽ 25°♒02′ in figs. 9.1 and 9.2) formed an opposition to Mars (♂ 01°♍38′ in figs. 9.1 and 9.2), indicating that she learned from experience that indiscreet words and actions create enemies. She lost opportunities and was careless (see "Delineating Planetary Aspects" in chapter 8).

Mars (♂ 01°♍38′ in figs. 9.1 and 9.2) formed a square to Venus (♀ 24°♉24′ in figs. 9.1 and 9.2), which suggests that she was careless and extravagant. She encountered losses through fire. Her problems stemmed from marriage, partnerships, or jealous friends (see "Delineating Planetary Aspects" in chapter 8).

The planet Mars (♂ 01°♍38′ in figs. 9.1 and 9.2) formed a sextile to Mercury (♀ 03°♋12′ in figs. 9.1 and 9.2), suggesting that she applied immense energy to music, design, art, chemistry, medicine, or engineering. Educators, professionals, scientists, and literary people aided in her personal development (see "Delineating Planetary Aspects" in chapter 8).

THE NEED FOR FULFILLMENT: DIANA'S MENTALITY AND ABILITY TO ACHIEVE PERSONAL DESIRES

Mentality and the desire to attain a higher education are subjects that are discussed in Western, Judaic, and Vedic astrology. Though she was shy and had a character suited to being an actor, dancer, or musician, Diana was also naturally inclined to politics and social affairs. She fulfilled her greatest desires, but she did not have a happy life. She struggled against mental laziness, and found herself in unwanted conflicts with religious or spiritual leaders. These elements of her mentality and her ability to fulfill her desires are disclosed in the prognostications that follow.

Western, Judaic, and Vedic House III rulers.   The House III ruler (18°♓21′ in fig. 9.1; 20°♓33′ in fig. 9.2) in both her Western and Judaic horoscopes is the zodiac sign Pisces (♓), which indicates that she was overly emotional in her communications. She was also intuitive, but mentally lazy (see "Delineating House Rulerships" in chapter 8). In real life, Diana never passed any of her ordinary- or advanced-level exams, and even failed those that she took twice.

Her Vedic House III ruler (10 [♐, Sagittarius] in fig. 9.3) suggested that she had limited communication skills. She was reluctant to express herself verbally. She had a limited or delayed education, but was mentally organized (see "Interpreting the House Rulers in the *Bhavacakra*" in chapter 5). In actuality, her education prior to her marriage to Prince Charles at the age of eighteen was limited. Swiss finishing schools offer no academic challenge—a fact that was evident when she returned to England and was unable to score a passing grade in any required secondary-school subjects.

Western, Judaic, and Vedic House IX rulers.   The House IX ruler (20°♍33′ in fig. 9.2; 18°♍21′ in fig. 9.1) in both her western and Judaic horoscopes is the zodiac sign Virgo (♍), which indicates that she was concerned with higher education, publishing, philosophy, religion, anthropology, and travel abroad. She had the potential to earn an advanced degree abroad (see "Delineating House Rulerships" in chapter 8).

Her Vedic House IX ruler (4 [♋, Cancer] in fig. 9.3) suggests that Diana had a strong emotional connection to higher education, culture, publishing, religion, and politics (see "Interpreting the House Rulers in the *Bhavacakra*" in chapter 5).

Planets in House III.   Neither Diana's Western nor her Judaic charts contained any planets in House III. But in her Vedic horoscope it was occupied by the Moon (☽ in fig. 9.3) and by the Moon's South Node (☋ in fig. 9.3). The Moon's placement suggests that she fulfilled her strong desires. It also intimates that she could have become a musician, dancer, writer, or actor. And it suggests that she had an unhappy life (see "Interpreting the Planetary Positions in a *Bhavacakra*" in chapter 5). Her musical talent, in real life, was well noted by her family and friends. The Moon's South Node placement indicates that she was eccentric, and she easily fulfilled her desires (see "Interpreting the Planetary Positions in a *Bhavacakra*" in chapter 5).

Planets in House IX.   Neither Diana's Western nor Judaic charts contained any planets in House IX. But her Vedic horoscope was occupied by Mars (♂ in fig. 9.3), and the Moon's North Node (☊ in fig. 9.3). Mars's (♂ in fig. 9.3) placement in this house indicates that she had conflicts with religious or spiritual teachers. According to reports, Diana was not a very religious person.

This placement also suggests that she was very ambitious and had a strong interest in religion. Diana did, in fact, meet with the headmaster of England's top Roman Catholic school on a number of occasions to learn about Catholicism, the religion her mother had adopted after she left Diana's father.

The position of the Moon's North Node (☊ in fig. 9.3) indicates that Diana had anarchistic and criminal tendencies. She craved philosophic or religious knowledge. If she had lived longer, her personal power would have increased during her forty-second year of life.

LOVE OF KIN: DIANA'S RELATIONSHIP WITH SIBLINGS

The relationship between an individual and his or her siblings and close relatives is a subject analyzed in Western, Judaic, Vedic, and Arabian astrologies.

(Neither Tibetan nor Chinese astrology yields any particular prognostications occurring in this area of Diana's life.) Diana had strong and long-lasting bonds to her siblings. She also felt a familial duty toward them, despite any pain and suffering they caused her. This facet is revealed in the material that follows.

Western, Judaic, and Vedic House III rulers.   As mentioned earlier, the House III ruler (18°♓21′ in fig. 9.1; 20°♓33′ in fig. 9.2) in both her Western and Judaic horoscopes is the zodiac sign Pisces (♓), which indicates that she was overly emotional in her communications. She also formed emotional ties to her brother and sisters (see "Delineating House Rulerships" in chapter 8).

Her Vedic House III ruler, Capricorn (10 in fig. 9.3), suggests that she felt responsibility for her siblings or formed extremely close relations with them (see "Interpreting the House Rulers in the *Bhavacakra*" in chapter 5).

Planets in House III.   Neither Diana's Western nor Judaic charts contained any planets in House III. But, as mentioned earlier, her Vedic horoscope was occupied by the Moon (☽ in fig. 9.3) and by the Moon's South Node (☋ in fig. 9.3). The Moon's placement suggests that she had many siblings and enjoyed happy relations with them (see "Interpreting the Planetary Positions in a *Bhavacakra*" in chapter 5). But the Moon's South Node placement indicates that she experienced suffering caused by her siblings (see "Interpreting the Planetary Positions in a *Bhavacakra*" in chapter 5).

The Arabian Part of Brethren and Part of the Love of Brethren.   Arabian astrology seems to uncover a weak spot in this realm. The Arabian Part of Brethren indicates an individual's relationship to siblings and close relatives. The Part is derived by adding the Western Ascendant's position (18°♐24′ in fig. 9.1) to Saturn's position (♄ 27°♑49′ in fig. 9.1) and subtracting Jupiter's position (♃ 05°♒05′ in fig. 9.1) from the sum. Diana's Arabian Part of Brethren (11°♐08′) is one sign apart from its traditional ruler, Jupiter (♃), indicating that she had only one sibling (see chapter 6, "The Part of Brethren"). In reality, however, Diana had two sisters—Sarah and Jane—and a brother, Charles.

The Arabian Part of Love of Brethren indicates an individual's relationship to siblings and close relatives. The Part is derived by adding the Western Ascendant's position (18°♐24′ in fig. 9.1) to Saturn's position (♄ 27°♑49′ in fig. 9.1) and subtracting the Sun's position (☉ 09°♋39′ in fig. 9.1) from the sum. Diana's Arabian Part of Love of Brethren (06°♋34′) conjuncts the Sun (☉ 09°♋39′ in fig. 9.1), which suggests that Diana's bonds with her siblings were strong and long-lasting (see "The Part of Love of Brethren" in chapter 6).

HEARTH AND HOME: DIANA'S DOMESTIC LIFE

With regard to Diana's home life, Arabian and Vedic astrology yielded more insights than did the Western and Judaic traditions. Born to a domineering parent and a confrontational home life, Diana was more influenced by her father than her mother (though later she identified with her mother). She experienced sudden, unexpected changes of residence, and was sometimes the perpetrator of household upsets. The material below demonstrates how this information was astrologically disclosed.

House IV Ruler in the Western, Judaic, and Vedic Charts.   In Diana's Western and Judaic natal charts, her House IV ruler (23°♈03′ in figs. 9.1 and 9.2) is in the zodiac sign Aries. This indicates that she had a domineering parent and a confrontational or active home life (see "Delineating House Rulerships" in chapter 8).

Diana's Vedic chart posits her House IV ruler in the zodiac sign Aquarius (11 in fig. 9.3). This placement suggests that unusual situations surrounded her childhood, parents, and domestic life. She had unexpected changes of residence and experienced sudden separation from her family or parents (see "Delineating House Rulerships" in chapter 8). For no apparent reason, Diana's mother, Frances Spencer, left her husband when Diana was six years old.

No planets occupied House IV in any of her charts, Western, Judaic, or Vedic. Therefore, no additional prognostications were disclosed.

The Arabian Part of the Father, Part of the Mother, and Part of Fortune in Husbandry.   The Arabian Part of the Father indicates an individual's relationship with his or her father. The Part is derived by adding the Western Ascendant's position (18°♐24′ in fig. 9.1) to the Sun's position (☉ 09°♋39′ in fig. 9.1) and subtracting Saturn's position (♄ 27°♑49′ in fig. 9.1) from the sum. Diana's Arabian Part of the Father (00°♊14′) trines Jupiter (♃ 05°♒05′ in fig. 9.1), which suggests that Diana's father exerted a strong influence on her personality (see "The Part of the Father" in chapter 6). In truth, she loved and trusted her father.

Similarly, the Arabian Part of the Mother indicates an individual's relationship with his or her mother. The Part is derived by adding the Western Ascendant's position (18°♐24′ in fig. 9.1) to the Moon's position (☽ 25°♒02′ in fig. 9.1) and subtracting Venus's position (♀ 24°♉24′ in fig. 9.1) from the sum. Diana's Arabian Part of the Mother (19°♍02′) trines Venus (♀ 24°♉24′ in fig. 9.1), which suggests that Diana formed strong identification bonds with her mother (see "The Part of the Mother" in chapter 6). In real life, Diana never forgave her mother for leaving her father. One biographer, Nicholas Davies, documented that Diana was closer to her father than to her mother. Perhaps, when her own marriage ended later in her life, she did identify strongly with her mother, even though they never mended their relationship.

The Arabian Part of Fortune in Husbandry not only indicates the person's ability to reap abundance from the land, but also prognosticates the general domestic environment and the person's ability to deal with household issues. The Part is derived by adding the Western Ascendant's position (18°♐24′ in fig. 9.1) to Saturn's position (♄ 27°♑49′ in fig. 9.1) and subtracting Venus's position (♀ 24° ♉24′ in fig. 9.1) from the sum. Diana's Arabian Part of Fortune in Husbandry (21°♌49′) opposed the Moon (☽ 25°♒02′ in fig. 9.1), which suggests that Diana was the perpetrator of household upsets (see "The Part of Fortune in Husbandry" in chapter 6). The tirades she aimed at the personal dressers, maids, and office staff employed at Kensington Palace were the subject of media attention even before the details of her failing marriage were known.

A LIFE DEVOTED TO CHILDREN:
DIANA'S POTENTIAL FOR BEARING CHILDREN

Western, Judaic, Vedic, and Arabian astrological traditions highlighted some activity with regard to Diana and her children. Diana had an excellent rapport with children. Though her two boys (as predicted by Arabian astrology) are very creative and she had a strong attachment to them, they were (or would have become) a source of emotional frustration. Once again, there are signs of extravagance, unexpected losses, and marital problems. All of these traits can be found in the prognostications that follow.

House V Ruler in the Western, Judaic, and Vedic Charts: Diana's House V ruler (16°♉03′ in fig. 9.1; 24°♉24′ in fig. 9.2) is Taurus (♉) in both her Western and Judaic charts, which indicates that she had an excellent rapport with all children (see "Delineating House Rulerships" in chapter 8). Diana's Vedic House V ruler, Pisces (12 in fig. 9.3), suggests that her children, Princes William and Harry, are very creative (see "Delineating House Rulerships" in chapter 8).

Planets in House V. Diana's Western and Judaic charts show that House V is occupied by Venus (♀ 24°♉24′ in figs. 9.1 and 9.2). This placement suggests that Diana had a strong attachment to her children. Since this planet was adversely aspected, she was also emotionally frustrated over her children (see "Delineating Planetary Positions by House and by Sign" in chapter 8). It's been reported that Diana feared losing her sons' affections to their nanny, Tiggy, or to Charles's mistress, Camilla Parker-Bowles.

Mars (♂ 01°♍38′ in figs. 9.1 and 9.2) forms a square to Venus (♀ 24°♉24′ in figs. 9.1 and 9.2), which suggests that Diana was careless and extravagant. Her problems stemmed from her marriage, partnerships, or jealous friends (see "Delineating Planetary Aspects" in chapter 8). Similarly, Uranus (♅ 23°♌20′ in figs. 9.1 and 9.2) forms a square to Venus (♀ 24°♉24′ in figs. 9.1 and 9.2), suggesting that Diana experienced losses through unexpected circumstances (see "Delineating Planetary Aspects" in chapter 8).

On the brighter side, Saturn (♄ 27°♑49′ in figs. 9.1 and 9.2), forms a trine to Venus (♀ 24°♉24′ in figs. 9.1 and 9.2), which suggests that Diana gained through elders, superiors, and investments (see "Delineating Planetary Aspects" in chapter 8).

The Arabian Part of Children and Part of Male Children. Diana's Arabian Part of Children (see "The Part of Children" in chapter 6) is derived by adding the Western Ascendant's position (18°♐24′ in fig. 9.1) to Jupiter's position (♃ 05° ♒05′ in fig. 9.1) and subtracting Saturn's position (♄ 27°♑49′ in fig. 9.1) from the sum. Diana's Part of Children (25°♐40′) was positioned one zodiac sign away from its planetary ruler, Jupiter (♃), which suggests that she bore only one child (see "The Part of Children" in chapter 6) In real life, she bore two.

Her Arabian Part of Male Children (see "The Part of Male Children" in chapter 6) is derived by adding the Western Ascendant's position (18°♐24′ in fig. 9.1) to Jupiter's position (♃ 05°♒05′ in fig. 9.1) and subtracting the Moon's position (☽ 25°♒02′ in Fig. 9.1) from the sum. Diana's Part of Male Children (28°♏27′) is positioned two zodiac signs away from its traditional planetary ruler, Mars (♂), suggesting that she bore two male children (see "The Part of Male Children" in chapter 6).

A Creative Outlet: Diana's Pursuit of Pleasure and the Arts

Because the same house and planets employed to determine Diana's ability to bear children are also assessed to disclose her artistic talents and pleasure interests, the Western, Judaic, and Vedic astrological traditions are the only astrologies that designate any activity in this area. Attractive to the opposite sex, and indulgent, she had secret love affairs. She was attracted to a member of a minority group, found pleasure on or near water, and had romantic happiness. However, she also faced marital problems as well as problems with jealous friends. Though she experienced some fidelity in marriage, hasty actions led to divorce. These details of Diana's life are disclosed in the delineations that follow.

Western, Judaic, and Vedic House V rulers. Diana's House V ruler (16°♉03′ in fig. 9.1; 24°♉24′ in fig. 9.2) in both her Western and Judaic charts is Taurus (♉), which indicates that she was highly artistic. She was attractive to the opposite sex and indulgent with her pleasures (see "Delineating House Rulerships" in chapter 8). Diana's Vedic House V ruler, Pisces (12 in fig. 9.3), on the other hand, suggests that she had secret love affairs or romantic deceptions. In 1986 the princess began an affair with Captain James Hewitt, which lasted three years. There were reports of two other liaisons taking place during the early 1990s.

This position also suggests that she was attracted to a person from a minority group or one who worked with the sea, medicine, or feet. She was occasionally lucky with speculative ventures. She also found pleasure on or near the water (see "Delineating House Rulerships" in chapter 8). One biographer reported that Diana enjoyed swimming.

Planets in House V.   Diana's Western and Judaic charts show that House V is occupied by Venus (♀ 24°♉24′ in figs. 9.1 and 9.2). This placement suggests that she had romantic happiness (see "Delineating Planetary Positions by House and by Sign" in chapter 8).

However, Mars (♂ 01°♍38′ in figs. 9.1 and 9.2) forms a square to Venus (♀ 24°♉24′ in figs. 9.1 and 9.2). As mentioned earlier, this suggests that Diana was careless and extravagant. Her problems stemmed from her marriage, partnerships, or jealous friends (see "Delineating Planetary Aspects" in chapter 8). Similarly, Uranus (♅ 23°♌20′ in figs. 9.1 and 9.2) formed a square to Venus (♀ 24°♉24′ in figs. 9.1 and 9.2), which suggests that Diana had trouble with the opposite sex, including jealousy during marriage or a love affair. Her hastiness led to divorce. She experienced losses through unexpected circumstances (see "Delineating Planetary Aspects" in chapter 8).

On the brighter side, Saturn (♄ 27°♑49′ in figs. 9.1 and 9.2) forms a trine to Venus (♀ 24°♉24′ in figs. 9.1 and 9.2), which suggests that Diana experienced some success and fidelity in marriage and love. And, as mentioned earlier, she gained through elders, superiors, and investments (see "Delineating Planetary Aspects" in chapter 8).

A HEALTH OBSESSION: DIANA'S PHYSICAL WELL-BEING

Western, Judaic, Arabian, and Tibetan astrology give varying prognostications as to the princess's general state of physical health. Careless and prone to fevers and stress-related illnesses from childhood, Diana was profoundly affected by her surroundings and circumstances, and experienced many mood swings. She also suffered from stomach or gastrointestinal-related illnesses, and faced an accidental and unexpected death. There was a potential for illness or injuries involving the head, eyes, breasts, and stomach. It is difficult to say whether she feared or was indifferent about dying, though the concepts of death and reincarnation held her curiosity. The material below demonstrates how this information is disclosed.

House VI Ruler in the Western, Judaic, and Vedic charts.   Diana's House VI ruler (03°♊17′ in fig. 9.1; 22°♊02′ in fig. 9.2) in both her Western and Judaic charts is Gemini (♊), which indicates that she had respiratory or nervous complaints (see "Delineating House Rulerships" in chapter 8). Diana's Vedic House VI ruler, Aries (1 in fig. 9.3), on the other hand, suggests that she was prone to fevers, rash, high blood pressure, headaches, or stress-related illnesses (see "Delineating House Rulerships" in chapter 8).

Planets in House VI.   No planets occupy House VI in Diana's Western horoscope. In her Judaic chart, however, this house is occupied by the Sun (☉ 09°♋39′ in fig. 9.2). This placement suggests that she was profoundly affected by her surroundings, and experienced many mood swings (see "Delineating Planetary Positions by House and by Sign" in chapter 8). Her well-documented tantrums, emotional rollercoaster rides, anorexic attacks, and episodes of self-mutilation lasted throughout her life.

The Sun (☉ 09°♋39′ in fig. 9.2) forms a conjunction to Mercury (☿ 03°♋12′ in fig. 9.2), suggesting that Diana desired to observe and learn (see "Delineating Planetary Aspects" in chapter 8). The Sun (☉ 09°♋39′ in fig. 9.2) forms a trine to Neptune (♆ 08°♏38′ in fig. 9.2), which suggests that Diana received benefits through mystical and spiritual subjects (see "Delineating Planetary Aspects" in chapter 8). The Sun (☉ 09°♋39′ in fig. 9.2) formed a sextile to Pluto (♇ 06°♍02′ in fig. 9.2), which suggests that Diana had influence over other people and was able to modify herself in order to attain personal goals (see "Delineating Planetary Aspects" in chapter 8).

Mercury (☿ 03°♋12′ in fig. 9.2) in this house suggests that she had a speech impediment or difficulties in childhood (see "Delineating Planetary Positions by House and by Sign" in chapter 8). Mars (♂ 01°♍38′ in fig. 9.2) forms a sextile to Mercury (☿ 03°♋12′ in fig. 9.2), which suggests that she applied immense energy to music, design, art, chemistry, medicine, or engineering. Educators, professionals, scientists, and literary people aided in her personal development (see "Delineating Planetary Aspects" in chapter 8).

Neptune (♆ 08°♏38′ in fig. 9.2) forms a trine to Mercury (☿ 03°♋12′ in fig. 9.2), which suggests that she succeeded with unconventional healing or hydrotherapy. Diana's interest in alternative therapies was also well known. She tried aromatherapy, acupuncture, hydrotherapy, reflexology, osteopathy, hypnotherapy, and even anger-release therapy. This aspect also suggests that she had good experiences associated with liquids, chemicals, drugs, the sea, hospitals, and private institutions (see "Delineating Planetary Aspects" in chapter 8). And Pluto (♇ 06°♍02′ in fig. 9.2) forms a sextile to Mercury (☿ 03°♋12′ in fig. 9.2), which suggests that she was adaptable and persuasive (see "Delineating Planetary Aspects" in chapter 8).

Western, Judaic, and Vedic House VIII rulers. House VIII (29°♋48′ in fig. 9.1) is ruled by Cancer (♋) in Diana's Western natal chart, indicating that she feared death (see "Delineating House Rulerships" in chapter 8). The zodiac sign Leo (♌)is also intercepted in House VIII (fig. 9.1), which suggests that she had a secret fear of death.

House VIII (18°♌54′ in fig. 9.2) in Diana's Judaic natal chart, however, suggests that she experienced only the Leonine influences mentioned above. House VIII's ruler, Leo (3 in fig. 9.3), in Diana's Vedic natal chart, on the other hand, suggests that she was indifferent to the concept of death.

Planets in the Western and Judaic charts' House VIII. House VIII in both Diana's Western and Judaic charts was occupied by Uranus (♅ 20°♌23′ in figs. 9.1 and 9.2) in Leo (♌), indicating that she strongly believed in physical moderation (see "Delineating Planetary Positions by House and by Sign" in Chapter 8).

As mentioned earlier, the Moon (☽ 25°♒02′ in figs. 9.1 and 9.2) forms an opposition to Uranus (♅ 23°♌20′ in figs. 9.1 and 9.2), indicating that she experienced mental disturbance, stomach distress, or gastrointestinal problems (see "Delineating Planetary Aspects" in Chapter 8).

Venus (♀ 24°♉24′ in figs. 9.1 and 9.2) forms a square to Uranus (♅ 23°♌20′ in figs. 9.1 and 9.2), indicating that she experienced losses through unexpected circumstances (see "Delineating Planetary Aspects" in chapter 8).

The planet Pluto (♇ 06°♍02′ in figs. 9.1 and 9.2) occupies House VIII in both Diana's Western and Judaic charts. This suggests that she was attracted to death and the concept of regeneration (see "Delineating Planetary Positions by House and by Sign" in chapter 8).

Pluto (♇ 06°♍02′ in figs. 9.1 and 9.2) forms a sextile to the Sun (☉ 09°♋39′ in figs. 9.1 and 9.2), indicating that she had influence over other people and was able to modify herself in order to attain personal goals. Pluto (♇ 06°♍02′ in figs. 9.1 and 9.2) forms a sextile to Mercury (☿ 03°♋12′ in figs. 9.1 and 9.2), indicating that she was adaptable and persuasive (see "Delineating Planetary Aspects" in chapter 8).

The planet Pluto (♇ 06°♍02′ in figs. 9.1 and 9.2) forms a conjunction to Mars (♂ 01°♍38′ in figs. 9.1 and 9.2), indicating that her goals were achieved through hard work, self-confidence, and a competitive spirit, and by attacking sponta-neously (see "Delineating Planetary Aspects" in chapter 8).

The planet Mars (♂ 01°♍38′ in figs. 9.1 and 9.2) occupies House VIII in both Diana's Western and Judaic charts. This suggests that she experienced an acciden-tal death (see "Delineating Planetary Positions by House and by Sign" in chapter 8). Its placement in the zodiac sign Virgo suggests that she also lost friends through misunderstandings, serious quarrels, or death (see "Delineating Planetary Positions by House and by Sign" in Chapter 8).

As mentioned earlier, the Moon (☽ 25°♒02′ in figs. 9.1 and 9.2) forms an op-position to Mars (♂ 01°♍38′ in figs. 9.1 and 9.2), indicating that she had poor health, affecting the head, eyes, breasts, stomach, or sex organs, and that she was careless (see "Delineating Planetary Aspects" in Chapter 8).

Mars (♂ 01°♍38′ in figs. 9.1 and 9.2) forms a square to Venus (♀ 24°♉24′ in figs. 9.1 and 9.2), which suggests that she was careless and extravagant (see "Delin-eating Planetary Aspects" in chapter 8). The planet Mars (♂ 01°♍38′ in figs. 9.1 and 9.2) forms a sextile to Mercury (☿ 03°♋12′ in figs. 9.1 and 9.2), suggesting that she was accident- and addiction-prone (see "Delineating Planetary Aspects" in chapter 8).

The Arabian Part of Sickness and Part of Death. The Arabian Part of Sickness signifies the person's physical weak points. The Part is derived by adding the Ascen-dant's position (18°♐24′ in fig. 9.1) to Mars's position (♂ 01°♍38′ in figs. 9.1 and 9.2) and subtracting Saturn's position (♄ 27°♑49′ in fig. 9.1). The final sum, Diana's Arabian Part of Sickness (22°♋13′), indicates that her physical weak-nesses were in her bladder, muscles, and genitals (see "The Part of Sickness" in chapter 6).

The Arabian Part of Death prognosticates the conditions of a person's death, the person's preoccupation with life and death, and how prone the person is to ac-cidents or violent crimes. According to modern Western astrologers, the Part is de-rived by adding the Ascendant's position (18°♐24′ in fig. 9.1) to the cusp of House VIII (29°♋48′ in fig. 9.1) and subtracting the Moon's position (☽ 25°♒02′ in fig. 9.1) from the sum. Diana's Arabian Part of Death (23°♉10′) forms a square to her Moon (☽ 25°♒02′ in fig. 9.1), indicating that she was obsessed with death and her health (see "The Part of Death" in chapter 6).

Tibetan health force. According to Tibetan astrology, Diana's *lü* (health force) was ruled by the earth element (see "Determining the *Wang*" in Chapter 4, and fig. 4.5). This element signifies a strong health focus on her flesh, mouth, and spleen.

THE MARRIAGE OF THE CENTURY: DIANA'S MARRIED LIFE

Western, Judaic, Arabian, and Vedic astrological prognostications indicate that marriage was of critical importance to Diana. She had a strong desire for marriage, and preferred a marriage partnership to being alone. Though she was destined to have a happy marriage, she was also fated to have more than one. She faced social differences in marriage, but was capable of taking advantage of opportunities that could arise through her spouse. She also faced the possibility of an intelligent but emotionally detached husband. The details of her marital life are disclosed in the delineations that follow.

Western, Judaic, and Vedic House VII rulers.   House VII (18°♊24′ in fig. 9.1) in Diana's Western natal chart indicates that she would possibly have had more than one marriage. Her spouse or partner might have been involved in teaching, writing, communications, publishing, or advertising (see "Delineating House Rulerships" in chapter 8).

Her Judaic House VII ruler (19°♋42′ in fig. 9.2) suggests that Diana had a close, caring relationship with partners or spouse. She wanted to maintain a strong emotional connection to a dominating spouse (see "Delineating House Rulerships" in chapter 8).

Diana's Vedic House VII ruler, Taurus (2 in fig. 9.3), suggests that she needed constant interaction with others. She preferred partnership to operating alone. And she had a stable, long-lasting, and happy marriage or partnership (see "Delineating House Rulerships" in chapter 8).

The planets in House VII.   The Sun (☉ 09°♋39′ in fig. 9.1) occupies House VII in Diana's Western chart. This suggests that she had a strong desire for marriage (see "Delineating Planetary Positions by House and by Sign" in chapter 8).

The Sun (☉ 09°♋39′ in fig. 9.1) forms a conjunction to Mercury (☿ 03°♋12′ in fig. 9.1), indicating that she was ambitious, intelligent, and desired to observe and learn (see "Delineating Planetary Aspects" in chapter 8). The Sun (☉ 09°♋39′ in fig. 9.1) also forms a trine to Neptune (♆ 08°♏38′ in fig. 9.1), indicating that she received benefits through mystical and spiritual subjects (see "Delineating Planetary Aspects" in chapter 8).

Mercury (☿ 03°♋12′ in fig. 9.1) occupies House VII in Diana's Western chart. This suggests that her marriage choice was influenced by intellect. It also indicates that she took advantage of opportunities offered through her marriage (see "Delineating Planetary Positions by House and by Sign" in chapter 8).

As mentioned earlier, Mars (♂ 01°♍38′ in fig. 9.1) forms a sextile to Mercury (☿ 03°♋12′ in fig. 9.1), which suggests that educators, professionals, scientists, and literary people aided in her personal development (see "Delineating Planetary Aspects" in chapter 8). And Neptune (♆ 08°♏ 38′ in fig. 9.1) forms a trine to Mercury (☿ 03°♋ 12′ in fig. 9.1), which suggests that she had prophetic dreams (see "Delineating Planetary Aspects" in chapter 8).

These same two planets also occupy House VII in Diana's Vedic chart. Their prognostications are different, however. The Vedic placement of the Sun (☉ in fig. 9.3) suggests that Diana had a strong desire for marriage and was preoccupied with her husband. It was a well-documented fact that Diana was head-over-heels in love with Prince Charles during the early years of their marriage.

This placement, however, also suggests that she had marital problems. And she had the potential for an insufficient dowry, religious differences, or social differences connected with her marriage (see "Interpreting the Planetary Positions in the *Bhavacakra*" in chapter 5).

The Vedic placement of Mercury (☿ in fig. 9.3) indicates that she had an intelligent but emotionally detached spouse. It also suggests that she had a low sex drive (see "Interpreting the Planetary Positions in the *Bhavacakra*" in chapter 5).

There are no planets situated in House VII of Diana's Judaic chart (fig. 9.2). Therefore, no additional prognostications would be made by a practitioner.

The Arabian Part of Marriage. The Arabian Part of Marriage signifies the person's potential for marital happiness. The Part is derived by adding the Ascendant's position (18°♐ 24′ in fig. 9.1) to the cusp of House VII (18°♊ 24′ in fig. 9.1) and subtracting Venus's position (♀ 24°♉ 24′ in fig. 9.1) from the sum. Diana's Arabian Part of Marriage (12°♑ 24′) forms a sextile with Neptune (♆ 08°♏ 38′ in fig. 9.1), which suggests that Diana's marriage had an optimistic bearing, filled with strong memories of the good times that propelled the couple through dark periods (see "The Part of Marriage" in chapter 5).

THE PEOPLE'S PRINCESS: DIANA'S SOCIAL AND PROFESSIONAL LIFE

Western, Judaic, Arabian, and Vedic astrologies yield a few insights into the princess's public image and public life, which was also her profession. Diana attracted attention through her beauty, talent, and social position. A parent was involved in her career choice. She excelled in politics, encountered great financial success, and was destined to travel extensively, but her career would ultimately prove to be unstable. These facets of Diana's professional life can be prognosticated by using the material that follows.

Western, Judaic, and Vedic House X rulers. House X (23°♎ 03′ in fig. 9.1) in Diana's Western and Judaic natal charts is ruled by Libra (♎), which indicates that she attracted attention because of her physical appearance, artistic talent, or social position. She needed to find a balance between her home and her career (see "Delineating House Rulerships" in chapter 8).

Her Vedic House X ruler, Leo (5 in fig. 9.3), suggests that her ego and mode of self-expression were closely related to her choice of profession. A parent was involved in her career choice. She sought a leadership or public role in her profession, and was potentially self-employed (see "Delineating House Rulerships" in chapter 8).

Planets in House X.   Neptune (♆ 08°♏ 38′ in fig. 9.1) occupied House X in Diana's Western and Judaic charts. This suggests that she had an unstable career or profession (see "Delineating Planetary Positions by House and by Sign" in chapter 8). Given her status as a major public figure and England's most famous ambassador, Diana's profession was inherently an unstable one.

As mentioned earlier, Neptune (♆ 08°♏ 38′ in fig. 9.1) forms a trine to Mercury (☿ 03°♋ 12′ in fig. 9.1), which suggests that she had prophetic dreams and had good experiences associated with liquids, chemicals, drugs, the sea, hospitals, and private institutions (see "Delineating Planetary Aspects" in chapter 8). Diana's work with charitable organizations and hospitals was frequently reported by media.

The Sun (☉ 09°♋ 39′ in fig. 9.1) forms a trine to Mercury (☿ 03°♋ 12′ in fig. 9.1), which suggests that she had a strong business aptitude. She was ambitious, intelligent, and desired to observe and learn (see "Delineating Planetary Aspects" in chapter 8). Jupiter (♃ 05°♒ 05′ in fig. 9.1) forms a square to Mercury (☿ 03°♋ 12′ in fig. 9.1), which suggests that Diana encountered general financial success as well as profits from her profession or government. It also implies that she experienced extensive change and travel (see "Delineating Planetary Aspects" in chapter 8). From the day she became the Princess of Wales, Diana encountered a whirlwind of lifestyle changes. The stresses of a harsh travel schedule and little time for acclimation to her new life were the subject of many media reports.

The Arabian Part of Magistery and Profession, Part of Honor, Part of Sudden Advancement.   The Arabian Part of Magistery and Profession signifies the person's potential professional interests, including the ability to acquire a political position. It is derived by adding the Ascendant's position (18°♐ 24′ in fig. 9.1) to the Moon's position (☽ 25°♒ 02′ in fig. 9.1) and subtracting Saturn's position (♄ 27°♑ 49′ in fig. 9.1) from the sum. Diana's Arabian Part of Magistery and Profession (15°♑ 37′) is placed in House II, which suggests that she achieved fame because she was a self-starter (see "The Part of Magistery and Profession" in chapter 6).

The Arabian Part of Honor signifies how an individual achieves professional fame or honors. It is derived by adding the Ascendant's position (18°♐24′ in fig. 9.1) to 03°00′ Taurus (03°♉00′) and subtracting the Sun's position (☉ 09°♋39′ in fig. 9.1) from the sum. Diana's Arabian Part of Honor (11°♎45′) is placed in House IX, which suggests that her fame came through higher education or religion (see "The Part of Honor" in chapter 6).

The Arabian Part of Honor focuses on a person's ability to climb the promotion ladder and to excel based on a particular skill or talent. The Part is derived by adding the Ascendant's position (18°♐24′ in fig. 9.1) to the Part of Fortune (03°♌46′ from above) and subtracting Saturn's position (♄ 27°♑49′ in fig. 9.1) from the sum. Diana's Arabian Part of Sudden Advancement (24°♊21′) was posited in House VII, indicating that she excelled through politics or sales (see "The Part of Sudden Advancement" in chapter 6).

NOT-SO-FAIR FRIENDSHIPS: DIANA'S FRIENDS AND ASSOCIATES

Western, Judaic, and Vedic astrologies are the only traditions that shed any light on the princess's ability to make friends. (Arabian astrology does contain Parts that pertain to friendship, but in this case the data was not particularly revealing.) Secrecy and mystery surrounded Diana's friendships, and she was destined to be betrayed by her friends. She was an active participant in organizations and societies, and many of her friends were associated with health and social services, or were in the arts. Diana's friendships are the subject of the astrological material that follows.

Western, Judaic, and Vedic House XI rulers. Diana's House XI ruler (16°♏03′ in fig. 9.1 and 9.2) in her Western and Judaic charts is Scorpio (♏), which indicates that she may have made new friends in a new environment to improve her life, social standing, or professional status. She was potentially victimized by friends. Secrecy or mystery was associated with her friendships (see "Delineating House Rulerships" in chapter 8). Confidences she shared with her sister-in-law, Sarah Ferguson, were kept secret until after Diana's death.

Diana's Vedic House XI ruler, Virgo (6 in fig. 9.3), suggests that there was a strong interchange of thoughts that Diana shared with her friends. She was an active participant in organizations and societies. Her friends were associated with health, social services, the arts, writing, or design. She had few close friends but many acquaintances. She accepted responsibility for her friends (see "Interpreting the House Rulers in the *Bhavacakra*" in chapter 5).

THE PERSON BEHIND THE MASK:
DIANA'S HIDDEN FEARS AND LIMITATIONS

Western, Judaic, Vedic, and Arabian astrologies are the traditions that disclose the dark side to Diana's nature. With her nervous temperament and strong intuition, Diana often had unrealistic worries and concerns. She may even have considered suicide. A lack of self-confidence stifled her ability to form long-term relationships. She also feared the loss of possessions. Diana's fears and limitations are disclosed through the material that follows.

Western, Judaic, and Vedic House XII rulers. Diana's House XII ruler (03° ♐17′ in fig. 9.1; 22°♐02′ in fig. 9.2) in her Western and Judaic charts is Sagittarius (♐), which indicates that she had an unrealistic inability to worry or to have concern. She received help from unknown sources, was intuitive, and had an interest in psychology and the occult (see "Delineating House Rulerships" in chapter 8).

Her Vedic House XII ruler, Libra (7 in fig. 9.3), suggests that she was extremely sensitive about relationships. A lack of self-confidence negatively affected the formation and maintenance of her relationships. She threatened suicide or fell victim to potentially suicidal people (see "Interpreting the House Rulers in the *Bhavacakra*" in chapter 5).

The Arabian Part of Private Enemies and Part of the Perilous and Most Dangerous Year. The Arabian Part of Private Enemies prognosticates the reasons why an individual encounters personal opposition. The Part is derived by adding the Ascendant's position (18°♐24′ in fig. 9.1) to the cusp of House XII (03°♐17′ in fig. 9.1) and subtracting House XII's planetary ruler, Jupiter (♃ 05°♒05′ in fig. 9.1) from the sum. Diana's Arabian Part of Private Enemies (16°♎36′) is placed in House IX, which indicates that there was a difference between Diana's lack of education and her desire to communicate with educated people (see "The Part of Private Enemies" in chapter 6).

The Arabian Part of the Perilous and Most Dangerous Year determines an individual's weak point in social relationships. This particular part is derived by adding the Ascendant's position (18°♐24′ in fig. 9.1) to House VIII's ruler, the Moon (☽ 25°♒02′ in fig. 9.1) and subtracting Saturn's position (♄ 27°♑49′ in fig. 9.1) from the sum. Diana's Arabian Part of the Perilous and Most Dangerous Year (15° ♑37′) is situated in House I, indicating that she was overconfident (see "The Part of the Perilous and Most Dangerous Year" in chapter 6).

The information in Diana Spencer's astrological charts did not change upon her death; her birth data revealed the same information when she was alive and consulting her own astrologers. Although for the purposes of this book, the subject of death is generally set aside, the Moon's South Node (☋) in House I of her Western and Judaic natal charts (figs. 9.1 and 9.2) implies that she experienced many personal trials and tribulations, including facial or eye injuries, during a short life span (see "The Moon's South Node" in chapter 8).

One point does become evident: the percentage of incidental correlation between the astrological delineations described above and the actual events in Diana's life is very high. And the methods used by astrological practitioners to derive this sort of information involve no more than the application of mathematics, astronomy, and logic.

Which
Tradition
Is Right
for You?

No comparative study of astrology could be considered complete if it failed to address the first question in the minds of both practitioners and their subjects. Is one form of astrology *better* than another? The answer is: Yes, without a doubt. But the answer as to which one is better depends entirely upon what sort of insights are sought. There is no single discipline that can provide all the material needed to develop a thorough delineation of a facet of life such as the outcome of a professional direction during a specific time period, the potential for marital bliss, or the influence of travel abroad upon one's given destiny.

Over the millennia, disparate societies have had varied reasons for applying the science of astrology. Practitioners within those societies have been called upon to aid in the management of crops and livestock; in the successful direction of business or governmental affairs; in the pursuit of spiritual enlightenment; in the determination of an individual's potential for personal gain, romance, and marriage; or even in the diagnosis and prevention of disease. It all depended upon their societies' interests. Successive generations of astrologers generally focused on concerns similar to their predecessors', rather than branching into areas where there was little cultural interest. Thus, aside from some remarkable commonalities, each form of astrology has developed unique strengths.

Chinese culture concerns itself with an individual's ability to achieve balanced relationships with family members, friends, the community, and nature within the context of present time. Thus, Chinese astrology (see chapter 3) focuses its attention on preserving universal harmony between the individual and his or her environs. Based on the year, month, day, and hour of an individual's birth, four "pillars" of destiny—the *Ssu Chu*—provide the foundation from which personality traits and the timing of events are derived. The *gen* (year pillar) defines an individual's behavioral pattern, general appearance, and emotional state. The *miao* (month pillar) represents an individual's fate or destiny. The *hua* (day pillar) represents an individual's ego. And the birth *guo* (hour pillar) determines what direction that destiny might take, and to what extent the individual has been blessed by fate.

The *miao* (month pillar) and *hua* (day pillar) are also used to develop a series of fate cycles that represent the individual's potential areas of interest during a ten-year period of his or her life. To ascertain the appropriate day in which to begin or end a large-scale project, to conduct a marriage or funeral, to ask for favors, or to travel, Chinese practitioners refer to the Moon's daily movements through the *sieu* (lunar mansions).

Tibetan astrology (see chapter 4) analyzes the harmonic nature of five natural forces that practitioners believe operate within each and every individual's personality. By identifying the hidden sources of emotional, spiritual, and physical energy that flow in and out of a person, as well as the portion of fate that an individual was allocated at birth by his or her deeds in a previous life, the balanced relationship of an individual to both other people and the environment is sought.

The *sok* (life force) determines an individual's motive for taking action or following a particular direction in life and is directly associated with the animal that rules the individual's year of birth. The person's *wang* (power force) determines how that person overcomes obstacles and achieves success. The *lung ta* (luck force) is based on the Asian belief that every person is provided with a portion of positive or negative fortune at birth. The *la* (spirit force) governs an individual's emotional state. And the source of physical health concerns is determined by the *lü* (health force).

The timing of events in this tradition takes on a more generalized nature. Based on the person's animal sign, which is determined at birth, practitioners derive an individual's auspicious and inauspicious days during the course of any given lunar month which are categorized by quality: foundation, success, power, obstacle, enemy, and disturbance. Another form of Tibetan predictive astrology reveals bad- or low-energy years that may occur during an individual's life.

More complex in both calculation and interpretation, Vedic astrology (see chapter 5) seeks to guide an individual toward spiritual enlightenment as well as appropriate secular interaction with family, friends, neighbors, and the community. In the same way that Indian culture focuses its attention on karmic debt, so does the Vedic astrological tradition. Interpretation and application of numerous charts and formulae determine the accumulation of good fortune based upon the individual's actions during a previous life as well as the present one.

A general personality profile—or *yoga* (union)—derived from the planetary positions disclosed by the calculation and construction of a *rasicakra* (sign chart) or *bhavacakra* (house chart) forms the basis from which the person's destiny and direction are assessed. A *sodasavarga* (subdivisional chart) is employed when the practitioner wishes to delve more deeply into a specific facet of the person's life, such as his or her ultimate direction in life, marriage prospects, or ability to acquire material wealth.

The *candralagna* (Moon chart) is a specialized chart that serves as a visual comparative to the prognostications of either the *rasicakra* (sign chart) or *bhavacakra* (house chart), providing additional confirmation of a person's dominant characteristics and qualities. The *candralagna* can also aid in uncovering otherwise unforeseen facets of an individual's personality. Vedic astrologers primarily refer to this secondary chart when creating a woman's personality profile. Since the Moon is feminine and represents the woman and the mother, the *candralagna* is also consulted to assess a woman's physical health, emotional makeup, and ability to bear children.

The form of personal chronology created by Vedic practitioners—the *vimsottari dasa*—is perhaps the most detailed of all astrological prognostications, timing critical events in an individual's life to within the year, month, day, or even hour of potential occurrence.

Reflecting early Near Eastern culture, Arabian astrology (see chapter 6) focuses on the secular concerns of the individual: his or her financial prospects, sex life, social status, and potential for success. This discipline employs two of the culture's greatest contributions to the world: refined mathematics and science. Arabian astrology not only applies the construction of a natal horoscope, which maps out the position of the Ascendant and the planets within the zodiac's orbital path, but also incorporates any number of the 143 equations used to ascertain very specific details about an individual's life.

The Judaic tradition (see chapter 7) focuses on the individual as an interactive entity in a larger spiritual community—a view shared by Chinese, Tibetan, and Vedic astrologies. How the person is perceived and interacts with his or her family, spouse, neighbors, friends, and spiritual brethren are the focal points of the Judaic astrologer's delineation. The data derived from a Judaic natal horoscope can be directed to aid the individual in living in accordance with Halachah (Jewish law), making it very similar to the practice of Vedic and Tibetan astrology.

As in modern Western and Vedic astrology, the Judaic Ascendant (House I) and its decanates (subdivisions of the Ascendant, which are 10°00′ each) are the keys to uncovering an individual's personality. Used as a key for spiritual guidance, an individual's personality is viewed for potential strengths that can be directed toward the betterment of all those who encounter the person. Weaknesses are treated as areas from which the individual may derive personal wisdom at a later date, or as elements that need the guidance of a spiritual counselor.

Relatively younger than its counterparts, Western astrology (see chapter 8) is decidedly secular and self-oriented. It concentrates its attention on the interplay of an individual's ego and id. It seeks to define the person that other people see, as well as the individual "behind the mask." As a mirror of the culture that created it, Western astrology focuses its attention on the ability of an individual to react within fixed parameters of activity with the mental, emotional, and physical tools he or she has been given at birth.

What can be learned from applying these diverse cultural views of the individual's role in society to the analysis of a single person's life? In the same way a patient learns more about his or her physical condition by consulting not only with a general practitioner but with any number of specialists, an individual who seeks self-knowledge through astrology can derive a wide variety of personal insights from the various traditions. Whether it's simply a desire to get a "second opinion" about a personality trait or the pursuit of a new course of action during a chaotic period, the information gained from multiple astrological readings can help paint a much more complete and clearer picture.

Following is a more detailed look at the comparative strengths of the various astrologies, showing some of the specific areas where deeper insights can be gained, and indicating which astrologies to combine to gain them. This is by no means a complete list, as that would fill volumes on its own, but it should serve as a starting point by addressing some common issues. Figure 10.1 provides a quick reference to the various procedures mentioned in the sections below, as well as to their locations in the previous chapters.

FIGURE 10.1. LOCATION OF PROCEDURES USED IN VARIOUS ASTROLOGICAL TRADITIONS

SUBJECT	DESCRIPTION	METHOD	TRADITION
Children	number of children potentially born to the person	Part of Children (see page 295)	Arabian
Children	number of female children potentially born to the person	Part of Female Children (see page 296)	Arabian
Children	number of male children potentially born to the person	Part of Male Children (see page 298)	Arabian
Children	potential for bearing children (for a woman)	*candralagna* (Moon chart) (see page 226)	Vedic
Children	potential for children	House V ruler (see page 182), planets occupying the house (see pages 413–35), aspects formed by planets (see page 436)	Judaic

Subject	Description	Method	Tradition
Children	potential for children	House V ruler (see page 182)	Vedic
Children	potential for children	House V ruler (see page 182), planets occupying the house (see pages 411–35), aspects formed by planets (see page 436)	Western
Domestic life and familial relationships	domestic environment	House IV ruler (see page 181)	Vedic
Domestic life and familial relationships	domestic life	Part of Fortune in Husbandry (see page 293)	Arabian
Domestic life and familial relationships	potential home environs, family life, and domestic situation	House IV ruler (see page 181), planets occupying the house (see pages 413–35), aspects formed by planets (see page 436)	Western
Domestic life and familial relationships	potential home environs, family life, and domestic situation	House IV ruler (see page 181), planets occupying the house (see pages 413–35), aspects formed by planets (see page 436)	Judaic
Domestic life and familial relationships	relationship with father	Part of the Father (see page 288)	Arabian
Domestic life and familial relationships	relationships with siblings and close relatives	Part of Brethren (see page 285)	Arabian
Domestic life and familial relationships	relationship with mother	Part of the Mother (see page 325)	Arabian
Domestic life and familial relationships	relationship with siblings	House III ruler (see page 180)	Vedic
Domestic life and familial relationships	relationship with siblings and close relatives	House III ruler (see page 180), planets occupying the house (see pages 413–35), aspects formed by planets (see page 436)	Western
Domestic life and familial relationships	relationship with siblings and close relatives	House III ruler (see page 180), planets occupying the house (see pages 413–35), aspects formed by planets (see page 436)	Judaic
Domestic life and familial relationships	relationship with siblings and close relatives	House IV ruler (see page 181), planets occupying the house (see pages 413–35), aspects formed by planets (see page 436)	Judaic
Domestic life and familial relationships	relationship with the family	House IV ruler (see page 181)	Vedic
Domestic life and familial relationships	relationship with the father	House IX ruler (see page 188)	Vedic

SUBJECT	DESCRIPTION	METHOD	TRADITION
Domestic life and familial relationships	relationship with the father (or parents)	House IV ruler (see page 181), planets occupying the house (see pages 413–35), aspects formed by planets (see page 436)	Western
Domestic life and familial relationships	relationship with the mother	House IV ruler (see page 181)	Vedic
Domestic life and familial relationships	relationship with the mother	House X ruler (see page 190), planets occupying the house (see pages 413–35), aspects formed by planets (see page 436)	Western
Domestic life and familial relationships	relationship with the mother	House X ruler (see page 190), planets occupying the house (see pages 413–35), aspects formed by planets (see page 436)	Judaic
Domestic life and familial relationships	sense of familial duty to siblings and close relatives	Part of Love of Brethren (see page 286)	Arabian
Education, mentality, and beliefs	ability to learn	House IX ruler (see page 188), planets occupying the house (see pages 413–35), aspects formed by planets (see page 436)	Judaic
Education, mentality, and beliefs	ability to learn	House IX ruler (see page 188), planets occupying the house (see pages 413–35), aspects formed by planets (see page 436)	Western
Education, mentality, and beliefs	general interest level in education	House IX ruler (see page 188), planets occupying the house (see pages 413–35), aspects formed by planets (see page 436)	Western
Education, mentality, and beliefs	advanced education	House IX ruler (see page 188)	Vedic
Education, mentality, and beliefs	cognitive abilities	House III ruler (see page 180), planets occupying the house (see pages 413–35), aspects formed by planets (see page 436)	Judaic
Education, mentality, and beliefs	cognitive abilities	House III ruler (see page 180), planets occupying the house (see pages 413–35), aspects formed by planets (see page 436)	Western
Education, mentality, and beliefs	general interest level in education	House IX ruler (see page 188), planets occupying the house (see pages 413–35), aspects formed by planets (see page 436)	Judaic
Education, mentality, and beliefs	inherent wisdom (reasoning power, imagination, speaking skills)	Part of Understanding (see page 273)	Arabian

Subject	Description	Method	Tradition
Education, mentality, and beliefs	intellectual interests	House III ruler (see page 180), planets occupying the house (see pages 413–35), aspects formed by planets (see page 436)	Judaic
Education, mentality, and beliefs	intellectual interests	House III ruler (see page 180), planets occupying the house (see pages 413–35), aspects formed by planets (see page 436)	Western
Education, mentality, and beliefs	level of intelligence	House V ruler (see page 182)	Vedic
Education, mentality, and beliefs	level of truthfulness the person conveys	House II ruler (see page 179)	Vedic
Education, mentality, and beliefs	overall education	House V ruler (see page 182)	Vedic
Education, mentality, and beliefs	person's belief system	Part of Faith (Religion) (see page 315)	Arabian
Education, mentality, and beliefs	prospects for advanced education	House IV ruler (see page 181)	Vedic
Education, mentality, and beliefs	relationships with employees and co-workers	Part of Servants (see page 301)	Arabian
Education, mentality, and beliefs	religious and philosophic beliefs	House IX ruler (see page 188), planets occupying the house (see pages 413–35), aspects formed by planets (see page 436)	Judaic
Education, mentality, and beliefs	religious and philosophic beliefs	House IX ruler (see page 188)	Vedic
Education, mentality, and beliefs	religious and philosophical beliefs	House IX ruler (see page 188), planets occupying the house (see pages 413–35), aspects formed by planets (see page 436)	Western
Education, mentality, and beliefs	speech and learning capabilities	House II ruler (see page 179)	Vedic
Education, mentality, and beliefs	spiritual nature	House XII ruler (see page 194)	Vedic
Education, mentality, and beliefs	who or what an individual serves	Part of Slavery and Bondage (see page 303)	Arabian
Finances and legacies	ability to acquire and accumulate material wealth	House II ruler (see page 179), planets occupying the house (see pages 413–35), aspects formed by planets (see page 436)	Western

SUBJECT	DESCRIPTION	METHOD	TRADITION
Finances and legacies	ability to acquire and accumulate material wealth	House II ruler (see page 179), planets occupying the house (see pages 413–35), aspects formed by planets (see page 436)	Judaic
Finances and legacies	familial wealth	House II ruler (see page 179)	Vedic
Finances and legacies	good or bad days for business	chart of good and bad days for each animal sign (see page 137)	Tibetan
Finances and legacies	good or bad days for business	*chien-ch'ü* (indicator) based on the relationship of the *hua* (day pillar) to the nearest *chieh* (festival) in the calendar year (see page 91)	Chinese
Finances and legacies	income from a profession, hobby, or side venture	House XI ruler (see page 192)	Vedic
Finances and legacies	joint financial life	House VIII ruler (see page 187)	Vedic
Finances and legacies	potential for discovering wealth	Part of Collection (see page 281)	Arabian
Finances and legacies	potential for inheritance	Part of Inheritances and Possessions (see page 290)	Arabian
Finances and legacies	potential for losing material wealth	Part of Sorrow (see page 282)	Arabian
Finances and legacies	potential for material wealth	Part of Goods (see page 278)	Arabian
Finances and legacies	the level of material comfort	House IV ruler (see page 181)	Vedic
Finances and legacies	unearned moneys such as insurance, inheritance, legacy, spouse's income, lotteries, and legal settlements	House VIII ruler (see page 187)	Vedic
Finances and legacies	ability to acquire and accumulate inheritances or legacies	House VIII ruler (see page 187), planets occupying the house (see pages 413–35), aspects formed by planets (see page 436)	Western
Finances and legacies	ability to acquire and accumulate inheritances or legacies	House VIII ruler (see page 187), planets occupying the house (see pages 413–35), aspects formed by planets (see page 436)	Judaic
Friends and associates	adversaries	House VI ruler (see page 184)	Vedic
Friends and associates	participation as a member of a community and ability to form friendships	House XI ruler (see page 192)	Vedic
Friends and associates	personal opposition	Part of Private Enemies (see page 329)	Arabian
Friends and associates	relationships with friends, associates, and mother	Part of Friends and Mother (see page 327)	Arabian
Friends and associates	social skills including the ability to make friends and associates	House XI ruler (see page 192), planets occupying the house, (see pages 413–35), aspects formed by planets (see page 436)	Judaic

SUBJECT	DESCRIPTION	METHOD	TRADITION
Friends and associates	social skills including the ability to make friends and associates	House XI ruler (see page 192), planets occupying the house, (see pages 413–35), aspects formed by planets (see page 436)	Western
Friends and associates	social status	House X ruler (see page 190), planets occupying the house (see pages 413–35), aspects formed by planets (see page 436)	Western
Friends and associates	social status	House X ruler (see page 190), planets occupying the house (see pages 413–35), aspects formed by planets (see page 436)	Judaic
Friends and associates	weaknesses in social relationships	Part of the Perilous and Most Dangerous Year (see page 330)	Arabian
Health and death	attitude toward death and potential events connected with an individual's death	House VIII ruler (see page 187), planets occupying the house (see pages 413–35), aspects formed by planets (see page 436)	Judaic
Health and death	attitude toward death and potential events connected with an individual's death	House VIII ruler (see page 187), planets occupying the house (see pages 413–35), aspects formed by planets (see page 436)	Western
Health and death	conditions of a person's death	Part of Death (see page 314)	Arabian
Health and death	overall health	*gen* (year pillar) (see page 49)	Chinese
Health and death	overall health	House VI ruler (see page 184), planets occupying the house (see pages 413–35), aspects formed by planets (see page 436)	Judaic
Health and death	overall health	House VI ruler (see page 184)	Vedic
Health and death	overall health	House VI ruler (see page 184), planets occupying the house (see pages 413–35), aspects formed by planets (see page 436)	Western
Health and death	physical health	*lü* (health force) (see page 132)	Tibetan
Health and death	physical health (for a woman)	*candralagna* (Moon chart) (see page 226)	Vedic
Health and death	physical weakness	Part of Sickness (see page 300)	Arabian
Health and death	potential for accidents or chronic illness; potential longevity	House VIII ruler (see page 187)	Vedic
Health and death	proneness to accidents or violent crimes	Part of Death (see page 314)	Arabian
Health and death	the person's preoccupation with life and death	Part of Death (see page 314)	Arabian

SUBJECT	DESCRIPTION	METHOD	TRADITION
Individuality and personality	behavioral pattern	chart shape (see page 397); predominant features (see page 403); placement of the Sun (see page 414); placement of the Ascendant (see page 178)	Western
Individuality and personality	behavioral pattern	*gen* (year pillar) (see page 49)	Chinese
Individuality and personality	behavioral pattern	placement of the Ascendant (see page 178); placement of the Sun (see page 414); predominant features (see page 403)	Judaic
Individuality and personality	behavioral pattern	*sok* (life force) (see page 129)	Tibetan
Individuality and personality	behavioral pattern	*yoga* based on planetary positions determined in the *rasicakra* or *bhavacakra* (see page 237)	Vedic
Individuality and personality	emotional makeup	placement of the Moon (see page 416)	Western
Individuality and personality	general appearance and demeanor	Ascendant's *naksatra* (lunar mansion) (see page 155)	Vedic
Individuality and personality	general appearance and demeanor	*gen* (year pillar) (see page 49)	Chinese
Individuality and personality	overall emotional state	*gen* (year pillar) (see page 49)	Chinese
Individuality and personality	overall emotional state	*la* (spirit force) (see page 132)	Tibetan
Individuality and personality	overall emotional state	Part of Life (see page 269)	Arabian
Individuality and personality	overall emotional state	*sok* (life force) (see page 129)	Tibetan
Individuality and personality	overall emotional state (for a woman)	*candralagna* (Moon chart) (see page 226)	Vedic
Individuality and personality	personal/spiritual motivation	Part of Spirit (Part of the Sun) (see page 267)	Arabian
Individuality and personality	physical appearance (overall demeanor)	Part of Durability (see page 275)	Arabian
Individuality and personality	way in which one overcomes obstacles	*wang* (power force) (see page 130)	Tibetan
Individuality and personality	way in which one overcomes obstacles	Part of Aptness (see page 272)	Arabian
Marriage and partnerships	marital happiness	Part of Marriage (see page 311)	Arabian
Marriage and partnerships	marital status and condition of the union	House VII ruler (see page 185), planets occupying the house (see pages 413–35), aspects formed by planets (see page 436)	Judaic
Marriage and partnerships	marital status and condition of the union	House VII ruler (see page 185)	Vedic

SUBJECT	DESCRIPTION	METHOD	TRADITION
Marriage and partnerships	marital status and condition of the union	House VII ruler (see page 185), planets occupying the house (see pages 413–35), aspects formed by planets (see page 436)	Western
Marriage and partnerships	potential for encountering difficulties in communications with a spouse	Part of Discord and Controversy (see page 310)	Arabian
Marriage and partnerships	sexual drive	Part of Sex (see page 308)	Arabian
Marriage and partnerships	type of person the individual finds sexually attractive	Part of Desire and Sexual Attraction (see page 307)	Arabian
Occupation and professional honors	ability to excel at a particular skill	Part of Sudden Advancement (see page 322)	Arabian
Occupation and professional honors	an individual's ideal profession, social and public standing, business acumen, and the father's financial condition	House X ruler (see page 190)	Vedic
Occupation and professional honors	ideal profession	House X ruler (see page 190), planets occupying the house (see pages 413–35), aspects formed by planets (see page 436)	Judaic
Occupation and professional honors	ideal profession	House X ruler (see page 190), planets occupying the house (see pages 413–35), aspects formed by planets (see page 436)	Western
Occupation and professional honors	ideal type of employment	House VI ruler (see page 184), planets occupying the house (see pages 413–35), aspects formed by planets (see page 436)	Judaic
Occupation and professional honors	ideal type of employment	House VI ruler (see page 184), planets occupying the house (see pages 413–35), aspects formed by planets (see page 436)	Western
Occupation and professional honors	potential for honors and awards	House X ruler (see page 190), planets occupying the house (see pages 413–35), aspects formed by planets (see page 436)	Judaic
Occupation and professional honors	potential for honors and awards	House X ruler (see page 190), planets occupying the house (see pages 413–35), aspects formed by planets (see page 436)	Western
Occupation and professional honors	potential for promoting ideas or goods	Part of Merchandise (see page 324)	Arabian
Occupation and professional honors	potential professional interests	Part of Magistery and Profession (see page 323)	Arabian
Occupation and professional honors	professional fame and honors	Part of Honor (see page 320)	Arabian

Subject	Description	Method	Tradition
Occupation and professional honors	work habits and desire to serve others	House VI ruler (see page 184)	Vedic
Personal chronology	chronological course of events	ten-year fate cycles (see pages 65–83)	Chinese
Personal chronology	chronological course of events	*vimsottari dasa* (see page 246)	Vedic
Personal destiny	chaos or problems encountered	placement of the Moon's South Node (see page 410)	Judaic
Personal destiny	chaos or problems encountered	placement of the Moon's South Node (see page 410)	Western
Personal destiny	direction of destiny	*yoga* (see page 237)	Vedic
Personal destiny	financial gain, professional success, receipt of favors	placement of the Moon's North Node (see page 409)	Judaic
Personal destiny	financial gain, professional success, receipt of favors	placement of the Moon's North Node (see page 409)	Western
Personal destiny	form of luck; direction of destiny	*guo* (hour pillar) in relation to the "Song of Four Seasons" (see page 95)	Chinese
Personal destiny	form of luck; direction of destiny	*lung ta* (luck force) (see page 131)	Tibetan
Personal destiny	person's general fortune or luck	House IX ruler (see page 188)	Vedic
Personal destiny	potential for success	Part of Fortune (Part of the Moon) (see page 264)	Arabian
Personal destiny	potential for success	Part of Fortune (Part of the Moon) (see page 264)	Western
Personal limitations and fulfillment of goals	fulfillment of goals and desires	House XI ruler (see page 192)	Vedic
Personal limitations and fulfillment of goals	limitations or personal restrictions	House XII ruler (see page 194), planets occupying the house (see pages 413–35), aspects formed by planets (see page 436)	Judaic
Personal limitations and fulfillment of goals	limitations or personal restrictions	House XII ruler (see page 194), planets occupying the house (see pages 413–35), aspects formed by planets (see page 436)	Western
Personal limitations and fulfillment of goals	obstacles	House VI ruler (see page 184)	Vedic
Personal limitations and fulfillment of goals	passions	House VII ruler (see page 185)	Vedic

SUBJECT	DESCRIPTION	METHOD	TRADITION
Personal limitations and fulfillment of goals	past-life karma	House V ruler (see page 182)	Vedic
Personal limitations and fulfillment of goals	personal courage, the fulfillment of personal desires	House III ruler (see page 180)	Vedic
Personal limitations and fulfillment of goals	things that an individual does not personally control	House XII ruler (see page 194)	Vedic
Pleasure and creativity	creative talent	House V ruler (see page 182), planets occupying the house (see pages 413–35), aspects formed by planets (see page 436)	Judaic
Pleasure and creativity	creative talent	House V ruler (see page 182), planets occupying the house (see pages 413–35), aspects formed by planets (see page 436)	Western
Pleasure and creativity	creative talent and interests	House III ruler (see page 180)	Vedic
Pleasure and creativity	creative talent and interests	House V ruler (see page 182)	Vedic
Pleasure and creativity	imagination	Part of Understanding (see page 273)	Arabian
Pleasure and creativity	passions (both sexual and emotional)	House VIII ruler (see page 187)	Vedic
Pleasure and creativity	romance and pursuit of pleasure	Part of Plays (see page 305)	Arabian
Pleasure and creativity	speculative ventures,	House V ruler (see page 182)	Vedic
Pleasure and creativity	speculative ventures, gambling, sports, and romance	House V ruler (see page 182), planets occupying the house (see pages 413–35), aspects formed by planets (see page 436)	Western
Pleasure and creativity	speculative ventures, gambling, sports, and romance	House V ruler (see page 182), planets occupying the house (see pages 413–35), aspects formed by planets (see page 436)	Judaic
Voyages and journeys	good or bad days for travel	chart of good and bad days for each animal sign (see page 137)	Tibetan
Voyages and journeys	good or bad days for travel	*chien-ch'ü* (indicator) based on the relationship of the *hua* (day pillar) to the nearest *chieh* (festival) in the calendar year (see page 91)	Chinese
Voyages and journeys	outcome of long-distance journeys	Part of Travel by Land (see page 318)	Arabian

Subject	Description	Method	Tradition
Voyages and journeys	outcome of short trips	House III ruler (see page 180), planets occupying the house (see pages 413–35), aspects formed by planets (see page 436)	Western
Voyages and journeys	outcome of short trips	House III ruler (see page 180), planets occupying the house (see pages 413–35), aspects formed by planets (see page 436)	Judaic
Voyages and journeys	potential for foreign travel	House IX ruler (see page 188), planets occupying the house (see pages 413–35), aspects formed by planets (see page 436)	Judaic
Voyages and journeys	potential for foreign travel	House IX ruler (see page 188)	Vedic
Voyages and journeys	potential for foreign travel	House IX ruler (see page 188), planets occupying the house (see pages 413–35), aspects formed by planets (see page 436)	Western
Voyages and journeys	potential for taking up residence in a foreign place	House VII ruler (see page 185)	Vedic
Voyages and journeys	safe passage by water	Part of Journeys by Water (see page 317)	Arabian

INDIVIDUALITY AND PERSONALITY

In Western astrology, a person's general physical appearance, inherent qualities, tendencies, and latent powers including the ability to acquire self-knowledge are viewed as the foundations of individuality. In fact, the character types (melancholic, sanguine, choleric, and phlegmatic) created and applied by early physicians and psychologists were based on Western astrological descriptions of people who had a predominance of earth-, air-, fire-, or water-based zodiac signs in their natal horoscopes (see "Analyzing the Predominant Features" in chapter 8). Arabian practitioners used similar generalizations, enhancing their delineations by calculating the Part of Life to confirm the individual's overall emotional makeup, the Part of Durability to define the person's general demeanor, the Part of Spirit to determine the source of personal and spiritual motivation, and the Part of Aptness to determine how he or she might overcome obstacles.

The profile presented by the overall shape of a person's Western horoscope, predominant features, placements of the Sun (character traits) and Moon (emotional makeup), and placement of the Ascendant or the House I ruler (the individual's persona) can be further enhanced by casting a Vedic natal chart such as a *rasicakra* (sign chart) or *bhavacakra* (house chart) and determining the existence of a specific *yoga* or personality type based on the placement of the planets within the chart. It is also accomplished by delineating the *naksatra* (lunar mansion) in which the Ascendant resides. The *candralagna* (Moon chart) is frequently applied by practitioners to confirm the strength of characteristics disclosed in the *rasicakra* or *bhavacakra,* and is commonly employed to review a woman's overall emotional makeup. A similar cross-examination can be made between a Vedic natal chart, using the elements described above, and a Judaic chart, which concentrates on the placements of the Ascendant, the Sun, the Moon, and predominant features as well.

A quicker comparison can be made by referring to the year in which the person was born and delineating the *gen* (year pillar): a procedure commonly used in Chinese astrology. The personality types described in this system might provide a different way in which to view the person's actions. For example, a seemingly quiet, taciturn Virgo—according to Western astrology—might be a blunt-speaking, secret control freak because he or she was born in a Chinese *lung* (Dragon) year.

Similarly, the year of birth can be used to interpret the person's character through Tibetan eyes. The same person mentioned above might be seen as a good listener, a dutiful person who does not spring into action, and a quick-tempered yet good-natured person, since this is how Dragon-sign people are perceived in Tibetan culture. That same person's *sok* (life force) stabilizes and strengthens the overall character because the Dragon is governed by the earth element. The *la* (spirit force) reinforces the prognostication that he or she is quick-tempered. The *wang* (power force) adds subtlety to this delineation by adding that because the person was born in a year subruled by the water element, the person acts with the smooth yet powerful force of a river.

Personal Chronology and Destiny
Developing a Chronology

By placing the person's ego within a timeline, both Vedic and Chinese astrology provide an alternative view of an otherwise linear perspective of personality. In many ways this is a much more realistic approach to the construction of a profile, since few people maintain a static personality throughout their lives.

In Chinese astrology, a chronology is created and analyzed by comparing the ever-changing relationship of the *hua* (day pillar)—which represents the ego—to the position of the progressed *miao* (month pillar). According to Chinese practitioners, this relationship proceeds in ten-year-long fate cycles during the course of the person's life. By focusing on the positive or negative nature of this pairing, one can see how the person in question might react to the events that are destined to occur during a specific cycle. For example, a person's progressed *miao* might be ruled by the water *hsing* (element) during one cycle. This would indicate that his or her communication skills and natural talents as an artisan or tradesperson would be accentuated during that time. If this progressed *miao* enters the first fate house during this cycle, it further suggests that the person's ultimate destiny or fate will be achieved during this same period, because this particular fate house governs individual destiny. Naturally, the positive or negative nature of that destiny would be determined by the relationship of the elements governing the progressed *miao* and the *hua*.

In Vedic astrology, this same process is executed by determining the placement of the Moon against the backdrop of the *naksatras* (lunar mansions) and constructing a timeline that can be divided into broad periods (years) or incremental segments (days). Called the *vimsottari dasa*, the influence of the various planets (as well as interaction between planets) upon an individual is placed within the context of time and personal destiny.

Unlike the equal time periods found in the Chinese fate cycles, the *dasas* (periods) of this chronology vary radically because each *dasa* is governed by a planet whose sphere of influence can last from seven to twenty years. For example, the person described in the previous paragraphs would discover that during the same Chinese fate cycle mentioned above, a Moon *dasa* governs a portion of that same period, marking it as a good time to start a new business, achieve success in publishing, and attain harmony in life. The individual's mother, spouse, or children will also be fortunate. During the balance of that period, the Mars *dasa* emerges, heralding a time to develop a new health and fitness regimen to bolster health. Travel, adventure, and action become possible. Determination can be applied to any undertaking, and assistance from friends is beneficial.

By comparing the indications of these two forms of chronology, all other questions that may arise concerning the person's domestic life and potential for marriage, children, or financial success can be placed in light of past, present, or future consequence.

Determining Personal Destiny

Destiny and *fate* are generally taboo terms in Western culture, implying as they do that there is a predetermined outcome of an individual's existence. Despite this misinterpretation, three prognosticators of personal destiny are applied in Western, Judaic, and Arabian astrology: the delineations of the Moon's North and South Nodes, and the Part of Fortune. The Moon's North Node (☊) determines the individual's potential for financial gain, professional success, or the receipt of favors, and the vehicle(s) by which these opportunities are obtained. In many cultures, this is known as the person's portion of good luck. Its converse, the Moon's South Node (☋), determines the precise forms of chaos or problems a person encounters in life, or the individual's portion of bad luck. The Arabian Part of Fortune (which is also used by Western astrologers) indicates the source of an individual's worldly success. For example, the placement of the Part of Fortune in House II of a natal horoscope suggests that worldly success is attained through property, employment, and business. Placed in House III, this same Part implies that fortunes are to be made from writings, publishing, advertising, brethren, and short journeys.

Vedic practitioners do not dwell as deeply upon general fortune as do those from other traditions, since fate is determined by one's accumulated karmic debt from previous lifetimes as well as the present. However, astrologers occasionally refer to the delineation of House IX if such a question does arise.

Luck plays a greater role in Chinese astrology. But one of the oldest methods for determining a person's good fortune provides a more general view of personal destiny, which involves locating the individual's *guo* (hour pillar) *ti chih* on one of four images depicting the Emperor Huang Ti. Chinese almanacs generally contain this series of images or "songs," called the "Song of the Four Seasons." Each image represents a particular season: spring, summer, autumn, or winter. The twelve *ti chih* are distributed in varying orders on the emperor's head, shoulders, belly, hands, groin, knees, and feet. Each position implies the form of fortune that befalls the individual in question. For example, if a person born during autumn had a *guo ti chih* placed on the emperor's head, this placement would indicate that his or her life would pass without worry, promising good luck and a good future. Promotion and advancement to top positions would also be possible. On the other hand, if the person had been born during the summer and had a *guo ti chih* placed on the emperor's groin, the prognostication would suggest that he or she would attain wealth. No destiny is unreachable or too farfetched for this individual. And the person might be awarded a very high position in older age, with his or her fortunes passed on to descendants.

Tibetan astrology offers a simpler and equally generalized way to determine the type of luck a person might possess. The *lung ta* (luck force) is the secondary element that governs the individual's animal sign, as opposed to the animal sign's *sok* (life force) or the element that governs the specific year of birth. For example, a person born in a *hBrul* (Dragon) year would have a *sok* ruled by the earth element. (The year of birth itself might be ruled by the water, earth, fire, metal, or wood element.) Because this person has a Dragon animal sign, his or her *lung ta* is ruled by wood.

The relationship between the *sok* and *lung ta* elements determines the positive or negative nature of that luck. For example, the relationship between earth and wood is very beneficial; therefore the person is deemed to enjoy good fortune throughout life. Both the Chinese and Tibetan methods can be used as quick confirmation of the delineation of the Moon's Nodes and Part of Fortune mentioned earlier.

Vedic practitioners determine the existence of a specific *yoga* or personality type based on the planets' placement within a fixed order in a natal horoscope. This apportionment of destiny is a key element of Vedic astrology because it represents the person's present direction in life. For example, if the planetary rulers of Houses I, II, V, IX, or XI physically occupy these same houses, the chart exhibits the *dhana-yoga*, which suggests that the person achieves material wealth in the areas represented by the affected houses. If three planets occupy the zodiac sign they also rule, the chart presents one of many *raj-yogas*, which indicate that the individual is extremely powerful and successful throughout his or her lifetime. All other elements of personality disclosed by the occupation of the remaining planets are weighed against this foundation. Once again, the delineation of a *yoga* can be combined with luck factors found in any of the other traditions, thereby providing a very rounded view of the person's destiny.

No matter which tradition is applied, general personality traits, individual chronology, and personal destiny are only the beginning of any profile. The subject in question often wants or needs to know more details about his or her strengths or weaknesses in a given area. The most frequent concerns center around finances and material gain, domestic life, children, pleasure, marriage and partnerships, health, travel, education, employment and profession, social status, friendships, and relationships with various family members.

Finances and Legacies

Western and Judaic practitioners determine a person's ability to acquire and accumulate money as well as his or her potential for receiving legacies, gifts, grants, and benefactions by delineating the House II and VIII rulers, any planets that occupy those same houses, and any aspects those planets form within the chart.

In the Vedic tradition, a practitioner might look to the House IV ruler for indications of the level of material comfort the person might experience if the question arises from an assessment of the individual's *yoga*. The House II ruler might also be addressed if there are indications in a person's *yoga* other than familial wealth. The

House XI ruler is sometimes consulted if there are concerns about the person's income from a profession, hobby, or side venture. Or the House VIII ruler might be consulted if joint financial ventures or unearned moneys (such as insurance, inheritance, lotteries, legacies, legal settlements, or the spouse's income) are at question.

Prognostications found in Western, Judaic, or Vedic readings can be confirmed by looking to Arabian astrology for the specific ways and means by which an individual derives wealth. For example, the Part of Goods indicates the potential for acquiring material wealth; the Part of Collection determines an individual's potential for discovering wealth; the modern-day Part of Sorrow discloses the potential for losing material wealth; and the Part of Inheritances and Possessions indicates the potential for receiving material legacies.

Chinese and Tibetan astrologies can aid someone seeking daily advice on the road to wealth and prosperity. In both cultures the pursuit of material wealth is not treated as a separate or detailed entity. One's ability to become wealthy is considered to be part of destiny, and the specific events related to that fate are determined by reviewing the individual chronology. But, once again, the apportionment of luck plays a key role.

Chinese astrologers determine good or bad days for the transaction of business by cross-referencing the person's birth *hua* (day pillar) with the nearest *chieh* (festivals) in the Chinese calendar to the date in question. The resulting *chien-ch'ü* (indicator) outlines the potential outcome of the day's events. For example, the *chien-ch'ü* for the day in question might advise that successful conclusions to large-scale social events, long-distance travel, and changes of residence can be achieved and routine tasks can be resumed. Personal opinions must be concealed, however, and the person must not meddle in other people's affairs.

Tibetan practitioners provide a more rigid view of the auspicious or inauspicious nature of individual days, based on a person's animal sign. As mentioned earlier, days are categorized by quality, allowing someone with minimal astrological knowledge to decide quickly if it is a good day to start a new business or finish projects. For example, a person born in a Dragon year would know that a Foundation Day (the best day for starting new projects) occurs three days after the beginning of the lunar month; a Success Day (the best day to finish a project) occurs seventeen days after the beginning of the lunar month; and a Power Day (the day when he or she is strongest) occurs twenty-four days after the beginning of the lunar month. At the opposite end of fortune, an Obstacle Day (a day when he or she may encounter delays or obstacles) occurs eight days after the beginning of the lunar month. An Enemy Day (a day when he or she may encounter opposition to projects) takes place eleven days after the beginning of the lunar month; and a Disturbance Day (a day when chaos may occur) happens nine days after the beginning of the lunar month.

Domestic Life and Familial Relationships

The questions of home environs, family life, and general domestic situation are determined in the Western and Judaic traditions by delineating the House IV ruler, any planets that occupy that house, and any aspects formed by those planets.

Relationships between the person and his or her siblings are determined in the Western and Judaic traditions by delineating the House III ruler, any planets that occupy that house, and any aspects formed by those planets. The interactions between the individual and his or her father are disclosed by interpreting the House IV ruler, any planets that occupy that house, and any aspects formed by those planets. And the interactions between the individual and his or her mother are determined by some Western astrologers by delineating the House X ruler, any planets that occupy that house, and any aspects formed by those planets.

In Arabian astrology, these basic facets of human existence are governed by the Part of Fortune in Husbandry, which can be employed to confirm or enhance prognostications found in other traditions. But other portions of family life, such as relationships among family members, are disclosed by other means. Arabian astrologers considered family relations to be a key element of a person's potential for success, providing the foundations for social status and professional advancement as well as the primary source for the initial acquisition of material wealth. Therefore the Part of the Father, the Part of Brethren, the Part of the Mother, and the Part of Love of Brethren all addressed those issues. These Parts can also be applied when confirmation or enhancement of other delineations is desired.

If questions about the person's family, domestic environment, or maternal relationship arise (pertinent concerns in Hindu culture), Vedic practitioners might review the House IV ruler. The House III ruler would be consulted concerning relationships among siblings. The House IX ruler would be assessed when questions arise concerning the person's relationship with his or her father. Once again, this information can be used to enhance an existing Western or Judaic profile of domestic life.

Pleasure and Creativity

Western, Judaic, and even Vedic astrologers determine an individual's interest in speculative ventures, romance, gambling, sports, and other pleasures by delineating the House V ruler, planets that occupy this same house, and any aspects formed by those planets. This material is also reviewed by those same astrologers as an indication of a person's creativity, especially if the person in question is a performing or visual artist. The House III ruler is also reviewed in Vedic astrology to determine the level of a person's creativity. And the House VIII ruler is consulted to disclose a person's sexual and emotional passions.

A combined reading of any two of the above traditions can be augmented by the calculation of one or more Arabian Parts if there is any question as to the strength of a person's imagination or desire for pleasure. Arabian practitioners determined an individual's level of creativity by assessing the Part of Understanding for his or her strength of imagination. Romance and the pursuit of pleasure are indicated in the Part of Plays.

Children

The promise of children in a person's chart is also determined by delineating the House V ruler, planets that occupy that same house, and any aspects formed by those planets in both Western and Judaic astrology. Vedic practitioners assess the same ruler, which they believe governs the promise of children. As mentioned earlier, a woman's potential for bearing children is also disclosed by the construction and delineation of a *candralagna* (Moon chart). This information can be used to enhance a Western or Judaic reading of the same subject.

Arabian practitioners applied the Part of Children to determine the number of children as well as the Part of Female Children and Part of Male Children if the number of each gender was questioned. However, the data derived from the Parts should only be used to compare the results with delineation from other traditions.

Marriage and Partnerships

In both Western and Judaic astrology, a person's marital status and the condition of a union are determined by delineating the House VII ruler, any planets that occupy that house, and any aspects formed by those planets. (This same procedure is also employed to determine the status of business or other partnerships.) Similarly, the House VII ruler is reviewed by Vedic practitioners seeking insight into either question. Naturally, the readings from Western, Judaic, or Vedic prognosticators can be compared with each other to enhance an interpretation.

Additionally, Arabian astrology can provide even more data. Practitioners can calculate the Part of Marriage to ascertain the state of marital happiness; the Part of Discord and Controversy to determine the potential for miscommunications with one's spouse; the Part of Sex to disclose the type of sexual drive the person has; and the modern-day Part of Desire and Sexual Attraction to determine the type of person the individual finds sexually attractive.

Health and Death

Western and Judaic practitioners determine a person's overall health, attitude toward death, and eventual demise by delineating the House VI and VIII rulers, any planets occupying those houses, and the aspects formed by those planets. Death is treated as the termination of life in Western civilization. Therefore the House VIII ruler, occupying planets, and aspects are sometimes consulted for the potential health, accidental, or criminal events connected with the end of a person's life. Additionally, the House VI ruler, occupying planets, and aspects are reviewed for indications of chronic or acute illness and the quality of the person's life. The House VI and VIII rulers, occupying planets, and aspects are reviewed by Vedic practitioners for the same reasons mentioned above. And a woman's physical health is further assessed by the delineation of a *candralagna* (Moon chart).

Combining the information disclosed by these traditions provides more than enough data to assess this area. And the Arabian Parts do little to enhance these prognostications. But if you choose to consult this particular tradition, the Part of Sickness determines physical weaknesses, according to Arabian astrologers. And the Part of Death discloses the person's proneness to accidents or violent crimes.

Similarly, Tibetan and Chinese astrologies provide little material that can be used outside of traditional Oriental medicine. The methods described below are provided purely for reference purposes.

Tibetan practitioners ascertain the source of physical health by assessing the *lü* (health force). To identify this force, astrologers employ the individual's animal sign and its "key element" as well as the person's *wang* (power force) to identify his or her *lü*. For example, a person born in a Dragon year has metal as his or her "key element." If that individual's *wang* is water, then the *lü* is also water. Using the same interpretative material applied to the element that governs the *sok* force, the astrologer determines that the person's bloodstream should be of primary concern in his or her overall health regimen. If, however, a person born in a Dragon year has a *wang* governed by wood, his or her *lü* is fire, which suggests that the heart and tongue should be primary health concerns.

In a similar fashion, the *hsing* that rules the *gen* (year pillar) in Chinese astrology indicates which area of the human body deserves attention in the development of a balanced health regimen. For example, a person who has a *gen* ruled by the earth and wood *hsing* (governing the *Ming Shu* sign and the year in question, respectively) would seek to nourish and harmonize the areas of the body controlled by his or her spleen and liver.

Voyages and Journeys

The outcome of long-distance or foreign journeys was of great concern to trade-oriented cultures in the past, as it is to industrialized cultures in the present. Western and Judaic astrologers determine an individual's potential for long-distance travel as well as the condition and outcome of short trips by delineating the House IX and III rulers respectively, as well as any planets that occupy those houses, and any aspects formed by those planets. Vedic practitioners assess the House IX ruler to ascertain the potential for foreign travel and the House VII ruler for the possibility that the person may make his or her home in a foreign place. Arabian astrologers consulted the Part of Travel by Land or the Part of Journeys by Water, depending on the circumstances. If this facet of life is of interest, any of the above methods can be applied in any combination to enhance a delineation.

The daily predictors used by Chinese astrologers are frequently consulted in that culture to determine the safety of travel on specific days (see "Finances and Legacies," page 544). More generally, the Tibetan chart of good and bad days can provide insight in this realm (see "Finances and Legacies," page 544).

Education, Mentality, and Beliefs
Level of Education and Intellect

An individual's ability to learn, as well as his or her general level of interest in education, including intellectual interests and the individual's cognitive abilities, is determined by Western and Judaic astrologers who delineate the zodiac signs that govern Houses IX and III respectively, any planets that occupy those same houses, and any aspects formed by those planets. Vedic practitioners have a unique take on this particular subject. They assess the House II ruler to determine the person's speech and learning capabilities as well as the level of truthfulness the person conveys; the House IV and IX rulers to determine his or her prospects for advanced education; and the House V ruler to review his or her education and level of intelligence. These methods can be used in any combination to enhance one's view of an individual's mentality.

The above can also be enhanced by calculating the Arabian Part of Understanding to confirm an individual's degree of inherent wisdom, which includes his or her reasoning power, level of imagination, and speaking skills. This is an area of human existence that is not specifically covered by the Chinese and Tibetan traditions discussed in this book. Therefore, no recommendations are available regarding these forms of astrology.

Religious and Philosophical Beliefs

According to Western and Judaic practitioners, an individual's ideological beliefs—both religious and philosophical—can be determined by a review of the House IX ruler, any planets that occupy that same house, and any aspects formed by those planets. Vedic astrologers assess the House IX ruler for insights into the person's religious or philosophical beliefs, and the House XII ruler if the person's spiritual nature needs to be determined as well. As with other facets of life, any of the above methods can be employed in any combination to enhance a profile.

Additionally, the Arabian Part of Faith can be calculated to disclose an individual's belief system. And the Part of Servants can be applied to reveal insights into who or what the individual serves, whether it's his or her own interests, senses, fame, the pursuit of pleasure, business, karmic debt, or spiritual improvement.

Once again, this is an area of human existence that is not specifically covered by the Chinese and Tibetan traditions discussed in this book. Therefore, no recommendations are available regarding these forms of astrology.

Occupation and Professional Honors

The ideal type of business, career, or employment for an individual, as well as the potential for receiving professional honors and awards, is determined by Western and Judaic practitioners who delineate the House VI and X rulers, any planets that occupy those houses, and any aspects formed by those planets. Vedic astrologers assess the House VI ruler to analyze an individual's work habits as well as the desire to serve others, and the House X ruler to ascertain an individual's profession, social and public standing, business acumen, and the father's financial condition (this last element plays an important role in one's professional life in Hindu culture). Once again, any of the above methods can be employed in any combination to enhance a professional prognostication.

Of great importance to Arabian practitioners, the Part of Sudden Advancement can be calculated to ascertain one's ability to excel at a particular skill; the Part of Merchandise can help determine one's potential for promoting ideas or goods; and the Part of Magistery and Profession can determine an individual's professional interests. On a similar note, the Part of Honor sheds light on professional honors as well as the potential for fame.

Since in Chinese and Tibetan cultures an individual's professional and work life are determined by familial legacy and cultural parameters, this aspect is not specifically covered by Chinese and Tibetan astrology. Therefore, no recommendations are available regarding these traditions.

Friends and Associates

A person's social skills, including the ability to develop friendships and associations within a particular social sphere, are determined by Western and Judaic practitioners who delineate the House XI ruler, any planets occupying that house, and any aspects formed by those planets (although one's social standing is determined by interpreting the House X ruler, occupying planets, and aspects). Vedic astrologers look to the House XI ruler to determine the person's participation as a member of the community as well as his or her ability to form friendships, while the House VI ruler provides insight into one's adversaries. Combining these traditions can enrich the prognostications in this realm.

Arabian astrology derives information regarding friendships and associations from the Part of Friends and Mother, while weaknesses in social relationships are determined by the calculation of the Part of the Perilous and Most Dangerous Year. Personal opposition, on the other hand, is ascertained through the calculation of the Part of Private Enemies.

Since friendships and associations are determined by cultural parameters, these are not specifically covered by Chinese and Tibetan astrology. Therefore, no recommendations are available regarding these traditions.

Personal Limitations and the Fulfillment of Goals

Personal fulfillment is surprisingly not an area specifically covered by Western, Judaic, Chinese, Arabian, or Tibetan astrology. A person's potential limitations or personal restrictions, however, are determined in Western and Judaic astrology by delineating the House XII ruler, any planets that occupy the house, and any aspects formed by those planets. Because little information is provided by these traditions, one should refer to Vedic astrology when questions arise as to an individual's ability to find fulfillment.

The Vedic tradition concentrates a great deal of attention in this area. Practitioners look to the House III ruler to ascertain the person's level of personal courage as well as his or her ability to fulfill personal desires. The House VI ruler is consulted to determine what sort of obstacles an individual might encounter, while the House VII ruler is reviewed to see what sort of passions lie beneath the surface. The House XI ruler is employed to determine if the person fulfills his or her goals and desires; and the House XII ruler provides insight into things that an individual cannot personally control. Since karmic debt from a previous lifetime is considered to be a prime protagonist in one's present existence, Vedic practitioners also refer to the House V ruler which points to person's past-life karma.

Although the recommendations for combining various world astrologies in this chapter is by no means complete, it at least provides a starting point from which customized formulae can be tested and adapted. Naturally, the further one delves into this incredibly rich subject, the more one finds to add to one's library of self-knowledge and expertise: a road that travels over many horizons.

Conclusion

Proficiency in any of the world's astrologies requires years of study and application. Consequently, it is impossible to detail within the confines of a single book the complete volumes of alternative mathematical, structural, and interpretative methods used by the world's practicing astrologers at the end of the twentieth century. (It would be even more hopeless to attempt to document the millennias-old oral traditions that gave birth to, and still contribute to, the evolution of the astrological sciences.) The foundations of natal and predictive astrology presented here, however, provide ample data to commence with the analysis and comparison of the various disciplines through application. To take it a step beyond is the life's work of most practicing astrologers.

It seems that the search for self-knowledge reaches critical crests when potential changes in the surrounding environments—home, neighborhood, nation, and the world—are perceived on the apparent horizon. The birth of theosophy and spiritualism during the late 1800s and the introduction in the West of numerous Eastern ideologies during the 1920s, 1940s, and 1960s are only a few recent examples of the rising tide of hunger to comprehend the meaning and purpose of life. The end of a decade, a century, and a millennium and the beginning of a new precessional age appear to trigger a desire to prepare for the unknown by seeking the meaning and purpose of self through both modern and ancient sources.

The revitalized interest in, and use of, the Arabian Parts by modern Western astrologers only hints at the continuing thirst for answers to tomorrow's questions: Will the economy continue along the same path next year or next decade? Is marriage or divorce possible? Are children in the offing? Is fame and glory coming soon? Will a secret goal finally be attained in the next month? The fascination with *feng shui*, the *I Ching*, and the Chinese concept of harmonic balance goes hand-in-hand with a desire to learn more about cosmic flow as presented in other Chinese and Tibetan practices such as *Tzu P'ing, Ming Shu,* and even t'ai chi, which have their basis in the fundamentals of Taoism, Confucianism, and Buddhism. Similarly, the rising interest in Vedic astrology, the Kabbala, and Mesoamerican astrology among New Age enthusiasts provides further evidence of modern, computerized society's thirst for answers to the hardest question of all: Why does humanity exist, and what is its purpose?

The evolution of global communications has opened the range of available information resources and shared wisdom on the potential causes and effects of natural phenomena as well as human behavior. Medical science has discovered how synapses operate in the brain. Behavioral science can explain why a misfiring of synaptic pulses or an imbalance of hormones may create socially undesirable actions in humans and other animals. Meteorological science knows how to predict climatic changes with a reasonable degree of accuracy. And in recent times, astrology's offspring—astronomical science—has presented modern civilization with its first hard evidence of the forces that create the stars themselves.

Few educated people in the civilized world can deny knowledge of these discoveries. Is it possible that, in light of the accumulating evidence, a practice as relatively unchanged and ancient as astrology will once again be accepted as a legitimate science—that one day the prejudice and negative stereotypes surrounding this study of the celestial bodies will be overshadowed by irrefutable proof that we are affected by the forces exerted by the heavens?

Glossary

Abhijit: The twenty-eighth Vedic *naksatra* (lunar mansion), which is only an intercalary and rarely used.

Akrab: Judaic term for the zodiac sign of Scorpio.

Anahibazon: Arabic term for the Moon's North Node (☊).

angles: The four major compass points of the horoscope: Ascendant, Nadir, Descendant, and Midheaven.

angular houses: Houses I, IV, VII, and X of the horoscope, which are positioned closest to the chart's primary angles: Ascendant, Nadir, Descendant, and Midheaven.

antardasa: Vedic term for the subdivision of a *bhukti* into nine equal parts or a *dasa* into eighty-one equal parts.

antiscia: Name given to each of two planets that are equally distant from any angle in a chart, forming a mundane parallel (see below).

Anuradha: The seventeenth Vedic *naksatra* (lunar mansion).

Aquarius: The eleventh sign of the Western zodiac (♒); the name of a constellation.

arcs of asterisms: Similar to constellations, four star groupings as observed by Chinese astrologers, named the Green Dragon or Azure Dragon, the Red Bird or Vermilion Bird, the White Tiger, and the Dark Warrior or Black Warrior.

Ardra: The sixth Vedic *naksatra* (lunar mansion).

Ari: Judaic term for the zodiac sign of Leo (♌); Vedic term meaning "enemy" which is House VI of the horoscope.

Aries: The first sign of the Western zodiac (♈); the name of a constellation.

Artha: Vedic term meaning "wealth" which is House II of the horoscope.

Ascendant (rising sign): The first of four major compass points of the horoscope, situated on the horizon near the cusp of House I, representing an individual's personality.

Aslesa: The ninth Vedic *naksatra* (lunar mansion).

aspect: The degree of arc created between a planet, corollary point, or cusp and another, similar entity.

asterism: A star cluster not necessarily associated with documented constellations.

Asvini: The first Vedic *naksatra* (lunar mansion).

athasastra: Vedic term meaning "study of government and politics," a major branch of Indian learning.

Aya: Vedic term meaning "gain" which is House XI of the horoscope.

ayanamsa: The fluctuating, apparent position of 00°♈00′ on the celestial ecliptic (versus static position of 00°♈00′ in the tropical ecliptic), which moves at a rate of precession of approximately 00°00′50″ per year.

azemene: A series of degrees said to indicate lifelong infirmity or terminal disease if the Ascendant, the Ascendant's ruler, or the luminaries (the Sun or the Moon) occupy 06°♉00′–10°♉00′;

09°♋00′–13°♋00′; 18°♌00′, 27°♌00′, and 28°♌00′; 19°♏00′ and 28°♏00′; 01°♐00′, 07°♐00′–08°♐00′, and 18°♐00′–19°♐00′, 26°♑00′–29°♑00′, and 18°♒00′–19°♒00′.

ba tze: Chinese term meaning "eight characters"; one of the ten *t'ien kan* or the twelve *ti chih*.

Bandhu: Vedic term meaning "kin" which is House IV of the horoscope.

bap-par: Tibetan term meaning "descending *parkha*," which is a progressed *parkha* used in astrological prediction.

Betulah: Judaic term for the zodiac sign of Virgo (♍).

Bharani: The second Vedic *naksatra* (lunar mansion).

bhava: Vedic term meaning "house," as in houses of the horoscope.

bhavacakra: Vedic term meaning "house chart."

Bhratr: Vedic term meaning "brothers" which is House III of the horoscope.

bhukti: Vedic term for the subdivision of a *dasa* into nine equal parts.

biquintile: An aspect created between two planets, corollary points, or cusps that has an arc of 144°00′.

brahmanas: Vedic term for the protocol for the execution of rituals by the priests.

Budha: Vedic term for the planet Mercury (☿).

By-bai: Tibetan term for the *Ming Shu* sign of the Rat.

Bya: Tibetan term for the *Ming Shu* sign of the Rooster.

cadent houses: Houses III, VI, IX, and XII of the horoscope.

Cancer: The fourth sign of the Western zodiac (♋); the name of a constellation.

Candra: Vedic term for the Moon.

candralagna: Vedic term meaning "Moon as Ascendant"; a Moon chart.

Capricorn: The tenth sign of the Western zodiac (♑); the name of a constellation.

Caput Draconis (Dragon's Head):   Latin term for the Moon's North Node (☊).

Cauda Draconis (Dragon's Tail):   Latin term for the Moon's South Node (☋).

ch'i: Chinese term meaning "breath," one of twenty-four divisions of the solar calendar.

Ch'io: Chinese term meaning "horn," the first *sieu* (lunar mansion).

chak: Tibetan term for the characteristics represented by the element metal.

Chaldean: Judaic term for "astrologer"; also one of many national groups settled in Mesopotamia.

Chang: Chinese term meaning "bow," the twenty-sixth *sieu* (lunar mansion).

Chen: Chinese term meaning "carriage," the twenty-eight *sieu* (lunar mansion).

chestabala: Vedic term for a planet's strength of motion as determined by its position in the northern latitudes of the zodiac.

Chi':   Chinese term for the *Ming Shu* sign of the Rooster.

Chi: Chinese term for the *Ming Shu* sign of the Pig; also a Chinese term meaning "basket," the seventh *sieu* (lunar mansion).

chieh: Chinese term meaning "monthly festival," one of twelve divisions of the solar calendar.

chien-ch'ü: Chinese term for one of twelve "indicators" used in predictive astrology.

Ching: Chinese term meaning "well," the twenty-second *sieu* (lunar mansion).

chu: Tibetan term for the characteristics represented by the element water.

Citra: The fourteenth Vedic *naksatra* (lunar mansion).

conjunction: An aspect (☌) created between two planets, corollary points, or cusps that has an arc of 00°00′.

Dagim: Judaic term for the zodiac sign of Pisces (♓).

Dark Warrior: Chinese term for the northern arc of asterisms.

dasa (mahadasa):   Vedic term for periods of ecliptical time measuring 13.33°00′ each.

decile (semi-quintile):   An aspect created between two planets, corollary points, or cusps that has an arc of 36°00′.

Deli: Judaic term for the zodiac sign of Aquarius (♒).

Descendant: The third of four major compass points of the horoscope situated on the horizon near the cusp of House VII.

Dharma: Vedic term meaning "proper way" which is House IX of the horoscope; in lowercase, the Vedic term for the way in which a person conducts his or her present life.

dharmasastra: Vedic term meaning "study of moral and ritual law," a major branch of Indian learning.

dikbala: Vedic term for a planet's strength of direction.

disturbance: One of the six qualities of monthly days used in Tibetan astrology.

drekkanacakra: Vedic term for "tenth-sign chart."

drigbala: Vedic term for the strength received by the aspects formed between the given planet and a planet that is either naturally benefic or is deemed benefic to the individual's Ascendant.

dun-Zur: Tibetan term for "opposite," used to define the relationship between zodiac signs.

dur-mik: Tibetan term meaning "death spot," used to indicate an inauspicious *bap-par* or a bad year.

Earth Planet: Chinese description of the planet Saturn (♄), embodying the natural characteristics of the earth element or *hsing*.

electional astrology: The astrological study that concentrates on the actual selection of the optimal time to take action on a particular issue or event.

elements: Characteristics embodied in natural elements such as fire, earth, water, air, metal, and wood in various astrologies.

enemy: One of the six qualities of monthly days used in Tibetan astrology.

ephemeris: A listing of the daily and monthly motions and locations of the Sun, the Moon, the planets, and some of the asteroids as they travel along the ecliptic.

esoteric astrology: The astrological study that concentrates on pseudoscientific subjects, such as the zodiac's hidden symbology; previous life studies; postmortem predictions; and the application of hypothetical planets, asteroids, and other psychically perceived entities.

Evening Star: Another term for the planet Venus (♀).

exact aspect (partile aspect):   An aspect that has no flexible orb of influence.

exoteric astrology: The astrological study that concentrates on the potential physical and emotional experiences in an individual's life, centering on the circumstances surrounding a person's birth (natal), general progress (predictive), specific future (horary), health (medical), and behavior as a member of a culture or other secular body (mundane).

extra-Saturnian planets: The seventh, eighth, and ninth planets of the solar system, discovered after the seventeenth century A.D.: Neptune (♆), Uranus (♅), and Pluto (♇).

Fang: Chinese term meaning "room," the fourth *sieu* (lunar mansion).

Fire Planet: Chinese description of the planet Mars (♂), embodying the natural characteristics of the fire element or *hsing*.

foundation: One of the six qualities of monthly days used in Tibetan astrology.

Gedi: Judaic term for the zodiac sign of Capricorn (♑).

Gemini: The third sign of the Western zodiac (♊); the name of a constellation.

gen: Chinese term meaning "year pillar," one of the *Ssu Chu.*

genethliacal astrology: Another term for natal astrology.

geocentric: A cosmological perception that places the Earth at the center of the universe.

gLan: Tibetan term for the *Ming Shu* sign of the Ox or Buffalo.

Green Dragon: Chinese name for the eastern arc of asterisms.

Greenwich Mean Time (GMT), also called Universal Time (UT):   Unit of measure that represents the time at the Prime Meridian located in Greenwich, England (00°00′ longitude).

guo: Chinese term meaning "hour pillar," one of the *Ssu Chu.*

Guru: Vedic term for the planet Jupiter (♃); alternately known as Brhaspati.

Halachah: Judaic term for Jewish law, meaning "the way to go."

Hasta: The thirteenth Vedic *naksatra* (lunar mansion).

hBrul: Tibetan term for the *Ming Shu* sign of the Dragon.

heliocentric: A cosmological perception that places the Sun at the center of the universe.

horacakra: Vedic term for "half-sign chart."

horary astrology: The astrological study that seeks to answer specific requests raised by an individual by casting a chart for an exact year, month, day, time, and location (if known).

Hou: Chinese term for the *Ming Shu* sign of the Monkey.

Hsin: Chinese term meaning "heart," the first *sieu* (lunar mansion).

Hsing: Chinese term meaning "star," the twenty-fifth *sieu* (lunar mansion); in lowercase, a Chinese term meaning "agent," used to describe one of the five natural elements.

Hsü: Chinese term meaning "void," the eleventh *sieu* (lunar mansion).

Hu: Chinese term for the *Ming Shu* sign of the Tiger.

hua: Chinese term meaning "day pillar," one of the *Ssu Chu.*

I: Chinese term meaning "wings," the twenty-seventh *sieu* (lunar mansion).

I Ching: A Chinese form of divination that applies a series of sixty-four predictive poems coordinated with eight linear images called trigrams, which are made up of a combination of three broken or unbroken lines.

iatromathematics: Another term for medical astrology.

jataka: Vedic term for natal astrology.

jung-tsi: Tibetan term for the spiritual side of astrology which is based on Chinese astrological methods.

Jyestha: The eighteenth Vedic *naksatra* (lunar mansion).

jyotisa: A Vedic term for astrology.

jyotisastra: Vedic term meaning "study of the heavenly bodies," which includes astrology, astronomy, and mathematics; a major branch of Indian learning.

K'ang: Chinese term meaning "neck," the second *sieu* (lunar mansion).

k'o: Chinese term for time periods.

K'uei: Chinese term meaning "astride," the fifteenth *sieu* (lunar mansion).

kalabala: Vedic term for a planet's strength of time.

Kalatra: Vedic term meaning "wife" which is House VII of the horoscope.

kamasastra: Vedic term meaning "study of the art of love and pleasure," a major branch of Indian learning.

kar-tsi: Tibetan term for the technical side of astrology, which is based on Hindu astrological methods.

Karma: Vedic term meaning "actions" or "work" which is House X of the horoscope; in lowercase, the Vedic term for past actions that affect an individual's fortunes or destiny in the present or future.

Kasshat: Judaic term for the zodiac sign of Sagittarius (♐).

kendra: Vedic term for Houses I, IV, VII, and X of the horoscope.

Ketu: Vedic term for the Moon's South Node (☋).

Khy: Tibetan term for the *Ming Shu* sign of the Dog.

Kou: Chinese term for the *Ming Shu* sign of the Dog.

Krttika: The third Vedic *naksatra* (lunar mansion).

Kuei: Chinese term meaning "ghosts," the twenty-third *sieu* (lunar mansion).

Kuja: Vedic term for the planet Mars (♂).

la: Tibetan term for "spirit force."

Lagna: Vedic term meaning "that which meets one" which is the Ascendant or House I of the horoscope; alternately known as Tanu (the Body).

leap year: A year that occurs every four years in which an intercalary day is inserted between February and March to accommodate for the 0.25-day deficit in the solar calendar.

Leo: The fifth sign of the Western zodiac (♌); the name of a constellation.

Libra: The seventh sign of the Western zodiac (♎); the name of a constellation.

Liu: Chinese term meaning "willow," the twenty-fourth *sieu* (lunar mansion).

lo shu: A Chinese form of numerological divination that employs a nine-digit magic square as its foundation.

logarithm (proportional logarithm): A mathematical device used to simplify multiplication and division problems by converting the equations into addition and subtraction problems.

Lou: Chinese term meaning "mound," the sixteenth *sieu* (lunar mansion).

lü: Tibetan term for "health force."

Lug: Tibetan term for the *Ming Shu* sign of the Ram or Sheep.

luminary: Term used to describe the Sun (☉) or the Moon (☽).

lunar mansion: Term used to describe one of twenty-eight fixed stars used by Chinese, Tibetan, Vedic, Arabian, and medieval European astrologers to determine the transiting of the Moon.

Lung: Chinese term for the *Ming Shu* sign of the Dragon.

lung ta: Tibetan term for "luck force."

luni-solar calendar: A calendar system similar to the Greek and Judaic nineteen-year Cycle of Meton, which rectifies the unequal orbital paths of the Sun and Moon into twelve segments of time, inserting intercalary moons into the annual cycle so that the vernal equinox always occurs during the second lunar month, the summer solstice always occurs during the fifth lunar month, the autumn equinox occurs during the eighth lunar month, and the winter solstice occurs during the eleventh lunar month.

Ma: Chinese term for the *Ming Shu* sign of the Horse.

Magha: The tenth Vedic *naksatra* (lunar mansion).

manazil: Arabic term meaning "lunar mansion."

Mao: Chinese term meaning "lights," the eighteenth *sieu* (lunar mansion).

me: Tibetan term for the characteristics represented by the fire element.

medical astrology: The astrological study of the effect of planetary influences on the health of the human body (also called *iatromathematics*).

Metal Planet: Chinese description of the planet Venus (♀), embodying the natural characteristics of the metal element or *hsing*.

mewa: Tibetan term for any one of nine magical squares similar to *lo shu* divination, used as a form of astrological prediction.

miao: Chinese term meaning "month pillar," one of the *Ssu Chu*.

Midheaven: The south of four major compass points of the horoscope, situated on the meridian near the cusp of House X.

Ming Shu: Chinese term for the zodiac "circle of animals."

Moon's North Node (Ascending Node, ☊): Event in which the Moon passes through the ecliptic from a southern to a northern latitude.

Moon's South Node (Descending Node, ☋): Event in which the Moon passes through the ecliptic from north to south.

Morning Star: Another term for the planet Venus.

Moznayim: Judaic term for the zodiac sign of Libra (♎).

Mrgasiras: The fifth Vedic *naksatra* (lunar mansion).

Mrtyu: Vedic term meaning "death," which is House VIII of the horoscope; alternately known as Randhra, which means "vital points."

muhurta: Vedic term for electional astrology.

Mula: The nineteenth Vedic *naksatra* (lunar mansion).

mulatrikona: Vedic term meaning "root triangle"; a planet's most powerful state.

mundane astrology: The astrological study that focuses on secular or world affairs and the acts of a society or culture as a whole.

mundane parallel: Condition created when two planets are equally distant from any angle in a chart.

Nadir: The second of four major compass points of the horoscope, situated on the meridian near the cusp of House IV.

naisargikabala: Vedic term for a planet's natural strengths.

naksatra: Vedic term meaning "constellation" or "lunar mansion."

naksatradasa: Vedic term for a system of *dasa* calculation based on the person's Moon *naksatra.*

navagrahas: Vedic term used to describe the nine planets: Surya (☉, Sun), Candra (☽, Moon), Kuja (♂, Mars), Budha (☿, Mercury), Guru (♃, Jupiter), Sukra (♀, Venus), Sani (♄, Saturn), Rahu (☊, the Moon's North Node), and Ketu (☋, the Moon's South Node).

navamsacakra: Vedic term for "ninth-sign chart."

Niu: Chinese term for the *Ming Shu* sign of the Ox or Buffalo; also a Chinese term meaning "Buffalo," the ninth *sieu* (lunar mansion).

Nü: Chinese term meaning "maiden," the tenth *sieu* (lunar mansion).

obstacle: One of the six qualities of monthly days used in Tibetan astrology.

opposition: An aspect (☍) created between two planets, corollary points, or cusps that has an arc of 180°00'.

parallel: A condition that is often treated as an aspect (//), in which two planets are equally distant from the celestial equator and have the same north or south declination.

parkha: Tibetan term for a Chinese trigram that comprises a combination of three broken or unbroken lines, and is used in astrological prediction.

Phag: Tibetan term for the *Ming Shu* sign of the Pig.

Pi: Chinese term meaning "wall," the fourteenth *sieu* (lunar mansion).

Pí: Chinese term meaning "net," the nineteenth *sieu* (lunar mansion).

Pisces: The twelfth sign of the Western zodiac; the name of a constellation.

Placidus house system: A time-oriented method of dividing the 360° 00' of a horoscope's circle into twelve unequal houses.

Pole Star: Term used to identity the fixed star that corresponds to the position of the terrestrial North Pole.

power: One of the six qualities of monthly days used in Tibetan astrology.

prasna: Vedic term for horary astrology.

predictive astrology: The astrological study of the potential impact of planetary forces on an individual during that person's life.

Prophetic Age (Astrological Age): In Judaic astrology, the name given to each of the twelve 2,160-year periods that make up the "Great Year."

Punarvasu: The seventh Vedic *naksatra* (lunar mansion).

Purvabhadrapada (Purvaprosthapada): The twenty-fifth Vedic *naksatra* (lunar mansion).

Purvaphalguni: The eleventh Vedic *naksatra* (lunar mansion).

Purvasadha: The twentieth Vedic *naksatra* (lunar mansion).

Pusya: The eighth Vedic *naksatra* (lunar mansion).

Putra: Vedic term meaning "sons" which is House V of the horoscope.

quincunx: An aspect created between two planets, corollary points, or cusps that has an arc of 150°00'.

quindecile: An aspect created between two planets, corollary points, or cusps that has an arc of 24°00'.

quintile: An aspect created between two planets, corollary points, or cusps that has an arc of 72°00'.

Rahu: Vedic term for the Moon's North Node (☊).

rapt parallel: A condition often treated as an aspect (∥), in which two planets are equally distant from the meridian at the point of the Midheaven.

rasi: Vedic term for zodiac sign.

rasicakra: Vedic term meaning "sign chart."

Red Bird: Chinese name for the southern arc of asterisms.

Revati: The twenty-seventh Vedic *naksatra* (lunar mansion).

Rohini: The fourth Vedic *naksatra* (lunar mansion).

rTa: Tibetan term for the *Ming Shu* sign of the Horse.

sa: Tibetan term for the characteristics represented by the earth element.

Sagittarius: The ninth sign of the Western zodiac (♐); the name of a constellation.

samhita: Vedic term for a form of divination that includes crow auguries, dream interpretation, and the observation of meteors and comets.

Sani: Vedic term for the planet Saturn (♄).

saptamsacakra: Vedic term for "seventh-sign chart."

Sarton: Judaic term for the zodiac sign of Cancer (♋).

Satabhisaj: The twenty-fourth Vedic *naksatra* (lunar mansion).

sBrul: Tibetan term for the *Ming Shu* sign of the Snake.

Scorpio: The eighth sign of the Western zodiac (♏); the name of a constellation.

semi-decile (vigintile):   An aspect created between two planets, corollary points, or cusps that has an arc of 18°00′.

semi-sextile: An aspect created between two planets, corollary points, or cusps that has an arc of 30°00′.

semi-square: An aspect created between two planets, corollary points, or cusps that has an arc of 45°00′.

sesquiquadrate: An aspect created between two planets, corollary points, or cusps that has an arc of 135°00′.

sextile: An aspect (✶) created between two planets, corollary points, or cusps that has an arc of 60°00′.

shadbala: Vedic term for the six sources from which a planet draws its strength.

She: Chinese term for the *Ming Shu* sign of the Snake.

Shen: Chinese term meaning "three associates," the twenty-first *sieu* (lunar mansion).

shi-shey: Tibetan term for "enemies," used to define the relationship between zodiac signs.

Shih: Chinese term meaning "house," the thirteenth *sieu* (lunar mansion).

shing: Tibetan term for the characteristics represented by the wood element.

Shor: Judaic term for the zodiac sign of Taurus (♉).

Shu: Chinese term for the *Ming Shu* sign of the Rat or Mouse.

sidereal day: A 24-hour period that is 00:03:55.91 shorter than the average calendar day, and is used to calculate the length of time on the ecliptic.

Sidpaho: A common Tibetan household accessory used to attract a positive flow of energy into most Tibetan homes.

sieu: Chinese term meaning "lunar mansion."

sodasavarga (varga):   Vedic term for the sixteen divisional charts used by astrologers to delve into facets of an individual's natal delineation.

sok: Tibetan term for "life force."

soma: Vedic term for an intoxicating sacred drink distilled from an unknown plant that was consumed by the gods and their worshipers.

Song of the Four Seasons: Four separate images depicting the Emperor Huang Ti, used in Chinese predictive astrology.

sPre: Tibetan term for the *Ming Shu* sign of the Monkey.

square (quartile):   An aspect (□) created between two planets, corollary points, or cusps that has an arc of 90°00′.

Sravana: The twenty-second Vedic *naksatra* (lunar mansion).

Sravistha: The twenty-third Vedic *naksatra* (lunar mansion).

Ssu Chu: Chinese term for the "Four Pillars of Destiny" that form the basis of Chinese astrology.

sTag: Tibetan term for the *Ming Shu* sign of the Tiger.

sthanabala: Vedic term for the *shadbala* drawn from a planet's position in a given house or sign and its compatibility with other planets and *navamsa*.

succedent houses: Houses II, V, VIII, and XI of the horoscope.

success: One of the six qualities of monthly days used in Tibetan astrology.

Sukra: Vedic term for the planet Venus (♀).

Surya: Vedic term for the Sun (☉).

Svati: The fifteenth Vedic *naksatra* (lunar mansion).

swakshetra: Vedic term meaning "sign of rulership"; a state in which a planet is in the sign that it rules.

synchronicity: An acausal parallelism of time and meaning between apparent and invisible events that cannot be reduced to a common scientific principle.

t'ien hsia: Chinese term meaning "that which is under Heaven" or "universe."

t'ien kan: Chinese term meaning "celestial stem," one of the *ba tze*.

T'u: Chinese term for the *Ming Shu* sign of the Hare or Rabbit.

Taleh: Judaic term for the zodiac sign of Aries (♈).

Talmud: The written embodiment of Jewish civil and religious law.

Talmudic "first hour":   Judaic term for 6:00 A.M. (06:00:00).

Taurus: The second sign of the Western zodiac (♉); the name of a constellation.

Teomin: Judaic term for the zodiac sign of Gemini (♊).

thun-sun: Tibetan term for "friends," used to define the relationship between zodiac signs.

ti chih: Chinese term meaning "terrestrial branch," one of the *ba tze*.

Ti: Chinese term meaning "base," the third *sieu* (lunar mansion).

Torah: Judaic term for the books of the Old Testament of the Bible.

Tou: Chinese term meaning "ladle," the eighth *sieu* (lunar mansion).

tredecile: An aspect created between two planets, corollary points, or cusps that has an arc of 108°00′.

trikona: Vedic term for Houses V and IX of the horoscope.

trine: An aspect (△) created between two planets, corollary points, or cusps that has an arc of 120°00′ or 240°00′.

triplicities: Characteristics embodied in the natural elements of fire, earth, water, and air.

Tsui: Chinese term meaning "beak," the twentieth *sieu* (lunar mansion).

Tzu P'ing: Chinese term for the form of fate calculation based on the *Ssu Chu*.

ucca: Vedic term for an exalted position. Surya (☉) is exalted in 10°♈00′. Candra (☽) is exalted in 03°♉00′. Kuja (♂) is exalted in 28°♑00′. Budha (☿) is exalted in 15°♍00′. Guru (♃) is exalted in 05°♋00′. Sukra (♀) is exalted in 27°♓00′. Sani (♄) is exalted in 20°♎00′. Rahu (☊) is exalted in 00°♉00′–30°♉00′; and Ketu (☋) is exalted in 00°♏00′–30°♏00′.

Uranian astrology: A branch of esoteric astrology that delineates the specific degree a planet occupies, rather than the elements and qualities that planet is said to exert in more conventional forms.

Uttarabhadrapada (Uttaraprosthapada):   The twenty-sixth Vedic *naksatra* (lunar mansion).

Uttaraphalguni: The twelfth Vedic *naksatra* (lunar mansion).

Uttarasadha: The twenty-first Vedic *naksatra* (lunar mansion).

varshaphala: Vedic term for predictive astrology.

Vedic: Another term for Hindu or Indian astrology; derived from the Vedas.

vernal equinox: A term meaning "equal night of spring"; the vernal equinox marks one of two moments in the course of a year in which the plane created by the apparent path of the Sun (the ecliptic) intersects the plane created by the Earth's equator.

vimsottari dasa: Vedic term for a 120-year timeline divided into *dasas.*

Virgo: The sixth sign of the Western zodiac; the name of a constellation.

Visakha: The sixteenth Vedic *naksatra* (lunar mansion).

vivaha: Vedic term for marital astrology.

Vyaya: Vedic term meaning "loss" which is House XII of the horoscope.

wang: Tibetan term for "power force."

Water Planet: Chinese description of the planet Mercury (☿), embodying the natural characteristics of the water element or *hsing.*

Wei: Chinese term meaning "roof," the twelfth *sieu* (lunar mansion); also a Chinese term meaning "stomach," the seventeen *sieu* (lunar mansion); also a Chinese term meaning "tail," the sixth *sieu* (lunar mansion).

White Tiger: Chinese name for the Western arc of asterisms.

wide aspect (platic aspect): An aspect that has an orb of influence that is 02°00′–08°00′ plus or minus an exact arc formation.

Wood Planet: Chinese description of the planet Jupiter (♃), embodying the natural characteristics of the wood element or *hsing.*

wu hsing (Five Agents): Five characteristics applied in Chinese and Tibetan astrology that are embodied in natural elements of fire, earth, water, metal, and wood.

yáng: Chinese term for the *Ming Shu* sign of the Ram or Sheep.

yang: A Chinese term for the energies generated by the heavens.

yatra: Vedic term for mundane astrology.

yin: Chinese term for the energies generated by the Earth.

yoga: Vedic term for a formula that prescribes a personality type by combining planetary positions in specific houses along with levels of *shadbala.*

Yos: Tibetan term for the *Ming Shu* sign of the Hare or Rabbit.

zodiac: "Circle of animals," the name given to the 360° 00′ arc of the ecliptic, which is divided into twelve segments.

zu chu: Chinese term meaning "day master," which is the *t'ien kan* for the day of birth.

Selected Bibliography

Albin, Michel. *Astrologies: Chinoise, Indienne, Arabe, Hebraïque & Occidentales.* Paris: Question de Albin Michel, 1979.

Ashmand, J. M., trans. *Ptolemy's Tetrabiblos or Quadripartite Being Four Books of the Influence of the Stars.* Chicago: Aries Press, 1936.

Baravalle, Carlos H., MAFA. "Diana, A Textbook Example of Tragedy." *Today's Astrologer* 59, no. 12 (29 November 1997): 417–18.

Beyer, Steve L. *The Star Guide: A Unique System for Identifying the Brightest Stars in the Night Sky.* Boston: Little, Brown, 1986.

Campion, Nicholas. *The Great Year: Astrology, Millenarism and History in the Western Tradition.* London: Penguin/Arkana, 1994.

Cassidy, William. "On the Origin of Chinese Divination: Of Time and Tortoises." http://209.1.162.9/astro/html/chineseorigin.html, 1998.

Chartrand, Mark R. *Skyguide: A Field Guide to the Heavens.* New York: Golden Books, 1990.

Cohen, Abraham. *Everyman's Talmud: The Major Teachings of the Rabbinic Sages.* New York: Schocken Books, 1995.

Cornu, Philippe. *Tibetan Astrology.* Translated by Hamish Gregor. Boston: Shambhala, 1997.

Croswell, Ken. *The Alchemy of the Heavens: Searching for Meaning in the Milky Way.* New York: Anchor Books, 1995.

Davies, Nicholas. *Diana: The People's Princess.* Secaucus, N.J.: Citadel Stars, 1997.

deVore, Nicholas. *Encyclopedia of Astrology.* Totowa, N.J.: Littlefield, Adams, 1976 (reprint; original edition published by Philosophical Library, 1947).

Dobin, Rabbi Joel C. *The Astrological Secrets of the Hebrew Sages: To Rule Both Day and Night.* Rochester, Vt.: Inner Traditions International, 1977.

Dreyer, Ronnie Gale. *Indian Astrology: A Western Approach to the Ancient Hindu Art.* Northamptonshire, England: Aquarian Press, 1990.

——. *Vedic Astrology: A Guide to the Fundamentals of Jyotish.* Foreword by James Braha. York Beach, Maine: Samuel Weiser, 1997.

Foulsham, W. *Raphael's Astronomical Ephemeris of Planets' Places for 1997.* Chippenham, England: W. Foulsham, 1996.

Frazer, Sir James George. *The Golden Bough: A Study in Magic and Religion.* 3rd edition. Part V: *Spirit of the Corn and of the Wild,* vol. 1. London: Macmillan, 1912.

George, Llewellyn. *The New A to Z Horoscope Maker and Delineator.* 13th edition. Revised and edited by Marylee Bytheriver. St. Paul, Minn.: Llewellyn Publications, 1910, 1981.

Gettings, Fred. *The Arkana Dictionary of Astrology.* London: Penguin Books, 1985, 1990.

Goldschneider, Gary, and Joost Elffers. *The Secret Language of Birthdays.* New York: Viking Studio Books, 1994.

Goravani, Das. *Vedic Astrology: Lessons 1–15.* Eugene, Ore.: Spiritweb, 1995. http://www.spiritweb.org.

Grasse, Ray, Robin Armstrong, Bill Watson, Michael Erlewine, Hart deFouw, Dennis Flaherty, James Braha, and Richard Houck. *Eastern System for Western Astrologers: An Anthology.* Introduction by Thomas Moore. York Beach, Maine: Samuel Weiser, 1997.

Hall, Manly Palmer. *The Story of Astrology.* Los Angeles: Phoenix Press, 1993.

Hamaker-Zondag, Karen. *Foundations of Personality: Combining Elements, Crosses, and Houses with Jungian Psychological Concepts in Horoscope Interpretation.* York Beach, Maine: Samuel Weiser, 1984, 1988.

Harwood, P. J. *Astrological Prediction.* Santa Fe: Sun Books, 1993.

Heald, Henrietta Grant, ed. *Chronicle of Britain.* Farnsborough, Hampshire, England: Chronicle Communications, 1992.

Hill, Victoria, MAFA. "Princess Diana: A Royal Tragedy." *Today's Astrologer* 59, no. 11 (31 October 1997): 370–73.

Holden, James H. *A History of Horoscopic Astrology.* Tempe, Ariz.: American Federation of Astrologers, 1996.

Huon de Kermadec, Jean-Michel. *The Way to Chinese Astrology: The Four Pillars of Destiny.* Translated by N. Derek Poulsen. Foreword by John Blofeld. London: Unwin Books, 1983.

Ibn Ezra, Abraham ben Meir. *Le Livre des Fondements Astrologiques.* Paris: Retz, Bibliotheca hermetica, 1977.

Jones, Marc Edmund. *Essentials of Astrological Analysis.* St. Paul, Minn.: Llewellyn Publications, 1960.

———. *Sabian Symbols in Astrology: Illustrated by One Thousand Horoscopes of Well-Known People.* Boulder, Colo.: Shambhala, 1953, 1969.

Jung, Carl G. "Synchronicity: An Acausal Connecting Principle" and "On Synchronicity." In *The Collected Works of Carl G. Jung,* vol. 8. New York: Bollingen-Pantheon, 1951.

Kwok, Man-Ho. *The Feng Shui Kit: The Chinese Way to Health, Wealth and Happiness at Home and at Work.* Boston: Charles E. Tuttle, 1995.

Lau, Kwan. *Secrets of Chinese Astrology: A Handbook for Self Discovery.* New York: Tengu Books, 1994.

Lau, Theodora. *The Handbook of Chinese Horoscopes.* New York: HarperPerennial, 1995.

Lewi, Grant. *Astrology for the Millions.* St. Paul, Minn.: Llewellyn Publications, 1990.

Lewis, James R. *The Astrology Encyclopedia.* Detroit: Gale Research, 1994.

Mayo, Elizabeth, LPMAFA. "The Death of Princess Diana." *Today's Astrologer* 59, no. 10 (1 October 1997): 328–30.

Paltrinieri, Mario, Elena Rader, and Dr. Rosanna Zerilli. *The Book of Practical Astrology.* New York: Collier Books, 1981.

Patel, P. A., MAFA. "Diana, Princess of Wales." *Today's Astrologer* 59, no. 13 (29 December 1997): 441–45.

Pegis, Anton C., ed. *The Basic Writing of Saint Thomas Aquinas,* vol. 2. New York: Random House, 1945.

Renshaw, Steve, and Saori Ihara. "The Lunar Calendar in Japan." http://www2.gol.com/users/stever/calendar.htm, 1997.

Roberts, Press, and Ima Roberts. *Transits in Plain English.* Seattle: Vulcan Books, 1976.

Roberts, Press, Ima Roberts, and Don Borkowski. *Signs and Parts in Plain English.* Seattle: Vulcan Books, 1976.

Roebuck, Valerie. *The Circle of Stars: An Introduction to Indian Astrology.* Shaftsbury, Dorset, England: Element Books, 1992.

Sakya, Jnan Bahadur. *Short Description of Gods, Goddesses, and Ritual Objects of Buddhism and Hinduism in Nepal.* Kathmandu, Nepal: Handicraft Association of Nepal, 1989.

Sargeant, Winthrop. *The Bhagavad Gita: An Interlinear Translation of the Sanskrit with Word-Word Transliteration and Translation, and Complete Grammatical Commentary as well as a Readable Prose Translation and Page-by-Page Vocabularies.* New York: Doubleday, 1979.

Sepharial. *Kabalistic Astrology: Being the Hebraic Method of Divination by the Power, Sound, Number, and Planetary Influence.* 3rd edition. North Hollywood, Calif.: Newcastle Publishing, 1981.

Sholem, Gershom G. *On the Kabbalah and Its Symbolism.* Translated by Ralph Manheim. New York: Schocken Books, 1969.

Tennant, Catherine. *The Lost Zodiac: 22 Ancient Star Signs.* Boston: Bulfinch Press/Little, Brown, 1995.

Tester, Jim. *A History of Western Astrology.* New York: Ballantine Books, 1987.

Walter, Derek. *Chinese Astrology: Interpreting the Revelations of the Celestial Messengers.* London: Aquarian Press, 1987, 1992.

Walter, Derek. *The Chinese Astrology Workbook: How to Calculate and Interpret Chinese Horoscopes.* Wellingborough, England: Aquarian Press, 1988.

Zoller, Robert. *The Arabic Parts in Astrology: A Lost Key to Prediction.* Rochester, Vt.: Inner Traditions International, 1980, 1989.

Index

Page numbers in **boldface type** refer to tables and charts.

ability to act appropriately, 272
acausal connection, 15. *See also* meaningful coincidence
accidentally exalted planet, 277
accidents and illnesses, 81–83, 187–88, 203, 300–1, 313, 419, 422, 423, 429, 430, 432, 474, 547. *See also* health
adoption, 39
ages: Astrological (Prophetic), 32n, 333, 334; of Aquarius, 334n; of Aries, 334; of Pisces, 334; of Taurus, 334; precessional, 333
alchemy. *See* divination
Alexander the Great. *See* emperors
Alice T.: Ascendant, 152, 161, 209, 212, 223, 343–44, 453; *bap-par*, 140; *bhavacakra*, 175, 195, 197, 207, 239; birth data, 44; birth *sieu*, 117; *dasas*, 253; Disturbance Day, 136; *drekkanacakra*, 220–21; Enemy Day, 136; fate cycle, 80, 102–3; fate house, 102–3; features, predominant, 451–53; Foundation Day, 136; *gen's ba tze* pair, 56, 101; *gen's t'ien kan*, 56, 78, 101; *gen's ti chih*, 56, 101; *guo's ba tze* pair, 95; *guo's t'ien kan*, 95; *guo's ti chih*, 95, 102; *horacakra*, **214**; horoscope, Western natal, 147; House I, 195, 485; House II, 195, 456–57;

House III, 195, 479, 480, 482, 483; House IV, 195, 461; House V, 195, 463–64, 468; House VI, 195, 473–74, 484–87; House VII, 195, 468–69; House VIII, 196, 456–59, 473, 474–77; House IX, 196, 263, 479–80, 483–84; House X, 196, 263, 487; House XI, 196, 488; House XII, 196, 489; house rulers, 177–78; houses, 451; *hsing*, year, 56, 101; *hua's ba tze* pair, 85, 101; *hua's t'ien kan*, 88–89, 95; *hua's ti chih*, 92; Jupiter (♃), 152, 176, 213, 214, 218, 221, 224, 228, 233; key element, 132; *la*, 132; *lü*, 132; *lung ta*, 131; Mars (♂), 153, 176, 213, 215, 218, 221, 224, 228, 233, 237, 468; Mercury (☿), 153, 176, 213, **218**, 221, 224, 228; *miao's ba tze* pair, 77, 79, 102; *miao's ti chih*, 81, 88–89 (progressed), 102; *Ming Shu* sign, 56, 65, 101; Moon (☾), 153, 176, 197, 198, 213, 215, 218, 221, 224, 228, 236, 247, 452; Moon's North Node (☊), 153, 175, 213, **218**, 221, 224, 228–29, 386, 453; Moon's South Node (☋), 153, 176, 212, **218**, 222, 224, 229, 386, 453; *naksatradasa*, 248–49; natal chart (horoscope), **259**, **364**; *navamsa* signs, 210; *navamsacakra*, 212, 215–16; Obstacle Day, 136; Part of Aptness, 272–73; Part of Brethren, 285–86; Part of Children, 295–96; Part of Collection,

character traits (*cont.*)

121, 163, 179, 340, 428, 431; seeks recognition, 59; self-assured, 168; self-centered, 62, 425; self-confident (confident), 56, 61, 62, 63, 164, 198, 403, 424; self-critical, 204; self-destructive, 121; self-disciplined, 62, 128; self-doubting, 158; self-indulgent, 199; self-interested, 128, 168, 420; self-praising, 343; self-protective, 404; self-reliant, 55, 162, 163, 340; self-sacrificing, 59, 62, 121, 179; self-satisfied, 159; selfish, 58, 168; sensible, 342; sensitive, 162, 420, 427, 430, 431; sensual, 158, 160, 161, 178; serious, 204, 428, 431; short-tempered, 170; showman, 63; shrewd, 54, 58, 61, 163, 171, 428; shy, 159, 161, 169; sickly as child, 158; sincere (candor; sincerity), 59, 63, 158, 167; single-minded, 63; skeptical, 163; slow, 121; sly, 342; smart, 62; social (sociable), 159, 164, 179, 341, 342; sophisticated, 63; spendthrift, 167, 203, 206; sports-minded, 162; stable, 64; steadfast, 60, 61, 65; stingy, 121; stoic, 206; strict, 63; strong, 158, 160, 340; strong convictions, 167; strong personal values, 59; strong-willed, 60, 61, 198; stubborn, 58, 62, 121, 163, 428; superficial, 179; superiority complex, 63; supportive, 160; suspicious, 166; sympathetic, 64, 164, 166, 167; systematic, 62; tactile, 178; talkative (loquacious), 121, 205, 338, 342, 418; temperamental, 60; tenacious, 163; theatrical, 179; thinks a great deal, 121; touchy, 60; traditional, 58; trusting, 179; trustworthy, 167; truthful, 201, 203; tyrannical, 340; unbiased, 165; uncomfortable with strangers, 158; uncompromising, 60; unconventional, 62, 164; understands group dynamics, 59; unhappy, 202; unkind, 158; unobtrusive, 160, 163; unpretentious,

164; unreliable, 342; unruly, 62; unstable, 62, 418; untrustworthy, 121; vacillating, 62; vain (vanity), 63; values cooperation, 60; vengeful, 128, 168; versatile, 427; vigorous, 55, 164; violent, 171, 179; virtuous (virtue), 60; volatile, 55, 62, 404; walks quickly, 121; wanderlust, 62; wants to please others, 62; warm, 63, 64; warm-hearted, 163; well-bred, 339; well-dressed, 158; well-educated, 428; well-mannered, 161; well-meaning, 121; well-spoken, 161, 339; willpower, 170; wise (wisdom), 55, 165, 170, 204, 341; witty, 61; worries, 171

charitable works, 81–83

Chen. *See* asterisms; *sieu*

Chi. *See* asterisms; *sieu*

chicken. *See* summer

chieh, 78, **79**, **91**, 92, 544; Ch'ing Mong, **79**; Ch'iu Fen, **79**; Ch'u Shu, **79**; Ch'un Fen, **79**; Ching Chih, **79**; Han Lu, **79**; Hsaio Man, **79**; Hsaio Shu, **79**; Hsia Chih, **79**; Hsiao Han, **79**; Hsiao Hsüeh, **79**; Ku Yu, **79**; Li Ch'iu, **79**; Li Ch'un, **79**; Li Hsia, **79**; Li Tung, **79**; Mang Chung, **79**; Pai Lu, **79**; Shuang Chiang, **79**; Ta Han, **79**; Ta Hsüeh, **79**; Ta Shu, **79**; Thung Chih, **79**; Yü Shui, **79**

chien-ch'ü, 90, **91**, 92, 544

children (offspring; sons; daughters), 28, 56, 81–83, 162, 167, 183–84, 222, 226, 259, 294–99, 415, 417, 420, 422, 424, 426, 427, 429, 432, 435, 450, 462–63, 495, 543, 546. *See also* Alice T.; Diana, Princess of Wales; Peter C.

Chinese mansions. *See sieu*

Ching. *See* asterisms; *sieu*

chronology, personal (life chronology), 65, 81, 141, 496, 540, 543, 544; Fate Cycles, 28, 46, 78–83 (*see also* fate); *vimsottari dasa* (*dasas*), 29, 81, 144, 246–54, 528, 541 (*see also* time). *See also* Alice T.; books; Diana, Princess of Wales; Peter C.

Circle of Animals. *See* zodiac

of the celestial river, 54; water of the ocean, 54; water which enters and fertilizes, 53; wood of cedar and pine, 53; wood of mulberry, 54; wood of pomegranate, 54; wood of poplar and willow, 53; wood of the plain, 53. *See also ba tze*

poets and philosophers: Aristotle, 14, 21; Confucius, 8; Li-Po, xx; Mencius, 6n; Plato, 21, 23; Saint Augustine, 21, 22; Saint Thomas Aquinas, 22, 345

Polaris. *See* fixed stars

Pole Star. *See* fixed stars

political astrology. *See* astrology: mundane

Polo, Marco, 8

pork. *See* winter

prasna. See astrology: horary

prediction: daily, 30, 107; Dominican and Franciscan orders, advent of, 23; Genghis Khan, birth of, 16; great storm, 15; human acts, 22; Jesus Christ, birth of, 13, 21; Magian religion, end of, 13; Mohammed, birth of, 13; Richard I, abduction of, 23; Saladin, fall of, 23; using the birth *hua* for daily, 90, **91**, 93; weather, 25; Zoroasterism, rise of, 13

predictive astrology. *See* astrology

presidents: Jefferson, Thomas, 25; Washington, George, 25

prime: meridian, 12, 351, 356, 366, 369; numbers, 119

princes and princesses: Arjuna, 11; Bhima, 11; Hun-shin Kun-ju (Kong Jo), 9, 121; Nakula, 11; Pandava, 11; Sahadeva, 11; Yudhisthira, 11. *See also* Diana, Princess of Wales

profession (occupation), 28, **81–83**, 190, 191, 199–200, 259, 320–21, 338–43, 396, 415, 417, 419, 421, 423, 425, 426, 430, 432, 450, 484, 495, 543, 549. *See also* Alice T.; Diana, Princess of Wales; Peter C.; success

projects, conclusion to, 109–16

Prophetic Ages. *See* ages

psychically perceived entities, 29, 30

punishment, 40

quadrants. *See* angles

quadratures, 416

radiation, xix

radix. *See* horoscope

real estate and real property (land), 181–82, 198, 200, 201, 202, 203, 204, 205, 206, 426. *See also* Alice T.; Diana, Princess of Wales; domestic life and residences; Peter C.

red, 55, 129. Bird (*see* arc of asterisms); Ruler (*see* Mars). *See also* summer

reincarnation, 18

relatives, close (brethren), **81–83**, 180–81, 205, 284. *See also* Alice T.; aunts; brothers and sisters; Diana, Princess of Wales; Peter C.; uncles

religions (ideologies), 21, 188–89, 259, 423, 426, 430, 432, 435, 549; Buddhism, 18, 35, 554; Catholic (Roman), 19, 23; Christian, 16, 21, 22; Confucianism, 554; Gnostic, 14; Hinduism, 4, 10, 11, 18, 33, 35, 141, 142 (*see also* Hindu gods; Hindu texts); Judaism, 17–19 (*see also* Jewish); Kabbala, 18, 19, 554; Khazarite, 15; Lamaism, 10; Magian, 15; Mahayana Buddhism, 10; Manichaean, 14; Mu'tazilah, 14; Muslim (Islam), 12; Shi'ite Islam, 14; Swedish Lutheran, 25; Tantric Buddhism, 10; Taoism, 558; Tibetan Buddhism, 10; Turkish Ghurid, 12. *See also* Alice T.; Diana, Princess of Wales; Peter C.

retrograde motion, 32, **151**, 450

reward, 40

romance and love, 60, 64, 167, 182–83, 198, 200, 201, 202, 203, 205–7, 415, 420, 422, 424, 426, 429, 431, 432, 435, 462–63. *See also* Alice T.; Diana, Princess of Wales; marriage; Peter C.; sex and sexual attraction

About the Authors

Anistatia R Miller is an astrological researcher and practitioner who has specialized in comparing and utilizing various forms of Eastern and Western astrology. She also maintains a Web site devoted to this study at http://members.aol.com/Anistatia/index.html and a mailing-list discussion group at worldastrology@coollist.com. She is a Research Member of the American Federation of Astrologers and a member of the International Society for Astrological Research.

Miller and her husband, Jared M. Brown, have written articles on modern iconography for *Icon: Thoughtstyle Magazine, Adobe Magazine, Wine Spectator,* and *Cigar Aficionado.* They have also written numerous books on subjects ranging from corporate trademarks and symbology in modern graphic design to a chronological review of historic events to Martinis.

In the past seven years, they have lived in Manhattan, Chicago, Vancouver, and San Francisco. They currently live and work in a fourteen-room Victorian house built in 1896 in Boise, Idaho, with their two nameless cats.